SECOND EDITION

RISK MANAGEMENT
AND
FINANCIAL INSTITUTIONS

SECOND EDITION

RISK MANAGEMENT AND FINANCIAL INSTITUTIONS

John C. Hull

Maple Financial Group Professor of Derivatives and Risk Management
Joseph L. Rotman School of Management
University of Toronto

PRENTICE HALL

Boston   Columbus   Indianapolis   New York   San Francisco   Upper Saddle River
Amsterdam   Cape Town   Dubai   London   Madrid   Milan   Munich   Paris   Montreal   Toronto
Delhi   Mexico City   São Paulo   Sydney   Hong Kong   Seoul   Singapore   Taipei   Tokyo

Editor in Chief: Donna Battista
Editorial Project Manager: Kerri McQueen
Marketing Manager: Elizabeth Averbeck
Marketing Coordinator: Ian Gold
Managing Editor: Jeffrey Holcomb
Production Supervisor: Heather McNally
Senior Manufacturing Buyer: Carol Melville
Senior Media Manufacturing Buyer: Ginny Michaud
Art Director: Jayne Conte
Cover Designer: Margaret Kenselaar
Cover Art: Getty Images, Inc.
Manager, Rights & Permissions: Shannon Barbe
Media Project Manager: Nicole Sackin
Composition: The Geometric Press

Credits and acknowledgments borrowed from other sources and reproduced, with permission, in this textbook appear on appropriate page within text.

Library of Congress Cataloging-in-Publication Data

Hull, John, 1946–
    Risk management and financial institutions / John Hull.—2nd ed.
        p. cm.
    Includes index.
    ISBN 978-0-13-610295-3 (alk. paper)
    1. Risk management. 2. Financial institutions—Management. I. Title.
    HD61.H83 2009
    332.1068′1–dc22
                                    2009015069

Prentice Hall
is an imprint of

PEARSON

www.pearsonhighered.com

ISBN 13: 978-0-13-610295-3
ISBN 10: 0-13-610295-6

10 9 8 7 6 5 4 3 2 1—HA—13 12 11 10 09

To
Michelle, Peter, and David

CONTENTS IN BRIEF

Contents

BUSINESS SNAPSHOTS

Preface

Much has happened in financial markets since the first edition of this book was published in 2006. Huge losses have been experienced by financial institutions throughout the world. Both financial institutions and their regulators have been re-evaluating risk management practices. Stress testing and liquidity risk are receiving more attention.

Risk Management and Financial Institutions has been expanded and updated to reflect these market developments. Like my popular text *Options, Futures, and Other Derivatives*, the book is designed to be useful to practicing managers as well as college students. Those studying for GARP and PRMIA qualifications will find the book particularly helpful.

The book is appropriate for elective courses in either risk management or financial institutions. It is not necessary for students to take a course on options and futures markets prior to taking a course based on this book. But if they have taken such a course, some of the material in the first seven chapters does not need to be covered.

The level of mathematical sophistication and the way material is presented has been managed carefully so that the book is accessible to as wide an audience as possible. For example, when covering copulas in Chapter 10, the intuition is presented first and then followed by a detailed numerical example; when covering maximum likelihood methods in Chapter 9 and extreme value theory in Chapter 12, numerical examples and sufficient details are provided for readers to develop their own Excel® spreadsheets. I have provided my own Excel spreadsheets for applications, where appropriate; these are available on my website.

This is a book about risk management, so there is relatively little material on the valuation of derivatives contracts. (This is the main focus of my other two books *Options, Futures, and Other Derivatives* and *Fundamentals of Futures and Options Markets*.) The appendices at the end of the book include material that summarizes some of the key results that are important to risk managers.

What's New in This Edition?

The second edition contains much new material. In particular:

1. There are three new chapters providing background material on financial institutions. These are Chapter 2 on banks, Chapter 3 on insurance companies and pension plans, and Chapter 4 on mutual funds and hedge funds.

2. There is a new chapter titled "ABSs, CDOs, and the Credit Crunch of 2007" (Chapter 16). This explains the events that led to the credit crisis of 2007–2009 and the lessons that can be learned from it.

3. There is a new chapter titled "Scenario Analysis and Stress Testing" (Chapter 17). This reflects the importance now placed on stress testing by both financial institutions and their regulators.

4. There are separate chapters on liquidity risk and model risk (Chapters 19 and 20). Both of these topics have assumed greater importance since 2007.

5. Value at risk is now introduced before Basel II is discussed (Chapter 8). This sequence was suggested to me as more logical by a number of instructors.

6. A sample portfolio with accompanying spreadsheets (available on the author's website) is used for explaining alternative approaches for calculating value at risk.

7. There are many more numerical examples.

8. The DerivaGem software (version 1.53) is included with the book.

DerivaGem Software

Version 1.53 of the widely acclaimed software DerivaGem is included with this book. An installation routine is provided with this version of the software. This loads files into correct folders, creates icons, and makes it easier for students to start using the software. DerivaGem consists of two Excel applications: the *Options Calculator* and the *Applications Builder*. The Options Calculator consists of easy-to-use software for valuing a wide range of options. The Applications Builder consists of a number of Excel functions from which users can build their own applications. It includes a number of sample applications that enable students to explore risk management issues. It also allows more interesting assignments to be designed. The software is described more fully at the end of the book. Updates to the software can be downloaded from the author's website:

www.rotman.utoronto.ca/~hull

PowerPoint Slides

Several hundred PowerPoint slides (ISBN 0-13-610332-4) can be downloaded from Pearson's Instructor Resource Center (www.pearsonhighered.com/irc) or from my own website. Adopting instructors are welcome to adapt the slides to meet their own needs.

Questions and Problems

End-of-chapter problems are divided into two groups: "Practice Questions and Problems" and "Further Questions." The solutions to the former are at the end of the book. Solutions to the latter are made available by the publisher to adopting instructors in the Instructor's Manual.

Instructor's Manual

The Instructor's Manual (ISBN 0-13-610329-4) is made available online to adopting instructors by Pearson. It contains solutions to the "Further Questions," notes on the teaching of each chapter, and some advice on course organization.

Acknowledgments

Many people have played a part in the production of this book. I have benefited from interactions with many academics and practicing risk managers. I would like to thank the students in my MBA and MFin courses at the University of Toronto, many of whom have made suggestions as to how the material could be improved. Eddie Mizzi from the Geometric Press did an excellent job editing the final manuscript and handling the page composition. Derrick Knie and Milena Litoiu provided excellent research assistance.

Alan White, a colleague at the University of Toronto, deserves a special acknowledgment. Alan and I have been carrying out joint research and consulting in the area of derivatives and risk management for over 25 years. During that time we have spent countless hours discussing key issues. Many of the new ideas in this book, and many of the new ways used to explain old ideas, are as much Alan's as mine. Alan has done most of the development work on the DerivaGem software.

Special thanks are due to many people at Pearson, particularly my editor Donna Battista, for their enthusiasm, advice, and encouragement.

I welcome comments on the book from readers. My e-mail address is:

hull@rotman.utoronto.ca

John Hull
Joseph L. Rotman School of Management
University of Toronto

CHAPTER 1

Introduction

Imagine you are the chief risk officer of a major corporation. The CEO wants your views on a major new venture. You have been inundated with reports showing that the new venture has a positive net present value and will enhance shareholder value. What sort of analysis and ideas is the CEO looking for from you?

As chief risk officer it is your job to consider how the new venture fits into the company's portfolio. What is the correlation of the performance of the new venture with the rest of the company's business? When the rest of the business is experiencing difficulties, will the new venture also provide poor returns, or will it have the effect of dampening the ups and downs in the rest of the business?

Companies must take risks if they are to survive and prosper. The risk management function's primary responsibility is to understand the portfolio of risks that the company is currently taking and the risks it plans to take in the future. It must decide whether the risks are acceptable and, if they are not acceptable, what action should be taken.

Most of this book is concerned with the ways risks are managed by banks and other financial institutions, but many of the ideas and approaches we will discuss are equally applicable to nonfinancial corporations. Risk management has become a progressively more important for all corporations in the last few decades. Financial institutions in particular are finding they have to increase the resources they devote to risk management. Large "rogue trader" losses such as those at Barings Bank in 1995, Allied Irish Bank in 2002, and Société Générale in 2007 would have been avoided if procedures used by the banks for collecting data on trading positions had more been more carefully developed. Huge "subprime" losses at banks such as Citigroup, UBS, and Merrill Lynch would have been less severe if risk management groups had been able to convince senior management that unacceptable risks were being taken.

This opening chapter sets the scene. It starts by reviewing the classical arguments concerning the risk–return trade-offs faced by an investor who is choosing a portfolio of stocks and bonds. It then considers whether the same arguments can be used by a company in choosing new projects and managing its risk exposure. The chapter concludes that there are reasons why companies—particularly financial institutions—should be concerned with the total risk they face, not just with the risk from the viewpoint of a well-diversified shareholder.

1

1.1 RISK vs. RETURN FOR INVESTORS

As all fund managers know, there is a trade-off between risk and return when money is invested. The greater the risks taken, the higher the return that can be realized. The trade-off is actually between risk and *expected return*, not between risk and actual return. The term "expected return" sometimes causes confusion. In everyday language an outcome that is "expected" is considered highly likely to occur. However, statisticians define the expected value of a variable as its mean value. Expected return is therefore a weighted average of the possible returns, where the weight applied to a particular return equals the probability of that return occurring. The possible returns and their probabilities can be either estimated from historical data or assessed subjectively.

Suppose, for example, that you have $100,000 to invest for one year. One alternative is to buy Treasury bills yielding 5% per annum. There is then no risk and the expected return is 5%. Another alternative is to invest the $100,000 in a stock. To simplify things a little we suppose that the possible outcomes from this investment are as shown in Table 1.1. There is a 0.05 probability that the return will be +50%, a 0.25 probability that the return will be +30%, and so on. Expressing the returns in decimal form, the expected return per year is:

$$0.05 \times 0.50 + 0.25 \times 0.30 + 0.40 \times 0.10 + 0.25 \times (-0.10) + 0.05 \times (-0.30) = 0.10$$

This shows that in return for taking some risk you are able to increase your expected return per annum from the 5% offered by Treasury bills to 10%. If things work out well, your return per annum could be as high as 50%. But the worst-case outcome is a -30% return or a loss of $30,000.

One of the first attempts to understand the trade-off between risk and expected return was by Markowitz (1952). Later Sharpe (1964) and others carried the Markowitz analysis a stage further by developing what is known as the capital asset pricing model. This is a relationship between expected return and what is termed systematic risk. In 1976, Ross developed arbitrage pricing theory which can be viewed as an extension of the capital asset pricing model to the situation where there are several sources of systematic risk. The key insights of these researchers have had a profound effect on the way portfolio managers think about and analyze the risk–return trade-offs that they face. In this section we review these insights.

Quantifying Risk

How do you quantify the risk you are taking when you choose an investment? A convenient measure that is often used is the standard deviation of return over one year.

Table 1.1 Return in one year from investing $100,000 in equities.

Probability	Return
0.05	+50%
0.25	+30%
0.40	+10%
0.25	−10%
0.05	−30%

This is

$$\sqrt{E(R^2) - [E(R)]^2}$$

where R is the return per annum. The symbol E denotes expected value, so that $E(R)$ is expected return per annum. In Table 1.1, as we have shown, $E(R) = 0.10$. To calculate $E(R^2)$, we must weight the alternative squared returns by their probabilities:

$$E(R^2) = 0.05 \times 0.50^2 + 0.25 \times 0.30^2 + 0.40 \times 0.10^2 + 0.25 \times (-0.10)^2 + 0.05 \times (-0.30)^2$$
$$= 0.046$$

The standard deviation of returns is therefore $\sqrt{0.046 - 0.1^2} = 0.1897$, or 18.97%.

Investment Opportunities

Suppose we choose to characterize every investment opportunity by its expected return and standard deviation of return. We can plot available risky investments on a chart such as Figure 1.1, where the horizontal axis is the standard deviation of return and the vertical axis is the expected return.

Once we have identified the expected return and the standard deviation of the return for individual investments, it is natural to think about what happens when we combine investments to form a portfolio. Consider two investments with returns R_1 and R_2. The return from putting a proportion w_1 of our money in the first investment and a proportion $w_2 = 1 - w_1$ in the second investment is

$$w_1 R_1 + w_2 R_2$$

The portfolio expected return is

$$\mu_P = w_1 \mu_1 + w_2 \mu_2 \tag{1.1}$$

Figure 1.1 Alternative risky investments.

Table 1.2 Expected return, μ_P, and standard deviation of return, σ_P, from a portfolio consisting of two investments. The expected returns from the investments are 10% and 15%, the standard deviation of the returns are 16% and 24%, and the correlation between returns is 0.2.

w_1	w_2	μ_P	σ_P
0.0	1.0	15%	24.00%
0.2	0.8	14%	20.09%
0.4	0.6	13%	16.89%
0.6	0.4	12%	14.87%
0.8	0.2	11%	14.54%
1.0	0.0	10%	16.00%

where μ_1 is the expected return from the first investment and μ_2 is the expected return from the second investment. The standard deviation of the portfolio return is given by

$$\sigma_P = \sqrt{w_1^2 \sigma_1^2 + w_2^2 \sigma_2^2 + 2\rho w_1 w_2 \sigma_1 \sigma_2} \tag{1.2}$$

where σ_1 and σ_2 are the standard deviations of R_1 and R_2 and ρ is the coefficient of correlation between the two.

Suppose that μ_1 is 10% per annum and σ_1 is 16% per annum while μ_2 is 15% per

Figure 1.2 Alternative risk–return combinations from two investments as calculated in Table 1.2.

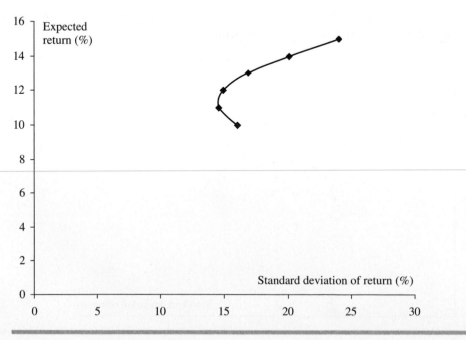

annum and σ_2 is 24% per annum. Suppose also that the coefficient of correlation, ρ, between the returns is 0.2 or 20%. Table 1.2 shows the values of μ_P and σ_P for a number of different values of w_1 and w_2. The calculations show that by putting part of your money in the first investment and part in the second investment a wide range of risk–return combinations can be achieved. These are plotted in Figure 1.2.

Most investors are risk-averse. They want to increase expected return while reducing the standard deviation of return. This means that they want to move as far as they can in a "northwest" direction in Figures 1.1 and 1.2. Figure 1.2 shows that forming a portfolio of the two investments we have been considering helps them do this. For example, by putting 60% in the first investment and 40% in the second, a portfolio with an expected return of 12% and a standard deviation of return equal to 14.87% is obtained. This is an improvement over the risk–return trade-off for the first investment. (The expected return is 2% higher and the standard deviation of the return is 1.13% lower.)

1.2 THE EFFICIENT FRONTIER

Let us now bring a third investment into our analysis. The third investment can be combined with any combination of the first two investments to produce new risk–return combinations. This enables us to move further in the northwest direction. We can then add a fourth investment. This can be combined with any combination of the first three investments to produce yet more investment opportunities. As we continue this process, considering every possible portfolio of the available risky investments, we obtain what is known as an *efficient frontier*. This represents the limit of how far we can move in a northwest direction and is illustrated in Figure 1.3. There is no investment that dominates a point on the efficient frontier, in the sense that it has both a higher expected return and a lower standard deviation of return. The area southeast of the

Figure 1.3 Efficient frontier obtainable from risky investments.

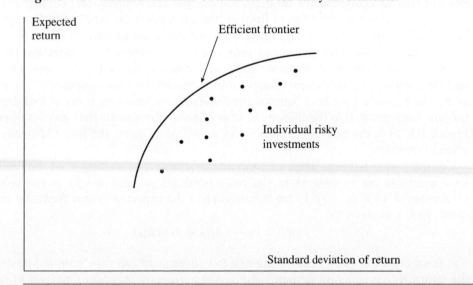

Figure 1.4 The efficient frontier of all investments. Point *I* is achieved by investing a percentage β_I of available funds in portfolio *M* and rest in a risk-free investment. Point *J* is achieved by borrowing $\beta_J - 1$ of available funds at the risk-free rate and investing everything in portfolio *M*.

efficient frontier represents the set of all investments that are possible. For any point in this area that is not on the efficient frontier, there is a point on the efficient frontier that has a higher expected return and lower standard deviation of return.

In Figure 1.3 we have considered only risky investments. What does the efficient frontier of all possible investments look like? Specifically, what happens when we include the risk-free investment? Suppose that the risk-free investment yields a return of R_F. In Figure 1.4 we have denoted the risk-free investment by point *F* and drawn a tangent from point *F* to the efficient frontier of risky investments that was developed in Figure 1.3. *M* is the point of tangency. As we will now show, the line *FM* is our new efficient frontier.

Consider what happens when we form an investment *I* by putting β_I of the funds we have available for investment in the risky portfolio *M*, and $1 - \beta_I$ in the risk-free investment *F* $(0 < \beta_I < 1)$. From equation (1.1) the expected return from the investment, $E(R_I)$, is given by

$$E(R_I) = (1 - \beta_I)R_F + \beta_I E(R_M)$$

and from equation (1.2), because the risk-free investment has zero standard deviation, the return R_I has standard deviation $\beta_I\sigma_M$, where σ_M is the standard deviation of return for portfolio M. This risk–return combination corresponds to the point labeled I in Figure 1.4. From the perspective of both expected return and standard deviation of return, point I is β_I of the way from F to M.

All points on the line FM can be obtained by choosing a suitable combination of the investment represented by point F and the investment represented by point M. The points on this line dominate all the points on the previous efficient frontier because they give a better risk–return combination. The straight line FM is therefore the new efficient frontier.

If we make the simplifying assumption that we can borrow at the risk-free rate of R_F as well as invest at that rate, we can create investments that are on the line from F to M but beyond M. Suppose, for example, that we want to create the investment represented by the point J in Figure 1.4, where the distance of J from F is β_J times the distance of M from F ($\beta_J > 1$). We borrow $\beta_J - 1$ of the amount that we have available for investment at rate R_F and then invest everything (the original funds and the borrowed funds) in the investment represented by point M. After allowing for the interest paid, the new investment has an expected return $E(R_J)$ given by

$$E(R_J) = \beta_J E(R_M) - (\beta_J - 1)R_F$$

and the standard deviation of the return is $\beta_J \sigma_M$. This shows that the risk and expected return combination corresponds to point J.

The argument that we have presented shows that, when the risk-free investment is considered, the efficient frontier must be a straight line. To put this another way, there should be linear trade-off between the expected return and the standard deviation of returns, as indicated in Figure 1.4. All investors should choose the same portfolio of risky assets. This is the portfolio represented by M. They should then reflect their appetite for risk by combining this risky investment with borrowing or lending at the risk-free rate.

It is a short step from here to argue that the portfolio of risky investments represented by M must be the portfolio of all risky investments. Suppose a particular investment is not in the portfolio. No investors would hold it and its price would have to go down so that its expected return increased and it became part of portfolio M. In fact we can go further than this. To ensure a balance between the supply and demand for each investment, the price of each risky investment must adjust so that the amount of that investment in portfolio M is proportional to the amount of that investment available in the economy. The investment represented by point M is therefore usually referred to as the *market portfolio*.

1.3 THE CAPITAL ASSET PRICING MODEL

How do investors decide on the expected returns they require for individual investments? Based on the analysis we have presented, the market portfolio should play a key role. The expected return required on an investment should reflect the extent to which the investment contributes to the risks of the market portfolio.

A common procedure is to use historical data to determine a best-fit linear relationship between returns from an investment and returns from the market portfolio. This relationship has the form:

$$R = a + \beta R_M + \epsilon \tag{1.3}$$

where R is the return from the investment, R_M is the return from the market portfolio, a and β are constants, and ϵ is a random variable equal to the regression error.

Equation (1.3) shows that there are two components to the risk in the investment's return:

1. A component βR_M, which is a multiple of the return from the market portfolio
2. A component ϵ, which is unrelated to the return from the market portfolio

The first component is referred to as *systematic risk*. The second component is referred to as *nonsystematic risk*.

Consider first the nonsystematic risk. If we assume that the ϵ's for different investments are independent of each other, the nonsystematic risk is almost completely diversified away in a large portfolio. An investor should not therefore be concerned about nonsystematic risk and should not require an extra return above the risk-free rate for bearing nonsystematic risk.

The systematic risk component is what should matter to an investor. When a large well-diversified portfolio is held, the systematic risk represented by βR_M does not disappear. An investor should require an expected return to compensate for this systematic risk.

We know how investors trade off systematic risk and expected return from Figure 1.4. When $\beta = 0$, there is no systematic risk and the expected return is R_F. When $\beta = 1$, we have the same systematic risk as the market portfolio, which is represented by point M, and the expected return should be $E(R_M)$. In general

$$E(R) = R_F + \beta[E(R_M) - R_F] \tag{1.4}$$

This is the *capital asset pricing model*. The excess expected return over the risk-free rate required on the investment is β times the excess expected return on the market portfolio. This relationship is plotted in Figure 1.5. The parameter β is the *beta* of the investment.

Example 1.1

Suppose that the risk-free rate is 5% and the return on the market portfolio is 10%. An investment with a beta of 0 should have an expected return of 5%. This is because all of the risk in the investment can be diversified away. An investment with a beta of 0.5 should have an expected return of

$$0.05 + 0.5 \times (0.1 - 0.05) = 0.075$$

or 7.5%. An investment with a beta of 1.2 should have an expected return of

$$0.05 + 1.2 \times (0.1 - 0.05) = 0.11$$

or 11%.

The parameter, β, is equal to $\rho\sigma/\sigma_M$ where ρ is the correlation between the return from the investment and the return from the market portfolio, σ is the standard deviation of the return from the investment, and σ_M is the standard deviation of the return from the market portfolio. Beta measures the sensitivity of the return from the investment to the return from the market portfolio. We can define the beta of any investment portfolio as in equation (1.3) by regressing its returns against the returns from the market portfolio. The capital asset pricing model in equation (1.4) should then apply with the return R defined as the return from the portfolio. In Figure 1.4 the market portfolio represented by M has a beta of 1.0 and the riskless portfolio represented by F has a beta of zero.

Figure 1.5 The capital asset pricing model.

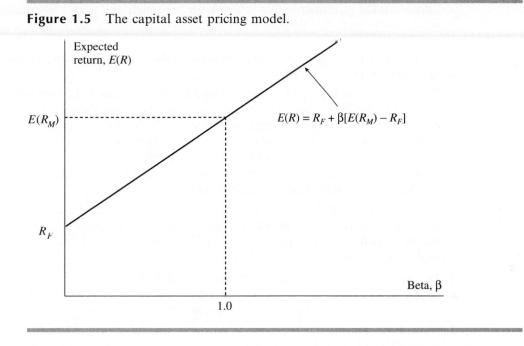

The portfolios represented by the points *I* and *J* have betas equal to equal to β_I and β_J, respectively.

Assumptions

The analysis we have presented leads to the surprising conclusion that all investors want to hold the same portfolios of assets (the portfolio represented by *M* in Figure 1.4.) This is clearly not true. Indeed, if it were true, markets would not function at all well because investors would not want to trade with each other! In practice, different investors have different views on the attractiveness of stocks and other risky investment opportunities. This is what causes them to trade with each other and it is this trading that leads to the formation of prices in markets.

The reason why the analysis leads to conclusions that do not correspond with the realities of markets is that, in presenting the arguments, we implicitly made a number of assumptions. In particular:

1. We assumed that investors care only about the expected return and the standard deviation of return of their portfolio. Another way of saying this is that investors look only at the first two moments of the return distribution. If returns are normally distributed, it is reasonable for investors to do this. However, the returns from many portfolios are non-normal. They have *skewness* and *excess kurtosis*. Skewness is related to the third moment of the distribution and kurtosis is related to the fourth moment. In the case of positive skewness, very high returns are more likely and very low returns are less likely than the normal distribution would predict; in the case of negative skewness, very low returns are more likely and very high returns are less likely than the normal distribution would predict. Excess

kurtosis leads to a distribution where both very high and very low returns are more likely than the normal distribution would predict. Most investors are concerned about the possibility of extreme negative outcomes. They are likely to want a higher expected return from investments with negative skewness or excess kurtosis.

2. We assumed that the ϵ's for different investments in equation (1.3) are independent. Equivalently we assumed the returns from investments are correlated with each other only because of their correlation with the market portfolio. This is clearly not true. Ford and General Motors are both in the automotive sector. There is likely to be some correlation between their returns that does not arise from their correlation with the overall stock market. This means that their ϵ's are not likely to be independent of each other.

3. We assumed that investors focus on returns over just one period and the length of this period is the same for all investors. This is also clearly not true. Some investors such as pension funds have very long time horizons. Others such as day traders have very short time horizons.

4. We assumed that investors can borrow and lend at the same risk-free rate. This is approximately true for a large financial institution in normal market conditions with a good credit rating. But it is not true for small investors.

5. We did not consider tax. In some jurisdictions, capital gains are taxed differently from dividends and other sources of income. Some investments get special tax treatment. Furthermore, not all investors are subject to the same tax rate. In practice, tax considerations have a part to play in the decisions of an investor. An investment that is appropriate for a pension fund that pays no tax might be quite inappropriate for a high-marginal-rate taxpayer living in New York, and vice versa.

6. Finally, we assumed that all investors make the same estimates of expected returns, standard deviations of returns, and correlations between returns for available investments. To put this another way, we assumed that investors have *homogeneous expectations*. This is clearly not true. Indeed, as indicated earlier, if we lived in a world of homogeneous expectations there would be no trading.

In spite of all this, the capital asset pricing model has proved to be a useful tool for portfolio managers. Estimates of the betas of stocks are readily available and the expected return on a portfolio estimated by the capital asset pricing model is a commonly used benchmark for assessing the performance of the portfolio manager, as we will now explain.

Alpha

When we observe a return of R_M on the market what do we expect the return on a portfolio with a beta of β to be? The capital asset pricing model relates the expected return on a portfolio to the expected return on the market. But it can also be used to relate the expected return on a portfolio to the actual return on the market:

$$E(R_P) = R_F + \beta(R_M - R_F)$$

where R_F is the risk-free rate and R_P is the return on the portfolio.

Figure 1.6   Relation between expected return on portfolio and the actual return on the market when portfolio beta is 0.6 and risk-free rate is 4%.

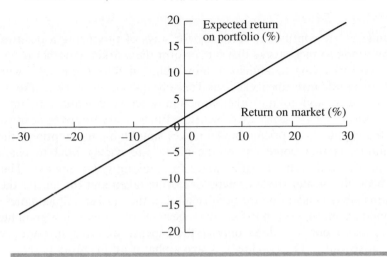

Example 1.2

Consider a portfolio with a beta of 0.6 when the risk-free interest rate is 4%. When the return from the market is 20%, the expected return on the portfolio is

$$0.04 + 0.6 \times (0.2 - 0.04) = 0.136$$

or 13.6%. When the return from the market is 10%, the expected return from the portfolio is

$$0.04 + 0.6 \times (0.1 - 0.04) = 0.076$$

or 7.6%. When the return from the market is −10%, the expected return from the portfolio is

$$0.04 + 0.6 \times (-0.1 - 0.04) = -0.044$$

or −4.4%. The relationship between the expected return on the portfolio and the return on the market is shown in Figure 1.6.

Suppose that the actual return on the portfolio is greater than the expected return:

$$R_P > R_F + \beta(R_M - R_F)$$

The portfolio manager has produced a superior return for the amount of systematic risk being taken. The extra return is

$$\alpha = R_P - R_F - \beta(R_M - R_F)$$

This is commonly referred to as the *alpha* created by the portfolio manager.

Example 1.3

A portfolio manager has a portfolio with a beta of 0.8. The one-year risk-free rate of interest is 5%, the return on the market during the year is 7% and the portfolio manager's return is 9%. The manager's alpha is

$$\alpha = 0.09 - 0.05 - 0.8 \times (0.07 - 0.05) = 0.024$$

or 2.4%.

Portfolio managers are continually searching for ways of producing a positive alpha. One way is by trying to pick stocks that outperform the market. Another is by *market timing*. This involves trying to anticipate movements in the market as a whole and moving funds from safe investments such as Treasury bills to the stock market when an upturn is anticipated and in the other direction when a downturn is anticipated. Chapter 4 explains other strategies used by hedge funds to try to create positive alpha.

Although the capital asset pricing model makes simplifying assumptions, the alpha and beta parameters that come out of the model are widely used to characterize investments. Beta describes the return obtained from taking systematic risk. The higher the value of beta, the greater the systematic risk being taken and the greater the extent to which returns are dependent on the performance of the market. Alpha represents the extra return made from superior portfolio management (or perhaps just good luck). An investor can make a positive alpha only at the expense of other investors who are making a negative alpha. The weighted average alpha of all investors is zero.

1.4   ARBITRAGE PRICING THEORY

Arbitrage pricing theory can be viewed as an extension of the capital asset pricing model. The return from an investment is assumed to depend on several factors. (These factors might involve variables such as the gross national product, the domestic interest rate, and the inflation rate.) By exploring ways in which investors can form portfolios that eliminate their exposure to the factors, arbitrage pricing theory shows that the expected return from an investment is linearly dependent on the factors.

The assumption that the ϵ's for different investments are independent in equation (1.3) ensures that there is just one factor driving expected returns (and therefore one source of systematic risk) in the capital asset pricing model. This is the return from the market portfolio. In arbitrage pricing theory there are several factors affecting investment returns. Each factor is a separate source of systematic risk. Unsystematic (i.e., diversifiable) risk in arbitrage pricing theory is the risk that is unrelated to all the factors.

1.5   RISK vs. RETURN FOR COMPANIES

We now move on to consider the trade-offs between risk and return made by a company. How should a company decide whether the expected return on a new investment project is sufficient compensation for its risks?

The ultimate owners of a company are its shareholders and a company should be managed in the best interests of its shareholders. It is therefore natural to argue that a new project undertaken by the company should be viewed as an addition to its shareholder's portfolio. The company should calculate the beta of the investment project and its expected return. If the expected return is greater than that given by the capital asset pricing model, it is a good deal for shareholders and the investment should be accepted. Otherwise it should be rejected.

The argument just given suggests that nonsystematic risks should not be considered when accept/reject decisions on new projects are taken. In practice of course, companies are concerned about nonsystematic as well as systematic risks. For example, most companies insure themselves against the risk of their buildings being burned down—even though this risk is entirely nonsystematic and can be diversified away by their shareholders. They try to avoid taking high risks and often hedge their exposures to exchange rates, interest rates, commodity prices, and other market variables. Earnings stability and the survival of the company are important managerial objectives. Companies do try and ensure that their the expected returns on new ventures are consistent with the risk–return trade-offs of their shareholders. But there is an over-riding constraint that the total risks taken should not be allowed to get too large.

Most investors are also concerned about the overall risk of the companies they invest in. They do not like surprises and prefer to invest in companies that show solid growth and meet earnings forecasts. They like companies to manage risks carefully and limit the overall amount of risk—both systematic and nonsystematic—they are taking.

The theoretical arguments we presented in Sections 1.1 to 1.4 suggest that investors should not behave in this way. They should hold a well diversified portfolio and encourage the companies they invest in to make high risk investments when the combination of expected return and systematic risk is favorable. Some of the companies in a shareholder's portfolio will go bankrupt, but others will do very well. The result should be an overall return to the shareholder that is satisfactory.

Are investors behaving suboptimally? Would their interests be better served if companies took more nonsystematic risks? There is an important argument to suggest that this is not necessarily the case. This argument is usually referred to as the "bankruptcy costs" argument. It is often used to explain why a company should restrict the amount of debt it takes on, but can be extended to apply to all risks.

Bankruptcy Costs

In a perfect world bankruptcy would be a fast affair where the company's assets (tangible and intangible) are sold at their fair market value and the proceeds are distributed to bond holders, shareholders, and other stake holders using well-defined rules. If we lived in such a perfect world the bankruptcy process itself would not destroy value for shareholders. Unfortunately the real world is far from perfect. By the time a company reaches the point of bankruptcy it is likely that its assets have lost some value. The bankruptcy process itself invariably reduces the value of its assets further. This further reduction in value is referred to as *bankruptcy costs*.

What is the nature of bankruptcy costs? Once a bankruptcy has been announced customers and suppliers become less inclined to do business with the company; assets sometimes have to be sold quickly at prices well below those that would be realized in an orderly sale; the value of important intangible assets such as the company's brand name and its reputation in the market are often destroyed; the company is no longer run in the best interests of shareholders; large fees are often paid to accountants and lawyers; and so on. The story in Business Snapshot 1.1 is representative of what often happens in practice. It illustrates how, when a high-risk decision works out badly, there can be disastrous bankruptcy costs.

Business Snapshot 1.1   The Hidden Costs of Bankruptcy

Several years ago a company had a market capitalization of $2 billion and $500 million of debt. The CEO decided to acquire a company in a related industry for $1 billion in cash. The cash was raised using a mixture of bank debt and bond issues. The price paid for the company was justified on the basis of potential synergies, but key threats to the profitability of the company were overlooked.

Many of the anticipated synergies were not realized. Furthermore, the company that was acquired was not profitable and proved to be a cash drain on the parent company. After three years the CEO resigned. The new CEO sold the acquisition for $100 million (10% of the price paid) and announced that the company would focus on its original core business. However, by then, the company was highly leveraged. A temporary economic downturn made it impossible for the company to service its debt and it declared bankruptcy.

The offices of the company were soon filled with accountants and lawyers representing the interests of the various parties (banks, different categories of bondholders, equity holders, the company, and the board of directors). These people directly or indirectly billed the company about $10 million per month in fees. The company lost sales that it would normally have made because nobody wants to do business with a bankrupt company. Key senior executives left. The company experienced a dramatic reduction in its market share.

After two years and three reorganization attempts, an agreement was reached between the various parties and a new company with a market capitalization of $700,000 was incorporated to continue the remaining profitable parts of the business. The shares in the new company were entirely owned by the banks and the bondholders. The shareholders got nothing.

We mentioned earlier that corporate survival is an important managerial objective and that shareholders like companies to avoid excessive risks. We now understand why this is so. Bankruptcy laws vary widely from country to country, but they all have the effect of destroying value as lenders and other creditors vie with each other to get paid. This value has often been painstakingly built up by the company over many years. It makes sense for a company that is operating in the best interests of its shareholders to limit the probability of this value destruction occurring. It does this by limiting the total risk (systematic and nonsystematic) that it takes.

When a major new investment is being contemplated, it is important to consider how well it fits in with other risks taken by the company. Relatively small investments can often have the effect of reducing the overall risks taken because of their diversification benefits. However, a large investment can dramatically increase these risks. Many spectacular corporate failures (such as the one in Business Snapshot 1.1) can be traced to CEOs who made large acquisitions (often highly leveraged) that did not work out.

1.6   RISK MANAGEMENT BY FINANCIAL INSTITUTIONS

Most of the rest of this book is concerned with financial institutions such as banks and insurance companies. Like other companies, these are concerned with providing a good trade-off between return and systematic risk for their investors. Like other companies, they are also concerned with total risks (systematic plus nonsystematic) because the bankruptcy costs arguments given in the previous section apply to them. However, there is another reason why most financial institutions carefully monitor total risks carefully. This is that regulators require them to do so.

Unlike most other companies, financial institutions are heavily regulated. Governments throughout the world want a stable financial sector. It is important that companies and private individuals have confidence in banks and insurance companies when they transact business. The regulations are designed to ensure that the probability of a bank or an insurance company experiencing severe financial difficulties is low. The bailouts of financial institutions in 2008 during the subprime crisis illustrate the reluctance of governments to let financial institutions fail.

Bankruptcy, of course, arises from losses being incurred. Regulators try to ensure that the capital held by a bank is sufficient to provide a cushion to absorb the losses with a high probability. Suppose for example that there is considered to be only a 0.1% probability that a financial institution will experience a loss of $2 billion or more in a year. Regulators might require the bank to hold equity capital equal to $2 billion. This would ensure that there is a 99.9% probability that the equity capital is sufficient to absorb the losses. The models used by regulators are discussed in more detail in later chapters.

The key point here is that regulators are concerned with total risks, not systematic risks. Their goal is to make bankruptcy a highly unlikely event.

How Risks Are Managed

There are two broad risk management strategies open to a financial institution (or any other organization). One approach is to identify risks one by one and handle each one separately. This is sometimes referred to as *risk decomposition*. The other is to reduce risks by being well diversified. This is sometimes referred to as *risk aggregation*. Both approaches are typically used by financial institutions.

Consider, for example, the market risks incurred by the trading room of a U.S. bank. These risks depend on the future movements in a multitude of market variables (exchange rates, interest rates, stock prices, and so on). To implement the risk decomposition approach, the trading room is organized so that traders are responsible for trades related to just one market variable (or perhaps a small group of market variables). For example, there could be one trader who is responsible for all trades involving the dollar–yen exchange rate. At the end of each day, the trader is required to ensure that certain risk measures are kept within limits specified by the bank. If the end of the day is approached and it looks as though one or more of the risk measures will be outside the specified limits, the trader must either get special permission to maintain the position or execute new hedging trades so that the limits are adhered to. (The risk measures and the way they are used are discussed in Chapter 6.)

The risk managers working in what is termed the "middle office" of a bank implement the risk aggregation approach for the market risks being taken. This involves calculating at the end of each day the total risk faced by the bank from movements in all market variables. Hopefully the bank is well diversified, so that its overall exposure to market movements is fairly small. If risks are unacceptably high, then the reasons must be determined and corrective action taken. The models used for the risk aggregation of market risks are given in Chapters 8, 12, and 13.

Risk aggregation is a key tool for insurance companies. Consider automobile insurance. The insurance company's payout on one particular automobile insurance policy is quite uncertain. However, the payout from 100,000 similar insurance policies can be predicted with reasonable accuracy.

Credit risks are also traditionally managed using risk aggregation. It is important for a financial institutions to be well diversified. If, for example, a bank lends 40% of its available funds to a single borrower, it is not well diversified and likely to be subject to unacceptable risks. If the borrower runs into financial difficulties and is unable to make interest and principal payments, the bank could become insolvent.

If the bank adopts a more diversified strategy of lending 0.01% of its available funds to each of 10,000 different borrowers, it is in a much safer position. Suppose that in a particular year the probability of any one borrower defaulting is 1%. We can expect that close to 100 borrowers will default in the year and the losses on these borrowers will be more than offset by the profits earned on the 99% of loans that perform well. To maximize the benefits of diversification, borrowers should be in different geographical regions and different industries. A large international bank with different types of borrowers all over the world is likely to be much better diversified than a small bank in Texas that lends entirely to oil companies. But however well diversified a bank is, it is still exposed to systematic risk. This is the risk that there will be an economic downturn and a resulting increase in the probability of default for all borrowers.

Since the late 1990s we have seen the emergence of an active market for credit derivatives. Credit derivatives allow banks to handle credit risks one by one (risk decomposition) rather than relying solely on risk diversification. They also allow banks to buy protection against the overall level of defaults in the economy. However, for every buyer of credit protection, there must be a seller. Many sellers of credit protection, whether on individual names or on portfolios, took huge losses during the credit crunch starting in 2007. Credit derivatives and the credit crunch are discussed further in Chapters 14 and 16.

SUMMARY

An important general principle in finance is that there is a trade-off between risk and return. Higher expected returns can usually be achieved only by taking higher risks. In theory, investors should not be concerned with risks they can diversify away. The extra return they demand should be for the amount of systematic (i.e., nondiversifiable) risk they are bearing.

For companies, investment decisions are more complicated. Companies are not in general as well diversified as investors, and survival is an important and legitimate objective. Both financing and investment decisions should be taken so that the possibility of financial distress is low. This is because financial distress leads to what are known as bankruptcy costs. These costs arise from the nature of the bankruptcy process and almost invariably lead to a reduction in shareholder value over and above the reduction that took place as a result of the adverse events leading to bankruptcy.

Two general approaches to risk management are risk decomposition and risk aggregation. Risk decomposition involves managing risks one by one. Risk aggregation involves relying on the power of diversification to reduce risks. Banks use both approaches to manage market risks. Credit risks have traditionally been managed using risk aggregation, but, with the advent of credit derivatives, the risk decomposition approach can be used.

FURTHER READING

Markowitz, H. "Portfolio Selection," *Journal of Finance*, 7, 1 (March 1952): 77–91.

Ross, S. "The Arbitrage Theory of Capital Asset Pricing," *Journal of Economic Theory*, 13, 3 (December 1976): 341–360.

Sharpe, W. "Capital Asset Prices: A Theory of Market Equilibrium," *Journal of Finance*, 19, 3 (September 1964): 425–442.

Smith, C. W., and R. M. Stulz, "The Determinants of a Firm's Hedging Policy," *Journal of Financial and Quantitative Analysis*, 20 (1985): 391–406.

Stulz, R. M., *Risk Management and Derivatives*. Southwestern, 2003.

PRACTICE QUESTIONS AND PROBLEMS (Answers at the End of the Book)

1.1. An investment has probabilities 0.1, 0.2, 0.35, 0.25, and 0.1 of giving returns equal to 40%, 30%, 15%, −5% and −15%. What is the expected return and the standard deviation of returns?

1.2. Suppose that there are two investments with the same probability distribution of returns as in Problem 1.1. The correlation between the returns is 0.15. What is the expected return and standard deviation of return from a portfolio where money is divided equally between the investments.

1.3. For the two investments considered in Figure 1.2 and Table 1.2, what are the alternative risk–return combinations if the correlation is (a) 0.3, (b) 1.0, and (c) –1.0

1.4. What is the difference between systematic and nonsystematic risk? Which is more important to an equity investor? Which can lead to the bankruptcy of a corporation?

1.5. Outline the arguments leading to the conclusion that all investors should choose the same portfolio of risky investments. What are the key assumptions?

1.6. The expected return on the market portfolio is 12% and the risk-free rate is 6%. What is the expected return on an investment with a beta of (a) 0.2, (b) 0.5, (c) 1.4?

1.7. "Arbitrage pricing theory is an extension of the capital asset pricing model." Explain this statement.

1.8. "The capital structure decision of a company is a trade-off between bankruptcy costs and the tax advantages of debt." Explain this statement.

1.9. What is meant by risk aggregation and risk decomposition? Which requires an in-depth understanding of individual risks? Which requires a detailed knowledge of the correlations between risks?

1.10. A bank's operational risk includes the risk of very large losses because of employee fraud, natural disasters, litigation, etc. Do you think operational risk best handled by risk decomposition or risk aggregation. (Operational risk will be discussed in Chapter 18.)

1.11. A bank's profit next year will be normally distributed with a mean of 0.6% of assets and a standard deviation of 1.5% of assets. The bank's equity is 4% of assets. What is the probability that the bank will have a positive equity at the end of the year? Ignore taxes.

1.12. Why do you think that banks are regulated to ensure that they do not take too much risk but most other companies (for example, those in manufacturing and retailing) are not?

1.13. List the bankruptcy costs incurred by the company in Business Snapshot 1.1.

1.14. The return from the market last year was 10% and the risk-free rate was 5%. A hedge fund manager with a beta of 0.6 has an alpha of 4%. What return did the hedge fund manager earn?

FURTHER QUESTIONS

1.15. Suppose that one investment has a mean return of 8% and a standard deviation of return of 14%. Another investment has a mean return of 12% and a standard deviation of return of 20%. The correlation between the returns is 0.3. Produce a chart similar to Figure 1.2 showing alternative risk–return combinations from the two investments.

1.16. The expected return on the market is 12% and the risk-free rate is 7%. The standard deviation of the return on the market 15%. One investor creates a portfolio on the efficient frontier with an expected return of 10%. Another creates a portfolio on the efficient frontier with an expected return of 20%. What is the standard deviation of the returns of the two portfolios?

1.17. A bank estimates that its profit next year is normally distributed with a mean of 0.8% of assets and the standard deviation of 2% of assets. How much equity (as a percentage of assets) does the company need to be (a) 99% sure that it will have a positive equity at the end of the year and (b) 99.9% sure that it will have positive equity at the end of the year. Ignore taxes.

1.18. A portfolio manager has maintained an actively managed portfolio with a beta of 0.2. During the last year, the risk-free rate was 5% and major equity indices performed very badly, providing returns of about −30%. The portfolio manager produced a return of −10% and claims that in the circumstances it was good. Discuss this claim.

2

Banks

The word "bank" originates from the Italian word "banco". This is a desk or bench, covered by a green tablecloth, that was used several hundred years ago by Florentine bankers. The traditional role of banks has been to take deposits and make loans. The interest charged on the loans is greater than the interest paid on deposits. The difference between the two has to cover administrative costs and loan losses (i.e., losses when borrowers fail to make the agreed payments of interest and principal), while providing a satisfactory return on equity.

Today, most large banks engage in both commercial and investment banking. *Commercial banking* involves, among other things, the deposit-taking and lending activities we have just mentioned. *Investment banking* is concerned with assisting companies in raising debt and equity, and providing advice on mergers and acquisitions, major corporate restructurings, and other corporate finance decisions. Large banks are also often involved in securities trading (e.g., by providing brokerage services).

Commercial banking can be classified as *wholesale banking* or *retail banking*. Retail banking, as its name implies, involves taking relatively small deposits from private individuals or small businesses and making relatively small loans to them. Wholesale banking involves the provision of banking services to medium and large corporate clients, fund managers, and other financial institutions. Both loans and deposits are much larger in wholesale banking than in retail banking. Sometimes banks fund their wholesale or retail lending by borrowing in financial markets themselves.

Typically the spread between the cost of funds and the lending rate is smaller for wholesale banking than for retail banking. However, this tends to be offset by lower costs. (When a certain dollar amount of wholesale lending is compared to the same dollar amount of retail lending, the expected loan losses and administrative costs are usually much less.) Banks that are heavily reliant on wholesale banking and fund their lending by borrowing in financial markets are often referred to as *money center banks*.

This chapter will review how commercial and investment banking have evolved over the last hundred years. It will examine the way the banks are regulated, consider the nature of the risks facing the banks, and look at the key role of capital in providing a cushion against losses.

2.1 COMMERCIAL BANKING

Commercial banking in virtually all countries has been subject to a great deal of regulation. This is because most national governments consider it important that individuals and companies have confidence in the banking system. Among the issues addressed by regulation is the capital that banks must keep, the activities they are allowed to engage in, deposit insurance, and the extent to which mergers and foreign ownership are allowed. The nature of bank regulation during the twentieth century has influenced the structure of commercial banking in different countries. To illustrate this, we consider the case of the United States.

The United States is unusual in that it has a large number of banks (7,450 in 2007). This leads to a relatively complicated payments system compared with those of other countries with fewer banks. There are a few large money center banks such as Citigroup and J. P. Morgan Chase. There are several hundred regional banks that engage in a mixture of wholesale and retail banking, and several thousand community banks that specialize in retail banking.

Table 2.1 summarizes the size distribution of banks in the US in 1994 and 2007. The number of banks declined by almost 50% between the two dates. In 2007, there were fewer small community banks and more large banks than in 1994. Although there were only 87 banks (1.2% of the total) with assets of $10 billion or more in 2007, they accounted for over 75% of the assets in the US banking system.

The structure of banking in the US is largely a result of regulatory restrictions on interstate banking. At the beginning of the twentieth century, most US banks had a

Table 2.1 Bank concentration in the US in 1984 and 2007.
Source: FDIC Quarterly Banking Profile, www.fdic.gov.

Size (assets)	1984			
	Number	Percent of total	Assets ($ billions)	Percent of total
Under $100 million	12,044	83.2	404.2	16.1
$100 million to $1 billion	2,161	14.9	513.9	20.5
$1 billion to $10 billion	254	1.7	725.9	28.9
Over $10 billion	24	0.2	864.8	34.5
Total	14,483		2,508.9	

Size (assets)	2007			
	Number	Percent of total	Assets ($ billions)	Percent of total
Under $100 million	3,331	44.7	173.9	1.8
$100 million to $1 billion	3,631	48.7	1,031.9	10.6
$1 billion to $10 billion	401	5.4	1,095.3	11.2
Over $10 billion	87	1.2	7,464.3	76.4
Total	7,450		9,765.4	

single branch from which they served customers. During the early part of the twentieth century, many of these banks expanded by opening more branches in order to serve their customers better. This ran into opposition from two quarters. First, small banks that still had only a single branch were concerned that they would lose market share. Second, large money center banks were concerned that the multibranch banks would be able to offer check-clearing and other payment services and erode the profits that they themselves made from offering these services. As a result, there was pressure to control the extent to which community banks could expand. Several states passed laws restricting the ability of banks to open more than one branch within a state.

The McFadden Act was passed in 1927 and amended in 1933. This act had the effect of restricting all banks from opening branches in more than one state. This restriction applied to nationally chartered as well as state-chartered banks. One way of getting round the McFadden Act was to establish a *multibank holding company*. This is a company that acquires more than one bank as a subsidiary. By 1956, there were 47 multibank holding companies. This led to the Douglas Amendment to the Bank Holding Company Act. This did not allow a multibank holding company to acquire a bank in a state that prohibited out-of-state acquisitions. However, acquisitions prior to 1956 were grandfathered (that is, multibank holding companies did not have to dispose of acquisitions made prior to 1956).

Banks are creative in finding ways around regulations—particularly when it is profitable for them to do so. After 1956, one approach was to form a one-bank holding company. This is a holding company with a just one bank as a subsidiary and a number of nonbank subsidiaries in different states from the bank. The nonbank subsidiaries offered financial services such as consumer finance, data processing, and leasing and were able to create a presence for the bank in other states.

The 1970 Bank Holding Companies Act restricted the activities of one-bank holding companies. They were only allowed to engage in activities that were closely related to banking, and acquisitions by them were subject to approval by the Federal Reserve. They had to divest themselves of acquisitions that did not conform to the act by 1980.

After 1970, the interstate banking restrictions started to disappear. Individual states passed laws allowing banks from other states to enter and acquire local banks. (Maine was the first to do so in 1978.) Some states allowed free entry of other banks. Some allowed banks from other states to enter only if there were reciprocal agreements. (This means that state A allowed banks from state B to enter only if state B allowed banks from state A to do so.) In some cases, groups of states developed regional banking pacts that allowed interstate banking.

In 1994, the US Congress passed the Riegel–Neal Interstate Banking and Branching Efficiency Act. This act led to full interstate banking becoming a reality. It permitted bank holding companies to acquire branches in other states. It invalidated state laws that allowed interstate banking on a reciprocal or regional basis. Starting in 1997, bank holding companies were allowed to convert out-of-state subsidiary banks into branches of a single bank. Many people argue that this type of consolidation is necessary to enable US banks to be large enough to compete internationally. The Riegel–Neal Act prepared the way for a wave of consolidation in the US banking system (for example, the acquisition by J.P. Morgan of banks formerly named Chemical, Chase, Bear Stearns, and Washington Mutual).

2.2 THE CAPITAL REQUIREMENTS OF A SMALL COMMERCIAL BANK

To illustrate the role of capital in banking, we consider a hypothetical small community bank named Deposits and Loans Corporation (DLC). DLC is primarily engaged in the traditional banking activities of taking deposits and making loans. A summary balance sheet for DLC at the end of 2009 is shown in Table 2.2 and a summary income statement for 2009 is shown in Table 2.3.

Table 2.2 shows that the bank has $100 million of assets. Most of the assets (80% of the total) are loans made by the bank to private individuals and small corporations. Cash and marketable securities account for a further 15% of the assets. The remaining 5% of the assets are fixed assets (i.e., buildings, equipment, etc.). A total of 90% of the funding for the assets comes from deposits of one sort or another from the bank's customers. A further 5% is financed by subordinated long-term debt. (These are bonds issued by the bank to investors that rank below deposits in the event of a liquidation.) The remaining 5% is financed by the bank's shareholders in the form of equity capital. The equity capital consists of the original cash investment of the shareholders and earnings retained in the bank.

Consider next the income statement for 2009 shown in Table 2.3. The first item on the income statement is net interest income. This is the excess of the interest earned over the interest paid and is 3% of the total assets in our example. It is important for the bank to be managed so that net interest income remains roughly constant regardless of movements in interest rates. We will discuss this in more detail in Chapter 7.

The next item is loan losses. This is 0.8% for the year in question. Clearly it is very important for management to quantify credit risks and manage them carefully. But however carefully a bank assesses the financial health of its clients before making a loan, it is inevitable that some borrowers will default. This is what leads to loan losses. The percentage of loans that default will tend to fluctuate from year to year with economic conditions. It is likely that in some years default rates will be quite low, while in others they will be quite high.

The next item, noninterest income, consists of income from all the activities of a bank other than lending money. This includes fees for the services the bank provides for its clients. In the case of DLC, noninterest income is 0.9% of assets.

The final item is noninterest expense and is 2.5% of assets in our example. This consists of all expenses other than interest paid. It includes salaries, technology-related costs, and other overheads. As in the case of all large businesses, these have a tendency

Table 2.2 Summary balance sheet for DLC at end of 2009 ($ millions).

Assets		Liabilities and net worth	
Cash	5	Deposits	90
Marketable securities	10	Subordinated long-term debt	5
Loans	80	Equity capital	5
Fixed assets	5		
Total	100	Total	100

Table 2.3 Summary income statement for DLC in 2009 ($ millions).

Net interest income	3.00
Loan losses	(0.80)
Noninterest income	0.90
Noninterest expense	(2.50)
Pre-tax operating income	0.60

to increase over time unless they are managed carefully. Banks must try to avoid large losses from litigation, business disruption, employee fraud, etc. The risk associated with these types of losses is known as *operational risk* and will be discussed in Chapter 18.

Capital Adequacy

Is the equity capital of 5% of assets in Table 2.2 adequate? Using an approach similar to that adopted by regulators and banks themselves, we consider an extreme scenario and determine whether the bank will survive. Suppose that there is a severe recession and as a result the bank's loan losses rise, by 3.2% of assets, to 4% next year. We assume that other items on the income statement in Table 2.3 are unaffected. The result will be a pretax net operating loss of 2.6% of assets ($0.6 - 3.2 = -2.6$). Assuming a tax rate of 30%, this would result in an after-tax loss of about 1.8% of assets.

In Table 2.2, equity capital is 5% of assets, and so an after-tax loss equal to 1.8% of assets, although not at all welcome, can be absorbed. It would result in a reduction of the equity capital to 3.2% of assets. Even a second bad year similar to the first would not totally wipe out the equity.

Suppose now that the bank has the more aggressive capital structure shown in Table 2.4. Everything is the same as Table 2.2 except that equity capital is 1% (rather than 5%) of assets and deposits are 94% (rather than 90%) of assets. In this case, one year where the loan losses are 4% of assets would totally wipe out equity capital and the bank would find itself in serious financial difficulties. It would no doubt try to raise additional equity capital, but it is likely to find this difficult when in such a weak financial position.

Table 2.4 Alternative balance sheet for a DLC bank at end of 2009 with equity only 1% of assets ($ millions).

Assets		Liabilities and net worth	
Cash	5	Deposits	94
Marketable securities	10	Subordinated long-term debt	5
Loans	80	Equity capital	1
Fixed assets	5		
Total	100	*Total*	100

It is possible that there would be a run on the bank (where all depositors decide to withdraw funds at the same time) and the bank would be forced into liquidation. If all assets could be liquidated for book value (a big assumption), the long-term debt-holders would likely receive about $4.2 billion rather than $5 billion (they would in effect absorb the negative equity) and the depositors would be repaid in full.

Clearly, it is inadequate for a bank to have only 1% of assets funded by equity capital. Maintaining equity capital equal to 5% of assets is more reasonable. Note that equity and subordinated long-term debt are both sources of capital. Equity provides the best protection against adverse events. (In our example, when the bank has $5 billion of equity capital rather than $1 billion, it stays solvent and is unlikely to be liquidated.) Subordinated long-term debt-holders rank below depositors in the event of default, but subordinated debt does not provide as good a cushion for the bank as equity because it does not prevent the bank's insolvency.

As we shall see in Chapter 11, bank regulators have tried to ensure that the capital a bank keeps is sufficient to cover the risks it takes. The risks include market risk, credit risk, and operational risk. Equity capital is categorized as "Tier 1 capital"; subordinated long-term debt is categorized as "Tier 2 capital".

2.3   DEPOSIT INSURANCE

To maintain confidence in banks, government regulators in many countries have introduced guaranty programs. These typically insure depositors against losses up to a certain level.

The United States with its large number of small banks is particularly prone to bank failures. After the stock market crash of 1929 the US experienced a major recession and about 10,000 banks failed between 1930 and 1933. Runs on banks and panics were common. In 1933, the United States government created the Federal Deposit Insurance Corporation (FDIC) to provide protection for depositors. Originally, the maximum level of protection provided was $2,500. This has been increased several times and became $250,000 per depositor per bank in October 2008. (It was scheduled to return to $100,000 for most accounts on January 1, 2010.) Banks pay a premium that is a percentage of their domestic deposits. In 2007, a system was introduced where the premium depends on the risk of the bank (as measured by its capital ratios).

Up to 1980, the system worked well. There were no runs on banks and few bank failures. However, between 1980 and 1990 bank failures in the US accelerated with the total number of failures during this decade being over 1,000 (larger than for the whole 1933 to 1979 period). There were several reasons for this. One was the way in which banks managed interest rate risk and we will talk about that in Chapter 7. Another reason was the reduction in oil and other commodity prices which led to many loans to oil, gas, and agricultural companies not being repaid.

A further reason for the bank failures was that the existence of deposit insurance allowed banks to follow risky strategies that would not otherwise be feasible. For example, they could increase their deposit base by offering high rates of interest to depositors and use the funds to make risky loans. Without deposit insurance, a bank could not follow this strategy, because their depositors would see what they were doing, decide that the bank was too risky, and withdraw their funds. With deposit insurance, it can follow the strategy because depositors know that, if the worst happens, they are protected under FDIC. This is an example of what is known as *moral hazard*. We will talk about moral hazard further in Chapter 3. It can be defined as the possibility that the existence of insurance changes the behavior of the insured party. The introduction of risk-based premiums referred to earlier reduces moral hazard to some extent.

During the 1980s, the funds of FDIC became seriously depleted and it had to borrow $30 billion from the US Treasury. In December 1991, Congress passed the FDIC Improvement Act to prevent any possibility of the fund becoming insolvent in the future. Between 1991 and 2006, bank failures in the United States were relatively rare and by 2006 the fund had reserves of about $50 billion. In 2008, defaults by banks such as IndyMac depleted FDIC funds, making premium increases inevitable.

2.4 INVESTMENT BANKING

The main activity of investment banking is raising debt and equity financing for corporations or governments. This involves originating the securities, underwriting them, and then placing them with investors. In a typical arrangement a corporation approaches an investment bank indicating that it wants to raise a certain amount of finance in the form of debt, equity, or hybrid instruments such as a convertible bonds. The securities are originated complete with legal documentation outlining the rights of the security holder. A prospectus is created outlining the company's past performance and future prospects. The risks faced by the company from such things as major lawsuits are itemized. There is a "road show" in which the investment bank and senior management from the company attempt to market the securities to large fund managers. A price for the securities is agreed between the bank and the corporation. The bank then sells the securities in the market.

There are a number a different types of arrangement between the investment bank and the corporation. Sometimes the issue takes the form of a *private placement* in which the securities are sold to a small number of large institutional investors such as life insurance companies or pension funds and the investment bank receives a fee. On other occasions it takes the form of a *public offering*, where securities are offered to the general public. A public offering may be on a *best efforts* or *firm commitment* basis. In the case of a best efforts public offering, the investment bank does as well as it can to place the securities with investors and is paid a fee that depends to some extent on its success. In the case of a firm commitment public offering, the investment bank agrees to buy the securities from the issuer at a particular price and then attempts to sell them in the market for a slightly higher price. It makes a profit equal to the difference between the price at which it sells the securities and the price it pays the issuer. If for any reason it is unable to sell the securities, it ends up owning them itself. The difference between the two types of deal is illustrated in Example 2.1.

Example 2.1

A bank has agreed to underwrite an issue of 50 million shares by ABC Corporation. In negotiations between the bank and the corporation the target net price to be received by the corporation has been set at $30 per share. This means that the corporation is expecting to raise 30×50 million dollars or $1.5 billion in total. The bank can either offer the client a best efforts arrangement where it charge a fee of \$0.30 per share sold so that, assuming all shares are sold, it obtains a total fee of $0.3 \times 50 = 15$ million dollars. Alternatively, it can offer a firm commitment where it agrees to buy the shares from ABC Corporation for \$30 per share.

The bank is confident that it will be able to sell the shares, but is uncertain about the price. As part of its procedures for assessing risk it considers two alternative scenarios. Under the first scenario, it can obtain a price of \$32 share; under the second, it is able to obtain only \$29 per share.

In a best-efforts deal, the bank obtains a fee of \$15 million in both cases. In a firm commitment deal its profit depends on the price it is able to obtain. If it sells the shares for \$32, it makes a profit of $(32 - 30) \times 50 = \$100$ million because it has agreed to pay ABC Corporation \$30 per share. However, if it can only sell the shares for \$29, it loses $(30 - 29) \times 50 = \$50$ million because it still has to pay ABC Corporation \$30 per share. The situation is summarized in the table below. The decision taken is likely to depend on the probabilities assigned by the bank to different outcomes and what is referred to as its "appetite for risk".

	Profits if best efforts	*Profits if firm commitment*
Can sell at \$29	+\$15 million	−\$50 million
Can sell at \$32	+\$15 million	+\$100 million

When equity financing is being raised and the company is already publicly traded, the investment bank can look at the prices at which the company's shares are trading a few days before the issue is to be sold as a guide to the issue price. Typically it will agree to attempt to issue new shares at a target price slightly below the current price. The main risk is then that the price of the company's shares will show a substantial decline before the new shares are sold.

IPOs

When the company wishing to issue shares is not publicly traded, the share issue is known as an *initial public offering* (IPO). These types of offering are typically made on a best efforts basis. The correct offering price is difficult to determine and depends on the investment bank's assessment of the company's value. The bank's best estimate of the market price is its estimate of the company's value divided by the number of shares currently outstanding. However, the bank will typically set the offering price below its best estimate of the market price. This is because does not want to take the chance that the issue will not sell. (It typically earns the same fee per share sold regardless of the offering price.)

Often there is a substantial increase in the share price immediately after shares are sold in an IPO (sometimes as much as 40%), indicating that the company could have raised more money if the issue price had been higher. As a result, IPOs are considered attractive buys by many investors. Banks frequently offer IPOs to the fund managers that are their best customers and to senior executives of large companies in the hope that they will provide them with business. (The latter is known as "spinning" and is frowned upon by regulators.)

Dutch Auction Approach

A few companies have used a Dutch auction approach for their IPOs. As for a regular IPO, a prospectus is issued and usually there is a road show. Individuals and companies bid by indicating the number of shares they want and the price they are prepared to pay. Shares are first issued to the highest bidder, then to the next highest bidder, and so on, until all the shares have been sold. The price paid by all successful bidders is the lowest bid that leads to a share allocation. This is illustrated in Example 2.2.

Example 2.2

A company wants to sell one million shares in an IPO. It decides to use the Dutch auction approach. The bidders are shown in the table below. In this case, shares are allocated first to C, then to F, then to E, then to H, then to A. At this point 800,000 shares have been allocated. Then next highest bidder is D, who has bid for 300,000 shares. Because only 200,000 remain unallocated, D's order is only two-thirds filled. The price paid by all the investors to whom shares are allocated (A, C, D, E, F, and H) is the price bid by D, or $29.00.

Bidder	Number of shares	Price
A	100,000	$30.00
B	200,000	$28.00
C	50,000	$33.00
D	300,000	$29.00
E	50,000	$30.50
F	300,000	$31.50
G	400,000	$25.00
H	200,000	$30.25

Dutch auctions potentially overcome two of the problems with a traditional IPO that we have mentioned. First, the price that clears the market ($29.00 in Example 2.2) should be the market price if all potential investors have participated in the bidding process. Second, the situations where investment banks offer IPOs only to favored clients are avoided. However, the company does not take advantage of the relationships that investment bankers have developed with large investors that usually enables the investment bankers to sell an IPO very quickly. One high-profile IPO that used a Dutch auction was the Google IPO in 2004. This is discussed in Business Snapshot 2.1.

Advisory Services

In addition to assisting companies with new issues of securities, investment banks offer advice to companies on mergers and acquisitions, divestments, major corporate restructurings, etc. They will assist in finding merger partners and takeover targets or help companies find buyers for divisions or subsidiaries of which they want to divest themselves. They will also advise the management of companies which are themselves merger or takeover targets. Sometimes they suggest steps they should take to avoid a merger or takeover. These are known as *poison pills*. Examples of poison pills are:

1. A potential target adds to its charter a provision where, if another company acquires one third of the shares, other shareholders have right to sell their shares to that company for twice the recent average share price.

Business Snapshot 2.1   Google's IPO

Google, developer of the the well-known internet search engine, decided to go public in 2004. It chose to use the Dutch auction approach. It was assisted by two investment banks, Morgan Stanley and Credit Suisse First Boston. The SEC gave approval for it to raise funds up to a maximum of $2,718,281,828. (Why the odd number? The mathematical constant e is 2.7182818...) The IPO method was not a pure Dutch auction because Google reserved to right to change the number of shares that would be issued and the percentage allocated to each bidder when it saw the bids.

Some investors expected the price of the shares to be as high as $120. But when Google saw the bids it decided that the number of shares offered would be 19,605,052 at a price of $85. This meant that the total value of the offering was 19,605,052 × $85, or $1.67 billion. Investors who had bid $85 or above obtained 74.2% of the shares they had bid for. The date of the IPO was August 19, 2004. Most companies would have given investors 100% of their allocation and raised $1.96 billion, instead of $1.67 billion. Perhaps Google (stock symbol: GOOG) correctly anticipated it would have no difficulty in selling further shares at a higher price later.

The initial market capitalization was $23.1 billion with over 90% of the shares being held by employees. These employees included the founders, Sergei Brin and Larry Page, and the CEO, Eric Schmidt. On the first day of trading, the shares closed at $100.34, 18% above the offer price and there was a further 7% increase on the second day. Google's issue therefore proved to be underpriced—but not as underpriced as some other IPOs of technology stocks where traditional IPO methods were used.

The cost of Google's IPO (fees paid to investment banks, etc) was 2.8% of the amount raised. This compares with an average of about 4% for a regular IPO.

There were some mistakes made and Google was lucky that these did not prevent the IPO from going ahead as planned. Sergei Brin and Larry Page gave an interview to *Playboy* magazine in April 2004. The interview appeared in the September issue. This violated SEC requirements that there be a "quiet period" with no promoting of the company's stock in the period leading up to an IPO. To avoid SEC sanctions Google had to include the *Playboy* interview (together with some factual corrections) in its SEC filings. Google also forgot to register 28 million shares and stock options.

Google's stock price rose rapidly in the period after the IPO. Approximately one year later (in September 2005), it was able to raise a further $4.18 billion by issuing an additional 14,159,265 shares at $295. (Why the odd number? The mathematical constant π is 3.14159265...)

---

2. A potential target grants to its key employees stock options that vest (i.e., can be exercised) in the event of a takeover. This is liable to create an exodus of key employees immediately after a takeover, leaving an empty shell for the new owner.

3. A potential target adds to its charter provisions making it impossible for a new owner to get rid of existing directors for one or two years after an acquisition.

4. A potential target issues preferred shares that automatically get converted to regular shares when there is a change in control.

> ## Business Snapshot 2.2 Peoplesoft's Poison Pill
>
> In 2003, the management of Peoplesoft, Inc., a company that provided human resource management systems, was concerned about a takeover by Oracle, a company specializing in database management systems. It took the unusual step of guaranteeing to its customers that, if it were acquired within two years and product support was reduced within four years, its customers would receive a refund of between two and five times the fees paid for their software licenses. The hypothetical cost to Oracle was estimated at $1.5 billion. The guarantee was opposed by Peoplesoft's shareholders. (It was clearly not in their interests!) Peoplesoft discontinued the guarantee in April 2004.
>
> Oracle did succeed in acquiring Peoplesoft in December 2004. Although some jobs at Peoplesoft were eliminated, Oracle maintained at least 90% of Peoplesoft's product development and support staff.

5. A potential target adds a provision where existing shareholders have the right to purchase shares at a discounted price during or after a takeover.

6. A potential target changes the voting structure so that shares owned by management have more votes than those owned by others.

Poison pills, which are illegal in many countries outside the US, have to be approved by a majority of shareholders. Often shareholders oppose poison pills because they see them as benefiting only management. An unusual poison pill, tried by Peoplesoft to fight a takeover by Oracle, is explained in Business Snapshot 2.2.

Valuation, strategy, and tactics are key aspects of the advisory services offered by an investment bank. For example, in advising Company A on a potential takeover of Company B, it is necessary for the investment bank to value Company B and help Company A assess possible synergies between the operations of the two companies. It must also consider whether it is better to offer Company B's shareholders cash or a share-for-share exchange (i.e., a certain number of shares in Company A in exchange for each share of Company B). What should the initial offer be? What does it expect the final offer that will close the deal to be? It must assess the best way to approach the senior managers of Company B and consider what the motivations of the managers will be. Will the takeover be a hostile one (opposed by the management of Company B) or friendly one (supported by the management of Company B)? In some instances there will be antitrust issues and approval from some branch of government may be required.

2.5 SECURITIES TRADING

Banks often get involved in securities trading, providing brokerage services, and making a market in individual securities. In so doing, they compete with smaller securities firms that do not offer other banking services.

A broker assists in the trading of securities by taking orders from clients and arranging for them to be carried out on an exchange. Some brokers operate nationally and some serve only a particular region. Some, known as full-service brokers, offer investment research and advice. Others, known as discount brokers, charge lower commissions, but provide no advice. Some offer online services and some, such as E-trade, provide a platform for customers to trade without a broker.

Market making involves quoting a bid (price at which you are prepared to buy) and offer (price at which you are prepared to sell). When asked for a price, a market maker will always quote both a bid and an offer without knowing whether the person asking for the price wants to buy or sell. The market maker makes a profit from the spread between the bid and the offer, but takes the risk that he or she will be left with an unacceptably high exposure.

Many exchanges on which stocks, options, and futures trade use market makers. Typically an exchange will specify a maximum level for the size of a market maker's bid–offer spread (the difference between the offer and the bid). In addition to exchanges, many instruments such as forward contracts, swaps, and options trade in the over-the-counter (OTC) market. (See Chapter 5 for a discussion of the over-the-counter market.) Most large investment banks are market makers for these instruments.

Trading is closely related to market making. Most large investment and commercial banks have extensive trading activities. The counterparties in their trading activities are typically other banks, corporations, and fund managers. Banks trade for three main reasons:

1. To meet the needs of its counterparties. For example, a bank may sell a foreign currency option to a corporate client to help it reduce its foreign exchange risk or buy a credit derivative from a hedge fund to help it implement a trading strategy.

2. To reduce its own risks. This will be discussed further in Chapter 6.

3. To take a speculative position in the hope of making a profit. This is referred to as trading for its own account or proprietary ("prop") trading.

2.6 POTENTIAL CONFLICTS OF INTEREST IN BANKING

There are many potential conflicts of interest between commercial banking, securities services, and investment banking when they are all conducted under the same corporate umbrella. For example:

1. A bank when asked for advice by an investor might be tempted to recommend securities that the investment banking part of its organization is trying to sell. When it has a fiduciary account (i.e., a customer account where the bank can choose trades for the customer), the bank can "stuff" difficult-to-sell securities into the account.

2. A bank when it lends money to a company often obtains confidential information about the company. It might be tempted to pass that information to the mergers and acquisitions arm of the investment bank to help it provide advice to one of its clients on potential takeover opportunities.

3. The research end of the securities business might be tempted to recommend a company's share as a "buy" in order to please the company's management and obtain investment banking business.

4. Suppose a commercial bank no longer wants a loan it has made to a company on its books because the confidential information it has obtained from the company leads it to believe that there is an increased chance of bankruptcy. It might be tempted to arrange for the investment bank to do a bond issue for the company, with the proceeds being used to pay off the loan. This would have the effect of replacing its loan with a loan made by investors who were less well informed.

As a result of these types of conflict of interest, some countries have in the past attempted to separate commercial banking from investment banking. The Glass–Steagall Act of 1933 in the United States limited the ability of commercial banks and investment banks to engage in each other's activities. Commercial banks were allowed to continue underwriting Treasury instruments and some municipal bonds. They were also allowed to do private placements. But they were not allowed to engage in other activities such as public offerings. Similarly, investment banks were not allowed to take deposits and make commercial loans.

In 1987, the Federal Reserve Board relaxed the rules somewhat and allowed banks to establish holding companies with two subsidiaries, one in investment banking and the other in commercial banking. The revenue of the investment banking subsidiary was restricted to being a certain percentage of the group's total revenue.

In 1997, the rules were relaxed further so that commercial banks could acquire existing investment banks. Finally, in 1999, the Financial Services Modernization Act was passed. This effectively eliminated all restrictions on the operations of banks, insurance companies, and securities firms. In 2007, there were five large investment banks in the United States that had no commercial banking interests. These were Goldman Sachs, Morgan Stanley, Merrill Lynch, Bear Stearns, and Lehman Brothers. In 2008, the credit crisis led to Lehman Brothers going bankrupt, Bear Stearns being taken over by J. P. Morgan Chase, and Merrill Lynch being taken over by Bank of America. Goldman Sachs and Morgan Stanley became bank holding companies with both commercial and investment banking interests. (As a result, they had to maintain lower leverage ratios and subject themselves to more regulatory scrutiny.) The year 2008 therefore marked the end of an era for investment banking in the United States.

2.7 TODAY'S LARGE BANKS

Today's large banks operate globally and transact business in many different areas. They are still engaged in the traditional commercial banking activities of taking deposits, making loans, and clearing checks (both nationally and internationally). They also offer retail customers credit cards, telephone banking, internet banking, and automatic teller machines (ATMs), and they provide payroll services to businesses.

Banks offer lines of credit to businesses and individual customers. They provide a range of services to companies when they are exporting goods and services. Companies can enter into variety of contracts with banks that are designed to hedge risks they face relating to foreign exchange, commodity prices, interest rates, and other market variables. These contracts will be discussed in later chapters. Even risks related to the weather can be hedged.

Banks do securities research and offer "buy", "sell", and "hold" recommendations on individual stocks. They offer brokerage services (discount and full service). They offer trust services where they are prepared to manage portfolios of assets for clients. They have economics departments that consider macroeconomic trends and actions likely to be taken by central banks. These departments produce forecasts on interest rates, exchange rates, commodity prices, and other variables. Banks offer a range of mutual funds and in some cases have their own hedge funds. Increasingly banks are offering insurance products.

The investment banking arm of a bank has complete freedom to underwrite securities for governments and corporations. It can provide advice to corporations on mergers and acquisitions and other topics relating to corporate finance.

To support these activities, large banks have huge trading operations. Some of a bank's trading is on exchanges, but most of it is in the over-the-counter (OTC) market. This is a huge market where traders working for financial institutions, fund managers, and large corporations agree to trades over the telephone (see Chapter 5).

How are the conflicts of interest outlined in Section 2.6 handled? There are internal barriers known as known as *Chinese walls*. These internal barriers prohibit the transfer of information from one part of the bank to another when this is not in the best interests of one or more of the bank's customers. There have been some well-publicized violations of conflict-of-interest rules by large banks. These have led to hefty fines and lawsuits. Top management has a big incentive to enforce Chinese walls. This is not only because of the fines and lawsuits. A bank's reputation is its most valuable asset. The adverse publicity associated with conflict-of-interest violations can lead to a loss of confidence in the bank and business being lost in many different areas.

Accounting

It is appropriate at this point to provide a brief discussion of how a bank calculates a profit or loss from its many diverse activities. Activities that generate fees, such as most investment banking activities, are straightforward. Accrual accounting rules similar to those that would be used by any other business apply.

For other banking activities there is an important distinction between the "banking book" and the "trading book". As its name implies, the trading book includes all the contracts the bank enters into as part of its trading operations. The value of the assets and liabilities in the trading book are *marked to market* daily. This means that the value of the book is adjusted on an almost continual basis to reflect changes in market prices. If a bank trader buys an asset for $100 on one day and the price falls to $60 the next day, the bank records an immediate loss of $40—even if it has no intention of selling the asset for some time. Sometimes it is not easy to estimate the value of a contract that has been entered into because there are no market prices for similar transactions. For example, there might be a lack of liquidity in the market or it might be the case that the transaction is a complex nonstandard derivative that does not trade sufficiently frequently for benchmark market prices to be available. Banks are nevertheless expected to come up with a market price in these circumstances. Often a model has to be assumed. The process of coming up with a "market price" is then sometimes termed *marking to model* because the banks must assume a model in determining the price. (Chapter 20 discusses model risk and accounting issues further.)

The banking book includes loans made to corporations and individuals. These are not marked to market. If a borrower is up to date on principal and interest payments on a loan, the loan is recorded in the bank's books at the principal amount owed plus

---

Business Snapshot 2.3 How to Keep Loans Performing

When a borrower is experiencing financial difficulties and is unable to make interest and principal payments as they become due, it is sometimes tempting to lend more money to the borrower so that the payments on the old loans can be kept up to date. This is an accounting game, sometimes referred to as *debt rescheduling*. It allows interest on the loans to be accrued and avoids (or at least defers) the recognition of loan losses.

In the 1970s banks in the United States and other countries lent huge amounts of money to Eastern European, Latin American and other less developed countries (LDCs). Some of the loans were made to help countries develop their infrastructure, but others were less justifiable (e.g., one was to finance the coronation of a ruler in Africa). Sometimes the money found its way into the pockets of dictators. For example, the Marcos family in the Philippines allegedly transferred billions of dollars into its own bank accounts.

In the early 1980s, many LDCs were unable to service their loans. One option for them was *debt repudiation*, but a more attractive alternative was debt rescheduling. In effect, this leads to the interest on the loans being capitalized and bank funding requirements for the loans to increase. Well-informed LDCs were aware of the desire of banks to keep their LDC loans performing so that profits looked strong. They were therefore in a strong negotiating position as their loans became 90 days overdue and banks were close to having to produce their quarterly financial statements.

In 1987, Citicorp (now Citigroup) took the lead in refusing to reschedule LDC debt and increased its loan loss reserves by $3 billion in recognition of expected losses on the debt. Other banks with large LDC exposures followed suit.

---

accrued interest. If payments due from the borrower are more than 90 days past due, the loan is usually classified as *nonperforming*. The bank does not then accrue interest on the loan when calculating its profit. When problems with the loan become more serious and it is clear that interest and principal will not be paid, the loan is classified as a loan loss.

A bank creates a reserve for loan losses. This is a charge against the income statement for an estimate of the loan losses that will be incurred. Periodically the reserve is increased or decreased. A bank can smooth out its income from one year to the next by over-estimating reserves in good years and underestimating them in bad years. Actual loan losses are charged against reserves. Occasionally, as described in Business Snapshot 2.3, a bank resorts to artificial ways of avoiding the recognition of loan losses.

The Originate-to-Distribute Model

DLC, the small hypothetical bank we looked at in Tables 2.2 to 2.4, took deposits and used them to finance loans. In recent years, banks have increasing assumed the role of originators of loans rather than keepers of loans. Typically pools of loans are packaged and tranches are sold to investors. This process is described in more detail in Chapter 16 and is referred to as the *originate-to-distribute* model for the operations of a bank.

The originate-to-distribute model has been used in the US mortgage market for some time. In order to increase the liquidity of the US mortgage market and facilitate the growth of home ownership, three government-backed agencies have been created: the Government National Mortgage Association (GNMA), or "Ginnie Mae", the Federal National Mortgage Association (FNMA), or "Fannie Mae", and the Federal Home Loan Mortgage Corporation (FHLMC), or "Freddie Mac". These buy pools of mortgages from banks and other mortgage originators, guarantee the timely repayment of interest and principal, and then package the cash flow streams and sell them to investors. The investors typically take what is known as *prepayment risk*. This is the risk that interest rates will decrease and mortgages will be paid off earlier than expected. However, they do not take any credit risk, because the mortgages are guaranteed by GNMA or FNMA or FHLMC. In 1999, FNMA and FHLMC started to guarantee subprime loans and as a result ran into serious financial difficulties.[1]

The originate-to-distribute model has—at least until the credit crunch of 2007—been used for many types of bank lending including student loans, commercial loans, commercial mortgages, residential mortgages, and credit card receivables. Except in the case of the mortgages guaranteed by the agencies mentioned above, it is usually the investors that bear the credit risk when the loans are packaged and sold.

The originate-to-distribute model is also termed *securitization* because securities are created from cash flow streams originated by the bank. It is an attractive model for banks. By securitizing its loans it gets them off the balance sheet and frees up funds to enable it to make more loans. It also frees up capital that can be used to cover risks being taken elsewhere in the bank. (This is particularly attractive if the bank feels that the capital required by regulators for a loan is too high.) A bank earns a fee for originating a loan and a further fee if it services the loan after it has been sold. As will be explained in Chapter 16, when loans with a total principal of $100 million are packaged, $75 million of top quality (AAA-rated) securities and $25 million of lower quality securities might be created.

As we will explain in Chapter 16, the originate-to-distribute model got out of control during the 2000 to 2006 period. Banks relaxed their mortgage lending standards and the credit quality of the instruments being originated declined sharply. This led to the credit crunch of 2007 and a period during which the originate-to-distribute model could not be used by banks because investors lost confidence in the securities that had been created.

2.8 THE RISKS FACING BANKS

A bank's operations give rise to many risks. Much of the rest of this book is devoted to considering these risks in detail.

Central bank regulators require banks to hold sufficient capital for the risks they are bearing. In 1987, international standards were developed for the determination of this capital. These standards and the way they have evolved since 1987 are discussed in Chapter 11. The Basel II rules, which were implemented in 2007, assign capital for each of three types of risk: credit risk, market risk, and operational risk. The total required

---

[1] GNMA has always been government owned, whereas FNMA and FHLMC used to be private corporations with shareholders. As a result of their financial difficulties in 2008, the US government had to step in and assume complete control of FNMA and FHLMC.

capital is the capital for credit risk plus the capital for market risk plus the capital for operational risk.

Credit risk is the risk that counterparties in loan transactions and derivatives transactions will default. This has traditionally been the greatest risk facing a bank and is usually the one for which the most regulatory capital is required. Market risk arises primarily from the bank's trading operations. It is the risk relating to the possibility that instruments in the bank's trading book will decline in value. Operational risk is the risk that losses are made because internal systems fail to work as intended or because of external events. The time horizon for considering losses from credit risks and operational risks is one year, whereas the time horizon for considering losses from market risks is ten days. The objective of regulators is to keep the total capital of a bank sufficiently high that the chance of a bank failure is very low. For example, in the case of credit risk and operational risk, the capital is chosen so that the chance of unexpected losses exceeding the capital in a year is 0.1%.

In addition to calculating regulatory capital, most large banks have systems in place for calculating what is termed *economic capital* (see Chapter 21). This is the capital that the bank, using its own models rather than those prescribed by regulators, thinks it needs. Economic capital is often less than regulatory capital. However, banks have no choice but to maintain their capital above the regulatory capital level. The form the capital can take (equity, subordinated debt, etc.) is prescribed by regulators. To avoid having to raise capital at short notice, banks try to keep their capital amounts well above the regulatory minimum.

When banks announced huge losses on their subprime mortgage portfolios in 2007 and 2008, many had to raise new equity capital in a hurry. *Sovereign wealth funds*, which are investment funds controlled by the government of a country, have provided some of this capital. For example, Citigroup, which reported losses in the region of $40 billion, raised $7.5 billion in equity from the Abu Dhabi Investment Authority in November 2007 and $14.5 billion from investors that included the governments of Singapore and Kuwait in January 2008. Later, Citigroup and many other banks required capital injections from their own governments to survive.

SUMMARY

Banks are complex global organizations engaged in many different types of activity. The traditional separation of commercial and investment banking has largely disappeared. Today, the world's large banks are engaged in taking deposits, making loans, underwriting securities, trading, providing brokerage services, providing fiduciary services, advising on a range of corporate finance issues, offering mutual funds, providing services to hedge funds, and so on. There are potential conflicts of interest and banks develop internal rules to avoid them. It is important that senior managers are vigilant in ensuring that employees obey these rules. The cost in terms of reputation, lawsuits, and fines from inappropriate behavior where one client (or the bank) is advantaged at the expense of another client can be very large.

There are now international agreements on the regulation of banks. This means that the capital banks are required to keep for the risks they are bearing does not vary too much from one country to another. Many countries have guaranty programs that protect small depositors from losses arising from bank failures. This has the effect of maintaining confidence in the banking system and avoiding mass withdrawals of deposits when there is negative news (or perhaps just a rumor) about problems faced by a particular bank.

FURTHER READING

Saunders, A., and M. M. Cornett, *Financial Institutions Management: A Risk Management Approach*, 6th edn. McGraw-Hill, 2008.

PRACTICE QUESTIONS AND PROBLEMS (Answers at the End of the Book)

2.1. How did concentration in the US banking system change between 1984 and 2007?

2.2. What government policies led to the large number of small community banks in the US?

2.3. What risks does a bank take if it funds long-term loans with short-term deposits?

2.4. Suppose that an out-of-control trader working for DLC bank (see Tables 2.2 and 2.3) loses $7 million trading foreign exchange. What do you think would happen?

2.5. What is meant by net interest income?

2.6. Which items on the income statement of DLC bank in Section 2.2 are most likely to be affected by (a) credit risk, (b) market risk, and (c) operational risk

2.7. Explain the terms "private placement" and "public offering"? What is the difference between "best efforts" and "firm commitment" for a public offering.

2.8. The bidders in a Dutch auction are as follows:

Bidder	Number of shares	Price
A	20,000	$100.00
B	30,000	$93.00
C	50,000	$110.00
D	70,000	$88.00
E	60,000	$80.00
F	10,000	$105.00
G	90,000	$70.00
H	80,000	$125.00

The number of shares being auctioned is 150,000. What is the price paid by investors? How many shares does each investor receive?

2.9. What is the attraction of a Dutch auction over the normal procedure for an IPO. In what ways was Google's IPO different from a standard Dutch auction?

2.10. Management sometimes argue that poison pills are in the best interests of shareholders because they enable management to extract a higher price from would-be acquirers. Discuss this argument.

2.11. Give three examples of the conflicts of interest in a large bank. How are conflicts of interest handled?

2.12. A loan for $10 million that pays 8% interest is classified as nonperforming. What is the impact of this on the income statement?

2.13. Explain how the loan loss provision account works.

2.14. What is the originate-to-distribute model? Why was it not used in the period following July 2007?

FURTHER QUESTIONS

2.15. Regulators calculate that DLC bank (see Section 2.2) will report a profit that is normally distributed with a mean of $0.6 million and a standard deviation of $2.0 million. How much equity capital in addition to that in Table 2.2 should regulators require for there to be a 99.9% chance of the capital not being wiped out by losses?

2.16. Explain the moral hazard problems with deposit insurance. How can they be overcome?

2.17. The bidders in a Dutch auction are as follows:

Bidder	Number of shares	Price
A	60,000	$50.00
B	20,000	$80.00
C	30,000	$55.00
D	40,000	$38.00
E	40,000	$42.00
F	40,000	$42.00
G	50,000	$35.00
H	50,000	$60.00

The number of share being auctioned is 210,000. What is the price paid by investors? How many shares does each investor receive?

2.18. An investment bank has been asked to underwrite an issue of 10 million shares by a company. It is trying to decide between a firm commitment where it buys the shares for $10 per share and a best efforts where it charges a fee of 20 cents for each share sold. Explain the pros and cons of the two alternatives.

CHAPTER 3

Insurance
Companies and
Pension Plans

The role of insurance companies is to provide protection against adverse events. The company or individual seeking protection is referred to as the *policyholder*. The policyholder makes regular payments, known as *premiums*, and receives payments from the insurance companies if certain specified events occur. Insurance is usually classified as *life* and *nonlife*, with health insurance often being considered to be a separate category. Nonlife insurance is also referred to as *property–casualty* insurance and this is the terminology we will use here.

A life insurance contract typically lasts a long time and provides payments to the policyholder that depend on when he or she dies. A property–casualty insurance contract typically lasts one year (although it may be renewed) and provides compensation for losses from accidents, fire, theft, and so on.

Insurance has existed for many years. As long ago as 200 BC, there was a form of life insurance in ancient Greece where an individual could make a lump sum payment (the amount dependent on his or her age) and obtain a monthly income for life. The Romans had a different sort of life insurance where an individual could purchase a contract that would provide a payment to relatives on his or her death. In ancient China, a form of property–casualty insurance existed between merchants where if the ship of one merchant sank the rest of the merchants would provide compensation.

A pension plan is a form of insurance arranged by a company for its employees. It is designed to provide the employees with income for the rest of their lives once they have retired. Typically both the company and its employees make regular monthly contributions to the plan and the funds in the plan are invested to provide income for current and futures retirees.

This chapter describes how the contracts offered by insurance companies work. It explains the risks that insurance companies face and the way they are regulated. It also discusses key issues associated with pension plans.

3.1 LIFE INSURANCE

In life insurance contracts the payments to the policyholder depend—at least to some extent—on when the policyholder dies. Outside the United States, the term *life*

39

assurance is often used to describe a contract where the event being insured against is certain to happen at some future time (e.g., a contract that will pay $100,000 on the policyholder's death). Life insurance is used to describe a contract where the event being insured against may never happen (e.g., a contract that provides a payoff in the event of the accidental death of the policyholder).[1] In the United States, all types of life policies are referred to as life insurance and this is the terminology that will be adopted here.

There are many different types of life insurance products. The products available vary from country to country. We will now describe some of the more common ones.

Term Life Insurance

Term life insurance (sometimes referred to as *temporary life insurance*) lasts a predetermined number of years. If the policyholder dies during the life of the policy, the insurance company makes a payment to the specified beneficiaries equal to the face amount of the policy. If the policyholder does not die during the term of the policy, no payments are made by the insurance company. The policyholder is required to make regular monthly or annual premium payments to the insurance company for the life of the policy or until the policyholder's death (whichever is earlier). The face amount of the policy typically stays the same or declines with the passage of time. The premium payments typically stay the same or increase with the passage of time. One type of policy where the premium payments increase is an *annual renewable term* policy. In this the insurance company guarantees to renew the policy from one year to the next at a rate reflecting the policyholder's age without regard to the policyholder's health.

A common reason for term life insurance is a mortgage. For example, a person aged 35 with a 25-year mortgage might choose to buy 25-year term insurance (with a declining face amount) to provide dependents with the funds to pay off the mortgage in the event of his or her death.

Whole Life Insurance

Whole life insurance (sometimes referred to as *permanent life insurance*) provides protection over the whole life of the policyholder. The policyholder is required to make regular monthly or annual payments until his or her death. The face value of the policy is then paid to the designated beneficiary. In the case of term life insurance there is no certainty that there will be a payout, but in the case of whole life insurance there is certain to be a payout providing the policyholder continues to make the agreed premium payments. The only uncertainty is when the payout will occur. Not surprisingly, whole life insurance requires considerably higher premiums than term life insurance policies. Usually, the payments and the face value of the policy both remain constant through time.

Policyholders can often redeem (surrender) whole life policies early or use the policies as collateral for loans. When a policyholder wants to redeem a whole life policy early, it is sometimes the case that an investor will buy the policy from the policyholder for more than the surrender value offered by the insurance company. The investor will then

---

[1] In theory, for a contract to be referred to as life assurance, it is the event being insured against that must be certain to occur. It does not need to be the case that a payout is certain. Thus a policy that pays out if the policyholder dies in the next 10 years is life assurance. In practice, this distinction is sometimes blurred.

Figure 3.1 Cost of life insurance per year compared with the annual premium in a whole life contract

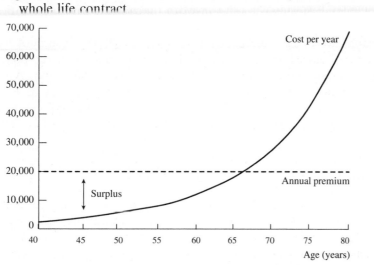

make the premium payments and collect the face value from the insurance company when the policyholder dies.

The annual premium for a year can be compared with the cost of providing term life insurance for that year. Consider a man who buys a $1 million whole life policy at the age of 40. Suppose that the premium is $20,000 per year. As we will see later, the probability of a male aged 40 dying within one year is about 0.0024 suggesting that a fair premium for one-year insurance is about $2,400. This means that there is a *surplus premium* of $17,600 available for investment from the first year's premium. The probability of a man aged 41 dying in one year is about 0.0026, suggesting that a fair premium for insurance during the second year is $2,600. This means that there is a $17,400 surplus premium available for investment from the second year's premium. The cost of a one-year policy continues to rise as the individual gets older, so that at some stage it is greater than the annual premium. In our example, this would have happened by the 30th year because the probability of a man aged 70 dying in one year is 0.0275. (A fair premium for the 30th year is $27,500, which is more than the $20,000 received.) The situation is shown in Figure 3.1. In the early years the insurance company invests the surplus premiums to make up the premium shortfall later on. Figure 3.1 shows that there is a savings element to whole life insurance. In the early years, the part of the premium not needed to cover the risk of a payout is invested on behalf of the policyholder by the insurance company.

There are tax advantages associated with life insurance policies in many jurisdictions. If the policyholder invested the surplus premiums, tax would be payable on the income as it was earned. But, when the surplus premiums are invested within the insurance policy, tax is payable only when the policyholder dies and cash is received by the policyholder's beneficiaries.[2] Life insurance policies therefore lead to a deferral of taxes. This is beneficial to the policyholder. The later the taxes are paid, the lower their present value.

---

[2] If the policyholder dies early, very little income has been earned from surpluses and very little tax is payable by the policyholder's beneficiaries. If the policyholder lives for a long time, a much larger part of the cash received from the insurance company is taxable.

Variable Life Insurance

Given that a whole life insurance policy involves funds being invested for the policy-holder, a natural development is to allow the policyholder to specify how the funds are invested. Variable life (VL) insurance is a form of whole life insurance where the surplus premiums discussed above are invested in a fund chosen by the policyholder. This could be an equity fund, a bond fund, or a money market fund. A minimum guaranteed payout on death is usually specified, but the payout can be more if the fund does well. Income earned from the investments can be applied toward the premiums, if desired. The policyholder can usually switch from one fund to another at any time.

Universal Life Insurance

Universal life (UL) insurance is also a form of whole life insurance. The policyholder can reduce the premium down to a specified minimum without the policy lapsing. The surplus premiums discussed above are invested by the insurance company in fixed income products such as bonds, mortgages, and money market instruments. The insurance company guarantees a certain minimum return, say 4%, on these funds. The policyholder can choose between two options. Under the first option, a fixed benefit is paid on death; under the second, the policyholder's beneficiaries receive more than the fixed benefit if the investment return is greater than the guaranteed minimum. Needless to say, premiums are lower for the first option.

Variable–Universal Life Insurance

Variable–universal life (VUL) insurance blends the features found in variable life insurance and universal life insurance. The policyholder can choose between a number of alternatives for the investment of surplus premiums. The insurance company guarantees a certain minimum death benefit and interest on the investments can be applied toward premiums. Premiums can be reduced down to a specified minimum without the policy lapsing.

Endowment Life Insurance

Endowment life insurance lasts for a specified period and pays a lump sum either when the policyholder dies or at the end of the period, whichever is first. There are many different types of endowment life insurance contracts. The amount that is paid out can be specified in advance as the same regardless of whether the policyholder dies or survives to the end of the policy. Sometimes the payout is also made if the policyholder has a critical illness. In a *with-profits* endowment life insurance policy, the insurance company declares periodic bonuses that depend on the performance of the insurance company's investments. These bonuses accumulate to increase the amount paid out to the policyholder assuming the policyholder lives beyond the end of the life of policy. In a unit-linked endowment, the amount paid out at maturity depends on the performance of a fund chosen by the policyholder. A *pure endowment* policy has the property that a payout occurs only if the policyholder survives to the end of the life of the policy.

Group Life Insurance

Group life insurance covers many people under a single policy. It is often purchased by a company for its employees. The policy may be *contributory* where the premium payments are shared by the employer and employee or *noncontributory* where the employer pays the whole of the cost. There are economies of scale in group life insurance. The selling and administration costs are lower. Whereas an individual is usually required to undergo medical tests when purchasing life insurance in the usual way, this may not be necessary for group life insurance. The insurance company knows that it will be taking on some better-than-average risks and some worse-than-average risks.

3.2   ANNUITY CONTRACTS

Many life insurance companies also offer annuity contracts. Whereas a life insurance contract has the effect of converting regular payments into a lump sum, an annuity contract has the opposite effect: that of converting a lump sum into regular payments. In a typical arrangement the policyholder makes a lump sum payment to the insurance company and the insurance company agrees to provide the policyholder with an annuity that starts at a particular date and lasts for the rest of the policyholder's life. In a *fixed annuity* contract the payments to be received by the policyholder every month are specified in advance. In some instances the annuity starts immediately after the lump sum payment by the policyholder. More usually, the lump sum payment is made by the policyholder several years ahead of the time when the annuity is to start and the insurance company invests the funds to create the annuity. (This is referred to as a *deferred annuity*.) Instead of a lump sum, the policyholder sometimes saves for the annuity by making regular monthly, quarterly, or annual payments to the insurance company. At a specified futures date (e.g., when the policyholder is 65 years old) the funds that have accumulated are converted to a lifetime annuity.

Variable Annuity Contracts

A *variable annuity* (VA) contract is a deferred annuity contract where the insurance company invests in equities, bonds, or other instruments chosen by the policyholder and the annual payments received by the policyholder are not fixed in advance. Typically they depend on the performance of the investments and the level of interest rates at the time the annuity starts.

As with life insurance, there can be tax deferral advantages to the policyholder because taxes usually have to be paid only when the annuity income is received. The value to which the funds invested by the insurance company on behalf of the policyholder have grown is referred to as the *accumulated value*. Funds can usually be withdrawn early, but there are liable to be penalties. In other words, the surrender value of an annuity contract is typically less than the accumulated value. This is because the insurance company has to recover selling and administration costs. Policies sometimes allow *penalty-free withdrawals*, where a certain percentage of the accumulated value or a certain percentage of the original investment can be withdrawn in a year without penalty. In the event that the policyholder dies before the start of the annuity

Business Snapshot 3.1   Equitable Life

Equitable Life was a British life insurance company founded in 1762 that at its peak had 1.5 million policyholders. Starting in the 1950s, Equitable Life sold annuity products where it guaranteed that the interest rate used to calculate the size of the annuity payments would be above a certain level. (This is known as a Guaranteed Annuity Option, GAO.) The guaranteed interest rate was gradually increased in response to competitive pressures and increasing interest rates. Toward the end of 1993, interest rates started to fall. Also, life expectancies were rising so that the insurance companies had to make increasingly high provisions for future payouts on contracts. Equitable Life did not take action. Instead, it grew by selling new products. In 2000, it was forced to close its doors to new business. A report issued by Ann Abraham in July 2008 was highly critical of regulators and urged compensation for policyholders.

An interesting aside to this is that regulators did at one point urge insurance companies that offered GAOs to hedge their exposures to an interest rate decline. As a result many insurance companies scrambled to enter into contracts with banks that paid off if long-term interest rates declined. The banks in turn hedged their risk by buying instruments such as bonds that increased in price when rates fell. This was done on such a massive scale that the extra demand for bonds caused long-term interest rates in the UK to decline sharply (increasing losses for insurance companies on the unhedged part of their exposures). This shows that, when large numbers of different companies have similar exposures, problems are created if they all decide to hedge at the same time. There are not likely to be enough investors willing to take on their risks without market prices changing.

(and sometimes in other circumstances such as when the policyholder is admitted to a nursing home), the full accumulated value can be withdrawn without penalty.

Some deferred annuity contracts in the United States have embedded options. The accumulated value is sometimes calculated so that it tracks a particular equity index such as the S&P 500. Lower and upper limits are specified. If the growth in the index in a year is less than the lower limit, the accumulated value grows at the lower limit rate; if it is greater than the upper limit, the accumulated value grows at the upper limit rate; otherwise it grows at the same rate as the S&P 500. Suppose that the lower limit is 2% and the upper limit is 8%. The policyholder is assured that the accumulated value will always grow by at least 2% in a year, but index growth rates in excess of 8% are given up. In these types of arrangement, the policyholder is typically not compensated for dividends that would be received from an investment in the stocks underlying the index, and the insurance company may be able to change parameters such as the lower and upper limit from one year to the next. These types of contract appeal to investors who want an exposure to the equity market but are reluctant to risk a decline in their accumulated value. Sometimes, the way the accumulated value grows from one year to the next is a quite complicated function of the performance of the index during the year.

In the United Kingdom, the annuity contracts offered by insurance companies used to guarantee a minimum level for the interest rate used for the calculation of the size of the annuity payments. Many insurance companies regarded this guarantee—an interest rate option granted to the policyholder—as a necessary marketing cost and did not calculate the cost of the option or hedge their risks. As interest rates declined and life expectancies increased, many insurance companies found themselves in financial difficulties, and, as described in Business Snapshot 3.1, one of them went bankrupt.

3.3   MORTALITY TABLES

Mortality tables are the key to valuing life insurance contracts. Table 3.1 shows an extract from the mortality rates estimated by the US Department of Social Security for 2004. To understand the table, consider the row corresponding to age 31. The second column shows that the probability of a man aged 31 dying within the next year is 0.001367 (or 0.1367%). The third column shows that the probability of a man surviving to age 31 is 0.97015 (or 97.015%). The fourth column shows that a man aged 31 has a remaining life expectancy of 45.64 years. This means that, on average, he will live to age 76.64. The remaining three columns show similar statistics for a woman. The probability of a 31-year-old woman dying within one year is 0.000659 (0.0659%), the probability of a woman surviving to age 31 is 0.98381 (98.381%), and the remaining life expectancy for a 31-year-old woman is 50.06 years.

The full table shows that the probability of death during the following year is a decreasing function of age for the first 10 years of life and then starts to increase. Mortality statistics for women are a little more favorable than for men. If a man is lucky enough to reach age 90, the probability of death in the next year is 18.2%. The full table shows that this probability is 37.0% at age 100, and it is 60.3% at age 110. For women, the corresponding probabilities are 14.1%, 31.6%, and 56.6%, respectively.

Some numbers in the table can be calculated from others. The third column of the table shows that the probability of a man surviving to 90 is 0.13988. The probability of the man surviving to 91 is 0.11445. It follows that the probability of a man dying between his 90th and 91st birthday is $0.13988 - 0.11445 = 0.02543$. Conditional on a man reaching the age of 90, the probability that he will die in the course of the following year is therefore

$$\frac{0.02543}{0.13988} = 0.1818$$

This is consistent with the number given in the second column of the table.

The probability of a man aged 90 dying in the second year (between ages 91 and 92) is the probability that he does not die in the first year multiplied by the probability that he does die in the second year. From the numbers in the second column of the table, this is

$$(1 - 0.181789) \times 0.199019 = 0.16284$$

Similarly, the probability that he dies in the third year (between ages 92 and 93) is

$$(1 - 0.181789) \times (1 - 0.199019) \times 0.217396 = 0.14247$$

These types of calculation enable the fourth column of the table to be calculated from the second column.

Table 3.1 Mortality table. (*Source*: US Department of Social Security, www.ssa.gov/OACT/STATS/table4c6.html.

Age (years)	Male			Female		
	Prob. death within 1 year	Prob. survival	Life expectancy	Prob. death within 1 year	Prob. survival	Life expectancy
0	0.007474	1.00000	74.83	0.006091	1.00000	79.96
1	0.000513	0.99253	74.40	0.000461	0.99391	79.45
2	0.000328	0.99202	73.43	0.000268	0.99345	78.49
3	0.000247	0.99169	72.46	0.000195	0.99318	77.51
⋮	⋮	⋮	⋮	⋮	⋮	⋮
30	0.001352	0.97146	46.58	0.000621	0.98442	51.05
31	0.001367	0.97015	45.64	0.000659	0.98381	50.08
32	0.001404	0.96882	44.70	0.000705	0.98316	49.11
33	0.001467	0.96746	43.76	0.000761	0.98247	48.14
⋮	⋮	⋮	⋮	⋮	⋮	⋮
40	0.002420	0.95526	37.28	0.001439	0.97559	41.46
41	0.002629	0.95294	36.36	0.001581	0.97418	40.52
42	0.002863	0.95044	35.46	0.001732	0.97264	39.58
43	0.003127	0.94772	34.56	0.001891	0.97096	38.65
⋮	⋮	⋮	⋮	⋮	⋮	⋮
50	0.005657	0.92077	28.46	0.003198	0.95449	32.25
51	0.006134	0.91557	27.62	0.003431	0.95144	31.35
52	0.006595	0.90995	26.79	0.003696	0.94818	30.46
53	0.007027	0.90395	25.96	0.003998	0.94467	29.57
⋮	⋮	⋮	⋮	⋮	⋮	⋮
60	0.011858	0.85045	20.36	0.007445	0.91048	23.53
61	0.012966	0.84037	19.60	0.008187	0.90370	22.71
62	0.014123	0.82947	18.85	0.008959	0.89630	21.89
63	0.015312	0.81776	18.11	0.009747	0.88827	21.08
⋮	⋮	⋮	⋮	⋮	⋮	⋮
70	0.027533	0.71055	13.27	0.018406	0.81136	15.72
71	0.030131	0.69098	12.64	0.020342	0.79643	15.01
72	0.032978	0.67016	12.01	0.022346	0.78023	14.31
73	0.036086	0.64806	11.41	0.024382	0.76279	13.62
⋮	⋮	⋮	⋮	⋮	⋮	⋮
80	0.068836	0.45747	7.62	0.047769	0.60405	9.22
81	0.075724	0.42598	7.15	0.053190	0.57520	8.65
82	0.083466	0.39372	6.70	0.059279	0.54460	8.11
83	0.092144	0.36086	6.26	0.066080	0.51232	7.59
⋮	⋮	⋮	⋮	⋮	⋮	⋮
90	0.181789	0.13988	3.80	0.140793	0.25660	4.60
91	0.199019	0.11445	3.54	0.155906	0.22047	4.28
92	0.217396	0.09167	3.29	0.172147	0.18610	3.97
93	0.236906	0.07174	3.06	0.189496	0.15406	3.70

Example 3.1

Assume that interest rates for all maturities are 4% and premiums are paid once a year at the beginning of the year. What is an insurance company's break-even premium for $100,000 of term life insurance for a man of average health aged 90? If the term insurance lasts one year, the expected payout is $0.181789 \times 100,000$, or $18,179. Assume that the payout occurs halfway through the year. (This is likely to be approximately true on average.) The premium is $18,179 discounted for six months at 4%. Assuming semiannual compounding, this is $18,179/1.02$, or $17,822.

Suppose next that the term insurance lasts two years. In this case the present value of expected payouts in the first year is $17,822 as before. The probability that the policyholder dies during the second year is $(1 - 0.181789) \times 0.199019 = 0.16284$, so that there is also an expected payout of $0.16284 \times 100,000$, or $16,284, during the second year. Assuming this happens at 18 months, the present value of the payout is $16,284/1.02^3$, or $15,345. The total present value of the payout is $17,822 + 15,345$, or $34,106.

Consider next the premium payments. We are certain that the first premium will be paid. The probability of the second premium payment being made at the beginning of the second year is the probability that the man does not die during the first year. This is $1 - 0.181789 = 0.818211$. When the premium is X dollars per year, the present value of the premium payments is

$$X + \frac{0.818211 \times X}{(1.02)^2} = 1.786439X$$

The break-even annual premium is given by the value of X that equates the present value of the expected premium payments to the present value of the expected payout. This is the value of X that solves

$$1.786439X = 34,106$$

or $X = 19,092$. The break-even premium payment is therefore $19,092.

3.4 LONGEVITY AND MORTALITY RISK

Longevity risk is the risk that advances in medical sciences and lifestyle changes will lead to people living longer. Increases in longevity adversely affect the profitability of most types of annuity contracts (because the annuity has to be paid for longer), but increases the profitability of most life insurance contracts (because the final payout is either delayed or, in the case of term insurance, less likely to happen). Life expectancy has been steadily increasing in most parts of the world. Average life expectancy of a child born in the United States in 2004 is estimated to be about 20 years higher than for a child born in 1929. Life expectancy varies from country to country.

Mortality risk is the risk that wars, epidemics such as AIDS, or pandemics such as Spanish flu will lead to people living less long than expected. This adversely affects the payouts on most types of life insurance contracts (because the insured amount has to be paid earlier than expected), but should increase the profitability of annuity contracts (because the annuity is not paid out for as long). In calculating the impact of mortality risk, it is important to consider the age groups within the population that are likely to be most affected by a particular event.

To some extent, the longevity and mortality risks in the annuity business of a life insurance company offset those in its regular life insurance contracts. Actuaries must carefully assess the insurance company's exposure under different scenarios. Longevity risk can be hedged with reinsurance contracts and with longevity derivatives. We now discuss longevity derivatives. Reinsurance is discussed later in this chapter.

Longevity Derivatives

A longevity derivative is designed to provide insurance companies and pension funds with compensation for the increased payments they have to make if individuals live longer than expected. A typical contract is a *longevity bond*, also known as a *survivor bond*, which first traded in the late 1990s. A population group is defined and the coupon on the bond at any given time is defined as being proportional to the number of individuals in the population that are still alive. Insurance companies and pension plans should find longevity derivatives attractive because they provide a hedge against the risks they face. But who will sell such bonds? The answer is some speculators find the bonds attractive because they have very little systematic risk (see Section 1.3). The bond payments depend on how long people live and this is largely uncorrelated with returns from the market.

3.5   PROPERTY–CASUALTY INSURANCE

Property–casualty insurance can be subdivided into property insurance and casualty insurance. Property insurance provides protection against loss of or damage to property (from fire, theft, water damage, etc.). Casualty insurance provides protection against legal liability exposures (from, for example, injuries caused to third parties). Casualty insurance might more accurately be referred to as liability insurance. Sometimes both types of insurance are included in a single policy. For example, a homeowner might buy insurance that provides protection against various types of loss, such as property damage and theft, as well as legal liabilities if others are injured while on the property. Similarly, car insurance typically provides protection against theft of, or damage to, one's own vehicle, as well as protection against claims brought by others.

Typically property–casualty policies are renewed from year to year and the insurance company will increase the premium if its assessment of the expected payout increases. (This is in contrast to life insurance, where premiums are typically set in advance for many years.) Because property–casualty insurance companies get involved in many different types of insurance there is some natural risk diversification. For some risks, the "law of large numbers" applies. For example, if an insurance company has written policies protecting 250,000 homeowners against losses from theft and fire damage, the expected payout can be predicted reasonably accurately. This is because the policies provide protection against a large number of (almost) independent events. (Of course, there are liable to be trends in the number of losses and the average size of a loss and the insurance company should keep track of these trends in determining year-to-year changes in the premiums.)

Property damage arising from natural disasters such as hurricanes give rise to payouts for an insurance company that are much less easy to predict. For example, Hurricane Katrina in the United States in the summer of 2005 and the a heavy storm in north-west Europe in January 2007 that measured 12 on the Beaufort scale proved to be very expensive. These are termed *catastrophic risks*. The problem with them is that the claims made by different policyholders are not independent. Either a hurricane happens in a year and the insurance company has to deal with a large number of claims for hurricane-related damage or there is no hurricane in the year and therefore no claims are made. Most large insurers have models based on geographical, seismographical, and meteorological information to estimate the probabilities of catastrophes and the losses resulting therefrom. This provides a basis for setting premiums, but it does not alter the "all-or-nothing" nature of these risks for insurance companies.

Liability insurance, like catastrophe insurance, gives rise to total payouts that vary from year to year and are difficult to predict. For example, claims arising from asbestos-related damages to workers' health have proved very expensive for insurance companies in the United States. A feature of liability insurance is what is known as *long-tail risk*. This is the possibility of claims being made several years after the insured period is over. In the case of asbestos, for example, the health risks were not realized until some time after exposure. As a result, the claims, when they were made, were under policies that had been in force several years previously. This creates a complication for actuaries and accountants. They cannot close the books soon after the end of each year and calculate a profit or loss. They must allow for the cost of claims that have not yet been made, but may be made some time in the future.

Claims made under property–casualty policies can be characterized, from the perspective of the insurance company, by their frequency and their severity. A general principle is that the total cost per year of high-frequency low-severity claims (such as claims arising from theft) is relatively easy to predict. By contrast, the total cost per year of low-frequency high-severity claims (such as those arising from catastrophic risks and liability insurance) are much less easy to predict.

CAT Bonds

The derivatives market has come up with a number of products for hedging catastrophic risk. The most popular is a CAT bond. This is a bond issued by a subsidiary of an insurance company that pays a higher-than-normal interest rate. In exchange for the extra interest, the holder of the bond agrees to cover payouts on a particular type of catastrophic risk that are in a certain range. Depending on the terms of the CAT bond, the interest or principal (or both) can be used to meet claims.

Suppose an insurance company has a $70 million exposure to California earthquake losses and wants protection for losses over $40 million. The insurance company could issue CAT bonds with a total principal of $30 million. In the event that the insurance company's California earthquake losses exceeded $40 million, bondholders would lose some or all of their principal. As an alternative, the insurance company could cover the same losses by making a much bigger bond issue where only the bondholders' interest is at risk. Yet another alternative is to make three separate bond issues covering losses in the range $40 to $50 million, $50 to $60 million, and $60 to $70 million, respectively. CAT bonds typically give a high probability of an above-normal rate of interest and a low-probability of a high loss.

Why would investors be interested in such instruments? The answer is that the return on CAT bonds, like the longevity bonds considered earlier, have no statistically significant correlations with market returns.[3] CAT bonds are therefore an attractive addition to an investor's portfolio. Their total risk can be completely diversified away in a large portfolio. If a CAT bond's expected return is greater than the risk-free interest rate (and typically it is), it has the potential to improve risk–return trade-offs.

Ratios Calculated by Property–Casualty Insurers

Insurance companies calculate a *loss ratio* for different types of insurance. This is the ratio of payouts made to premiums earned in a year. Loss ratios are typically in the 60% to 80% range. Statistics published by A. M. Best show that loss ratios in the United States have tended to increase through time. The *expense ratio* for an insurance company is the ratio of expenses to premiums earned in a year. The two major sources of expenses are loss adjustment expenses and selling expenses. Loss adjustment expenses are those expenses related to determining the validity of a claim and how much the policyholder should be paid. Selling expenses include the commissions paid to brokers and other expenses concerned with the acquisition of business. Expense ratios in the United States are typically in the 25–30% range and have tended to decrease through time.

The *combined ratio* is the sum of the loss ratio and the expense ratio. Suppose that for a particular category of policies in a particular year the loss ratio is 75% and the expense ratio is 30%. The combined ratio is then 105%. Sometimes a small dividend is paid to policyholders. Suppose that this is 1% of premiums. When this is taken into account we obtain what is referred to as the *combined ratio after dividends*. This is 106% in our example. This number suggests that the insurance company has lost 6% before tax on the policies being considered. In fact, this may not be the case. Premiums are generally paid by policyholders at the beginning of a year and payouts on claims are made during the year, or after the end of the year. The insurance company is therefore able to earn interest on the premiums during the time that elapses between the receipt of premiums and payouts. Suppose that, in our example, investment income is 9% of premiums received. When the investment income is taken into account, a ratio of $106 - 9 = 97\%$ is obtained. This is referred to as the *operating ratio*. Table 3.2 summarizes the example.

3.6 HEALTH INSURANCE

Health insurance has some of the attributes of property–casualty insurance and some of the attributes of life insurance. It is sometimes considered to be a totally separate category of insurance. The extent to which health care is provided by the government varies from country to country. In the United States publicly funded health care is limited, and health insurance is therefore an important consideration for most people. About 16% of the population have no health care coverage. Canada is at the other extreme: nearly all health care needs are provided by a publicly funded system, and doctors are not permitted to offer most services privately. The main role of health

---

[3] See R. H. Litzenberger, D. R. Beaglehole, and C. E. Reynolds, "Assessing Catastrophe Reinsurance-Linked Securities as a New Asset Class," *Journal of Portfolio Management*, Winter 1996: 76–86.

Table 3.2 Example showing calculation of operating ratio for a property–casualty insurance company.

Loss ratio	75%
Expense ratio	30%
Combined ratio	105%
Dividends	1%
Combined ratio after dividends	106%
Investment income	(9%)
Operating ratio	97%

insurance in Canada is to cover prescription costs and dental care, which are not funded publicly. In most other countries there is a mixture of public and private health care. The United Kingdom, for example, has a publicly funded health care system, but some individuals buy insurance to have access to a private system that operates side by side with the public system. (The main advantage of private health insurance is a reduction in waiting times for routine elective surgery.)

As with other forms of insurance, the policyholder makes regular premium payments and payouts are triggered by events. In the case of health insurance, examples of such events might be the policyholder's need for an examination by a doctor, or for prescription medication, or for treatment at a hospital. Typically the premiums increase because of overall increases in the costs of providing health care. However, they usually cannot increase because the health of the policyholder deteriorates. It is interesting to compare health insurance with auto insurance and life insurance in this respect. An auto insurance premium can increase (and usually does) if the policyholder's driving record indicates that expected payouts have increased and if the costs of repairs to automobiles have increased. Life insurance premiums do not increase—even if the policyholder is diagnosed with a health problem that significantly reduces life expectancy. Health insurance premiums are like life insurance premiums in that changes to the insurance company's assessment of the risk of a payout do not lead to an increase in premiums. However, it is like auto insurance in that increases in the overall costs of meeting claims do lead to premium increases.

Of course, when a policy is first issued, an insurance company does its best to determine the risks it is taking on. In the case of life insurance, questions concerning the policyholders health have to be answered, pre-existing medical conditions have to be declared, and physical examinations may be required. In the case of auto insurance, the policyholders driving record is investigated. In both of these cases, insurance can be refused. In the case of health insurance, legislation sometimes determines the circumstances under which insurance can be refused. For example, an insurance company in the United States may be able to refuse an application for health insurance based on a pre-existing medical condition diagnosed in the last year, but not one diagnosed earlier.

Health insurance is often provided by the *group health insurance plans* of employers. These plans typically cover the employee and the employee's family. Usually, the employee cannot be refused insurance because of pre-existing medical conditions and the cost of the health insurance is often split between the employer and employee. The expenses that are covered vary from plan to plan. In the United States, most plans cover basic medical needs such as medical check-ups, physicals, treatments for common disorders, surgery, and hospital stays. Pregnancy costs may or may not be covered. Procedures such as cosmetic surgery are usually not covered.

3.7 MORAL HAZARD AND ADVERSE SELECTION

We now consider two key risks facing insurance companies: moral hazard and adverse selection.

Moral Hazard

Moral hazard is the risk that the existence of insurance will cause the policyholder to behave differently than he or she would without the insurance. This different behavior increases the risks and the expected payouts of the insurance company. Examples of moral hazard are:

1. A car owner buys insurance to protect against the car being stolen. As a result of the insurance, he or she becomes less likely to lock the car.

2. An individual purchases health insurance. As a result of the existence of the policy, more health care is demanded than previously.

3. A bank takes more risks as a result of a government-sponsored deposit insurance plan because it knows that it is less likely to lose depositors. (This was discussed in Section 2.3.)

Moral hazard is not a big problem in life insurance. Insurance companies have traditionally dealt with moral hazard in property–casualty and health insurance in a number of ways. Typically there is a *deductible*. This means that the policyholder is responsible for bearing the first part of any loss. Sometimes there is a *co-insurance provision* in a policy. The insurance company then pays a predetermined percentage (less than 100%) of losses in excess of the deductible. In addition there is nearly always a *policy limit* (i.e., an upper limit to the payout). The effect of these provisions is to align the interests of the policyholder more closely with those of the insurance company.

Adverse Selection

Adverse selection is the phrase used to describe the problems an insurance company has when it cannot distinguish between good and bad risks. It offers the same price to everyone and inadvertently attracts more of the bad risks. If an insurance company is not able to distinguish good drivers from bad drivers and offers the same auto insurance premium to both, it is likely to attract more bad drivers. If it is not able to distinguish healthy from unhealthy people and offers the same life insurance premiums to both, it is likely to attract more unhealthy people.

To lessen the impact of adverse selection, an insurance company tries to find out as much as possible about the policyholder before committing itself. Before offering life insurance, it often requires the policyholder to undergo a physical examination by an approved doctor. Before offering auto insurance to an individual, it will try to obtain as much information as possible about the individual's driving record. In the case of auto insurance, it will continue to collect information on the driver's risk (number of accidents, number of speeding tickets, etc.) and make year-to-year changes to the premium to reflect this.

Adverse selection can never be completely overcome. It is interesting that, in spite of the physical examinations that are required, individuals buying life insurance tend to die earlier than mortality tables would suggest. But individuals who purchase annuities tend to live longer than mortality tables would suggest.

3.8 REINSURANCE

Reinsurance is an important way in which an insurance company can protect itself against large losses by entering into contracts with another insurance company. For a fee, the second insurance company agrees to be responsible for some of the risks that have been insured by the first company. Reinsurance allows insurance companies to write more policies than they would otherwise be able to do. Some of the counterparties in reinsurance contracts are other insurance companies or rich private individuals; others are companies that specialize in reinsurance such as Swiss Re and Warren Buffett's company, Berkshire Hathaway.

Reinsurance contracts can take a number of forms. Suppose that an insurance company has an exposure of $100 million to hurricanes in Florida and wants to limit this to $50 million. One alternative is to enter into annual reinsurance contracts that cover on a pro rata basis 50% of its exposure. (The reinsurer would then probably receive 50% of the premiums.) If hurricane claims in a particular year total $70 million, the costs to the insurance company would be only $0.5 \times \$70$, or $35 million, and the reinsurance company would pay the other $35 million.

Another more popular alternative, involving lower reinsurance premiums, is to buy a series of reinsurance contracts covering what are known as *excess cost layers*. The first layer might provide indemnification for losses between $50 million and $60 million, the next layer might cover losses between $60 million and $70 million, and so on. Each reinsurance contract is known as an *excess-of-loss* reinsurance contract.

3.9 CAPITAL REQUIREMENTS

The balance sheets for life insurance and property–casualty insurance companies are different because the risks taken and reserves that must be set aside for future payouts are different.

Life Insurance Companies

Table 3.3 shows an abbreviated balance sheet for a life insurance company. Most of the life insurance company's investments are in corporate bonds. The insurance company tries to match the maturity of its assets with the maturity of liabilities. However, it takes on credit risk because the default rate on the bonds may be higher than expected.

Unlike a bank, an insurance company has exposure on the liability side of the balance sheet as well as on the asset side. The loss reserves (80% of assets in this case) are estimates (usually conservative) of actuaries for the payouts on the policies that have been written. The estimates may prove to be low if the holders of life insurance policies

Table 3.3 Abbreviated balance sheet for life insurance company.

Assets		Liabilities and net worth	
Investments	90	Policy reserves	80
Other assets	10	Subordinated long-term debt	10
		Equity capital	10
Total	100	Total	100

die earlier than expected or the holders of annuity contract live longer than expected. The 10% equity on the balance sheet includes the original equity contributed and retained earnings, and it provides a cushion. If payouts are greater than loss reserves by an amount equal to 5% of assets, equity will decline, but the life insurance company will survive.

Property–Casualty Insurance Companies

Table 3.4 shows an abbreviated balance sheet for a property–casualty life insurance company. A key difference between Tables 3.3 and 3.4 is that the equity in Table 3.4 is much higher. This reflects the differences in the risks taken by the two sorts of insurance companies. The payouts for a property–casualty company are much less easy to predict than those for a life insurance company. Who knows when a hurricane will hit Miami or how large payouts will be for the next asbestos-like liability problem? The unearned premiums item on the liability side represents premiums that have been received, but apply to future time periods. If a policyholder pays $2,500 for house insurance on June 30 of a year, only $1,250 has been earned by December 31 of the year. The investments in Table 3.4 consist largely of liquid bonds with shorter maturities than the bonds in Table 3.3.

3.10 THE RISKS FACING INSURANCE COMPANIES

The most obvious risk for an insurance company is that the policy reserves are not sufficient to meet the claims of policyholders. Although the calculations of actuaries are

Table 3.4 Abbreviated balance sheet for property–casualty insurance company.

Assets		Liabilities and net worth	
Investments	90	Policy reserves	45
Other assets	10	Unearned premiums	15
		Subordinated long-term debt	10
		Equity capital	30
Total	100	Total	100

usually fairly conservative, there is always the chance that payouts much higher than anticipated will be required. Insurance companies also face risks concerned with the performance of their investments. Many of these investments are in corporate bonds. If defaults on corporate bonds are above average, the profitability of the insurance company will suffer. It is important that an insurance company's bond portfolio be diversified by business sector and geographical region. An insurance company also needs to monitor the liquidity risks associated with its investments. Illiquid bonds (e.g., those the insurance company might buy in a private placement) tend to provide higher yields than bonds that are publicly owned and actively traded. However, they cannot be as readily converted into cash to meet unexpectedly high claims. Insurance companies enter into transactions with banks and reinsurance companies. This exposes them to credit risk. Like banks, insurance companies are also exposed to operational risks and business risks.

Regulators specify minimum capital requirements for an insurance company to provide a cushion that reflects the risks to which it is exposed. Insurance companies, like banks, have also developed their own procedures for calculating economic capital. (This is their own internal estimate of required capital (see Chapter 21).

3.11 REGULATION

The ways in which insurance companies are regulated in the United States and Europe are quite different.

The United States

In the United States, the McCarran–Ferguson Act of 1945 confirmed that insurance companies are regulated at the state level rather than the federal level. (Banks, by contrast, are regulated at the federal level.) This means that a large insurance company that operates throughout the United States has to deal with 50 different regulatory authorities. From time to time there have been suggestions that a federal regulatory body be set up. The National Association of Insurance Commissioners (NAIC) provides some services to state regulatory commissions. For example, it provides statistics on the loss ratios of property–casualty insurers. This helps state regulators identify those insurers for which the ratios are outside normal ranges.

Insurance companies are required to file detailed annual financial statements with state regulators, and the state regulators conduct periodic on-site reviews. Capital requirements are determined by regulators using risk-based capital standards determined by NAIC. These capital levels reflect the risk that policy reserves are inadequate, that counterparties in transactions default, and that the income on investments is less than expected.

The policyholder is protected against an insurance company becoming insolvent (and therefore unable to make payouts on claims) by insurance guaranty associations. An insurer is required to be a member of the guaranty association in a state as a condition of being licensed to conduct business in the state. When there is an insolvency by another insurance company operating in the state, each insurance company operating in the state has to contribute an amount to the state guaranty fund that is dependent on the premium income it collects in the state. The fund is used to pay the small policyholders of the insolvent insurance company. (The definition of a small policyholder varies from state to state.) There may be a cap on the amount the insurance company has to contribute to the state guaranty fund in a year. This can lead to the policyholder having to wait several years before the guaranty fund is in a position to make a full payout on its claims. In the case of life insurance, where policies last for many years, the policyholders of insolvent companies are usually taken over by other insurance companies. However, there may be some change to the terms of the policy so that the policyholder is somewhat worse off than before.

The guaranty system for insurance companies in the United States is therefore different from that for banks. In the case of banks, there is a permanent fund created from premiums paid by banks on their domestic deposits. In the case of insurance companies there is no permanent fund. Insurance companies have to make contributions after an insolvency has occurred. An exception to this is property–casualty companies in New York state where a permanent fund does exist.

Europe

In Europe, insurance companies are regulated by the European Union. This means that in theory the same regulatory framework applies to insurance companies throughout Europe. The framework that has existed since the 1970s is now known as Solvency I. It was heavily influenced by research carried out by Professor Campagne from the Netherlands, who showed that, with a capital equal to 4% of policy provisions, life insurance companies have a 95% chance of surviving. Investment risks are not explicitly considered by Solvency I.

A number of countries, such as the UK, the Netherlands, and Switzerland, have developed their own plans to overcome some of the weaknesses in Solvency I. The European Union is working on Solvency II, which assigns capital for a wider set of risks than Solvency I. Both Solvency I and Solvency II are discussed further in Chapter 11.

3.12 PENSION PLANS

Pension plans are set up by companies for their employees. Typically, contributions are made to a pension plan by both the employee and the employer while the employee is working for the company. When the employee retires, he or she receives a pension for the rest of his or her life. A pension fund therefore involves the creation of a lifetime annuity from regular contributions and has similarities to some of the products offered by life insurance companies. There are two types of pension plan: defined benefit and defined contribution.

In a *defined benefit plan* the pension that the employee will receive on retirement is defined by the plan. Typically it is calculated by a formula that is based on the number of years of employment and the employee's salary. For example, the pension per year might equal the employee's average earnings per year during the last three years of employment multiplied the number of years of employment multiplied by 2%. The employee's spouse may continue to receive a (usually reduced) pension if the employee dies before the spouse. In the event of the employee's death while still employed, a lump sum is often payable to dependents and a monthly income may be payable to a spouse or dependent children. Sometimes pensions are adjusted for inflation. This is known as indexation. For example, the indexation in a defined benefit plan might lead to pensions being increased each year by 75% of the increase in the consumer price index.

In a *defined contribution plan* the employer and employee contributions are invested on behalf of the employee. When employees retire, there are typically a number of options open to them. The amount to which the contributions have grown can be converted to a lifetime annuity. In some cases, the employee can opt to receive a lump sum instead of an annuity. The key difference between a defined contribution and a defined benefit plan is that, in the former, the funds are identified with individual employees. An account is set up for each employee and the pension is calculated only from the funds contributed to that account. By contrast, in a defined benefit plan, all contributions are pooled and payments to retirees are made out of the pool. In the United States, a 401(k) plan is a form of defined contribution plan where the employee elects to have some portion of his or her income directed to the plan (with possibly some employer matching) and can choose between a number of investment alternatives (e.g., stocks, bonds, and money market instruments).

A key aspect of both defined benefit and defined contribution plans is the fact that income tax is deferred. No taxes are payable on money contributed to the plan by the employee and contributions by a company are deductible. Taxes are payable only when pension income is received.

Defined contribution plans involve no risks for employers. If the performance of the plan's investments is less than anticipated, the employee bears the cost. By contrast, defined benefit plans impose significant risks on employers because they are ultimately responsible for paying the promised benefits. Let us suppose that the assets of a defined benefit plan total $100 million and that actuaries calculate the present value of the obligations to be $120 million. The plan is $20 million underfunded and the employer is required to make up the shortfall (usually over a number of years). The risks posed by defined benefit plans have led some companies to convert defined benefit plans to defined contribution plans.

Estimating the present value of the liabilities in defined benefit plans is not easy. An important issue is the discount rate used. The higher the discount rate, the lower are the pension plan liabilities. A common approach used for discounting estimated future payments at the average rate of return on the assets of the pension plan. This encourages the pension plan to invest in equities because the average return on equities is higher than the average return on bonds, making the value of the liabilities look low. Accounting standards now recognize that the liabilities of pension plans are obligations similar to bonds and require the liabilities to be discounted at AA-rated bond yields. The difference between the value of the assets of a defined benefit plan and that of its liabilities must be recorded as an asset or liability on the balance sheet of the company. Thus, if a company's defined benefit plan is underfunded, the company's shareholder equity is reduced. A "perfect storm" is created when the assets of a pension plan decline sharply in value and the discount rate for its liabilities decreases sharply (see Business Snapshot 3.2).

Are Defined Benefit Plans Viable?

A typical defined benefit plan provides the employee with about 70% of final salary as a pension and includes some indexation for inflation. What percentage of the employee's income during his or her working life should be set aside for providing the pension? The answer depends on a assumptions about interest rates, how fast the employee's

---

Business Snapshot 3.2   A Perfect Storm

During the period December 31, 1999, to December 31, 2002, the S&P 500 declined by about 40% from 1469.25 to 879.82 and 20-year Treasury rates in the US declined by 200 basis points from 6.83% to 4.83%. The impact of the first of these events was that the market value of the assets of pension plans declined sharply. The impact of the second of the two events was that the discount rate used by defined benefit plans for their liabilities decreased so that the fair value of the liabilities calculated by actuaries increased. This created a "perfect storm" for defined benefit pension plans. Many funds that had been overfunded became underfunded. Funds that had been slightly underfunded became much more seriously underfunded. A combination of negative equity returns and declining interest rates, such as occurred during the three-year period just considered is a nightmare for all managers of defined benefit plans.

New accounting rules requiring pension plan overfunding (underfunding) to be recorded as an asset (liability) on the balance sheet will make the impact of perfect storms much more transparent. It is not surprising that many companies have tried to replace defined benefit pension plans with defined contribution plans.

---

income rises, and so on. But, if an insurance company were asked to provide a quote for the sort of defined benefit plan we are considering, the required contribution rate would be about 25% of income each year (see Problems 3.15 and 3.19 for an indication of calculations that can be carried out). The insurance company would invest the premiums in corporate bonds (in the same way that it does the premiums for life insurance and annuity contracts) because this provides the best way of matching the investment income with the payouts.

The contributions to defined benefit plans (employer plus employee) are much less than 25% of income. In a typical defined benefit plan, the employer and employee each contribute around 5%. The total contribution is therefore only 40% of what an insurance actuary would calculate the required premium to be. It is not surprising that many pension plans are underfunded!

Unlike insurance companies, pension funds choose to invest a significant proportion of their assets in equities. (A typical portfolio mix for a pension plan is 60% equity and 40% debt.) By investing in equities, the pension fund is creating the situation where there is some chance that the pension plan will be fully funded. But there is also some chance of severe underfunding. If equity markets do well, as they have done from 1960 to 2000 in many parts of the world, defined benefit plans find they can afford their liabilities. But if equity markets perform badly, and since 2000 the performance has been less than stellar, there are likely to be problems.

This raises an interesting question: who is responsible for underfunding in defined benefit plans? In the first instance it is the company's shareholders that bear the cost. If the company declares bankruptcy, the cost may be borne by the government via insurance that is offered.[4] In either case there is a transfer of wealth to retirees from the next generation.

---

[4] For example, in the United States the Pension Benefit Guaranty Corporation (PBGC) insures private defined benefit plans. If the premiums the PBGC receives from plans are not sufficient to meet claims, presumably the government would have to step in.

A similar issue applies to the pension plans that are sponsored by governments (such as Social Security in the United States). These are similar to defined benefit plans in that they require regular contributions and provide lifetime pensions.

Many people argue that wealth transfers from one generation to the previous one are not viable. A 25% contribution rate to pension plans is also unacceptable. If defined benefit plans are to continue, there must be modifications to the terms of the plan so that there is some risk sharing between retirees and the next generation. If equity markets perform badly during their working life, retirees must be prepared to accept a lower pension. If equity markets perform well, retirees can receive a full pension and some of the benefits can be passed on to the next generation.

Longevity risk is a major concern for pension plans. We mentioned earlier that life expectancy increased by 20 years between 1929 and 2004. If this trend continues, and life expectancy increases by a further 4.25 years by 2020, the underfunding problems of defined benefit plans (both those administered by companies and those administered by national governments) will become more severe. It is not surprising that, in many jurisdictions, individuals have the right to work past the normal retirement age. This helps solve the problems faced by pension plans. An individual who retires at 70 rather than 65 makes an extra five years of pension contributions and the period of time for which the pension is received is shorter by five years.

SUMMARY

There are two main types of insurance company: life and property–casualty. Life insurance companies offer a number of products that provide a payoff when the policyholder dies. Term life insurance provides a payoff only if the policyholder dies during a certain period. Whole life insurance provides a payoff on the death on the insured, regardless of when this is. There is a savings element to whole life insurance. Typically, the portion of the premium not required to meet expected payouts in the early years of the policy is invested and this is used to finance expected payouts in later years. Whole life insurance policies can give rise to tax benefits because tax is deferred on the investment returns until there is a payout on the policy.

Life insurance companies also offer annuity contracts. These are contracts that, in return for a lump sum payment, provide the policyholder with an annual income from a certain date for the rest of his or her life. Mortality tables provide important information for the valuation of the life insurance contracts and annuities. However, actuaries must consider (a) longevity risk (the possibility that people will live longer than expected) and (b) mortality risk (the possibility that epidemics such as AIDS or Spanish flu will reduce life expectancy for some segments of the population).

Property–casualty insurance is concerned with providing protection against a loss of, or damage to, property. It also protects individuals and companies from legal liabilities. The most difficult payouts to predict are those where the same event is liable to trigger claims by many policyholders at about the same time. Examples of such events are hurricanes or earthquakes. Payouts arising from legal liabilities are also difficult to predict.

Health insurance has some of the features of life insurance and some of the features of property–casualty insurance. Health insurance premiums are like life insurance premiums in that changes to the company's assessment of the risk of payouts do not lead to an increase in premiums. However, it is like property–casualty insurance in that increases in the overall costs of providing health care can lead to increases in premiums.

Two key risks in insurance are moral hazard and adverse selection. Moral hazard is the risk that the behavior of an individual or corporation with an insurance contract will be different from the behavior without the insurance contract. Adverse selection is the risk that the individuals and companies who buy a certain type of policy are those for which expected payouts are relatively high. Insurance companies take steps to reduce these two types of risk, but they cannot eliminate them altogether.

Insurance companies are different from banks, such as the one considered in Section 2.2, in that their liabilities as well as their assets are subject to risk. A property–casualty insurance company must typically keep more equity capital, as a percent of total assets, than a life insurance company. In the United States, insurance companies are regulated at the state level rather than at the federal level. In Europe, insurance companies are regulated by the European Union and by national governments. The European Union is currently working on a new set of capital requirements known as Solvency II.

There are two types of pension plan: defined benefit plans and defined contribution plans. Defined contribution plans are straightforward. Contributions made by an employee and contributions made by the company on behalf of the employee are kept in a separate account, invested on behalf of the employee, and converted into a lifetime annuity when the employee retires. In a defined benefit plan, contributions from all employees and the company are pooled and invested. Retirees receive a pension that is based on the salary they earned while working. The viability of defined benefit plans is questionable. Many are underfunded and need superior returns from equity markets to pay promised pensions to both current retirees and future retirees.

FURTHER READING

Ambachtsheer, K. P., *Pension Revolution: A Solution to the Pensions Crisis.* Wiley, 2007.

Canter, M. S., J. B. Cole, and R. L. Sandor, "Insurance Derivatives: A New Asset Class for the Capital Markets and a New Hedging Tool for the Insurance Industry," *Journal of Applied Corporate Finance*, Autumn 1997: 69–83.

Doff, R., *Risk Management for Insurers: Risk Control, Economic Capital, and Solvency II*. Risk Books, 2007.

Froot, K. A., "The Market for Catastrophe Risk: A Clinical Examination," *Journal of Financial Economics*, 60 (2001): 529–571.

Froot, K. A., *The Financing of Catastrophe Risk*. University of Chicago Press, 1999.

Geman, H. "CAT Calls," *Risk*, September 1994: 86–89.

Hanley, M. "A Catastrophe Too Far," *Risk Supplement on Insurance*, July 1998.

Litzenberger, R. H., D. R. Beaglehole, and C. E. Reynolds. "Assessing Catastrophe Reinsurance-Linked Securities as a New Asset Class," *Journal of Portfolio Management*, Winter 1996: 76–86.

PRACTICE QUESTIONS AND PROBLEMS (Answers at the End of the Book)

3.1. What is the difference between term life insurance and whole life insurance? Explain the tax advantages of whole life insurance.

3.2. Explain the meaning of variable life insurance and universal life insurance.

3.3. A life insurance company offers whole life and annuity contracts. In which contracts does it have exposure to (a) longevity risk and (b) mortality risk?

3.4. "Equitable Life gave its policyholders a free option." Explain the nature of the option.

3.5. Use Table 3.1 to calculate the minimum premium an insurance company should charge for a $1 million two-year term life insurance policy issued to a woman aged 50. Assume that the premium is paid at the beginning of each year and that the interest rate is zero.

3.6. From Table 3.1 what is the probability that a man aged 30 will live to 90? What is the same probability for a woman aged 30?

3.7. What features of the policies written by a property–casualty insurance company give rise to the most risk?

3.8. Explain how CAT bonds work.

3.9. Consider two bonds that have the same coupon, time to maturity, and price. One is a B-rated corporate bond. The other is a CAT bond. An analysis based on historical data shows that the expected losses on the two bonds in each year of their life is the same. Which bond would you advise a portfolio manager to buy and why?

3.10. How does health insurance in the United States differ from that in Canada and the United Kingdom?

3.11. An insurance company decides to offer individuals insurance against losing their jobs. What problems is it likely to encounter?

3.12. Why do property–casualty insurance companies hold more capital than life insurance companies?

3.13. Explain what is meant by "loss ratio" and "expense ratio" for a property–casualty insurance company. "If an insurance company is profitable, it must be the case that the loss ratio plus the expense ratio is less than 100%." Discuss this statement.

3.14. What is the difference between a defined benefit and a defined contribution pension plan?

3.15. Suppose that in a certain defined benefit pension plan
(a) Employees work for 40 years earning wages that increase with inflation.
(b) They retire with a pension equal to 75% of their final salary. This pension also increases with inflation.
(c) The pension is received for 20 years.
(d) The pension fund's income is invested in bonds which earn the inflation rate.

Estimate the percentage of an employee's salary that must be contributed to the pension plan if it is to remain solvent. [*Hint*: Do all calculations in real rather than nominal dollars.]

FURTHER QUESTIONS

3.16. Use Table 3.1 to calculate the minimum premium an insurance company should charge for a $5 million three-year term life insurance contract issued to a man aged 60. Assume that the premium is paid at the beginning of each year and death always takes place halfway through a year. The risk-free interest rate is 6% per annum (with semiannual compounding).

3.17. An insurance company's losses of a particular type are to a reasonable approximation normally distributed with a mean of $150 million and a standard deviation of $50 million. (Assume no difference between losses in a risk-neutral world and losses in the real world.) The one-year risk-free rate is 5%. Estimate the cost of the following:
    (a) A contract that will pay in one-year's time 60% of the insurance company's costs on a pro rata basis;
    (b) A contract that pays $100 million in one-year's time if losses exceed $200 million.

3.18. During a certain year, interest rates fall by 200 basis points (2%) and equity prices are flat. Discuss the effect of this on a defined benefit pension plan that is 60% invested in equities and 40% invested in bonds.

3.19. Suppose that in a certain defined benefit pension plan:
    (a) Employees work for 45 years earning wages that increase at a real rate of 2%.
    (b) They retire with a pension equal to 70% of their final salary. This pension increases at the rate of inflation minus 1%.
    (c) The pension is received for 18 years.
    (d) The pension fund's income is invested in bonds which earn the inflation rate plus 1.5%.

    Estimate the percentage of an employee's salary that must be contributed to the pension plan if it is to remain solvent. [*Hint*: Do all calculations in real rather than nominal dollars.]

C H A P T E R

Mutual Funds
and Hedge Funds

Mutual funds and hedge funds invest cash on behalf of individuals and companies. The funds from different investors are pooled and investments are chosen by the fund manager in an attempt to meet specified objectives. Mutual funds, which are called "unit trusts" in some countries, serve the needs of relatively small investors, while hedge funds seek to attract funds from wealthy individuals and large investors such as pension funds. Hedge funds are subject to much less regulation than mutual funds. They are free to use a wider range of trading strategies than mutual funds and are usually more secretive about what they do.

This chapter describes the types of mutual fund and hedge fund that exist. It examines how they are regulated and the fees they charge. It also looks at how successful they have been at producing good returns for investors.

4.1 MUTUAL FUNDS

One of the attractions of mutual funds for the small investor is the diversification opportunities they offer. As we saw in Chapter 1, diversification improves an investor's risk–return trade-off. However, it can be difficult for a small investor to hold enough stocks to be well diversified. In addition, maintaining a well-diversified portfolio can lead to high transaction costs. A mutual fund provides a way in which the resources of many small investors are pooled so that the benefits of diversification are realized at a relatively low cost.

Mutual funds have grown very fast in since the Second World War. Table 4.1 shows estimates of the assets managed by mutual funds in the United States since 1940. These assets were over $10 trillion by 2008. About 50% of US households own mutual funds. Some mutual funds are offered by firms that specialize in asset management, such as Fidelity. Others are offered by banks such as J. P. Morgan Chase. Some insurance companies also offer mutual funds. For example, in 2001, the large US insurance company State Farm began offering ten mutual funds throughout the United States. They can be purchased on the internet or over the phone through State Farm agents.

Table 4.1 Growth of assets of mutual funds
in the United States. *Source*: Investment
Company Institute.

Year	Assets ($ billions)
1940	0.5
1960	17.0
1980	134.8
2000	6,964.6
2008	10,630.7

Mutual funds are regulated by the SEC. They are required to state their objectives in a prospectus that is available to potential investors. A number of different types of fund have been created, such as:

1. Bond funds that invest in fixed income securities with a life of more than one year

2. Equity funds that invest in common and preferred stock

3. Hybrid funds that invest in stocks, bonds, and other securities

4. Money market funds that invest in interest-bearing instruments with a life of less than one year

Equity mutual funds are by far the most popular.

An investor in a mutual fund owns a certain number of shares in the fund. The most common type of mutual fund is *open-ended*. This means that the total number of shares outstanding goes up as investors buy more shares and down as shares are redeemed. Mutual funds are valued at 4 p.m. each day. This involves the mutual fund manager calculating the market value of each asset in the portfolio so that the total value of the fund is determined. This total value is divided by the number of shares outstanding to obtain the value of each share. The latter is referred to as the *net asset value* (NAV) of the fund. Shares in the fund can be bought from the fund or sold back to the fund at any time. When an investor issues instructions to buy or sell shares, it is the next-calculated NAV that applies to the transaction. For example, if an investor decides to buy at 2 p.m. on a particular business day, the NAV at 4 p.m. on that day determines the amount paid by the investor.

The investor usually pays tax as though he or she owned the securities in which the fund has invested. Thus, when the fund receives a dividend, an investor in the fund has to pay tax on the investor's share of the dividend, even if the dividend is reinvested in the fund for the investor. When the fund sells securities, the investor is deemed to have realized an immediate capital gain or loss, even if the investor has not sold any of his or her shares in the fund. Suppose the investor buys shares at $100 and the trading by the fund leads to a capital gain of $20 per share in the first year and a capital loss of $25 in the second year. The investor has to declare a capital gain of $20 in the first year and a loss of $25 in the second year. When the investor sells the shares, there is also a capital gain or loss. To avoid double counting, the purchase price of the shares is adjusted to reflect the capital gains and losses that have already accrued to the investor. Thus, if in our example the investor sold shares in the fund after the end of the first year, the purchase price would be assumed to be \$120 for the purpose of calculating capital gains or losses on the transaction; if the investor sold the shares in the fund after the end of the second year, the purchase price would be assumed to be \$95 for the purpose of calculating capital gains or losses on the transaction.

Index Funds

Some funds are designed to track a particular equity index such as the S&P 500 and the FTSE 100. The tracking can most simply be achieved by buying all the shares in the index in amounts that reflect their weight. For example, if IBM has 1% weight in a particular index, 1% of the tracking portfolio for the index would be invested in IBM stock. Another way of achieving tracking is to choose a smaller portfolio of representative shares that has been shown by research to track the chosen portfolio closely. Yet another way is to use index futures.

One of the first index funds was launched in the United States on December 31, 1975, by John Bogle to track the S&P 500. It started with only \$11 million of assets and was initially ridiculed as being "un-American" and "Bogle's folly". However, it was later renamed the Vanguard 500 Index Fund and the assets under administration reached \$100 billion in November 1999.

How accurately do index funds track the index? Some funds, including the Vanguard 500 Index Fund, come very close to matching the index year after year. But others do not do as well. A survey by the organization Morningstar, which monitors mutual funds, found that index funds had tracking errors that averaged 38 basis points in 2003. This means that the difference between the return on the index fund and the return on the index averaged 0.38%.

Costs

Mutual funds incur a number of different costs. These include management expenses, sales commissions, accounting and other administrative costs, transactions costs on trades, and so on. To recoup these costs, and to make a profit, fees are charged to investors. A *front-end load* is a fee charged when an investor first buys shares in a mutual fund. Not all funds charge this type of fee. Those that do are referred to as *front-end loaded*. In the United States front-end loads are restricted to being less than 8.5% of the investment. Some funds charge fees when an investor sells shares. These are referred to as a *back-end load*. Typically the back-end load declines with the length of time the shares in the fund have been held. All funds charge an annual fee. There may be separate fees to cover management expenses, distribution costs, and so on. The *total expense ratio* is the total of the annual fees charged per share divided by the value of the share.

Khorana *et al.* compare the mutual fund fees in 18 different countries.[1] They assume in their analysis that a fund is kept for five years. The *total shareholder cost* per year is calculated as

$$\text{Total expense ratio} + \frac{\text{Front-end load}}{5} + \frac{\text{Back-end load}}{5}$$

---

[1] See A. Khorana, H. Servaes, and P. Tufano, "Mutual Fund Fees Around the World," *Review of Financial Studies*, 22 (March 2009): 1279–1310.

Table 4.2 Average total cost per year when mutual fund is held for five years (% of assets). *Source*: Khorana, Servaes, and Tufano, "Mutual Fund Fees Around the World," *Review of Financial Studies*.

Country	Bond funds	Equity funds
Australia	0.75	1.41
Austria	1.55	2.37
Belgium	1.60	2.27
Canada	1.84	3.00
Denmark	1.91	2.62
Finland	1.76	2.77
France	1.57	2.31
Germany	1.48	2.29
Italy	1.56	2.58
Luxembourg	1.62	2.43
Netherlands	1.73	2.46
Norway	1.77	2.67
Spain	1.58	2.70
Sweden	1.67	2.47
Switzerland	1.61	2.40
United Kingdom	1.73	2.48
United States	1.05	1.53
Average	1.39	2.09

Their results are summarized in Table 4.2. The average fees for equity funds vary from 1.41% in Australia to 3.00% in Canada. Fees for equity funds are on average about 50% higher than for bond funds. Index funds tend to have lower fees than regular funds, because no highly paid stock pickers or analysts are required. For some index funds in the United States, fees are as low as 0.15% per year.

Closed-End Funds

The funds we have talked about so far are open-ended funds. These are by far the most common type of fund. The number of shares outstanding varies from day to day as individuals choose to invest in the fund or redeem their shares. Closed-end funds are like regular corporations and have a fixed number of shares outstanding. The shares of the fund are traded on a stock exchange. For closed-end funds, two NAVs can be calculated. One is the price at which the shares of the fund are trading. The other is the market value of the fund's portfolio divided by the number of shares outstanding. The latter can be referred to as the *fair market value*. Usually a closed-end fund's share price is less than its fair market value. A number of researchers have investigated the reason for this. Research by Ross suggests that the fees paid to fund managers provide the explanation.[2]

[2] See S. Ross, "Neoclassical Finance, Alternative Finance, and the Closed End Fund Puzzle," *European Financial Management*, 8 (2002): 129–137.

ETFs

Exchange-traded funds (ETFs) have existed in the United States since 1993 and in Europe since 1999. They usually track an index and so are an alternative to an index fund for investors who are comfortable earning a return that mirrors the index. In a survey of investment professionals conducted in March 2008, 67% called ETFs the most innovative investment vehicle of the last two decades and 60% reported that ETFs have fundamentally changed the way they construct investment portfolios. In 2008, the SEC in the United States authorized the creation of actively managed ETFs. (However, it required the way they are managed to be transparent.)

ETFs are created by institutional investors. Typically an institutional investor deposits a block of securities with the ETF and obtains shares in the ETF (known as *creation units*) in return. Some or all of the shares in the ETF are then sold on a stock exchange. This gives ETFs the characteristics of a closed-end fund rather than an open-ended fund. However, a key feature of ETFs is that institutional investors can exchange large blocks of shares in the ETF for the assets underlying the shares at that time. They can give up shares they hold in the ETF and receive the assets or they can deposit new assets and receive new shares. This ensures that there is never any appreciable difference between the price at which shares in the ETF are trading on the stock exchange and their fair market value. This is a key difference between ETFs and closed-end funds and makes ETFs more attractive to investors than closed-end funds.

ETFs have a number of advantages over open-end mutual funds. ETFs can be bought or sold at any time of the day. They can be shorted in the same way that shares in any stock are shorted. (See Chapter 5 for a discussion of short selling.) ETF holdings are disclosed twice a day, giving investors full knowledge of the assets underlying the fund. Mutual funds by contrast only have to disclose their holdings relatively infrequently. When shares in a mutual fund are sold, managers often have to sell the stocks in which the fund has invested to raise the cash that is paid to the investor. When shares in the ETF are sold, this is not necessary as another investor is providing the cash. This means that transactions costs are saved and there are less unplanned capital gains and losses passed on to shareholders. Finally, the expense ratios of ETFs tend to be less than those of mutual funds.

Mutual Fund Returns

Do actively managed mutual funds outperform stock indices such as the S&P 500? Some funds in some years do very well, but this could be the result of good luck rather good investment management. Two key questions for researchers are:

1. Do actively managed funds outperform stock indices on average?
2. Do funds that outperform the market in one year continue to do so?

The answer to both questions appears to be no. In a classic study, Jensen performed tests on mutual fund performance using 10 years of data on 115 funds.[3] He calculated the alpha for each fund in each year. (As explained in Section 1.3, alpha is the return earned in excess of that predicted by the capital asset pricing model.) The average alpha of all funds was slightly negative, even before management costs were taken into account.

---

[3] See M.C. Jensen, "Risk, the Pricing of Capital Assets and the Evaluation of Investment Portfolios," *Journal of Business*, 42 (April 1969): 167–247.

Table 4.3 Consistency of good performance by mutual funds.

Number of consecutive years of positive alpha	Number of observations	Percentage of observations when next alpha is positive
1	574	50.4
2	312	52.0
3	161	53.4
4	79	55.8
5	41	46.4
6	17	35.3

Jensen tested whether funds with positive alphas tended to continue to earn positive alphas. His results are summarized in Table 4.3. The first row shows that 574 positive alphas were observed from the 1,150 observations (close to 50%). Of these positive alphas, 50.4% were followed by another year of positive alpha. Row two shows that, when two years of positive alphas have been observed, there is a 52% chance that the next year will have a positive alpha, and so on. The results show that, when a manager has achieved above average returns for one year (or several years in a row), there is still only a probability of about 50% of achieving above average returns the next year. The results suggest that managers who obtain positive alphas do so because of luck rather than skill. It is possible that there are some managers who are able to perform consistently above average, but they are a very small percentage of the total. More recent studies have confirmed Jensen's conclusions. On average mutual fund managers do not beat the market and past performance is not a good guide to future performance. The success of index funds shows that this research has influenced the views of many investors.

Mutual funds frequently advertise impressive returns. However, the fund being featured might be one fund, out of many offered by the same organization, that happens to have produced returns well above the average for the market. Distinguishing between good luck and good performance is always tricky. Suppose an asset management company has 32 funds following different trading strategies and assume that the fund managers have no particular skills, so that the return of each fund has a 50% chance of being greater than the market each year. The probability of a particular fund beating the market every year for the next five years is $(1/2)^5$, or 1/32. This means that by chance one out of the 32 funds will show a great performance over the five-year period!

One point should be made about the way returns over several years are expressed. One mutual fund might advertise: "The average of the returns per year that we have achieved over the last five years is 15%." Another might say: "If you had invested your money in our mutual fund for the last five years your money would have grown at 15% per year." These statements sound the same, but are actually different, as illustrated by Business Snapshot 4.1. In many countries, regulators have strict rules to ensure that mutual fund returns are not reported in a misleading way.

Regulation and Mutual Fund Scandals

Because they solicit funds from small retail customers, many of whom are unsophisticated, mutual funds are heavily regulated. The SEC is the primary regulator of mutual

---

Business Snapshot 4.1 Mutual Fund Returns Can Be Misleading

Suppose that the following is a sequence of returns per annum reported by a mutual fund manager over the last five years (measured using annual compounding):

$$15\%, \quad 20\%, \quad 30\%, \quad -20\%, \quad 25\%$$

The arithmetic mean of the returns, calculated by taking the sum of the returns and dividing by 5, is 14%. However, an investor would actually earn less than 14% per annum by leaving the money invested in the fund for five years. The dollar value of $100 at the end of the five years would be

$$100 \times 1.15 \times 1.20 \times 1.30 \times 0.80 \times 1.25 = \$179.40$$

By contrast, a 14% return (with annual compounding) would give

$$100 \times 1.14^5 = \$192.54$$

The return that gives $179.40 at the end of five years is 12.4%. This is because

$$100 \times (1.124)^5 = 179.40$$

What average return should the fund manager report? It is tempting for the manager to make a statement such as: "The average of the returns per year that we have realized in the last five years is 14%." Although true, this is misleading. It is much less misleading to say: "The average return realized by someone who invested with us for the last five years is 12.4% per year." In some jurisdictions regulations require fund managers to report returns the second way.

   This phenomenon is an example of a result that is well known by mathematicians. The geometric mean of a set of numbers (not all the same) is always less than the arithmetic mean. In our example, the return multipliers each year are 1.15, 1.20, 1.30, 0.80, and 1.25. The arithmetic mean of these numbers is 1.140, but the geometric mean is only 1.124. An investor who keeps an investment for several years earns the geometric mean of the returns per year, not the arithmetic mean.

---

funds in the United States. Mutual funds must file a registration document with the SEC. Full and accurate financial information must be provided to prospective fund purchasers in a prospectus. There are rules to prevent conflicts of interest, fraud, and excessive fees.

   Despite the regulations, there have been a number of scandals involving mutual funds. One of these involves *late trading*. As mentioned earlier in this chapter, if a request to buy or sell mutual fund shares is placed by an investor with a broker by 4 p.m. on any given business day, it is the NAV of the fund at 4 p.m. that determines the price that is paid or received by the investor. In practice, for various reasons, an order to buy or sell is sometimes not passed from a broker to a mutual fund until later than 4 p.m. This allows brokers to collude with investors and submit new orders or change existing orders after 4 p.m. The NAV of the fund at 4 p.m. still applies the investors— even though they may be using information on market movements (particularly movements in overseas markets) after 4 p.m. Late trading is not permitted under SEC regulations, and there were a number of prosecutions in the early 2000s that led to multi-million-dollar payments and employees being fired.

Another scandal is known as *market timing*. This is a practice where favored clients are allowed to buy and sell mutual funds shares frequently (e.g., every few days) without penalty. One reason why they might want to do this is because they are indulging in the illegal practice of late trading. Another reason is that they are analyzing the impact of stocks whose prices have not been updated recently on the fund's NAV. Suppose that the price of a stock has not been updated for several hours. (This could be because it does not trade frequently or because it trades on an exchange in a country in a different time zone.) If the US market has gone up (down) in the last few hours, the calculated NAV is likely to understate (overstate) the value of the underlying portfolio and there is a short-term trading opportunity. Taking advantage of this is not necessarily illegal. However, it may be illegal for the mutual fund to offer special trading privileges to favored customers because the costs (such as those associated with providing the liquidity necessary to accommodate frequent redemptions) are borne by all customers.

Other scandals have involved *front running* and *directed brokerage*. Front running occurs when a mutual fund is planning a big trade that is expected to move the market. It informs favored customers or partners before executing the trade, allowing them to trade for their own account first. Directed brokerage involves an improper arrangement between a mutual fund and a brokerage house where the brokerage house recommends the mutual fund to clients in return for receiving orders from the mutual fund for stock and bond purchases.

4.2 HEDGE FUNDS

Hedge funds are different from mutual funds in that they are subject to very little regulation. This is because they accept funds only from financially sophisticated individuals and organizations. Examples of the regulations that affect mutual funds are the requirements that:

1. Shares be redeemable at any time
2. NAV be calculated daily
3. Investment policies be disclosed
4. The use of leverage be limited
5. No short positions be taken

Hedge funds are largely free from these regulations. This gives them a great deal of freedom to develop sophisticated, unconventional, and proprietary investment strategies. Hedge funds are sometimes referred to as *alternative investments*.

The first hedge fund, A. W. Jones & Co., was created by Alfred Winslow Jones in the United States in 1949. It was structured as a general partnership to avoid SEC regulations. Jones combined long positions in stocks considered to be undervalued with short positions in stocks considered to be overvalued. He used leverage to magnify returns. A performance fee equal to 20% of profits was charged to investors. The fund performed well and the term "hedge fund" was coined in a newspaper article written about A. W. Jones & Co. by Carol Loomis in 1966. The article showed that the fund's performance after allowing for fees was better than the most successful mutual funds. Not surprisingly, the article led to great deal of interest in hedge funds and their investment approach. Other hedge fund pioneers were George Soros, Walter J. Schloss, and Julian Robertson.[4]

The term "hedge fund" implies that risks are being hedged. The trading strategy of Jones did involve hedging. He had little exposure to the overall direction of the market because his long position (in stocks considered to be undervalued) at any given time was about the same size as his short position (in stocks considered to be overvalued). However, for some hedge funds, the word "hedge" is inappropriate because they take aggressive bets on the future direction of the market with no particular hedging policy.

Hedge funds have grown in popularity over the years. The year 2008 was not a good year for hedge fund returns, but it is estimated that at the end of the year over $1 trillion was still invested with hedge fund managers throughout the world. Many hedge funds are registered in tax-favorable jurisdictions. For example, over 30% of hedge funds are domiciled in the Cayman Islands. *Funds of funds* have been set up to allocate funds to different hedge funds. Hedge funds are difficult to ignore. It has been estimated that they account for 40–50% of the daily turnover on the New York and London stock exchanges, 70% of the volume of convertible bond trading, 20–30% of the volume of credit default swap trading, 82% of the volume of trading in US distressed debt, and 33% of the trading in non-investment-grade bonds, and that they control 70% of US exchange-traded funds.

Fees

One characteristic of hedge funds that distinguishes them from mutual funds is that fees are higher and dependent on performance. An annual management fee that is usually between 1% and 3% of assets under management is charged. This is designed to meet operating costs—but there may be an additional fee for such things as audits, account administration, and trader bonuses. Moreover, an incentive fee that is usually between 15% and 30% of realized profits (if any) is charged. This fee structure is designed to attract the most talented and sophisticated investment managers. Thus, a typical hedge fund fee schedule might be expressed as "2 plus 20%", indicating that the fund charges 2% per year of assets under management and 20% of profit. On top of high fees there is usually a lock up period of at least one year during which invested funds cannot be withdrawn. Some hedge funds with good track records have charged much more than the average. Steve Cohen's SAC Capital Partners has charged "3 plus 35%" and Jim Simons's Renaissance Technologies Corp. has charged "5 plus 44%". Poor performance in 2008, however, has led some hedge funds to reduce their fees.

The agreements offered by hedge funds may include clauses that make the incentive fees more palatable. For example:

1. There is sometimes a *hurdle rate*. This is the minimum return necessary for the incentive fee to be applicable.
2. There is sometimes a *high water mark clause*. This states that any previous losses must be recouped by new profits before an incentive fee applies. Because different

---

[4] The famous Warren Buffett of Omaha can also be considered to be a hedge fund pioneer. In 1956 he started Buffett partnership LP with seven limited partners and $100,100. Buffett charged his partners 25% of profits above a hurdle rate of 25%. He specialized in special situations, merger arbitrage, spin-offs, and distressed debt opportunities and earned an average of 29.5% per year. The partnership was disbanded 1969 and Berkshire Hathaway (a holding company, not a hedge fund) was formed.

investors place money with the fund at different times, the high water mark is not necessarily the same for all investors. There may be a *proportional adjustment clause* stating that, if funds are withdrawn by investors, the amount of previous losses that has to be recouped is adjusted proportionally. Suppose a fund worth $200 million loses $40 million and $80 million of funds are withdrawn. The high water mark clause on its own would require $40 million of profits on the remaining $80 million to be achieved before the incentive fee applied. The proportional adjustment clause would reduce this to $20 million because the fund is only half as big as it was when the loss was incurred.

3. There is sometimes a *clawback clause* that allows investors to recover losses by the return of previously paid incentive fees. A portion of the incentive fees paid by the investor each year are retained in a *recovery account*. The account is used to compensate investors for a percentage of any future losses.

Some hedge fund managers have become very rich from the generous fee schedules. In 2007, the top 50 hedge fund managers earned a combined $29 billion. Five managers were reported as earning more than $1 billion. These were John Paulson of Safronov & Co., Philip Falcone of Harbinger Capital Partners, Jim Simons of Renaissance Technologies (a former mathematics professor), Steve Cohen of SAC Capital Advisers, and Kenneth Griffin of Citadel Investment Group.

A typical fee charged by a fund of hedge funds used to be 1% of assets under management and 10% of profits. This is less than the fees charged by a hedge fund. However, a fund of hedge funds has to pay the normal fees charged by the hedge funds in which it chooses to invest. Investors are therefore subject to quite high fees in total. Suppose a fund of hedge funds divides its money equally between 10 hedge funds. All charge 2 plus 20% and the fund of hedge funds charges 1 plus 10%. It sounds as though the investor pays 3 plus 30%—but it can be much more than this. Suppose that five of the hedge funds lose 40% and the other five make 40%. The fund of funds earns an overall return of zero and the investor pays 3% in management fees. In addition it must pay 20% of 40%, or 8%, to the funds that showed a profit. Half of the money invested attracts this additional fee of 8%, so that the total fee paid as a percent of total funds invested is $0.5 \times 8 + 3 = 7\%$. The net return of the investor is -7%. (This is 7% less than the return on the underlying assets before fees.) The fees charged by funds of hedge funds have declined sharply as a result of poor hedge fund performance in 2008.

Incentives of Hedge Fund Managers

The fee structure gives hedge fund managers an incentive to make a profit. But it also encourages them to take risks. The hedge fund manager has a call option on the assets of the fund. As is well known, the value of a call option increases as the volatility of the underlying assets increases. This means that the hedge fund manager can increase the value of the option by taking risks that increase the volatility of the fund's assets.

Suppose that a hedge fund manager is presented with an opportunity where there is a 0.4 probability of a 60% profit and a 0.6 probability of a 60% loss, with the fees earned by the hedge fund manager being 2 plus 20%. The expected return of the investment is

$$0.4 \times 60 + 0.6 \times (-60)$$

or -12%.

Table 4.4 Return from a high-risk investment where returns of +60% and −60% have probabilities of 0.4 and 0.6, respectively. The hedge fund charges 2 plus 20%.

Expected return to hedge fund	6.8%
Expected return to investors	−18.8%
Overall expected return	−12.0%

Even though this is a terrible expected return, the hedge fund manager might be tempted to accept the investment. If the investment produces a 60% profit, the hedge fund's fee is $2 + 0.2 \times 60$, or 14%. If the investment produces a 60% loss, the hedge fund's fee 2%. The expected fee to the hedge fund is therefore

$$0.4 \times 14 + 0.6 \times 2 = 6.8$$

or 6.8% of the funds under administration. The expected management fee is 2% and the expected incentive fee is 4.8%.

To the investors in the hedge fund the expected return is

$$0.4 \times (0.8 \times 60 + 2) + 0.6 \times (-60 - 2) = -18.8$$

or −18.8%.

The example is summarized in Table 4.4. It shows that the fee structure of a hedge fund gives its managers an incentive to take high risks even when expected returns are negative. The incentives may be reduced by hurdle rates, high water mark clauses, and clawback clauses. However, these clauses are not always as useful to investors as they sound. One reason is that investors have to continue to invest with the fund to take advantage of them. Another is that, as losses mount up for a hedge fund, the managers have an incentive to wind up the hedge fund and start a new one.

The incentives we are talking about here are real. Imagine how you would feel as an investor in the hedge fund, Amaranth. One of its traders, Brian Hunter, liked to make huge bets on the price of natural gas. Until 2006 his bets were largely right and as a result he was regarded as a star trader. His remuneration including bonuses is reputed to have been close to $100 million in 2005. During 2006, his bets proved wrong and Amaranth, which had about $9 million of assets under administration, lost a massive $6.5 billion. (This was even more that the loss of Long-Term Capital Management in 1998.) Brian Hunter did not have to return the bonuses he had previously earned. Instead he left Amaranth and tried to start his own hedge fund.

It is interesting to note that, in theory, two individuals can create a money machine as follows. One starts a hedge fund with a certain high risk (and secret) investment strategy. The other starts a hedge fund with an investment strategy that is the opposite of that followed by the first hedge fund. For example, if the first hedge fund decides to buy $1 million of silver, the second hedge fund shorts this amount of silver. At the time they start the funds, the two individuals enter into an agreement to share the incentive fees. One hedge fund (we do not know which one) will do well and earn good incentive fees. The other will do badly and earn no incentive fees. Provided that they can find investors for their funds, they have a money machine!

Prime Brokers

Prime brokers are the banks that offer services to hedge funds. Typically a hedge fund when it is first started will choose a single prime broker. This broker handles the hedge fund's trades (which may be with the prime broker or with other broker dealers), nets trades off against each other to determine the collateral the hedge fund has to post, borrows securities for the hedge fund when it wants to take short positions, provides cash management and portfolio reporting services, and makes loans to the hedge fund. In some cases, the prime broker provides risk management and consulting services and introduces the hedge fund to potential investors. The prime broker has a good understanding of the hedge fund's portfolio and will typically carry out stress tests on the portfolio to decide how much leverage it is prepared to offer the fund.

As a hedge fund gets larger, it is likely to use more than one prime broker. This means that no one bank sees all its trades and has a complete understanding of its portfolio. The opportunity of transacting business with more than one prime broker gives a hedge fund more negotiating clout to reduce the fees it pays. Goldman Sachs, Morgan Stanley, and many other large banks offer prime broker services to hedge funds and find them to be an important contributor to their profits.[5]

Although a hedge fund is not regulated, it does have to answer to its prime broker. A hedge fund is often highly leveraged and posts the minimum amount of collateral with its prime brokers. When it loses money, more collateral has to be posted. If it cannot post more collateral, it has no choice but to close out its trades. One thing the hedge fund has to think about is the possibility that it will enter into a trade that is correct in the long term, but loses money in the short term. Consider a hedge fund that in early 2008 thinks credit spreads are too high. It might be tempted to take a highly leveraged position where BBB-rated bonds are bought and Treasury bonds are shorted. However, there is the danger that credit spreads will increase before they decrease. In this case, the hedge fund might run out of collateral and be forced to close out its position at a huge loss.

4.3 HEDGE FUND STRATEGIES

In this section we will discuss some of the strategies followed by hedge funds. Our classification is similar to the one used by Credit Suisse/Tremont. Not all hedge funds can be classified in the way indicated. Some follow more than one of the strategies mentioned and some follow strategies that are not listed. (For example, there are funds specializing in weather derivatives.)

Long/Short Equity

As described earlier, long/short equity strategies were used by hedge fund pioneer Alfred Winslow Jones. They continue to be among the most popular of hedge fund strategies. The hedge fund manager identifies a set of stocks that are considered to be undervalued by the market and a set that are considered to be overvalued. The manager takes a long position in the first set and a short position in the second set. Typically the

---

[5] Although a bank is taking some risks when it lends to a hedge fund, it is also true that a hedge fund is taking some risks when it chooses a prime broker. Many hedge funds that chose Lehman Brothers as their prime broker found that they could not access their assets when Lehman Brothers went bankrupt in 2008.

hedge fund has to pay the prime broker 1% per year to rent the shares that are borrowed for the short position. (See Chapter 5 for a discussion of short selling.)

Long/short equity strategies are all about stock picking. If the overvalued and undervalued stocks have been picked well, the strategies should give good returns in both bull and bear markets. Hedge fund managers often concentrate on smaller stocks that are not well covered by analysts and research the stocks extensively using fundamental analysis, as pioneered by Benjamin Graham. The hedge fund manager may choose to maintain a net long bias where the shorts are of smaller magnitude than the longs or a net short bias where the reverse is true. Alfred Winslow Jones maintained a net long bias in his successful use of long/short equity strategies.

An *equity-market-neutral* fund uses a long/short strategy, but has no net long or net short bias. A *dollar-neutral* fund is an equity-market-neutral fund where the dollar amount of the long position equals the dollar amount of the short position. A *beta-neutral fund* is more sophisticated equity-market-neutral fund where the weighted average beta of the shares in the long portfolio equals the weighted average beta of the shares in the short portfolio so that the overall beta of the portfolio is zero. If the capital asset pricing model is true, the beta-neutral fund should be totally insensitive to market movements. Long and short positions in index futures are sometimes used to maintain a beta-neutral position.

Sometimes equity market neutral funds go one step further. They maintain *sector neutrality*, where long and short positions are balanced by industry sectors, or *factor neutrality*, where the exposure to factors such as the price of oil, the level of interest rates, or the rate of inflation is neutralized.

Dedicated Short

Managers of dedicated short funds look exclusively for overvalued companies and sell them short. They are attempting to take advantage of the fact that brokers and analysts are reluctant to issue sell recommendations—even though one might reasonably expect the number of companies overvalued by the stock market to be approximately the same as the number of companies undervalued at any given time. Typically the companies chosen are those with weak financials, those that change their auditors regularly, those that delay filing reports with the SEC, companies in industries with overcapacity, companies suing or attempting to the silence their short sellers, and so on.

Distressed Securities

Bonds with credit ratings of BB or lower are known as "non-investment-grade" or "junk" bonds. Those with a credit rating of CCC are referred to as "distressed" and those with a credit rating of D are in default. Typically, distressed bonds sell at a big discounts to their par value and provide a yield that is over 1,000 basis points (10%) more than the yield on Treasury bonds. Of course, an investor only earns this yield if the required interest and principal payments are actually made.

The managers of funds specializing in distressed securities calculate carefully a fair value for distressed securities by considering possible future scenarios and their probabilities. Distressed debt cannot usually be shorted and so they are searching for debt that is undervalued by the market. Bankruptcy proceedings usually lead to a reorganization or liquidation of a company. The fund managers understand the legal system, know priorities in the event of liquidation, estimate recovery rates, consider actions likely to be taken by management, and so on.

Some funds are passive investors. They buy distressed debt when the price is below its fair value and wait. Other hedge funds adopt an active approach. They might purchase a sufficiently large position in outstanding debt claims that they have the right to influence a reorganization proposal. In Chapter 11 reorganizations in the US, each class of claims must approve a reorganization proposal with a two-thirds majority. This means that one-third of an outstanding issue can be suffcient to stop a reorganization proposed by management or other stakeholders. In a reorganization of a company, the equity is often worthless and the outstanding debt is converted into new equity. Sometimes, the goal of an active manager is to buy more than one-third of the debt, obtain control of a target company, and then find a way to extract wealth from it.

Merger Arbitrage

Merger arbitrage involves trading after a merger or acquisition is announced in the hope that the announced deal will take place. There are two main types of merger and acquisition: cash deals and share-for-share exchanges.

Consider first cash deals. Suppose that Company A announces that it is prepared to acquire all the shares of Company B for $30 per share. Suppose the shares of Company B were trading at $20 prior to the announcement. Immediately after the announcement its share price might jump to $28. It does not jump immediately to $30 because (a) there is some chance that the deal will not go through and (b) it may take some time for the full impact of the deal to be reflected in market prices. Merger arbitrage hedge funds buy the shares in company B for $28 and wait. If the acquisition goes through at $30, the fund makes a profit of $2 per share. If it goes through at a higher price the profit is bigger. However, if for any reason the deal does not go through, the hedge fund will take a loss.

Consider next a share-for-share exchange. Suppose that Company A announces that it is willing to exchange one its shares for four of Company B shares. Assume that Company B's shares were trading at 15% of the price of company A's shares prior to the announcement. After the announcement, Company B's share price might rise to 22% of Company A's share price. A merger-arbitrage hedge fund would buy a certain amount of Company B's stock and at the same time short a quarter as much of company A's stock. This strategy generates a profit if the deal goes ahead at the announced share-for-share exchange ratio or one that is more favorable to Company B.

Merger arbitrage hedge funds can generate steady, but not stellar, returns. It is important to distinguish merger arbitrage from the activities of Ivan Boesky and others who used inside information to trade before mergers became public knowledge.[6] Trading on inside information is illegal. Ivan Boesky was sentenced to three years in prison and fined $100 million.

Convertible Arbitrage

Convertible bonds are bonds that can be converted into the equity of the bond issuer at certain specified future times with the number of shares received in exchange for a bond possibly depending on the time of the conversion. The issuer usually has the right to

---

[6] The Michael Douglas character of Gordon Gekko in the award-winning movie *Wall Street* was based on Ivan Boesky.

call the bond (i.e., buy it back a prespecified price) in certain circumstances. Usually, the issuer announces its intention to call the bond as a way of forcing the holder to convert the bond into equity immediately. (If the bond is not called, the holder is liable to postpone the decision to convert it into equity for as long as possible.)

A convertible arbitrage hedge fund has typically developed a sophisticated model for valuing convertible bonds. The convertible bond price depends in a complex way on the price of the underlying equity, its volatility, the level of interest rates, and the chance of the issuer defaulting. Many convertible bonds trade at prices below their fair value. Hedge fund managers buy the bond and then hedge their risks by shorting the stock. (This is an application of delta hedging that will be discussed in Chapter 6.) Interest rate and credit risk can be hedged by shorting nonconvertible bonds issued by the company that issued the convertible. Alternatively, the managers can take positions in interest rate futures contracts, asset swaps, and credit default swaps to accomplish this hedging.

Fixed Income Arbitrage

The basic tool of fixed income trading is the zero-coupon yield curve, the construction of which is discussed in Appendix B. One strategy followed by hedge funds that engage in fixed income arbitrage is a *relative value* strategy, where they buy bonds that the zero-coupon yield curve indicates are undervalued by the market and sell bonds that it indicates are overvalued. *Market-neutral* strategies are similar to relative value strategies except that the hedge fund manager tries to ensure that the fund has no exposure to interest rate movements.

Some fixed-income hedge fund managers follow directional strategies where they take a position based on a belief that a certain spread between interest rates, or interest rates themselves, will move in a certain direction. Usually they have a lot of leverage. They are therefore taking the risk that they are right in the long term, but the market moves against them in the short term so that they are forced to close out their positions at a loss. This is what happened to Long-Term Capital Management (see Business Snapshot 15.1).

Emerging Markets

Emerging market hedge funds specialize in investments associated with developing countries. Some of these funds focus on equity investments. They screen emerging market companies looking for shares that are overvalued or undervalued. They gather information by traveling, attending conferences, meeting with analysts, talking to management, and employing consultants. Usually they invest in securities trading on the local exchange, but sometimes they use American Depository Receipts (ADRs). ADRs are certificates issued in the US and traded on a US exchange. They are backed by shares of a foreign company. ADRs may have better liquidity and lower transactions costs than the underlying foreign shares. Sometimes there are price discrepancies between ADRs and the underlying shares giving rise to arbitrage opportunities.

Another type of investment is debt issued by an emerging market country. Brady bonds are dollar-denominated bonds issued by a less developed country and backed by the US Treasury. Eurobonds are bonds issued by the country and denominated in a hard currency such as the US dollar or the euro. Local currency bonds are bonds denominated in the local currency. Hedge funds invest in all three types of bond. Both

Eurobonds and local currency bonds are risky. Countries such as Russia, Argentina, Brazil, and Venezuela have defaulted many times on their debt.

Global Macro

Global macro is the hedge fund strategy use by star managers such as George Soros and Julian Robertson. Global macro hedge fund managers carry out trades that reflect global macroeconomic trends. They look for situations where markets have for whatever reason moved away from equilibrium and place large bets that they will move back into equilibrium. Often the bets are on exchange rates and interest rates. A global macro strategy was used in 1992 when George Soros's Quantum Fund gained $1 billion by betting that the British pound would decrease in value. More recently, hedge funds have (with mixed results) placed bets that the huge US balance of payments would cause the value of the US dollar to decline. The main problem for global macro funds is that they do not know when equilibrium will be restored. World markets can for various reasons be in disequilibrium for long periods of time.

Managed Futures

Hedge fund managers that use managed futures strategies attempt to predict future movements in commodity prices. Some rely on on the manager's judgment; others use computer programs to generate trades. Some managers base their trading on technical analysis, which analyzes past price patterns to predict the future. Others use fundamental analysis, which involves calculating a fair value for the commodity from economic, political, and other relevant factors.

When technical analysis is used, trading rules are usually first tested on historical data. This is known as back-testing. If (as is often the case) a trading rule has come from an analysis of past data, trading rules should be tested out of sample (that is, on data that are different from the data used to generate the rules). Analysts should be aware of the perils of data mining. Analysts have been known to generate thousands of different trading rules and then test them on historical data. Just by chance a few of the trading rules will perform very well—but this does not mean that they will perform well in the future.

4.4 HEDGE FUND RETURNS

It is not as easy to assess hedge fund returns as it is to assess mutual fund returns. There is no data set that records the returns of all hedge funds. For the Tass hedge funds database, which is available to researchers, participation by hedge funds is voluntary. Small hedge funds and those with poor track records often do not report their returns and are therefore not included in the data set. When returns are reported by a hedge fund, the database is usually backfilled with the fund's previous returns. This creates a bias in the returns that are in the data set because, as just mentioned, the hedge funds that decide to start providing data are likely to be the ones doing well. When this bias is removed, some researchers have argued, hedge fund returns are no better than mutual fund returns.[7]

---

[7] See, for example, N. Posthuma and P.J. van der Sluis, "A Reality Check on Hedge Fund Returns," Working Paper, Free University, Amsterdam, 2003.

Table 4.5 Hedge fund performance. (The Sharpe ratio is the ratio of the mean of $r - r_f$ to its standard deviation, where r is the realized return and r_f is the risk-free rate.) *Source*: Credit Suisse/Tremont.

Category	2008 return per annum	2004–2008 return per annum	SD of monthly returns (annualized)	Sharpe ratio
Convertible arbitrage	−31.59%	5.45%	6.84%	0.24
Dedicated short bias	14.87%	−0.78%	16.96%	−0.27
Emerging markets	−30.41%	6.70%	15.85%	0.18
Equity market neutral	−40.32%	5.57%	11.03%	0.16
Event driven	−17.74%	9.60%	6.11%	0.95
Fixed-income arbitrage	−28.82%	3.47%	6.00%	−0.06
Global macro	−4.62%	12.47%	10.57%	0.82
Long/short equity	−19.76%	9.72%	10.22%	0.58
Managed futures	18.33%	7.21%	11.91%	0.29
Multi-strategy	−23.63%	7.12%	5.46%	0.60
Hedge fund index	−19.07%	8.73%	7.96%	0.62

Arguably, hedge funds can improve the risk–return trade-offs available to pension plans. This is because pension plans cannot (or choose not to) take short positions, obtain leverage, invest in derivatives, and engage in many of the complex trades that are favored by hedge funds. Investing in a hedge fund is a simple way in which a pension fund can (for a fee) expand the scope of its investing. This may improve its efficient frontier. (See Section 1.2 for a discussion of efficient frontiers.)

It is not uncommon for hedge funds to report good returns for a few years and then "blow up". Long-Term Capital Management reported returns (before fees) of 28%, 59%, 57%, and 17% in 1994, 1995, 1996, and 1997, respectively. In 1998 it lost virtually all its capital. Some people have argued that hedge fund returns are like the returns from writing out-of-the-money options. Most of the time, the options cost nothing, but every so often they are very expensive.

This may be unfair. Advocates of hedge funds would argue that hedge fund managers search for profitable opportunities that other investors do not have the resources or expertise to find. They would point to John Paulson as an example of a hedge fund manager that has been successful at finding these opportunities.

The year 2008 was a very bad one for hedge funds and for the stock market generally. The Credit Suisse/Tremont hedge fund index was down 19.07% for the year, although it produced a return of 8.73% per annum on average over the five-year period leading up to December 31, 2008. The S&P 500 index performed worse than the Credit Suisse/Tremont hedge fund index. It declined by 38.5% during 2008 and lost 4.1% per year on average over the five-year period leading up to December 31, 2008. However, these statistics may be misleading because they do not take account of dividends on the S&P 500, and there may be biases in the hedge fund data, as mentioned above.

The performance of different sectors is shown in Table 4.5.

SUMMARY

Mutual funds offer a way small investors can capture the benefits of diversification. Overall, the evidence is that actively managed funds do not outperform the market and this has led many investors to choose funds that are designed to track a market index such as the S&P 500. Mutual funds are highly regulated. They cannot take short positions or use leverage and must allow investors to redeem their shares in the mutual fund at any time. Most mutual funds are open-ended, so that the number of shares in the fund increases (decreases) as investors contribute (withdraw) funds. An open-end mutual fund calculates the net asset value of shares in the fund at 4 p.m. each business day, and this is the price used for all buy and sell orders placed in the previous 24 hours. A closed-end fund has a fixed number of shares that trade in the same way as the shares of any other corporation.

Exchange-traded funds are proving to be popular alternatives to open- and closed-ended funds. The shares held by the fund are known at any given time. Large institutional investors can exchange shares in the fund at any time for the assets underlying the shares at that time. This ensures that the shares in the ETF (unlike shares in a closed-end fund) trade at a price very close to the funds's net asset value. Shares in an ETF can be traded at any time (not just at 4 p.m.) and shares in an ETF (unlike shares in an open-end mutual fund) can be shorted.

Hedge funds cater to the needs of large investors. They are subject to very little regulation and are able to use trading strategies that mutual funds are not allowed to use. For example, they can borrow money and short securities. Hedge funds charge investors much higher fees than mutual funds. The fee for a typical fund is "2 plus 20%". This means that the fund charges a management fee of 2% per year and receives 20% of the profits (if any) generated by the fund. Hedge fund managers have a call options on the assets of the fund and, as a result, may have an incentive to take high risks.

Among the strategies followed by hedge funds are long/short equity, dedicated short, distressed securities, merger arbitrage, convertible arbitrage, fixed income arbitrage, emerging markets, global macro, and managed futures. The jury is still out on whether hedge funds on average provide superior risk–return trade-offs to index funds after fees. There is a tendency for hedge funds to provide excellent returns for a number of years and then report a disastrous loss.

FURTHER READING

Khorana, A., H. Servaes, and P. Tufano, "Mutual Fund Fees Around the World," *Review of Financial Studies*, 22 (March 2009): 1279–1310.

Jensen, M.C., "Risk, the Pricing of Capital Assets, and the Evaluation of Investment Portfolios," *Journal of Business*, 42, 2 (April 1969): 167–247.

Lhabitant, F.-S., *Handbook of Hedge Funds*. Chichester: Wiley, 2006.

Ross, S., "Neoclassical Finance, Alternative Finance, and the Closed End Fund Puzzle," *European Financial Management*, 8 (2002), 129–137.

PRACTICE QUESTIONS AND PROBLEMS (Answers at the End of the Book)

4.1. What is the difference between an open-end and closed-end mutual fund?

4.2. How is the NAV of an open-end mutual fund calculated? When is it calculated?

4.3. An investor buys 100 shares in a mutual fund on January 1, 2009, for $30 each. The fund makes capital gains in 2009 and 2010 of $3 per share and $1 per share, respectively, and earns no dividends. The investor sells the shares in the fund during 2011 for $32 per share. What capital gains or losses is the investor deemed to have made in 2009, 2010, and 2011.

4.4. What is an index fund? How is it created?

4.5. What is a mutual fund's (a) front-end load and (b) back-end load?

4.6. Explain how an exchange-traded fund that tracks the S&P 500 works. What is the advantage of an exchange-traded fund over (a) an open-end mutual fund and (b) a closed-end mutual fund?

4.7. What is the difference between the geometric mean and the arithmetic mean of a set of numbers? Why is the difference relevant to the reporting of mutual fund returns?

4.8. Explain the meaning of (a) late trading, (b) market timing, (c) front running, and (d) directional brokerage.

4.9. Give four examples of the trading restrictions that apply to mutual fund trading, but do not apply to hedge fund trading.

4.10. "If 70% of convertible bond trading is by hedge funds, I would expect the profitability of that strategy to decline." Discuss this viewpoint.

4.11. Explain the meanings of the terms hurdle rate, high water mark clause, and clawback clause when used in connection with the incentive fees of hedge funds.

4.12. A hedge fund charges 3 plus 30%. Investors want a return after fees of 20%. How much does the hedge fund have to earn before fees to provide investors with this return?

4.13. "It is important for a hedge fund to be right in the long term. Short-term gains and losses do not matter." Discuss this statement.

4.14. "The risks that hedge funds take are regulated by their prime brokers." Discuss this statement.

FURTHER QUESTIONS

4.15. An investor buys 100 shares in a mutual fund on January 1, 2009, for $50 each. The fund earns dividends of $2 and $3 per share during 2009 and 2010. These are reinvested in the fund. Its capital gains in 2009 and 2010 are $5 per share and $3 per share, respectively. The investor sells the shares in the fund during 2011 for $59 per share. Explain how the investor is taxed.

4.16. Good years are followed by equally bad years for a mutual fund. It earns +8%, −8%, +12%, −12% in successive years. What is the investor's overall return for the four years?

4.17. A fund of funds divides its money between five hedge funds that earn −5%, 1%, 10%, 15%, and 20% before fees in a particular year. The fund of funds charges 1 plus 10%

and the hedge funds charge 2 plus 20%. What is the overall return on the investments? How is it divided between the fund of funds, the hedge funds, and investors in the fund of funds?

4.18. A hedge funds charges 2 plus 20%. A pension fund invests in the hedge fund. Plot the return to the pension fund as a function of the return to the hedge fund.

Financial Instruments

Financial institutions do a huge volume of trading involving a wide range of different financial instruments. There are a number of reasons for this. Some trades are designed to satisfy the needs of their clients, some are to manage their own risks, some are to exploit arbitrage opportunities, and some are to reflect their own views on the direction in which market prices will move.

We will discuss the approaches a financial institution uses to manage its trading risks in later chapters. The purpose of this chapter is to set the scene by describing the instruments that trade, how they trade, and the ways they are used.

5.1 THE MARKETS

There are two markets for trading financial instruments. These are known as the *exchange-traded* market and the *over-the-counter* (or OTC) market.

Exchange-Traded Markets

Exchanges have been used to trade financial products for many years. Some exchanges such as the New York Stock Exchange (NYSE; www.nyse.com) focus on the trading of stocks. Others such as the Chicago Board of Trade (CBOT; www.cbot.com) and the Chicago Board Options Exchange (CBOE; www.cboe.com) are concerned with the trading of derivatives such as futures and options.

The role of the exchange is to define the contracts that trade and organize trading so that market participants can be sure that the trades they agree to will be honored. Traditionally individuals have met at the exchange and agreed on the prices for trades, often by using an elaborate system of hand signals. Most exchanges have now moved wholly or partly to *electronic trading*. This involves traders entering their desired trades at a keyboard and a computer being used to match buyers and sellers. Not everyone agrees that the shift to electronic trading is desirable. Electronic trading is less physically demanding than traditional floor trading. However, in some ways, it is also less exciting. Traders do not have the opportunity to attempt to predict short-term market trends from the behavior and body language of other traders.

Sometimes trading is facilitated with market makers. These are individuals or companies who are always prepared to quote both a *bid price* (price at which they are prepared to buy) and an *offer price* (price at which they are prepared to sell). For example, at the request of a trader, a market maker might quote "bid 30.3, offer 30.5" for a particular share, indicating a willingness to buy at $30.30 and sell at $30.50. At the time quotes are provided, the market maker does not know whether the trader wishes to buy or sell. Typically the exchange will specify an upper bound for the spread between a market maker's bid and offer prices. The market maker earns its profit from this spread, but must manage its inventories carefully to limit its exposure to price changes.

Over-the-Counter Markets

The OTC market is a telephone- and computer-linked network of traders who work for financial institutions, large corporations, or fund managers. Most of the trading by banks is in the OTC market. Banks often act as market makers for the more commonly traded instruments. For example, many banks are prepared to provide bid and offer quotes on exchange rates for corporations planning large transactions.

A key advantage of the over-the-counter market is that the terms of a contract do not have to be those specified by an exchange. Market participants are free to negotiate any mutually attractive deal. Phone conversations in the over-the-counter market are usually taped. If there is a dispute over what was agreed, the tapes are replayed to resolve the issue. Trades in the over-the-counter market are typically much larger than trades in the exchange-traded market.

Credit Risk

One difference between exchange-traded markets and OTC markets concerns credit risk. A transaction between two parties often involves agreements to make payments in the future. If one of the parties to the transaction goes out of business before all payments have been made, it will not fulfill its obligations and the other party may lose money. As we will explain, exchanges have organized themselves so that credit risk is almost completely eliminated. Steps are usually taken to reduce credit risk in OTC trades, but some credit risk always remains. When Lehman Brothers went bankrupt in 2008, it defaulted on a multitude of contracts that it had entered into, leading to losses by some of its counterparties.

Regulators are concerned about what is known as *systemic risk*. This is the risk that a default by one bank creates losses by other banks that have traded with it. This, in turn, may lead to more bankruptcies and severe problems for the financial system. This is one reason why regulators chose to bail out many financial institutions in 2008, rather letting them go bankrupt.

5.2   LONG AND SHORT POSITIONS IN ASSETS

The simplest type of trade is the purchase of an asset for cash or the sale of an asset that is owned for cash. Examples of such trades are:

1. The purchase of 100 IBM shares
2. The sale of 1 million British pounds for dollars

3. The purchase of 1,000 ounces of gold

4. The sale of $1 million worth of bonds issued by General Motors

The first of these trades would typically be done on an exchange; the other three would be done in the over-the-counter market. The trades are sometimes referred to as *spot trades* because they lead to almost immediate (on the spot) delivery of the asset.

Short Sales

In some markets it is possible to sell an asset that you do not own with the intention of buying it back later. This is referred to as shorting the asset. We will illustrate how it works by considering a short sale of shares of a stock.

Suppose an investor instructs a broker to short 500 shares of a certain stock. The broker will carry out the instructions by borrowing the shares from another client and selling them on an exchange in the usual way. (A small fee may be charged for the borrowed shares.) The investor can maintain the short position for as long as desired, provided there are always shares available for the broker to borrow. At some stage, however, the investor will close out the position by purchasing 500 shares. These are then replaced in the account of the client from whom the shares were borrowed. The investor takes a profit if the stock price has declined and a loss if it has risen. If, at any time while the contract is open, the broker runs out of shares to borrow, the investor is *short-squeezed* and is forced to close out the position immediately, even if not ready to do so.

An investor with a short position must pay to the broker any income, such as dividends or interest, that would normally be received on the asset that has been shorted. The broker will transfer this to the client account from which the asset has been borrowed. Suppose a trader shorts 500 shares in April when the price per share is $120 and closes out the position by buying them back in July when the price per share is $100. Suppose further that a dividend of $1 per share is paid in May. The investor receives $500 \times \$120 = \$60,000$ in April when the short position is initiated. The dividend leads to a payment by the investor of $500 \times \$1 = \$500$ in May. The investor also pays $500 \times \$100 = \$50,000$ for shares when the position is closed out in July. The

Table 5.1 Cash flows from short sale and purchase of shares.

Purchase of Shares	
April: Purchase 500 shares for $120	−$60,000
May: Receive dividend	+$500
July: Sell 500 shares for $100 per share	+$50,000
Net profit = −$9,500	

Short Sale of Shares	
April: Borrow 500 shares and sell them for $120	+$60,000
May: Pay dividend	−$500
July: Buy 500 shares for $100 per share and replace borrowed shares to close short position	−$50,000
Net profit = +$9,500	

net gain is therefore

$$\$60,000 - \$500 - \$50,000 = \$9,500$$

Table 5.1 illustrates this example and shows that (assuming no fee is charged for borrowing the shares) the cash flows from the short sale are the mirror image of the cash flows from purchasing the shares in April and selling them in July.

An investor entering into a short position is required to maintain a *margin account* with the broker to guarantee that future obligations will be met. Margin accounts are discussed later in the chapter.

From time to time regulations are changed on short selling. The SEC abolished the uptick rule in the United States in July 2007 and reintroduced it in April 2009. (The effect of the rule is to allow shorting only when the most recent movement in the price of the stock is an increase.) On September 19, 2008, in an attempt to halt the slide in bank stock prices, the SEC imposed a temporary ban on the short selling of 799 financial companies. This was similar to a ban imposed by the UK Financial Services authority (FSA) the day before.

5.3 DERIVATIVES MARKETS

A derivative is an instrument whose value depends on (or derives from) other more basic market variables. A stock option, for example, is a derivative whose value is dependent on the price of a stock.

Derivatives trade in both the exchange-traded and OTC markets. Both markets are huge. Although the statistics that are collected for the two markets are not exactly comparable, it is clear that the over-the-counter derivatives market is much larger than the exchange-traded derivatives market. The Bank for International Settlements (www.bis.org) started collecting statistics on the markets in 1998. Figure 5.1 compares

Figure 5.1   Size of over-the-counter and exchange-traded derivatives markets.

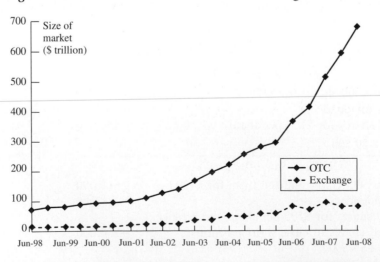

(a) the estimated total principal amounts underlying transactions that were outstanding in the over-the-counter markets between June 1998 and June 2008 and (b) the estimated total value of the assets underlying exchange-traded contracts during the same period. Using these measures, by June 2008, the over-the-counter market had grown to $683.7 trillion and the exchange-traded market had grown to $84.3 trillion.

In interpreting these numbers, we should bear in mind that the principal (or value of assets) underlying a derivatives transaction is not the same as its value. An example of an over-the-counter contract is an agreement to buy 100 million US dollars with British pounds at a predetermined exchange rate in one year. The total principal amount underlying this transaction is $100 million. However, the value of the contract might be only $1 million. The Bank for International Settlements estimates the gross market value of all OTC contracts outstanding in June 2008 to be about $20.3 trillion.[1]

5.4 PLAIN VANILLA DERIVATIVES

This section discusses the standard, or commonly traded, contracts in derivatives markets. They are known as a *plain vanilla* derivatives products.

Forward Contracts

A forward contract is an agreement to buy an asset in the future for a certain price. Forward contracts trade in the over-the-counter market. One of the parties to a forward contract assumes a *long position* and agrees to buy the underlying asset on a certain specified future date for a certain specified price. The other party assumes a *short position* and agrees to sell the asset on the same date for the same price.

Forward contracts on foreign exchange are very popular. Table 5.2 provides quotes on the exchange rate between the British pound (GBP) and the US dollar (USD) that might be provided by a large international bank on August 5, 2008. The quotes are for the number of USD per GBP. The first row indicates that the bank is prepared to buy GBP (also known as sterling) in the spot market (i.e., for virtually immediate delivery) at the rate of $1.8356 per GBP and sell sterling in the spot market at $1.8360 per GBP; the second row indicates that the bank is prepared to buy sterling in one month at $1.8314 per GBP and sell sterling in one month at $1.8319 per GBP; and so on.

Table 5.2 Spot and forward quotes for the USD–GBP exchange rate, August 27, 2008 (GBP = British pound; USD = US dollar; quote is number of USD per GBP).

	Bid	*Offer*
Spot:	1.8356	1.8360
1-month forward:	1.8314	1.8319
3-month forward:	1.8237	1.8242
6-month forward:	1.8127	1.8133

[1] A contract that is worth $1 million to one side and −$1 million to the other side would be counted as having a gross market value of $1 million.

Forward contracts can be used to hedge foreign currency risk. Suppose that on August 27, 2008, the treasurer of a US corporation knows that the corporation will pay £1 million in six months (on February 27, 2009) and wants to hedge against exchange rate moves. The treasurer can agree to buy £1 million six months forward at an exchange rate of 1.8133 by trading with the bank providing the quotes in Table 5.2. The corporation then has a long forward contract on GBP. It has agreed that on February 27, 2009, it will buy £1 million from the bank for $1,813,300. The bank has a short forward contract on GBP. It has agreed that on February 27, 2009, it will sell £1 million for $1,813,300. Both the corporation and the bank have made a binding commitment.

What are the possible outcomes in the trade we have just described? The forward contract obligates the corporation to purchase 1 million pounds for an exchange rate of 1.8133 in six months. If the spot exchange rate rose to, say, 1.9000 at the end of the six months, the forward contract leads to 1 million pounds being purchased by the corporation for an exchange rate of 1.8133 rather than at the spot exchange rate of

Figure 5.2   Payoffs from forward contracts: (a) long position, (b) short position.

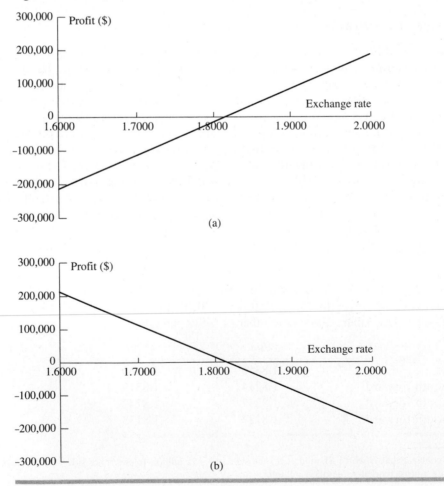

1.9000. This is worth \$86,700 (= (1.9000 − 1.8133) × \$1,000,000) to the corporation. Of course, it may also happen that the contract will have a negative final value to the corporation. If the exchange rate falls to 1.7000 by the end of the six months, the forward contract leads to \$1 million pounds being purchased by the corporation for an exchange rate of 1.8133 rather than at the 1.7000 available in the market. This costs the corporation \$113,300 (= (1.8133 − 1.7000) × \$1,000,000). This example shows that a long forward contract can lead to a payoff that is a gain or loss. The payoff is the spot price of the assets underlying the forward contract minus the agreed delivery price for the assets and is shown in Figure 5.2(a).

The bank in our example has entered into a short forward contract. Its position is the mirror image of that of the corporation. It has agreed to sell \$1 million pounds for an exchange rate of 1.8133 in six months. If the spot exchange rate rose to 1.9000, at the end of the six months the forward contract leads to \$1 million pounds being sold by the bank for an exchange rate of 1.8133 rather than at the spot exchange rate of 1.9000. This costs the bank \$86,700. If the exchange rate falls to 1.7000 by the end of the six months, the forward contract leads to \$1 million pounds being sold by the bank for an exchange rate of 1.8133 rather than 1.7000. This is worth \$113,300 to the bank. The payoff is the agreed delivery price for the assets underlying the forward contract minus spot price and is shown in Figure 5.2(b).

Futures Contracts

Futures contracts, like forward contracts, are agreements to buy an asset at a future time. Unlike forward contracts, futures are traded on an exchange. This means that the contracts that trade are standardized. The exchange defines the amount of the asset underlying one contract, when delivery can be made, exactly what can be delivered, and so on. Contracts are referred to by their delivery month. For example, the September 2010 gold futures is a contract where delivery is made in September 2010. Whereas only one delivery day is usually specified for a forward contract, a futures contract can often be delivered on several days during the delivery month. Alternative delivery times, delivery locations, etc., are defined by the exchange. It is the party with the short position that initiates the delivery process and chooses between the alternatives.

Most futures contracts trade actively with the futures price at any given time being determined by supply and demand. If there are more buyers than sellers at a time when the September 2010 price of gold is \$780 per ounce, the price goes up. Similarly, if there are more sellers than buyers, the price goes down.

One of the attractive features of futures contracts is that it is easy to close out a position. If you buy (i.e., take a long position in) a September 2010 gold futures contract in March 2009, you can exit in June 2009 by selling (i.e., taking a short position in) the same contract. Closing out a position in a forward contract is not as easy as closing out a position in a futures contract. As a result, forward contracts usually lead to final delivery of the underlying assets, whereas futures contracts are usually closed out before the delivery month is reached. Business Snapshot 5.1 is an amusing story showing that the assets underlying futures contracts do get delivered if mistakes are made in the close out.

Futures traders maintain a cash balance known as a *margin account* with their brokers and the balance in the margin account is adjusted for daily gains and losses. Margin accounts are discussed later in the chapter.

Business Snapshot 5.1   The Unanticipated Delivery of a Futures Contract

This story (which may well be apocryphal) was told to the author of this book by a senior executive of a financial institution. It concerns a new employee of the financial institution who had not previously worked in the financial sector. One of the clients of the financial institution regularly entered into a long futures contract on live cattle for hedging purposes and issued instructions to close out the position on the last day of trading. (Live cattle futures contracts trade on the Chicago Mercantile Exchange and each contract is on 40,000 pounds of cattle.) The new employee was given responsibility for handling the account.

When the time came to close out a contract the employee noted that the client was long one contract and instructed a trader at the exchange go long (not short) one contract. The result of this mistake was that the financial institution ended up with a long position in two live cattle futures contracts. By the time the mistake was spotted trading in the contract had ceased.

The financial institution (not the client) was responsible for the mistake. As a result it started to look into the details of the delivery arrangements for live cattle futures contracts—something it had never done before. Under the terms of the contract, cattle could be delivered by the party with the short position to a number of different locations in the United States during the delivery month. Because it was long, the financial institution could do nothing but wait for a party with a short position to issue a *notice of intention to deliver* to the exchange and for the exchange to assign that notice to the financial institution.

It eventually received a notice from the exchange and found that it would receive live cattle at a location 2,000 miles away the following Tuesday. The new employee was dispatched to the location to handle things. It turned out that the location had a cattle auction every Tuesday. The party with the short position that was making delivery bought cattle at the auction and then immediately delivered them. Unfortunately the cattle could not be resold until the next cattle auction the following Tuesday. The employee was therefore faced with the problem of making arrangements for the cattle to be housed and fed for a week. This was a great start to a first job in the financial sector!

Futures contracts are administered by what is known as the *exchange clearinghouse*. The contracts are settled once a day at the close of trading. If the futures price increases from the close of trading on one day to the close of trading on the next day, money flows from traders with short positions to the clearinghouse and from the clearinghouse to traders with long positions. If the futures price decreases from the close of trading on one day to the close of trading on the next day, money flows from traders with long positions to the clearinghouse and from the clearinghouse to traders with short positions. Consider what happens when you buy one September gold futures contract on the Chicago Board of Trade when the futures price is $780 per ounce. The contract is on 100 ounces of gold. If during the first day the futures price moves up to $785, you make a gain of $(785 - 780) \times 100 = \$500$ and receive this amount from the clearinghouse. If on the next day it moves down to $778, you take a loss of $(785 - 778) \times 100 = \$700$ and this amount is paid to the clearinghouse.

> **Business Snapshot 5.2** A Systems Error?
>
> A foreign exchange trader working for a bank enters into a long forward contract to buy 1 million pounds sterling at an exchange rate of 1.6000 in three months. At the same time, another trader on the next desk takes a long position in 16 three-month futures contracts on sterling. The futures price is 1.6000 and each contract is on 62,500 pounds. The positions taken by the forward and futures traders are therefore the same. Within minutes of the positions being taken, the forward and the futures prices both increase to 1.6040. The bank's systems show that the futures trader has made a profit of $4,000 while the forward trader has made a profit of only $3,900. The forward trader immediately calls the bank's systems department to complain. Does the forward trader have a valid complaint?
>
> The answer is no! The daily settlement of futures contracts ensures that the futures trader realizes an almost immediate profit corresponding to the increase in the futures price. If the forward trader closed out the position by entering into a short contract at 1.6040, the forward trader would have contracted to buy 1 million pounds at 1.6000 in three months and sell 1 million pounds at 1.6040 in three months. This would lead to a $4,000 profit—but in three months, not today. The forward trader's profit is the present value of $4,000.
>
> The forward trader can gain some consolation from the fact that gains and losses are treated symmetrically. If the forward/futures prices dropped to 1.5960 instead of rising to 1.6040 the futures trader would take a loss of $4,000 while the forward trader would take a loss of only $3,900. Also, over the three-month contract life, the total gain or loss from the futures contract and the forward contract will be the same.

The futures price of an asset is usually very similar to its forward price. Appendix C at the end of the book gives the relationship between the futures/forward price of an asset and its spot price. Because a futures contract is settled daily whereas a forward contract is settled at the end of its life, the timing of the realization of gains and losses is different for the two contracts. This sometimes causes confusion, as indicated in Business Snapshot 5.2. Table 5.3 summarizes the difference between forward and futures contracts.

Table 5.3 Comparison of forward and futures contracts.

Forward	*Futures*
Private contract between two parties	Traded on an exchange
Not standardized	Standardized contract
Usually one specified delivery date	Range of delivery dates
Settled at end of contract	Settled daily
Delivery or final cash settlement usually takes place	Contract is usually closed out prior to maturity
Some credit risk	Virtually no credit risk

Swaps

The first swap contracts were negotiated in the early 1980s. Since then the market has seen phenomenal growth. Swaps now occupy a position of central importance in the over-the-counter derivatives market.

A swap is an agreement between two companies to exchange cash flows in the future. The agreement defines the dates when the cash flows are to be paid and the way in which they are to be calculated. Usually the calculation of the cash flows involves the future values of interest rates, exchange rates, or other market variables.

A forward contract can be viewed as a simple example of a swap. Suppose that it is March 1, 2010, and a company enters into a forward contract to buy 100 ounces of gold for $800 per ounce in one year. The company can sell the gold in one year as soon as it is received. The forward contract is therefore equivalent to a swap where the company agrees that on March 1, 2011, it will swap 100 times the spot price of gold for $80,000.

Whereas a forward contract is equivalent to the exchange of cash flows on just one future date, swaps typically lead to cash flow exchanges taking place on several future dates. The most common swap is a "plain vanilla" interest rate swap where a fixed rate of interest is exchanged for LIBOR.[2] Both interest rates are applied to the same notional principal. A swap where company A pays a fixed rate of interest of 5% and receives LIBOR is shown in Figure 5.3. Suppose that in this contract interest rates are reset every six months, the notional principal is $100 million, and the swap lasts for three years. Table 5.4 shows the cash flows to company A if six-month LIBOR interest rates prove to be those shown in the second column of the table. The swap is entered into on March 5, 2010. The six-month interest rate on that date is 4.2% per year or 2.1% per six months. As a result the floating-rate cash flow received six months later on September 5, 2010, is 0.021×100 or $2.1 million. Similarly the six-month interest rate of 4.8% per annum (or 2.4% per six months) on September 5, 2010, leads to the floating cash flow received six months later (on March 5, 2011) being $2.4 million; and so on. The fixed rate cash flow paid is always $2.5 million (5% of $100 million applied to a six-month period).[3] Note that the timing of cash flows corresponds to the usual way interest rates such as LIBOR work. The interest is observed at the beginning of the period to which it applies and paid at the end of the period.

Plain vanilla interest rate swaps are very popular because they can be used for many purposes. For example, the swap in Figure 5.3 could be used by company A to transform borrowings at a floating rate of LIBOR plus 1% to borrowings at a fixed

Figure 5.3   A plain vanilla interest rate swap.

---

[2] LIBOR is the London Interbank Offered Rate. It is the rate at which a bank offers to make large wholesale deposits with another bank and will be discussed in Chapter 7.

[3] Note that we have not taken account of day count conventions, holiday calendars, etc., in Table 5.4.

Table 5.4 Example of cash flows (millions of dollars) to company A in the swap shown in Figure 5.3. Swap lasts three years and has a principal of $100 million.

Date	Six-month LIBOR rate (%)	Floating cash flow received	Fixed cash flow paid	Net cash flow
Mar. 5, 2010	4.20			
Sept. 5, 2010	4.80	+2.10	−2.50	−0.40
Mar. 5, 2011	5.30	+2.40	−2.50	−0.10
Sept. 5, 2011	5.50	+2.65	−2.50	+0.15
Mar. 5, 2012	5.60	+2.75	−2.50	+0.25
Sept. 5, 2012	5.90	+2.80	−2.50	+0.30
Mar. 5, 2013	6.40	+2.95	−2.50	+0.45

rate of 6%. The combination of

1. Pay interest at LIBOR plus 1% under loan agreement
2. Receive LIBOR under swap agreement
3. Pay 5% under the swap agreement

nets out to a fixed payment of 6%. It can also be used by company A to transform an investment earning a fixed rate of 4.5% to an investment earning LIBOR minus 0.5%. The combination of

1. Receive 4.5% on the investment
2. Receive LIBOR under swap agreement
3. Pay 5% under the swap agreement

nets out to a floating income at the rate of LIBOR plus 0.5%.

Example 5.1

Suppose a bank has floating-rate deposits and five-year fixed-rate loans. As will be discussed in Chapter 7, this exposes the bank to significant risks. If rates rise, the deposits will be rolled over at high rates and the bank's net interest income will contract. The bank can hedge its risks by entering into the swap in Figure 5.3 (taking the role of Company A). The swap can be viewed as transforming the floating-rate deposits to fixed-rate deposits. Alternatively, it can be viewed as transforming the fixed-rate loans to floating-rate loans.

Many banks are market makers in swaps. Table 5.5 shows quotes for US dollar swaps that might be posted by a bank.[4] The first row shows that the bank is prepared to enter into a two-year swap where it pays a fixed rate of 6.03% and receives LIBOR. It is also prepared to enter into a swap where it receives 6.06% and pays LIBOR. The bid–offer spread in Table 5.5 is 3 or 4 basis points. The average of the bid and offer fixed rates is known as the *swap rate*. This is shown in the final column of the table.

---

[4] The standard swap in the United States is one where fixed payments made every six months are exchanged for floating LIBOR payments made every three months. In Table 5.4, we assumed that fixed and floating payments are exchanged every six months.

Table 5.5 Swap quotes made by a market maker (percent per annum).

Maturity (years)	Bid	Offer	Swap rate
2	6.03	6.06	6.045
3	6.21	6.24	6.225
4	6.35	6.39	6.370
5	6.47	6.51	6.490
7	6.65	6.68	6.665
10	6.83	6.87	6.850

The trading of swaps and other over-the-counter derivatives is facilitated by ISDA, the International Swaps and Derivatives Association. This organization has developed standard contracts that are widely used by market participants. Swaps can be designed so that the periodic cash flows depend on the future value of any well-defined variable. Swaps dependent on interest rates, exchange rates, commodity prices, and equity indices are popular. Sometimes there are embedded options in a swap. For example, one side might have the option to terminate a swap early or to choose between a number of different ways of calculating cash flows. One bizarre swap entered into between Bankers Trust and Procter and Gamble will be discussed later in the chapter (see Business Snapshot 5.4). The valuation of swaps is discussed in Appendix D at the end of this book.

Options

Options are traded both on exchanges and in the over-the-counter market. There are two basic types of option. A *call option* gives the holder the right to buy the underlying asset by a certain date for a certain price. A *put option* gives the holder the right to sell the underlying asset by a certain date for a certain price. The price in the contract is known as the *exercise price* or *strike price*; the date in the contract is known as the *expiration date* or *maturity*. *American options* can be exercised at any time up to the expiration date. *European options* can be exercised only on the expiration date itself.[5] Most of the options that are traded on exchanges are American. In the exchange-traded equity option market, one contract is usually an agreement to buy or sell 100 shares. European options are generally easier to analyze than American options, and some of the properties of an American option are frequently deduced from those of its European counterpart.

An *at-the-money* option is an option where the strike price is close to the price of the underlying asset. An *out-of-the-money* option is a call option where the strike price is above the price of the underlying asset or a put option where the strike price is below this price. An *in-the-money* option is a call option where the strike price is below the price of the underlying asset or a put option where the strike price is above this price.

It should be emphasized that an option gives the holder the right to do something. The holder does not have to exercise this right. By contrast, in a forward and futures contract, the holder is obligated to buy or sell the underlying asset. Note that, whereas

---

[5] Note that the terms *American* and *European* do not refer to the location of the option or the exchange. Some options trading on North American exchanges are European.

it costs nothing to enter into a forward or futures contract, there is a cost to acquiring an option. This cost is referred to as the *option premium*.

The largest exchange in the world for trading stock options is the Chicago Board Options Exchange (CBOE; www.cboe.com). Table 5.6 gives the closing prices of some of the American options trading on Intel (ticker INTC) on August 27, 2008. The option strike prices are $22, $23, $24, and $25. The maturities are September 2008, October 2008, and January 2009. The September options have an expiration date of September 20, 2008; the October options have an expiration date of October 18, 2008; and the January options have an expiration date of January 17, 2009.[6] Intel's stock price at the close of trading on August 27, 2008, was $23.45.

Suppose an investor instructs a broker to buy one October call option contract on Intel with a strike price of $24. The broker will relay these instructions to a trader at the CBOE. This trader will then find another trader who wants to sell one October call contract on Intel with a strike price of $24, and a price will be agreed upon. We assume that the price is $0.92, as indicated in Table 5.6. This is the price for an option to buy one share. In the United States, one stock option contract is a contract to buy or sell 100 shares. Therefore, the investor must arrange for $92 to be remitted to the exchange through the broker. The exchange will then arrange for this amount to be passed on to the party on the other side of the transaction.

In our example the investor has obtained at a cost of $92 the right to buy 100 Intel shares for $24 each. The party on the other side of the transaction has received $92 and has agreed to sell 100 Intel shares for $24 per share if the investor chooses to exercise the option. If the price of Intel does not rise above $24 before October 18, 2008, the option is not exercised and the investor loses $92. But if the Intel share price does well and the option is exercised when it is $30, the investor is able to buy 100 shares at $24 per share when they are worth $30 per share. This leads to a gain of $600, or $508 when the initial cost of the options is taken into account.

If the investor is bearish on Intel, an alternative trade would be the purchase of one January put option contract with a strike price of $24. From Table 5.6 we see that this would cost 100×2.21, or $221. The investor would obtain at a cost of $221 the right to sell 100 Intel shares for $24 per share prior to January, 2009. If the Intel share price moves above $24, then the option is not exercised and the investor loses $221. But if the investor exercises when the stock price is $15, the investor makes a gain of $900 by buying 100 Intel shares at $15 and selling them for $24. The net profit after the cost of the option is taken into account is $679.

Table 5.6   Prices of options on Intel, August 27, 2008; stock price = $23.45.

Strike price ($)	Calls			Puts		
	Sept08	Oct08	Jan09	Sept08	Oct08	Jan09
22	1.65	2.10	n.a.	0.21	0.63	n.a.
23	0.90	1.44	n.a.	0.47	0.97	n.a.
24	0.39	0.92	1.69	0.96	1.45	2.21
25	0.12	0.54	1.27	1.68	2.06	2.78

[6] The exchange chooses the expiration date as the Saturday following the third Friday of the delivery month.

Figure 5.4   Net profit from (a) purchasing a contract consisting of 100 Intel October call options with a strike price of $24 and (b) purchasing a contract consisting of 100 Intel January put options with a strike price of $24.

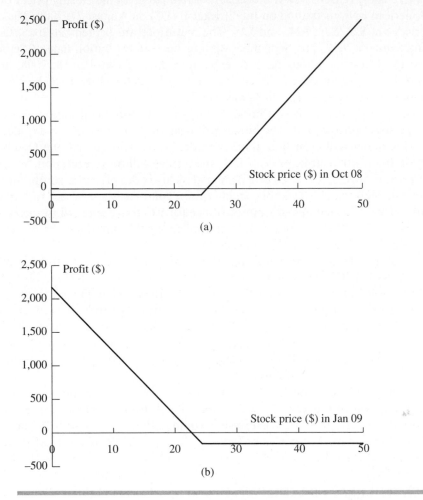

The options trading on the CBOE are American. If we assume for simplicity that they are European, so that they can be exercised only at maturity, the investor's profit as a function of the final stock price for the Intel options we have been considering is shown in Figure 5.4.

There are four types of trade in options markets:

1. Buying a call
2. Selling a call
3. Buying a put
4. Selling a put

Buyers are referred to as having *long positions*; sellers are referred to as having *short positions*. Selling an option is also known as *writing the option*.

Options trade very actively in the over-the-counter market as well as on exchanges. The underlying assets include stocks, currencies, and stock indices. Indeed the over-the-counter market for options is now larger than the exchange-traded market. Whereas exchange-traded options tend to be American, options trading in the over-the-counter market are frequently European. The advantage of the over-the-counter market is that maturity dates, strike prices, and contract sizes can be tailored to meet the precise needs of a client. They do not have to correspond to those specified by the exchange. The sizes of option trades in the over-the-counter are usually much greater than those on exchanges.

Valuation formulas and numerical procedures for options on a variety of assets are in Appendices E and F at the end of this book.

Interest Rate Options

Important interest rate options that trade in the over-the-counter market are *caps*, *floors*, and *swap options*. Whereas a swap exchanges a sequence of floating rates for a fixed rate, as indicated in Table 5.4, a cap, as its name implies, caps the floating rate. It is a series of call options on a floating rate (usually LIBOR). If the floating rate is greater than the strike rate (also known cap rate), there is a payoff equal to the excess of the floating rate over the cap rate; if the floating rate is less than the cap rate, there is no payoff. As in the case of swaps, payoffs are made at the end of the period covered by an interest rate.

There is usually no payoff for the first period covered, because the rate for that period is known when the contract is entered into. Consider a trader who on March 5, 2010, buys a three-year cap on six-month LIBOR with a cap rate of 5.2% and a principal of $100 million. If rates proved to be those indicated in the second column of Table 5.4, there would be no payoff on March 5, 2011. The payoff on September 5, 2011, would be $0.5 \times (0.0530 - 0.0520) \times 100$, or $0.05 million. Similarly there would be payoffs of $0.15 million, $0.20 million, and $0.35 on March 5, 2012, September 5, 2012, and March 5, 2013.

A floor is similarly a series of put options on floating rates. If the instrument we have just been considering were a floor rather than a cap, then the payoff would be $0.5 \times (0.0520 - 0.0480) \times 100$, or $0.20 million on March 5, 2011. Similarly, it would be zero on the other dates.

A swap option is an option to enter into a swap at some future time where the fixed rate is the strike rate. There are two types of swap option. One is an option to pay the strike rate and receive LIBOR; the other is an option to pay LIBOR and receive the strike rate.

5.5   MARGINS

It is appropriate at this stage to explain margins. *Margin* consists of cash or securities posted by a trader with a broker or counterparty. There are two main reasons for margins:

1. The trader is borrowing money to buy an asset. This is referred to a *buying on margin*. The margin is the amount provided by the trader toward the cost of the assets.

2. The trader is entering into a contract that could lead to him or her owing money in the future. In this case the margin can be regarded as collateral for the trade. By posting margin the trader is saying "I am good for this trade. The margin I have posted can be used to cover any losses."

Trades involving margins are monitored daily. Sometimes an initial margin has to be posted. If the market moves against the trader, there may be a *margin call* requesting that additional margin be posted. If the margin is not posted within a reasonable amount of time (usually 24 hours), the trader's position is closed out. The most common type of margin is cash. However, securities that are owned by the trader are sometimes used. For example, Treasury bills might be marginable at 90% of their face value. This means that they are credited to the trader's margin account at 90% of their face value. Shares of a stock might be marginable at 50% of their value.

Margins are used in both the exchange-traded and OTC markets. For example, exchanges require margins on futures contracts, short option positions, and short sales of stock. In the OTC market, banks often require their counterparties to post margins on contracts such as forwards and swaps. Hedge funds, which were discussed in Chapter 4, use a great deal of leverage, some of it through margin agreements. There are many different ways in which margin accounts operate. This section gives a few examples.

Buying on Margin

Many assets can be bought on margin. As an example we consider the situation where a trader buys 1,000 shares for $120 per share on margin using a broker. The broker states that the *initial margin* is 50% and the *maintenance margin* is 25%. The initial margin is the minimum percentage of the cost of the trade that has to be provided by trader. Therefore, in this case, the trader has to deposit at least $60,000 in cash or in the form of marginable securities with the broker. We suppose that the trader deposits $60,000 in cash. The remaining $60,000 that is required to buy the shares is borrowed from the broker (with the broker keeping the shares as collateral). Initially, therefore, the balance in the margin account is $60,000 and the amount borrowed is $60,000. Gains and losses on the shares (as well as interest charged by the broker) are reflected in the margin account balance, which can also be viewed as the trader's equity in the position.

The *maintenance margin* (25% in this case) is the minimum margin balance as a percentage of the value of the shares purchased. If the margin balance drops below this minimum, there is a margin call requiring the trader to provide additional margin bringing the balance up to the maintenance margin level.

Suppose that the price of the share declines by $10. The balance in the margin account falls to $50,000 and the value of the shares purchased is $110,000. The amount borrowed from the broker remains at $60,000. The margin as a percent of the value of the shares purchased is 50,000/110,000. This is more than 25% and so there is no margin call. (The calculations here ignore the interest that would be charged by the broker.) Suppose that, a short time later, the price of the share falls to $78. The loss on the position is 120,000 − 78,000, or $42,000. The balance in the margin account falls to $60,000 − $42,000 = $18,000 and the value of the shares is $78,000. The balance in the margin account has now fallen to 18,000/78,000 = 23.1% of the value of the shares. Because this is less than 25% there is a margin call. The trader is required to bring the margin balance up to 25% of the value of the shares. This means that $0.25 \times 78,000 - 18,000 = \$1,500$ of additional margin must be provided. If it is not provided, the broker sells the shares. If it is provided, the position is maintained and the amount borrowed from the broker falls to \$58,500.

Margins for Short Sales

When sales are shorted, a typical initial margin is 150% of the value of the shares. Suppose that a trader shorts 100 shares when the price is \$60. As explained in Section 5.2, the shares are borrowed and sold in the market. The proceeds of the sale, \$6,000, belong to the trader. However, the margin that must be initially posted is 150% of \$6,000, or \$9,000 in total. The trader must therefore post margin equal to the proceeds of the sale plus an additional \$3,000. In this case, when the value of the shares declines, the balance in the margin account increases. When the value of the shares increases, the balance in the margin account decreases.

Suppose that the maintenance margin is 125%. This means that, when the balance in the margin account falls below 125% of the value of the shares, there is a margin call requiring that the balance be brought up to 125% of the value of the shares. Suppose that the share price rises to \$70. The value of the shares that have been shorted is \$7,000 and the maintenance margin is $1.25 \times 7,000$, or \$8,750. The \$9,000 initial margin covers this. However, if the share price rises again to \$80, the maintenance margin is $1.25 \times 8,000$, or \$10,000. There is a \$1,000 margin call. If it is not met, the position is closed out.

Note one important difference between this example and the earlier one. In the earlier example, \$60,000 was borrowed from the broker and the trader has to pay interest to the broker on it. In this example the initial margin, and any additional margin contributed, belongs to the trader, and, if the trader has a good broker, interest will be paid on the funds by the broker.

Margins for Futures Trades

Consider the trader we looked at earlier who buys one contract (100 ounces) of September gold for \$780. Suppose that the initial margin is \$2,000 per contract and the maintenance margin is \$1,500 per contract. The trader must post \$2,000 of margin with the broker at the time of the trade. Losses on the futures contract are charged to the margin account. Suppose the price of gold falls to \$778. The trader loses \$200. (Gold which the trader agreed to buy for \$780 can now only be sold for \$778.) The balance in the margin account is reduced from \$2,000 to \$1,800. Because the maintenance margin has not been reached, there is no margin call. If the next day the price of gold falls to \$774, the trader loses a further \$400 and the balance in the margin account is reduced to \$1,400. This is below the maintenance margin level. The trader is then required to bring the balance in the margin account up to the initial margin level. The margin call is therefore \$600. If the margin is not provided within 24 hours, the broker will close out the position. Note a difference between this arrangement and the arrangements discussed above for buying on margin and short sales. Here the trader has to bring the balance in the margin account up to the initial margin level. In the other cases, it is sufficient for the trader to bring the balance up to the maintenance margin level.

The initial margins and maintenance margins for futures traders who are selling are similar to those for futures traders who are buying. Traders earn interest on the balance in their margin accounts. As indicated earlier, the daily settlement procedures mean that funds flow from the margin accounts of traders with short positions to the margin accounts of traders with long positions when the futures price increases and in the other direction when it decreases.

Margins for Options Trading

When a trader purchases options for cash, there are no margin requirements because there are no circumstances under which the trader will have a liability in the future. Options on stocks and stock indices that last longer than nine months can be bought on margin in the US. The initial and maintenance margin is 75% of the value of the option.

When options are sold, there are potential future liabilities and margin must be posted. When a call option on a stock is written, the initial and maintenance margin in the US is the greater of

1. 100% of the value of the option plus 20% of the underlying share price less the amount, if any, by which the option is out of the money
2. 100% of the value of the option plus 10% of the share price

When a put option is written, it is the greater of

1. 100% of the value of the option plus 20% of the underlying share price less the amount, if any, by which the option is out of the money
2. 100% of the value of the option plus 10% of the exercise price

These margin requirements may be reduced if the trader has other positions in the stock. For example, if the trader has a fully covered position (where the trader has sold call options on a certain number of share and owns the same number of shares), there is no margin requirement on the short option position.

Margins in the OTC Market

A bank often requires counterparties to post margin on OTC contracts such as forwards and swaps. This is sometimes referred to a collateralizing the trades. Suppose that a bank has entered into an interest rate swap with a particular corporation. This trade is worth zero to both sides when first entered into, but after time has passed it is likely to have a positive value to one side and a negative value to the other side.

The arrangement might be that the bank will give the corporation a certain amount of credit (say, $5 million), so that no margin is required provided that the swap is worth less than $5 million to the bank. But, when the value to the bank exceeds $5 million (so that it is a liability of over $5 million to the corporation), the bank requires the corporation to post margin. For example, when the value is −$7 million to the corporation and +$7 million to the bank, $2 million of margin would have to be posted by the corporation. (Interest is paid by the bank on the margin.) The value of the transactions would be monitored regularly (e.g., every day) and the required margin adjusted.

In a two-way arrangement, the bank would have to post margin with the corporation if value of the swap moved in the corporation's favor by more than a certain amount.

Hedge funds have always tried to obtain two-way arrangements. With the failure of Lehman Brothers and problems experienced by other banks, nonfinancial corporations are increasingly seeking two-way arrangements. In another development, regulators are pushing for clearinghouses to handle margins and settlement on some OTC trades.

Collateralization agreements and the way in which multiple trades with the same counterparty are handled are discussed in more detail Chapter 15.

5.6 NONTRADITIONAL DERIVATIVES

Whenever there are risks in the economy, financial engineers have attempted to develop derivatives to allow entities with exposures to the risks to trade with either (a) entities that have opposite exposures to the risks or (b) speculators who are willing to assume the risks. This section gives examples of derivatives that have been developed to meet specific needs.

Weather Derivatives

Many companies are in the position where their performance is liable to be adversely affected by the weather.[7] It makes sense for these companies to consider hedging their weather risk in much the same way as they hedge foreign exchange or interest rate risks.

The first over-the-counter weather derivatives were introduced in 1997. To understand how they work, we explain two variables:

HDD: Heating degree days

CDD: Cooling degree days

A day's HDD is defined as

$$HDD = \max(0, 65 - A)$$

and a day's CDD is defined as

$$CDD = \max(0, A - 65)$$

where A is the average of the highest and lowest temperature during the day at a specified weather station, measured in degrees Fahrenheit. For example, if the maximum temperature during a day (midnight to midnight) is $68°$ Fahrenheit and the minimum temperature is $44°$ Fahrenheit, $A = 56$. The daily HDD is then 9 and the daily CDD is 0.

A typical over-the-counter product is a forward or option contract providing a payoff dependent on the cumulative HDD or CDD during a month (that is, the total of the HDDs or CDDs for every day in the month). For example, a dealer could in January 2009 sell a client a call option on the cumulative HDD during February 2010 at the Chicago O'Hare Airport weather station with a strike price of 700 and a payment rate of $10,000 per degree day. If the actual cumulative HDD is 820, the payoff is $1.2 million. Often contracts include a payment cap. If the cap in our example is $1.5 million, the client's position is equivalent to a long call option on cumulative HDD with a strike price of 700 and a short call option with a strike price of 850.

---

[7] The US Department of Energy has estimated that one-seventh of the US economy is subject to weather risk.

A day's HDD is a measure of the volume of energy required for heating during the day. A day's CDD is a measure of the volume of energy required for cooling during the day. Most weather derivative contracts are entered into by energy producers and energy consumers. But retailers, supermarket chains, food and drink manufacturers, health service companies, agriculture companies, and companies in the leisure industry are also potential users of weather derivatives. The Weather Risk Management Association (www.wrma.org) has been formed to serve the interests of the weather risk management industry.

In September 1999, the Chicago Mercantile Exchange began trading weather futures and European options on weather futures. The contracts are on the cumulative HDD and CDD for a month observed at a weather station.[8] The contracts are settled in cash just after the end of the month once the HDD and CDD are known. One futures contract is on \$100 times the cumulative HDD or CDD. The HDD and CDD are calculated by a company, Earth Satellite Corporation, using automated data collection equipment.

Oil Derivatives

Crude oil is one of the most important commodities in the world with global demand amounting to about 80 million barrels daily. Ten-year fixed-price supply contracts have been commonplace in the over-the-counter market for many years. These are swaps where oil at a fixed price is exchanged for oil at a floating price.

In the 1970s, the price of oil was highly volatile. The 1973 war in the Middle East led to a tripling of oil prices. Following the fall of the Shah of Iran in the late 1970s, oil prices increased again. These events led oil producers and users to a realization that they needed more sophisticated tools for managing oil price risk. In the 1980s both the over-the-counter market and the exchange-traded market developed products to meet this need. These products were heavily used to hedge risks in 2007 and 2008, a period of particularly high oil-price volatility.

In the over-the-counter market, virtually any derivative that is available on common stocks or stock indices is now available with oil as the underlying asset. Swaps, forward contracts, and options are popular. Contracts sometimes require settlement in cash and sometimes require settlement by physical delivery (i.e., by delivery of the oil).

Exchange-traded contracts on oil are also popular. The New York Mercantile Exchange (NYMEX) and the International Petroleum Exchange (IPE) trade a number of oil futures and futures options contracts. Some of the futures contracts are settled in cash; others are settled by physical delivery. For example, the Brent crude oil futures traded on the IPE has cash settlement based on the Brent index price; the light sweet crude oil futures traded on NYMEX require physical delivery. In both cases, the amount of oil underlying one contract is 1,000 barrels. NYMEX also trades popular contracts on two refined products: heating oil and gasoline. In both cases, one contract is for the delivery of 42,000 gallons.

Natural Gas Derivatives

The natural gas industry throughout the world has been going through a period of deregulation and the elimination of government monopolies. The supplier of natural

---

[8] The CME has introduced contracts for 10 different weather stations (Atlanta, Chicago, Cincinnati, Dallas, Des Moines, Las Vegas, New York, Philadelphia, Portland, and Tucson).

gas is now not necessarily the same company as the producer of the gas. Suppliers are faced with the problem of meeting daily demand.

A typical over-the-counter contract is for the delivery of a specified amount of natural gas at a roughly uniform rate over a one-month period. Forward contracts, options, and swaps are available in the over-the-counter market. The seller of gas is usually responsible for moving the gas through pipelines to the specified location.

NYMEX trades a contract for the delivery of 10,000 million British thermal units of natural gas. The contract, if not closed out, requires physical delivery to be made during the delivery month at a roughly uniform rate to a particular hub in Louisiana. The IPE trades a similar contract in London.

Electricity Derivatives

Electricity is an unusual commodity because it cannot easily be stored.[9] The maximum supply of electricity in a region at any moment is determined by the maximum capacity of all the electricity-producing plants in the region. In the United States there are 140 regions known as *control areas*. Demand and supply are first matched within a control area, and any excess power is sold to other control areas. It is this excess power that constitutes the wholesale market for electricity. The ability of one control area to sell power to another control area depends on the transmission capacity of the lines between the two areas. Transmission from one area to another involves a transmission cost, charged by the owner of the line, and there are generally some energy transmission losses.

A major use of electricity is for air-conditioning systems. As a result, the demand for electricity, and therefore its price, is much greater in the summer months than in the winter months. The nonstorability of electricity causes occasional very large movements in the spot price. Heat waves have been known to increase the spot price by as much as 1,000% for short periods of time.

Like natural gas, electricity has been going through a period of deregulation and the elimination of government monopolies. This has been accompanied by the development of an electricity derivatives market. NYMEX now trades a futures contract on the price of electricity, and there is an active over-the-counter market in forward contracts, options, and swaps. A typical contract (exchange traded or over the counter) allows one side to receive a specified number of megawatt-hours for a specified price at a specified location during a particular month. In a 5 × 8 contract, power is received for five days a week (Monday to Friday) during the off-peak period (11 p.m. to 7 a.m.) for the specified month. In a 5 × 16 contract, power is received five days a week during the on-peak period (7 a.m. to 11 p.m.) for the specified month. In a 7 × 24 contract, it is received around the clock every day during the month. Option contracts have either daily exercise or monthly exercise. In the case of daily exercise, the option holder can choose on each day of the month (by giving one day's notice) to receive the specified amount of power at the specified strike price. When there is monthly exercise, a single decision on whether to receive power for the whole month at the specified strike price is made at the beginning of the month.

---

[9] Electricity producers with spare capacity sometimes use it to pump water to the top of their hydroelectric plants so that it can be used to produce electricity at a later time. This is the closest they can get to storing this commodity.

An interesting contract in electricity and natural gas markets is what is known as a *swing option* or *take-and-pay option*. In this contract, a minimum and maximum for the amount of power that must be purchased at a certain price by the option holder is specified for each day during a month and for the month in total. The option holder can change (or swing) the rate at which the power is purchased during the month, but usually there is a limit on the total number of changes that can be made.

5.7 EXOTIC OPTIONS AND STRUCTURED PRODUCTS

Many different types of exotic options and structured products trade in the over-the-counter market. Although the amount of trading in them is small compared with the trading in the plain vanilla derivatives discussed in Section 5.4, they are important to a bank because the profit on trades in exotic options and structured products tends to be much higher than on plain vanilla options or swaps.

Here are a few examples of exotic options:

Asian options: Whereas regular options provide a payoff based on the final price of the underlying asset at the time of exercise, Asian options provide a payoff based on the average of the price of the underlying asset over some specified period. An example is an *average price call option* that provides a payoff in one year equal to $\max(\bar{S} - K, 0)$ where $\bar{S}$ is the average asset price during the year and K is the strike price.

Barrier options: These are options that come into existence or disappear when the price of the underlying asset reaches a certain barrier. For example a knock-out call option with a strike price of $30 and a barrier of $20 is a regular call option that ceases to exist if the asset price falls below $20.

Basket options: These are options on a portfolio of assets rather than options on a single asset.

Binary options: These are options that provide a fixed dollar payoff, or a certain amount of the underlying asset, if some condition is satisfied. An example is an option that provides a payoff in one year of $1,000 if a stock price is greater than $20.

Compound options: These are options on options. There are four types: a call on a call, a call on a put, a put on a call, and a put on a put. An example of a compound option is an option to buy an option on a stock currently worth $15. The first option expires in one year and has a strike price of $1. The second option expires in three years and has a strike price of $20.

Lookback options: These are options that provide a payoff based on the maximum or minimum price of the underlying asset over some period. An example is an option that provides a payoff in one year equal to $S_T - S_{\min}$, where S_T is the asset price at the end of the year and $S_{\min}$ is the minimum asset price during the year.

Exotic options are sometimes more appropriate for hedging than plain vanilla options. As explained in Business Snapshot 5.3, Microsoft uses Asian options on a basket for some of its foreign currency hedging.

Structured products are products created by banks to meet the needs of investors or corporate treasurers. One example of a structured product is a principal protected note, where a bank offers an investor the opportunity to earn a certain percentage of the return provided by the S&P 500 with a guarantee that the return will not be negative. Another example of a (highly) structured product is the 5/30 transaction described in

---

Business Snapshot 5.3 Microsoft's Hedging

Microsoft actively manages its foreign exchange exposure. In some countries (e.g., Europe, Japan, and Australia), it bills in the local currency and converts its net revenue to US dollars monthly. For these currencies there is a clear exposure to exchange rate movements. In other countries (e.g., those in Latin America, Eastern Europe, and Southeast Asia), it bills in US dollars. The latter appears to avoid any foreign exchange exposure—but it does not.

Suppose the US dollar strengthens against the currency of a country in which it is billing in US dollars. People in the country will find Microsoft's products more expensive because it takes more of the local currency to buy $1. As a result Microsoft is likely to find it necessary to reduce its (US dollar) price in the country or face a decline in sales. Microsoft therefore has a foreign exchange exposure—both when it bills in US dollars and when it bills in the local currency. (This shows that it is important for a company to consider the big picture when assessing its exposure.)

Microsoft likes to use options for hedging. Suppose it chooses a one-year time horizon. Microsoft recognizes that its exposure to an exchange rate (say, the Japanese yen–US dollar exchange rate) is an exposure to the average of the exchange rates at the end of each month during the year. This is because approximately the same amount of Japanese yen is converted to US dollars each month. Asian options rather than regular options are appropriate to hedge its exposure. What is more, Microsoft's total foreign exchange exposure is a a weighted average of the exchange rates in all the countries in which it does business. This means that a basket option, where the option is on a portfolio of currencies, is an appropriate tool for hedging. A contract it likes to negotiate with banks is therefore an Asian basket option. The cost of this option is much less than a portfolio of put options, one for each month and each exchange rate (see Problem 5.23), but it gives Microsoft exactly the protection it wants.

Microsoft faces other financial risks. For example, it is exposed to interest rate risk on its bond portfolio. (When rates rise the portfolio loses money.) It also has two sorts of exposure to equity prices. It is exposed to the equity prices of the companies in which it invests. It is also exposed to its own equity price because it regularly repurchases it own shares as part of its stock awards program. It sometimes uses sophisticated option strategies to hedge these risks.

Business Snapshot 5.4.[10] (In the case of this product, it is debatable whether Bankers Trust was meeting a client need or selling the client a product it did not need!)

5.8 RISK MANAGEMENT CHALLENGES

Instruments such as futures, forwards, swaps, options, and structured products are versatile. They can be used for hedging, for speculation, and for arbitrage. (Hedging involves reducing risks; speculation involves taking risks; and arbitrage involves

---

[10] The details of this transaction are in the public domain because it later became the subject of litigation. See D.J. Smith, "Aggressive Corporate Finance: A Close Look at the Procter and Gamble–Bankers Trust Leveraged Swap," *Journal of Derivatives*, 4, 4 (Summer 1997): 67–79.

Business Snapshot 5.4   Procter and Gamble's Bizarre Deal

A particularly bizarre swap is the so-called "5/30" swap entered into between Bankers Trust (BT) and Procter and Gamble (P&G) on November 2, 1993. This was a five-year swap with semiannual payments. The notional principal was $200 million. BT paid P&G 5.30% per annum. P&G paid BT the average 30-day CP (commercial paper) rate minus 75 basis points plus a spread. The average commercial paper rate was calculated by taking observations on the 30-day commercial paper rate each day during the preceding accrual period and averaging them.

The spread was zero for the first payment date (May 2, 1994). For the remaining nine payment dates it was

$$\max\left[0, \frac{98.5\left(\dfrac{\text{5-year CMT\%}}{5.78\%}\right) - (\text{30-year TSY price})}{100}\right]$$

In this, five-year CMT is the constant maturity Treasury yield (i.e., the yield on a five-year Treasury note, as reported by the US Federal Reserve). The 30-year TSY price is the midpoint of the bid and offer cash bond prices for the 6.25% Treasury bond maturing on August 2023. Note that the spread calculated from the formula is a decimal interest rate. It is not measured in basis points. If the formula gives 0.1 and the CP rate is 6%, the rate paid by P&G is 15.25%.

P&G were hoping that the spread would be zero and the deal would enable it to exchange fixed-rate funding at 5.30% for funding at 75 basis points less than the commercial paper rate. In fact, interest rates rose sharply in early 1994, bond prices fell, and the swap proved very, very expensive (see Problem 5.36).

---

attempting to lock in a profit by simultaneously trading in two or more markets.) It is this very versatility that can cause problems. Sometimes traders who have a mandate to hedge risks or follow an arbitrage strategy become (consciously or unconsciously) speculators. The results can be disastrous. One example of this is provided by the activities of Nick Leeson at Barings Bank (see Business Snapshot 5.5).[11]

To avoid the type of problem Barings encountered is an important risk management challenge. Both financial and nonfinancial corporations must set up controls to ensure that derivatives are being used for their intended purpose. Risk limits should be set and the activities of traders should be monitored daily to ensure that the risk limits are adhered to. We will be discussing this in later chapters.

SUMMARY

There are two types of market in which financial products trade: the exchange-traded market and the over-the-counter market. This chapter has reviewed spot trades, forwards, futures, swaps, and options contracts. A forward or futures contract involves an obligation to buy or sell an asset at a certain time in the future for a certain price. A swap

---

[11] The movie *Rogue Trader* provides a good dramatization of the failure of Barings Bank.

Business Snapshot 5.5   The Barings Bank Disaster

Derivatives are very versatile instruments. They can be used for hedging, speculation, and arbitrage. One of the risks faced by a company that trades derivatives is that an employee who has a mandate to hedge or to look for arbitrage opportunities may become a speculator.

Nick Leeson, an employee of Barings Bank in the Singapore office in 1995, had a mandate to look for arbitrage opportunities between the Nikkei 225 futures prices on the Singapore exchange and the Osaka exchange. Over time Leeson moved from being an arbitrageur to being a speculator without anyone in the Barings London head office fully understanding that he had changed the way he was using derivatives. He began to make losses, which he was able to hide. He then began to take bigger speculative positions in an attempt to recover the losses, but only succeeded in making the losses worse.

In the end, Leeson's total loss was close to 1 billion dollars. As a result, Barings—a bank that had been in existence for 200 years—was wiped out. One of the lessons from the Barings disaster is that it is important to define unambiguous risk limits for traders and then carefully monitor their activities to make sure that the limits are adhered to.

---

is an agreement to exchange cash flows in the future in amounts dependent on the values of one or more market variables. There are two types of option: calls and puts. A call option gives the holder the right to buy an asset by a certain date for a certain price. A put option gives the holder the right to sell an asset by a certain date for a certain price.

Forward, futures, and swap contracts have the effect of locking in the prices that will apply to future transactions. Options by contrast provide insurance. They ensure that the price applicable to a future transaction will not be worse than a certain level. Exotic options and structured products are tailored to the particular needs of corporate treasurers. For example, as shown in Business Snapshot 5.3, Asian basket options can allow a company such as Microsoft to hedge its net exposure to several risks over a period of time.

Margin is cash or marketable securities deposited by a trader in a margin account with either a broker or a counterparty. Margin accounts are used when a trader wishes to borrow money for trading or when the trading may give rise to future liabilities. The trader's position is monitored daily and there may be margin calls requesting further margin. If the trader does not satisfy a margin call within 24 hours the trader's position is usually closed out.

Derivatives now trade on a wide variety of variables. This chapter has reviewed those that provide payoffs dependent on the weather, oil, natural gas, and electricity. It has also discussed exotic options and structured products.

FURTHER READING

Boyle, P., and F. Boyle, *Derivatives: The Tools That Changed Finance*. London: Risk Books, 2001.

Flavell, R., *Swaps and Other Instruments*. Chichester: Wiley, 2002.

Geczy, C., B. A. Minton, and C. Schrand, "Why Firms Use Currency Derivatives," *Journal of Finance*, 52, 4 (1997): 1323–54.

Litzenberger, R. H., "Swaps: Plain and Fanciful," *Journal of Finance*, 47, 3 (1992): 831–50.

Miller, M. H. "Financial Innovation: Achievements and Prospects," *Journal of Applied Corporate Finance*, 4 (Winter 1992): 4–11.

Warwick B., F. J. Jones, and R. J. Teweles, *The Futures Games*, 3rd edn. New York: McGraw-Hill, 1998.

PRACTICE QUESTIONS AND PROBLEMS (Answers at the End of the Book)

5.1. What is the difference between a long forward position and a short forward position?

5.2. Explain carefully the difference between hedging, speculation, and arbitrage.

5.3. What is the difference between entering into a long forward contract when the forward price is $50 and taking a long position in a call option with a strike price of $50?

5.4. Explain carefully the difference between selling a call option and buying a put option.

5.5. An investor enters into a short forward contract to sell 100,000 British pounds for US dollars at an exchange rate of 1.9000 US dollars per pound. How much does the investor gain or lose if the exchange rate at the end of the contract is (a) 1.8900 and (b) 1.9200?

5.6. A trader enters into a short cotton futures contract when the futures price is 50 cents per pound. The contract is for the delivery of 50,000 pounds. How much does the trader gain or lose if the cotton price at the end of the contract is (a) 48.20 cents per pound and (b) 51.30 cents per pound?

5.7. Suppose you write a put contract with a strike price of $40 and an expiration date in three months. The current stock price is $41 and the contract is on 100 shares. What have you committed yourself to? How much could you gain or lose?

5.8. What is the difference between the over-the-counter market and the exchange-traded market? Which of the two markets do the following trade in: (a) a forward contract, (b) a futures contract, (c) an option, (d) a swap, and (e) an exotic option?

5.9. You would like to speculate on a rise in the price of a certain stock. The current stock price is $29, and a three-month call with a strike of $30 costs $2.90. You have $5,800 to invest. Identify two alternative strategies, one involving an investment in the stock and the other involving investment in the option. What are the potential gains and losses from each?

5.10. Suppose that you own 5,000 shares worth $25 each. How can put options be used to provide you with insurance against a decline in the value of your holding over the next four months?

5.11. When first issued, a stock provides funds for a company. Is the same true of a stock option? Discuss.

5.12. Suppose that a March call option to buy a share for $50 costs $2.50 and is held until March. Under what circumstances will the holder of the option make a profit? Under what circumstances will the option be exercised?

5.13. Suppose that a June put option to sell a share for $60 costs $4 and is held until June. Under what circumstances will the seller of the option (i.e., the party with the short position) make a profit? Under what circumstances will the option be exercised?

5.14. A company knows that it is due to receive a certain amount of a foreign currency in four months. What type of option contract is appropriate for hedging?

5.15. A United States company expects to have to pay 1 million Canadian dollars in six months. Explain how the exchange rate risk can be hedged using (a) a forward contract and (b) an option.

5.16. In the 1980s, Bankers Trust developed index currency option notes (ICONs). These are bonds in which the amount received by the holder at maturity varies with a foreign exchange rate. One example was its trade with the Long Term Credit Bank of Japan. The ICON specified that if the yen–US dollar exchange rate S_T is greater than 169 yen per dollar at maturity (in 1995), the holder of the bond receives \$1,000. If it is less than 169 yen per dollar, the amount received by the holder of the bond is

$$1,000 - \max\left[0,\ 1,000\left(\frac{169}{S_T} - 1\right)\right]$$

When the exchange rate is below 84.5, nothing is received by the holder at maturity. Show that this ICON is a combination of a regular bond and two options.

5.17. Suppose that USD–sterling spot and forward exchange rates are as follows:

Spot	1.6080
90-day forward	1.6056
180-day forward	1.6018

What opportunities are open to an arbitrageur in the following situations: (a) a 180-day European call option to buy £1 for \$1.57 costs 2 cents, and (b) a 90-day European put option to sell £1 for \$1.64 costs 2 cents?

5.18. A company has money invested at 5% for five years. It wishes to use the swap quotes in Table 5.5 to convert its investment to a floating rate investment. Explain how it can do this.

5.19. A company has borrowed money for five years at 7%. Explain how it can use the quotes in Table 5.5 to convert this to a floating-rate liability.

5.20. A company has a floating-rate liability that costs LIBOR plus 1%. Explain how it can use the quotes in Table 5.5 to convert this to a three-year fixed-rate liability.

5.21. A corn farmer argues: "I do not use futures contracts for hedging. My real risk is not the price of corn. It is that my whole crop gets wiped out by the weather." Discuss this viewpoint. Should the farmer estimate his or her expected production of corn and hedge to try to lock in a price for expected production?

5.22. An airline executive has argued: "There is no point in our hedging the price of jet fuel. There is just as much chance that we will lose from doing this as that we will gain." Discuss the executive's viewpoint.

5.23. Why is the cost of an Asian basket put option to Microsoft considerably less than the cost of a portfolio of put options, one for each currency and each maturity (see Business Snapshot 5.3)?

5.24. A United States investor writes five call option contracts. The option price is \$3.50, the strike price is \$60, and the stock price is \$57. What is the initial margin requirement?

5.25. "Oil, gas, and electricity exhibit mean reversion." What do you think is meant by this statement? Which energy source is likely to have the highest rate of mean reversion? Which is likely to have the lowest?

5.26. Does a knockout barrier call option become more or less valuable as the frequency with which the barrier is observed is increased?

5.27. Suppose that each day during July the minimum temperature is 68° Fahrenheit and the maximum temperature is 82° Fahrenheit. What is the payoff from a call option on the cumulative CDD during July with a strike of 250 and a payment rate of $5,000 per degree day?

5.28. Explain how a 5×8 option contract on electricity for May 2010 with daily exercise works. Explain how a 5×8 option contract on electricity for May 2010 with monthly exercise works. Which is worth more?

5.29. A trader shorts 500 shares of a stock when the price is $50. The initial margin is 160% and the maintenance margin is 130%. How much cash is required from the trader initially? How high does the price of the stock have to rise for there to be a margin call?

FURTHER QUESTIONS

5.30. A company enters into a short futures contract to sell 5,000 bushels of wheat for 250 cents per bushel. The initial margin is $3,000 and the maintenance margin is $2,000. What price change would lead to a margin call? Under what circumstances could $1,500 be withdrawn from the margin account?

5.31. The current price of a stock is $94, and three-month European call options with a strike price of $95 currently sell for $4.70. An investor who feels that the price of the stock will increase is trying to decide between buying 100 shares and buying 2,000 call options ($= 20$ contracts). Both strategies involve an investment of $9,400. What advice would you give? How high does the stock price have to rise for the option strategy to be more profitable?

5.32. A bond issued by Standard Oil worked as follows. The holder received no interest. At the bond's maturity the company promised to pay $1,000 plus an additional amount based on the price of oil at that time. The additional amount was equal to the product of 170 and the excess (if any) of the price of a barrel of oil at maturity over $25. The maximum additional amount paid was $2,550 (which corresponds to a price of $40 per barrel). Show that the bond is a combination of a regular bond, a long position in call options on oil with a strike price of $25, and a short position in call options on oil with a strike price of $40.

5.33. The price of gold is currently $500 per ounce. The forward price for delivery in one year is $700. An arbitrageur can borrow money at 10% per annum. What should the arbitrageur do? Assume that the cost of storing gold is zero and that gold provides no income.

5.34. A company's investments earn LIBOR minus 0.5%. Explain how it can use the quotes in Table 5.5 to convert them to (a) three-year, (b) five-year, and (c) ten-year fixed-rate investments.

5.35. What position is equivalent to a long forward contract to buy an asset at K on a certain date and a long position in a European put option to sell it for K on that date?

5.36. Estimate the interest rate paid by P&G on the 5/30 swap in Business Snapshot 5.4 if (a) the CP rate is 6.5% and the Treasury yield curve is flat at 6%, and (b) the CP rate is 7.5% and the Treasury yield curve is flat at 7% with semiannual compounding.

5.37. A trader buys 200 shares of a stock on margin. The price of the stock is $20. The initial margin is 60% and the maintenance margin is 30%. How much money does the trader have to provide initially? For what share price is there a margin call?

CHAPTER **6**

How Traders Manage Their Exposures

The trading function within a financial institution is referred to as the *front office*; the part of the financial institution that is concerned with the overall level of the risks being taken, capital adequacy, and regulatory compliance is referred to as the *middle office*; the record keeping function is referred to as the *back office*. As explained in Section 1.6, there are two levels within a financial institution at which trading risks are managed. First, the front office hedges risks by ensuring that exposures to individual market variables are not too great. Second, the middle office aggregates the exposures of all traders to determine whether the total risk is acceptable. In this chapter we focus on the hedging activities of the front office. In later chapters we will consider how risks are aggregated in the middle office.

This chapter explains what are termed the "Greek letters" or simply the Greeks. Each of the Greeks measures a different aspect of the risk in a trading position. Traders calculate their Greeks at the end of each day and are required to take action if the internal risk limits of the financial institution they work for are exceeded. Failure to take this action is liable to lead to immediate dismissal.

6.1 DELTA

Imagine that you are a trader working for a US bank and responsible for all trades involving gold. The current price of gold is $800 per ounce. Table 6.1 shows a summary of your portfolio (known as your "book"). How can you manage your risks?

The value of your portfolio is currently $117,000. One way of investigating the risks you face is to revalue the portfolio on the assumption that there is a small increase in the price of gold from $800 per ounce to $800.10 per ounce. Suppose that the new value of the portfolio is $116,900. A $0.1 increase in the price of gold decreases the value of your portfolio by $100. The sensitivity of the portfolio to the price of gold is therefore

$$\frac{-100}{0.1} = -1,000$$

This is referred to as the *delta* of the portfolio. The portfolio loses value at a rate of about $1,000 per $1 increase in the price of gold. Similarly, it gains value at a rate of about $1,000 per $1 decrease in the price of gold.

113

Table 6.1 Summary of gold portfolio.

Position	Value ($)
Spot gold	180,000
Forward contracts	−60,000
Futures contracts	2,000
Swaps	80,000
Options	−110,000
Exotics	25,000
Total	117,000

In general, the *delta*, Δ, of a portfolio P with respect to a market variable S is

$$\frac{\Delta P}{\Delta S}$$

where ΔS is a small increase in the value of the variable and ΔP is the resultant change in the value of the portfolio. Using calculus terminology, delta is the partial derivative of the portfolio value with respect to the value of the variable:

$$\text{Delta} = \frac{\partial P}{\partial S}$$

In our example the trader can eliminate the delta exposure by buying 1,000 ounces of gold. This is because the delta of a long position in 1,000 ounces of gold is 1,000. (The position gains value at the rate of $1,000 per $1 increase in the price of gold.) When this trade is combined with the existing portfolio, the resultant portfolio has a delta of zero. Such a portfolio is referred to as a *delta-neutral* portfolio.

Linear Products

A linear product is one whose value at any given time is linearly dependent on the value of the underlying market variable (see Figure 6.1). Forward contracts, futures contracts, and swaps are linear products; options are not.

A linear product can be hedged relatively easily. As a simple example, consider a US bank that enters into a forward contract with a corporate client where it agrees to sell the client one million euros for $1.3 million in one year. Assume that the euro and dollar interest rates are 4% and 3% with annual compounding. This means that the present value of a 1 million euro cash flow in one year is $1,000,000/1.04 = 961,538$ euros. The present value of a $1.3 million dollars in one year is $1,300,000/1.03 = 1,262,136$ dollars. Suppose that S is the value of 1 euro in dollars today. The value of the contract today in dollars is[1]

$$1,262,136 - 961,538S$$

This shows that the delta of the contract is −961,538. It can be hedged by buying 961,538 euros.

---

[1] See Appendix C for more information on the valuation of forward contracts.

Figure 6.1 A linear product.

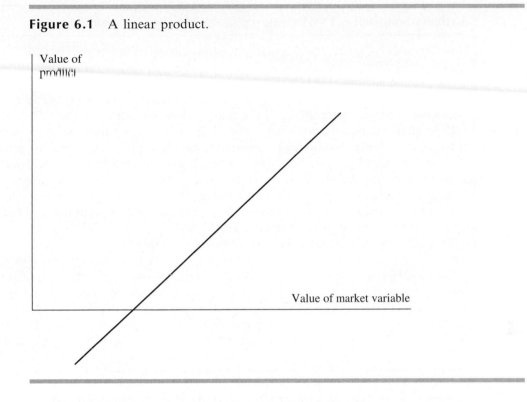

To see that the hedge works, note that the 961,538 euros that are purchased can be invested at 3% for one year so that they grow to exactly 1 million euros in one year. This is what the bank will need to make payment under the terms of the forward contract.

When the bank enters into the opposite transaction and agrees to buy 1 million euros in one year the value of the contract is

$$961,538S - 1,262,136$$

It has a delta of +961,538. It must hedge by shorting 961,538 euros. It does this by borrowing the euros today at 4% and immediately converting them to US dollars. The 1 million euros received in one year are used to repay the loan.

Shorting assets to hedge forward contracts is sometimes tricky. Gold is an interesting case in point. Financial institutions often find that they enter into very large forward contracts to buy gold from gold producers. This means that they need to borrow large quantities of gold to create a short position for hedging. As outlined in Business Snapshot 6.1, central banks are the source of the borrowed gold. A fee known as the gold lease rate is charged by central banks for lending the gold.

Nonlinear Products

Options and other more complex derivatives are nonlinear products. The relationship between the value of the product and the value of the underlying market variable at any given time is nonlinear. This nonlinearity makes them more difficult to hedge.

Business Snapshot 6.1   Hedging by Gold Mining Companies

It is natural for a gold mining company to consider hedging against changes in the price of gold. Typically it takes several years to extract all the gold from a mine. Once a gold mining company decides to go ahead with production at a particular mine, it has a big exposure to the price of gold. Indeed a mine that looks profitable at the outset could become unprofitable if the price of gold plunges.

Gold mining companies are careful to explain their hedging strategies to potential shareholders. Some gold mining companies do not hedge. They tend to attract shareholders who buy gold stocks because they want to benefit when the price of gold increases and are prepared to accept the risk of a loss from a decrease in the price of gold. Other companies choose to hedge. They estimate the number of ounces they will produce each month for the next few years and enter into futures or forward contracts to lock in the price that will be received.

Suppose you are Goldman Sachs and have just entered into a forward contract with a gold mining company where you agree to buy a large amount of gold at a fixed price. How do you hedge your risk? The answer is that you borrow gold from a central bank and sell it at the current market price. (The central banks of some of the countries that hold large amounts of gold are prepared to lend gold for a fee known as the gold lease rate.) At the end of the life of the forward contract you buy gold from the gold mining company under the terms of the forward contract and use it to repay the central bank.

Consider as an example a trader who sells 100,000 European call options on a non-dividend-paying stock when:

1. The stock price is $49
2. The strike price is $50
3. The risk-free interest rate is 5%
4. The stock price volatility is 20% per annum
5. The time to option maturity is 20 weeks

We suppose that the amount received for the options is $300,000 and that the trader has no other positions dependent on the stock.

The value of one option as a function of the underlying stock price is shown in Figure 6.2. The delta of one option changes with the stock price in the way shown in Figure 6.3.[2] At the time of the trade the value of an option to buy one share of the stock is $2.40 and the delta of the option is 0.522. Because the trader is short 100,000 options, the value of the trader's portfolio is −$240,000 and the delta of the portfolio is −$52,200. The trader can feel pleased that the options have been sold for $60,000 more than their theoretical value, but is faced with the problem of hedging the risk in the portfolio.

Immediately after the trade, the trader's portfolio can be made delta neutral by buying 52,200 shares of the underlying stock. If there is a small decrease (increase) in

---

[2] Figures 6.2 and 6.3 were produced with the DerivaGem software that accompanies this book. The Black–Scholes model was selected by choosing "Analytic:European" as the option type.

Figure 6.2 Value of option as a function of stock price.

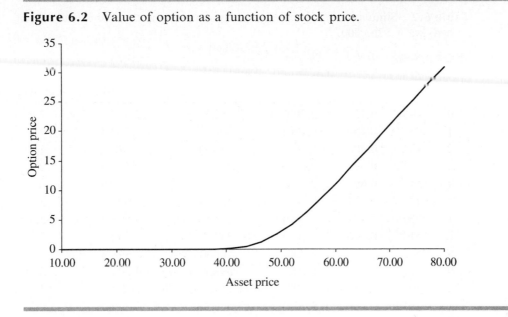

the stock price the gain (loss) to the trader of the short option position should be offset by the loss (gain) on the shares. For example, if the stock price increases from $49 to $49.10, the value of the options will decrease by about $52,200 \times 0.10 = \$5,220$, while the value of the shares will increase by this amount.

In the case of linear products, once the hedge has been set up, it does not need to be changed. This is not the case for nonlinear products. To preserve delta neutrality the hedge has to be adjusted periodically. This is known as *rebalancing*.

Figure 6.3 Delta of option as a function of stock price.

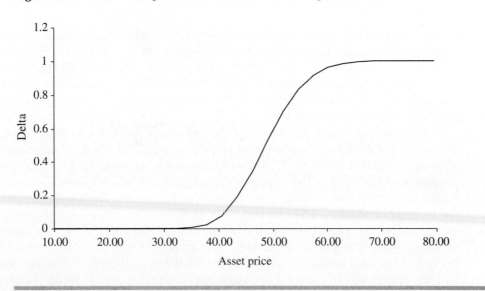

Table 6.2 Simulation of delta hedging. Option closes in the money and cost of hedging is $263,300.

Week	Stock price	Delta	Shares purchased	Cost of shares purchased ($000)	Cumulative cost including interest ($000)	Interest cost ($000)
0	49.00	0.522	52,200	2,557.8	2,557.8	2.5
1	48.12	0.458	(6,400)	(308.0)	2,252.3	2.2
2	47.37	0.400	(5,800)	(274.7)	1,979.8	1.9
3	50.25	0.596	19,600	984.9	2,966.6	2.9
4	51.75	0.693	9,700	502.0	3,471.5	3.3
5	53.12	0.774	8,100	430.3	3,905.1	3.8
6	53.00	0.771	(300)	(15.9)	3,893.0	3.7
7	51.87	0.706	(6,500)	(337.2)	3,559.5	3.4
8	51.38	0.674	(3,200)	(164.4)	3,398.5	3.3
9	53.00	0.787	11,300	598.9	4,000.7	3.8
10	49.88	0.550	(23,700)	(1,182.2)	2,822.3	2.7
11	48.50	0.413	(13,700)	(664.4)	2,160.6	2.1
12	49.88	0.542	12,900	643.5	2,806.2	2.7
13	50.37	0.591	4,900	246.8	3,055.7	2.9
14	52.13	0.768	17,700	922.7	3,981.3	3.8
15	51.88	0.759	(900)	(46.7)	3,938.4	3.8
16	52.87	0.865	10,600	560.4	4,502.6	4.3
17	54.87	0.978	11,300	620.0	5,126.9	4.9
18	54.62	0.990	1,200	65.5	5,197.3	5.0
19	55.87	1.000	1,000	55.9	5,258.2	5.1
20	57.25	1.000	0	0.0	5,263.3	0.0

Tables 6.2 and 6.3 provide two examples of how rebalancing might work in our example. Rebalancing is assumed to be done weekly. As mentioned, the initial value of delta for a single option is 0.522, and the delta of the portfolio is −52,200. This means that, as soon as the option is written, $2,557,800 must be borrowed to buy 52,200 shares at a price of $49. The rate of interest is 5%. An interest cost of approximately $2,500 is therefore incurred in the first week.

In Table 6.2, the stock price falls by the end of the first week to $48.12. The delta declines to 0.458. A long position in 45,800 shares is now required to hedge the option position. Therefore 6,400 (= 52,200 − 45,800) shares are sold to maintain the delta neutrality of the hedge. The strategy realizes $308,000 in cash, and the cumulative borrowings at the end of Week 1 are reduced to $2,252,300. During the second week, the stock price reduces to $47.37 and delta declines again. This leads to 5,800 shares being sold at the end of the second week. During the third week, the stock price increases to over $50 and delta increases. This leads to 19,600 shares being purchased at the end of the third week. Toward the end of the life of the option, it becomes apparent that the option will be exercised and delta approaches 1.0. By Week 20, therefore, the

Table 6.3 Simulation of delta hedging. Option closes out of the money and cost of hedging is $256,600.

Week	Stock price	Delta	Shares purchased	Cost of shares purchased ($000)	Cumulative cost including interest ($000)	Interest cost ($000)
0	49.00	0.522	52,200	2,557.8	2,557.8	2.5
1	49.75	0.568	4,600	228.9	2,789.2	2.7
2	52.00	0.705	13,700	712.4	3,504.3	3.4
3	50.00	0.579	(12,600)	(630.0)	2,877.7	2.8
4	48.38	0.459	(12,000)	(580.6)	2,299.9	2.2
5	48.25	0.443	(1,600)	(77.2)	2,224.9	2.1
6	48.75	0.475	3,200	156.0	2,383.0	2.3
7	49.63	0.540	6,500	322.6	2,707.9	2.6
8	48.25	0.420	(12,000)	(579.0)	2,131.5	2.1
9	48.25	0.410	(1,000)	(48.2)	2,085.4	2.0
10	51.12	0.658	24,800	1,267.8	3,355.2	3.2
11	51.50	0.692	3,400	175.1	3,533.5	3.4
12	49.88	0.542	(15,000)	(748.2)	2,788.7	2.7
13	49.88	0.538	(400)	(20.0)	2,771.4	2.7
14	48.75	0.400	(13,800)	(672.7)	2,101.4	2.0
15	47.50	0.236	(16,400)	(779.0)	1,324.4	1.3
16	48.00	0.261	2,500	120.0	1,445.7	1.4
17	46.25	0.062	(19,900)	(920.4)	526.7	0.5
18	48.13	0.183	12,100	582.4	1,109.6	1.1
19	46.63	0.007	(17,600)	(820.7)	290.0	0.3
20	48.12	0.000	(700)	(33.7)	256.6	0.0

hedger owns 100,000 shares. The hedger receives $5 million (= 100,000 × $50) for these shares when the option is exercised, so that the total cost of writing the option and hedging it is $263,300.

Table 6.3 illustrates an alternative sequence of events where the option closes out of the money. As it becomes clear that the option will not be exercised, delta approaches zero. By Week 20 the hedger therefore has no position in the underlying stock. The total costs incurred are $256,600.

In Tables 6.2 and 6.3, the costs of hedging the option, when discounted to the beginning of the period, are close to, but not exactly the same as, the theoretical (Black–Scholes) price of $240,000. If the hedging scheme worked perfectly, the cost of hedging would, after discounting, be exactly equal to the Black–Scholes price for every simulated stock price path. The reason for the variation in the cost of delta hedging is that the hedge is rebalanced only once a week. As rebalancing takes place more frequently, the variation in the cost of hedging is reduced. Of course, the examples in Tables 6.2 and 6.3 are idealized in that they assume the model underlying the Black–Scholes formula to be exactly correct and that there are no transaction costs.

Delta hedging aims to keep the value of the financial institution's position as close to unchanged as possible. Initially, the value of the written option is $240,000. In the situation depicted in Table 6.2, the value of the option can be calculated as $414,500 in Week 9. Thus, the financial institution has lost $414,500 − 240,000 = $174,500$ on its short option position. Its cash position, as measured by the cumulative cost, is $1,442,900 worse in Week 9 than in Week 0. The value of the shares held has increased from $2,557,800 to $4,171,100 for a gain of $1,613,300. The net effect is that the value of the financial institution's position has changed by only $4,100 during the nine-week period.

Where the Cost Comes From

The delta-hedging procedure in Tables 6.2 and 6.3 in effect creates a long position in the option synthetically to neutralize the trader's short option position. As the tables illustrate, the scheme tends to involve selling stock just after the price has gone down and buying stock just after the price has gone up. It might be termed a buy-high, sell-low scheme! The cost of $240,000 comes from the average difference between the price paid for the stock and the price realized for it.

Transaction Costs

Maintaining a delta-neutral position in a single option and the underlying asset, in the way that has just been described, is liable to be prohibitively expensive because of the transaction costs incurred on trades. Maintaining delta neutrality is more feasible for a large portfolio of derivatives dependent on a single asset because only one trade in the underlying asset is necessary to zero out delta for the whole portfolio. The hedging transactions costs are absorbed by the profits on many different trades.

6.2 GAMMA

The *gamma* (Γ) of a portfolio of options on an underlying asset is the rate of change of the portfolio's delta with respect to the price of the underlying asset. It is the second

Figure 6.4   Hedging error introduced by nonlinearity.

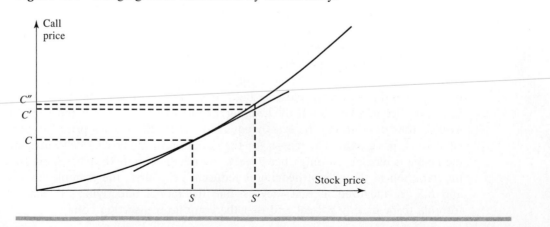

Figure 6.5   Relationship between gamma of an option and price of underlying asset. *K* is the option's strike price.

partial derivative of the portfolio with respect to asset price:

$$\text{Gamma} = \frac{\partial^2 P}{\partial S^2}$$

If gamma is small, delta changes slowly, and adjustments to keep a portfolio delta neutral need to be made only relatively infrequently. However, if gamma is large in absolute terms, delta is highly sensitive to the price of the underlying asset. It is then quite risky to leave a delta-neutral portfolio unchanged for any length of time. Figure 6.4 illustrates this point. When the stock price moves from S to S', delta hedging assumes that the option price moves from C to C', when in fact it moves from C to C''. The difference between C' and C'' leads to a hedging error. This error depends on the curvature of the relationship between the option price and the stock price. Gamma measures this curvature.[3]

Gamma is positive for a long position in an option. The general way in which gamma varies with the price of the underlying asset is shown in Figure 6.5. Gamma is greatest for options where the stock price is close to the strike price K.

Making a Portfolio Gamma Neutral

A linear product has zero gamma and cannot be used to change the gamma of a portfolio. What is required is a position in an instrument, such as an option, that is not linearly dependent on the underlying asset price.

Suppose that a delta-neutral portfolio has a gamma equal to Γ, and a traded option has a gamma equal to Γ_T. If the number of traded options added to the portfolio is w_T, the gamma of the portfolio is

$$w_T \Gamma_T + \Gamma$$

Hence, the position in the traded option necessary to make the portfolio gamma neutral is $w_T = -\Gamma/\Gamma_T$. Including the traded option is likely to change the delta of the

---

[3] Indeed, the gamma of an option is sometimes referred to as its *curvature* by practitioners.

portfolio, so the position in the underlying asset then has to be changed to maintain delta neutrality. Note that the portfolio is gamma neutral only for a short period of time. As time passes, gamma neutrality can be maintained only if the position in the traded option is adjusted so that it is always equal to $-\Gamma/\Gamma_T$.

Making a delta-neutral portfolio gamma neutral can be regarded as a first correction for the fact that the position in the underlying asset cannot be changed continuously when delta hedging is used. Delta neutrality provides protection against relatively small stock price moves between rebalancing. Gamma neutrality provides protection against larger movements in this stock price between hedge rebalancing. Suppose that a portfolio is delta neutral and has a gamma of $-3,000$. The delta and gamma of a particular traded call option are 0.62 and 1.50, respectively. The portfolio can be made gamma neutral by including in the portfolio a long position of

$$\frac{3,000}{1.5} = 2,000$$

in the call option. (The gamma of the portfolio is then $-3000 + 1.5 \times 2,000 = 0$.) However, the delta of the portfolio will then change from zero to $2,000 \times 0.62 = 1,240$. Therefore 1,240 units of the underlying asset must be sold to keep it delta neutral.

6.3   VEGA

Another source of risk in derivatives trading is the possibility that volatility will change. The volatility of a market variable measures our uncertainty about the future value of the variable. (It will be discussed more fully in Chapter 9.) In option valuation models volatilities are often assumed to be constant, but in practice they do change through time. Spot positions, forwards, and swaps do not depend on the volatility of the underlying market variable, but options and more complicated derivatives do. Their values are liable to change because of movements in volatility as well as because of changes in the asset price and the passage of time.

The *vega* ($\mathcal{V}$) of a portfolio is the rate of change of the value of the portfolio with respect to the volatility of the underlying market variable.[4]

$$\mathcal{V} = \frac{\partial P}{\partial \sigma}$$

If vega is high in absolute terms, the portfolio's value is very sensitive to small changes in volatility. If vega is low in absolute terms, volatility changes have relatively little impact on the value of the portfolio.

The vega of a portfolio can be changed by adding a position in a traded option. If $\mathcal{V}$ is the vega of the portfolio and $\mathcal{V}_T$ is the vega of a traded option, a position of $-\mathcal{V}/\mathcal{V}_T$ in the traded option makes the portfolio instantaneously vega neutral. Unfortunately, a portfolio that is gamma neutral will not, in general, be vega neutral, and vice versa. If a hedger requires a portfolio to be both gamma and vega neutral, at least two traded derivatives dependent on the underlying asset must usually be used.

---

[4] Vega is the name given to one of the "Greek letters" in option pricing, but it is not one of the letters in the Greek alphabet.

Example 6.1

Consider a portfolio that is delta neutral, with a gamma of $-5,000$ and a vega of $-8,000$. The options shown in the table below can be traded. The portfolio could be made vega neutral by including a long position in 4,000 of Option 1. This would increase delta to 2,400 and require that 2,400 units of the asset be sold to maintain delta neutrality. The gamma of the portfolio would change from $-5,000$ to $-3,000$.

	Delta	Gamma	Vega
Portfolio	0	-5,000	-8,000
Option 1	0.6	0.5	2.0
Option 2	0.5	0.8	1.2

To make the portfolio gamma and vega neutral, both Option 1 and Option 2 can be used. If w_1 and w_2 are the quantities of Option 1 and Option 2 that are added to the portfolio, we require that

$$-5,000 + 0.5w_1 + 0.8w_2 = 0$$
$$-8,000 + 2.0w_1 + 1.2w_2 = 0$$

The solution to these equations is $w_1 = 400$, $w_2 = 6,000$. The portfolio can therefore be made gamma and vega neutral by including 400 of Option 1 and 6,000 of Option 2. The delta of the portfolio after the addition of the positions in the two traded options is $400 \times 0.6 + 6,000 \times 0.5 = 3,240$. Hence, 3,240 units of the asset would have to be sold to maintain delta neutrality.

The vega of a long position in an option is positive. The variation of vega with the price of the underlying asset is similar to that for gamma and is shown in Figure 6.6. Gamma neutrality protects against large changes in the price of the underlying asset between hedge rebalancing. Vega neutrality protects against variations in volatility.

The volatilities of short-dated options tend to be more variable than the volatilities of long-dated options. The vega of a portfolio is therefore often calculated by changing the volatilities of short-dated options by more than that of long-dated options. One way of doing this is discussed in Section 9.9.

Figure 6.6 Variation of vega of an option with price of underlying asset. K is option's strike price.

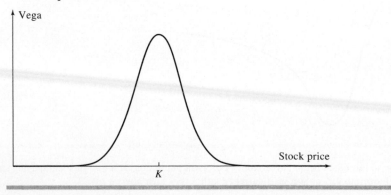

6.4 THETA

The *theta* (Θ) of a portfolio is the rate of change of the value of the portfolio with respect to the passage of time with all else remaining the same. Theta is sometimes referred to as the *time decay* of the portfolio.

Theta is usually negative for an option.[5] This is because as the time to maturity decreases with all else remaining the same, the option tends to become less valuable. The general way in which Θ varies with stock price for a call option on a stock is shown in Figure 6.7. When the stock price is very low, theta is close to zero. For an at-the-money call option, theta is large and negative. Figure 6.8 shows typical patterns for the variation of Θ with the time to maturity for in-the-money, at-the-money, and out-of-the-money call options.

Theta is not the same type of Greek letter as delta. There is uncertainty about the future stock price, but there is no uncertainty about the passage of time. It makes sense to hedge against changes in the price of the underlying asset, but it does not make any sense to hedge against the effect of the passage of time on an option portfolio. In spite of this, many traders regard theta as a useful descriptive statistic for a portfolio. In a delta-neutral portfolio, when theta is large and positive, gamma tends to be large and negative, and vice versa.

6.5 RHO

The final Greek letter we consider is rho. Rho is the rate of change of a portfolio with respect to the level of interest rates. Currency options have two rhos, one for the domestic interest rate and one for the foreign interest rate. When bonds and interest rate derivatives are part of the portfolio, traders usually consider carefully the ways in which the whole term structure of interest rates can change. We discuss this in the next chapter.

Figure 6.7 Variation of theta of a European call option with stock price.

---

[5] An exception to this could be an in-the-money European put option on a non-dividend-paying stock or an in-the-money European call option on a currency with a very high interest rate.

Figure 6.8 Typical patterns for variation of theta of a European call option with time to maturity.

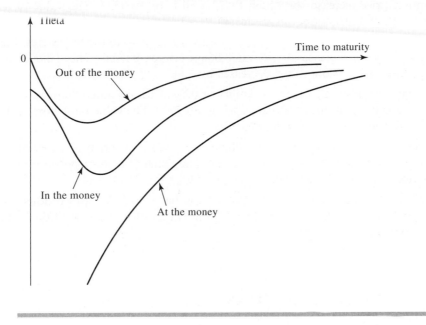

6.6 CALCULATING GREEK LETTERS

Appendices E and F explain how Greek letters can be calculated. The software DerivaGem that accompanies this book can be used for European and American options. Consider again the European call option in Section 6.1. The stock price is $49, the strike price is $50, the risk-free rate is 5%, the stock price volatility is 20% and the time to exercise is 20 weeks or 20/52 years. Table 6.4 shows delta, gamma, vega, theta, and rho for the option (i.e., for a long position in one option) and for a short position in 100,000 options, which was the position considered in Tables 6.2 and 6.3.

Table 6.4 Greek letters calculated using DerivaGem: $S = 49$, $K = 50$, $r = 5\%$, $\sigma = 20\%$, and $T = 20$ weeks.

	Single option	Short position in 100,000 options
Value ($)	2.40	−240,000
Delta (per $)	0.522	−52,200
Gamma (per $ per $)	0.066	−6,600
Vega (per %)	0.121	−12,100
Theta (per day)	−0.012	1,200
Rho (per %)	0.089	−8,900

Here are some examples of how these numbers can be interpreted:

1. When there is an increase of \$0.1 in the stock price with no other changes, the option price increases by about $0.522 \times \$0.1$, or \$0.0522. The value of a short position in 100,000 options decreases by \$5,220.

2. When there is an increase \$0.1 in the stock price with no other changes, the delta of the option increases by about 0.066×0.1, or 0.0066. The delta of a short position in 100,000 options decreases by 660.

3. When there is an increase in volatility of 0.5% with no other changes, the option price increases by about $\$0.121 \times 0.5$, or \$0.0605. The value of a short position in 100,000 options decreases by \$6,050.

4. When one day goes by with no changes to the stock price or its volatility, the option price decreases by about \$0.012. The value of a short position in 100,000 options increases by \$1,200.

5. When interest rates increase by 1% (or 100 basis points) with no other changes, the option price increases by \$0.089. The value of a short position in 100,000 options decreases by \$8,900.

6.7   TAYLOR SERIES EXPANSIONS

Taylor series expansions are explained in Appendix G. They can be used to show how the change in the portfolio value in a short period of time depends on the Greek letters. Consider a portfolio dependent on a single market variable S. If the volatility of the underlying asset and interest rates are assumed to be constant, the value P of the portfolio is a function of S and time t. The Taylor series expansion gives

$$\Delta P = \frac{\partial P}{\partial S}\Delta S + \frac{\partial P}{\partial t}\Delta t + \frac{1}{2}\frac{\partial^2 P}{\partial S^2}\Delta S^2 + \frac{1}{2}\frac{\partial^2 P}{\partial t^2}\Delta t^2 + \frac{\partial^2 P}{\partial S \partial t}\Delta S\,\Delta t + \cdots \qquad (6.1)$$

where ΔP and ΔS are the change in P and S in a small time interval Δt. The first term is delta times ΔS. The second term, which is theta times Δt, is nonstochastic. The third term can be made zero by ensuring that the portfolio is gamma neutral as well as delta neutral. Arguments from stochastic calculus show that ΔS is of order $\sqrt{\Delta t}$. This means that third term on the right-hand side is of order Δt. Later terms in the Taylor series expansion are of higher order than Δt.

For a delta-neutral portfolio, the first term on the right-hand side of equation (6.1) is zero, so that

$$\Delta P = \Theta\,\Delta t + \tfrac{1}{2}\Gamma\,\Delta S^2 \qquad (6.2)$$

when terms of higher order than Δt are ignored. The relationship between the change in the portfolio value and the change in the stock price is quadratic as shown in Figure 6.9. When gamma is positive, the holder of the portfolio gains from large movements in the market variable and loses when there is little or no movement. When gamma is negative, the reverse is true, so that a large positive or negative movement in the market variable leads to severe losses.

Figure 6.9 Alternative relationships between ΔP and ΔS for a delta-neutral portfolio: (a) slightly positive gamma, (b) large positive gamma, (c) slightly negative gamma, and (d) large negative gamma.

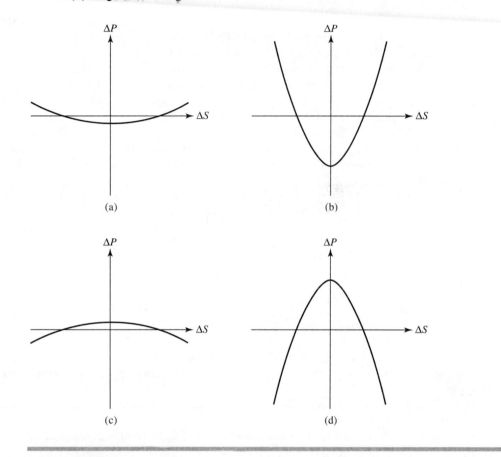

Example 6.2

Suppose that the gamma of a delta-neutral portfolio of options on an asset is $-10,000$ and that a change of $+2$ in the price of the asset occurs over a short period of time (for which Δt can be assumed to be zero). Equation (6.2) shows that there is an unexpected decrease in the value of the portfolio of approximately $0.5 \times 10,000 \times 2^2 = \$20,000$. Note that the same unexpected decrease would occur if there were a change of -2.

When the volatility of the underlying asset is uncertain, P is a function of σ, S, and t. Equation (6.1) then becomes

$$\Delta P = \frac{\partial P}{\partial S} \Delta S + \frac{\partial P}{\partial \sigma} \Delta \sigma + \frac{\partial P}{\partial t} \Delta t + \frac{1}{2} \frac{\partial^2 P}{\partial S^2} \Delta S^2 + \frac{1}{2} \frac{\partial^2 P}{\partial \sigma^2} \Delta \sigma^2 + \cdots$$

where $\Delta \sigma$ is the change in σ in time Δt. In this case, delta hedging eliminates the first term on the right-hand side. The second term is eliminated by making the portfolio

---

Business Snapshot 6.2   Dynamic Hedging in Practice

In a typical arrangement at a financial institution, the responsibility for a portfolio of derivatives dependent on a particular underlying asset is assigned to one trader or to a group of traders working together. For example, one trader at Goldman Sachs might be assigned responsibility for all derivatives dependent on the value of the Australian dollar. A computer system calculates the value of the portfolio and Greek letters for the portfolio. Limits are defined for each Greek letter and special permission is required if a trader wants to exceed a limit at the end of a trading day.

The delta limit is often expressed as the equivalent maximum position in the underlying asset. For example, the delta limit of Goldman Sachs on Microsoft might be $10 million. If the Microsoft stock price is $50 this means that the absolute value of delta as we have calculated it can be no more that 200,000. The vega limit is usually expressed as a maximum dollar exposure per 1% change in the volatility.

As a matter of course, options traders make themselves delta neutral—or close to delta neutral—at the end of each day. Gamma and vega are monitored, but are not usually managed on a daily basis. Financial institutions often find that their business with clients involves writing options and that as a result they accumulate negative gamma and vega. They are then always looking out for opportunities to manage their gamma and vega risks by buying options at competitive prices.

There is one aspect of an options portfolio that mitigates problems of managing gamma and vega somewhat. Options are often close to the money when they are first sold so that they have relatively high gammas and vegas. But after some time has elapsed, the underlying asset price has often changed enough for them to become deep out of the money or deep in the money. Their gammas and vegas are then very small and of little consequence. The nightmare scenario for an options trader is where written options remain very close to the money as the maturity date is approached.

---

vega neutral. The third term is nonstochastic. The fourth term is eliminated by making the portfolio gamma neutral.

Traders often define other "Greek letters" to correspond to higher-order terms in the Taylor series expansion. For example, $\partial^2 P/\partial\sigma^2$ is sometimes referred to as "gamma of vega".

6.8   THE REALITIES OF HEDGING

In an ideal world traders working for financial institutions would be able to rebalance their portfolios very frequently in order to maintain a zero delta, a zero gamma, a zero vega, and so on. In practice, this is not possible. When managing a large portfolio dependent on a single underlying asset, traders usually make delta zero or close to zero at least once a day by trading the underlying asset. Unfortunately a zero gamma and a zero vega are less easy to achieve, because it is difficult to find options or other nonlinear derivatives that can be traded in the volume required at competitive prices (see the discussion of dynamic hedging in Business Snapshot 6.2).

Figure 6.10 Static options replication. A replicating portfolio *P* is chosen so that it has the same value as the exotic option portfolio at a number of points on a boundary.

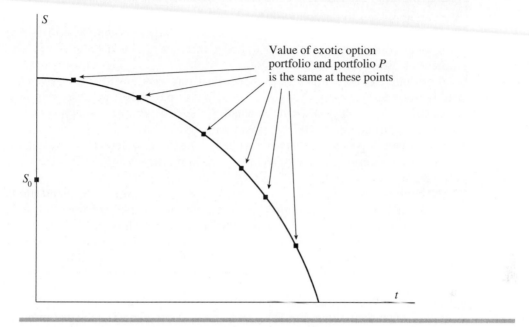

There are large economies of scale in being an options trader. As noted earlier, maintaining delta neutrality for an individual option on an asset by trading the asset daily would be prohibitively expensive. But it is realistic to do this for a portfolio of several hundred options on the asset. This is because the cost of daily rebalancing is covered by the profit on many different trades.

6.9 HEDGING EXOTIC OPTIONS

Exotic options can often be hedged using the approach we have outlined. As explained in Business Snapshot 6.3, delta hedging is sometimes easier for exotics and sometimes more difficult. When delta hedging is not feasible for a portfolio of exotic options, an alternative approach known as *static options replication* is sometimes used. This is illustrated in Figure 6.10. Suppose that *S* denotes the asset price and *t* denotes time, with the current ($t = 0$) value of *S* being S_0. Static options replication involves choosing a boundary in $\{S, t\}$ space that will eventually be reached, and then finding a portfolio of regular options that is worth the same as the portfolio of exotic options at a number of points on the boundary. The portfolio of exotic options is hedged by shorting the portfolio of regular options. Once the boundary is reached, the hedge is unwound.

The theory underlying static options replication is that, if two portfolios are worth the same at all $\{S, t\}$ points on the boundary, then they must be worth the same at all the $\{S, t\}$ points that can be reached prior to the boundary. In practice, values of the original portfolio of exotic options and the replicating portfolio of regular options are matched at some, but not all, points on the boundary. The procedure therefore relies on the idea that,

---

Business Snapshot 6.3   Is Delta Hedging Easier or More Difficult
   for Exotics?

We can approach the hedging of exotic options by creating a delta-neutral position
and rebalancing frequently to maintain delta neutrality. When we do this, we find
that some exotic options are easier to hedge than plain vanilla options and some are
more difficult.

An example of an exotic option that is relatively easy to hedge is an average price
call option (see Asian options in Section 5.7). As time passes, we observe more of the
asset prices that will be used in calculating the final average. This means that our
uncertainty about the payoff decreases with the passage of time. As a result, the
option becomes progressively easier to hedge. In the final few days, the delta of the
option always approaches zero because price movements during this time have very
little impact on the payoff.

By contrast, barrier options (see Section 5.7) are relatively difficult to hedge.
Consider a knock-out call option on a currency when the exchange rate is 0.0005
above the barrier. If the barrier is hit, the option is worth nothing. If the barrier is
not hit, the option may prove to be quite valuable. The delta of the option is
discontinuous at the barrier, making conventional hedging very difficult.

---

if two portfolios have the same value at a reasonably large number of points on the
boundary, then their values are likely to be close at other points on the boundary.

6.10   SCENARIO ANALYSIS

In addition to monitoring risks such as delta, gamma, and vega, option traders often
also carry out a scenario analysis. The analysis involves calculating the gain or loss on
their portfolio over a specified period under a variety of different scenarios. The time
period chosen is likely to depend on the liquidity of the instruments. The scenarios can
be either chosen by management or generated by a model.

Consider a trader with a portfolio of options on a particular foreign currency. There
are two main variables on which the value of the portfolio depends. These are the
exchange rate and the exchange rate volatility. Suppose that the exchange rate is
currently 1.0000 and its volatility is 10% per annum. The bank could calculate a table

Table 6.5   Profit or loss realized in two weeks under
different scenarios ($ millions).

Volatility	*Exchange rate*						
	0.94	0.96	0.98	1.00	1.02	1.04	1.06
8%	+102	+55	+25	+6	−10	−34	−80
10%	+80	+40	+17	+2	−14	−38	−85
12%	+60	+25	+9	−2	−18	−42	−90

such as Table 6.5 showing the profit or loss experienced during a two-week period under different scenarios. This table considers seven different exchange rates and three different volatilities.

In Table 6.5, the greatest loss is in the lower-right corner of the table. The loss corresponds to the volatility increasing to 12% and the exchange rate moving up to 1.06. Usually the greatest loss in such a table occurs at one of the corners, but this is not always so. For example, as we saw in Figure 6.9, when gamma is positive, the greatest loss is experienced when the underlying market variable stays where it is.

SUMMARY

A trader working for a bank, who is responsible for all the trades involving a particular market variable, monitors a number of Greek letters and ensures that they are kept within the limits specified by the bank.

The delta of a portfolio is the rate of change of its value with respect to the price of the underlying asset. Delta hedging involves creating a position with zero delta (sometimes referred to as a delta-neutral position). Because the delta of the underlying asset is 1.0, one way of hedging the portfolio is to take a position of $-\Delta$ in the underlying asset. For portfolios involving options and more complex derivatives, the position taken in the underlying asset has to be changed periodically. This is known as rebalancing.

Once a portfolio has been made delta neutral, the next stage is often to look at its gamma. The gamma of a portfolio is the rate of change of its delta with respect to the price of the underlying asset. It is a measure of the curvature of the relationship between the portfolio and the asset price. Another important hedge statistic is vega. This measures the rate of change of the value of the portfolio with respect to changes in the volatility of the underlying asset. Gamma and vega can be changed by trading options on the underlying asset.

In practice, derivatives traders usually rebalance their portfolios at least once a day to maintain delta neutrality. It is usually not feasible to maintain gamma and vega neutrality on a regular basis. Typically a trader monitors these measures. If they get too large, either corrective action is taken or trading is curtailed.

FURTHER READING

Derman, E., D. Ergener, and I. Kani, "Static Options Replication," *Journal of Derivatives*, 2, 4 (Summer 1995), 78–95.

Taleb, N. N., *Dynamic Hedging: Managing Vanilla and Exotic Options*. New York: Wiley, 1996.

PRACTICE QUESTIONS AND PROBLEMS (Answers at the End of the Book)

6.1. The delta of a derivatives portfolio dependent on the S&P 500 index is −2,100. The S&P 500 index is currently 1000. Estimate what happens to the value of the portfolio when the index increases to 1005.

6.2. The vega of a derivatives portfolio dependent on the dollar–sterling exchange rate is 200 ($ per %). Estimate the effect on the portfolio of an increase in the volatility of the exchange rate from 12% to 14%.

6.3. The gamma of a delta-neutral portfolio is 30 (per $ per $). Estimate what happens to the value of the portfolio when the price of the underlying asset (a) suddenly increases by $2 and (b) suddenly decreases by $2.

6.4. What does it mean to assert that the delta of a call option is 0.7? How can a short position in 1,000 options be made delta neutral when the delta of a long position in each option is 0.7?

6.5. What does it mean to assert that the theta of an option position is −100 per day? If a trader feels that neither a stock price nor its implied volatility will change, what type of option position is appropriate?

6.6. What is meant by the gamma of an option position? What are the risks in the situation where the gamma of a position is large and negative and the delta is zero?

6.7. "The procedure for creating an option position synthetically is the reverse of the procedure for hedging the option position." Explain this statement.

6.8. A company uses delta hedging to hedge a portfolio of long positions in put and call options on a currency. Which of the following would lead to the most favorable result: (a) a virtually constant spot rate or (b) wild movements in the spot rate? How does your answer change if the portfolio contains short option positions?

6.9. A bank's position in options on the dollar–euro exchange rate has a delta of 30,000 and a gamma of −80,000. Explain how these numbers can be interpreted. The exchange rate (dollars per euro) is 0.90. What position would you take to make the position delta neutral? After a short period of time, the exchange rate moves to 0.93. Estimate the new delta. What additional trade is necessary to keep the position delta neutral? Assuming the bank did set up a delta-neutral position originally, has it gained or lost money from the exchange-rate movement?

6.10. "Static options replication assumes that the volatility of the underlying asset will be constant." Explain this statement.

6.11. Suppose that a trader using the static options replication technique wants to match the value of a portfolio of exotic derivatives with the value of a portfolio of regular options at 10 points on a boundary. How many regular options are likely to be needed? Explain your answer.

6.12. Why is an Asian option easier to hedge than a regular option?

6.13. Explain why there are economies of scale in hedging options.

6.14. Consider a six-month American put option on a foreign currency when the exchange rate (domestic currency per foreign currency) is 0.75, the strike price is 0.74, the domestic risk-free rate is 5%, the foreign risk-free rate is 3%, and the exchange-rate volatility is 14% per annum. Use the DerivaGem software (binomial tree with 100 steps) to calculate the price, delta, gamma, vega, theta, and rho of the option. Verify that delta is correct by changing the exchange rate to 0.751 and recomputing the option price.

FURTHER QUESTIONS

6.15. The gamma and vega of a delta-neutral portfolio are 50 per $ per $ and 25 per %, respectively. Estimate what happens to the value of the portfolio when there is a shock to the market causing the underlying asset price to decrease by $3 and its volatility to increase by 4%.

6.16. Consider a one-year European call option on a stock when the stock price is $30, the strike price is $30, the risk-free rate is 5%, and the volatility is 25% per annum. Use the DerivaGem software to calculate the price, delta, gamma, vega, theta, and rho of the option. Verify that delta is correct by changing the stock price to $30.1 and recomputing the option price. Verify that gamma is correct by recomputing the delta for the situation where the stock price is $30.1. Carry out similar calculations to verify that vega, theta, and rho are correct.

6.17. A financial institution has the following portfolio of over-the-counter options on sterling:

Type	Position	Delta of option	Gamma of option	Vega of option
Call	−1,000	0.50	2.2	1.8
Call	−500	0.80	0.6	0.2
Put	−2,000	−0.40	1.3	0.7
Call	−500	0.70	1.8	1.4

A traded option is available with a delta of 0.6, a gamma of 1.5, and a vega of 0.8.

(a) What position in the traded option and in sterling would make the portfolio both gamma neutral and delta neutral?

(b) What position in the traded option and in sterling would make the portfolio both vega neutral and delta neutral?

6.18. Consider again the situation in Problem 6.17. Suppose that a second traded option with a delta of 0.1, a gamma of 0.5, and a vega of 0.6 is available. How could the portfolio be made delta, gamma, and vega neutral?

6.19. Reproduce Table 6.2. (In Table 6.2 the stock position is rounded to the nearest 100 shares.) Calculate the gamma and theta of the position each week. Using the DerivaGem Applications Builders to calculate the change in the value of the portfolio each week (before the rebalancing at the end of the week) and check whether equation (6.2) is approximately satisfied. [*Note*: DerivaGem produces a value of theta "per calendar day". The theta in equation (6.2) is "per year".]

CHAPTER

7

Interest Rate Risk

Interest rate risk is more difficult to manage than the risk arising from market variables such as equity prices, exchange rates, and commodity prices. One complication is that there are many different interest rates in any given currency (Treasury rates, interbank borrowing and lending rates, mortgage rates, deposit rates, prime borrowing rates, and so on). Although these tend to move together, they are not perfectly correlated. Another complication is that we need more than a single number to describe the interest rate environment. We need a function describing the variation of the rate with maturity. This is known as the *interest rate term structure* or the *yield curve*.

Consider, for example, the situation of a US government bond trader. The trader's portfolio is likely to consist of many bonds with different maturities. There is an exposure to movements in the one-year rate, the two-year rate, the three-year rate, and so on. The trader's delta exposure is therefore more complicated than that of the gold trader in Table 6.1. He or she must be concerned with all the different ways in which the US Treasury yield curve can change its shape through time.

This chapter starts with a description of traditional approaches used by a financial institution to manage interest rate risk. It explains the importance of LIBOR and swap rates to financial institutions. It then covers duration and convexity measures. These can be regarded as the interest rate equivalents of the delta and gamma measures considered in the previous chapter. A number of different approaches to managing the risks of nonparallel shifts are then presented. These include the use of partial durations, the calculation of multiple deltas, and the use of principal components analysis.

7.1 THE MANAGEMENT OF NET INTEREST INCOME

As explained in Section 2.2, the net interest income of a bank is the excess of interest received over interest paid. It is the role of the asset–liability management function within the bank to ensure that net interest income remains roughly constant through time. This section considers the traditional way of doing this.

How can fluctuations in net interest income occur? Consider a simple situation where a bank offers consumers a one-year and a five-year deposit rate as well as a one-year and five-year mortgage rate. The rates are shown in Table 7.1. We make the simplifying assumption that market participants expect the one-year interest rate for future time

Table 7.1 Example of rates offered by a bank to its customers.

Maturity (years)	Deposit rate	Mortgage rate
1	3%	6%
5	3%	6%

periods to equal the one-year rates prevailing in the market today. Loosely speaking, this means that the market considers interest rate increases to be just as likely as interest rate decreases. As a result, the rates in Table 7.1 are "fair" in that they reflect the market's expectations. Investing money for one year and reinvesting for four further one-year periods lead to an uncertain return. But, given our assumptions, the expected overall return is the same as a single five-year investment. Similarly, borrowing money for one year and refinancing each year for the next four years leads to the same expected financing costs as a single five-year loan.

Suppose you have money to deposit and agree with the prevailing view that interest rate increases are just as likely as interest rate decreases. Would you choose to deposit your money for one year at 3% per annum or for five years at 3% per annum? The chances are that you would choose one year because this gives you more financial flexibility. It ties up your funds for a shorter period of time.

Now suppose that you want a mortgage. Again you agree with the prevailing view that interest rate increases are just as likely as interest rate decreases. Would you choose a one-year mortgage at 6% or a five-year mortgage at 6%? The chances are that you would choose a five-year mortgage because it fixes your borrowing rate for the next five years and subjects you to less refinancing risk.

When the bank posts the rates shown in Table 7.1, it is likely to find that the majority of its depositors opt for a one-year maturity and the majority of the customers seeking mortgages opt for a five-year maturity. This creates an asset–liability mismatch for the bank and subjects its net interest income to risks. The deposits that are financing the five-year 6% mortgages are rolled over every year. There is no problem if interest rates fall. After one year, the bank will find itself financing the five-year 6% mortgages with deposits that cost less than 3% and net interest income will increase. However, if interest rates rise, the deposits that are financing the 6% mortgages will cost more than 3% and net interest income will decline. Suppose that there is a 3% rise in interest rates during the first two years. This would reduce net interest income for the third year to zero.

Table 7.2 Five-year rates are increased in an attempt to match maturities of assets and liabilities.

Maturity (years)	Deposit rate	Mortgage rate
1	3%	6%
5	4%	7%

Business Snapshot 7.1   Expensive Failures of Financial Institutions in the US

Throughout the 1960s, 1970s, and 1980s Savings and Loans (S&Ls) in the United States failed to manage interest rate risk well. They tended to take short-term deposits and make long-term fixed-rate mortgages. As a result they were seriously hurt by interest rate increases in 1966, 1969–70, 1974, and the killer period 1979–82. S&Ls were protected by government guarantees. Over 1,700 failed in the 1980s. A major reason for the failures was their inadequate interest rate risk management. The total cost to the US tax payer of the failures has been estimated to be between $100 and $500 billion.

The failure of Contintental Illinois, a large US bank, in the 1980s can also be attributed to poor management of interest rate risk. During the period 1980 to 1983 its assets (i.e., loans) with maturities over a year totaled between $7 and $8 billion, whereas its liabilities (i.e., deposits) with maturities over a year were between $1.4 and $2.5 billion. Continental failed in 1984 and was the subject of an expensive government bailout.

It is the job of the asset–liability management group to ensure that this type of interest rate risk is minimized. One way of doing this is to ensure that the maturities of the assets on which interest is earned and the maturities of the liabilities on which interest is paid are matched. In our example, the matching can be achieved by increasing the five-year rate on both deposits and mortgages. For example, the bank could move to the situation in Table 7.2 where the five-year deposit rate is 4% and the five-year mortgage rate 7%. This would make five-year deposits relatively more attractive and one-year mortgages relatively more attractive. Some customers who chose one-year deposits when the rates were as in Table 7.1 will choose five-year deposits when rates are as in Table 7.2. Some customers who chose five-year mortgages when the rates were as in Table 7.1 will choose one-year mortgages. This may lead to the maturities of assets and liabilities being matched. If there is still an imbalance with depositors tending to choose a one-year maturity and borrowers a five-year maturity, five-year deposit and mortgage rates could be increased even further. Eventually the imbalance will disappear.

The net result of all banks behaving in the way we have just described is that long-term rates tend to be higher than those predicted by expected future short-term rates. This phenomenon is referred to as *liquidity preference theory*. It leads to long-term rates being higher than short-term rates much of the time. Even when the market expects a small decline in short-term rates, liquidity preference theory is likely to cause long-term rates to be higher than short-term rates. Only when a steep decline in interest rates is expected will long-term rates be less than short-term rates.

Many banks now have sophisticated systems for monitoring the decisions being made by customers so that, when they detect small differences between the maturities of the assets and liabilities being chosen, they can fine-tune the rates they offer. Sometimes derivatives such as interest rate swaps are also used to manage their exposures (see Example 5.1 in Section 5.4). The result of all this is that net interest income is very stable and does not lead to significant risks. However, as indicated in Business Snapshot 7.1, this has not always been the case.

7.2 LIBOR AND SWAP RATES

A key interest rate for banks is LIBOR, the *London interbank offered rate*. This is the rate at which a bank is prepared to lend to another bank.[1] Many loans to corporations and governments, as well as some mortgages, have floating rates that are reset to LIBOR periodically. For example, a loan in sterling to a corporation might be quoted as "three-month LIBOR plus 40 basis points". The rate of interest would then be set equal to three-month sterling LIBOR plus 40 basis points every three months. The British Bankers Association (BBA; www.bba.org.uk) provides LIBOR quotes in different currencies for maturities of one, three, six, and twelve months at 11 a.m. every business day. These rates are based on information provided to the BBA by large banks.[2]

A bank must satisfy certain creditworthiness criteria to qualify for receiving LIBOR deposits (i.e, a LIBOR loan) from another bank. Typically it must have to have a AA credit rating.[3] LIBOR rates are therefore the one-month to twelve-month borrowing rates for banks that have AA credit ratings. How can the LIBOR yield curve be extended beyond one year? There are two possible approaches:

1. Create a yield curve to represent the rates at which AA-rated companies can borrow for periods of time longer than one year.

2. Create a yield curve to represent the future short-term borrowing rates for AA-rated companies.

It is important to understand the difference. Suppose that the yield curve is 4% for all maturities. If it is created in the first way, this means that AA-rated companies can today lock in an interest rate of 4% regardless of how long they want to borrow. If it is created in the second way, the forward interest rate that the market assigns to the short-term borrowing rates of AA-rated companies at future times is 4%. (See Appendix C for how forward rates are defined and calculated.) When the yield curve is created in the first way, it gives the forward short-term borrowing rate for a company that is AA-rated today. When it is created in the second way, it gives the forward short-term borrowing rate for a company that will be AA at the beginning of the period covered by the forward contract.

In practice, the LIBOR yield curve is extended using the second approach. Swap rates (see Table 5.5) are used to extend the LIBOR yield curve, as described in Appendix B.[4] The resulting yield curve is sometimes called the LIBOR yield curve, sometimes the swap yield curve, and sometimes the LIBOR/swap yield curve. To understand why swap rates can be used to extend the LIBOR yield curve when the second approach is

---

[1] Banks also quote LIBID, the London interbank bid rate. The is the rate at which a bank is prepared to accept deposits from another bank. The LIBOR quote is slightly higher than the LIBID quote, reflecting the bank's bid–offer spread.

[2] In 2008, during the credit crisis, there is some evidence that banks understated LIBOR when providing information to the BBA because they did not want to reveal how high their true borrowing costs were.

[3] The best credit rating given to a company by the rating agency S&P is AAA. The second best is AA. The corresponding ratings from the rival rating agency Moody's are Aaa and Aa, respectively. Credit ratings are discussed further in Chapter 14.

[4] Eurodollar futures, which are contracts on the future value of LIBOR, can also be used to extend the LIBOR yield curve.

used, note that a bank can convert a series of short-term LIBOR loans to a swap rate using the swap market. For example, it can:

1. Lend a certain principal for six months to a AA borrower and relend it for nine successive six month periods to AA borrowers; and
2. Enter into a swap to exchange the LIBOR for the five-year swap rate.

LIBOR vs. Treasury Rate

The risk-free rate is important in the pricing of financial contracts. The usual practice among financial institutions is to assume that the LIBOR/swap yield curve provides the risk-free rate. Treasury rates are regarded as too low to be used as risk-free rates because:

1. Treasury bills and Treasury bonds must be purchased by financial institutions to fulfill a variety of regulatory requirements. This increases demand for these Treasury instruments, driving their prices up and their yields down.
2. The amount of capital a bank is required to hold to support an investment in Treasury bills and bonds is substantially smaller than the capital required to support a similar investment in other very-low-risk instruments.
3. In the United States, Treasury instruments are given a favorable tax treatment compared with most other fixed-income investments because they are not taxed at the state level.

As we have seen, the credit risk in the LIBOR/swap yield curve corresponds to the credit risk in a series of short-term loans to AA-rated borrowers. It is therefore not a perfect proxy for the risk-free yield curve. There is a small chance that a AA borrower will default during the life of a short-term loan. But traders feel it is the best proxy for them to use. There is some evidence that, in normal market conditions, a true risk-free yield curve, uninfluenced by the factors affecting Treasury rates that we have just mentioned, is about 10 basis points (= 0.1%) below the LIBOR/swap yield curve.[5]

The amount by which the three-month LIBOR rate exceeds the three-month Treasury rate is known as the *TED spread*. In normal market conditions the TED spread averages about 30 basis points. During the credit crisis starting in July 2007, banks were reluctant to lend to each other because they were concerned about their own liquidity and about the creditworthiness of other banks. During the second half of 2007 and during 2008, the TED spread was regularly in the 100 to 200 basis point range, and on October 10, 2008, reached a record 464 basis points.

7.3 DURATION

Duration is a widely used measure of a portfolio's exposure to yield curve movements. Suppose y is a bond's yield and B is its market price. The duration D of the bond is

---

[5] See J. Hull, M. Predescu, and A. White, "The Relationship Between Credit Default Swap Spreads, Bond Yields, and Credit Rating Announcements," *Journal of Banking and Finance*, 28 (November 2004): 2789–2811.

given by

$$\frac{\Delta B}{B} = -D\,\Delta y$$

or equivalently

$$\Delta B = -DB\,\Delta y \tag{7.1}$$

where Δy is a small change in the bond's yield and ΔB is the corresponding change in its price. Duration measures the sensitivity of percentage changes in the bond's price to changes in its yield. Using calculus notation, we can write

$$D = -\frac{1}{B}\frac{dB}{dy} \tag{7.2}$$

Consider a bond that provides cash flows $c_1, c_2, \ldots, c_n$ at times $t_1, t_2, \ldots, t_n$. (The cash flows consist of the coupon and principal payments on the bond.) The bond yield y is defined as the discount rate that equates the bond's theoretical price to its market price. If the yield on the bond is measured with continuous compounding (see Appendix A), it follows that the relationship between the price B of the bond and its yield y is

$$B = \sum_{i=1}^{n} c_i e^{-yt_i}$$

From this, it follows that

$$D = \sum_{i=1}^{n} t_i \left(\frac{c_i e^{-yt_i}}{B} \right) \tag{7.3}$$

The term in parentheses in equation (7.3) is the ratio of the present value of the cash flow at time t_i to the bond price. The bond price is the present value of all the cash flows. The duration is therefore a weighted average of the times when payments are made, with the weight applied to time t_i being equal to the proportion of the bond's total present value provided by the cash flow at time t_i. (The sum of the weights is 1.0.) This explains where the term "duration" comes from. Duration is a measure of how long the bondholder has to wait for cash flows. A zero-coupon bond that lasts n years has a duration of n years. However, a coupon-bearing bond lasting n years has a duration of less than n years, because the holder receives some of the cash payments prior to year n.

Consider a three-year 10% coupon bond with a face value of $100. Suppose that the yield on the bond is 12% per annum with continuous compounding. This means that $y = 0.12$. Coupon payments of $5 are made every six months. Table 7.3 shows the calculations necessary to determine the bond's duration. The present values of the bond's cash flows, using the yield as the discount rate, are shown in column 3. (For example, the present value of the first cash flow is $5e^{-0.12 \times 0.5} = 4.709$.) The sum of the numbers in column 3 is the bond's market price, 94.213. The weights are calculated by dividing the numbers in column 3 by 94.213. The sum of the numbers in column 5 gives the duration as 2.653 years.

Small changes in interest rates are often measured in *basis points*. A basis point is 0.01% per annum. The following example investigates the accuracy of the duration relationship in equation (7.1).

Table 7.3   Calculation of duration.

Time (years)	Cash flow ($)	Present value	Weight	Time × weight
0.5	5	4.709	0.050	0.025
1.0	5	4.435	0.047	0.047
1.5	5	4.176	0.044	0.066
2.0	5	3.933	0.042	0.083
2.5	5	3.704	0.039	0.098
3.0	105	73.256	0.778	2.333
Total	130	94.213	1.000	2.653

Example 7.1

For the bond in Table 7.3, the bond price B is 94.213 and the duration D is 2.653, so that equation (7.1) gives

$$\Delta B = -94.213 \times 2.653 \Delta y$$

or

$$\Delta B = -249.95 \Delta y$$

When the yield on the bond increases by 10 basis points ($= 0.1\%$), $\Delta y = +0.001$. The duration relationship predicts that $\Delta B = -249.95 \times 0.001 = -0.250$, so that the bond price goes down to $94.213 - 0.250 = 93.963$. How accurate is this? When the bond yield increases by 10 basis points to 12.1%, the bond price is

$$5e^{-0.121 \times 0.5} + 5e^{-0.121 \times 1.0} + 5e^{-0.121 \times 1.5} + 5e^{-0.121 \times 2.0}$$
$$+ 5e^{-0.121 \times 2.5} + 105e^{-0.121 \times 3.0} = 93.963$$

which is (to three decimal places) the same as that predicted by the duration relationship.

Modified Duration

The definition of duration in equation (7.3) was suggested by Macaulay in 1938. It is referred to as *Macaulay's duration*. When the yield y on the bond is measured with continuous compounding, it is equivalent to the definition in equation (7.1) or (7.2). When duration is defined using equations (7.1) or (7.2) and other compounding frequencies are used for y, a small adjustment is necessary to Macaulay's duration. When y is measured with annual compounding, it can be shown that the expression for D in equation (7.3) must be divided by $1 + y$. More generally, when y is expressed with a compounding frequency of m times per year, it must be divided by $1 + y/m$. Duration defined with these adjustments to equation (7.3) is referred to as *modified duration*.

Example 7.2

The bond in Table 7.3 has a price of 94.213 and a duration of 2.653. The yield, expressed with semiannual compounding is 12.3673% (see Appendix A). The (modified) duration appropriate for calculating sensitivity to the yield when it is expressed with semiannual compounding is

$$\frac{2.653}{1 + 0.123673/2} = 2.4985$$

From equation (7.1),

$$\Delta B = -94.213 \times 2.4985 \Delta y$$

or

$$\Delta B = -235.39 \Delta y$$

When the yield (semiannually compounded) increases by 10 basis points ($= 0.1\%$), $\Delta y = +0.001$. The duration relationship predicts that we expect ΔB to be $-235.39 \times 0.001 = -0.235$, so that the bond price goes down to $94.213 - 0.235 = 93.978$. How accurate is this? When the bond yield (semiannually compounded) increases by 10 basis points to 12.4673% (or to 12.0941% with continuous compounding), an exact calculation similar to that in the previous example shows that the bond price becomes 93.978. This suggests that the modified duration is accurate for small yield changes.

Dollar Duration

The dollar duration of a bond is defined as the product of its duration and its price. If $D_\$$ is dollar duration, it follows from equation (7.1) that

$$\Delta B = -D_\$ \Delta y$$

or using calculus notation

$$D_\$ = -\frac{dB}{dy}$$

Whereas duration relates proportional changes in a bond's price to its yield, dollar duration relates actual changes in the bond's price to its yield. Dollar duration is similar to the delta measure discussed in Chapter 6.

7.4 CONVEXITY

The duration relationship measures exposure to small changes in yields. This is illustrated in Figure 7.1, which shows the relationship between the percentage change in value and change in yield for two bonds with the same duration. The gradients of the two curves are the same at the origin. This means that both portfolios change in value by the same percentage for small yield changes, as predicted by equation (7.1). For large yield changes, the bonds behave differently. Bond X has more curvature in its relationship with yields than bond Y. A factor known as *convexity* measures this curvature and can be used to improve the relationship between bond prices and yields.

The convexity for a bond is

$$C = \frac{1}{B}\frac{d^2 B}{dy^2} = \frac{\sum_{i=1}^{n} c_i t_i^2 e^{-y t_i}}{B}$$

where y is the bond's yield measured with continuous compounding. This is the

Figure 7.1 Two bonds with the same duration.

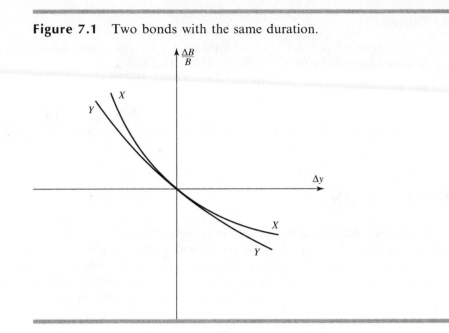

weighted average of the square of the time to the receipt of cash flows. From Appendix G, a second-order approximation to the change in the bond price is

$$\Delta B = \frac{dB}{dy}\Delta y + \frac{1}{2}\frac{d^2 B}{dy^2}(\Delta y)^2$$

This leads to

$$\frac{\Delta B}{B} = -D\,\Delta y + \frac{1}{2}C(\Delta y)^2 \qquad (7.4)$$

Example 7.3

Consider again the bond in Table 7.3. The bond price B is 94.213 and the duration D is 2.653. The convexity is

$$0.05 \times 0.5^2 + 0.047 \times 1.0^2 + 0.044 \times 1.5^2$$
$$+ 0.042 \times 2.0^2 + 0.039 \times 2.5^2 + 0.779 \times 3.0^2 = 7.570$$

The convexity relationship in equation (7.4) is therefore

$$\frac{\Delta B}{B} = -2.653\Delta y + \frac{1}{2} \times 7.570 \times (\Delta y)^2$$

Consider a 2% change in the bond yield from 12% to 14%. The duration relationship predicts that the dollar change in the value of the bond will be $-94.213 \times 2.653 \times 0.02 = -4.999$. The convexity relationship predicts that it will be

$$-94.213 \times 2.653 \times 0.02 + 0.5 \times 94.213 \times 7.570 \times 0.02^2 = -4.856$$

The actual change in the value of the bond is -4.859. This shows that the convexity relationship gives much more accurate results than duration for a large change in the bond yield.

Dollar Convexity

The *dollar convexity* $C_\$$ of a bond can be defined analogously to dollar duration as the product of convexity and the value of the portfolio. This means that

$$C_\$ = \frac{d^2 B}{dy^2}$$

and shows that dollar convexity is similar to the gamma measure introduced in Chapter 6.

7.5   GENERALIZATION

So far we have used duration and convexity to measure the sensitivity of the price of a single bond to interest rates. The definitions of duration and convexity can be generalized so that they apply to a portfolio of bonds—or to any portfolio of interest-rate-dependent instruments. We define a parallel shift in the zero-coupon yield curve as a shift where all zero-coupon interest rates change by the same amount, as indicated in Figure 7.2.

Suppose that P is the value of the portfolio of interest-rate-dependent securities. We can make a small parallel shift in the zero-coupon yield curve and observe the change ΔP in P. Duration is defined as

$$D = -\frac{1}{P} \frac{\Delta P}{\Delta y} \tag{7.5}$$

where Δy is size of the small parallel shift.[6] Equation (7.5) is equivalent to

$$\frac{\Delta P}{P} = -D \, \Delta y \tag{7.6}$$

Figure 7.2   A parallel shift in zero rates by Δy.

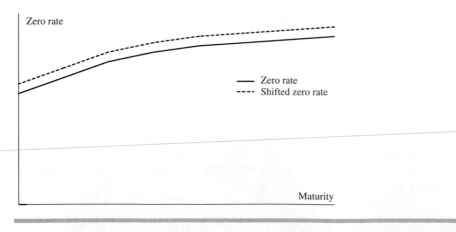

---

[6] A small parallel shift of Δy in the zero-coupon yield curve leads to the yield of all bonds changing by approximately Δy.

Suppose a portfolio consists of a number of interest-rate-dependent assets. The ith asset is worth X_i and has a duration D_i $(i = 1, 2, \ldots, n)$. Define ΔX_i as the change in the value of X_i arising from the yield curve shift Δy. It follows that $P = \sum_{i=1}^{n} X_i$ and $\Delta P = \sum_{i=1}^{n} \Delta X_i$, so that from equation (7.5) the duration of the portfolio is given by

$$D = -\frac{1}{P} \sum_{i=1}^{n} \frac{\Delta X_i}{\Delta y}$$

The duration of the ith asset is

$$D_i = -\frac{1}{X_i} \frac{\Delta X_i}{\Delta y}$$

Hence

$$D = \sum_{i=1}^{n} \frac{X_i}{P} D_i$$

This shows that the duration D of a portfolio is the weighted average of the durations of the individual assets comprising the portfolio, with the weight assigned to an asset being proportional to the value of the asset.

The dollar duration $D_\$$ of a portfolio can be defined as the duration of the portfolio times the value of the portfolio:

$$D_\$ = -\frac{\Delta P}{\Delta y}$$

This is a measure of the delta of the portfolio with respect to interest rates. The dollar duration of a portfolio consisting of a number of interest-rate-dependent assets is the sum of the dollar durations of the individual assets.

The convexity measure can be generalized in the same way as duration. For any interest-rate-dependent portfolio whose value is P, we define the convexity C as $1/P$ times the second partial derivative of the value of the portfolio with respect to a parallel shift in the zero-coupon yield curve. Equation (7.4) is correct with B replaced by P:

$$\frac{\Delta P}{P} = -D\,\Delta y + \tfrac{1}{2}C(\Delta y)^2 \tag{7.7}$$

The relationship between the convexity of a portfolio and the convexity of the assets comprising the portfolio is similar to that for duration: the convexity of the portfolio is the weighted average of the convexities of the assets with the weights being proportional to the value of the assets. The convexity of a bond portfolio tends to be greatest when the portfolio provides payments evenly over a long period of time. It is least when the payments are concentrated around one particular point in time.

The dollar convexity for a portfolio worth P can be defined as P times the convexity This a measure of the gamma of the portfolio with respect to interest rates. The dollar convexity of a portfolio consisting of a number of interest-rate-dependent assets is the sum of the dollar convexities of the individual assets.

Portfolio Immunization

A portfolio consisting of long and short positions in interest-rate-dependent assets can be protected against relatively small parallel shifts in the yield curve by ensuring that its duration is zero. It can be protected against relatively large parallel shifts in the yield curve by ensuring that its duration and convexity are both zero or close to zero.

7.6   NONPARALLEL YIELD CURVE SHIFTS

Unfortunately the basic duration relationship in equation (7.6) only quantifies exposure to parallel yield curve shifts. The duration plus convexity relationship in equation (7.7) allows the shift to be relatively large, but it is still a parallel shift.

Some researchers have attempted to extend duration measures so that nonparallel shifts can be considered. Reitano suggests a partial duration measure where just one point on the zero-coupon yield curve is shifted and all other points remain the same.[7] Suppose that the zero curve is as shown in Table 7.4 and Figure 7.3. Shifting the five-year point involves changing the zero curve as indicated in Figure 7.4.[8]

Suppose that there are n points on the zero curve The partial duration D_i for the ith point is

$$D_i = -\frac{1}{P}\frac{\Delta P_i}{\Delta y_i} \tag{7.8}$$

where P is the value of the portfolio, Δy_i is the size of a small change made to the ith point on the zero curve, and ΔP_i is the resulting change in the portfolio value. The variable Δy_i is measured as a change in the interest rate when it is expressed in decimal form. Thus, $\Delta y_i = 0.001$ is a 10-basis-point increase in the ith point on the zero curve. From equation (7.8), the proportional change in the portfolio value arising

Table 7.4   Zero-coupon yield curve (rates continuously compounded).

Maturity (years):	1	2	3	4	5	7	10
Rate (%):	4.0	4.5	4.8	5.0	5.1	5.2	5.3

Figure 7.3   The zero-coupon yield curve in Table 7.4.

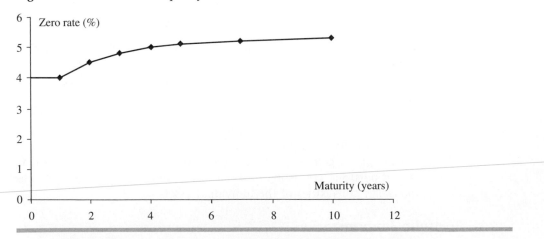

[7] See R. Reitano, "Non-Parallel yield curve shifts and Immunization," Journal of Portfolio Management, Spring 1992: 36–43.

[8] When the ith point on the zero curve is shifted, the other points are not shifted and rates on the shifted yield curve are calculated using linear interpolation, as indicated in Figure 7.4.

Figure 7.4 Change in zero-coupon yield curve when one point is shifted.

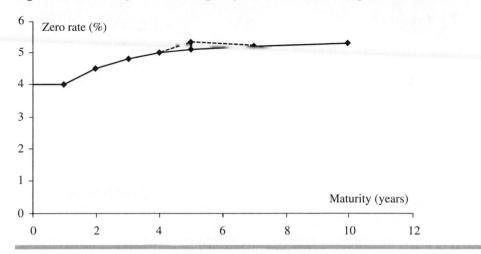

from a change Δy_i in the ith point on the zero curve is

$$\frac{\Delta P_i}{P} = -D_i \,\Delta y_i \tag{7.9}$$

Example 7.4

The partial durations for a portfolio worth $5 million are shown in Table 7.5. When the one-year rate increases by 10 basis points, the value of the portfolio increases by

$$-2 \times 5,000,000 \times 0.001 = -10,000$$

(a decrease of $10,000). When the four-year rate increases by 5 basis points, the value of the portfolio increases by

$$-0.2 \times 5,000,000 \times 0.0005 = -500$$

(a decrease of $500). When the ten-year rate increases by 2 basis points, the value of the portfolio increases by

$$1.9 \times 5,000,000 \times 0.0002 = 1,900$$

or $1,900.

The sum of all the partial durations equals the usual duration measure. This is because the sum of equal changes such as those in Figure 7.4 for all points on the zero curve is a parallel shift in the zero curve. In the example in Table 7.5, the sum of the partial durations is 0.2, so that the usual duration measure is 0.2. This means that the portfolio is relatively insensitive to parallel shifts in the yield curve. However, the durations for

Table 7.5 Partial durations for a portfolio.

Maturity (years):	1	2	3	4	5	7	10	*Total*
Duration:	2.0	1.6	0.6	0.2	−0.5	−1.8	−1.9	0.2

Figure 7.5 A rotation of the yield curve.

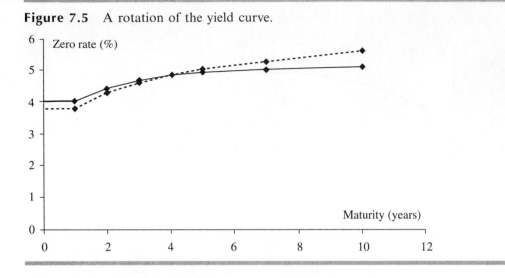

short maturities are positive, while those for long maturities are negative. This means that the portfolio loses (gains) in value when short rates rise (fall). It gains (loses) in value when long rates rise (fall).

We are now in a position to go one step further and calculate the sensitivity of a portfolio value to any nonparallel shifts. Suppose that, in the case of the yield curve shown in Figure 7.3, we define a rotation where the changes to the 1-year, 2-year, 3-year, 4-year, 5-year, 7-year, 10-year maturities are $-3e$, $-2e$, $-e$, 0, e, $3e$, $6e$, where $e = 0.0001$, or 1 basis point. This is illustrated in Figure 7.5. From the partial durations in Table 7.5 and equation (7.9), the proportional change in the value of the portfolio arising from the change in the one-year rate is

$$-2.0 \times (-3e) = 6e$$

The proportional change in the value of the portfolio arising from the change in the two-year rate is

$$-1.6 \times (-2e) = 3.2e$$

and so on. The proportional change in the value of the portfolio arising from the changes in all rates is $27.1e$. For a parallel shift of e in the yield curve, the percentage change in the value of the portfolio is $-0.2e$. This shows that a portfolio that gives rise to the partial durations in Table 7.5 is much more heavily exposed to a rotation of the yield curve than to a parallel shift.

7.7 INTEREST RATE DELTAS IN PRACTICE

In practice, a number of different approaches are used to calculate interest rate deltas. One approach is to define delta as the dollar duration. This is the sensitivity of the portfolio to a parallel shift in the zero-coupon yield curve. A measure related to this definition of delta is DV01. This is the impact of a 1-basis-point increase in all rates. It is the dollar duration multiplied by 0.0001. Alternatively, it is the duration of the portfolio multiplied by the value of the portfolio multiplied by 0.0001.

Table 7.6 Deltas for portfolio in Table 7.5. Value of portfolio is $1 million. The dollar impact of a 1-basis-point shift in points on the zero curve is shown.

Maturity (years):	1	2	3	4	5	7	10	*Total*
Delta.	200	160	60	20	50	−180	−190	20

In practice, analysts like to calculate several deltas to reflect their exposures to all the different ways in which the yield curve can move. There are a number of different ways this can be done. One approach corresponds to the partial duration approach that we outlined in the previous section. It involves computing the impact of a 1-basis-point change similar to the one illustrated in Figure 7.4 for each point on the zero-coupon yield curve. This delta is the partial duration calculated in Table 7.5 multiplied by the value of the portfolio multiplied by 0.0001. The sum of the deltas for all the points on the yield curve equals the DV01. Suppose that the portfolio in Table 7.5 is worth $1 million. The deltas are shown in Table 7.6.

A variation on this approach is to divide the yield curve into a number of segments or "buckets" and calculate for each bucket the impact of changing all the zero rates corresponding to the bucket by 1 basis point while keeping all other zero rates unchanged. This approach is often used in asset–liability management (see Section 7.1) and is referred to as *GAP management*. Figure 7.6 shows the type of change that would be considered for the segment of the zero curve between 2.0 and 3.0 years in Figure 7.3. As with the partial duration approach, the sum of the deltas for all the segments equals the DV01.

Calculating Deltas to Facilitate Hedging

One of the problems with the delta measures that we have considered so far is that they are not designed to make hedging easy. Consider the deltas in Table 7.6. If we plan to hedge our portfolio with zero-coupon bonds, we can calculate the position in a one-year

Figure 7.6 Change considered to yield curve when bucketing approach is used.

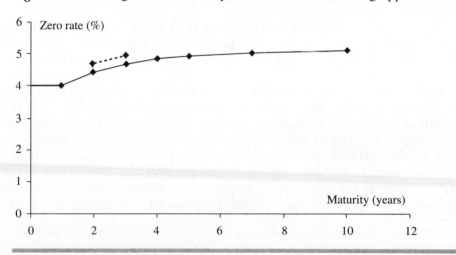

zero-coupon bond to zero out the $200 per basis point exposure to the one-year rate, the position in a two-year zero-coupon bond to zero out the exposure to the two-year rate, and so on. But, if other instruments are used, a much more complicated analysis is necessary.

In practice, traders tend to use positions in the instruments that have been used to construct the zero curve to hedge their exposure. For example, a government bond trader is likely to take positions in the actively traded government bonds that were used to construct the Treasury zero curve when hedging. A trader of instruments dependent on the LIBOR/swap yield curve is likely take position in LIBOR deposits, Eurodollar futures, and swaps when hedging.

To facilitate hedging, traders therefore often calculate the impact of small changes in the quotes for each of the instruments used to construct the zero curve. The quote for the instrument is changed by a small amount, the zero-coupon yield curve is recomputed, and the portfolio revalued. Consider a trader responsible for interest rate caps and swap options. Suppose that, when there is a 1-basis-point change in a Eurodollar futures quote, the portfolio value increases by $500. Each Eurodollar futures contract changes in value by $25 for a 1-basis-point change in the Eurodollar futures quote. It follows that the traders exposure can be hedged with 20 contracts. Suppose that the exposure to a 1-basis-point change in the five-year swap rate is $4,000 and that a five-year swap with a notional principal of $1 million changes in value by $400 for a 1-basis-point change in the five-year swap rate. The exposure can be hedged by trading swaps with a notional principal of $10 million.

7.8   PRINCIPAL COMPONENTS ANALYSIS

The approaches we have just outlined can lead to analysts calculating 10 to 15 different deltas for every zero curve. This seems like overkill because the variables being considered are quite highly correlated with each other. For example, when the yield on a five-year bond moves up by a few basis points, most of the time the yield on a ten-year bond moves in a similar way. Arguably a trader should not be worried when a portfolio has a large positive exposure to the five-year rate and a similar large negative exposure to the ten-year rate.

One approach to handling the risk arising from groups of highly correlated market variables is principal components analysis. This takes historical data on movements in the market variables and attempts to define a set of components or factors that explain the movements.

Principal components analysis is a standard statistical tool that has many applications in risk management. The mathematics underlying principal components analysis is explained in Appendix I. The approach is best illustrated with an example. The market variables we will consider are ten US Treasury rates with maturities between 3 months and 30 years. Tables 7.7 and 7.8 show results produced by Frye for these market variables using 1,543 daily observations between 1989 and 1995.[9] The first column in Table 7.7 shows the maturities of the rates that were considered. The remaining ten columns in the table show the ten factors (or principal components) describing the rate

---

[9] See J. Frye, "Principals of Risk: Finding VAR through Factor-Based Interest Rate Scenarios," in: *VAR: Understanding and Applying Value at Risk.* London: Risk Publications, 1997, pp. 275–288.

Table 7.7 Factor loadings for US Treasury data.

Maturity	PC1	PC2	PC3	PC4	PC5	PC6	PC7	PC8	PC9	PC10
3m	0.21	−0.57	0.50	0.47	−0.39	−0.02	0.01	0.00	0.01	0.00
6m	0.26	−0.49	0.23	0.37	0.70	0.01	−0.04	0.02	−0.01	0.00
12m	0.32	−0.32	−0.37	−0.58	−0.52	−0.23	−0.04	−0.05	0.00	0.01
2y	0.35	−0.10	−0.38	0.17	0.04	0.59	0.56	0.12	−0.12	−0.05
3y	0.36	0.02	−0.30	0.27	0.07	0.24	−0.79	0.00	−0.09	−0.00
4y	0.36	0.14	−0.12	0.25	0.16	−0.63	0.15	0.55	−0.14	−0.08
5y	0.36	0.17	−0.04	0.14	0.08	−0.10	0.09	−0.26	0.71	0.48
7y	0.34	0.27	0.15	0.01	0.00	−0.12	0.13	−0.54	0.00	−0.68
10y	0.31	0.30	0.28	−0.10	−0.06	0.01	0.03	−0.23	−0.63	0.52
30y	0.25	0.33	0.46	−0.34	−0.18	0.33	−0.09	0.52	0.26	−0.13

moves. The first factor, shown in the column labeled PC1, corresponds to a roughly parallel shift in the yield curve. When we have one unit of that factor, the three-month rate increases by 0.21 basis points, the six-month rate by 0.26 basis points, and so on. The second factor is shown in the column labeled PC2. It corresponds to a "twist" or change of slope of the yield curve. Rates between 3 months and 2 years move in one direction; rates between 3 years and 30 years move in the other direction. The third factor corresponds to a "bowing" of the yield curve. Rates at the short end and long end of the yield curve move in one direction; rates in the middle move in the other direction. The interest rate move for a particular factor is known as *factor loading*. In our example, the first factor's loading for the three-month rate is 0.21.[10]

Because there are ten rates and ten factors, the interest rate changes observed on any given day can always be expressed as a linear sum of the factors by solving a set of ten simultaneous equations. The quantity of a particular factor in the interest rate changes on a particular day is known as the *factor score* for that day.

The importance of a factor is measured by the standard deviation of its factor score. The standard deviations of the factor scores in our example are shown in Table 7.8 and the factors are listed in order of their importance. A quantity of the first factor equal to one standard deviation corresponds to the three-month rate moving by $0.21 \times 17.49 = 3.67$ basis points, the six-month rate moving by $0.26 \times 17.49 = 4.55$ basis points, and so on.

The factors have the property that the factor scores are uncorrelated across the data. For instance, in our example, the first factor score (amount of parallel shift) is uncorrelated with the second factor score (amount of twist) across the 1,543 days. The variances of the factor scores have the property that they add up to the total

Table 7.8 Standard deviation of factor scores.

PC1	PC2	PC3	PC4	PC5	PC6	PC7	PC8	PC9	PC10
17.49	6.05	3.10	2.17	1.97	1.69	1.27	1.24	0.80	0.79

---

[10] The factor loadings have the property that the sum of their squares for each factor is 1.0.

Figure 7.7   The three most important factors driving yield curve movements.

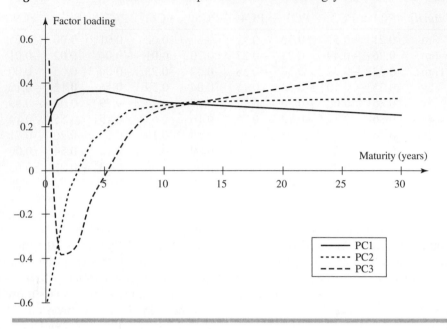

variance of the data. From Table 7.8, the total variance of the original data (that is, sum of the variance of the observations on the three-month rate, the variance of the observations on the six-month rate, and so on) is

$$17.49^2 + 6.05^2 + 3.10^2 + \cdots + 0.79^2 = 367.9$$

From this it can be seen that the first factor accounts for $17.49^2/367.9 = 83.1\%$ of the variance in the original data; the first two factors account for

$$(17.49^2 + 6.05^2)/367.9 = 93\%$$

of the variance in the data; the third factor accounts for a further 2.6% of the variance. This shows that most of the risk in interest rate moves is accounted for by the first two or three factors. It suggests that we can relate the risks in a portfolio of interest rate dependent instruments to movements in these factors instead of considering all ten interest rates. The three most important factors from Table 7.7 are plotted in Figure 7.7.[11]

Using Principal Components Analysis to Calculate Deltas

To illustrate how a principal components analysis can provide an alternative way of calculating deltas, suppose we have a portfolio with the exposures to interest rate moves shown in Table 7.9. A 1-basis-point change in the one-year rate causes the portfolio value to increase by $10 million; a 1-basis-point change in the two-year rate causes it to increase by $4 million; and so on. We use the first two factors to model

[11] Results similar to those described here, concerning the nature of the factors and the amount of the total risk they account for, are obtained when a principal components analysis is used to explain the movements in almost any yield curve in any country.

Table 7.9 Change in portfolio value for a 1-basis-point rate move ($ millions).

Rate:	1-year	2-year	3-year	4-year	5-year
Change:	+10	+4	8	−1	+2

rate moves. (As mentioned earlier, this captures over 90% of the uncertainty in rate moves.) Using the data in Table 7.7, our delta exposure to the first factor (measured in millions of dollars per factor score basis point) is

$$10 \times 0.32 + 4 \times 0.35 - 8 \times 0.36 - 7 \times 0.36 + 2 \times 0.36 = -0.08$$

and our delta exposure to the second factor is

$$10 \times (-0.32) + 4 \times (-0.10) - 8 \times 0.02 - 7 \times 0.14 + 2 \times 0.17 = -4.40$$

The approach being used here is similar to the approach described in Section 7.6 where partial durations were used to estimate the impact of a particular type of shift in the yield curve. The advantage of using a principal components analysis is that it tells you which are the most appropriate shifts to consider. It also provides information on the relative importance of different shifts. In the example we have considered, our exposure to the second shift is about 50 times greater than our exposure to the first shift. However, the first shift is about three times as important in terms of the extent to which it occurs. (This last statement is based on the standard deviation of factor scores reported in Table 7.8.)

7.9 GAMMA AND VEGA

When several delta measures are calculated, there are many possible gamma measures. Suppose that ten instruments are used to compute the zero curve and that we measure deltas with respect to changes in the quotes for each of these. Gamma is a second partial derivative of the form $\partial^2 P/\partial x_i \partial x_j$ where P is the portfolio value. We have ten choices for x_i and ten choices for x_j and a total of 55 different gamma measures. This may be "information overload". One approach is to ignore cross-gammas and focus on the ten partial derivatives where $i = j$. Another is to calculate a single gamma measure as the second partial derivative of the value of the portfolio with respect to a parallel shift in the zero curve. (This is dollar convexity.) A further possibility is to calculate gammas with respect to the first two factors in a principal components analysis.

The vega of a portfolio of interest rate derivatives measures its exposure to volatility changes. Different volatilities are used to price different interest rate derivatives. One approach is to make the same small change to all volatilities and calculate the effect on the value of the portfolio. Another is to carry out a principal components analysis to calculate factors that reflect the patterns of volatility changes across different instruments (caps, swaptions, bond options, etc.) that are traded. Vega measures can then be calculated for the first two or three factors.

SUMMARY

A bank's net interest income is the excess of the interest earned over the interest paid. There are now well-established asset–liability management procedures to ensure that this remains roughly constant from year to year. These involve adjusting the rates offered to customers to ensure that the maturities of assets and liabilities are matched.

LIBOR is an important interest rate that governs the rates paid on many floating-rate loans throughout the world. The LIBOR rate is a short-term borrowing rate for AA-rated financial institutions. A complete LIBOR term structure of interest rates is constructed from LIBOR rates, Eurodollar futures, and swap rates. Forward interest rates calculated from this term structure are the forward borrowing rates for companies that will be AA rated at the beginning of the period covered by the forward contract— not companies that are AA rated today. The LIBOR/swap term structure of interest rates is used as a proxy for the term structure of risk-free interest rates by most financial institutions.

An important concept in interest rate markets is duration. Duration measures the sensitivity of the value of a portfolio to a small parallel shift in the zero-coupon yield curve. The relationship is

$$\Delta P = -PD\,\Delta y$$

where P is the value of the portfolio, D is the duration of the portfolio, Δy is the size of a small parallel shift in the zero curve, and ΔP is the resultant effect on the value of the portfolio. A more precise relationship is

$$\Delta P = -PD\,\Delta y + \tfrac{1}{2}CP(\Delta y)^2$$

where C is the convexity of the portfolio. This relationship is accurate for relatively large parallel shifts in the yield curve but does not quantify the exposure to nonparallel shifts.

To quantify exposure to all the different ways the yield curve can change through time, several duration or delta measures are necessary. There are a number of ways these can be defined. A principal components analysis can be a useful alternative to calculating multiple deltas. It shows that the yield curve shifts that occur in practice are to a large extent a linear sum of two or three standard shifts. If a portfolio manager is hedged against these standard shifts, he or she is therefore also well hedged against the shifts that occur in practice.

FURTHER READING

Duffie, D., "Debt Management and Interest Rate Risk," in: W. Beaver and G. Parker (eds.), *Risk Management: Challenges and Solutions*. New York: McGraw-Hill, 1994.

Fabozzi, F. J., *Duration, Convexity, and Other Bond Risk Measures*. Frank J. Fabozzi Associates, 1999.

Frye, J., "Principals of Risk: Finding VAR through Factor-Based Interest Rate Scenarios," in: *VAR: Understanding and Applying Value at Risk*. London: Risk Publications, 1997, pp. 275–288.

Jorion, P., *Big Bets Gone Bad: Derivatives and Bankruptcy in Orange County*. New York: Academic Press, 1995.

Reitano, R., "Non-Parallel Yield Curve Shifts and Immunization," *Journal of Portfolio Management*, Spring 1992: 36–43.

PRACTICE QUESTIONS AND PROBLEMS (Answers at the End of the Book)

7.1. Explain carefully the risks faced by Continental Illinois in the 1980–83 period based on the data in Business Snapshot 7.1.

7.2. Explain carefully why interest rate risks contributed to the expensive S&L failures in the United States.

7.3. Suppose that a bank has $5 billion of one-year loans and $20 billion of five-year loans. These are financed by $15 billion of one-year deposits and $10 billion of five-year deposits. Explain the impact on the bank's net interest income of interest rates increasing by 1% every year for the next three years.

7.4. Explain why long-term rates are higher than short-term rates most of the time. Under what circumstances would you expect long-term rates to be lower than short-term rates?

7.5. Why are US Treasury rates significantly lower that other rates that are close to risk-free?

7.6. What does duration tell you about the sensitivity of a bond portfolio to interest rates. What are the limitations of the duration measure?

7.7. A five-year bond with a yield of 11% (continuously compounded) pays an 8% coupon at the end of each year.
(a) What is the bond's price?
(b) What is the bond's duration?
(c) Use the duration to calculate the effect on the bond's price of a 0.2% decrease in its yield.
(d) Recalculate the bond's price on the basis of a 10.8% per annum yield and verify that the result is in agreement with your answer to (c).

7.8. Repeat Problem 7.7 on the assumption that the yield is compounded annually. Use modified durations.

7.9. A six-year bond with a continuously compounded yield of 4% provides a 5% coupon at the end of each year. Use duration and convexity to estimate the effect of a 1% increase in the yield on the price of the bond. How accurate is the estimate?

7.10. Explain three ways in which multiple deltas can be calculated to manage nonparallel yield curve shifts.

7.11. Estimate the delta of the portfolio in Table 7.6 with respect to the first two factors in Table 7.7.

7.12. Use the partial durations in Table 7.5 to calculate the impact of a shift in the yield curve on a $10 million portfolio where the 1-, 2-, 3-, 4-, 5-, 7-, and 10-year rates increase by 10, 8, 7, 6, 5, 3, and 1 basis points respectively.

7.13. How are "dollar duration" and "dollar convexity" defined?

7.14. What is the relationship between (a) the duration, (b) the partial durations, and (c) the DV01 of a portfolio?

FURTHER QUESTIONS

7.15. Suppose that a bank has $10 billion of one-year loans and $30 billion of five-year loans. These are financed by $35 billion of one-year deposits and $5 billion of five-year deposits. The bank has equity totaling $2 billion and its return on equity is currently 12%. Estimate what change in interest rates next year would lead to the bank's return on equity being reduced to zero. Assume that the bank is subject to a tax rate of 30%.

7.16. Portfolio A consists of a one-year zero-coupon bond with a face value of $2,000 and a ten-year zero-coupon bond with a face value of $6,000. Portfolio B consists of a 5.95-year zero-coupon bond with a face value of $5,000. The current yield on all bonds is 10% per annum (continuously compounded):
   (a) Show that both portfolios have the same duration.
   (b) Show that the percentage changes in the values of the two portfolios for a 0.1% per annum increase in yields are the same.
   (c) What are the percentage changes in the values of the two portfolios for a 5% per annum increase in yields?

7.17. What are the convexities of the portfolios in Problem 7.16? To what extent does (a) duration and (b) convexity explain the difference between the percentage changes calculated in part (c) of Problem 7.16?

7.18. When the partial durations are as in Table 7.5, estimate the effect of a shift in the yield curve where the ten-year rate stays the same, the one-year rate moves up by $9e$, and the movements in intermediate rates are calculated by interpolation between $9e$ and 0. How could your answer be calculated from the results for the rotation calculated in Section 7.6?

7.19. Suppose that the change in a portfolio value for a 1-basis-point shift in the 3-month, 6-month, 1-year, 2-year, 3-year, 4-year, and 5-year rates are (in $ million) +5, −3, −1, +2, +5, +7, and +8, respectively. Estimate the delta of the portfolio with respect to the first three factors in Table 7.7. Quantify the relative importance of the three factors for this portfolio.

8

Value at Risk

Chapters 6 and 7 describe how a trader responsible for a financial institution's exposure to a particular market variable (e.g., an equity index, an interest rate, or a commodity price) quantifies and manages risks by calculating measures such as delta, gamma, and vega. Often a financial institution's portfolio depends on hundreds, or even thousands, of market variables. A huge number of these types of risk measures are therefore produced each day. While very useful to traders, the risk measures do not provide senior management and the individuals that regulate financial institutions with a measure of the total risk to which a financial institution is exposed.

Value at Risk (VaR) is an attempt to provide a single number that summarizes the total risk in a portfolio. It was pioneered by J. P. Morgan (see Business Snapshot 8.1) and has become widely used by corporate treasurers and fund managers as well as by financial institutions. As we shall see in Chapter 11, it is the measure regulators have chosen to use for many of the calculations they carry out concerned with the setting of capital requirements for market risk, credit risk, and operational risk.

This chapter introduces the VaR measure and discusses its strengths and weaknesses. Chapters 12 and 13 discuss how VaR is calculated for market risk, while Chapter 15 does the same for credit risk.

8.1 DEFINITION OF VaR

When using the value-at-risk measure, we are interested in making a statement of the following form:

"We are X percent certain that we will not lose more than V dollars in time T."

The variable V is the VaR of the portfolio. It is a function of two parameters: the time horizon, T, and the confidence level, X percent. It is the loss level during a time period of length T that we are $X\%$ certain will not be exceeded.

VaR can be calculated from either the probability distribution of gains during time T or the probability distribution of losses during time T. (In the former case, losses are negative gains; in the latter case, gains are negative losses.) When the distribution of gains is used, VaR is equal to minus the gain at the $(100 - X)$th percentile of the

---

Business Snapshot 8.1 Historical Perspectives on VaR

J. P. Morgan is credited with helping to make VaR a widely used measure. The Chairman, Dennis Weatherstone, was dissatisfied with the long risk reports he received every day. These contained a huge amount of detail on the Greek letters for different exposures, but very little that was really useful to top management. He asked for something simpler that focused on the bank's total exposure over the next 24 hours measured across the bank's entire trading portfolio. At first his subordinates said this was impossible, but eventually they adapted the Markowitz portfolio theory (see Section 1.1) to develop a VaR report. This became known as the 4:15 report because it was placed on the chairman's desk at 4:15 p.m. every day after the close of trading.

Producing the report entailed a huge amount of work involving the collection of data daily on the positions held by the bank around the world, the handling of different time zones, the estimation of correlations and volatilities, and the development of computer systems. The work was completed in about 1990. The main benefit of the new system was that senior management had a better understanding of the risks being taken by the bank and were better able to allocate capital within the bank. Other banks had been working on similar approaches for aggregating risks and by 1993 VaR was established as an important risk measure.

Banks usually keep the details about the models they develop internally a secret. However, in 1994 J. P. Morgan made a simplified version of their own system, which they called RiskMetrics, available on the internet. RiskMetrics included variances and covariances for a very large number of different market variables. This attracted a lot of attention and led to debates about the pros and cons of different VaR models. Software firms started offering their own VaR models, some of which used the RiskMetrics database. After that, VaR was rapidly adopted as a standard by financial institutions and some nonfinancial corporations. The BIS Amendment, which was based on VaR (see Section 11.6), was announced in 1996 and implemented in 1998. Later the RiskMetrics group within J. P. Morgan was spun off as a separate company. This company developed CreditMetrics for handling credit risks in 1997 and CorporateMetrics for handling the risks faced by nonfinancial corporations in 1999.

---

distribution, as illustrated in Figure 8.1. When the distribution of losses is used, VaR is equal to the loss at the Xth percentile of the distribution, as indicated in Figure 8.2. For example, when T is five days and $X = 97\%$, VaR is minus the third percentile of the distribution of gains in the value of the portfolio over the next five days. Alternatively, it is the 97th percentile of the distribution of losses in the value of the portfolio over the next five days.

8.2 EXAMPLES OF THE CALCULATION OF VaR

This section provides four simple examples to illustrate the calculation of VaR. In the first two examples the probability distribution of the gain (or loss) is a continuous distribution. In the last two examples, it is a discrete distribution.

Figure 8.1 Calculation of VaR from the probability distribution of the gain in the portfolio value during time T. Losses are negative gains; confidence level is $X\%$; VaR level is V.

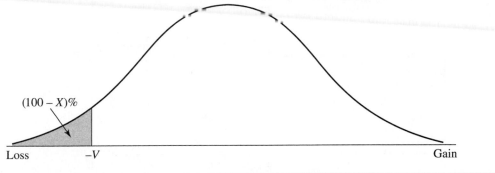

Example 8.1

Suppose that the gain from a portfolio during six months is normally distributed with a mean of $2 million and a standard deviation of $10 million. From the properties of the normal distribution, the one-percentile point of this distribution is $2 - 2.33 \times 10$, or $-$21.3 million. The VaR for the portfolio with a time horizon of six months and confidence level of 99% is therefore $21.3 million.

Example 8.2

Suppose that for a one-year project all outcomes between a loss of $50 million and a gain of $50 million are considered equally likely. In this case the loss from the project has a uniform distribution extending from $-$50 million to $+$50 million. There is a 1% chance that there will be a loss greater than $49 million. The VaR with a one-year time horizon and a 99% confidence level is therefore $49 million.

Figure 8.2 Calculation of VaR from the probability distribution of the loss in the portfolio value during time T. Gains are negative losses; confidence level is $X\%$; VaR level is V.

Figure 8.3   Cumulative loss distribution for Examples 8.3 and 8.4.

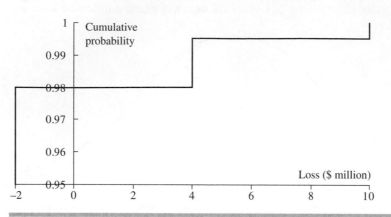

Example 8.3

A one-year project has a 98% chance of leading to a gain of $2 million, a 1.5% chance of leading to a loss of $4 million and a 0.5% chance of leading to a loss of $10 million. The cumulative loss distribution is shown in Figure 8.3. The point on this cumulative distribution that corresponds to a cumulative probability of 99% is $4 million. It follows that VaR with a confidence level of 99% and a one-year time horizon is $4 million.

Example 8.4

Consider again the situation in Example 8.3. Suppose that we are interested in calculating a VaR using a confidence level of 99.5%. In this case, Figure 8.3 shows that all losses between $4 and $10 million have a cumulative probability of 99.5% of not being exceeded. There is a probability of 0.5% of a loss equal to V dollars being exceeded for this range of values of V. VaR is therefore not uniquely defined. A sensible convention in this type of situation is to set VaR equal to the midpoint of the range of possible VaR values. This means that, in this case, VaR would be set equal to $7 million.

8.3   VaR vs. EXPECTED SHORTFALL

VaR is an attractive measure because it is easy to understand. In essence, it asks the simple question: "How bad can things get?" This is the question all senior managers want answered. They are very comfortable with the idea of compressing all the Greek letters for all the market variables underlying a portfolio into a single number. VaR is also relatively easy to back-test, as we will see later in this chapter.

However, when VaR is used in an attempt to limit the risks taken by a trader, it can lead to undesirable results. Suppose that a bank tells a trader that the one-day 99% VaR of the trader's portfolio must be kept at less than $10 million. The trader can construct a portfolio where there is a 99.1% chance that the daily loss is less than

Figure 8.4 Probability distribution for gain in portfolio value during time *T*; confidence level is *X*%. Portfolio has the same VaR level, *V*, as in Figure 8.1, but a large loss is more likely.

$10 million and a 0.9% chance that it is $500 million. The trader is satisfying the risk limits imposed by the bank but is clearly taking unacceptable risks.

This type of behavior by a trader is not as unlikely as it seems. Many traders like taking high risks in the hope of realizing high returns. If they can find ways of taking high risks without violating risk limits, they will do so. To quote one trader the author has talked to: "I have never met a risk control system that I cannot trade around." The sort of probability distribution of gains that the trader might aim for is shown in Figure 8.4. The VaR in Figure 8.4 is the same as the VaR in Figure 8.1. However, the portfolio in Figure 8.4 is much riskier than the portfolio in Figure 8.1 because a large loss is more likely.

Expected Shortfall

A measure that can produce better incentives for traders than VaR is *expected shortfall*. This is also sometimes referred to as *conditional VaR, conditional tail expectation*, or *tail loss*. Whereas VaR asks the question: "How bad can things get?", expected shortfall asks: "If things do get bad, what is the expected loss?" Expected shortfall, like VaR, is a function of two parameters: *T* (the time horizon) and *X* (the confidence level). It is the expected loss during time *T*, conditional on the loss being greater than the *X*th percentile of the loss distribution. For example, suppose that *X* = 99, *T* is ten days, and the VaR is $64 million. The expected shortfall is the average amount lost over a ten-day period assuming that the loss is greater $64 million.

As shown in the next section, expected shortfall has better properties than VaR in that it encourages diversification. One disadvantage is that it does not have the simplicity of VaR and, as a result, is more difficult to understand. Another is that it is more difficult to back-test a procedure for calculating expected shortfall than it is to back-test a procedure for calculating VaR. (Back-testing, as will be explained, later is a way of looking at historical data to test the reliability of a particular methodology for calculating a risk measure.)

In spite of its weaknesses, VaR has become the most popular measure of risk among both regulators and risk managers. Therefore, in most of our discussions in this chapter and the chapters that follow, we will focus on how VaR can be measured and used. Many of the points we make apply equally to expected shortfall and other risk measures.

8.4   VaR AND CAPITAL

As we will describe in later chapters, VaR is used by regulators of financial institutions and by financial institutions themselves to determine the amount of capital they should keep. Regulators calculate the capital required for market risk as a multiple of the VaR calculated using a ten-day time horizon and a 99% confidence level. They calculate capital for credit risk and operational risk as the VaR using a one-year time horizon and a 99.9% confidence level.

Suppose that the VaR of a portfolio for a confidence level of 99.9% and a time horizon of one year is $50 million. This means that in extreme circumstances (theoretically, once every thousand years) the financial institution is expected to lose more than $50 million in a year. It also means that if it keeps $50 million in capital it will have a 99.9% probability of not running out of capital in the course of one year.

Suppose we are trying to design a risk measure that will equal the capital a financial institution is required to keep. Is VaR (with an appropriate time horizon and an appropriate confidence level) the best measure? Artzner *et al.* have examined this question. They first proposed a number of properties that such a risk measure should have.[1] These are:

1. *Monotonicity*: If a portfolio produces a worse result than another portfolio for every state of the world, its risk measure should be greater.

2. *Translation invariance*: If an amount of cash K is added to a portfolio, its risk measure should go down by K.

3. *Homogeneity*: Changing the size of a portfolio by a factor λ, while keeping the relative amounts of different items in the portfolio the same, should result in the risk measure being multiplied by λ.

4. *Subadditivity*: The risk measure for two portfolios after they have been merged should be no greater than the sum of their risk measures before they were merged.

The first condition is straightforward. If one portfolio always gives us a worse result than another portfolio, it clearly should be viewed as more risky and require more capital. The second condition is also reasonable. If we add an amount of cash equal to K to a portfolio, this provides a buffer against losses and should reduce the capital requirement by K. The third condition is also reasonable. If we double the size of a portfolio, presumably we should require twice as much capital. The fourth condition states that diversification helps reduce risks. When we aggregate two portfolios, the total should either decrease or stay the same.

VaR satisfies the first three conditions. However, it does not always satisfy the fourth one, as is illustrated by the following two examples.

Example 8.5

Suppose each of two independent projects has a probability of 0.02 of a loss of $10 million and a probability of 0.98 of a loss of $1 million during a one-year period. The one-year, 97.5% VaR for each project is $1 million. When the projects are put in the same portfolio there is a $0.02 \times 0.02 = 0.0004$ probability of a loss of $20 million, a $2 \times 0.02 \times 0.98 = 0.0392$ probability of a loss of

---

[1] See P. Artzner, F. Delbaen, J.-M. Eber, and D. Heath, "Coherent Measures of Risk," *Mathematical Finance*, 9 (1999): 203–228.

$11 million, and a $0.98 \times 0.98 = 0.9604$ probability of a loss of $2 million. The one-year 97.5% VaR for the portfolio is $11 million. The total of the VaRs of the projects considered separately is $2 million. The VaR of the portfolio is therefore greater than the sum of the VaRs of the projects by $9 million. This violates the subadditivity condition.

Example 8.6

A bank has two $10 million one-year loans, each of which has a 1.25% chance of defaulting. If a default occurs, all losses between 0% and 100% of the principal are equally likely. If the loan does not default, a profit of $0.2 million is made. To simplify matters, we suppose that if one loan defaults it is certain that the other loan will not default.[2]

Consider first a single loan. This has a 1.25% chance of defaulting. When a default occurs, the loss experienced is evenly distributed between zero and $10 million. This means that there is a 1.25% chance that a loss greater than zero will be incurred; there is a 0.625% chance that a loss greater than $5 million is incurred; there is no chance of a loss greater than $10 million. The loss level that has a probability of 1% of being exceed is $2 million. (Conditional on a loss being made, there is an 80% (0.8) chance that the loss will be greater than $2 million. Because the probability of a loss is 1.25% (0.0125), the unconditional probability of a loss greater than $2 million is $0.8 \times 0.0125 = 0.01$ or 1%.) The one-year, 99% VaR is therefore $2 million.

Consider next the portfolio of two loans. Each loan defaults 1.25% of the time and they never default together. There is therefore a 2.5% probability that a default will occur. As before, the loss experienced on a defaulting loan is evenly distributed between zero and $10 million. The VaR in this case turns out to be $5.8 million. This is because there is a 2.5% (0.025) chance of one of the loans defaulting and conditional on this event there is an 40% (0.4) chance that the loss on the loan that defaults is greater than $6 million. The unconditional probability of a loss from a default being greater than $6 million is therefore $0.4 \times 0.025 = 0.01$, or 1%. In the event that one loan defaults, a profit of $0.2 million is made on the other loan, showing that the one-year 99% VaR is $5.8 million.

The total VaR of the loans considered separately is $2 + 2 = $4 million. The total VaR after they have been combined in the portfolio is $1.8 million greater at $5.8 million. This shows that the subadditivity condition is violated. (This is in spite of the fact that there are clearly very attractive diversification benefits from combining the loans into a single portfolio.)

8.5 COHERENT RISK MEASURES

Risk measures satisfying all four conditions given above are referred to as coherent. Examples 8.5 and 8.6 illustrate that VaR is not coherent. In contrast, it can be shown that the expected shortfall measure is coherent. The following examples illustrate this.

---

[2] This is to simplify the calculations. If the loans default independently of each other, so that two defaults can occur, the numbers are slightly different and the VaR of the portfolio is still greater than the sum of the VaRs of the individual loans.

Example 8.7

Consider again the situation in Example 8.5. The VaR for one of the projects considered on its own is $1 million. To calculate the expected shortfall for a 97.5% confidence level we note that, of the 2.5% tail of the loss distribution, 2% corresponds to a loss is $10 million and a 0.5% to a loss of $1 million. (Note that the other 97.5% of the distribution also corresponds to a loss of $1 million.) Conditional that we are in the 2.5% tail of the loss distribution, there is therefore an 80% probability of a loss of $10 million and a 20% probability of a loss of $1 million. The expected loss is $0.8 \times 10 + 0.2 \times 1$, or $8.1 million.

When the two projects are combined, of the 2.5% tail of the loss distribution, 0.04% corresponds to a loss of $20 million and 2.46% corresponds to a loss of $11 million. Conditional that we are in the 2.5% tail of the loss distribution, the expected loss is therefore $(0.04/2.5) \times 20 + (2.46/2.5) \times 11$, or $11.144 million.

Because $8.1 + 8.1 > 11.144$, the expected shortfall measure does satisfy the subadditivity condition for this example.

Example 8.8

Consider again the situation in Example 8.6. We showed that the VaR for a single loan is $2 million. The expected shortfall from a single loan when the time horizon is one year and the confidence level is 99% is therefore the expected loss on the loan conditional on a loss greater than $2 million. Given that losses are uniformly distributed between zero and $10 million, the expected loss conditional on a loss greater than $2 million is halfway between $2 million and $10 million, or $6 million.

The VaR for a portfolio consisting of the two loans was calculated in Example 8.6 as $5.8 million. The expected shortfall from the portfolio is therefore the expected loss on the portfolio conditional on the loss being greater than $5.8 million. When one loan defaults, the other (by assumption) does not and outcomes are uniformly distributed between a gain of $0.2 million and a loss of $9.8 million. The expected loss, given that we are in the part of the distribution between $5.8 million and $9.8 million, is $7.8 million. This is therefore the expected shortfall of the portfolio.

Because $7.8 million is less than $2 \times$ $6 million, the expected shortfall measure does satisfy the subadditivity condition.

The subadditivity condition is not of purely theoretical interest. It is not uncommon for a bank to find that, when it combines two portfolios (e.g., its equity portfolio and its fixed income portfolio), the total VaR goes up.

A risk measure can be characterized by the weights it assigns to quantiles of the loss distribution.[3] VaR gives a 100% weighting to the Xth quantile and zero to other quantiles. Expected shortfall gives equal weight to all quantiles greater than the Xth quantile and zero weight to all quantiles below the Xth quantile. We can define what is known as a *spectral risk measure* by making other assumptions about the weights assigned to quantiles. A general result is that a spectral risk measure is coherent (i.e., it satisfies the subadditivity condition) if the weight assigned to the qth quantile of the loss distribution is a nondecreasing function of q. Expected shortfall satisfies this condition.

---

[3] Quantiles are also referred to as percentiles or fractiles.

Figure 8.5 Weights as a function of quantiles for (a) expected shortfall when $X = 90\%$, (b) exponential spectral risk measure with $\gamma = 0.15$, and (c) exponential spectral risk measure with $\gamma = 0.05$.

However, VaR does not, because the weights assigned to quantiles greater than X are less than the weight assigned to the Xth quantile. Some researchers have proposed measures where the weights assigned to the qth quantile of the loss distribution increase relatively fast with q. One idea is to make the weight assigned to the qth quantile proportional to $e^{-(1-q)/\gamma}$, where γ is a constant. This is referred to as the *exponential spectral risk measure*. Figure 8.5 shows the weights assigned to loss quantiles for expected shortfall and for the exponential spectral risk measure when γ has two different values.

8.6 CHOICE OF PARAMETERS FOR VaR

We now return to considering VaR. The user must choose two parameters: the time horizon and the confidence level. A common (though not very good) assumption is that the change in the portfolio value over the time horizon is normally distributed. The mean change in the portfolio value is usually assumed to be zero. These assumptions are convenient because they lead to a simple formula for VaR:

$$\text{VaR} = \sigma N^{-1}(X) \tag{8.1}$$

where X is the confidence level, σ is the standard deviation of the portfolio change over the time horizon, and $N^{-1}(\cdot)$ is the inverse cumulative normal distribution (which can be calculated using NORMSINV in Excel). This equation shows that, regardless of the time horizon, VaR for a particular confidence level is proportional to σ.

Example 8.9

Suppose that the change in the value of a portfolio over a ten-day time horizon is normal with a mean of zero and a standard deviation of $20 million. The ten-day 99% VaR is $20 N^{-1}(0.99) = 46.5$, or $46.5 million.

The Time Horizon

An appropriate choice for the time horizon depends on the application. The trading desks of banks calculate the profit and loss daily. When their positions are fairly liquid and actively managed, it therefore makes sense to calculate a VaR over a time horizon of one trading day. If the VaR turns out to be unacceptable, the portfolio can be adjusted fairly quickly. Also, a VaR with a longer time horizon might not be meaningful because of changes in the composition of the portfolio.

For an investment portfolio held by a pension fund, a time horizon of one month is often chosen. This is because the portfolio is traded less actively and some of the instruments in the portfolio are less liquid. Also the performance of pension fund portfolios is often monitored monthly.

Whatever the application, when market risks are being considered, analysts almost invariably start by calculating VaR for a time horizon of one day. The usual assumption is

$$T\text{-day VaR} = 1\text{-day VaR} \times \sqrt{T} \tag{8.2}$$

This formula is exactly true when the changes in the value of the portfolio on successive days have independent identical normal distributions with mean zero. In other cases it is an approximation. The formula follows from equation (8.1) and the following results:

1. The standard deviation of the sum on T independent identically distributions is $\sqrt{N}$ times the standard deviation of each distribution
2. The sum of independent normal distributions is normal.

Impact of Autocorrelation

In practice, the changes in the value of a portfolio from one day to the next are not always totally independent. Define ΔP_i as the change in the value of a portfolio on day i. A simple assumption is first-order autocorrelation, where the correlation between ΔP_i and ΔP_{i-1} is ρ for all i. Suppose that the variance of ΔP_i is σ^2 for all i. Using the usual formula for the variance of the sum of two variables, the variance of $\Delta P_{i-1} + \Delta P_i$ is

$$\sigma^2 + \sigma^2 + 2\rho\sigma^2 = 2(1 + \rho)\sigma^2$$

The correlation between ΔP_{i-j} and ΔP_i is ρ^j. This leads to the following formula for the variance of $\sum_{i=1}^{T} \Delta P_i$ (see Problem 8.11):

$$\sigma^2[T + 2(T - 1)\rho + 2(T - 2)\rho^2 + 2(T - 3)\rho^3 + \cdots + 2\rho^{T-1}] \tag{8.3}$$

Table 8.1 shows the impact of autocorrelation on the relationship between the T-day VaR and the one-day VaR. It assumes that the distribution of daily changes in the portfolio are identical normals with mean zero. Note that the ratio of the T-day VaR to the one-day VaR does not depend on the daily standard deviation, σ, or the confidence level. This follows from the result in equation (8.1) and the property of equation (8.3) that the T-day standard deviation is proportional to the one-day standard deviation. Comparing the $\rho = 0$ row in Table 8.1 with the other rows shows that the existence of autocorrelation results in the VaR estimates calculated from equation (8.1) being too low.

Table 8.1 Ratio of *T*-day VaR to one-day VaR for different values of *T* when there is first-order correlation; distribution of change in portfolio value each day is assumed to have the same normal distribution with mean zero; ρ is the autocorrelation parameter.

ρ	$T = 1$	$T = 2$	$T = 5$	$T = 10$	$T = 50$	$T = 250$
0	1.00	1.41	2.24	3.16	7.07	15.81
0.05	1.00	1.45	2.33	3.31	7.43	16.62
0.1	1.00	1.48	2.42	3.46	7.80	17.47
0.2	1.00	1.55	2.62	3.79	8.62	19.35

Example 8.10

Suppose that the standard deviation of daily changes in the portfolio value is \$3 million and the first-order autocorrelation of daily changes is 0.1. From equation (8.3), the variance of the change in the portfolio value over five days is

$$3^2[5 + 2 \times 4 \times 0.1 + 2 \times 3 \times 0.1^2 + 2 \times 2 \times 0.1^3 + 2 \times 1 \times 0.1^4] = 52.7778$$

The standard deviation of the change in the value of the portfolio over five days is $\sqrt{52.7778}$ or 7.265. The five-day 95% VaR is therefore $7.265 \times N^{-1}(0.95) = 11.95$, or \$11.95 million. Note that the ratio of the five-day standard deviation of portfolio changes to the one-day standard is $7.265/3 = 2.42$. Because VaRs are proportional to standard deviations under the assumptions we are making, this is the number in Table 8.1 for $\rho = 0.1$ and $T = 5$.

Confidence Level

The confidence level chosen for VaR is likely to depend on a number of factors. Suppose that a bank wants to maintain a AA credit rating and calculates that companies with this credit rating have a 0.03% chance of defaulting over a one-year period. It might choose to use a 99.97% confidence level in conjunction with a one-year time horizon for internal risk management purposes. Suppose that the one-year 99.97% VaR across all exposures is \$5 billion. This means that with \$5 billion of capital the bank will have a 0.03% chance of becoming insolvent (i.e., running out of equity) during one year. This type of analysis might be communicated by banks to rating agencies in an attempt to convince the rating agency that the bank deserves its AA rating.

The confidence level that is actually used for the first VaR calculation is often much less than the one that is eventually reported. This is because it is very difficult to estimate a VaR directly when the confidence level is very high. If daily portfolio changes are assumed to be normally distributed with zero mean, we can use equation (8.1) to convert a VaR calculated with one confidence level to a VaR with another confidence level. Suppose that σ is the standard deviation of the change in the portfolio value over a certain time horizon and that the expected change in the portfolio value is zero. Denote VaR for a confidence level of X by VaR(X). From equation (8.1),

$$\text{VaR}(X) = \sigma N^{-1}(X)$$

for all confidence levels X. It follows that a VaR with a confidence level of X^* can be calculated from a VaR with a lower confidence level of X using

$$\mathrm{VaR}(X^*) = \mathrm{VaR}(X)\frac{N^{-1}(X^*)}{N^{-1}(X)} \qquad\qquad (8.4)$$

Unfortunately this formula is critically dependent on the shape of the tails of the loss distribution being normal. When the distribution is not normal, the formula may be quite a bad approximation. Extreme value theory which will be covered in Chapter 12 provides an alternative way of extrapolating tails of loss distributions.

Equation (8.4) assumes that the two VaR measures have the same time horizon. If we want to change the time horizon and are prepared to assume a normal distribution, we can use equation (8.4) in conjunction with equation (8.2) or (8.3).

Example 8.11

Suppose that the one-day VaR with a confidence level of 95% is $1.5 million. Using the assumption that the distribution of changes in portfolio value is normal with mean zero, equation (8.4) gives the one-day 99% VaR as

$$1.5 \times \frac{2.326}{1.645} = 2.12$$

or $2.12 million. If we assume that daily changes are independent, then the ten-day 99% VaR is $\sqrt{10}$ times this, or $6.71 million, and the 250-day VaR is $\sqrt{250}$ times this, or $33.54 million.

8.7   MARGINAL VaR, INCREMENTAL VaR, AND COMPONENT VaR

Analysts often calculate additional measures in order to understand VaR. Consider a portfolio with a number of subportfolios where the investment in the ith subportfolio is x_i. The *marginal VaR* is the sensitivity of VaR to the size of the ith subportfolio. It is

$$\frac{\partial\mathrm{VaR}}{\partial x_i}$$

For a portfolio of investments, marginal VaR is closely related to the capital asset pricing model's beta (see Section 1.1). If a subportfolio's beta is high, its marginal VaR will tend to be high. If its beta is low, the marginal VaR tends to be low. In some circumstances marginal VaR is negative, indicating that increasing the weighting of a particular subportfolio reduces the risk of the portfolio.

Incremental VaR is the incremental effect on VaR of the ith subportfolio. It asks the question: "What is the difference between VaR with and without the subportfolio?" One way of calculating incremental VaR is by "brute force". This involves calculating VaR with and without the subporfolio. Unfortunately, this is liable to be computationally time-consuming. If a subportfolio is small in relation to the size of a portfolio, it may be reasonable to assume that the marginal VaR remains constant as x_i is reduced all the way to zero. This leads to the following approximate formula for the incremental

VaR of the ith subportfolio:

$$\frac{\partial \text{VaR}}{\partial x_i} x_i \tag{8.5}$$

A result known as Euler's theorem shows that[4]

$$\text{VaR} = \sum_{i=1}^{N} \frac{\partial \text{VaR}}{\partial x_i} x_i$$

where N is the number of subportfolios. The *component VaR* for the ith subportfolio is defined as

$$C_i = \frac{\partial \text{VaR}}{\partial x_i} x_i \tag{8.6}$$

This has two desirable properties:

1. The ith component VaR for a large portfolio is approximately equal to the incremental VaR for the ith subportfolio.
2. The sum of all the component VaRs equals the portfolio VaR.

Interestingly, the definition of C_i in equation (8.6) is equivalent to the alternative definition that C_i is the expected loss on the ith subportfolio conditional on the loss on the portfolio equaling the VaR level. Component VaR is often used to allocate the total VaR to subportfolios—or even to individual trades.

Marginal, incremental, and component expected shortfall can be defined analogously to marginal, incremental, and component VaR. Euler's theorem applies, so that component expected shortfall can be defined by equation (8.5) with VaR replaced by expected shortfall.

8.8 BACK-TESTING

Whatever the method used for calculating VaR, an important reality check is *back-testing*. It involves testing how well the VaR estimates would have performed in the past. Suppose that we have developed a procedure for calculating a one-day 99% VaR. Back-testing involves looking at how often the loss in a day would have exceeded the one-day 99% VaR when it is calculated using the procedure. Days when the actual change exceeds VaR are referred to as *exceptions*. If exceptions happen on about 1% of the days, we can feel reasonably comfortable with the methodology for calculating VaR. If they happen on, say, 7% of days, the methodology is suspect and it is likely that VaR is under-estimated. From a regulatory perspective, the capital calculated using the VaR estimation procedure is then too low. On the other hand, if exceptions happen on, say, 0.3% of days, it is likely that the procedure is overestimating VaR and the capital calculated is too high.

One issue in back-testing a one-day VaR is whether we take account of changes made in the portfolio during a day. There are two possibilities. The first is to compare VaR with the hypothetical change in the portfolio value over the next day, calculated on the assumption that the composition of the portfolio remains unchanged during the day. The other is to compare VaR to the actual change in the value of the portfolio during

---

[4] The condition that we need for Euler's theorem is that, when each of the x_i are multiplied by λ, the portfolio VaR is multiplied by λ. This condition is known as linear homogeneity and is clearly satisfied.

the day. The assumption underlying the the calculation of VaR is usually that the portfolio will remain unchanged, so the first comparison based on hypothetical changes is more logical. However, it is actual changes in the portfolio value that we are ultimately interested in. In practice, risk managers usually compare VaR to both hypothetical portfolio changes and actual portfolio changes (and regulators insist on seeing the results of back-testing using actual changes as well as hypothetical changes). The actual changes are adjusted for items unrelated to the market risk, such as fee income and profits from trades carried out at prices different from the mid-market.

Suppose that the confidence limit for a one-day VaR is $X\%$. If the VaR model used is accurate, the probability of the VaR being exceeded on any given day is $p = 1 - X/100$. Suppose also that we look at a total of n days and we observe that the VaR level is exceeded on m of the days, where $m/n > p$. Should we reject the model for producing values of VaR that are too low? Expressed formally we can consider two alternative hypotheses:

1. The probability of an exception on any given day is p.
2. The probability of an exception on any given day is greater than p.

From the properties of the binomial distribution, the probability of the VaR level being exceeded on m or more days is

$$\sum_{k=m}^{n} \frac{n!}{k!\,(n-k)!} p^k (1-p)^{n-k}$$

This can be calculated using the BINOMDIST function in Excel. An often-used confidence level in statistical tests is 5%. If the probability of the VaR level being exceeded on m or more days is less than 5%, we reject the first hypothesis that the probability of an exception is p. If the probability of the VaR level being exceeded on m or more days is greater than 5%, the hypothesis is not rejected.

Example 8.12

Suppose that we back-test a VaR model using 600 days of data. The VaR confidence level is 99% and we observe nine exceptions. The expected number of exceptions is six. Should we reject the model? The probability of nine or more exceptions can be calculated in Excel as $1 - \text{BINOMDIST}(8,600,0.01,\text{TRUE})$. It is 0.152. So, at a 5% confidence level, we should not reject the model. However, if the number of exceptions had been 12, we would have calculated the probability of 12 or more exceptions as 0.019 and rejected the model. The model is rejected when the number of exceptions is 11 or more. (The probability of ten or more exceptions is greater than 5%, but the probability of 11 or more is less than 5%.)

When the number of exceptions, m, is lower than the expected number of exceptions, we can similarly test whether the true probability of an exception is 1%. (In this case, our alternative hypothesis is that the true probability of an exception is less than 1%.) The probability of m or less exceptions is

$$\sum_{k=0}^{m} \frac{n!}{k!\,(n-k)!} p^k (1-p)^{n-k}$$

and this is compared with the 5% threshold.

Example 8.13

Suppose again that we back-test a VaR model using 600 days of data when the VaR confidence level is 99% and we observe one exception, well below the expected number of six. Should we reject the model? The probability of one or zero exceptions can be calculated in Excel as BINOMDIST(1,600,0.01,TRUE). It is 0.017. At a 5% confidence level, we should therefore reject the model. However, if the number of exceptions had been two or more, we would not have rejected the model.

The tests we have considered so far have been one-tailed tests. In Example 8.12 we assumed that the true probability of an exception was either 1% or greater than 1%. In Example 8.13 we assumed that it was 1% or less than 1%. Kupiec has proposed a relatively powerful two-tailed test.[5] If the probability of an exception under the VaR model is p and m exceptions are observed in n trials, then

$$-2\ln[(1-p)^{n-m}p^m] + 2\ln[(1-m/n)^{n-m}(m/n)^m] \qquad (8.7)$$

should have a chi-square distribution with one degree of freedom. Values of the statistic are high for either very low or very high numbers of exceptions. There is a probability of 5% that the value of a chi-square variable with one degree of freedom will be greater than 3.84. It follows that we should reject the model whenever the expression in equation (8.7) is greater than 3.84.

Example 8.14

Suppose that, as in the previous two examples, we back-test a VaR model using 600 days of data when the VaR confidence level is 99%. The value of the statistic in equation (8.7) is greater that 3.84 when the number of exceptions, m, is one or less and when the number of exceptions is 12 or more. We therefore accept the VaR model when $2 \leqslant m \leqslant 11$ and reject it otherwise.

Generally speaking, the difficulty of back-testing a VaR model increases as the VaR confidence level increases. This is an argument in favor of not using very high confidence levels for VaR.

Bunching

A separate issue from the number of exceptions is *bunching*. If daily portfolio changes are independent, exceptions should be spread evenly throughout the period used for back-testing. In practice, they are often bunched together, suggesting that losses on successive days are not independent. One approach to testing for bunching is to use the following statistic suggested by Christoffersen[6]

$$-2\ln[(1-\pi)^{u_{00}+u_{10}}\pi^{u_{01}+u_{11}}] + 2\ln[(1-\pi_{01})^{u_{00}}\pi_{01}^{u_{01}}(1-\pi_{11})^{u_{10}}\pi_{11}^{u_{11}}]$$

where u_{ij} is the number of observations in which we go from a day where we are in state i to a day where we are in state j. This statistic is chi-square with one degree of freedom

[5] See P. Kupiec, "Techniques for Verifying the Accuracy of Risk Management Models," *Journal of Derivatives*, 3 (1995): 73–84.

[6] See P. F. Christoffersen, "Evaluating Interval Forecasts," *International Economic Review*, 39 (1998): 841–862.

if there is no bunching. State 0 is a day where there is no exception while state 1 is a day where there is an exception. Also,

$$\pi = \frac{u_{01} + u_{11}}{u_{00} + u_{01} + u_{10} + u_{11}}$$

$$\pi_{01} = \frac{u_{01}}{u_{00} + u_{01}}$$

$$\pi_{11} = \frac{u_{11}}{u_{10} + u_{11}}$$

SUMMARY

A value at risk (VaR) calculation is aimed at making a statement of the form: "We are X percent certain that we will not lose more than V dollars in time T." The variable V is the VaR, X percent is the confidence level, and T is the time horizon. It has become a very popular risk measure. An alternative measure that has rather better theoretical properties is *expected shortfall*. This is the expected loss conditional on the loss being greater than the VaR level.

When changes in a portfolio value are normally distributed, a VaR estimate with one confidence level can be used to calculate a VaR level with another confidence level. Also, if one-day changes have independent normal distributions, an N-day VaR equals the one-day VaR multiplied by $\sqrt{N}$. When the independence assumption is relaxed, other somewhat more complicated formulas can be used to go from the one-day VaR to the N-day VaR.

Consider the situation where a portfolio has a number of subportfolios. The marginal VaR with respect to the ith subporfolio is the partial derivative of VaR with respect to the size of the subporfolio. The incremental VaR with respect to a particular subportfolio is the incremental effect of that subportfolio on VaR. There is a formula that can be used for dividing VaR into components that correspond to the positions taken in the subportfolios. The component VaRs sum to VaR and each component is, for a large portfolio of relatively small positions, approximately equal to the corresponding incremental VaR.

Back-testing is an important part of a VaR system. It examines how well the VaR model would have performed in the past. There are two ways in which back-testing may indicate weaknesses in a VaR model. One is in the percentage of exceptions, that is, the percentage of times the actual loss exceeds VaR. The other is in the extent to which exceptions are bunched. There are statistical tests to determine whether a VaR model should be rejected because of the percentage of exceptions or the amount of bunching. As we will see in Chapter 11, regulators have rules for increasing the VaR multiplier when market risk capital is calculated if they consider the results from back-testing over 250 days to be unsatisfactory.

FURTHER READING

Artzner P., F. Delbaen, J.-M. Eber, and D. Heath, "Coherent Measures of Risk," *Mathematical Finance*, 9 (1999): 203–228.

Basak, S., and A. Shapiro, "Value-at-Risk-Based Risk Management: Optimal Policies and Asset Prices," *Review of Financial Studies*, 14, 2 (2001): 371–405.

Beder, T., "VaR: Seductive but Dangerous," *Financial Analysts Journal*, 51, 5 (1995): 12–24.

Boudoukh, J., M. Richardson, and R. Whitelaw, "The Best of Both Worlds," *Risk*, May 1998: 64–67.

Dowd, K., *Measuring Market Risk*, 2nd edn. New York: Wiley, 2005.

Duffie, D., and J. Pan, "An Overview of Value at Risk." *Journal of Derivatives*, 4, 3 (Spring 1997): 7–49.

Hopper, G., "Value at Risk: A New Methodology for Measuring Portfolio Risk," *Business Review*, Federal Reserve Bank of Philadelphia, July–August 1996: 19–29.

Hua P., and P. Wilmott, "Crash Courses," *Risk*, June 1997: 64–67.

Jackson, P., D.-J. Maude, and W. Perraudin, "Bank Capital and Value at Risk," *Journal of Derivatives*, 4, 3 (Spring 1997): 73–90.

Jorion, P., *Value at Risk*, 2nd edn. McGraw-Hill, 2001.

Longin, F. M., "Beyond the VaR," *Journal of Derivatives*, 8, 4 (Summer 2001): 36–48.

Marshall, C., and M. Siegel, "Value at Risk: Implementing a Risk Measurement Standard," *Journal of Derivatives* 4, 3 (Spring 1997): 91–111.

PRACTICE QUESTIONS AND PROBLEMS (Answers at the End of the Book)

8.1. What is the difference between expected shortfall and VaR? What is the theoretical advantage of expected shortfall over VaR?

8.2. What is a spectral risk measure? What conditions must be satisfied by a spectral risk measure for the subadditivity condition in Section 8.3 to be satisfied?

8.3. A fund manager announces that the fund's one-month 95% VaR is 6% of the size of the portfolio being managed. You have an investment of $100,000 in the fund. How do you interpret the portfolio manager's announcement?

8.4. A fund manager announces that the fund's one-month 95% expected shortfall is 6% of the size of the portfolio being managed. You have an investment of $100,000 in the fund. How do you interpret the portfolio manager's announcement?

8.5. Suppose that each of two investments has a 0.9% chance of a loss of $10 million, a 99.1% of a loss of $1, and 0% chance of a profit. The investments are independent of each other.
   (a) What is the VaR for one of the investments when the confidence level is 99%?
   (b) What is the expected shortfall for one of the investments when the confidence level is 99%?
   (c) What is the VaR for a portfolio consisting of the two investments when the confidence level is 99%?
   (d) What is the expected shortfall for a portfolio consisting of the two investments when the confidence level is 99%?
   (e) Show that in this example VaR does not satisfy the subadditivity condition whereas expected shortfall does.

8.6. Suppose that the change in the value of a portfolio over a one-day time period is normal with a mean of zero and a standard deviation of $2 million. What is (a) the one-day 97.5% VaR, (b) the five-day 97.5% VaR, and (c) the five-day 99% VaR?

8.7. What difference does it make to your answer to Problem 8.6 if there is first-order daily autocorrelation with correlation parameter equal to 0.16?

8.8. Explain carefully the differences between marginal VaR, incremental VaR, and component VaR for a portfolio consisting of a number of assets.

8.9. Suppose that we back-test a VaR model using 1,000 days of data. The VaR confidence level is 99% and we observe 17 exceptions. Should we reject the model at the 5% confidence level? Use a one-tailed test.

8.10. Explain what is meant by bunching.

8.11. Prove equation (8.3).

FURTHER QUESTIONS

8.12. Suppose that each of two investments has a 4% chance of a loss of $10 million, a 2% chance that of a loss of $1 million, and a 94% chance of a profit of $1 million. They are independent of each other.
(a) What is the VaR for one of the investments when the confidence level is 95%?
(b) What is the expected shortfall when the confidence level is 95%?
(c) What is the VaR for a portfolio consisting of the two investments when the confidence level is 95%?
(d) What is the expected shortfall for a portfolio consisting of the two investments when the confidence level is 95%?
(e) Show that, in this example, VaR does not satisfy the subadditivity condition whereas expected shortfall does.

8.13. Suppose that daily changes for a portfolio have first-order correlation with correlation parameter 0.12. The ten-day VaR, calculated by multiplying the one-day VaR by $\sqrt{10}$, is $2 million. What is a better estimate of the VaR that takes account of autocorrelation?

8.14. Suppose that we back-test a VaR model using 1,000 days of data. The VaR confidence level is 99% and we observe 15 exceptions. Should we reject the model at the 5% confidence level. Use Kupiec's two-tailed test.

Volatility

It is important for a financial institution to monitor the volatilities of the market variables (interest rates, exchange rates, equity prices, commodity prices, etc.) on which the value of its portfolio depends. This chapter describes the procedures it can use to do this.

The chapter starts by defining volatility. It then explains how volatility can be implied from option prices or estimated from historical data. It examines the common assumption that percentage returns from market variables are normally distributed and presents the power law as an alternative. After that it moves on to consider models with imposing names such as exponentially weighted moving average (EWMA), autoregressive conditional heteroscedasticity (ARCH), and generalized autoregressive conditional heteroscedasticity (GARCH). The distinctive feature of these models is that they recognize that volatility is not constant. During some periods, volatility is relatively low, while during other periods it is relatively high. The models attempt to keep track of variations in volatility through time.

9.1 DEFINITION OF VOLATILITY

A variable's volatility σ is defined as the standard deviation of the return provided by the variable per unit of time when the return is expressed using continuous compounding. (See Appendix A for a discussion of compounding frequencies.) When volatility is used for option pricing, the unit of time is usually one year, so that volatility is the standard deviation of the continuously compounded return per year. However, when volatility is used for risk management, the unit of time is usually one day, so that volatility is the standard deviation of the continuously compounded return per day.

In general $\sigma\sqrt{T}$ is equal to the standard deviation of

$$\ln\frac{S_T}{S_0}$$

where S_T is the value of the market variable at time T and S_0 is its value today. The expression $\ln(S_T/S_0)$ equals the total return (not the return per unit time) earned in time T expressed with continuous compounding. If σ is per day, then T is measured in days; if σ is per year, then T is measured in years.

When T is small, the continuously compounded percentage return of a market variable during time T is the close to the percentage increase in the variable during time T. It follows that, for small T, $\sigma\sqrt{T}$ is approximately equal to the standard deviation of the percentage change in the market variable in time T. Suppose, for example, that a stock price is \$50 and its volatility is 30% per year. The standard deviation of the percentage change in the stock price in one week is approximately

$$30 \times \sqrt{\frac{1}{52}} = 4.16\%$$

A 1-standard-deviation move in the stock price in one week is therefore approximately 50×0.0416, or \$2.08.

When the time horizons considered are fairly short, our uncertainty about a future stock price, as measured by its standard deviation, increases—at least approximately—with the square root of how far ahead we are looking. For example, the standard deviation of the stock price in four weeks is approximately twice the standard deviation in one week. This is consistent with the adage "uncertainty increases with the square root of time".

Variance Rate

Risk managers often focus on the variance rate rather than the volatility. The *variance rate* is defined as the square of the volatility. The variance rate per year is the variance of the continuously compounded return in one year. The variance rate per day is the variance of the continuously compounded return in one day. Whereas the standard deviation of the return in time T increases with the square root of time, the variance of this return increases linearly with time. If we wanted to be pedantic, we could say that it is correct to talk about the variance rate per day, but volatility is "per square root of day".

Trading Days vs. Calendar Days

When volatilities are calculated and used, an issue that crops up is whether time should be measured in calendar days or trading days. As shown in Business Snapshot 9.1, research shows that volatility is much higher when the exchange is open for trading than when it is closed. As a result, analysts tend to ignore days when the exchange is closed when estimating volatility from historical data. The usual assumption is that there are 252 days per year.

Define σ_{year} as the volatility per year of a certain asset while σ_{day} is the equivalent volatility per day of the asset. The standard deviation of the continuously compounded return on the asset in one year is either σ_{year} or $\sigma_{\text{day}}\sqrt{252}$. It follows that

$$\sigma_{\text{year}} = \sigma_{\text{day}}\sqrt{252}$$

or

$$\sigma_{\text{day}} = \frac{\sigma_{\text{year}}}{\sqrt{252}}$$

showing that the daily volatility is about 6% of annual volatility.

Business Snapshot 9.1 What Causes Volatility?

It is natural to assume that the volatility of a stock is caused by new information reaching the market. This new information causes people to revise their opinions about the value of the stock. The price of the stock changes and volatility results. However, this view of what causes volatility is not supported by research.

With several years of daily stock price data, researchers can calculate:

1. The variance of stock price returns between the close of trading on one day and the close of trading on the next day when there are no intervening nontrading days

2. The variance of the stock price returns between the close of trading on Friday and the close of trading on Monday

The second variance is the variance of returns over a three-day period. The first is a variance over a one-day period. We might reasonably expect the second variance to be three times as great as the first variance. Fama (1965), French (1980), and French and Roll (1986) show that this is not the case. These three research studies estimate the second variance to be, respectively, 22%, 19% and 10.7% higher than the first variance.

At this stage you might be tempted to argue that these results are explained by more news reaching the market when the market is open for trading. But research by Roll (1984) does not support this explanation. Roll looked at the prices of orange juice futures. By far the most important news for orange juice futures prices is news about the weather and news about the weather is equally likely to arrive at any time. When Roll did a similar analysis to that just described for stocks, he found that the second (Friday-to-Monday) variance is only 1.54 times the first variance.

The only reasonable conclusion from all this is that volatility is to a large extent caused by trading itself. (Traders usually have no difficulty accepting this conclusion!)

9.2 IMPLIED VOLATILITIES

As shown in Appendix E at the end of this book, the one parameter in option pricing formulas that cannot be directly observed is the volatility of the asset price. This allows traders to imply a volatility from option prices.

To illustrate how implied volatilities are calculated, suppose that the market price of a three-month European call option on a non-dividend-paying stock is $1.875 when the stock price is $21, the strike price is $20, and the risk-free rate is 10%. The implied volatility is the value of volatility that, when substituted into the Black–Scholes option pricing formula, gives an option price of $1.875. Unfortunately, it is not possible to invert the Black–Scholes formula so that volatility is expressed as a function of the option price and other variables. However, an iterative search procedure can be used to find the implied volatility σ. For example, we can start by trying $\sigma = 0.20$. This gives a value for the option price equal to $1.76, which is less than the market price of $1.875. Because the option price is an increasing function of σ, a higher value of σ is required. We can next try $\sigma = 0.3$. This gives a value for the option price equal to $2.10, which is too high and means that σ must lie between 0.20 and 0.30. Next, a value of 0.25 can be tried for σ. This also proves to be too high, showing that the implied volatility lies between 0.20 and 0.25. Proceeding in this way, the range for σ can be halved at each iteration and the correct value of σ can be calculated to any required accuracy.[1] In this example, the implied volatility is 0.235, or 23.5% per annum. A similar procedure can be used in conjunction with binomial trees to find implied volatilities for American options (see Appendix F for a discussion of American options).

Implied volatilities are used extensively by traders. However, risk management is largely based on historical volatilities. Later in this chapter we will present procedures for monitoring volatility using historical data.

The VIX Index

The CBOE publishes indices of implied volatility. The most popular index, the SPX VIX, is an index of the implied volatility of 30-day options on the S&P 500 calculated from a wide range of calls and puts.[2] Trading in futures on the VIX started in 2004 and trading in options on the VIX started in 2006. A trade involving options on the S&P 500 is a bet on both the future level of the S&P 500 and the volatility of the S&P 500. By contrast, a futures or options contract on the VIX is a bet only on volatility. One contract is on 1,000 times the index. Figure 9.1 shows the VIX index between 2004 and 2008. It can be seen that volatilities were very high in the last few months of 2008. This was a reflection of market uncertainties following the collapse of Lehman Brothers.

Example 9.1

Suppose that a trader buys an April futures contract on the VIX when the futures price is 18.5 (corresponding to a 30-day S&P 500 volatility of 18.5%) and closes

Figure 9.1 The VIX index, January 2004 to December 2008.

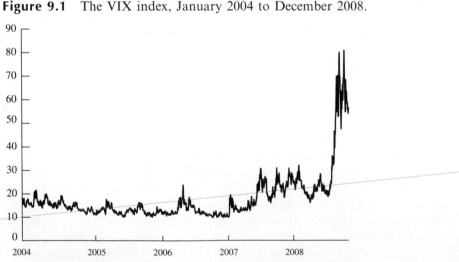

---

[1] This method is presented for illustration. Other, more powerful, search procedures are used to calculate implied volatilities in practice.

[2] Similarly, the VXN is an index of the volatility of the NASDAQ 100 index and the VXD is an index of the volatility of the Dow Jones Industrial Average.

out the contract when the futures price is 19.3 (corresponding to an S&P 500 volatility of 19.3%). The trader makes a gain of $800.

9.3 ESTIMATING VOLATILITY FROM HISTORICAL DATA

When the volatility of a variable is estimated using historical data, the value of the variable is usually observed at fixed intervals of time (e.g., every day, week, or month).
Define:

$n + 1$: Number of observations

S_i: Value of variable at end of ith interval ($i = 0, 1, \ldots, n$)

τ: Length of time interval

and let the return during the ith interval be

$$u_i = \ln \left(\frac{S_i}{S_{i-1}} \right)$$

for $i = 1, 2, \ldots, n$.

The usual estimate s of the standard deviation of the u_i is given by

$$s = \sqrt{\frac{1}{n-1} \sum_{i=1}^{n} (u_i - \bar{u})^2}$$

or

$$s = \sqrt{\frac{1}{n-1} \sum_{i=1}^{n} u_i^2 - \frac{1}{n(n-1)} \left(\sum_{i=1}^{n} u_i \right)^2}$$

where $\bar{u}$ is the mean of the u_i.

As explained in Section 9.1, the standard deviation of the u_i is $\sigma\sqrt{\tau}$, where σ is the volatility of the variable. The variable s is therefore an estimate of $\sigma\sqrt{\tau}$. It follows that σ itself can be estimated as $\hat{\sigma}$, where

$$\hat{\sigma} = \frac{s}{\sqrt{\tau}}$$

The standard error of this estimate can be shown to be approximately $\hat{\sigma}/\sqrt{2n}$. If τ is measured in years, the volatility calculated is a volatility per year. If τ is measured in days, then the volatility is a daily volatility.

Example 9.2

Table 9.1 shows a possible sequence of stock prices during 21 consecutive trading days. In this case

$$\sum u_i = 0.09531 \quad \text{and} \quad \sum u_i^2 = 0.00326$$

and the estimate of the standard deviation of the daily return is

$$\sqrt{\frac{0.00326}{19} - \frac{0.09531^2}{380}} = 0.01216$$

Table 9.1 Computation of volatility.

Day	Closing stock price ($)	Price relative S_i/S_{i-1}	Daily return $u_i = \ln(S_i/S_{i-1})$
0	20.00		
1	20.10	1.00500	0.00499
2	19.90	0.99005	−0.01000
3	20.00	1.00503	0.00501
4	20.50	1.02500	0.02469
5	20.25	0.98780	−0.01227
6	20.90	1.03210	0.03159
7	20.90	1.00000	0.00000
8	20.90	1.00000	0.00000
9	20.75	0.99282	−0.00720
10	20.75	1.00000	0.00000
11	21.00	1.01205	0.01198
12	21.10	1.00476	0.00475
13	20.90	0.99052	−0.00952
14	20.90	1.00000	0.00000
15	21.25	1.01675	0.01661
16	21.40	1.00706	0.00703
17	21.40	1.00000	0.00000
18	21.25	0.99299	−0.00703
19	21.75	1.02353	0.02326
20	22.00	1.01149	0.01143

or 1.216%. To calculate a daily volatility, we set $\tau = 1$ and obtain a volatility of 1.216%. To calculate a volatility per year, we set $\tau = 1/252$, and the data give an estimate for the volatility per annum of $0.01216\sqrt{252} = 0.193$, or 19.3%. The standard error of the daily volatility estimate is

$$\frac{0.01216}{\sqrt{2 \times 20}} = 0.0019$$

or 0.19% per day. The standard error of the volatility per year is

$$\frac{0.193}{\sqrt{2 \times 20}} = 0.031$$

or 3.1% per annum.

9.4 ARE DAILY PERCENTAGE CHANGES IN FINANCIAL VARIABLES NORMAL?

The Black–Scholes model and its extensions (see Appendix E) make the assumption that asset prices change continuously and have constant volatility. This means that the return in a short period of time Δt always has a normal distribution with a standard deviation of $\sigma\sqrt{\Delta t}$. Suppose that the volatility of an exchange rate is estimated as 12%

Table 9.2 Percentage of days when absolute size of daily exchange rate moves is greater than 1, 2, ..., 6 standard deviations (SD = standard deviation of percentage daily change).

No. of standard deviations	Real world (%)	Normal model (%)
>1 SD	25.04	31.73
>2 SD	5.27	4.55
>3 SD	1.34	0.27
>4 SD	0.29	0.01
>5 SD	0.08	0.00
>6 SD	0.03	0.00

per year. This corresponds to $12/\sqrt{252}$ or 0.756% per day. Assuming normally distributed returns, the tables at the end of this book show that the probability that the value of the foreign currency will change by more than 1 standard deviation—that is, by more than 0.756%—in one day is 31.73%; the probability that the exchange rate will change by more than 2 standard deviations—that is, by more than 1.512%—is 4.55%; the probability that it will change by more than 3 standard deviations—that is, by more than 2.268%—is 0.27%; and so on.

In practice, exchange rates, and most other market variables, tend to have heavier tails than the normal distribution. Table 9.2 illustrates this by examining the daily movements in 12 different exchange rates over a ten-year period.[3] The first step in the production of the table is to calculate the standard deviation of daily percentage changes

Figure 9.2 Comparison of normal distribution with a heavy-tailed distribution. The two distributions have the same mean and standard deviation.

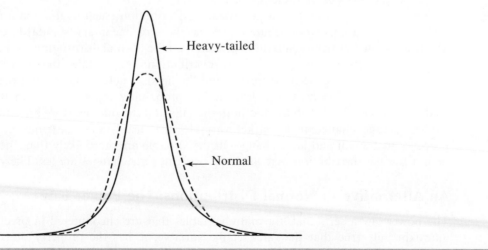

[3] This table is taken from J. C. Hull and A. White, "Value at Risk When Daily Changes in Market Variables Are Not Normally Distributed," *Journal of Derivatives*, 5, 3 (Spring 1998): 9–19.

Business Snapshot 9.2 Making Money from Foreign Currency Options

Suppose that most market participants think that exchange rates are lognormally distributed. They will be comfortable using the same volatility to value all options on a particular exchange rate. You have just done the analysis in Table 9.2 and know that the lognormal assumption is not a good one for exchange rates. What should you do?

The answer is that you should buy deep-out-of-the-money call and put options on a variety of different currencies—and wait. These options will be relatively inexpensive and more of them will close in the money than the lognormal model predicts. The present value of your payoffs will on average be much greater than the cost of the options.

In the mid-1980s a few traders knew about the heavy tails of foreign exchange probability distributions. Everyone else thought that the lognormal assumption of Black–Scholes was reasonable. The few traders who were well informed followed the strategy we have described—and made lots of money. By the late 1980s everyone realized that out-of-the-money options should have a higher implied volatility than at-the-money options and the trading opportunities disappeared.

---

in each exchange rate. The next stage is to note how often the actual percentage changes exceeded 1 standard deviation, 2 standard deviations, and so on. These numbers are then compared with the corresponding numbers for the normal distribution.

Daily percentage changes exceed three standard deviations on 1.34% of the days. The normal model for returns predicts that this should happen on only 0.27% of days. Daily percentage changes exceed 4, 5, and 6 standard deviations on 0.29%, 0.08%, and 0.03% of days, respectively. The normal model predicts that we should hardly ever observe this happening. The table, therefore, provides evidence to support the existence of heavy tails. Business Snapshot 9.2 shows how you could have made money if you had done the analysis in Table 9.2 in 1985!

Figure 9.2 compares a typical heavy-tailed distribution (such as the one for foreign exchange) with a normal distribution that has the same mean and standard deviation.[4] The heavy-tailed distribution is more peaked than the normal distribution. In Figure 9.2 we can distinguish three parts of the distribution: the middle, the tails, and the intermediate parts (between the middle and the tails). When we move from the normal distribution to the heavy-tailed distribution, probability mass shifts from the intermediate parts of the distribution to both the tails and the middle. If we are considering the percentage change in a market variable, the heavy-tailed distribution has the property that small and large changes in the variable are more likely than they would be if a normal distribution were assumed. Intermediate changes are less likely.

An Alternative to Normal Distributions: The Power Law

The power law asserts that, for many variables that are encountered in practice, it is approximately true that the value of the variable, v, has the property that, when x

---

[4] *Kurtosis* measures the size of a distribution's tails. A *leptokurtic distribution* has heavier tails than the normal distribution. A *platykurtic distribution* has less heavy tails than the normal distribution; a distribution with the same sized tails as the normal distribution is termed *mesokurtic*.

is large,

$$\text{Prob}(v > x) = Kx^{-\alpha} \qquad (9.1)$$

where K and α are constants. The equation has been found to be approximately true for variables as diverse as the income of individuals, the size of cities, and the number of visits to websites in a day.

Example 9.3

Suppose that we know from experience that $\alpha = 3$ for a particular financial variable and we observe that the probability that $v > 10$ is 0.05. Equation (9.1) gives

$$0.05 = K \times 10^{-3}$$

so that $K = 50$. The probability that $v > 20$ can now be calculated as

$$50 \times 20^{-3} = 0.00625$$

The probability that $v > 30$ is

$$50 \times 30^{-3} = 0.0019$$

and so on.

Equation (9.1) implies that

$$\ln[\text{Prob}(v > x)] = \ln K - \alpha \ln x$$

We can therefore do a quick test of whether it holds by plotting $\ln[\text{Prob}(v > x)]$ against $\ln x$. In order to do this for the data in Table 9.2, define x as the number of standard deviations by which the exchange rate increases in one day. We assume that the probabilities reported in Table 9.2 come from observations that are evenly divided between positive and negative exchange rate moves. For example, it is assumed that the 0.08% probability of an exchange rate move of more than 5 standard deviations is a result of a probability of 0.04% of the daily move being more that $+5$ standard deviations and a probability of 0.04% of the daily move being less than -5 standard deviations.

The values of $\ln x$ and $\ln[\text{Prob}(v > x)]$ are calculated in Table 9.3. The data in Table 9.3 are plotted in Figure 9.3. This shows that the logarithm of the probability of the exchange rate increasing by more than x standard deviations is approximately linearly dependent on $\ln x$ for $x > 3$. This is evidence that the power law holds for this

Table 9.3   Values calculated from Table 9.2.

x	$\ln x$	$\text{Prob}(v > x)$	$\ln[\text{Prob}(v > x)]$
1	0.000	0.12520	-2.078
2	0.693	0.02635	-3.636
3	1.099	0.00670	-5.006
4	1.386	0.00145	-6.536
5	1.609	0.00040	-7.824
6	1.792	0.00015	-8.805

Figure 9.3 Log–log plot for exchange rate increases: x is number of standard deviations; v is the exchange rate increase.

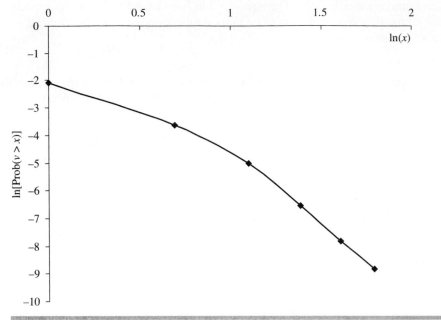

data. Using data for $x = 3$, 4, 5, and 6, a regression analysis gives the best-fit relationship as

$$\text{Prob}(v > x) = 1.06 - 5.51 \ln x$$

showing that estimates for K and α are as follows: $K = e^{1.06} = 2.88$ and $\alpha = 5.51$. An estimate for the probability of an increase greater than 4.5 standard deviations is

$$2.88 \times 4.5^{-5.51} = 0.00073$$

This means there is a probability of $2 \times 0.00073 = 0.00146$ that there will be a change (positive or negative) or more than 4.5 standard deviations. An estimate for the probability of an increase greater than 7 standard deviations is

$$2.88 \times 7^{-5.51} = 0.000064$$

This means there is a probability of $2 \times 0.000064 = 0.000128$ that there will be a change (positive or negative) or more than 7 standard deviations.

We will examine the power law more formally and explain better procedures for estimating the parameters when we consider extreme value theory in Chapter 12. We will also explain how it can be used in the assessment of operational risk in Chapter 18.

9.5 MONITORING DAILY VOLATILITY

Risk managers cannot assume that asset prices are well behaved with a constant volatility. It is important for them to monitor volatility on a daily basis.

Define σ_n as the volatility of a market variable on day n, as estimated at the end of day $n-1$. The variance rate is σ_n^2. Suppose that the value of the market variable at the end of day i is S_i. As in Section 9.3, we define the variable u_i as the continuously compounded return during day i (between the end of day $i-1$ and the end of day i), so that

$$u_i = \ln\left(\frac{S_i}{S_{i-1}}\right)$$

One approach to estimating σ_n is to set it equal to the historical volatility as calculated in Section 9.3. When m days of observations on the u_i are used, this approach gives

$$\sigma_n^2 = \frac{1}{m-1}\sum_{i=1}^{m}(u_{n-i} - \bar{u})^2 \tag{9.2}$$

where $\bar{u}$ is the mean of the u_i:

$$\bar{u} = \frac{1}{m}\sum_{i=1}^{m} u_{n-i}$$

For risk management purposes, the formula in equation (9.2) is usually changed in a number of ways:

1. u_i is defined as the percentage change in the market variable between the end of day $i-1$ and the end of day i, so that

$$u_i = \frac{S_i - S_{i-1}}{S_{i-1}} \tag{9.3}$$

   This makes very little difference to the values of u_i that are computed.

2. $\bar{u}$ is assumed to be zero. The justification for this is that the expected change in a variable in one day is very small when compared with the standard deviation of changes.

3. $m-1$ is replaced by m. This moves us from an unbiased estimate of the volatility to a maximum likelihood estimate (see Section 9.9).

These three changes allow the formula for the variance rate to be simplified to

$$\sigma_n^2 = \frac{1}{m}\sum_{i=1}^{m} u_{n-i}^2 \tag{9.4}$$

where u_i is given by equation (9.3).

Weighting Schemes

Equation (9.4) gives equal weight to all $u_{n-1}^2, u_{n-2}^2, \ldots, u_{n-m}^2$. Our objective is to estimate the volatility σ_n on day n. It therefore makes sense to give more weight to recent data. A model that does this is

$$\sigma_n^2 = \sum_{i=1}^{m} \alpha_i u_{n-i}^2 \tag{9.5}$$

The variable α_i is the amount of weight given to the observation i days ago. The α's are positive. If we choose them so that $\alpha_i < \alpha_j$ when $i > j$, less weight is given to older observations. The weights must sum to unity, so that

$$\sum_{i=1}^{m} \alpha_i = 1$$

An extension of the idea in equation (9.5) is to assume that there is a long-run average variance rate and that this should be given some weight. This leads to the model that takes the form

$$\sigma_n^2 = \gamma V_L + \sum_{i=1}^{m} \alpha_i u_{n-i}^2 \tag{9.6}$$

where V_L is the long-run variance rate and γ is the weight assigned to V_L. Because the weights must sum to unity, we have

$$\gamma + \sum_{i=1}^{m} \alpha_i = 1$$

This is known as an ARCH(m) model. It was first suggested by Engle.[5] The estimate of the variance is based on a long-run average variance and m observations. The older an observation, the less weight it is given. Defining $\omega = \gamma V_L$, the model in equation (9.6) can be written

$$\sigma_n^2 = \omega + \sum_{i=1}^{m} \alpha_i u_{n-i}^2 \tag{9.7}$$

In the next two sections we discuss two important approaches to monitoring volatility using the ideas in equations (9.5) and (9.6).

9.6   THE EXPONENTIALLY WEIGHTED MOVING AVERAGE MODEL

The exponentially weighted moving average (EWMA) model is a particular case of the model in equation (9.5) where the weights α_i decrease exponentially as we move back through time. Specifically, $\alpha_{i+1} = \lambda \alpha_i$, where λ is a constant between zero and one.

It turns out that this weighting scheme leads to a particularly simple formula for updating volatility estimates. The formula is

$$\sigma_n^2 = \lambda \sigma_{n-1}^2 + (1 - \lambda) u_{n-1}^2 \tag{9.8}$$

The estimate σ_n of the volatility for day n (made at the end of day $n - 1$) is calculated from σ_{n-1} (the estimate that was made at the end of day $n - 2$ of the volatility for day $n - 1$) and u_{n-1} (the most recent daily percentage change).

---

[5] See R. Engle "Autoregressive Conditional Heteroscedasticity with Estimates of the Variance of UK Inflation," *Econometrica*, 50 (1982), 987–1008. Robert Engle won the Nobel prize for economics in 2003 for his work on ARCH models.

To understand why equation (9.8) corresponds to weights that decrease exponentially, we substitute for σ_{n-1}^2 to get

$$\sigma_n^2 = \lambda[\lambda\sigma_{n-2}^2 + (1 - \lambda)u_{n-2}^2] + (1 - \lambda)u_{n-1}^2$$

or

$$\sigma_n^2 = (1 - \lambda)(u_{n-1}^2 + \lambda u_{n-2}^2) + \lambda^2\sigma_{n-2}^2$$

Substituting in a similar way for σ_{n-2}^2 gives

$$\sigma_n^2 = (1 - \lambda)(u_{n-1}^2 + \lambda u_{n-2}^2 + \lambda^2 u_{n-3}^2) + \lambda^3\sigma_{n-3}^2$$

Continuing in this way, we see that

$$\sigma_n^2 = (1 - \lambda)\sum_{i=1}^{m} \lambda^{i-1}u_{n-i}^2 + \lambda^m\sigma_{n-m}^2$$

For a large m, the term $\lambda^m\sigma_{n-m}^2$ is sufficiently small to be ignored, so that equation (9.8) is the same as equation (9.5) with $\alpha_i = (1 - \lambda)\lambda^{i-1}$. The weights for the u's decline at rate λ as we move back through time. Each weight is λ times the previous weight.

Example 9.4

Suppose that λ is 0.90, the volatility estimated for a market variable for day $n - 1$ is 1% per day, and during day $n - 1$ the market variable increased by 2%. This means that $\sigma_{n-1}^2 = 0.01^2 = 0.0001$ and $u_{n-1}^2 = 0.02^2 = 0.0004$. Equation (9.8) gives

$$\sigma_n^2 = 0.9 \times 0.0001 + 0.1 \times 0.0004 = 0.00013$$

The estimate σ_n of the volatility for day n is, therefore, $\sqrt{0.00013}$, or 1.14% per day. Note that the expected value of u_{n-1}^2 is σ_{n-1}^2, or 0.0001. In this example, the realized value of u_{n-1}^2 is greater than the expected value, and as a result our volatility estimate increases. If the realized value of u_{n-1}^2 had been less than its expected value, our estimate of the volatility would have decreased.

The EWMA approach has the attractive feature that relatively few data need to be stored. At any given time, we need to remember only the current estimate of the variance rate and the most recent observation on the value of the market variable. When we get a new observation on the value of the market variable, we calculate a new daily percentage change and use equation (9.8) to update our estimate of the variance rate. The old estimate of the variance rate and the old value of the market variable can then be discarded.

The EWMA approach is designed to track changes in the volatility. Suppose there is a big move in the market variable on day $n - 1$, so that u_{n-1}^2 is large. From equation (9.8), this causes our estimate of the current volatility to move upward. The value of λ governs how responsive the estimate of the daily volatility is to the most recent daily percentage change. A low value of λ leads to a great deal of weight being given to the u_{n-1}^2 when σ_n is calculated. In this case, the estimates produced for the volatility on successive days are themselves highly volatile. A high value of λ (i.e., a value close to 1.0) produces estimates of the daily volatility that respond relatively slowly to new information provided by the daily percentage change.

The RiskMetrics database, which was originally created by J. P. Morgan and made publicly available in 1994, uses the EWMA model with $\lambda = 0.94$ for updating daily volatility estimates in its RiskMetrics database. The company found that, across a range of different market variables, this value of λ gives forecasts of the variance rate that come closest to the realized variance rate.[6]

9.7   THE GARCH(1,1) MODEL

We now move on to discuss what is known as the GARCH(1,1) model, proposed by Bollerslev in 1986.[7] The difference between the GARCH(1,1) model and the EWMA model is analogous to the difference between equation (9.5) and equation (9.6). In GARCH(1,1), σ_n^2 is calculated from a long-run average variance rate, V_L, as well as from σ_{n-1} and u_{n-1}. The equation for GARCH(1,1) is

$$\sigma_n^2 = \gamma V_L + \alpha u_{n-1}^2 + \beta \sigma_{n-1}^2 \tag{9.9}$$

where γ is the weight assigned to V_L, α is the weight assigned to u_{n-1}^2, and β is the weight assigned to σ_{n-1}^2. Because the weights must sum to one:

$$\gamma + \alpha + \beta = 1$$

The EWMA model is a particular case of GARCH(1,1) where $\gamma = 0$, $\alpha = 1 - \lambda$, and $\beta = \lambda$.

The "(1,1)" in GARCH(1,1) indicates that σ_n^2 is based on the most recent observation of u^2 and the most recent estimate of the variance rate. The more general GARCH(p,q) model calculates σ_n^2 from the most recent p observations on u^2 and the most recent q estimates of the variance rate.[8] GARCH(1,1) is by far the most popular of the GARCH models.

Setting $\omega = \gamma V_L$, the GARCH(1,1) model can also be written

$$\sigma_n^2 = \omega + \alpha u_{n-1}^2 + \beta \sigma_{n-1}^2 \tag{9.10}$$

This is the form of the model that is usually used for the purposes of estimating the parameters. Once ω, α, and β have been estimated, we can calculate γ as $1 - \alpha - \beta$. The long-term variance V_L can then be calculated as ω/γ. For a stable GARCH(1,1) process, we require $\alpha + \beta < 1$. Otherwise, the weight applied to the long-term variance is negative.

---

[6] See J. P. Morgan, *RiskMetrics Monitor*, Fourth Quarter, 1995. We will explain an alternative (maximum likelihood) approach to estimating parameters later in the chapter. The realized variance rate on a particular day was calculated as an equally weighted average of the u_i^2 on the subsequent 25 days (see Problem 9.20).

[7] See T. Bollerslev, "Generalized Autoregressive Conditional Heteroscedasticity," *Journal of Econometrics*, 31 (1986): 307–327.

[8] Other GARCH models have been proposed that incorporate asymmetric news. These models are designed so that σ_n depends on the sign of u_{n-1}. Arguably, the models are more appropriate than GARCH(1,1) for equities. This is because the volatility of an equity's price tends to be inversely related to the price, so that a negative u_{n-1} should have a bigger effect on σ_n than the same positive u_{n-1}. For a discussion of models for handling asymmetric news, see D. Nelson, "Conditional Heteroscedasticity and Asset Returns: A New Approach," *Econometrica*, 59 (1990): 347–370 and R. F. Engle and V. Ng, "Measuring and Testing the Impact of News on Volatility," *Journal of Finance*, 48 (1993), 1749–1778.

Example 9.5

Suppose that a GARCH(1,1) model is estimated from daily data as

$$\sigma_n^2 = 0.000002 + 0.13u_{n-1}^2 + 0.86\sigma_{n-1}^2$$

This corresponds to $\alpha = 0.13$, $\beta = 0.86$, and $\omega = 0.000002$. Because $\gamma = 1 - \alpha - \beta$, it follows that $\gamma = 0.01$, and because $\omega = \gamma V_L$, it follows that $V_L = 0.0002$. In other words, the long-run average variance per day implied by the model is 0.0002. This corresponds to a volatility of $\sqrt{0.0002} = 0.014$, or 1.4% per day.

Suppose that the estimate of the volatility on day $n - 1$ is 1.6% per day, so that $\sigma_{n-1}^2 = 0.016^2 = 0.000256$, and that on day $n - 1$ the market variable decreased by 1%, so that $u_{n-1}^2 = 0.01^2 = 0.0001$. Then

$$\sigma_n^2 = 0.000002 + 0.13 \times 0.0001 + 0.86 \times 0.000256 = 0.00023516$$

So the new estimate of the volatility is $\sqrt{0.00023516} = 0.0153$, or 1.53% per day.

The Weights

Substituting for σ_{n-1}^2 in equation (9.10), we obtain

$$\sigma_n^2 = \omega + \alpha u_{n-1}^2 + \beta(\omega + \alpha u_{n-2}^2 + \beta\sigma_{n-2}^2)$$

or

$$\sigma_n^2 = \omega + \beta\omega + \alpha u_{n-1}^2 + \alpha\beta u_{n-2}^2 + \beta^2\sigma_{n-2}^2$$

Substituting for σ_{n-2}^2, we get

$$\sigma_n^2 = \omega + \beta\omega + \beta^2\omega + \alpha u_{n-1}^2 + \alpha\beta u_{n-2}^2 + \alpha\beta^2 u_{n-3}^2 + \beta^3\sigma_{n-3}^2$$

Continuing in this way, we see that the weight applied to u_{n-i}^2 is $\alpha\beta^{i-1}$. The weights decline exponentially at rate β. The parameter β can be interpreted as a "decay rate". It is similar to λ in the EWMA model. It defines the relative importance of the observations on the u_i in determining the current variance rate. For example, if $\beta = 0.9$, u_{n-2}^2 is only 90% as important as u_{n-1}^2; u_{n-3}^2 is 81% as important as u_{n-1}; and so on. The GARCH(1,1) model is the same as the EWMA model except that, in addition to assigning weights that decline exponentially to past u^2, it also assigns some weight to the long-run average variance rate.

9.8 CHOOSING BETWEEN THE MODELS

In practice, variance rates do tend to be pulled back to a long-run average level. This is known as *mean reversion*. The GARCH(1,1) model incorporates mean reversion, whereas the EWMA model does not. GARCH(1,1) is, therefore, theoretically more appealing than the EWMA model.

In the next section, we will discuss how best-fit parameters ω, α, and β in GARCH(1,1) can be estimated. When the parameter ω is zero, the GARCH(1,1) reduces to EWMA. In circumstances where the best-fit value of ω turns out to be negative, the GARCH(1,1) model is not stable and it makes sense to switch to the EWMA model.

9.9   MAXIMUM LIKELIHOOD METHODS

It is now appropriate to discuss how the parameters in the models we have been considering are estimated from historical data. The approach used is known as the *maximum likelihood method*. It involves choosing values for the parameters that maximize the chance (or likelihood) of the data occurring.

To illustrate the method, we start with a very simple example. Suppose that we sample ten stocks at random on a certain day and find that the price of one of them declined on that day and the prices of the other nine either remained the same or increased. What is our best estimate of the probability of a price decline? The natural answer is 0.1. Let us see if this is the result given by maximum likelihood methods.

Suppose that the probability of a price decline is p. The probability that one particular stock declines in price and the other nine do not is $p(1 - p)^9$. (There is a probability p that it will decline and $1 - p$ that each of the other nine will not.) Using the maximum likelihood approach, the best estimate of p is the one that maximizes $p(1 - p)^9$. Differentiating this expression with respect to p and setting the result equal to zero, we find that $p = 0.1$ maximizes the expression. This shows that the maximum likelihood estimate of p is 0.1, as expected.

Estimating a Constant Variance

As our next example of maximum likelihood methods, we consider the problem of estimating a variance of a variable X from m observations on X when the underlying distribution is normal. We assume that the observations are $u_1, u_2, \ldots, u_m$ and that the mean of the underlying normal distribution is zero. Denote the variance by v. The likelihood of u_i being observed is the probability density function for X when $X = u_i$. This is

$$\frac{1}{\sqrt{2\pi v}} \exp\left(\frac{-u_i^2}{2v}\right)$$

The likelihood of m observations occurring in the order in which they are observed is

$$\prod_{i=1}^{m} \left[\frac{1}{\sqrt{2\pi v}} \exp\left(\frac{-u_i^2}{2v}\right) \right] \tag{9.11}$$

Using the maximum likelihood method, the best estimate of v is the value that maximizes this expression.

Maximizing an expression is equivalent to maximizing the logarithm of the expression. Taking logarithms of the expression in equation (9.11) and ignoring constant multiplicative factors, it can be seen that we wish to maximize

$$\sum_{i=1}^{m} \left[-\ln v - \frac{u_i^2}{v} \right] \tag{9.12}$$

or

$$-m \ln v - \sum_{i=1}^{m} \frac{u_i^2}{v}$$

Differentiating this expression with respect to v and setting the result equation to zero, we see that the maximum likelihood estimator of v is

$$\frac{1}{m}\sum_{i=1}^{m} u_i^2$$

This maximum likelihood estimator is the one we used in equation (9.4). The corresponding unbiased estimator is the same with m replaced by $m-1$.

Estimating GARCH(1,1) or EWMA Parameters

We now consider how the maximum likelihood method can be used to estimate the parameters when GARCH(1,1) or some other volatility updating scheme is used. Define $v_i = \sigma_i^2$ as the estimate of the variance for day i. We assume that the probability distribution of u_i conditional on the variance is normal. A similar analysis to the one just given shows the best parameters are the ones that maximize

$$\prod_{i=1}^{m}\left[\frac{1}{\sqrt{2\pi v_i}}\exp\left(\frac{-u_i^2}{2v_i}\right)\right]$$

Taking logarithms, we see that this is equivalent to maximizing

$$\sum_{i=1}^{m}\left[-\ln(v_i)-\frac{u_i^2}{v_i}\right] \tag{9.13}$$

This is the same as the expression in equation (9.12), except that v is replaced by v_i. We search iteratively to find the parameters in the model that maximize the expression in equation (9.13).

The spreadsheet in Table 9.4 indicates how the calculations could be organized for the GARCH(1,1) model. The table analyzes data on the Japanese yen exchange rate between January 6, 1988, and August 15, 1997. The numbers in the table are based on trial estimates of the three GARCH(1,1) parameters: ω, α, and β. The first column in the table records the date. The second column counts the days. The third column shows the exchange rate S_i at the end of day i. The fourth column shows the proportional change in the exchange rate between the end of day $i-1$ and the end of day i. This is $u_i = (S_i - S_{i-1})/S_{i-1}$. The fifth column shows the estimate of the variance rate $v_i = \sigma_i^2$ for day i made at the end of day $i-1$. On day 3, we start things off by setting the variance equal to u_2^2. On subsequent days, equation (9.10) is used. The sixth column tabulates the likelihood measure $-\ln(v_i) - u_i^2/v_i$. The values in the fifth and sixth columns are based on the current trial estimates of ω, α, and β. We are interested in choosing ω, α, and β to maximize the sum of the numbers in the sixth column. This involves an iterative search procedure.[9]

In our example, the optimal values of the parameters turn out to be

$$\omega = 0.00000175, \quad \alpha = 0.0618, \quad \beta = 0.899$$

and the maximum value of the function in equation (9.13) is 22,063.5833. The numbers

---

[9] As discussed later, a general purpose algorithm such as Solver in Microsoft's Excel can be used. Alternatively, a special-purpose algorithm, such as Levenberg–Marquardt, can be used. See, for example, W.H. Press, B.P. Flannery, S.A. Teukolsky, and W.T. Vetterling. *Numerical Recipes in C: The Art of Scientific Computing*, Cambridge University Press, 1988.

Table 9.4 Estimation of parameters in GARCH(1,1) model.

Date	Day i	S_i	u_i	$v_i = \sigma_i^2$	$-\ln v_i - u_i^2/v_i$
06-Jan-88	1	0.007728			
07-Jan-88	2	0.007779	0.006599		
08-Jan-88	3	0.007746	−0.004242	0.00004355	9.6283
11-Jan-88	4	0.007816	0.009037	0.00004198	8.1329
12-Jan-88	5	0.007837	0.002687	0.00004455	9.8568
13-Jan-88	6	0.007924	0.011101	0.00004220	7.1529
⋮	⋮	⋮	⋮	⋮	⋮
13-Aug-97	2421	0.008643	0.003374	0.00007626	9.3321
14-Aug-97	2422	0.008493	−0.017309	0.00007092	5.3294
15-Aug-97	2423	0.008495	0.000144	0.00008417	9.3824
					22,063.5833

Trial Estimates of GARCH Parameters

ω	α	β
0.00000175	0.0618	0.899

shown in Table 9.4 were calculated on the final iteration of the search for the optimal ω, α, and β.

The long-term variance rate V_L in our example is

$$\frac{\omega}{1 - \alpha - \beta} = \frac{0.00000175}{0.0383} = 0.0000442$$

The long-term volatility is $\sqrt{0.0000442}$, or 0.665% per day.

Figure 9.4 shows the way in which the GARCH(1,1) volatility for the Japanese yen changed over the ten-year period covered by the data. Most of the time, the volatility was between 0.4% and 0.8% per day, but volatilities over 1% were experienced during some periods.

An alternative, more robust approach to estimating parameters in GARCH(1,1) is known as *variance targeting*.[10] This involves setting the long-run average variance rate V_L equal to the sample variance calculated from the data (or to some other value that is believed to be reasonable). The value of ω then equals $V_L(1 - \alpha - \beta)$ and only two parameters have to be estimated. For the data in Table 9.4, the sample variance is 0.00004341, which gives a daily volatility of 0.659%. Setting V_L equal to the sample variance, the values of α and β that maximize the objective function in equation (9.13) are 0.0607 and 0.8990, respectively. The value of the objective function is 22,063.5274, only marginally below the value of 22,063.5833 obtained using the earlier procedure.

When the EWMA model is used, the estimation procedure is relatively simple. We set $\omega = 0$, $\alpha = 1 - \lambda$, and $\beta = \lambda$, and only one parameter has to be estimated. In the data in Table 9.4, the value of λ that maximizes the objective function in equation (9.13) is 0.9686 and the value of the objective function is 21,995.8377.

---

[10] See R. Engle and J. Mezrich, "GARCH for Groups," *Risk*, August 1996: 36–40.

Figure 9.4   Daily volatility of the yen–USD exchange rate, 1988–1997.

Both GARCH(1,1) and the EWMA method can be implemented by using the Solver routine in Excel to search for the values of the parameters that maximize the likelihood function. The routine works well provided that we structure our spreadsheet so that the parameters we are searching for have roughly equal values. For example, in GARCH(1,1) we could let cells A1, A2, and A3 contain $\omega \times 10^5$, α, and 0.1β. We could then set $B1 = A1/100,000$, $B2 = A2$, and $B3 = 10 * A3$. We would then use B1, B2, and B3 to calculate the likelihood function, but we would ask Solver to calculate the values of A1, A2, and A3 that maximize the likelihood function.

How Good Is the Model?

The assumption underlying a GARCH model is that volatility changes with the passage of time. During some periods, volatility is relatively high; during others, it is relatively low. To put this another way, when u_i^2 is high, there is a tendency for u_{i+1}^2, u_{i+2}^2, ... to be high; when u_i^2 is low, there is a tendency for u_{i+1}^2, u_{i+2}^2, ... to be low. We can test how true this is by examining the autocorrelation structure of the u_i^2.

Let us assume that the u_i^2 do exhibit autocorrelation. If a GARCH model is working well, it should remove the autocorrelation. We can test whether it has done this by considering the autocorrelation structure for the variables u_i^2/σ_i^2. If these show very little autocorrelation, our model for σ_i has succeeded in explaining autocorrelations in the u_i^2.

Table 9.5 shows results for the yen–dollar exchange rate data referred to earlier. The first column shows the lags considered when the autocorrelation is calculated. The second column shows autocorrelations for u_i^2; the third column shows autocorrelations for u_i^2/σ_i^2.[11] The table shows that the autocorrelations are positive for u_i^2 for all lags between 1 and 15. In the case of u_i^2/σ_i^2, some of the autocorrelations are positive and some are negative. They are nearly always much smaller in magnitude than the autocorrelations for u_i^2.

---

[11] For a series x_i, the autocorrelation with a lag of k is the coefficient of correlation between x_i and x_{i+k}.

Table 9.5 Autocorrelations before and after the use of a GARCH model.

Time lag	Autocorrelation for u_i^2	Autocorrelation for u_i^2/σ_i^2
1	0.072	0.000
2	0.041	−0.010
3	0.057	0.005
4	0.107	0.000
5	0.075	0.011
6	0.066	0.009
7	0.019	−0.034
8	0.085	0.015
9	0.054	0.009
10	0.030	−0.022
11	0.038	−0.004
12	0.038	−0.021
13	0.057	−0.001
14	0.040	0.004
15	0.007	−0.026

The GARCH model appears to have done a good job in explaining the data. For a more scientific test, we can use what is known as the Ljung–Box statistic.[12] If a certain series has m observations the Ljung–Box statistic is

$$m \sum_{k=1}^{K} w_k \eta_k^2$$

where η_k is the autocorrelation for a lag of k, K is the number of lags considered, and

$$w_k = \frac{m+2}{m-k}$$

For $K = 15$, zero autocorrelation can be rejected with 95% confidence when the Ljung–Box statistic is greater than 25.

From Table 9.5, the Ljung–Box statistic for the u_i^2 series is about 123. This is strong evidence of autocorrelation. For the u_i^2/σ_i^2 series, the Ljung–Box statistic is 8.2, suggesting that the autocorrelation has been largely removed by the GARCH model.

9.10 USING GARCH(1,1) TO FORECAST FUTURE VOLATILITY

The variance rate estimated at the end of day $n-1$ for day n, when GARCH(1,1) is used, is

$$\sigma_n^2 = (1 - \alpha - \beta)V_L + \alpha u_{n-1}^2 + \beta \sigma_{n-1}^2$$

---

[12] See G. M. Ljung and G. E. P. Box. "On a Measure of Lack of Fit in Time Series Models," *Biometrica*, 65 (1978): 297–303.

so that

$$\sigma_n^2 - V_L = \alpha(u_{n-1}^2 - V_L) + \beta(\sigma_{n-1}^2 - V_L)$$

On day $n + t$ in the future, we have

$$\sigma_{n+t}^2 - V_L = \alpha(u_{n+t-1}^2 - V_L) + \beta(\sigma_{n+t-1}^2 - V_L)$$

The expected value of u_{n+t-1}^2 is σ_{n+t-1}^2. Hence,

$$E[\sigma_{n+t}^2 - V_L] = (\alpha + \beta)E[\sigma_{n+t-1}^2 - V_L]$$

where E denotes expected value. Using this equation repeatedly yields

$$E[\sigma_{n+t}^2 - V_L] = (\alpha + \beta)^t(\sigma_n^2 - V_L)$$

or

$$E[\sigma_{n+t}^2] = V_L + (\alpha + \beta)^t(\sigma_n^2 - V_L) \tag{9.14}$$

This equation forecasts the volatility on day $n + t$ using the information available at the end of day $n - 1$. In the EWMA model, $\alpha + \beta = 1$ and equation (9.14) shows that the expected future variance rate equals the current variance rate. When $\alpha + \beta < 1$, the final term in the equation becomes progressively smaller as t increases. Figure 9.5 shows the expected path followed by the variance rate for situations where the current variance rate is different from V_L. As mentioned earlier, the variance rate exhibits mean reversion with a reversion level of V_L and a reversion rate of $1 - \alpha - \beta$. Our forecast of the future variance rate tends toward V_L as we look further and further ahead. This analysis emphasizes the point that we must have $\alpha + \beta < 1$ for a stable GARCH(1,1) process. When $\alpha + \beta > 1$, the weight given to the long-term average variance is negative and the process is "mean fleeing" rather than "mean reverting".

In the yen–dollar exchange rate example considered earlier $\alpha + \beta = 0.9617$ and $V_L = 0.0000442$. Suppose that our estimate of the current variance rate per day is 0.00006 (corresponding to a volatility of 0.77% per day). In ten days, the expected

Figure 9.5 Expected path for the variance rate when (a) current variance rate is above long-term variance rate and (b) current variance rate is below long-term variance rate.

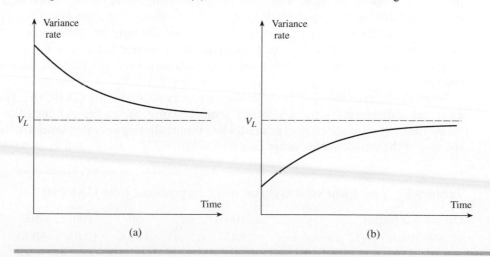

variance rate is

$$0.0000442 + 0.9617^{10}(0.00006 - 0.0000442) = 0.00005476$$

The expected volatility per day is $\sqrt{0.00005476}$, or 0.74%, still well above the long-term volatility of 0.665% per day. However, the expected variance rate in 100 days is

$$0.0000442 + 0.9617^{100}(0.00006 - 0.0000442) = 0.00004451$$

and the expected volatility per day is 0.667%, very close the long-term volatility.

Volatility Term Structures

Suppose it is day n. Define

$$V(t) = E(\sigma_{n+t}^2)$$

and

$$a = \ln \frac{1}{\alpha + \beta}$$

so that equation (9.14) becomes

$$V(t) = V_L + e^{-at}[V(0) - V_L]$$

Here, $V(t)$ is an estimate of the instantaneous variance rate in t days. The average variance rate per day between today and time T is

$$\frac{1}{T} \int_0^T V(t)\, dt = V_L + \frac{1 - e^{-aT}}{aT}[V(0) - V_L]$$

The longer the life of the option, the closer this is to V_L. Define $\sigma(T)$ as the volatility per annum that should be used to price a T-day option under GARCH(1,1). Assuming 252 days per year, $\sigma(T)^2$ is 252 times the average variance rate per day, so that

$$\sigma(T)^2 = 252\left\{ V_L + \frac{1 - e^{-aT}}{aT}[V(0) - V_L] \right\} \tag{9.15}$$

The relationship between the volatilities of options and their maturities is referred to as the *volatility term structure*. The volatility term structure is usually calculated from implied volatilities, but equation (9.15) provides an alternative approach for estimating it from the GARCH(1,1) model. Although the volatility term structure estimated from GARCH(1,1) is not the same as that calculated from implied volatilities, it is often used to predict the way that the actual volatility term structure will respond to volatility changes.

When the current volatility is above the long-term volatility, the GARCH(1,1) model estimates a downward-sloping volatility term structure. When the current volatility is below the long-term volatility, it estimates an upward-sloping volatility term structure. In the case of the yen–dollar exchange rate, $a = \ln(1/0.9617) = 0.0391$ and $V_L = 0.0000442$.

Table 9.6   Yen–dollar volatility term structure predicted from GARCH(1,1).

Option life (days):	10	30	50	100	500
Option volatility (% per annum):	12.02	11.61	11.35	11.02	10.65

Table 9.7 Impact of 1% change in the instantaneous volatility predicted from GARCH(1,1).

Option life (days):	10	30	50	100	500
Increase in volatility (%):	0.85	0.62	0.48	0.28	0.06

Suppose that the current variance rate per day, $V(0)$, is estimated as 0.00006 per day. It follows from equation (9.15) that

$$\sigma(T)^2 = 252\left[0.0000442 + \frac{1 - e^{-0.0391T}}{0.0391T}(0.00006 - 0.0000442)\right]$$

where T is measured in days. Table 9.6 shows the volatility per year for different values of T.

Impact of Volatility Changes

Equation (9.15) can be written as

$$\sigma(T)^2 = 252\left\{V_L + \frac{1 - e^{-aT}}{aT}\left[\frac{\sigma(0)^2}{252} - V_L\right]\right\}$$

When $\sigma(0)$ changes by $\Delta\sigma(0)$, $\sigma(T)$ changes by approximately

$$\frac{1 - e^{-aT}}{aT}\frac{\sigma(0)}{\sigma(T)}\Delta\sigma(0) \tag{9.16}$$

Table 9.7 shows the effect of a volatility change on options of varying maturities for our yen–dollar exchange rate example. We assume as before that $V(0) = 0.00006$, so that the daily volatility is $\sqrt{0.0006} = 0.0077$, or 0.77%, and $\sigma(0) = \sqrt{252} \times 0.77\% = 12.30\%$. The table considers a 100-basis-point change in the instantaneous volatility from 12.30% per year to 13.30% per year. This means that $\Delta\sigma(0) = 0.01$, or 1%.

Many financial institutions use analyses such as this when determining the exposure of their books to volatility changes. Rather than consider an across-the-board increase of 1% in implied volatilities when calculating vega, they relate the size of the volatility increase that is considered to the maturity of the option. Based on Table 9.7, a 0.84% volatility increase would be considered for a 10-day option, a 0.61% increase for a 30-day option, a 0.46% increase for a 50-day option, and so on.

SUMMARY

In option pricing we define the volatility of a variable as the standard deviation of its continuously compounded return per year. Volatilities are either estimated from historical data or implied from option prices. In risk management, the daily volatility of a market variable is defined as the standard deviation of the percentage daily change in the market variable. The daily variance rate is the square of the daily volatility. Volatility tends to be much higher on trading days than on nontrading days. As a result nontrading days are ignored in volatility calculations. It is tempting to assume that daily changes in market variables are normally distributed. In fact, this is far from true. Most market variables have distributions for percentage daily changes with much heavier tails than the normal distribution. The power law has been found to be a good description of the tails of many distributions that are encountered in practice.

Most popular option pricing models, such as Black–Scholes, assume that the volatility of the underlying asset is constant. This assumption is far from perfect. In practice, the volatility of an asset, like its price, is a stochastic variable. However, unlike the asset price, it is not directly observable. This chapter has discussed methods for attempting to keep track of the current level of volatility.

We define u_i as the percentage change in a market variable between the end of day $i - 1$ and the end of day i. The variance rate of the market variable (that is, the square of its volatility) is calculated as a weighted average of the u_i^2. The key feature of the methods that have been discussed here is that they do not give equal weight to the observations on the u_i^2. The more recent an observation, the greater the weight assigned to it. In the EWMA model and the GARCH(1,1) model, the weights assigned to observations decrease exponentially as the observations become older. The GARCH(1,1) model differs from the EWMA model in that some weight is also assigned to the long-run average variance rate. Both the EWMA and GARCH(1,1) models have structures that enable forecasts of the future level of the variance rate to be produced relatively easily.

Maximum likelihood methods are usually used to estimate parameters in GARCH(1,1) and similar models from historical data. These methods involve using an iterative procedure to determine the parameter values that maximize the chance or likelihood that the historical data will occur. Once its parameters have been determined, a model can be judged by how well it removes autocorrelation from the u_i^2.

The GARCH(1,1) model can be used to estimate a volatility for options from historical data. This analysis is often used to calculate the impact of a shock to volatility on the implied volatilities of options of different maturities.

FURTHER READING

On the Causes of Volatility

Fama, E. F., "The Behavior of Stock Market Prices," *Journal of Business*, 38 (January 1965): 34–105.

French, K. R., "Stock Returns and the Weekend Effect," *Journal of Financial Economics*, 8 (March 1980): 55–69.

French, K. R., and R. Roll, "Stock Return Variances: The Arrival of Information and the Reaction of Traders," *Journal of Financial Economics*, 17 (September 1986): 5–26.

Roll, R., "Orange Juice and Weather," *American Economic Review*, 74, 5 (December 1984): 861–880.

On GARCH

Bollerslev, T., "Generalized Autoregressive Conditional Heteroscedasticity," *Journal of Econometrics*, 31 (1986): 307–327.

Cumby, R., S. Figlewski, and J. Hasbrook, "Forecasting Volatilities and Correlations with EGARCH Models," *Journal of Derivatives*, 1, 2 (Winter 1993), 51–63.

Engle, R. F., "Autoregressive Conditional Heteroscedasticity with Estimates of the Variance of UK Inflation," *Econometrica*, 50 (1982), 987–1008.

Engle, R. F., and J. Mezrich, "Grappling with GARCH," *Risk*, September 1995: 112–117.

Engle, R. F., and V. Ng, "Measuring and Testing the Impact of News on Volatility," *Journal of Finance*, 48 (1993), 1749–1778.

Nelson, D., "Conditional Heteroscedasticity and Asset Returns; A New Approach," *Econometrica*, 59 (1990): 347–370.

Noh, J., R. F. Engle, and A. Kane, "Forecasting Volatility and Option Prices of the S&P 500 Index," *Journal of Derivatives*, 2 (1994): 17–30.

PRACTICE QUESTIONS AND PROBLEMS (Answers at the End of the Book)

9.1. The volatility of a stock price is 30% per annum. What is the standard deviation of the percentage price change in one week?

9.2. The volatility of an asset is 25% per annum. What is the standard deviation of the percentage price change in one trading day. Assuming a normal distribution with zero mean, estimate 95% confidence limits for the percentage price change in one day.

9.3. Why do traders assume 252 rather than 365 days in a year when using volatilities?

9.4. What is implied volatility? What does it mean if different options on the same asset have different implied volatilities?

9.5. Suppose that observations on an exchange rate at the end of the last 11 days have been 0.7000, 0.7010, 0.7070, 0.6999, 0.6970, 0.7003, 0.6951, 0.6953, 0.6934, 0.6923, 0.6922. Estimate the daily volatility using both the approach in Section 9.3 and the simplified approach in equation (9.4).

9.6. The number of visitors to websites follows the power law in equation (9.1) with $\alpha = 2$. Suppose that 1% of sites get 500 or more visitors per day. What percentage of sites get (a) 1,000 and (b) 2,000 or more visitors per day?

9.7. Explain the exponentially weighted moving average (EWMA) model for estimating volatility from historical data.

9.8. What is the difference between the exponentially weighted moving average model and the GARCH(1,1) model for updating volatilities?

9.9. The most recent estimate of the daily volatility of an asset is 1.5% and the price of the asset at the close of trading yesterday was $30.00. The parameter λ in the EWMA model is 0.94. Suppose that the price of the asset at the close of trading today is $30.50. How will this cause the volatility to be updated by the EWMA model?

9.10. A company uses an EWMA model for forecasting volatility. It decides to change the parameter λ from 0.95 to 0.85. Explain the likely impact on the forecasts.

9.11. Assume that S&P 500 at close of trading yesterday was 1,040 and the daily volatility of the index was estimated as 1% per day at that time. The parameters in a GARCH(1,1) model are $\omega = 0.000002$, $\alpha = 0.06$, and $\beta = 0.92$. If the level of the index at close of trading today is 1,060, what is the new volatility estimate?

9.12. The most recent estimate of the daily volatility of the US dollar–sterling exchange rate is 0.6% and the exchange rate at 4:00 p.m. yesterday was 1.5000. The parameter λ in the

EWMA model is 0.9. Suppose that the exchange rate at 4:00 p.m. today proves to be 1.4950. How would the estimate of the daily volatility be updated?

9.13. A company uses the GARCH(1,1) model for updating volatility. The three parameters are ω, α, and β. Describe the impact of making a small increase in each of the parameters while keeping the others fixed.

9.14. The parameters of a GARCH(1,1) model are estimated as $\omega = 0.000004$, $\alpha = 0.05$, and $\beta = 0.92$. What is the long-run average volatility and what is the equation describing the way that the variance rate reverts to its long-run average? If the current volatility is 20% per year, what is the expected volatility in 20 days?

9.15. Suppose that the daily volatility of the FTSE 100 stock index (measured in pounds sterling) is 1.8% and the daily volatility of the dollar–sterling exchange rate is 0.9%. Suppose further that the correlation between the FTSE 100 and the dollar–sterling exchange rate is 0.4. What is the volatility of the FTSE 100 when it is translated to US dollars? Assume that the dollar–sterling exchange rate is expressed as the number of US dollars per pound sterling. [*Hint*: When $Z = XY$, the percentage daily change in Z is approximately equal to the percentage daily change in X plus the percentage daily change in Y.]

9.16. Suppose that GARCH(1,1) parameters have been estimated as $\omega = 0.000003$, $\alpha = 0.04$, and $\beta = 0.94$. The current daily volatility is estimated to be 1%. Estimate the daily volatility in 30 days.

9.17. Suppose that GARCH(1,1) parameters have been estimated as $\omega = 0.000002$, $\alpha = 0.04$, and $\beta = 0.94$. The current daily volatility is estimated to be 1.3%. Estimate the volatility per annum that should be used to price a 20-day option.

FURTHER QUESTIONS

9.18. Suppose that observations on a stock price (in dollars) at the end of each of 15 consecutive weeks are as follows:

> 30.2, 32.0, 31.1, 30.1, 30.2, 30.3, 30.6, 33.0, 32.9, 33.0, 33.5, 33.5, 33.7, 33.5, 33.2

Estimate the stock price volatility. What is the standard error of your estimate?

9.19. Suppose that the price of gold at close of trading yesterday was $300 and its volatility was estimated as 1.3% per day. The price at the close of trading today is $298. Update the volatility estimate using:
(a) The EWMA model with $\lambda = 0.94$
(b) The GARCH(1,1) model with $\omega = 0.000002$, $\alpha = 0.04$, and $\beta = 0.94$.

9.20. An Excel spreadsheet containing over 900 days of daily data on a number of different exchange rates and stock indices can be downloaded from the author's website: http://www.rotman.utoronto.ca/~hull. Choose one exchange rate and one stock index. Estimate the value of λ in the EWMA model that minimizes the value of

$$\sum_i (v_i - \beta_i)^2$$

where v_i is the variance forecast made at the end of day $i - 1$ and β_i is the variance calculated from data between day i and day $i + 25$. Use the Solver tool in Excel. To start the EWMA calculations, set the variance forecast at the end of the first day equal to the square of the return on that day.

9.21. Suppose that the parameters in a GARCH(1,1) model are $\alpha = 0.03$, $\beta = 0.95$, and $\omega = 0.000002$.
   (a) What is the long-run average volatility?
   (b) If the current volatility is 1.5% per day, what is your estimate of the volatility in 20, 40, and 60 days?
   (c) What volatility should be used to price 20-, 40-, and 60-day options?
   (d) Suppose that there is an event that increases the current volatility by 0.5 percentage points to 2% per day. Estimate the effect on the volatility in 20, 40, and 60 days.
   (e) Estimate by how much the event increases the volatilities used to price 20-, 40-, and 60-day options.

9.22. Use the data source of Problem 9.20 and maximum likelihood methods to estimate for the TSE and S&P indices the best-fit parameters in an EWMA model and a GARCH(1,1) model for the variance rate.

9.23. The probability that the loss from a portfolio will be greater than \$10 million in one month is estimated to be 5%.
   (a) What is the one-month 99% VaR assuming that the change in value of the portfolio is normally distributed with zero mean?
   (b) What is the one-month 99% VaR assuming that the power law applies with $\alpha = 3$?

10

Correlations and Copulas

Suppose that a company has an exposure to two different market variables. In the case of each variable, it gains $10 million if there is a 1-standard-deviation increase and loses $10 million if there is a 1-standard-deviation decrease. If changes in the two variables have a high positive correlation, the company's total exposure is very high; if they have a correlation of zero, the exposure is less but still quite large; if they have a high negative correlation, the exposure is quite low because a loss on one of the variables is likely to be offset by a gain on the other. This example shows that it is important for a risk manager to estimate correlations between the changes in market variables as well as their volatilities when assessing risk exposures.

This chapter explains how correlations can be monitored in a similar way to volatilities. It also covers what are known as copulas. These are tools that provide a way of defining a correlation structure between two or more variables, regardless of the shapes of their probability distributions. Copulas have a number of applications in risk management. They are a convenient way of modeling default correlation and, as we will show in this chapter, can be used to develop a simple model for estimating the value at risk on a portfolio of loans. (The Basel II capital requirements, which will be discussed in the next chapter, use this simple model.) Copulas are also used to value credit derivatives and for the calculation of economic capital.

10.1 DEFINITION OF CORRELATION

The coefficient of correlation, ρ, between two variables V_1 and V_2 is defined as

$$\rho = \frac{E(V_1 V_2) - E(V_1)E(V_2)}{SD(V_1)SD(V_2)} \tag{10.1}$$

where $E(\cdot)$ denotes expected value and $SD(\cdot)$ denotes standard deviation. If there is no correlation between the variables, $E(V_1 V_2) = E(V_1)E(V_2)$ and $\rho = 0$. If $V_1 = V_2$, both the numerator and the denominator in the expression for ρ equal the variance of V_1. As we would expect, $\rho = 1$ in this case.

The *covariance* between V_1 and V_2 is defined as

$$\text{cov}(V_1, V_2) = E(V_1 V_2) - E(V_1)E(V_2) \tag{10.2}$$

so that the correlation can be written

$$\rho = \frac{\text{cov}(V_1, V_2)}{SD(V_1)SD(V_2)}$$

Although it is easier to develop intuition about the meaning of a correlation than a covariance, it is covariances that will prove to be the fundamental variables of our analysis. An analogy here is that variance rates were the fundamental variables for the EWMA and GARCH methods in Chapter 9, even though volatilities are easier to understand.

Correlation vs. Dependence

Two variables are defined as statistically independent if knowledge about one of them does not affect the probability distribution for the other. Formally, V_1 and V_2 are independent if

$$f(V_2 \mid V_1 = x) = f(V_2)$$

for all x, where $f(\cdot)$ denotes the probability density function.

Figure 10.1 Examples of ways in which V_2 can be dependent on V_1.

(a)   (b)

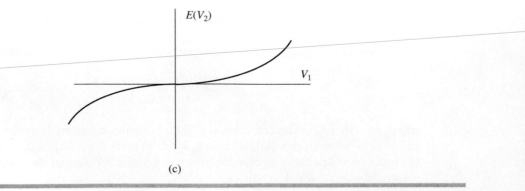

(c)

If the coefficient of correlation between two variables is zero, does this mean that there is no dependence between the variables? The answer is no. We can illustrate this with a simple example. Suppose that there are three equally likely values for V_1: -1, 0, and $+1$. If $V_1 = -1$ or $V_1 = +1$, then $V_2 = 1$. If $V_1 = 0$, then $V_2 = 0$. In this case there is clearly a dependence between V_1 and V_2. If we observe the value of V_1, we know the value of V_2. Also, a knowledge of the value of V_2 will cause us to change our probability distribution for V_1. However, the coefficient of correlation between V_1 and V_2 is zero.

This example emphasizes the point that the coefficient of correlation measures one particular type of dependence between two variables. This is linear dependence. There are many other ways in which two variables can be related. We can characterize the nature of the dependence between V_1 and V_2 by plotting $E(V_2)$ against V_1. Three examples are shown in Figure 10.1. Figure 10.1(a) shows linear dependence where the expected value of V_2 depends linearly on V_1. Figure 10.1(b) shows a V-shaped relationship between the expected values of V_2 and V_1. (This is similar to the example we have just considered; a symmetrical V-shaped relationship, however strong, leads to zero coefficient of correlation.) Figure 10.1(c) shows a type of dependence that is often seen when V_1 and V_2 are percentage changes in financial variables. For the values of V_1 normally encountered, there is very little relation between V_1 and V_2. However, extreme values of V_1 tend to lead to extreme values of V_2. To quote one commentator: "During a crisis the correlations all go to one."

Another aspect of the way in which V_2 depends on V_1 is the standard deviation of V_2 conditional on V_1. As we will see later, this is constant when V_1 and V_2 have a bivariate normal distribution. But, in other situations, the standard deviation of V_2 is liable to depend on the value of V_1.

10.2 MONITORING CORRELATION

Chapter 9 explained how exponentially weighted moving average and GARCH methods can be developed to monitor the variance rate of a variable. Similar approaches can be used to monitor the covariance rate between two variables. The variance rate per day of a variable is the variance of daily returns. Similarly the *covariance rate* per day between two variables is defined as the covariance between the daily returns of the variables.

Suppose that X_i and Y_i are the values of two variables X and Y at the end of day i. The returns on the variables on day i are

$$x_i = \frac{X_i - X_{i-1}}{X_{i-1}}, \qquad y_i = \frac{Y_i - Y_{i-1}}{Y_{i-1}}$$

The covariance rate between X and Y on day n is, from equation (10.2),

$$\text{cov}_n = E(x_n y_n) - E(x_n)E(y_n)$$

In Section 9.5 we explained that risk managers assume that expected daily returns are zero when the variance rate per day is calculated. They do the same when calculating the covariance rate per day. This means that the covariance rate per day between X and Y on day n is assumed to be

$$\text{cov}_n = E(x_n y_n)$$

Using equal weights for the last m observations on x_i and y_i gives the estimate

$$\text{cov}_n = \frac{1}{m} \sum_{i=1}^{m} x_{n-i} y_{n-i} \tag{10.3}$$

A similar weighting scheme for variances gives an estimate for the variance rate on day n for variable X as

$$\text{var}_{x,n} = \frac{1}{m} \sum_{i=1}^{m} x_{n-i}^2$$

and for variable Y as

$$\text{var}_{y,n} = \frac{1}{m} \sum_{i=1}^{m} y_{n-i}^2$$

The correlation estimate on day n is

$$\frac{\text{cov}_n}{\sqrt{\text{var}_{x,n} \text{var}_{y,n}}}$$

EWMA

Most risk managers would agree that observations from long ago should not have as much weight as recent observations. In Chapter 9, we discussed the use of the exponentially weighted moving average (EWMA) model for variances. We saw that it leads to weights that decline exponentially as we move back through time. A similar weighting scheme can be used for covariances. The formula for updating a covariance estimate in the EWMA model is similar to that in equation (9.8) for variances:

$$\text{cov}_n = \lambda \text{cov}_{n-1} + (1 - \lambda) x_{n-1} y_{n-1}$$

A similar analysis to that presented for the EWMA volatility model shows that the weight given to $x_{n-i} y_{n-i}$ declines as i increases (i.e., as we move back through time). The lower the value of λ, the greater the weight that is given to recent observations.

Example 10.1

Suppose that $\lambda = 0.95$ and that the estimate of the correlation between two variables X and Y on day $n - 1$ is 0.6. Suppose further that the estimate of the volatilities for X and Y on day $n - 1$ are 1% and 2%, respectively. From the relationship between correlation and covariance, the estimate of the covariance rate between X and Y on day $n - 1$ is

$$0.6 \times 0.01 \times 0.02 = 0.00012$$

Suppose that the percentage changes in X and Y on day $n - 1$ are 0.5% and 2.5%, respectively. The variance rates and covariance rate for day n would be updated as follows:

$$\sigma_{x,n}^2 = 0.95 \times 0.01^2 + 0.05 \times 0.005^2 = 0.00009625$$

$$\sigma_{y,n}^2 = 0.95 \times 0.02^2 + 0.05 \times 0.025^2 = 0.00041125$$

$$\text{cov}_n = 0.95 \times 0.00012 + 0.05 \times 0.005 \times 0.025 = 0.00012025$$

The new volatility of X is $\sqrt{0.00009625} = 0.981\%$ and the new volatility of Y is $\sqrt{0.00041125} = 2.028\%$. The new correlation between X and Y is

$$\frac{0.00012025}{0.00981 \times 0.02028} = 0.6044$$

GARCH

GARCH models can also be used for updating covariance rate estimates and forecasting the future level of covariance rates. For example, the GARCH(1,1) model for updating a covariance rate between X and Y is

$$\mathrm{cov}_n = \omega + \alpha x_{n-1} y_{n-1} + \beta\, \mathrm{cov}_{n-1}$$

This formula, like its counterpart in equation (9.10) for updating variances, gives some weight to a long-run average covariance, some to the most recent covariance estimate, and some to the most recent observation on covariance (which is $x_{n-1}y_{n-1}$). The long-term average covariance rate is $\omega/(1 - \alpha - \beta)$. Formulas similar to those in equations (9.14) and (9.15) can be developed for forecasting future covariance rates and calculating the average covariance rate during a future time period.

Consistency Condition for Covariances

Once variance and covariance rates have been calculated for a set of N market variables, an $N \times N$ variance–covariance matrix can be constructed. When $i \neq j$, the (i, j) element of this matrix shows the covariance rate between variable i and variable j. When $i = j$, it shows the variance rate of variable i. (See Section 13.3.)

Not all variance–covariance matrices are internally consistent. The condition for an $N \times N$ variance–covariance matrix Ω to be internally consistent is

$$w^{\mathsf{T}} \Omega\, w \geqslant 0 \qquad\qquad (10.4)$$

for all $N \times 1$ vectors w, where w^{T} is the transpose of w. A matrix that satisfies this property is known as *positive-semidefinite*.

To understand why the condition (10.4) holds, suppose that w is the (column) vector $(w_1, w_2, \ldots, w_N)$. Then $w^{\mathsf{T}} \Omega w$ is the variance rate of $w_1 z_1 + w_2 z_2 + \cdots + w_N z_N$, where z_i is the value of variable i. As such, it cannot be negative.

To ensure that a positive-semidefinite matrix is produced, variances and covariances should be calculated consistently. For example, if variance rates are calculated by giving equal weight to the last m data items, the same should be done for covariance rates. If variance rates are updated using an EWMA model with $\lambda = 0.94$, the same should be done for covariance rates. Using a GARCH model to update a variance–covariance matrix in a consistent way is trickier and requires a multivariate GARCH model.[1]

An example of a variance–covariance matrix that is not internally consistent is

$$\begin{bmatrix} 1 & 0 & 0.9 \\ 0 & 1 & 0.9 \\ 0.9 & 0.9 & 1 \end{bmatrix}$$

---

[1] See R. Engle and J. Mezrich, "GARCH for Groups," *Risk*, August 1996: 36–40, for a discussion of alternative approaches.

The variance of each variable is 1.0 and so the covariances are also coefficients of correlation in this case. The first variable is highly correlated with the third variable and the second variable is also highly correlated with the third variable. However, there is no correlation at all between the first and second variables. This seems strange. When we set w equal to $(1, 1, -1)$, we find that the condition in equation (10.4) is not satisfied, proving that the matrix is not positive-semidefinite.[2]

If we make a small change to a positive-semidefinite matrix that is calculated from observations on three variables (e.g., for the purposes of doing a sensitivity analysis), it is likely that the matrix will remain positive-semidefinite. However, if we do the same thing for observations on 1,000 variables, we have to be much more careful. An arbitrary small change to a positive-semidefinite $1,000 \times 1,000$ matrix is quite likely to lead to it no longer being positive-semidefinite.

10.3 MULTIVARIATE NORMAL DISTRIBUTIONS

Multivariate normal distributions are well understood and relatively easy to deal with. As we will explain in the next section, they can be useful tools for specifying the correlation structure between variables, even when the distributions of the variables are not normal.

We start by considering a bivariate normal distribution where there are only two variables, V_1 and V_2. Suppose that we know V_1. Conditional on this, the value of V_2 is normal with mean

$$\mu_2 + \rho\sigma_2 \frac{V_1 - \mu_1}{\sigma_1}$$

and standard deviation

$$\sigma_2\sqrt{1 - \rho^2}$$

Here μ_1 and μ_2 are the unconditional means of V_1 and V_2, σ_1 and σ_2 are their unconditional standard deviations, and ρ is the coefficient of correlation between V_1 and V_2. Note that the expected value of V_2 conditional on V_1 is linearly dependent on the value of V_1. This corresponds to Figure 10.1(a). Also, the standard deviation of V_2 conditional on the value of V_1 is the same for all values of V_1.

Generating Random Samples from Normal Distributions

Most programming languages have routines for sampling a random number between zero and one, and many have routines for sampling from a normal distribution.[3] If no routine for sampling from a standardized normal distribution is readily available, an approximate random sample can be calculated as

$$\epsilon = \sum_{i=1}^{12} R_i - 6 \tag{10.5}$$

---

[2] It can be shown that the condition for a 3×3 matrix of correlations to be internally consistent is

$$\rho_{12}^2 + \rho_{13}^2 + \rho_{23}^2 - 2\rho_{12}\rho_{13}\rho_{23} \leqslant 1$$

where ρ_{ij} is the coefficient of correlation between variables i and j.

[3] In Excel the instruction =NORMSINV(RAND()) gives a random sample from a normal distribution.

where the R_i $(1 \leqslant i \leqslant 12)$ are independent random numbers between 0 and 1, and ϵ is the required sample. This approximation is satisfactory for most purposes.

When samples ϵ_1 and ϵ_2 (with zero mean and unit variance) from a bivariate normal distribution are required, an appropriate procedure is as follows. Independent samples z_1 and z_2 from a univariate standardized normal distribution are obtained. The required samples ϵ_1 and ϵ_2 are then calculated as follows:

$$\epsilon_1 = z_1$$
$$\epsilon_2 = \rho z_1 + z_2 \sqrt{1 - \rho^2}$$

where ρ is the coefficient of correlation between ϵ_1 and ϵ_2.

Consider next the situation where we require n correlated samples from standardized normal distributions and the coefficient of correlation between variable i and variable j is ρ_{ij}. We first sample n independent variables z_i $(1 \leqslant i \leqslant n)$ from univariate standardized normal distributions. The required samples are ϵ_i $(1 \leqslant i \leqslant n)$, where

$$\epsilon_i = \sum_{k=1}^{i} \alpha_{ik} z_k$$

and the α_{ik} are parameters chosen to give the correct variances and the correct correlations for the ϵ's. For i $(1 \leqslant i \leqslant n)$, we must have

$$\sum_{k=1}^{i} \alpha_{ik}^2 = 1$$

and, for all $j < i$,

$$\sum_{k=1}^{j} \alpha_{ik} \alpha_{jk} = \rho_{ij}$$

The first sample, ϵ_1, is set equal to z_1. These equations for the α's can be solved, so that ϵ_2 is calculated from z_1 and z_2, ϵ_3 is calculated from z_1, z_2, and z_3, and so on. The procedure is known as the *Cholesky decomposition*.

If we find ourselves trying to take the square root of a negative number when using the Cholesky decomposition, the variance–covariance matrix assumed for the variables is not internally consistent. As explained in Section 10.2, this is equivalent to saying that the matrix is not positive-semidefinite.

Factor Models

Sometimes the correlations between normally distributed variables are defined using a factor model. Suppose that $U_1, U_2, \ldots, U_N$ have standard normal distributions (i.e., normal distributions with mean 0 and standard deviation 1). In a one-factor model, each U_i has a component dependent on a common factor F and a component that is uncorrelated with the other variables. Formally,

$$U_i = a_i F + \sqrt{1 - a_i^2}\, Z_i \qquad \text{(10.6)}$$

where F and the Z_i have a standard normal distributions and a_i is a constant between -1 and $+1$. The Z_i are uncorrelated with each other and uncorrelated with F. In this model, all the correlation between U_i and U_j arises from their dependence on the common factor F. The coefficient of correlation between U_i and U_j is $a_i a_j$.

A one-factor model imposes some structure on the correlations (and the resulting correlation matrix is always positive-semidefinite). Without assuming a factor model, the number of correlations that have to be estimated for the N variables is $\frac{1}{2}N(N-1)$. With the one-factor model we need only estimate N parameters: $a_1, a_2, \ldots, a_N$. An example of a one-factor model from the world of investments is the capital asset pricing model, where the return on a stock has a component dependent on the return from the market and an idiosyncratic (nonsystematic) component that is independent of the return on other stocks (see Section 1.1).

The one-factor model can be extended to a two-factor, three-factor, or M-factor model. In the M-factor model,

$$U_i = a_{i1}F_1 + a_{i2}F_2 + \cdots + a_{iM}F_M + \sqrt{1 - a_{i1}^2 - a_{i2}^2 - \cdots - a_{iM}^2}\, Z_i \qquad (10.7)$$

The factors $F_1, F_2, \ldots, F_M$ have uncorrelated standard normal distributions and the Z_i are uncorrelated both with each other and with the F's. In this case the correlation between U_i and U_j is

$$\sum_{m=1}^{M} a_{im}a_{jm}$$

10.4 COPULAS

Consider two correlated variables V_1 and V_2. The *marginal distribution* of V_1 (sometimes also referred to as the unconditional distribution) is its distribution assuming we know nothing about V_2; similarly, the marginal distribution of V_2 is its distribution assuming we know nothing about V_1. Suppose we have estimated the marginal distributions of V_1 and V_2. How can we make an assumption about the correlation structure between the two variables to define their joint distribution?

If the marginal distributions of V_1 and V_2 are normal, a convenient and easy-to-work-with assumption is that the joint distribution of the variables is bivariate normal.[4] (The correlation structure between the variables is then as described in Section 10.3.) Similar assumptions are possible for some other marginal distributions. But often there is no natural way of defining a correlation structure between two marginal distributions. This is where copulas come in.

As an example of the application of copulas, suppose that the variables V_1 and V_2 have the triangular probability density functions shown in Figure 10.2. Both variables have values between 0 and 1. The density function for V_1 peaks at 0.2. The density function for V_2 peaks at 0.5. For both density functions, the maximum height is 2.0. To use what is known as a *Gaussian copula*, we map V_1 and V_2 into new variables U_1 and U_2 that have standard normal distributions. (A standard normal distribution is a normal distribution with mean 0 and standard deviation 1) The mapping is accomplished on a percentile-to-percentile basis. The 1-percentile point of the V_1 distribution is mapped to the 1-percentile point of the U_1 distribution. The 10-percentile point of

---

[4] Although the bivariate normal assumption is a convenient one, it is not the only one that can be made. There are many other ways in which two normally distributed variables can be dependent on each other. For example, we could have $V_2 = V_1$ for $V_1 \leqslant k$ and $V_2 = -V_1$ for $V_1 > k$. See also Problem 10.11.

Figure 10.2 Triangular distributions for V_1 and V_2.

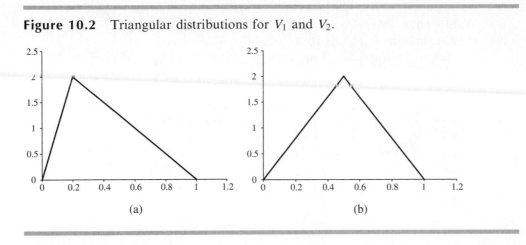

(a)   (b)

the V_1 distribution is mapped to the 10-percentile point of the U_1 distribution, and so on. The variable V_2 is mapped into U_2 in a similar way. Table 10.1 shows how values of V_1 are mapped into values of U_1, and similarly Table 10.2 shows how values of V_2 are mapped into values of U_2. Consider the $V_1 = 0.1$ calculation in Table 10.1. The cumulative probability that V_1 is less than 0.1 is (by calculating areas of triangles) $0.5 \times 0.1 \times 1 = 0.05$, or 5%. The value 0.1 for V_1 therefore gets mapped to the 5-percentile point of the standard normal distribution. This is -1.64.[5]

The variables U_1 and U_2 have normal distributions. We assume that they are jointly bivariate normal. This in turn implies a joint distribution and a correlation structure between V_1 and V_2. The essence of copulas therefore is that, instead of defining a correlation structure between V_1 and V_2 directly, we do so indirectly. We map V_1 and V_2 into other variables which have "well-behaved" distributions and for which it is easy to define a correlation structure.

Table 10.1 Mapping of V_1, which has the triangular distribution in Figure 10.2(a), to U_1, which has a standard normal distribution.

V_1 value	Percentile of distribution	U_1 value
0.1	5.00	-1.64
0.2	20.00	-0.84
0.3	38.75	-0.29
0.4	55.00	0.13
0.5	68.75	0.49
0.6	80.00	0.84
0.7	88.75	1.21
0.8	95.00	1.64
0.9	98.75	2.24

[5] It can be calculated using Excel: NORMSINV(0.05) = -1.64.

Table 10.2 Mapping of V_2, which has the triangular distribution in Figure 10.2(b), to U_2, which has a standard normal distribution.

V_2 value	Percentile of distribution	U_2 value
0.1	2.00	−2.05
0.2	8.00	−1.41
0.3	18.00	−0.92
0.4	32.00	−0.47
0.5	50.00	0.00
0.6	68.00	0.47
0.7	82.00	0.92
0.8	92.00	1.41
0.9	98.00	2.05

Suppose that we assume the correlation between U_1 and U_2 to be 0.5. The joint cumulative probability distribution between V_1 and V_2 is shown in Table 10.3. To illustrate the calculations, consider the first one where we are calculating the probability that $V_1 < 0.1$ and $V_2 < 0.1$. From Tables 10.1 and 10.2, this is the same as the probability that $U_1 < -1.64$ and $U_2 < -2.05$. From the cumulative bivariate normal distribution, this is 0.006 when $\rho = 0.5$.[6] (Note that the probability would be only $0.02 \times 0.05 = 0.001$ if $\rho = 0$.)

The correlation between U_1 and U_2 is referred to as the *copula correlation*. This is not, in general, the same as the correlation between V_1 and V_2. Because U_1 and U_2 are bivariate normal, the conditional mean of U_2 is linearly dependent on U_1 and the conditional standard deviation of U_2 is constant (as discussed in Section 10.3). However, a similar result does not in general apply to V_1 and V_2.

Expressing the Approach Algebraically

The way in which a Gaussian copula defines a joint distribution is illustrated in Figure 10.3. For a more formal description of the model, suppose that G_1 and G_2 are the cumulative marginal probability distribution of V_1 and V_2. We map $V_1 = v_1$ to $U_1 = u_1$ and $V_2 = v_2$ to $U_2 = u_2$, where

$$G_1(v_1) = N(u_1) \quad \text{and} \quad G_2(v_2) = N(u_2)$$

and N is the cumulative normal distribution function. This means that

$$u_1 = N^{-1}[G_1(v_1)], \quad u_2 = N^{-1}[G_2(v_2)], \quad v_1 = G_1^{-1}[N(u_1)], \quad v_2 = G_2^{-1}[N(u_2)]$$

The variables U_1 and U_2 are then assumed to be bivariate normal. The key property of a copula model is that it preserves the marginal distributions of V_1 and V_2 (however unusual these may me) while defining a correlation structure between them.

---

[6] An Excel function for calculating the cumulative bivariate normal distribution is on the author's website: www.rotman.utoronto.ca/~hull.

Figure 10.3 The way in which a copula model defines a joint distribution.

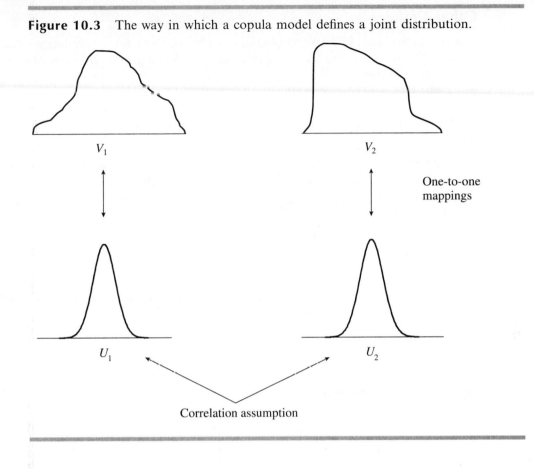

Table 10.3 Cumulative joint probability distribution for V_1 and V_2 in the Gaussian copula model. Correlation parameter = 0.5. The table shows the joint probability that V_1 and V_2 are less than the specified values.

V_1	V_2								
	0.1	0.2	0.3	0.4	0.5	0.6	0.7	0.8	0.9
0.1	0.006	0.017	0.028	0.037	0.044	0.048	0.049	0.050	0.050
0.2	0.013	0.043	0.081	0.120	0.156	0.181	0.193	0.198	0.200
0.3	0.017	0.061	0.124	0.197	0.273	0.331	0.364	0.381	0.387
0.4	0.019	0.071	0.149	0.248	0.358	0.449	0.505	0.535	0.548
0.5	0.019	0.076	0.164	0.281	0.417	0.537	0.616	0.663	0.683
0.6	0.020	0.078	0.173	0.301	0.456	0.600	0.701	0.763	0.793
0.7	0.020	0.079	0.177	0.312	0.481	0.642	0.760	0.837	0.877
0.8	0.020	0.080	0.179	0.318	0.494	0.667	0.798	0.887	0.936
0.9	0.020	0.080	0.180	0.320	0.499	0.678	0.816	0.913	0.970

Other Copulas

The Gaussian copula is just one copula that can be used to define a correlation structure between V_1 and V_2. There are many other copulas leading to many other correlation structures. One that is sometimes used is the *Student t-copula*. This works in the same way as the Gaussian copula except that the variables U_1 and U_2 have a bivariate Student t-distribution instead of a bivariate normal distribution. To sample from a bivariate Student t-distribution with f degrees of freedom and correlation ρ, the steps are as follows:

1. Sample from the inverse chi-square distribution to get a value χ. (In Excel the CHIINV function can be used. The first argument is RAND() and the second is f.)
2. Sample from a bivariate normal distribution with correlation ρ as described in Section 10.3.
3. Multiply the normally distributed samples by $\sqrt{f/\chi}$.

Tail Correlation

Figure 10.4 shows plots of 5,000 random samples from a bivariate normal, while Figure 10.5 does the same for the bivariate Student t. The correlation parameter is 0.5 and the number of degrees of freedom for the Student t is 4. Define a "tail value" of a distribution as a value in the left or right 1% tail of the distribution. There

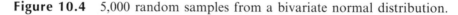

Figure 10.4   5,000 random samples from a bivariate normal distribution.

Figure 10.5 5,000 random samples from a bivariate Student *t*-distribution with four degrees of freedom.

is a tail value for the normal distribution when the variable is greater than 2.33 or less than −2.33. Similarly there is a tail value in the *t*-distribution when the value of the variable is greater than 3.75 or less than −3.75. Vertical and horizontal lines in the figures indicate where tail values occur. The figures illustrate that it is more common for the variables to have tail values at the same time in the bivariate *t*-distribution than in the bivariate normal distribution. To put this another way, the *tail correlation* is higher in a bivariate *t*-distribution than in a bivariate normal distribution. We made the point earlier that correlations between market variables tend to increase in extreme market conditions, so that Figure 10.1(c) is sometimes a better description of the correlation structure between two variables than Figure 10.1(a). This has led some researchers to argue that the Student *t*-copula provides a better description of the joint behavior of market variables than the Gaussian copula.

Multivariate Copulas

Copulas can be used to define a correlation structure between more than two variables. The simplest example of this is the multivariate Gaussian copula. Suppose that there are N variables, $V_1, V_2, \ldots, V_N$, and that we know the marginal distribution of each variable. For each i ($1 \leqslant i \leqslant N$), we transform V_i into U_i, where U_i has a standard normal distribution. (As described above, the transformation is accomplished on a percentile-to-percentile basis.) We then assume that the U_i have a multivariate normal distribution.

A Factor Copula Model

In multivariate copula models, analysts often assume a factor model for the correlation structure between the U's. When there is only one factor, equation (10.6) gives

$$U_i = a_i F + \sqrt{1 - a_i^2}\, Z_i \qquad\qquad (10.8)$$

where F and the Z_i have a standard normal distributions. The Z_i are uncorrelated with each other and with F. Other factor copula models are obtained by choosing F and the Z_i to have other zero-mean unit-variance distributions. For example, if Z_i is normal and F has a Student t-distribution, we obtain a multivariate Student t-distribution for U_i. These distributional choices affect the nature of the dependence between the U's, and therefore that between the V's.

10.5 APPLICATION TO LOAN PORTFOLIOS

We now present an application of the one-factor Gaussian copula that will prove useful in understanding the Basel II capital requirements in Chapter 11. Consider a portfolio of loans to companies. Define T_i as the time when company i defaults. (We assume that all companies will default eventually, but the default time may be many years in the future.) Denote the cumulative probability distribution of T_i by Q_i.

In order to define a correlation structure between the T_i using the one-factor Gaussian copula model, we map, for each i, the default time T_i to a variable U_i that has a standard normal distribution on a percentile-to-percentile basis. We assume the factor model in equation (10.8) for the correlation structure between the U_i:

$$U_i = a_i F + \sqrt{1 - a_i^2}\, Z_i \qquad\qquad (10.9)$$

where the variables F and Z_i have independent standard normal distributions. The mappings between the U_i and T_i imply

$$\mathrm{Prob}(U_i < U) = \mathrm{Prob}(T_i < T)$$

when

$$U = N^{-1}[Q_i(T)] \qquad\qquad (10.10)$$

From equation (10.9),

$$Z_i = \frac{U_i - a_i F}{\sqrt{1 - a_i^2}}$$

The probability that $U_i < U$ conditional on the factor value F is

$$\mathrm{Prob}(U_i < U \mid F) = \mathrm{Prob}\!\left(Z_i < \frac{U - a_i F}{\sqrt{1 - a_i^2}}\right) = N\!\left[\frac{U - a_i F}{\sqrt{1 - a_i^2}}\right]$$

This is also Prob($T_i < T \mid F$). Hence,

$$\text{Prob}(T_i < T \mid F) = N\left(\frac{N^{-1}[Q_i(T)] - a_i F}{\sqrt{1 - a_i^2}}\right) \tag{10.11}$$

To simplify matters, we suppose that the distribution of time to default, Q_i, is the same for all i and equal to Q. We also assume that the copula correlation between the default times of any two companies is the same and equals ρ. This means that $a_i = \sqrt{\rho}$ for all i. Equation (10.11) becomes

$$\text{Prob}(T_i < T \mid F) = N\left(\frac{N^{-1}[Q(T)] - \sqrt{\rho} F}{\sqrt{1 - \rho}}\right)$$

[handwritten: $\beta = \sqrt{\rho}$ $\beta^2 = \rho$]

For a large portfolio of loans, this equation provides a good estimate of the percentage of loans defaulting by time T conditional on F. We will refer to this as the default rate.

As F decreases, the default rate increases. How bad can the default rate become? Because F has a normal distribution, the probability that F will be less than $N^{-1}(Y)$ is Y. There is therefore a probability of Y that the default rate will be greater than

$$N\left(\frac{N^{-1}[Q(T)] - \sqrt{\rho}\, N^{-1}(Y)}{\sqrt{1 - \rho}}\right)$$

Define WCDR(T, X) as the "worst-case default rate" for a time horizon T and a confidence level X. This is the default rate that we are $X\%$ certain will not be exceeded in time T. It is obtained by substituting $Y = 1 - X$ into the above expression. Because $N^{-1}(X) = -N^{-1}(1 - X)$, we obtain

$$\text{WCDR}(T, X) = N\left(\frac{N^{-1}[Q(T)] + \sqrt{\rho}\, N^{-1}(X)}{\sqrt{1 - \rho}}\right) \tag{10.12}$$

This result was first developed by Vasicek in 1987. The right-hand side of the equation can easily be calculated using the NORMSDIST and NORMSINV functions in Excel.[7] Suppose that the dollar size of the loan portfolio is L and the proportional amount recovered in the event of a default is R. The value at risk for the loan portfolio with a time horizon of T and a confidence level of X is

$$\text{VaR}(T, X) = L \times (1 - R) \times \text{WCDR}(T, X)$$

Example 10.2

Suppose that a bank has a total of $100 million of retail exposures. The one-year probability of default averages 2% and the recovery rate averages 60%. The copula correlation parameter is estimated as 0.1. In this case,

$$\text{WCDR}(1, 0.999) = N\left(\frac{N^{-1}(0.02) + \sqrt{0.1}\, N^{-1}(0.999)}{\sqrt{1 - 0.1}}\right) = 0.128$$

---

[7] See O. Vasicek "Probability of Loss on a Loan Portfolio," Working Paper, KMV, 1987. Vasicek's results were published in *Risk* magazine in December 2002 under the title "Loan Portfolio Value".

showing that the 99.9% worst-case default rate is 12.8%. Losses when this worst-case loss rate occur are $100 \times 0.128 \times (1 - 0.6)$, or \$5.13 million. This is an estimate of the value at risk with a one-year time horizon and a 99.9% confidence level.

SUMMARY

Risk managers use correlations or covariances to describe the relationship between two variables. The daily covariance rate is the correlation between the daily returns on the variables multiplied by the product of their daily volatilities. The methods for monitoring a covariance rate are similar to those described in Chapter 9 for monitoring a variance rate. Risk managers often try to keep track of a variance–covariance matrix for all the variables to which they are exposed.

The marginal distribution of a variable is the unconditional distribution of the variable. Very often an analyst is in a situation where he or she has estimated the marginal distributions of a set of variables and wants to make an assumption about their correlation structure. If the marginal distributions of the variables happen to be normal, it is natural to assume that the variables have a multivariate normal distribution. In other situations copulas are used. The marginal distributions are transformed on a percentile-to-percentile basis to normal distributions (or to some other distribution for which there is a multivariate counterpart). The correlation structure between the variables of interest is then defined indirectly from an assumed correlation structure between the transformed variables.

When there are many variables, analysts often use a factor model. This is a way of reducing the number of correlation estimates that have to be made. The correlation between any two variables is assumed to derive solely from their correlations with the factors. The default correlation between different companies can be modeled using a factor-based Gaussian copula model of their times to default.

An important application of copulas for risk managers is to the calculation of value at risk for loan portfolios. Analysts often assume that a one-factor copula model relates the probability distributions of the times to default for different loans. The percentiles of the distribution of the number of defaults on a large portfolio can then be calculated from the percentiles of the probability distribution of the factor. As we will see in the next chapter, this is the approach used in determining credit risk capital requirements for banks under Basel II.

FURTHER READING

Cherubini, U., E. Luciano, and W. Vecchiato, *Copula Methods in Finance*. Wiley, 2004.

Demarta, S., and A. J. McNeil, "The *t* Copula and Related Copulas," Working paper, Department of Mathematics, ETH Zentrum, Zurich, Switzerland.

Engle, R. F. and J. Mezrich, "GARCH for Groups," *Risk*, August 1996: 36–40.

Vasicek, O., "Probability of Loss on a Loan Portfolio," Working Paper, KMV, 1987. Published in *Risk* magazine in December 2002 under the title "Loan Portfolio Value".

PRACTICE QUESTIONS AND PROBLEMS (Answers at the End of the Book)

10.1. If you know the correlation between two variables, what extra information do you need to calculate the covariance?

10.2. What is the difference between correlation and dependence? Suppose that $y = x^2$ and x is normally distributed with mean 0 and standard deviation 1. What is the correlation between x and y?

10.3. What is a factor model? Why are factor models useful when defining a correlation structure between large numbers of variables?

10.4. What is meant by a positive-semidefinite matrix? What are the implications of a coviariance matrix not being positive-semidefinite.

10.5. Suppose that the current daily volatilities of asset A and asset B are 1.6% and 2.5%, respectively. The prices of the assets at close of trading yesterday were $20 and $40, and the estimate of the coefficient of correlation between the returns on the two assets made at that time was 0.25. The parameter λ used in the EWMA model is 0.95.
(a) Calculate the current estimate of the covariance between the assets.
(b) On the assumption that the prices of the assets at close of trading today are $20.50 and $40.50, update the correlation estimate.

10.6. Suppose that the current daily volatilities of asset X and asset Y are 1.0% and 1.2%, respectively. The prices of the assets at close of trading yesterday were $30 and $50, and the estimate of the coefficient of correlation between the returns on the two assets made at this time was 0.50. Correlations and volatilities are updated using a GARCH(1,1) model. The estimates of the model's parameters are $\alpha = 0.04$ and $\beta = 0.94$. For the correlation $\omega = 0.000001$, and for the volatilities $\omega = 0.000003$. If the prices of the two assets at close of trading today are $31 and $51, how is the correlation estimate updated?

10.7. Suppose that in Problem 9.15 the correlation between the S&P 500 index (measured in dollars) and the FTSE 100 index (measured in sterling) is 0.7, the correlation between the S&P 500 index (measured in dollars) and the dollar–sterling exchange rate is 0.3, and the daily volatility of the S&P 500 index is 1.6%. What is the correlation between the S&P 500 index (measured in dollars) and the FTSE 100 index when it is translated to dollars? [*Hint*: For three variables X, Y, and Z, the covariance between $X + Y$ and Z equals the covariance between X and Z plus the covariance between Y and Z.]

10.8. Suppose that two variables V_1 and V_2 have uniform distributions where all values between 0 and 1 are equally likely. Use a Gaussian copula to define the correlation structure between V_1 and V_2 with a copula correlation of 0.3. Produce a table similar to Table 10.3 considering values of 0.25, 0.5, and 0.75 for V_1 and V_2. (A spreadsheet for calculating the cumulative bivariate normal distribution is on the author's website: www.rotman.utoronto.ca/~hull.

10.9. Assume that you have independent random samples z_1, z_2, and z_3 from a standard normal distribution and want to convert them to samples ϵ_1, ϵ_2, and ϵ_3 from a trivariate normal distribution using the Cholesky decomposition. Derive three formulas expressing ϵ_1, ϵ_2, and ϵ_3 in terms of z_1, z_2, and z_3 and the three correlations that are needed to define the trivariate normal distribution.

10.10. Explain what is meant by tail dependence. How can you vary tail dependence by the choice of copula?

10.11. Suppose that the marginal distributions of V_1 and V_2 are standard normal distributions but that a Student t-copula with four degrees of freedom and a correlation parameter of 0.5 is used to define the correlation between the variables. How would you construct a chart showing samples from the joint distribution.

10.12. In Table 10.3 what is the probability density function of V_2 conditional on $V_1 < 0.1$. Compare it with the unconditional distribution of V_2.

10.13. What is the median of the distribution of V_2 when V_1 equals 0.2 in the example in Tables 10.1 and 10.2?

10.14. Suppose that a bank has made a large number of loans of a certain type. The total amount lent is $500 million. The one-year probability of default on each loan is 1.5% and the recovery rate is 30%. The bank uses a Gaussian copula for time to default. The copula correlation parameter is 0.2. Estimate the value at risk for the portfolio with a one-year time horizon and a confidence level of 99.5%.

FURTHER QUESTIONS

10.15. Suppose that the price of gold at close of trading yesterday was $300 and its volatility was estimated as 1.3% per day. The price of gold at the close of trading today is $298. Suppose further that the price of silver at the close of trading yesterday was $8, its volatility was estimated as 1.5% per day, and its correlation with gold was estimated as 0.8. The price of silver at the close of trading today is unchanged at $8. Update the volatility of gold and silver and the correlation between gold and silver using:
(a) The EWMA model with $\lambda = 0.94$
(b) The GARCH(1,1) model with $\omega = 0.000002$, $\alpha = 0.04$, and $\beta = 0.94$

In practice, is the ω parameter likely to be the same for gold and silver?

10.16. The probability density function for an exponential distribution is $\lambda e^{-\lambda x}$, where x is the value of the variable and λ is a parameter. The cumulative probability distribution is $1 - e^{-\lambda x}$. Suppose that two variables V_1 and V_2 have exponential distributions with λ's of 1.0 and 2.0, respectively. Use a Gaussian copula to define the correlation structure between V_1 and V_2 with a copula correlation of -0.2. Produce a table similar to Table 10.3 using values of 0.25, 0.5, 0.75, 1, 1.25, and 1.5 for V_1 and V_2. (A spreadsheet for calculating the cumulative bivariate normal distribution is on the author's website: www.rotman.utoronto.ca/~hull.

10.17. Create an Excel spreadsheet to produce a chart similar to Figure 10.5 showing samples from a bivariate Student t-distribution with four degrees of freedom where the correlation is 0.5. Next suppose that the marginal distributions of V_1 and V_2 are Student t with four degrees of freedom but that a Gaussian copula with a copula correlation parameter of 0.5 is used to define the correlation between the two variables. Construct a chart showing samples from the joint distribution. Compare the two charts you have produced.

10.18. Suppose that a bank has made a large number loans of a certain type. The one-year probability of default on each loan is 1.2%. The bank uses a Gaussian copula for time to default. It is interested in estimating a "99.97% worst case" for the percentage of loans that default on the portfolio. Show how this varies with the copula correlation.

11

Regulation, Basel II, and Solvency II

Chapters 2, 3, and 4 describe the activities of different types of financial institution and provide an introduction to the way they are regulated. This chapter provides more details about the regulatory environment. The main focus of the chapter is on banks. This is because bank regulators have taken the lead in developing a methodology for setting capital requirements for financial institutions.

The chapter starts by reviewing the evolution of bank regulation between the 1980s and 2000. It explains the 1988 Basel Accord (now known as Basel I), netting provisions, and the 1996 Amendment. It then discusses Basel II, a new initiative that was implemented by banks throughout the world between 2007 and 2009. Finally, it reviews Solvency II, a new regulatory framework for insurance companies that is broadly similar to Basel II and is expected to be implemented by the European Union in 2012.

11.1 THE REASONS FOR REGULATING BANKS

The purpose of bank regulation is to ensure that a bank keeps enough capital for the risks it takes. It is not possible to eliminate altogether the possibility of a bank failing, but governments want to make the probability of default for any given bank very small. By doing this, they hope to create a stable economic environment where private individuals and businesses have confidence in the banking system.

It is tempting to argue: "Bank regulation is unnecessary. Even if there were no regulations, banks would manage their risks prudently and would strive to keep a level of capital that is commensurate with the risks they are taking." Unfortunately, history does not support this view. There is little doubt that regulation has played an important role in increasing bank capital and making banks more aware of the risks they are taking.

As discussed in Section 2.3, governments provide deposit insurance programs to protect depositors. Without deposit insurance, banks that took excessive risks relative to their capital base would find it difficult to attract deposits. However, the impact of deposit insurance is to create an environment where depositors are less discriminating. A bank can take large risks without losing its deposit base.[1] The last thing a government

---

[1] As mentioned in Chapter 2, this is an example of what insurance companies term moral hazard. The existence of an insurance contract changes the behavior of the insured party.

> **Business Snapshot 11.1**   Systemic Risk
>
> Systemic risk is the risk that a default by one financial institution will create a "ripple effect" that leads to defaults by other financial institutions and threatens the stability of the financial system. There are huge numbers of over-the-counter transactions between banks. If Bank A fails, Bank B may take a huge loss on the transactions it has with Bank A. This in turn could lead to Bank B failing. Bank C that has many outstanding transactions with both Bank A and Bank B might then take a large loss and experience severe financial difficulties; and so on.
>
> The financial system has survived defaults such as Drexel in 1990 very well, but regulators continue to be concerned. During the market turmoil of 2007 and 2008, many large financial institutions were bailed out, rather than being allowed to fail, because governments were concerned about systemic risk.

wants is to create a deposit insurance program that results in banks taking more risks. It is therefore essential that deposit insurance be accompanied by regulation concerned with capital requirements.

A major concern of governments is what is known as *systemic risk*. This is the risk that a failure by a large bank will lead to failures by other large banks and a collapse of the financial system. The way this can happen is described in Business Snapshot 11.1. When a bank or other large financial institution does get into financial difficulties governments have a difficult decision to make. If they allow the financial institution to fail, they are putting the financial system at risk. If they bail out the financial institution, they are sending the wrong signals to the market. There is a danger that large financial institutions will be less vigilant in controlling risks because they know that they are "too big to fail" and the government will always bail them out.

During the market turmoil of 2007 and 2008, the decision was taken to bail out many large financial institutions in the United States and Europe. However, Lehman Brothers was allowed to fail in September, 2008. Possibly the United States government wanted to make it clear to the market that bailouts for large financial institutions were not automatic. However, the decision to let Lehman Brothers fail has been criticized because it made the credit crisis worse. It led to banks becoming much more cautious in their lending to other banks and to nonfinancial corporations.

11.2 BANK REGULATION PRE-1988

Prior to 1988, bank regulators tended to regulate bank capital by setting minimum levels for the ratio of capital to total assets. However, definitions of capital and the ratios considered acceptable varied from country to country. Some countries enforced their regulations more diligently than other countries. Increasingly, banks were competing globally, and a bank operating in a country where capital regulations were slack was considered to have a competitive edge over one operating in a country with tighter and more strictly enforced capital regulations. In addition, the huge exposures of the major international banks to less developed countries such as Mexico, Brazil, and Argentina, as well as the accounting games sometimes used for those exposures (see Business Snapshot 2.3), were starting to raise questions about the adequacy of capital levels.

Another problem was that the types of transaction entered into by banks were becoming more complicated. The over-the-counter derivatives market for products such as interest rate swaps, currency swaps, and foreign exchange options was growing fast. These contracts increase the credit risks being taken by a bank. Consider, for example, an interest rate swap. If the counterparty in the interest rate swap transaction defaults when the swap has a positive value to the bank and a negative value to the counterparty, the bank is liable to lose money. Many of these newer transactions were "off balance sheet". This means that they had no effect on the level of assets reported by a bank. As a result, they had no effect on the amount of capital the bank was required to keep. It became apparent to regulators that total assets were no longer a good indicator of the total risks being taken. A more sophisticated approach than that of setting minimum levels for the ratio of capital to total balance-sheet assets was needed.

These problems led supervisory authorities for Belgium, Canada, France, Germany, Italy, Japan, Luxembourg, the Netherlands, Sweden, Switzerland, the United Kingdom, and the United States to form the Basel Committee on Banking Supervision. The committee met regularly in Basel, Switzerland, under the patronage of the Bank for International Settlements. The first major result of these meetings was a document entitled "International Convergence of Capital Measurement and Capital Standards". This was referred to as "The 1988 BIS Accord" or just "The Accord". More recently, it has come to be known as Basel I.

11.3 THE 1988 BIS ACCORD

The 1988 BIS Accord was the first attempt to set international risk-based standards for capital adequacy. It has been subject to much criticism as being too simple and somewhat arbitrary. In fact, the Accord was a huge achievement. It was signed by all 12 members of the Basel Committee and paved the way for significant increases in the resources banks devote to measuring, understanding, and managing risks.

The BIS Accord defined two requirements that bank capital had to satisfy. The first was that the ratio of a bank's assets to its capital had to be less than 20. (This requirement was similar to that existing prior to 1988 in many countries.) The second requirement involves what is known as the Cooke ratio.[2] For most banks there was no problem in satisfying the capital multiple requirement. The Cooke ratio was the key regulatory requirement.

The Cooke Ratio

In calculating the Cooke ratio, both on-balance-sheet and off-balance-sheet items are considered. They are used to calculate what is known as the bank's total *risk-weighted assets* (also sometimes referred to as the *risk-weighted amount*). It is a measure of the bank's total credit exposure.

Consider first on-balance-sheet items. Each on-balance-sheet item is assigned a risk weight reflecting its credit risk. A sample of the risk weights specified in the Accord are shown in Table 11.1. Cash and securities issued by OECD governments are considered to have virtually zero risk and have a risk weight of zero. Loans to corporations have a

---

[2] The ratio is named after Peter Cooke from the Bank of England.

Table 11.1 Risk weights for on-balance-sheet items.

Risk weight (%)	Asset category
0	Cash, gold bullion, claims on OECD governments such as Treasury bonds or insured residential mortgages
20	Claims on OECD banks and OECD public sector entities such as securities issued by US government agencies or claims on municipalities
50	Uninsured residential mortgage loans
100	All other claims such as corporate bonds and less-developed country debt, claims on non-OECD banks Real estate, premises, plant, and equipment

risk weight of 100%. Loans to OECD banks and government agencies have a risk weight of 20%. Uninsured residential mortgages have a risk weight of 50%. The total of risk-weighted assets for N on-balance-sheet items equals

$$\sum_{i=1}^{N} w_i L_i$$

where L_i is the principal amount of the ith item and w_i is its risk weight.

Example 11.1

The assets of a bank consist of $100 million of corporate loans, $10 million of OECD government bonds, and $50 million of residential mortgages. The total of risk-weighted assets is

$$1.0 \times 100 + 0.0 \times 10 + 0.5 \times 50 = 125$$

or $125 million.

Off-balance-sheet items are expressed as a *credit equivalent amount*. Loosely speaking, the credit equivalent amount is the loan principal that is considered to have the same credit risk. For nonderivatives the credit equivalent amount is calculated by applying a conversion factor to the principal amount of the instrument. Instruments that from a credit perspective are considered to be similar to loans, such as bankers' acceptances, have a conversion factor of 100%. Others, such as note issuance facilities (where a bank agrees that a company can issue short-term paper on preagreed terms in the future), have lower conversion factors.

For an over-the-counter derivative, such as an interest rate swap or a forward contract, the credit equivalent amount is calculated as

$$\max(V, 0) + aL \tag{11.1}$$

where V is the current value of the derivative to the bank, a is an *add-on factor*, and L is the principal amount. The first term in equation (11.1) is the current exposure. If the counterpart defaults today and V is positive, the contract is an asset to the bank and the bank is liable to lose V. If the counterparty defaults today and V is negative, the contract is an asset to the counterparty and there will be neither a gain nor a loss to the

Table 11.2 Add-on factors as a percentage of principal for derivatives.

Remaining maturity (years)	Interest rate	Exchange rate and gold	Equity	Precious metals except gold	Other commodities
< 1	0.0	1.0	6.0	7.0	10.0
1–5	0.5	5.0	8.0	7.0	12.0
> 5	1.5	7.5	10.0	8.0	15.0

bank. The bank's exposure is therefore $\max(V, 0)$. The add-on amount, aL, is an allowance for the possibility of the exposure increasing in the future. Examples of the add-on factor a are shown in Table 11.2.

Example 11.2

A bank has entered into a $100 million interest rate swap with a remaining life of four years. The current value of the swap is $2.0 million. In this case the add-on amount is 0.5% of the principal, so that the credit equivalent amount is $2.0 million plus $0.5 million, or $2.5 million.

The credit equivalent amount for an off-balance-sheet item is multiplied by the risk weight for the counterparty to calculate the risk-weighted assets. The risk weights for off-balance-sheet items are similar to those in Table 11.1, except that the risk weight for a corporation is 0.5 rather than 1.0 when off-balance-sheet items are considered.

Example 11.3

Consider again the bank in Example 11.2. If the interest rate swap is with a corporation, the risk-weighted assets are 2.5×0.5, or $1.25 million. If it is with an OECD bank, the risk-weighted assets are 2.5×0.2, or $0.5 million.

Putting all this together, the total risk-weighted assets for a bank with N on-balance-sheet items and M off-balance-sheet items is

$$\sum_{i=1}^{N} w_i L_i + \sum_{j=1}^{M} w_j^* C_j \tag{11.2}$$

Here, L_i is the principal of the ith on-balance-sheet item and w_i is its risk weight for the counterparty; C_j is the credit equivalent amount for the jth off-balance-sheet item and w_j^* is the risk weight for the counterparty.

Capital Requirement

The Accord required banks to keep capital equal to at least 8% of the risk-weighted assets. The capital had two components:

1. *Tier 1 Capital.* This consists of items such as equity and noncumulative perpetual preferred stock[3] net of goodwill.

---

[3] Noncumulative perpetual preferred stock is preferred stock lasting forever where there is a predetermined dividend rate. Unpaid dividends do not cumulate (i.e., the dividends for one year are not carried forward to the next year).

2. *Tier 2 Capital.* This is sometimes referred to as *supplementary capital.* It includes instruments such as cumulative perpetual preferred stock[4], certain types of 99 year debenture issues, and subordinated debt (i.e., debt subordinated to depositors) with an original life of more than five years.

At least 50% of the required capital (i.e., 4% of the risk-weighted assets) must be in Tier 1. The Basel committee updated its definition of instruments that are eligible for Tier 1 capital in 1998.

Although the risk-weighted capital calculations have changed over the years, the capital requirements as a percentage of risk-weighted assets have remained much the same. The bank supervisors in some countries require banks to hold more capital than the minimum specified by the Basel Committee and the banks themselves often have a target for the capital they will hold that is higher than that specified by their bank supervisors.

11.4 THE G-30 POLICY RECOMMENDATIONS

In 1993, a working group consisting of end-users, dealers, academics, accountants, and lawyers involved in derivatives published a report that contained 20 risk management recommendations for dealers and end-users of derivatives and four recommendations for legislators, regulators, and supervisors. The report was based on a detailed survey of 80 dealers and 72 end-users worldwide. The survey involved both questionnaires and in-depth interviews. The report is not a regulatory document, but it has been influential in the development of risk management practices.

A brief summary of the important recommendations is as follows:

1. A company's policies on risk management should be clearly defined and approved by senior management, ideally at the board of directors level. Managers at all levels should enforce the policies.

2. Derivatives positions should be marked to market at least once a day.

3. Derivatives dealers should measure market risk using a consistent measure such as value at risk. Limits to the market risks that are taken should be set.

4. Derivatives dealers should carry out stress tests to determine potential losses under extreme market conditions.

5. The risk management function should be set up so that it is independent of the trading operation.

6. Credit exposures arising from derivatives trading should be assessed based on the current replacement value of existing positions and potential future replacement costs.

7. Credit exposures to a counterparty should be aggregated in a way that reflects enforceable netting agreements. (We talk about netting in the next section.)

8. The individuals responsible for setting credit limits should be independent of those involved in trading.

---

[4] In cumulative preferred stock, unpaid dividends cumulate. Any backlog of dividends must be paid before dividends are paid on the common stock.

9. Dealers and end-users should assess carefully both the costs and benefits of credit risk mitigation techniques such as collateralization and downgrade triggers. In particular, they should assess their own capacity and that of their counterparties to meet the cash flow requirement of downgrade triggers. (Credit mitigation techniques are discussed in Chapter 15.)

10. Only individuals with the appropriate skills and experience should be allowed to have responsibility for trading derivatives, supervising the trading, carrying out back office functions in relation to the trading, etc.

11. There should be adequate systems in place for data capture, processing, settlement, and management reporting.

12. Dealers and end-users should account for the derivatives transactions used to manage risks so as to achieve a consistency of income recognition treatment between those instruments and the risks being managed.

11.5 NETTING

The term *netting* refers to a clause in the master agreement between two companies. It states that, if one of the companies defaults on one transaction that is covered by the master agreement, it must default on all transactions covered by the master agreement.

Netting can have the effect of substantially reducing credit risk. Consider a bank that has three swap transactions outstanding with a particular counterparty. The transactions are worth +$24 million, −$17 million, and +$8 million to the bank. Suppose that the counterparty experiences financial difficulties and defaults on its outstanding obligations. To the counterparty, the three transactions have values of −$24 million, +$17 million, and −$8 million, respectively. Without netting, the counterparty would default on the first transaction, keep the second transaction, and default on the third transaction. Assuming no recovery, the loss to the bank would be $32 (= 24 + 8) million. With netting, the counterparty is required to default on the second transaction as well. The loss to bank is then $15 (= 24 − 17 + 8) million.[5]

Suppose that a financial institution has a portfolio of N derivatives outstanding with a particular counterparty and that the current value of the ith derivative is V_i. Without netting, the financial institution's exposure in the event of a default today is

$$\sum_{i=1}^{N} \max(V_i, 0)$$

With netting, it is

$$\max\left(\sum_{i=1}^{N} V_i, 0\right)$$

Without netting, the exposure is the payoff from a portfolio of options. With netting, the exposure is the payoff from an option on a portfolio

The 1988 Accord did not take netting into account in setting capital requirements. From equation (11.1), the credit equivalent amount for a portfolio of derivatives with a

---

[5] Note that if the second transaction had been worth −$40 million to the bank then the counterparty would be better off if it chose not to default on its transactions with the bank.

counterparty under the Accord was

$$\sum_{i=1}^{N}[\max(V_i, 0) + a_i L_i]$$

where a_i and L_i are the add-on factor and the principal for the ith transaction.

By 1995, netting had been successfully tested in the courts in many jurisdictions. As a result, the 1988 Accord was modified to allow banks to reduce their credit equivalent totals when enforceable bilateral netting agreements were in place. The first step was to calculate the net replacement ratio, NRR. This is the ratio of the current exposure with netting to the current exposure without netting:

$$\text{NRR} = \frac{\max\left(\sum_{i=1}^{N} V_i,\, 0\right)}{\sum_{i=1}^{N} \max(V_i,\, 0)}$$

The credit equivalent amount was modified to

$$\max\left(\sum_{i=1}^{N} V_i,\, 0\right) + (0.4 + 0.6 \times \text{NRR}) \sum_{i=1}^{N} a_i L_i$$

Example 11.4

Consider the example in the table below, which shows a portfolio of three derivatives that a bank has with a particular counterparty. The third column shows the current marked-to-market values of the transactions and the fourth column shows the add-on amount calculated from Table 11.2. The current exposure with netting is $-60 + 70 + 55 = 65$. The current exposure without netting is $0 + 70 + 55 = 125$.

Transaction	Principal, L_i	Current value, V_i	Table 11.2 add-on amount, $a_i L_i$
3-year interest rate swap	1,000	−60	5
6-year foreign exchange forward	1,000	70	75
9-month option on a stock	500	55	30

The net replacement ratio is given by

$$\text{NRR} = \frac{65}{125} = 0.52$$

The total of the add-on amounts, $\sum a_i L_i$, is $5 + 75 + 30 = 110$. The credit equivalent amount when netting agreements are in place is

$$65 + (0.4 + 0.6 \times 0.52) \times 110 = 143.32$$

Without netting agreements, the credit equivalent amount is $125 + 110 = 235$. Suppose that the counterparty is an OECD bank, so that the risk weight is 0.2. This means that the risk-weighted assets with netting is $0.2 \times 143.32 = 28.66$. Without netting, it is $0.2 \times 235 = 47$.

11.6 THE 1996 AMENDMENT

In 1995, the Basel Committee issued a consultative proposal to amend the 1988 Accord. This became known as the "1996 Amendment". It was implemented in 1998 and was then sometimes referred to as "BIS 98". The amendment involves keeping capital for assets and liabilities that are held for trading.

Marking to market is the practice of revaluing assets and liabilities daily. It also known as *fair-value accounting*. Banks are required to use fair-value accounting for all assets and liabilities that are held for trading purposes. This includes most derivatives, marketable equity securities, foreign currencies, and commodities. These items constitute what is referred to as the bank's *trading book*. Banks are not required to use fair-value accounting for assets that are expected to be held for the whole of their life for investment purposes. These assets, which include loans and some debt securities, constitute what is referred to as the *banking book*. Unless there is reason to believe that repayment of the principal will not be made, they are held at historical cost (see Section 2.7).

Under the 1996 Amendment, the credit risk capital charge in the 1988 Accord continued to apply to all on-balance-sheet and off-balance-sheet items in the trading and banking book, except positions in the trading book that consisted of (a) debt and equity traded securities and (b) positions in commodities and foreign exchange. In addition, there was a market risk capital charge for all items in the trading book whether they were on balance sheet or off balance sheet.[6]

The 1996 Amendment outlined a standardized approach for measuring the capital charge for market risk. The standardized approach assigned capital separately to each of debt securities, equity securities, foreign exchange risk, commodities risk, and options. No account was taken of correlations between different types of instrument. The more sophisticated banks with well-established risk management functions were allowed to use an "internal model-based approach" for setting market risk capital. This involved calculating a value-at-risk measure and converting it into a capital requirement using a formula specified in the 1996 amendment. Most large banks preferred to use the internal model-based approach because it better reflected the benefits of diversification and led to lower capital requirements.

The value-at-risk measure used in the internal model-based approach is calculated with a ten-day time horizon and a 99% confidence level. It is the loss that has a 1% chance of being exceeded over a ten-day period. The capital requirement is

$$k \times \text{VaR} + \text{SRC} \tag{11.3}$$

where k is a multiplicative factor, and SRC is a specific risk charge. The measure of value at risk used here, VaR, is the greater of the previous day's value at risk and the average value at risk over the last 60 days. The minimum value for k is 3. Higher values may be chosen by regulators for a particular bank if tests reveal inadequacies in the bank's value-at-risk model, as will be explained shortly.

The specific risk charge, SRC, is a capital charge for the idiosyncratic risks related to individual companies. One security that gives rise to idiosyncratic risk is a corporate bond. There are two components to the risk of this security: interest rate risk and the credit risk of the corporation issuing the bond. The interest rate risk is captured by the

---

[6] Certain nontrading book positions that are used to hedge positions in the trading book can be included in the calculation of the market risk capital charge.

bank's market value-at-risk measure; the credit spread is captured by the specific risk charge.[7] The 1996 Amendment proposed standard methods for assessing a specific risk capital charge, but allowed banks to use internal models for arriving at a capital charge for specific risk similarly to the way they calculate a capital charge for market risks. The SRC is calculated using a ten-day time horizon and a 99% confidence limit.

The total capital a bank was required to keep after the implementation of the 1996 Amendment was (for banks adopting the internal model-based approach) the sum of (a) credit risk capital equal to 8% of the total risk-weighted assets (RWA) as given by equation (11.2), and (b) market risk capital as given by equation (11.3). For convenience, an RWA for market risk capital is defined as 12.5 multiplied by the amount given in equation (11.3). This means that the total capital required for credit and market risk is given by

$$\text{Total capital} = 0.08 \times (\text{Credit risk RWA} + \text{Market risk RWA}) \qquad \textbf{(11.4)}$$

A bank has more flexibility in the type of capital it uses for market risk. It can use Tier 1 or Tier 2 capital. It can also use what is termed Tier 3 capital. This consists of short-term subordinated debt with an original maturity of at least two years that is unsecured and fully paid up.

One-Day vs. Ten-Day VaR

Banks almost invariably calculate a one-day 99% VaR in the first instance. Regulators explicitly state that the ten-day 99% VaR can be calculated as $\sqrt{10}$ times the one-day 99% VaR. This means that, when the capital requirement for a bank is specified as k times the ten-day 99% VaR, it is to all intents and purposes $k \times \sqrt{10} = 3.16k$ times the one-day 99% VaR.

Back-testing

The BIS Amendment requires the one-day 99% VaR that a bank calculates to be back-tested over the previous 250 days. As described in Section 8.8, this involves using the bank's current procedure for estimating VaR for each of the most recent 250 days. If the actual loss that occurred on a day is greater than the VaR level calculated for that day, an "exception" is recorded. Calculations are typically carried out (a) including changes that were made to the portfolio during the day being considered and (b) assuming that no changes were made to the portfolio during the day being considered. (Regulators pay most attention to the first set of calculations.)

If the number of exceptions during the previous 250 days is less than 5, k is normally set equal to 3. If the number of exceptions is 5, 6, 7, 8, and 9, the value of the k is set equal to 3.4, 3.5, 3.65, 3.75, and 3.85, respectively. The bank supervisor has some discretion as to whether the higher multipliers are used. The penalty will normally apply when the reason for the exceptions is identified as a deficiency in the VaR model being used. If changes in the bank's positions during the day result in exceptions, the higher multiplier should be considered, but does not have to be used. When the only reason that is identified is bad luck, no guidance is provided for the supervisor. In circumstances where the number of exceptions is 10 or more, the Basel Amendment requires

---

[7] As mentioned earlier, the 1988 credit risk capital charge did not apply to debt securities in the trading book under the 1996 Amendment.

the multiplier to be set at 4. Problem 11.18 considers these guidelines in the context of the statistical tests we discussed in Section 8.8.

11.7 BASEL II

The 1988 Basel Accord improved the way capital requirements were determined, but it does have significant weaknesses. Under the 1988 Basel Accord, all loans by a bank to a corporation have a risk weight of 100% and require the same amount of capital. A loan to corporation with a AAA credit rating is treated in the same way as one to a corporation with a B credit rating.[8] Also, in Basel I there was no model of default correlation.

In June 1999, the Basel Committee proposed new rules that have become known as Basel II. These were revised in January 2001 and April 2003. A number of quantitative impact studies (QISs) were carried out to test the application of the new rules and the amount of capital that will be required. A final set of rules agreed to by all members of the Basel committee was published in June 2004. This was updated in November 2005. Implementation of the rules began in 2007 after a further QIS.[9]

The Basel II capital requirements apply to "internationally active" banks. In the United States, there are many small regional banks and the US regulatory authorities have decided that Basel II will not apply to them. (These banks are regulated under what is termed Basel IA, which is similar to Basel I.) Some of the larger regional banks are voluntarily implementing Basel II, possibly to signal to their shareholders that they manage risks in a sophisticated way. In Europe, all banks, large or small, are regulated under Basel II. Furthermore, the European Union requires the Basel II rules to be applied to securities companies as well as banks.

Basel II is based on three "pillars":

1. Minimum capital requirements
2. Supervisory review
3. Market discipline

In Pillar 1 the minimum capital requirement for credit risk in the banking book is calculated in a new way that reflects the credit ratings of counterparties. The capital requirement for market risk remains unchanged from the 1996 Amendment and there is a new capital charge for operational risk. The general requirement in Basel I that banks hold a total capital equal to 8% of risk-weighted assets (RWA) remains unchanged. When the capital requirement for a risk is calculated in a way that does not involve RWAs, it is multiplied by 12.5 to convert it to an RWA. As a result, it is always the case that

Total capital =

$$0.08 \times (\text{Credit risk RWA} + \text{Market risk RWA} + \text{Operational risk RWA}) \quad \textbf{(11.5)}$$

Pillar 2, which is concerned with the supervisory review process, allows regulators in different countries some discretion in how rules are applied (so that they can take

---

[8] Credit ratings are discussed in Chapter 14.

[9] One point to note about the QIS studies is that they do not take account of changes banks may choose to make to their portfolios to minimize their capital requirements once Basel II is implemented.

account of local conditions), but seeks to achieve overall consistency in the application of the rules. It places more emphasis on early intervention when problems arise. Supervisors are required to do far more than just ensuring that the minimum capital required under Basel II is held. Part of their role is to encourage banks to develop and use better risk management techniques and to evaluate these techniques. They should evaluate risks that are not covered by Pillar 1 and enter into an active dialogue with banks when deficiencies are identified.

Pillar 3, market discipline, requires banks to disclose more information about the way they allocate capital and the risks they take. The idea here is that banks will be subjected to added pressure to make sound risk management decisions if shareholders and potential shareholders have more information about those decisions.

11.8 CREDIT RISK CAPITAL UNDER BASEL II

For credit risk, banks have three choices under Basel II:

1. The standardized approach
2. The foundation internal ratings based (IRB) approach
3. The advanced IRB approach

However, the United States (which, as mentioned earlier, is only applying Basel II to large banks) has decided that only the IRB approach can be used.

The Standardized Approach

The standardized approach is used by banks that are not sufficiently sophisticated (in the eyes of the regulators) to use the internal ratings approaches. The standardized approach is similar to Basel I except for the calculation of risk weights.[10] Some of the new rules here are summarized in Table 11.3. Comparing Table 11.3 with Table 11.1, we see that the OECD status of a bank or a country is no longer considered important under Basel II. The risk weight for a country (sovereign) exposure ranges from 0% to 150%, and the risk weight for an exposure to another bank or a corporation ranges from 20% to 150%. In Table 11.1, OECD banks were implicitly assumed to be lesser credit risks than corporations. An OECD bank attracted a risk weight of 20%, while a corporation attracted a risk weight of 100%. Table 11.3 treats banks and corporation much more equitably. An interesting observation from Table 11.3 for a country, corporation, or bank that wants to borrow money is that it may be better to have no credit rating at all than a very poor credit rating! Supervisors are allowed to apply lower risk weights (20% rather than 50%, 50% rather than 100%, and 100% rather than 150%) when exposures are to the country in which the bank is incorporated or to that country's central bank.

For claims on banks, the rules are somewhat complicated. Instead of using the risk weights in Table 11.3, national supervisors can choose to base capital requirements on the rating of the country in which the bank is incorporated. The risk weight assigned to the bank will be 20% if the country of incorporation has a rating between AAA and AA−, 50% if it is between A+ and A−, 100% if it is between BBB+ and B−, 150% if

---

[10] Ratios calculated using the new weights are sometimes referred to as McDonough ratios after William McDonough, the head of the Basel Committee.

Table 11.3 Risk weights as a percent of principal for exposures to countries, banks, and corporations with different ratings under Basel II's standardized approach.

	AAA to AA−	A+ to A−	BBB+ to BBB−	BB+ to BB−	B+ to B−	Below B−	Unrated
Country*	0	20	50	100	100	150	100
Banks**	20	50	50	100	100	150	50
Corporations	20	50	100	100	150	150	100

* Includes exposures to the country's central bank.
** National supervisors have options as outlined in the text.

it is below B−, and 100% if it is unrated. Another complication is that, if national supervisors elect to use the rules in Table 11.3, they can choose to treat claims with a maturity less than three months more favorably, so that the risk weights are 20% if the rating is between AAA+ and BBB−, 50% if it is between BB+ and B−, 150% if it is below B−, and 20% if it is unrated.

The standard rule for retail lending is that a risk weight of 75% be applied. (This compares to 100% in the 1988 Accord.) When claims are secured by a residential mortgage the risk weight is 35%. (This compares with 50% in the 1988 Accord.) Because of poor historical loss experience, the risk weight for claims secured by commercial real estate is 100%.

Example 11.5

Suppose that the assets of a bank consist of $100 million of loans to corporations rated A, $10 million of government bonds rated AAA, and $50 million of residential mortgages. Under the Basel II standardized approach, the total risk-weighted assets is

$$0.5 \times 100 + 0.0 \times 10 + 0.35 \times 50 = 67.5$$

or $67.5 million. This compares with $125 million under Basel I (see Example 11.1).

Adjustments for Collateral

There are two ways banks can adjust risk weights for collateral. The first is termed the *simple approach* and is similar to an approach used in Basel I. The second is termed the *comprehensive approach*. Banks have a choice as to which approach is used in the banking book, but they must use the comprehensive approach to calculate capital for counterparty credit risk in the trading book.

Under the simple approach, the risk weight of the counterparty is replaced by the risk weight of the collateral for the part of the exposure covered by the collateral. (The exposure is calculated after netting.) For any exposure not covered by the collateral, the risk weight of the counterparty is used. The minimum level for the risk weight applied to the collateral is 20%.[11] A requirement is that the collateral must be revalued at least every six months and must be pledged for at least the life of the exposure.

---

[11] An exception is when the collateral consists of cash or government securities with the currency of the collateral being the same as the currency of the exposure.

Under the comprehensive approach, banks adjust the size of their exposure upward to allow for possible increases in the exposure and adjust the value of the collateral downward to allow for possible decreases in the value of the collateral.[12] (The adjustments depend on the volatility of the exposure and the collateral.) A new exposure equal to the excess of the adjusted exposure over the adjusted value of the collateral is calculated and the counterparty's risk weight is applied to this exposure. The adjustments applied to the exposure and the collateral can be calculated using rules specified in Basel II or, with regulatory approval, using a bank's internal models. Where netting arrangements apply, exposures and collateral are separately netted and the adjustments made are weighted averages.

Example 11.6

Suppose that an $80 million exposure to a particular counterparty is secured by collateral worth $70 million. The collateral consists of bonds issued by an A-rated company. The counterparty has a rating of B+. The risk weight for the counterparty is 150% and the risk weight for the collateral is 50%. The risk-weighted assets applicable to the exposure using the simple approach is

$$0.5 \times 70 + 1.50 \times 10 = 50$$

or $50 million.

Consider next the comprehensive approach. Assume that the adjustment to exposure to allow for possible future increases in the exposure is +10% and the adjustment to the collateral to allow for possible future decreases in its value is −15%. The new exposure is

$$1.1 \times 80 - 0.85 \times 70 = 28.5$$

or $28.5 million, and a risk weight of 150% is applied to this exposure to give risk-adjusted assets equal to $42.75 million.

The IRB Approach

The model underlying the IRB approach is shown in Figure 11.1. Regulators base the capital requirement on the value at risk calculated using a one-year time horizon and a 99.9% confidence level. They recognize that expected losses are usually covered by the way a financial institution prices its products. (For example, the interest charged by a bank on a loan is designed to recover expected loan losses.) The capital required is therefore the value at risk minus the expected loss.

The value at risk is calculated using the one-factor Gaussian copula model of time to default that we discussed in Section 10.5. Assume that a bank has a very large number of obligors, all of which have the same one-year probability of default, equal to PD. The copula correlation between each pair of obligors is ρ.[13] Equation (10.12) shows that there is a probability of 99.9% that the percentage of defaults during a one-year period

---

[12] An adjustment to the exposure is not likely to be necessary on a loan, but is likely to be necessary on an over-the-counter derivative. The adjustment is in addition to the add-on factor.

[13] Note that the Basel Committee publications use R, not ρ, to denote the copula correlation.

Figure 11.1 The loss probability density function and the capital required by a financial institution.

will be less than

$$\text{WCDR} = N\left[\frac{N^{-1}(\text{PD}) + \sqrt{\rho}\, N^{-1}(0.999)}{\sqrt{1-\rho}}\right] \qquad (11.6)$$

WCDR denotes the "worst-case default rate" that we are 99.9% certain will not be exceeded next year. It follows that, for a large portfolio of instruments (loans, loan commitments, derivatives, etc.) that have the same PD and ρ, there is a 99.9% chance that the loss on the portfolio will be less than

$$\sum_i \text{EAD}_i \times \text{LGD}_i \times \text{WCDR}$$

where EAD_i is the exposure at default of the ith counterparty and LGD_i is the loss given default for the ith counterparty. The variable EAD_i is the dollar amount that is expected to be owed by the ith counterparty at the time of default. If there is a single loan outstanding to the ith counterparty, this is likely to equal the principal amount outstanding on the loan. If there is a single swap or other derivative, a credit equivalent amount must be estimated (see Section 11.3 for the standard ways of doing this in Basel I). When there are several transactions with the ith counterparty, netting calculations similar to those in Section 11.5 must be carried out to determine EAD_i. The variable LGD_i is the proportion of EAD_i that is expected to be lost in the event of default. For example, if a bank expects to recover 30% of the amount owed in the event of default, then $\text{LGD}_i = 0.7$.

The expected loss from defaults is

$$\sum_i \text{EAD}_i \times \text{LGD}_i \times \text{PD}$$

The capital required in Figure 11.1 is the excess of the 99.9% worst-case loss minus the

Table 11.4 Dependence of WCDR on PD and ρ.

ρ	PD = 0.1%	PD = 0.5%	PD = 1%	PD = 1.5%	PD = 2.0%
0.0	0.1%	0.5%	1.0%	1.5%	2.0%
0.2	2.8%	9.1%	14.6%	18.9%	22.6%
0.4	7.1%	21.1%	31.6%	39.0%	44.9%
0.6	13.5%	38.7%	54.2%	63.8%	70.5%
0.8	23.3%	66.3%	83.6%	90.8%	94.4%

expected loss:

$$\sum_i \text{EAD}_i \times \text{LGD}_i \times (\text{WCDR} - \text{PD})$$

When counterparties have different PDs and different ρ's, an extension of the copula model can be use to show that the capital required in Figure 11.1 is

$$\sum_i \text{EAD}_i \times \text{LGD}_i \times (\text{WCDR}_i - \text{PD}_i) \tag{11.7}$$

where PD_i and WCDR_i are PD and WCDR for the ith counterparty.

Table 11.4 shows how WCDR depends on PD and ρ. When the correlation ρ is zero, WCDR = PD because in that case there is no default correlation and the percentage of loans defaulting can be expected to be the same in all years. As ρ increases, WCDR increases.

Corporate, Sovereign, and Bank Exposures

In the case of corporate, sovereign, and bank exposures, Basel II assumes a relationship between the correlation parameter ρ and the probability of default PD in equation (11.6) based on empirical research.[14] The formula is

$$\rho = 0.12\frac{1 - \exp(-50 \times \text{PD})}{1 - \exp(-50)} + 0.24\left[1 - \frac{1 - \exp(-50 \times \text{PD})}{1 - \exp(-50)}\right]$$

Because $\exp(-50)$ is a very small number, this formula to all intents and purposes reduces to

$$\rho = 0.12\left(1 + e^{-50 \times \text{PD}}\right) \tag{11.8}$$

As PD increases, ρ decreases. The reason usually given for this inverse relationship is as follows. As a company becomes less creditworthy, its PD increases and its probability of default becomes more idiosyncratic and less affected by overall market conditions.

Combining equation (11.8) with equation (11.6), we obtain the relationship between WCDR and PD in Table 11.5. WCDR is, as one would expect, an increasing function of PD. However, it does not increase as fast as it would if ρ were assumed to be independent of PD.

[14] See J. Lopez, "The Empirical Relationship Between Average Asset Correlation, Firm Probability of Default and Asset Size," *Journal of Financial Intermediation*, 13, 2 (2004): 265–283.

Table 11.5 Relationship between WCDR and PD for corporate, sovereign, and bank exposures.

PD:	0.1%	0.5%	1.0%	1.5%	2.0%
WCDR:	3.4%	9.8%	14.0%	16.9%	19.0%

We now drop the subscripts in equation (11.7) and define for a counterparty

PD: The probability that the counterparty will default within one year (expressed as a decimal)

EAD: The exposure at default (in dollars)

LGD: The loss given default or the proportion of the exposure that is lost if there is a default (expressed as a decimal)

The formula for the capital required is

$$\text{EAD} \times \text{LGD} \times (\text{WCDR} - \text{PD}) \times \text{MA} \tag{11.9}$$

The meaning of the first three terms in this expression should be clear from our earlier discussion leading to equation (11.7). The variable MA is the maturity adjustment and is defined as

$$\text{MA} = \frac{1 + (M - 2.5) \times b}{1 - 1.5 \times b} \tag{11.10}$$

where

$$b = [0.11852 - 0.05478 \times \ln(\text{PD})]^2$$

and M is the maturity of the exposure. The maturity adjustment is designed to allow for the fact that, if an instrument lasts longer than one year, there is a one-year credit exposure arising from a possible decline in the creditworthiness of the counterparty as well as from a possible default by the counterparty. (Note that, when $M = 1$, MA is 1.0 and has no effect.) As mentioned in Section 11.7 (see equation (11.5)), the risk-weighted assets (RWA) are calculated as 12.5 times the capital required

$$\text{RWA} = 12.5 \times \text{EAD} \times \text{LGD} \times (\text{WCDR} - \text{PD}) \times \text{MA}$$

so that the capital is 8% of RWA, 4% of which must be Tier 1.

Under the foundation IRB approach, banks supply PD while LGD, EAD, and M are supervisory values set by the Basel Committee. PD is subject to a floor of 0.03% for bank and corporate exposures. LGD is set at 45% for senior claims and 75% for subordinated claims. When there is eligible collateral, in order to correspond to the comprehensive approach that we described earlier, LGD is reduced by the ratio of the adjusted value of the collateral to the adjusted value of the exposure, both calculated using the comprehensive approach. The EAD is calculated in a manner similar to the credit equivalent amount in Basel I and includes the impact of netting. M is set at 2.5 in most circumstances.

Under the advanced IRB approach, banks supply their own estimates of the PD, LGD, EAD, and M for corporate, sovereign, and bank exposures. The PD can be reduced by credit mitigants such as credit triggers. (As in the case of the foundation IRB approach, it is subject to a floor of 0.03% for bank and corporate exposures.) The two main factors influencing the LGD are the seniority of the debt and the collateral. In calculating EAD, banks can with regulatory approval use their own estimates of credit conversion factors.

The capital given by equation (11.9) is intended to be sufficient to cover unexpected losses over a one-year period that we are 99.9% certain will not be exceeded. (As discussed earlier, the expected losses should be covered by a bank in the way it prices its products.) The WCDR is the probability of default that (theoretically) happens once every thousand years. The Basel committee reserves the right to apply a scaling factor (less than or greater than 1.0) to the result of the calculations in equation (11.9) if it finds that the aggregate capital requirements are too high or low. A typical scaling factor is 1.06.

Example 11.7

Suppose that the assets of a bank consist of $100 million of loans to A-rated corporations. The PD for the corporations is estimated as 0.1% and the LGD is 60%. The average maturity is 2.5 years for the corporate loans. This means that

$$b = [0.11852 - 0.05478 \times \ln(0.001)]^2 = 0.247$$

so that

$$MA = \frac{1}{1 - 1.5 \times 0.247} = 1.59$$

From Table 11.5, the WCDR is 3.4%. Under the Basel II IRB approach, the risk-weighted assets for the corporate loans are

$$12.5 \times 100 \times 0.6 \times (0.034 - 0.001) \times 1.59 = 39.3$$

or $39.3 million. This compares with $100 million under Basel I and $50 million under the standardized approach of Basel II (see Examples 11.1 and 11.5, where a $100 million corporate loan is part of the portfolio).

Retail Exposures

The model underlying the calculation of capital for retail exposures is similar to that underlying the calculation of corporate, sovereign, and banking exposures. However, the foundation IRB and advanced IRB approaches are merged, and all banks using the IRB approach provide their own estimates of PD, EAD, and LGD. There is no maturity adjustment. The capital requirement is therefore

$$EAD \times LGD \times (WCDR - PD)$$

and the risk-weighted assets are

$$RWA = 12.5 \times EAD \times LGD \times (WCDR - PD)$$

WCDR is calculated as in equation (11.6). For residential mortgages, ρ is set equal to 0.15 in this equation. For qualifying revolving exposures, ρ is set equal to 0.04. For all other retail exposures, a relationship between ρ and PD is specified for the calculation

Table 11.6 Relationship between WCDR and PD for retail exposures.

PD:	0.1%	0.5%	1.0%	1.5%	2.0%
WCDR:	2.1%	6.3%	9.1%	11.0%	12.3%

of WCDR. This is

$$\rho = 0.03\frac{1 - \exp(-35 \times PD)}{1 - \exp(-35)} + 0.16\left[1 - \frac{1 - \exp(-35 \times PD)}{1 - \exp(-35)}\right]$$

Because $\exp(-35)$ is a very small number, this formula to all intents and purposes reduces to

$$\rho = 0.03 + 0.13e^{-35 \times PD} \tag{11.11}$$

Comparing equation (11.11) with equation (11.8), we see that correlations are assumed to be much lower for retail exposures. Table 11.6 is the table corresponding to Table 11.5 for retail exposures.

Example 11.8

Suppose that the assets of a bank consist of $50 million of residential mortgages where the PD is 0.005 and the LGD is 20%. In this case, $\rho = 0.15$ and

$$WCDR = N\left[\frac{N^{-1}(0.005) + \sqrt{0.15}N^{-1}(0.999)}{\sqrt{1 - 0.15}}\right] = 0.067$$

The risk-weighted assets are

$$12.5 \times 50 \times 0.2 \times (0.067 - 0.005) = 7.8$$

or $7.8 million. This compares with $25 million under Basel I and $17.5 million under the standardized approach of Basel II (see Examples 11.1 and 11.5, where $50 million of residential mortgages is part of the portfolio).

Guarantees and Credit Derivatives

The approach traditionally taken by the Basel Committee for handling guarantees is the credit substitution approach. Suppose that a AA-rated company guarantees a loan to a BBB-rated company. For the purposes of calculating capital, the credit rating of the guarantor is substituted for the credit rating of the borrower, so that capital is calculated as though the loan had been made to the AA-rated company. This overstates the credit risk because, for the lender to lose money, both the guarantor and the borrower must default (with the guarantor defaulting before the borrower).[15] The Basel Committee has addressed this issue. In July 2005 it published a document concerned with the treatment of double defaults under Basel II.[16] As an alternative to using the

---

[15] Credit default swaps, which we will discuss in Chapter 14, provide a type of insurance against default and are handled in a similar way to guarantees for regulatory purposes.

[16] See "The Application of Basel II to Trading Activities and the Treatment of Double Defaults," July 2005, available at www.bis.org.

credit substitution approach, the capital requirement can be calculated as the capital that would be required without the guarantee multiplied by $0.15 + 160 \times PD_g$, where PD_g is the one-year probability of default of the guarantor.

11.9 OPERATIONAL RISK CAPITAL UNDER BASEL II

In addition to changing the way banks calculate credit risk capital, Basel II requires banks to keep capital for operational risk. This is the risk of losses from situations where the bank's procedures fail to work as they are supposed to or where there is an adverse external event such as a fire in a key facility. The impact of the Basel II credit risk calculation is to reduce the credit risk capital requirements for most banks and the capital charge for operational risk has the effect of restoring the total level of capital in the banking system to roughly where it was under Basel I.

There are three approaches to calculating capital for operational risk:

1. The basic indicator approach
2. The standardized approach
3. The advanced measurement approach

Which of these is used depends on the sophistication of the bank. The simplest approach is the basic indicator approach. This sets the operational risk capital equal to the bank's average annual gross income over the last three years multiplied by 0.15.[17] The standardized approach is similar to the basic indicator approach except that a different factor is applied to the gross income from different business lines. In the advanced measurement approach, the bank uses its own internal models to calculate the operational risk loss that it is 99.9% certain will not be exceeded in one year. One advantage of the advanced measurement approach is that it allows banks to recognize the risk-mitigating impact of insurance contracts subject to certain conditions. The calculation of operational risk is discussed further in Chapter 18.

11.10 PILLAR 2: SUPERVISORY REVIEW

Pillar 2 of Basel II is concerned with the supervisory review process. Four key principles of supervisory review are specified:

1. Banks should have a process for assessing their overall capital adequacy in relation to their risk profile and a strategy for maintaining their capital levels.
2. Supervisors should review and evaluate banks' internal capital adequacy assessments and strategies, as well as their ability to monitor and ensure compliance with regulatory capital ratios. Supervisors should take appropriate supervisory action if they are not satisfied with the result of this process.
3. Supervisors should expect banks to operate above the minimum regulatory capital and should be able to require banks to hold capital in excess of this minimum.

---

[17] Gross income defined as net interest income plus noninterest income. Net interest income is the excess of income earned on loans over interest paid on deposits and other instruments that are used to fund the loans. Years where gross income is negative are not included in the calculations.

4. Supervisors should seek to intervene at an early stage to prevent capital from falling below the minimum levels required to support the risk characteristics of a particular bank and should require rapid remedial action if capital is not maintained or restored.

The Basel Committee suggests that regulators pay particular attention to interest rate risk in the banking book, credit risk, and operational risk. Key issues in credit risk are stress tests used, default definitions used, credit risk concentration, and the risks associated with the use of collateral, guarantees, and credit derivatives.

The Basel Committee also stresses that there should be transparency and accountability in the procedures used by bank supervisors. This is particularly important when a supervisor exercises discretion in the procedures used or sets capital requirements above the minimum specified in Basel II.

11.11 PILLAR 3: MARKET DISCIPLINE

Pillar 3 of Basel II is concerned with increasing the disclosure by a bank of its risk assessment procedures and capital adequacy. The extent to which regulators can force banks to increase their disclosure varies from jurisdiction to jurisdiction. However, banks are unlikely to ignore directives on this from their supervisors, given the potential of supervisors to make their life difficult. Moreover, banks sometimes have to increase their disclosure in order to be allowed to use particular methodologies for calculating capital.

Regulatory disclosures are likely to be different in form from accounting disclosures and need not be made in annual reports. It is largely left to the bank to choose disclosures that are material and relevant. Among the items that banks should disclose are:

1. The entities in the banking group to which Basel II is applied and adjustments made for entities to which it is not applied
2. The terms and conditions of the main features of all capital instruments
3. A list of the instruments constituting Tier 1 capital and the amount of capital provided by each item
4. The total amount of Tier 2 and Tier 3 capital
5. Capital requirements for credit, market, and operational risk
6. Other general information on the risks to which a bank is exposed and the assessment methods used by the bank for different categories of risk
7. The structure of the risk management function and how it operates

11.12 REVISIONS TO BASEL II

Following the huge losses of banks in 2007 and 2008, the Basel Committee has taken a number of actions. It has revised its guidance for bank supervisors on the assessment of the adequacy of a bank's liquidity risk management framework (see Chapter 19) and has also issued guidance on scenario analysis and stress testing (see Chapter 17) and proposed increased capital requirements for resecuritizations (see Chapter 16).

CHAPTER 11

Business Snapshot 11.2   Basel III?

As explained in Section 11.12, the Basel Committee has already proposed a number of changes to Basel II as a result of the huge losses experienced during the credit crisis that started in 2007. At some stage it is likely that there will be another major overhaul of the regulation of banks. The replacement of Basel I by Basel II marked a trend towards self-regulation. It is likely that Basel III will lead to this trend being reversed. The crisis that started in 2007 suggests that banks, left to their own devices, tend to take too many risks. It is likely that banks will lose some of the freedom they have been given in Basel II to assess capital requirements for the risks being taken. It is also possible that there will be a new capital charge for liquidity risk and that bank supervisors will be more proactive in using stress testing as a determinant of a bank's capital requirements. Indeed, the proposed use of stressed VaR (see Section 11.12) to determine market risk capital is a move in this direction.

Over-the-counter derivatives are being subject to scrutiny, and clearinghouses similar to those used by exchanges have been formed for credit default swaps. Monitoring systemic risk will clearly be a priority for regulators in the future. Regulators need to have complete information on all derivatives exposures, both of banks and of nonbank financial institutions. They need to make sure that all market participants, regardless of their credit rating, post margin on their over-the-counter derivatives transactions. This can be done either by using clearinghouses or by using two-way collateralization agreements with no threshold (see Section 15.2).

A major proposal is the introduction of what is referred to as the *incremental risk charge* (IRC) for the trading book. In 2005 the Basel Committee became concerned that banks were reducing their capital requirements by shifting exposures from the banking book to the trading book. Structured products whose values depended on the creditworthiness of companies were increasingly put in the trading book (see Chapter 16 for a discussion of these products). The products were less liquid than other instruments in the trading book. The ten-day, 99% confidence calculation that had been used to determine a capital charge for the trading book was considered to be inappropriate for the products. Regulators proposed an "incremental default risk charge" (IDRC) that would be calculated with a 99.9% confidence level and a one-year time horizon for instruments in the trading book that were sensitive to default risk. These instruments would therefore be treated in much the same way as similar instruments in the banking book.

In 2008 the Basel Committee recognized that most of the losses sustained in the credit market turmoil of 2007 and 2008 were from changes in credit ratings, widening of credit spreads, and loss of liquidity, rather than solely as a result of defaults. It therefore amended its previous proposals so that these risks were included. The IDRC became the IRC and is expected to be implemented during 2010 and 2011. It is likely to lead to higher minimum capital requirements for large banks that trade structured credit products.

Another proposal involves what is termed *stressed VaR*. As will be explained in Chapter 12, the usual approach for calculating VaR is based on how market variables behaved over the most recent two to four years. A stressed VaR is calculated from the movements in market variables during a one-year period of significant losses (such as

2007 or 2008). The Basel Committee proposes that the capital for market risk be the sum of the results of the calculation in Section 11.6 and a similar calculation involving stressed VaR. This will at least double the capital banks have to keep for market risks. The scheduled implementation date for this proposal (assuming it survives the consultation period) is December 31, 2010.

The emphasis in Basel II is on self-regulation. Banks are allowed to use internal models to handle many aspects of the assessment of capital requirements. The financial crisis starting in August 2007 and the bail-outs of banks that became necessary has led many people to question whether Basel II's reliance on internal models should be reduced. Business Snapshot 11.2 speculates on changes that could be proposed by the Basel Committee in the future.

11.13 SOLVENCY II

As discussed in Section 3.11, there are no international standards for the regulation of insurance companies. In the United States, insurance companies are regulated at the state level rather than the federal level, with some help being provided to state regulatory commissions by the National Association of Insurance Commissioners. In Europe, the regulation of insurance companies is handled by the European Union. The long-standing regulatory framework in the European Union, known as Solvency I, is in the process of being replaced by Solvency II. Quantitative impact studies are being carried out and it is expected that Solvency II will be implemented in 2012. Whereas Solvency I calculates capital only for underwriting risks, Solvency II will consider investment risks and operational risks as well.

Solvency II has many similarities to Basel II. There are three pillars. Pillar 1 is concerned with the calculation of capital requirements and the types of capital that are eligible, Pillar 2 with the supervisory review process, and Pillar 3 with the disclosure of risk management information to the market. The three pillars are therefore similar to the three pillars of Basel II.

Pillar 1 of Solvency II specifies a *minimum capital requirement* (MCR) and a *solvency capital requirement* (SCR). If its capital falls below the SCR level, an insurance company should at minimum deliver to the supervisor a plan to restore capital to above the SCR level. The supervisor might require the insurance company to take particular measures to correct the situation. The MCR is regarded as an absolute minimum level of capital. If capital drops below the MCR level, supervisors are likely to prevent the insurance company from taking new business. It might force the insurance company into liquidation, transferring its policies to another company.

There are two ways to calculate the SCR: the standardized approach and the internal models approach. The internal models approach involves a VaR calculation with a one-year time horizon and a 99.5% confidence limit. (The confidence level is therefore less than the 99.9% confidence level used in Pillar 1 of Basel II.) Longer time horizons with lower confidence levels are also allowed when the protection provided is considered equivalent. The SCR involves a capital charge for investment risk, underwriting risk, and operational risk. Investment risk is subdivided into market risk and credit risk, while underwriting risk is subdivided into risk arising from life insurance, nonlife insurance (i.e., property and casualty), and health insurance.

Capital should be adequate to deal with large adverse events. Examples of the events considered in quantitative impact studies are:

1. A 32% decrease in global stock markets
2. A 20% decrease in real estate prices
3. A 20% change in foreign exchange rates
4. Specified catastrophic risk scenarios affecting property and casualty payouts
5. Health care costs increasing by a factor times the historical standard deviation of costs
6. A 10% increase in mortality rates
7. A 25% decrease in mortality rates
8. A 10% increase in expenses

The internal models are required to satisfy three tests. The first is a statistical quality test. This is a test of the soundness of the data and methodology used in calculating VaR. The second is a calibration test. This is a test of whether risks has been assessed in accordance with a common SCR target criterion. The third is a use test. This is a test of whether the model is genuinely relevant to and used by risk mangers.

A number of possible approaches for calculating MCR are being considered. One is to set MCR as a percentage of SCR. Another is to calculate MCR in the same way as SCR, but with a lower confidence level than 99.5%.

There are three types of capital in Solvency II. Tier 1 capital consists of equity capital, retained earnings, and other equivalent funding sources. Tier 2 capital consists of liabilities that are subordinated to policyholders and satisfy certain criteria concerning their availability in wind-down scenarios. Tier 3 capital consists of liabilities that are subordinated to policyholders and do not satisfy these criteria. As in Basel II, it is expected that limits will be specified on the amount of SCR can be satisfied with the different types of capital.

SUMMARY

This chapter has provided an overview of capital requirements for banks throughout the world. The way in which regulators calculate the minimum capital a bank is required to hold has changed dramatically since the 1980s. Prior to 1988, regulators determined capital requirements by specifying minimum ratios for capital to assets or maximum ratios for assets to capital. In the late 1980s, both bank supervisors and the banks themselves agreed that changes were necessary. Off-balance-sheet derivatives trading was increasing fast. Also banks were competing globally and it was considered important to create a level playing field by making regulations uniform throughout the world.

The 1988 Basel Accord assigned capital for credit risk both on and off the balance sheet. This involved calculating a risk-weighted asset for each item. The risk-weighted assets for an on-balance-sheet loan were calculated by multiplying the principal by a risk weight for the counterparty. In the case of derivatives such as swaps, banks were first required to calculate credit equivalent amounts. The risk-weighted assets were obtained by multiplying the credit equivalent amount by a risk weight for the counterparty. Banks were required to keep capital equal to 8% of the total risk weighted assets. In

1995, the capital requirements for credit risk were modified to incorporate netting. In 1996, the Accord was modified to include a capital charge for market risk. Sophisticated banks could base the capital charge on a value-at-risk calculation.

Basel II was proposed in 1999 and implemented between 2007 and 2009. It led to no immediate change to the capital requirement for market risk. Credit risk capital was calculated in a more sophisticated way than previously to reflect either (a) the credit ratings of obligors or (b) a bank's own internal estimates of default probabilities. There was also a capital charge for operational risk. An extra charge known as the incremental risk charge is expected to be introduced for banks trading structured credit products.

Solvency II is a regulatory framework for insurance companies expected to be implemented by the European Union in 2012. It will prescribe minimum capital levels for investment risk, underwriting risk, and operational risk. The overall structure of Solvency II is similar to Basel II.

FURTHER READING

Bank for International Settlements, "Basel II: International Convergence of Capital Measurement and Capital Standards: A Revised Framework," November 2005, www.bis.org.

Bank for International Settlements, "Guidelines for Computing Capital for Incremental Risk in the Trading Book," January 2009.

Bank for International Settlements, "Proposed Enhancements to the Basel II Framework," January 2009.

Bank for International Settlements, "Revisions to the Basel II Market Risk Framework," January 2009.

Crouhy, M., D. Galai, and R. Mark, *Risk Mangement*. New York: McGraw-Hill, 2001.

Gordy, M. B., "A Risk-factor Model Foundation for Ratings-Based Bank Capital Ratios," *Journal of Financial Intermediation*, 12 (2003), 199–232.

Lopez, J. A., "The Empirical Relationship Between Average Asset Correlation, Firm Probability of Default, and Asset Size," *Journal of Financial Intermediation*, 13, 2 (2004), 265–283.

PRACTICE QUESTIONS AND PROBLEMS (Answers at the End of the Book)

11.1. "When a steel company goes bankrupt, other companies in the same industry benefit because they have one less competitor. But when a bank goes bankrupt other banks do not necessarily benefit." Explain this statement.

11.2. "The existence of deposit insurance makes it particularly important for there to be regulations on the amount of capital banks hold." Explain this statement.

11.3. An interest rate swap involves the exchange of a fixed rate of interest for a floating rate of interest, with both being applied to the same principal. The principals are not exchanged. What is the nature of the credit risk for a bank when it enters into a five-year interest rate swap with a notional principal of $100 million? Assume that the swap is worth zero initially.

11.4. In a currency swap, interest on a principal in one currency is exchanged for interest on a principal in another currency. The principals in the two currencies are exchanged at the end of the life of the swap. Why is the credit risk on a currency swap greater than that on an interest rate swap?

11.5. A four-year interest rate swap currently has a negative value to a financial institution. Is the financial institution exposed to credit risk on the transaction? Explain your answer. How would the capital requirement be calculated under Basel I?

11.6. Estimate the capital required under Basel I for a bank that has the following transactions with a corporation (assume no netting):
   (a) A nine-year interest rate swap with a notional principal of $250 million and a current market value of −$2 million
   (b) A four-year interest rate swap with a notional principal of $100 million and a current value of $3.5 million
   (c) A six-month derivative on a commodity with a principal of $50 million that is currently worth $1 million.

11.7. What is the capital required in Problem 11.6 under Basel I assuming that the 1995 netting amendment applies?

11.8. All the transactions a bank has with a corporate client are loans to the client. What is the value to the bank of netting provisions in its master agreement with the client?

11.9. Explain why the final stage in the Basel II calculations for credit risk (IRB), market risk, and operational risk is to multiply by 12.5.

11.10. What is the difference between the trading book and the banking book for a bank? A bank currently has a loan of $10 million dollars to a corporate client. At the end of the life of the loan, the client would like to sell debt securities to the bank instead of borrowing. How does this potentially change affect the nature of the bank's regulatory capital calculations?

11.11. Under Basel I, banks do not like lending to highly creditworthy companies and prefer to help them issue debt securities. Why is this? Do you expect the banks' attitude to this type of lending to change under Basel II?

11.12. Banks sometimes use what is referred to as regulatory arbitrage to reduce their capital. What do you think this means?

11.13. Equation (11.9) gives the formula for the capital required under Basel II. It involves four terms being multiplied together. Explain each of these terms.

11.14. Explain the difference between the simple and the comprehensive approach for adjusting capital requirements for collateral.

11.15. Explain the difference between the standardized approach, the IRB approach, and the advanced IRB approach for calculating credit risk capital under Basel II.

11.16. Explain the difference between the basic indicator approach, the standardized approach, and the advanced measurement approach for calculating operational risk capital under Basel II.

11.17. Suppose that the assets of a bank consist of $200 million of retail loans (not mortgages). The PD is 1% and the LGD is 70%. What are the risk-weighted assets under the Basel II IRB approach? What are the Tier 1 and Tier 2 capital requirements.

11.18. Section 8.8 discusses how statistics can be used to accept or reject a VaR model. Section 11.6 discusses guidelines for bank supervisors in setting the VaR multiplier k. It explains that, if the number of exceptions in 250 trials is 5 or more, then k is increased. What is the chance of 5 or more exceptions if the VaR model is working well?

FURTHER QUESTIONS

11.19. Why is there an add-on amount in Basel I for derivatives transactions? "Basel I could be improved if the add-on amount for a derivatives transaction depended on the value of the transaction." How would you argue this viewpoint?

11.20. Estimate the capital required under Basel I for a bank that has the following transactions with another bank (assume no netting):
(a) A two-year forward contract on a foreign currency, currently worth $2 million, to buy foreign currency worth $50 million
(b) A long position in a six-month option on the S&P 500, with a principal of $20 million and a current value of $4 million
(c) A two-year swap involving oil, with a principal of $30 million and a current value of −$5 million.

What difference does it make if the netting amendment applies?

11.21. A bank has the following transaction with a AA-rated corporation:
(a) A two-year interest rate swap with a principal of $100 million that is worth $3 million
(b) A nine-month foreign exchange forward contract with a principal of $150 million that is worth −$5 million
(c) A long position in a six-month option on gold, with a principal of $50 million that is worth $7 million.

What is the capital requirement under Basel I if there is no netting? What difference does it make if the netting amendment applies? What is the capital required under Basel II when the standardized approach is used?

11.22. Suppose that the assets of a bank consist of $500 million of loans to BBB-rated corporations. The PD for the corporations is estimated as 0.3%. The average maturity is three years and the LGD is 60%. What are the risk-weighted assets for credit risk under the Basel II advanced IRB approach? What are the Tier 1 and Tier 2 capital requirements? How does this compare with the capital required under the Basel II standardized approach and under Basel I?

12

Market Risk VaR: The Historical Simulation Approach

In this chapter and the next, we cover the two main approaches to calculating VaR for market risk. The approach we consider in this chapter is known as historical simulation and is the one usually used by banks. It involves using the day-to-day changes in the values of market variables that have been observed in the past in a direct way to estimate the probability distribution of the change in the value of the current portfolio between today and tomorrow.

After describing the mechanics of the historical simulation approach, the chapter explains how to calculate the standard error of the VaR estimate, how the procedure can be modified so that recent data are given more weight, and how volatility data can be incorporated into the VaR estimates that are made. Finally, it covers extreme value theory. This is a tool that can be used to improve VaR estimates and deal with situations where the required VaR confidence level is very high.

All the models covered in this chapter are illustrated with a portfolio consisting of an investment in four different stock indices. Historical data on the indices and VaR calculations can be found at www.rotman.utoronto.ca/~hull/VaRExample.

12.1 THE METHODOLOGY

Historical simulation involves using past data as a guide to what will happen in the future. Suppose that we want to calculate VaR for a portfolio using a one-day time horizon, a 99% confidence level, and 501 days of data. (The time horizon and confidence level are those typically used for a market risk VaR calculation; 501 is a popular choice for the number of days of data used because, as we shall see, it leads to 500 scenarios being created.) The first step is to identify the market variables affecting the portfolio. These will typically be exchange rates, equity prices, interest rates, and so on. Data are then collected on movements in these market variables over the most recent 501 days. This provides 500 alternative scenarios for what can happen between today and tomorrow. Denote the first day for which we have data as Day 0, the second day as Day 1, and so on. Scenario 1 is where the percentage changes in the values of all

249

variables are the same as they were between Day 0 and Day 1, Scenario 2 is where they are the same as between Day 1 and Day 2, and so on. For each scenario, the dollar change in the value of the portfolio between today and tomorrow is calculated. This defines a probability distribution for daily loss (gains are negative losses) in the value of our portfolio. The 99th percentile of the distribution can be estimated as the fifth-worst loss.[1] The estimate of VaR is the loss when we are at this 99th percentile point. We are 99% certain that we will not take a loss greater than the VaR estimate if the changes in market variables in the last 500 days are representative of what will happen between today and tomorrow.

To express the approach algebraically, define v_i as the value of a market variable on Day i and suppose that today is Day n. The ith scenario in the historical simulation approach assumes that the value of the market variable tomorrow will be

$$\text{Value under }i\text{th scenario} = v_n \frac{v_i}{v_{i-1}} \tag{12.1}$$

Illustration

To illustrate the calculations underlying the approach, suppose that an investor owns, on September 25, 2008, a portfolio worth $10 million consisting of investments in four stock indices: the Dow Jones Industrial Average (DJIA) in the US, the FTSE 100 in the UK, the CAC 40 in France, and the Nikkei 225 in Japan. The value of the investment in each index on September 25, 2008, is shown in Table 12.1. An Excel spreadsheet containing 501 days of historical data on the closing prices of the four indices and a complete set of VaR calculations are on the author's website: www.rotman.utoronto.ca/~hull/VaRExample.[2] An extract from this data is shown in Table 12.2.

September 25, 2008, is an interesting date to choose in evaluating an equity investment. The turmoil in credit markets, which started in August 2007, was over a year old.

Table 12.1 Investment portfolio used for VaR calculations.

Index	Portfolio value ($000s)
DJIA	$4,000
FTSE 100	$3,000
CAC 40	$1,000
Nikkei 225	$2,000
Total	$10,000

---

[1] There are alternatives here. A case can be made for using the fifth-worst loss, the sixth-worst loss, or an average of the two. In Excel's PERCENTILE function, when there are n observations and k is an integer, the $k/(n-1)$ percentile is the observation ranked $k+1$. Other percentiles are calculated using linear interpolation.

[2] To keep the example as straightforward as possible, only days when all four indices traded were included in the compilation of the data. This is why the 501 items of data extend from August 7, 2006 to September 25, 2008. In practice, if the analysis were carried out by a US financial institution, an attempt might well be made to fill in data for days that were not US holidays.

Table 12.2 Data on stock indices for historical simulation calculation.

Day	Date	DJIA	FTSE 100	CAC 40	Nikkei 225
0	Aug. 7, 2006	11,219.38	5,828.8	4,956.34	15,154.06
1	Aug. 8, 2006	11,173.59	5,818.1	4,967.95	15,464.66
2	Aug. 9, 2006	11,076.18	5,860.5	5,025.15	15,656.59
3	Aug. 10, 2006	11,124.37	5,823.4	4,976.64	15,630.91
⋮	⋮	⋮	⋮	⋮	⋮
499	Sept. 24, 2008	10,825.17	5,095.6	4,114.54	12,115.03
500	Sept. 25, 2008	11,022.06	5,197.0	4,226.81	12,006.53

Equity prices had been declining for several months. Volatilities were increasing. Lehman Brothers had filed for bankruptcy ten days earlier. The Treasury Secretary's $700 billion Troubled Asset Relief Program (TARP) had not yet been passed by the United States Congress.

Table 12.3 shows the values of the market variables on September 26, 2008, for the scenarios considered. Scenario 1 (the first row in Table 12.3) shows the values of market variables on September 26, 2008, assuming that their percentage changes between September 25 and September 26, 2008, are the same as they were between August 7 and August 8, 2006; Scenario 2 (the second row in Table 12.3) shows the values of market variables on September 26, 2008, assuming these percentage changes are the same as those between August 8 and August 9, 2006; and so on. In general, Scenario i assumes that the percentage changes in the indices between September 25 and September 26 are the same as they were between Day $i - 1$ and Day i for $1 \leqslant i \leqslant 500$. The 500 rows in Table 12.3 are the 500 scenarios considered.

The DJIA was 11,022.06 on September 25, 2008. On August 8, 2006, it was 11,173.59, down from 11,219.38 on August 7, 2006. Therefore the value of the DJIA under Scenario 1 is

$$11,022.06 \times \frac{11,173.59}{11,219.38} = 10,977.08$$

Similarly, the values of the FTSE 100, the CAC 40, and the Nikkei 225 are 5,187.46,

Table 12.3 Scenarios generated for September 26, 2008, using data in Table 12.2.

Scenario number	DJIA	FTSE 100	CAC 40	Nikkei 225	Portfolio value ($000s)	Loss ($000s)
1	10,977.08	5,187.46	4,236.71	12,252.62	10,021.502	−21.502
2	10,925.97	5,234.87	4,275.48	12,155.54	10,023.327	−23.327
3	11,070.01	5,164.10	4,186.01	11,986.84	9,985.478	14.522
⋮	⋮	⋮	⋮	⋮	⋮	
499	10,831.43	5,057.36	4,117.75	12,030.80	9,828.450	171.550
500	11,222.53	5,300.42	4,342.14	11,899.00	10,141.826	−141.826

4,236.71, and 12,252.62, respectively. Therefore the value of the portfolio under Scenario 1 is (in $000s)

$$4,000 \times \frac{10,977.08}{11,022.06} + 3,000 \times \frac{5,187.46}{5,197.0}$$

$$+ 1,000 \times \frac{4,236.71}{4,226.81} + 2,000 \times \frac{12,252.62}{12,006.53} = 10,021.502$$

The portfolio therefore has a gain of $21,502 under Scenario 1. A similar calculation is carried out for the other scenarios. A histogram for the losses is shown in Figure 12.1. (The bars on the histogram represent losses ($000s) in the ranges 450 to 550, 350 to 450, 250 to 350, and so on.)

The losses for the 500 different scenarios are then ranked. An extract from the results of doing this is shown in Table 12.4. The worst scenario is number 494 (where indices are assumed to change in the same way that they did at the time of the bankruptcy of Lehman Brothers). The one-day 99% value at risk can be estimated as the fifth-worst loss. This is $247,571.

As explained in Section 11.6, the ten-day 99% VaR is usually calculated as $\sqrt{10}$ times the one-day 99% VaR. In this case the ten-day VaR would therefore be

$$\sqrt{10} \times 247,571 = 782,889$$

or $782,889.

Each day the VaR estimate in our example would be updated using the most recent 501 days of data. Consider, for example, what happens on September 26, 2008

Figure 12.1 Histogram of losses for the scenarios considered between September 25 and September 26, 2008.

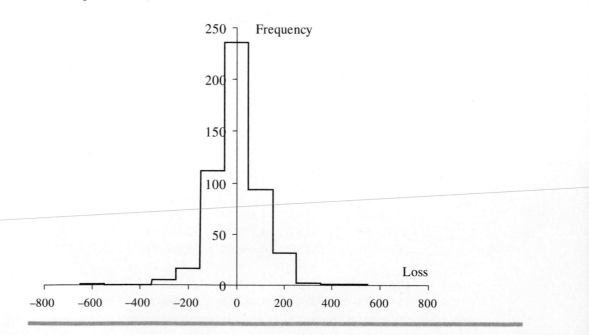

Table 12.4 Losses ranked from highest to lowest for 500 scenarios.

Scenario number	Loss ($000s)
494	499.395
339	359.440
329	341.366
299	251.943
487	247.571
131	241.712
227	230.265
495	227.332
441	225.051
376	217.945
306	211.797
365	202.970
242	200.116
238	199.467
477	188.758
⋮	⋮

(Day 501). We find out new values for all the market variables and are able to calculate a new value for our portfolio. We then go through the procedure we have outlined to calculate a new VaR. Data on the market variables from August 8, 2006, to September 26, 2008 (Day 1 to Day 501) are used in the calculation. (This gives us the required 500 observations on the percentage changes in market variables; the August 7, 2006, Day 0, values of the market variables are no longer used.) Similarly, on the next trading day September 29, 2008 (Day 502), data from August 9, 2006, to September 29, 2008 (Day 2 to Day 502) are used to determine VaR, and so on.

In practice, a bank's portfolio is, of course, considerably more complicated than the one we have considered here. It is likely to consist of thousands or tens of thousands of positions. Some of the bank's positions are typically in forward contracts, options, and other derivatives. A procedure known as *partial simulation*, which will be described in Section 13.8, is sometimes used to speed up the valuations for the scenarios. If a bank's trading leads to a riskier portfolio, the ten-day 99% VaR typically increases; if it leads to a less risky portfolio, the VaR typically decreases. The VaR on any given day is calculated on the assumption that the portfolio will remain unchanged over the next business day.

The market variables that have to be considered in a VaR calculation include exchange rates, commodity prices, and interest rates. In the case of interest rates, a bank typically needs the Treasury and LIBOR/swap term structure of zero-coupon interest rates in a number of different currencies in order to value its portfolio. The market variables that are considered are the ones from which these term structures are calculated (see Appendix B). There might be as many as ten market variables for each zero curve to which the bank is exposed.

12.2 ACCURACY

The historical simulation approach estimates the distribution of portfolio changes from a finite number of observations. As a result, the estimates of quantiles of the distribution are subject to error.

Kendall and Stuart describe how to calculate a confidence interval for the quantile of a probability distribution when it is estimated from sample data.[3] Suppose that the q-quantile of the distribution is estimated as x. The standard error of the estimate is

$$\frac{1}{f(x)} \sqrt{\frac{(1-q)q}{n}}$$

where n is the number of observations and $f(x)$ is an estimate of the probability density function of the loss evaluated at x. The probability density $f(x)$ can be determined by fitting the empirical data to an appropriate standard distribution.

Example 12.1

Suppose we are interested in estimating the 0.99 quantile (= the 99th percentile) of a loss distribution from 500 observations, so that $n = 500$ and $q = 0.99$. We can estimate $f(x)$ by approximating the actual empirical distribution with a standard distribution. Suppose that a normal distribution is chosen as the standard distribution and the best-fit mean and standard deviation are 0 and \$10 million, respectively. Using Excel, the 0.99 quantile is NORMINV(0.99,0,10), or 23.26. The value of $f(x)$ is NORMDIST(23.26,0,10,FALSE), or 0.0027. The standard error of the estimate that is made is

$$\frac{1}{0.0027} \times \sqrt{\frac{0.01 \times 0.99}{500}} = 1.67$$

If the estimate of the 0.99 quantile using historical simulation is \$25 million, a 95% confidence interval is from $25 - 1.96 \times 1.67$ to $25 + 1.96 \times 1.67$, that is, from \$21.7 million to \$28.3 million.

As Example 12.1 illustrates, the standard error of a VaR estimated using historical simulation tends to be quite high. It decreases as the VaR confidence level is decreased. For example, if in Example 12.1 the VaR confidence level had been 95% instead of 99%, the standard error would be \$0.95 million instead of \$1.67 million. The standard error declines as the sample size is increased—but only as the square root of the sample size. If we quadrupled the sample size in Example 12.1 from 500 to 2000 observations, the standard error halves from \$1.67 million to about \$0.83 million.

Additionally, we should bear in mind that historical simulation assumes that the joint distribution of daily changes in market variables is stationary through time. This is unlikely to be exactly true and creates additional uncertainty about VaR.

In the case of the data considered in Tables 12.1 to 12.4, when the loss is measured in \$000s, the mean is 1.280 and the standard deviation is \$97.555. If a normal distribution

---

[3] See M. G. Kendall and A. Stuart, *The Advanced Theory of Statistics, Vol. 1: Distribution Theory*, 4th edn. London: Charles Griffin and Co., 1972.

is assumed, a calculation similar to that in Example 12.1 gives $f(x)$ as 0.0002732, and the standard error of the estimate (in $000s) is

$$\frac{1}{0.0002732} \times \sqrt{\frac{0.01 \times 0.99}{500}} = 16.287$$

The VaR is $247,257. This shows that a 95% confidence interval for the VaR is about $215,000 to $280,000.

The normal distribution is not a particularly good assumption for the loss distribution, because the losses have heavier tails than the normal distribution. (The excess kurtosis is 4.2 for the loss distribution and zero for a normal distribution.) For a more sophisticated analysis, $f(x)$ could be estimated assuming a Pareto distribution, as will be discussed later in this chapter.

12.3 EXTENSIONS

The key assumption underlying the historical simulation approach is that the history is in some sense a good guide to the future. More precisely, it is that the empirical probability distribution estimated for a market variables over the last few years is a good guide to the behavior of the market variables over the next day. Unfortunately, the behavior of market variables is nonstationary. Sometimes the volatility of a market variable is high; sometimes it is low. In this section we cover extensions of the basic historical simulation approach in Section 12.1 that are designed to adjust for nonstationarity.

Weighting of Observations

The basic historical simulation approach assumes that each day in the past is given equal weight. More formally, if we have observations for n day-to-day changes, each of them is given a weighting of $1/n$. Boudoukh *et al.* suggest that more recent observations should be given more weight because they are more reflective of current volatilities and current macroeconomic conditions.[4] The natural weighting scheme to use is one where weights decline exponentially. (We used this in Section 9.6 when developing the exponentially weighted moving average model for monitoring volatility.) The weight assigned to Scenario 1 (which is the one calculated from the most distant data) is λ times that assigned to Scenario 2. This in turn is λ times that given to Scenario 3, and so on. So that the weights add up to 1, the weight given to Scenario i is

$$\frac{\lambda^{n-i}(1 - \lambda)}{1 - \lambda^n}$$

where n is the number of scenarios. As λ approaches 1, this approaches the basic historical simulation approach where all observations are given a weight of $1/n$ (see Problem 12.2).

---

[4] See J. Boudoukh, M. Richardson, and R. Whitelaw, "The Best of Both Worlds: A Hybrid Approach to Calculating Value at Risk," *Risk*, 11 (May 1998): 64–67.

Table 12.5 Losses ranked from highest to lowest for 500 scenarios with weights.

Scenario number	Loss ($000s)	Weight	Cumulative weight
494	499.395	0.00528	0.00528
339	359.440	0.00243	0.00771
329	341.366	0.00231	0.01002
299	251.943	0.00255	0.01258
487	247.571	0.00510	0.01768
131	241.712	0.00086	0.01853
227	230.265	0.00139	0.01992
495	227.332	0.00531	0.02523
441	225.051	0.00405	0.02928
⋮	⋮	⋮	⋮

VaR is calculated by ranking the observations from the worst outcome to the best. Starting at the worst outcome, weights are summed until the required quantile of the distribution is reached. For example, if we are calculating be VaR with a 99% confidence level, we continue summing weights until the sum just exceeds 0.01. We have then reached the 99% VaR level. The parameter λ can be chosen by experimenting to see which value back-tests best. One disadvantage of the exponential weighting approach relative to the basic historical simulation approach is that the effective sample size is reduced. However, we can compensate for this by using a larger value of n. Indeed, it is not really necessary to discard old days as we move forward in time, because they are given relatively little weight.

Table 12.5 show the results of using this procedure for the portfolio considered in Section 12.1 with $\lambda = 0.995$. The VaR when the confidence level is 99% is now the third-worst loss, $341,366 (not the fifth-worst loss of $247,571). The reason for this result is that recent observations are given more weight and the largest losses have occurred relatively recently. The standard calculation in Section 12.1 gives all observations a weighting of $1/500 = 0.002$. The highest loss occurred on Scenario 494 and this scenario has a weight of

$$\frac{(0.995^6) \times 0.005}{1 - 0.995^{500}} = 0.00528$$

Incorporating Volatility Updating

Hull and White suggest a way of incorporating volatility updating into the historical simulation approach.[5] A volatility-updating procedure, such as EWMA or GARCH(1,1) (both of which were described in Chapter 9) is used in parallel with the historical simulation approach for all market variables. Suppose that the daily volatility for a particular market variable estimated at the end of day $i - 1$ is σ_i. This is an estimate of the daily volatility between the end of day $i - 1$ and the end of day i.

---

[5] See J. Hull and A. White, "Incorporating Volatility Updating into the Historical Simulation Method for Value at Risk," *Journal of Risk*, Fall 1998: 5–19.

Suppose that it is now day n. The current estimate of the volatility of the market variable is σ_{n+1}. This applies to the time period between today and tomorrow, which is the time period over which we are calculating VaR.

Suppose that σ_{n+1} is twice σ_i. This means that we estimate the daily volatility of this particular market variable to be twice as great today as on day $i-1$. This means that we expect to see changes between today and tomorrow that are twice as big as changes between day $i-1$ and day i. When carrying out the historical simulation and creating a sample of what could happen between today and tomorrow based on what happened between day $i-1$ and day i, it therefore makes sense to multiply the latter by 2. In general, when this approach is used, the expression in equation (12.1) for the value of a market variable under the ith scenario becomes

$$\text{Value under } i\text{th scenario} = v_n \frac{v_{i-1} + (v_i - v_{i-1})\sigma_{n+1}/\sigma_i}{v_{i-1}} \qquad (12.2)$$

Each market variable is handled in the same way.

This approach takes account of volatility changes in a natural and intuitive way and produces VaR estimates that incorporate more current information. The VaR estimates can be greater than any of the historical losses that would have occurred for the current portfolio during the historical period considered. Hull and White produce evidence using exchange rates and stock indices to show that this approach is superior to traditional historical simulation and to the exponential weighting scheme described earlier. More complicated models can be developed, where observations are adjusted for the latest information on correlations as well as for the latest information on volatilities.

For the data in Table 12.2, the daily volatility estimates, calculated using a value of λ equal to 0.94, are shown in Table 12.6.[6] The ratios of the volatility estimated for September 26, 2008 (last row of table) to the volatility estimated for August 8, 2008 (first row of table) are 2.00, 2.34, 2.23, and 1.40 for DJIA, FTSE 100, CAC 40, and Nikkei 225, respectively. These are used as multipliers for the actual changes in the indices between August 7 and August 8, 2006. Similarly, the ratios of the volatility estimated for September 26, 2008 (last row of table) to the volatility estimated for

---

Table 12.6 Volatilities (% per day) estimated for the following day using EWMA with $\lambda = 0.94$.

Day	Date	DJIA	FTSE 100	CAC 40	Nikkei 225
0	Aug. 7, 2006	1.11	1.29	1.34	1.47
1	Aug. 8, 2006	1.08	1.25	1.30	1.51
2	Aug. 9, 2006	1.07	1.22	1.29	1.50
3	Aug. 10, 2006	1.04	1.19	1.28	1.45
⋮	⋮	⋮	⋮	⋮	⋮
499	Sept. 24, 2008	2.24	3.03	3.02	2.12
500	Sept. 25, 2008	2.21	3.01	3.00	2.06

---

[6] A decision must be made on how to start the variance time series. Any reasonable approach can be used. It makes little difference to the results that are obtained. The initial variance for the calculations reported here was the sample variance calculated over the whole time period.

Table 12.7 Volatility-adjusted losses ranked
from highest to lowest for 500 scenarios.

Scenario number	Loss ($000s)
131	1310.556
494	807.535
329	695.186
227	693.314
339	601.767
441	538.778
74	499.981
193	492.333
292	465.708
⋮	⋮

August 9, 2008 (second row of table) are 2.05, 2.41, 2.30, and 1.36 for DJIA, FTSE 100, CAC 40, and Nikkei 225, respectively. These are used as multipliers for the actual changes in the indices between August 8 and August 9, 2006. Multipliers for the other 498 daily changes are calculated in the same way.

Because volatilities were highest at the end of the historical period, the effect of the volatility adjustments is to create more variability in the gains and losses for the 500 scenarios. Table 12.7 shows an extract from a table that ranks losses from the highest to the lowest. Comparing this with Table 12.4, we see that the losses are much higher. The one-day 99% VaR is $601,767, over twice as high as the VaR given by the standard calculations.

In this particular case, the volatility of the stock indices remained high for the rest of 2008, with daily changes of between 5% and 10% in the indices being not uncommon. Estimating VaR using the volatility-adjusted approach would have worked better than using the standard approach.

Bootstrap Method

The bootstrap method is a variation on the basic historical simulation approach, aimed at calculating a confidence interval. It involves creating a set of changes in the portfolio value based on historical movements in market variables in the usual way. We then sample with replacement from these changes to create many new similar data sets. We calculate the VaR for each of the new data sets. Our 95% confidence interval for VaR is the range between the 2.5 percentile point and the 97.5 percentile point of the distribution of the VaRs calculated from the data sets.

Suppose, for example, that we have 500 days of data. We could sample with replacement 500,000 times from the data to obtain 1,000 different sets of 500 days of data. We calculate the VaR for each set. We then rank the VaRs. Suppose that the 25th largest VaR is $5.3 million and the 975th largest VaR is $8.9 million. The 95% confidence limit for VaR is $5.3 million to $8.9 million. Usually the 95% confidence range calculated for VaR using the bootstrap method is less than that calculated using the procedure in Section 12.2.

12.4 EXTREME VALUE THEORY

Section 9.4 introduced the power law and explained that it can be used to estimate the tails of a wide range of distributions. We now provide the theoretical underpinnings for the power law and present estimation procedures more sophisticated than those used in Section 9.4. *Extreme value theory* (EVT) is the term used to describe the science of estimating the tails of a distribution. EVT can be used to improve VaR estimates and to help in situations where analysts want to estimate VaR with a very high confidence level. It is a way of smoothing and extrapolating the tails of an empirical distribution.

The Key Result

The key result in EVT was proved by Gnedenko in 1943.[7] It shows that the tails of a wide range of different probability distributions share common properties.

Suppose that $F(v)$ is the cumulative distribution function for a variable v (such as the loss on a portfolio over a certain period of time) and that u is a value of v in the right-hand tail of the distribution. The probability that v lies between u and $u + y$ ($y > 0$) is $F(u + y) - F(u)$. The probability that v is greater than u is $1 - F(u)$. Define $F_u(y)$ as the probability that v lies between u and $u + y$ conditional on $v > u$. This is

$$F_u(y) = \frac{F(u + y) - F(u)}{1 - F(u)}$$

The variable $F_u(y)$ defines the right tail of the probability distribution. It is the cumulative probability distribution for the amount by which v exceeds u given that it does exceed u.

Gnedenko's result states that, for a wide class of distributions $F(v)$, the distribution of $F_u(y)$ converges to a generalized Pareto distribution as the threshold u is increased. The generalized Pareto (cumulative) distribution is

$$G_{\xi,\beta}(y) = 1 - \left(1 + \xi\frac{y}{\beta}\right)^{-1/\xi} \tag{12.3}$$

The distribution has two parameters that have to be estimated from the data. These are ξ and β. The parameter ξ is the shape parameter and determines the heaviness of the tail of the distribution. The parameter β is a scale parameter.

When the underlying variable v has a normal distribution, the parameter $\xi = 0$.[8] As the tails of the distribution become heavier, the value of ξ increases. For most financial data, ξ is positive and in the range 0.1 to 0.4.[9]

Estimating ξ and β

The parameters ξ and β can be estimated using maximum likelihood methods (see Section 9.9 for a discussion of maximum likelihood methods). The probability density

---

[7] D. V. Gnedenko, "Sur la distribution limité du terme d'une série aléatoire," *Ann. Math.*, 44 (1943): 423–453.

[8] When $\xi = 0$, the generalized Pareto distribution becomes $G_{\xi,\beta}(y) = 1 - \exp(-y/\beta)$.

[9] One of the properties of the distribution in equation (12.3) is that the kth moment $E(v^k)$ of v is infinite for $k \geqslant 1/\xi$. For a normal distribution, all moments are finite. When $\xi = 0.25$, only the first three moments are finite; when $\xi = 0.5$, only the first moment is finite; and so on.

function $g_{\xi,\beta}(y)$ of the cumulative distribution in equation (12.3) is calculated by differentiating $G_{\xi,\beta}(y)$ with respect to y. It is

$$g_{\xi,\beta}(y) = \frac{1}{\beta}\left(1 + \frac{\xi y}{\beta}\right)^{-1/\xi - 1}$$

We first choose a value for u (a value close to the 95 percentile point of the empirical distribution usually works well). We then rank the observations on v from the highest to the lowest and focus our attention on those observations for which $v > u$. Suppose there are n_u such observations and they are v_i $(1 \leqslant i \leqslant n_u)$. The likelihood function (assuming that $\xi \neq 0$) is

$$\prod_{i=1}^{n_u} \frac{1}{\beta}\left(1 + \frac{\xi(v_i - u)}{\beta}\right)^{-1/\xi - 1}$$

Maximizing this function is the same as maximizing its logarithm:

$$\sum_{i=1}^{n_u} \ln\left[\frac{1}{\beta}\left(1 + \frac{\xi(v_i - u)}{\beta}\right)^{-1/\xi - 1}\right] \tag{12.4}$$

Standard numerical procedures can be used to find the values of ξ and β that maximize this expression. Excel's Solver produces good results.

Estimating the Tail of the Distribution

The probability that $v > u + y$ conditional on $v > u$ is $1 - G_{\xi,\beta}(y)$. The probability that $v > u$ is $1 - F(u)$. The unconditional probability that $v > x$ $(x > u)$ is therefore

$$[1 - F(u)][1 - G_{\xi,\beta}(x - u)]$$

If n is the total number of observations, an estimate of $1 - F(u)$, calculated from the empirical data, is n_u/n. The unconditional probability that $v > x$ is therefore

$$\text{Prob}(v > x) = \frac{n_u}{n}[1 - G_{\xi,\beta}(x - u)] = \frac{n_u}{n}\left(1 + \xi\frac{x - u}{\beta}\right)^{-1/\xi} \tag{12.5}$$

Equivalence to the Power Law

If we set $u = \beta/\xi$, equation (12.5) reduces to

$$\text{Prob}(v > x) = \frac{n_u}{n}\left(\frac{\xi x}{\beta}\right)^{-1/\xi}$$

This is

$$Kx^{-\alpha}$$

where

$$K = \frac{n_u}{n}\left(\frac{\xi}{\beta}\right)^{-1/\xi}$$

and $\alpha = 1/\xi$. This shows that equation (12.5) is consistent with the power law introduced in Section 9.4.

The Left Tail

The analysis so far has assumed that we are interested in the right tail of the probability distribution of a variable v. If we are interested in the left tail of the probability distribution, we can work with $-v$ instead of v. Suppose, for example, that an oil company has collected data on daily percentage increases in the price of oil and wants to estimate a VaR that is the one-day percentage decline in the price of oil that has a 99.9% probability of not being exceeded. This is a statistic calculated from the left tail of the probability distribution of oil price increases. The oil company would change the sign of each data item (so that the data was measuring oil price decreases rather than increases) and then use the methodology that has been presented.

Calculation of VaR and Expected Shortfall

To calculate VaR with a confidence level of q, it is necessary to solve the equation

$$F(\text{VaR}) = q$$

From equation (12.5), we have

$$q = 1 - \frac{n_u}{n}\left(1 + \xi\frac{\text{VaR} - u}{\beta}\right)^{-1/\xi}$$

so that

$$\text{VaR} = u + \frac{\beta}{\xi}\left[\left(\frac{n}{n_u}(1 - q)\right)^{-\xi} - 1\right] \tag{12.6}$$

The expected shortfall (see Section 8.3) is given by

$$\text{Expected shortfall} = \frac{\text{VaR} + \beta - \xi u}{1 - \xi} \tag{12.7}$$

12.5 APPLICATIONS

Consider again the data in Tables 12.1 to 12.4. When $u = 200$, it can be seen from Table 12.4 that $n_u = 13$ (i.e., there are 13 scenarios where the loss in $000s is greater than 200). Table 12.8 shows calculations for the trial values $\beta = 40$ and $\xi = 0.3$. The value of the log-likelihood function in equation (12.4) is -66.98.

When Excel's Solver is used to search for the values of β and ξ that maximize the log-likelihood function, it gives

$$\beta = 43.526, \quad \xi = 0.371$$

and the maximum value of the log-likelihood function is -66.88.[10]

Suppose that we wish to estimate the probability that the portfolio loss between September 25 and September 26, 2008, will be more that $300,000 (or 3% of its value). From equation (12.5), this is

$$\frac{13}{500}\left(1 + 0.371 \times \frac{300 - 200}{43.526}\right)^{-1/0.371} = 0.0049$$

---

[10] As mentioned in Section 9.9, the Solver routine works best when the spreadsheet is set up so that the values being searched for are similar in magnitude.

Table 12.8 Extreme value theory calculations for Table 12.4: $u = 200$, $\beta = 40$, $\xi = 0.3$.

Scenario number	Loss ($000s)	Rank	$\ln\left[\dfrac{1}{\beta}\left(1 + \dfrac{\xi(v_i - u)}{\beta}\right)^{-1/\xi - 1}\right]$
494	499.395	1	−8.79
339	359.440	2	−7.10
329	341.366	3	−6.82
299	251.943	4	−5.11
487	247.571	5	−5.01
131	241.712	6	−4.87
227	230.265	7	−4.58
495	227.332	8	−4.50
441	225.051	9	−4.43
376	217.945	10	−4.24
306	211.797	11	−4.06
365	202.970	12	−3.78
242	200.116	13	−3.69
Total			−66.98

Trial estimates of EVT parameters

ξ	β
0.3	40

This is more accurate than counting observations. The probability that the portfolio loss will be more than $500,000 (or 5% of its value) is similarly 0.00085.

From equation (12.6), the value of VaR with a 99% confidence limit is

$$200 + \frac{43.526}{0.371}\left[\left(\frac{500}{13}(1 - 0.99)\right)^{-0.371} - 1\right] = 249.9$$

or $249,900. (In this instance, the VaR estimate is fairly close to the fifth-worst loss. This is not always the case.) When the confidence level is increased to 99.9%, VaR becomes

$$200 + \frac{43.526}{0.371}\left[\left(\frac{500}{13}(1 - 0.999)\right)^{-0.371} - 1\right] = 475.8$$

or $475,800.

The formula in equation (12.7) can provide a useful application of EVT because it is often difficult to estimate expected shortfall directly with any accuracy. In our example, when the confidence level is 99%, the expected shortfall is

$$\frac{249.9 + 43.526 - 0.371 \times 200}{1 - 0.371} = 348.5$$

or \$348,500. When the confidence level is 99.9%, the expected shortfall is

$$\frac{475.8 + 43.526 - 0.371 \times 200}{1 - 0.371} = 707.7$$

or \$707,700.

EVT can also be used in a straightforward way in conjunction with the volatility-updating procedure in Section 12.3 (see Problem 12.11). It can also be used in conjunction with the weighting-of-observations procedure in Section 12.3. In this case, the terms being summed in equation (12.4) must be multiplied by the weights applicable to the underlying observations.

A final calculation can be used to refine the confidence level for the 99% VaR estimate in Section 12.2. From equation (12.4), the probability density function evaluated at the VaR level for the probability distribution of the loss, conditional on it being greater than 200, is

$$0.01 \times \frac{1}{43.526}\left(1 + \frac{0.371 \times (249{,}900 - 200{,}000)}{43.526}\right)^{-1/0.371-1} = 0.0062$$

The unconditional probability density function evaluated at the VaR level is $n_u/n = 13/500$ times this, or 0.00016. This can be used as the $f(x)$ estimate in Section 12.2. It leads to the confidence interval for VaR increasing by about 70%.

Choice of u

A natural question is: how do the results depend on the choice of u? It is often found that values of ξ and β do depend on u, but the estimates of $F(x)$ remain roughly the same. (Problem 12.10 considers what happens when u is changed from 200 to 175 in the example we have been considering.) We want u to be sufficiently high that we are truly investigating the shape of the tail of the distribution, but sufficiently low that the number of data items included in the maximum likelihood calculation is not too low. More data lead to more accuracy in the assessment of the shape of the tail. We have applied the procedure with 500 data items. Ideally more data would be used.

A rule of thumb is that u should be approximately equal to the 95th percentile of the empirical distribution. (In the case of the data we have been looking at, the 95th percentile of the empirical distribution is 168.6.) In the search for the optimal values of ξ and β, both variables should be constrained to be positive. If the optimizer tries to set ξ negative, it is likely to be a sign that either (a) the tail of the distribution is not heavier than the normal distribution or (b) an inappropriate value of u has been chosen.

SUMMARY

Historical simulation is a very popular approach for estimating VaR. It involves creating a database consisting of the daily movements in all market variables over a period of time. The first simulation trial assumes that the percentage change in each market variable is the same as that on the first day covered by the database, the second simulation trial assumes that the percentage changes are the same as those on the second day, and so on. The change in the portfolio value is calculated for each simulation trial, and VaR is calculated as the appropriate percentile of the probability distribution of this change. The standard error for a VaR that is estimated using historical simulation tends to be quite high. The higher the VaR confidence level required, the higher the standard error.

There are a number of extensions of the basic historical simulation approach. The weights given to observations can be allowed to decrease exponentially as the observations become older. Volatility updating procedures can be used to take account of differences between the volatilities of market variables today and their volatilities at different times during the period covered by the historical data.

Extreme value theory is a way of smoothing the tails of the probability distribution of portfolio daily changes calculated using historical simulation. It leads to estimates of VaR that reflect the whole shape of the tail of the distribution, not just the positions of a few losses in the tails. Extreme value theory can also be used to estimate VaR when the VaR confidence level is very high. For example, even if we have only 500 days of data, it could be used to come up with an estimate of VaR for a VaR confidence level of 99.9%.

FURTHER READING

Boudoukh, J., M. Richardson, and R. Whitelaw, "The Best of Both Worlds," *Risk*, May 1998: 64–67.

Embrechts, P., C. Kluppelberg, and T. Mikosch, *Modeling Extremal Events for Insurance and Finance*. New York: Springer, 1997.

Hendricks, D., "Evaluation of Value-at-Risk Models Using Historical Data," *Economic Policy Review*, Federal Reserve Bank of New York, Vol. 2 (April 1996): 39–69.

Hull, J.C., and A. White, "Incorporating Volatility Updating into the Historical Simulation Method for Value at Risk," *Journal of Risk*, 1, 1 (1998): 5–19.

McNeil, A.J., "Extreme Value Theory for Risk Managers," in: *Internal Modeling and CAD II*. London: Risk Books, 1999. See also www.math.ethz.ch/~mcneil.

Neftci, S.N., "Value at Risk Calculations, Extreme Events and Tail Estimation," *Journal of Derivatives*, 7, 3 (Spring 2000): 23–38.

PRACTICE QUESTIONS AND PROBLEMS (Answers at the End of the Book)

12.1. What assumptions are being made when VaR is calculated using the historical simulation approach and 500 days of data?

12.2. Show that, when λ approaches 1, the weighting scheme in Section 12.3 approaches the basic historical simulation approach.

12.3. Suppose we estimate the one-day 95% VaR from 1,000 observations as $5 million. By fitting a standard distribution to the observations, the probability density function of the loss distribution at the 95% point is estimated to be 0.01. What is the standard error of the VaR estimate?

12.4. The one-day 99% VaR is calculated in Section 12.1 as $247,571. Look at the underlying spreadsheets on the author's website and calculate: (a) the one-day 95% VaR and (b) the one-day 97% VaR.

12.5. Use the spreadsheets on the author's website to calculate the one-day 99% VaR, using the basic methodology in Section 12.1, if the portfolio in Section 12.1 is equally divided between the four indices.

12.6. The "weighting-of-observations" procedure in Section 12.3 gives the one-day 99% VaR equal to $341,336 for the example considered. Use the spreadsheets on the author's website to calculate the one-day 99% VaR when the λ parameter in this procedure is changed from 0.995 to 0.99.

12.7. The "volatility updating" procedure in Section 12.3 gives the one-day 99% VaR equal to $601,767 for the example considered. Use the spreadsheets on the author's website to calculate the one-day 99% VaR when the λ parameter in this procedure is changed from 0.94 to 0.96.

12.8. In the application of EVT in Section 12.4, what is the probability that the loss will exceed $400,000?

12.9. In the application of EVT in Section 12.4, what is the one-day VaR with a confidence level of 97%?

12.10. Change u from 200 to 175 in the application of EVT in Section 12.4. How does this change the maximum likelihood estimates of ξ and β? How does it change the one-day 99% VaR when the confidence limit is (a) 99% and (b) 99.9%?

12.11. Carry out an extreme value theory analysis on the data from the volatility-updating procedure in Table 12.8 and on the author's website. Use $u = 400$. What are the best-fit values of ξ and β? Calculate the one-day 99% VaR with a 99% and 99.9% confidence level. What is the probability of a loss greater than $600,000?

FURTHER QUESTIONS

12.12. Suppose that a one-day 97.5% VaR is estimated as $13 million from 2,000 observations. The one-day changes are approximately normal with mean 0 and standard deviation $6 million. Estimate a 99% confidence interval for the VaR estimate.

12.13. Suppose that the portfolio considered in Section 12.1 has (in $000s) 3,000 in DJIA, 3,000 in FTSE, 1,000 in CAC 40 and 3,000 in Nikkei 225. Use the spreadsheet on the author's website to calculate what difference this makes to:
(a) The one-day 99% VaR that is calculated in Section 12.1
(b) The one-day 99% VaR that is calculated using the weighting-of-observations procedure in Section 12.3
(c) The one-day 99% VaR that is calculated using the volatility-updating procedure in Section 12.3
(d) The one-day 99% VaR that is calculated using extreme value theory in Section 12.4

12.14. Investigate the effect of applying extreme value theory to the volatility-adjusted results in Section 12.3, with $u = 350$.

12.15. The "weighting-of-observations" procedure in Section 12.3 gives the one-day 99% VaR equal to \$341,336. Use the spreadsheets on the author's website to calculate the one-day 99% VaR when the λ parameter in this procedure is changed from 0.995 to 0.985.

12.16. The "volatility-updating" procedure in Section 12.3 gives the one-day 99% VaR equal to \$601,767. Use the spreadsheets on the author's website to calculate the one-day 99% VaR when the λ parameter in this procedure is changed from 0.94 to 0.92.

12.17. Values for the NASDAQ composite index during the 1,500 days preceding March 10, 2006, can be downloaded from the author's website. Calculate the one-day 99% VaR on March 10, 2006, for a \$10 million portfolio invested in the index using:

(a) The basic historical simulation approach

(b) The exponential weighting scheme in Section 12.3 with $\lambda = 0.995$

(c) The volatility-updating procedure in Section 12.3 with $\lambda = 0.94$ (assume that the volatility is initially equal to the standard deviation of daily returns calculated from the whole sample)

(d) Extreme value theory with $u = 0.03$

(e) A model where daily returns are assumed to be normally distributed (use both constant weights and the EWMA approach with $\lambda = 0.94$ to estimate the standard deviation of daily returns)

Discuss the reasons for the differences between the results you get.

13

Market Risk VaR: The Model-Building Approach

An alternative to the historical simulation approach that is sometimes used by portfolio managers is what is known as the *model-building approach*, sometimes also referred to as the *variance–covariance approach*. This involves assuming a model for the joint distribution of changes in market variables and using historical data to estimate the model parameters.

The model-building approach is ideally suited to a portfolio consisting of long and short positions in stocks, bonds, commodities, and other products. It is based on Harry Markowitz's pioneering work in portfolio theory (see Section 1.1). The mean and standard deviation of the value of a portfolio can be calculated from the mean and standard deviation of the returns on the underlying products and the correlations between those returns. If, and it is a big if, daily returns on the investments are assumed to be multivariate normal, the probability distribution for the change in the value of the portfolio over one day is also normal. This makes it very easy to calculate value at risk.

As we shall see, the model-building approach is much more difficult to use when a portfolio involves nonlinear products such as options. It is also difficult to relax the assumption that returns are normal without a big increase in computation time.

13.1 THE BASIC METHODOLOGY

We start by considering how VaR is calculated using the model-building approach in a very simple situation where the portfolio consists of a position in a single stock. The portfolio we consider is one consisting of shares in Microsoft valued at $10 million. We suppose that the time horizon is ten days and the VaR confidence level is 99%, so that we are interested in the loss level over ten days that we are 99% confident will not be exceeded. Initially, we consider a one-day time horizon.

We assume that the volatility of Microsoft is 2% per day (corresponding to about 32% per year).[1] Because the size of the position is $10 million, the standard deviation of daily changes in the value of the position is 2% of $10 million, or $200,000.

---

[1] As discussed in Section 9.1, in VaR calculations volatility is usually measured per day, whereas in option pricing it is measured per year. A volatility per day can be converted to a volatility per year by multiplying by $\sqrt{252}$, or about 16.

It is customary in the model-building approach to assume that the expected change in a market variable over the time period considered is zero. This is not exactly true, but it is a reasonable assumption. The expected change in the price of a market variable over a short time period is generally small when compared to the standard deviation of the change. Suppose, for example, that Microsoft has an expected return of 20% per annum. Over a one-day period, the expected return is 0.20/252, or about 0.08%, whereas the standard deviation of the return is 2%. Over a ten-day period, the expected return is 0.08×10, or about 0.8%, whereas the standard deviation of the return is $2\sqrt{10}$, or about 6.3%.

So far, we have established that the change in the value of the portfolio of Microsoft shares over a one-day period has a standard deviation of $200,000 and (at least approximately) a mean of zero. We assume that the change is normally distributed.[2] Since $N(-2.33) = 0.01$, this means that there is a 1% probability that a normally distributed variable will decrease in value by more than 2.33 standard deviations. Equivalently, it means that we are 99% certain that a normally distributed variable will not decrease in value by more than 2.33 standard deviations. The one-day 99% VaR for our portfolio consisting of a $10 million position in Microsoft is therefore

$$2.33 \times 200,000 = \$466,000$$

Assuming that the changes in Microsoft's stock price on successive days are independent, the N-day VaR is calculated as $\sqrt{N}$ times the one-day VaR. The ten-day 99% VaR for Microsoft is therefore

$$466,000 \times \sqrt{10} = \$1,473,621$$

Consider next a portfolio consisting of a $5 million position in AT&T, and suppose the daily volatility of AT&T is 1% (approximately 16% per year). A similar calculation to that for Microsoft shows that the standard deviation of the change in the value of the portfolio in one day is

$$5,000,000 \times 0.01 = 50,000$$

Assuming that the change is normally distributed, the one-day 99% VaR is

$$50,000 \times 2.33 = \$116,500$$

and the ten-day 99% VaR is

$$116,500 \times \sqrt{10} = \$368,405$$

Two-Asset Case

Now consider a portfolio consisting of both $10 million of Microsoft shares and $5 million of AT&T shares. We suppose that the returns on the two shares have a bivariate normal distribution with a correlation of 0.3. A standard result in statistics tells us that, if two variables X and Y have standard deviations equal to σ_X and σ_Y with the coefficient of correlation between them being equal to ρ, then the standard deviation of $X + Y$ is given by

$$\sigma_{X+Y} = \sqrt{\sigma_X^2 + \sigma_Y^2 + 2\rho\sigma_X\sigma_Y}$$

[2] We could assume that the price of Microsoft is lognormal tomorrow. Because one day is such a short period of time, this is almost indistinguishable from the assumption we do make—that the change in the stock price between today and tomorrow is normal.

To apply this result, we set X equal to the change in the value of the position in Microsoft over a one-day period and Y equal to the change in the value of the position in AT&T over a one-day period, so that

$$\sigma_X = 200{,}000, \qquad \sigma_Y = 50{,}000$$

The standard deviation of the change in the value of the portfolio consisting of both stocks over a one-day period is therefore

$$\sqrt{200{,}000^2 + 50{,}000^2 + 2 \times 0.3 \times 200{,}000 \times 50{,}000} = 220{,}227$$

The mean change is assumed to be zero. The change is normally distributed. (This is because of the bivariate normal assumption.) So the one-day 99% VaR is therefore

$$220{,}227 \times 2.33 = \$513{,}129$$

The ten-day 99% VaR is $\sqrt{10}$ times this or \$1,622,657.

The Benefits of Diversification

In the example we have just considered:

1. The ten-day 99% VaR for the portfolio of Microsoft shares is \$1,473,621.
2. The ten-day 99% VaR for the portfolio of AT&T shares is \$368,405.
3. The ten-day 99% VaR for the portfolio of both Microsoft and AT&T shares is \$1,622,657.

The amount
$$(1{,}473{,}621 + 368{,}405) - 1{,}622{,}657 = \$219{,}369$$

represents the benefits of diversification. If Microsoft and AT&T were perfectly correlated, the VaR for the portfolio of both Microsoft and AT&T would equal the VaR for the Microsoft portfolio plus the VaR for the AT&T portfolio. Less than perfect correlation leads to some of the risk being "diversified away".[3]

13.2 GENERALIZATION

The examples we have just considered are simple illustrations of the use of the linear model for calculating VaR. Suppose that we have a portfolio worth P consisting of n assets with an amount α_i being invested in asset i ($1 \leqslant i \leqslant n$). Define Δx_i as the return on asset i in one day. The dollar change in the value of our investment in asset i in one day is $\alpha_i \, \Delta x_i$ and

$$\Delta P = \sum_{i=1}^{n} \alpha_i \, \Delta x_i \tag{13.1}$$

where ΔP is the dollar change in the value of the whole portfolio in one day.

---

[3] As discussed in Section 8.4, VaR does not always reflect the benefits of diversification. For nonnormal distributions, the VaR of two portfolios considered jointly can be greater than the sum of their VaRs.

In the example considered in the previous section, \$10 million was invested in the first asset (Microsoft) and \$5 million was invested in the second asset (AT&T), so that (in millions of dollars) $\alpha_1 = 10$, $\alpha_2 = 5$, and

$$\Delta P = 10\Delta x_1 + 5\Delta x_2$$

If we assume that the Δx_i in equation (13.1) are multivariate normal, then ΔP is normally distributed. To calculate VaR, we therefore need to calculate only the mean and standard deviation of ΔP. We assume, as discussed in the previous section, that the expected value of each Δx_i is zero. This implies that the mean of ΔP is zero.

To calculate the standard deviation of ΔP, we define σ_i as the daily volatility of the ith asset and ρ_{ij} as the coefficient of correlation between returns on asset i and asset j.[4] This means that σ_i is the standard deviation of Δx_i, and ρ_{ij} is the coefficient of correlation between Δx_i and Δx_j. The variance of ΔP, which we will denote by σ_P^2, is given by

$$\sigma_P^2 = \sum_{i=1}^{n} \sum_{j=1}^{n} \rho_{ij} \alpha_i \alpha_j \sigma_i \sigma_j \qquad (13.2)$$

This equation can also be written as

$$\sigma_P^2 = \sum_{i=1}^{n} \alpha_i^2 \sigma_i^2 + 2 \sum_{i=1}^{n} \sum_{j<i} \rho_{ij} \alpha_i \alpha_j \sigma_i \sigma_j$$

The standard deviation of the change over N days is $\sigma_P\sqrt{N}$, and the 99% VaR for an N-day time horizon is $2.33\sigma_P\sqrt{N}$.

The portfolio return in one day is $\Delta P/P$. From equation (13.2), the variance of this is

$$\sum_{i=1}^{n} \sum_{j=1}^{n} \rho_{ij} w_i w_j \sigma_i \sigma_j$$

where $w_i = \alpha_i/P$ is the weight of the ith investment in the portfolio. This result was produced by Markowitz in 1952 (see Chapter 1).

In the example considered in the previous section, $\sigma_1 = 0.02$, $\sigma_2 = 0.01$, and $\rho_{12} = 0.3$. As already noted, $\alpha_1 = 10$ and $\alpha_2 = 5$, so that

$$\sigma_P^2 = 10^2 \times 0.02^2 + 5^2 \times 0.01^2 + 2 \times 10 \times 5 \times 0.3 \times 0.02 \times 0.01 = 0.0485$$

and $\sigma_P = 0.220$. This is the standard deviation of the change in the portfolio value per day (in millions of dollars). The ten-day 99% VaR is $2.33 \times 0.220 \times \sqrt{10} = \$1.623$ million. This agrees with the calculation in the previous section.

13.3 CORRELATION AND COVARIANCE MATRICES

A correlation matrix is a matrix where the entry in the ith row and jth column is the correlation ρ_{ij} between variable i and j. It is shown in Table 13.1. Since a variable is always perfectly correlated with itself, the diagonal elements of the correlation matrix

---

[4] The ρ_{ij} are sometimes calculated using a factor model. See Section 10.3.

Table 13.1   A correlation matrix: ρ_{ij} is the correlation between variable i and variable j.

$$
\begin{bmatrix}
1 & \rho_{12} & \rho_{13} & \cdots & \rho_{1n} \\
\rho_{21} & 1 & \rho_{23} & \cdots & \rho_{2n} \\
\rho_{31} & \rho_{32} & 1 & \cdots & \rho_{3n} \\
\vdots & \vdots & \vdots & \vdots & \vdots \\
\rho_{n1} & \rho_{n2} & \rho_{n3} & \cdots & 1
\end{bmatrix}
$$

are 1. Furthermore, because $\rho_{ij} = \rho_{ji}$, the correlation matrix is symmetric. The correlation matrix, together with the daily standard deviations of the variables, enables the portfolio variance to be calculated using equation (13.2).

Instead of working with correlations and volatilities, analysts often use variances and covariances. The daily variance var_i of variable i is the square of its daily volatility:

$$\text{var}_i = \sigma_i^2$$

The covariance cov_{ij} between variable i and variable j is the product of the daily volatility of variable i, the daily volatility of variable j, and the correlation between i and j:

$$\text{cov}_{ij} = \sigma_i \sigma_j \rho_{ij}$$

The equation for the variance of the portfolio in equation (13.2) can be written

$$\sigma_P^2 = \sum_{i=1}^{n} \sum_{j=1}^{n} \text{cov}_{ij} \, \alpha_i \alpha_j \tag{13.3}$$

In a *covariance matrix*, the entry in the ith row and jth column is the covariance between variable i and variable j. As just mentioned, the covariance between a variable and itself is its variance. The diagonal entries in the matrix are therefore variances (see Table 13.2). For this reason, the covariance matrix is sometimes called the *variance–covariance matrix*. (Like the correlation matrix, it is symmetric.) Using matrix notation, the equation for the standard deviation of the portfolio in equation (13.3) becomes

$$\sigma_P^2 = \boldsymbol{\alpha}^\mathsf{T} C \boldsymbol{\alpha}$$

Table 13.2   A variance–covariance matrix: cov_{ij} is the covariance between variable i and variable j. Diagonal entries are variance: $\text{cov}_{ii} = \text{var}_i$.

$$
\begin{bmatrix}
\text{var}_1 & \text{cov}_{12} & \text{cov}_{13} & \cdots & \text{cov}_{1n} \\
\text{cov}_{21} & \text{var}_2 & \text{cov}_{23} & \cdots & \text{cov}_{2n} \\
\text{cov}_{31} & \text{cov}_{32} & \text{var}_3 & \cdots & \text{cov}_{3n} \\
\vdots & \vdots & \vdots & \vdots & \vdots \\
\text{cov}_{n1} & \text{cov}_{n2} & \text{cov}_{n3} & \cdots & \text{var}_n
\end{bmatrix}
$$

Table 13.3 Correlation matrix with same weight for all data: variable 1 is DJIA; variable 2 is FTSE 100; variable 3 is CAC 40; variable 4 is Nikkei 225.

$$
\begin{bmatrix}
1 & 0.534 & 0.569 & 0.124 \\
0.534 & 1 & 0.926 & 0.402 \\
0.569 & 0.926 & 1 & 0.409 \\
0.124 & 0.402 & 0.409 & 1
\end{bmatrix}
$$

where $\boldsymbol{\alpha}$ is the (column) vector whose ith element is α_i, C is the variance–covariance matrix, and $\boldsymbol{\alpha}^{\mathrm{T}}$ is the transpose of $\boldsymbol{\alpha}$.

The variances and covariances are generally calculated from historical data. One approach is to calculate them in the standard way by giving equal weight to all data. Another is to use the exponentially weighted moving average method. In this case, the same λ should be used for all calculations in order to ensure a positive-semidefinite matrix (see Section 10.2 for a discussion of the positive-semidefinite condition). GARCH methods can also be used, but ensuring consistency so that a positive-semidefinite matrix is produced is then more complicated.

Example Involving Four Investments

We now return to the example considered in Chapter 12. This involved a portfolio on September 25, 2008, consisting of a \$4 million investment in the Dow Jones Industrial Average, a \$3 million investment in the FTSE 100, a \$1 million investment in the CAC 40, and a \$2 million investment in the Nikkei 225. Daily returns were collected over 500 days ending on September 25, 2008. Data and all calculations presented here are on: www.rotman.utoronto.ca/~hull/VaRExample.

The correlation matrix, when calculations are carried out in the usual way with the same weight for all 500 returns, is shown in Table 13.3. The FTSE 100 and CAC 40 are very highly correlated. The Dow Jones Industrial Average is moderately highly correlated with both the FTSE 100 and the CAC 40. The correlation of the Nikkei 225 with other indices is less high. The covariance matrix is in Table 13.4.

From equation (13.3) this variance–covariance matrix gives the variance of the portfolio losses (\$000s) as 9,498.014. The standard deviation is the square root of this, or 97.46. The one-day 99% VaR is therefore $2.33 \times 97.46 = 226{,}721$, or \$226,721. This

Table 13.4 Covariance matrix with same weight for all data: variable 1 is DJIA; variable 2 is FTSE 100; variable 3 is CAC 40; variable 4 is Nikkei 225.

$$
\begin{bmatrix}
0.0001227 & 0.0000760 & 0.0000845 & 0.0000202 \\
0.0000760 & 0.0001649 & 0.0001594 & 0.0000757 \\
0.0000845 & 0.0001594 & 0.0001795 & 0.0000804 \\
0.0000202 & 0.0000757 & 0.0000804 & 0.0002156
\end{bmatrix}
$$

Table 13.5 Covariance matrix when EWMA with $\lambda = 0.94$ is used: variable 1 is DJIA; variable 2 is FTSE 100; variable 3 is CAC 40; variable 4 is Nikkei 225.

$$
\begin{bmatrix}
0.0004896 & 0.0004324 & 0.0004379 & 0.0000763 \\
0.0004324 & 0.0009006 & 0.0008801 & 0.0004202 \\
0.0004379 & 0.0008801 & 0.0008986 & 0.0003902 \\
0.0000763 & 0.0004202 & 0.0003902 & 0.0004232
\end{bmatrix}
$$

compares with \$247,571, calculated using the basic historical simulation approach in Chapter 12.

Use of EWMA

Instead of calculating variances and covariances by giving equal weight to all observed returns, we now use the exponentially weighted moving average method with $\lambda = 0.94$. This gives the variance–covariance matrix in Table 13.5.[5] From equation (13.3), the variance of portfolio losses (\$000s) is 45,570.235. The standard deviation is the square root of this, or 213.472. The one-day 99% VaR is therefore

$$2.33 \times 213.472 = 496.610$$

or \$496,610. This is over twice as high as the value given when returns are equally weighted. Tables 13.6 and 13.7 show the reasons. The standard deviation of a portfolio

Table 13.6 Volatilities (% per day) using equal weighting and EWMA.

	DJIA	FTSE 100	CAC 40	Nikkei 225
Equal weighting:	1.11	1.28	1.34	1.47
EWMA:	2.21	3.01	3.00	2.06

Table 13.7 Correlation matrix when EWMA method is used: variable 1 is DJIA; variable 2 is FTSE 100; variable 3 is CAC 40; variable 4 is Nikkei 225.

$$
\begin{bmatrix}
1 & 0.649 & 0.660 & 0.168 \\
0.649 & 1 & 0.975 & 0.678 \\
0.660 & 0.975 & 1 & 0.633 \\
0.168 & 0.678 & 0.633 & 1
\end{bmatrix}
$$

---

[5] In the EWMA calculations, the variance is initially set equal to the population variance. But all reasonable starting variances give essentially the same result because in this case all we are interested in is the final variance.

consisting of long positions in securities increases with the standard deviations of security returns and also with the correlations between security returns. Table 13.6 shows that the estimated daily standard deviations are much higher when EWMA is used than when data are equally weighted. This is because volatilities were much higher during the period immediately preceding September 25, 2008, than during the rest of the 500 days covered by the data. Comparing Table 13.7 with Table 13.3, we see that correlations had also increased.[6]

13.4 HANDLING INTEREST RATES

It is out of the question to define a separate market variable for every single bond price or interest rate to which a company is exposed. Some simplifications are necessary when the model-building approach is used. One possibility is to assume that only parallel shifts in the yield curve occur. It is then necessary to define only one market variable: the size of the parallel shift. The changes in the value of bond portfolio can then be calculated using the approximate duration relationship in equation (7.6):

$$\Delta P = -DP\,\Delta y$$

where P is the value of the portfolio, ΔP is the change in P in one day, D is the modified duration of the portfolio, and Δy is the parallel shift in one day. This approach gives a linear relationship between ΔP and Δy, but does not usually give enough accuracy because the relationship is not exact and it does not take account of nonparallel shifts in the yield curve.

The procedure usually followed is to choose as market variables the prices of zero-coupon bonds with standard maturities: 1 month, 3 months, 6 months, 1 year, 2 years, 5 years, 7 years, 10 years, and 30 years. For the purposes of calculating VaR, the cash flows from instruments in the portfolio are mapped into cash flows occurring on the standard maturity dates.

Consider a $1 million position in a Treasury bond lasting 0.8 years that pays a coupon of 10% semiannually. A coupon is paid in 0.3 years and 0.8 years and the principal is paid in 0.8 years. This bond is therefore, in the first instance, regarded as a $50,000 position in 0.3-year zero-coupon bond plus a $1,050,000 position in a 0.8-year zero-coupon bond. The position in the 0.3-year bond is then replaced by an equivalent position in 3-month and 6-month zero-coupon bonds, and the position in the 0.8-year bond is replaced by an equivalent position in 6-month and 1-year zero-coupon bonds. The result is that the position in the 0.8-year coupon-bearing bond is for VaR purposes regarded as a position in zero-coupon bonds having maturities of 3 months, 6 months, and 1 year. This procedure is known as *cash-flow mapping*.

Illustration of Cash-Flow Mapping

We now illustrate how cash-flow mapping works by continuing with the example we have just introduced. It should be emphasized that the procedure we use is just one of several that have been proposed.

---

[6] This is an example of the phenomenon that correlations tend to increase in adverse market conditions.

Table 13.8 Data to illustrate cash-flow mapping procedure.

	3 months	6 months	1 year
Zero rate (% with annual compounding):	5.50	6.00	7.00
Bond price volatility (% per day):	0.06	0.10	0.20

Correlation between daily returns

	3-month bond	6-month bond	1-year bond
3-month bond	1.0	0.9	0.6
6-month bond	0.9	1.0	0.7
1-year bond	0.6	0.7	1.0

Consider first the $1,050,000 that will be received in 0.8 years. We suppose that zero rates, daily bond price volatilities, and correlations between bond returns are as shown in Table 13.8. The first stage is to interpolate between the 6-month rate of 6.0% and the 1-year rate of 7.0% to obtain a 0.8-year rate of 6.6%. (Annual compounding is assumed for all rates.) The present value of the $1,050,000 cash flow to be received in 0.8 years is

$$\frac{1,050,000}{1.066^{0.8}} = 997,662$$

We also interpolate between the 0.1% volatility for the 6-month bond and the 0.2% volatility for the 1-year bond to get a 0.16% volatility for the 0.8-year bond.

Suppose we allocate α of the present value to the 6-month bond and the remaining $1 - \alpha$ to the 1-year bond. Using equation (13.2) and matching variances, we obtain

$$0.0016^2 = 0.001^2\alpha^2 + 0.002^2(1 - \alpha)^2 + 2 \times 0.7 \times 0.001 \times 0.002\alpha(1 - \alpha)$$

This is a quadratic equation that can be solved in the usual way to give $\alpha = 0.320337$. This means that 32.0337% of the value should be allocated to a 6-month zero-coupon bond and 67.9663% of the value should be allocated to a 1-year zero-coupon bond. The 0.8-year bond worth $997,662 is therefore replaced by a 6-month bond worth

$$997,662 \times 0.320337 = \$319,589$$

and a 1-year bond worth

$$997,662 \times 0.679663 = \$678,074$$

This cash-flow mapping scheme has the advantage that it preserves both the value and the variance of the cash flow. Also, it can be shown that the weights assigned to the two adjacent zero-coupon bonds are always positive.

For the $50,000 cash flow received at 0.3 years, we can carry out similar calculations (see Problem 13.7). It turns out that the present value of the cash flow is $49,189. This can be mapped to a position worth $37,397 in a 3-month bond and a position worth $11,793 in a 6-month bond.

The results of the calculations are summarized in Table 13.9. The 0.8-year coupon-bearing bond is mapped to a position worth $37,397 in a 3-month bond, a position worth $331,382 in a 6-month bond, and a position worth $678,074 in a 1-year bond.

Table 13.9   The cash-flow mapping result.

	$50,000 received in 0.3 years	$1,050,000 received in 0.8 years	Total
Position in 3-month bond ($)	37,397		37,397
Position in 6-month bond ($)	11,793	319,589	331,382
Position in 1-year bond ($)		678,074	678,074

Using the volatilities and correlations in Table 13.9, equation (13.2) gives the variance of the change in the price of the 0.8-year bond with $n = 3$, $\alpha_1 = 37{,}397$, $\alpha_2 = 331{,}382$, $\alpha_3 = 678{,}074$; $\sigma_1 = 0.0006$, $\sigma_2 = 0.001$, $\sigma_3 = 0.002$; and $\rho_{12} = 0.9$, $\rho_{13} = 0.6$, $\rho_{23} = 0.7$. This variance is 2,628,518. The standard deviation of the change in the price of the bond, therefore, is $\sqrt{2{,}628{,}518} = 1{,}621.3$. Since we are assuming that the bond is the only instrument in the portfolio, the 10-day 99% VaR is

$$1{,}621.3 \times \sqrt{10} \times 2.33 = 11{,}946$$

or about $11,950.

Principal Components Analysis

As we explained in Section 7.8, a principal components analysis (PCA) can be used to reduce the number of deltas that are calculated for movements in a zero-coupon yield curve. A PCA can also be used (in conjunction with cash-flow mapping) to handle interest rates when VaR is calculated using the model-building approach. For any given portfolio, we can convert a set of delta exposures, such as those given in Table 7.9, into a delta exposure to the first PCA factor, a delta exposure to the second PCA factor, and so on. The way this is done is explained in Section 7.8. Consider the data in Table 13.10. These are the same as in Table 7.9. In Section 7.8, the exposure to the first factor for these data is calculated as -0.08 and the exposure to the second factor is calculated as -4.40. (The first two factors capture over 90% of the variation in interest rates.)

Suppose that f_1 and f_2 are the factor scores. The change in the portfolio value is approximately

$$\Delta P = -0.08 f_1 - 4.40 f_2$$

The factor scores in a PCA are uncorrelated. From Table 7.8 the standard deviations of the first two factors are 17.49 and 6.05. The standard deviation of ΔP, therefore, is

$$\sqrt{0.08^2 \times 17.49^2 + 4.40^2 \times 6.05^2} = 26.66$$

Table 13.10   Change in portfolio value for a 1-basis-point rate move ($ millions).

1-year rate	2-year rate	3-year rate	4-year rate	5-year rate
+10	+4	−8	−7	+2

The 1-day 99% VaR is therefore $26.66 \times 2.33 = 62.12$. Note that the portfolio we are considering has very little exposure to the first factor and significant exposure to the second factor. Using only one factor would significantly understate VaR (see Problem 13.9). The duration-based method for handling interest rates would also significantly understate VaR in this case as it considers only parallel shifts in the yield curve.

13.5 APPLICATIONS OF THE LINEAR MODEL

The simplest application of the linear model is to a portfolio with no derivatives consisting of positions in stocks, bonds, foreign exchange, and commodities. In this case, the change in the value of the portfolio is linearly dependent on the percentage changes in the prices of the assets that make up the portfolio. Note that, for the purposes of VaR calculations, all asset prices are measured in the domestic currency. The market variables considered by a large bank in the United States are therefore likely to include the value of the Nikkei 225 index measured in dollars, the price of a 10-year sterling zero-coupon bond measured in dollars, and so on.

Examples of derivatives that can be handled by the linear model are forward contracts on foreign exchange and interest rate swaps. Suppose a forward foreign exchange contract matures at time T. It can be regarded as the exchange of a foreign zero-coupon bond maturing at time T for a domestic zero-coupon bond maturing at time T. For the purposes of calculating VaR, the forward contract is therefore treated as a long position in the foreign bond combined with a short position in the domestic bond. (As just mentioned, the foreign bond is valued in the domestic currency.) Each bond can be handled using a cash-flow mapping procedure, so that it is a linear combination of bonds with standard maturities.

Consider next an interest rate swap. This can be regarded as the exchange of a floating-rate bond for a fixed-rate bond. The fixed-rate bond is a regular coupon-bearing bond (see Appendix D). The floating-rate bond is worth par just after the next payment date. It can be regarded as a zero-coupon bond with a maturity date equal to the next payment date. The interest rate swap, therefore, reduces to a portfolio of long and short positions in bonds and can be handled using a cash-flow mapping procedure.

13.6 LINEAR MODEL AND OPTIONS

We now consider how the linear model can be used when there are options. Consider first a portfolio consisting of options on a single stock whose current price is S. Suppose that the delta of the position (calculated in the way described in Chapter 6) is δ.[7] Because δ is the rate of change of the value of the portfolio with S, it is approximately true that

$$\delta = \frac{\Delta P}{\Delta S}$$

---

[7] In Chapter 6 we denote the delta and gamma of a portfolio by Δ and Γ. In this section and the next, we use the lowercase Greek letters δ and γ to avoid overworking Δ.

or

$$\Delta P = \delta \, \Delta S \tag{13.4}$$

where ΔS is the dollar change in the stock price in one day and ΔP is, as usual, the dollar change in the portfolio in one day. We define Δx as the return on the stock in one day, so that

$$\Delta x = \frac{\Delta S}{S}$$

It follows that an approximate relationship between ΔP and Δx is

$$\Delta P = S \delta \, \Delta x$$

When we have a position in several underlying market variables that includes options, we can derive an approximate linear relationship between ΔP and the Δx_i similarly. This relationship is

$$\Delta P = \sum_{i=1}^{n} S_i \delta_i \, \Delta x_i \tag{13.5}$$

where S_i is the value of the ith market variable and δ_i is the delta of the portfolio with respect to the ith market variable. This is equation (13.1) with $\alpha_i = S_i \delta_i$:

$$\Delta P = \sum_{i=1}^{n} \alpha_i \, \Delta x_i \tag{13.6}$$

Equation (13.6) can therefore be used to calculate the standard deviation of ΔP.

Example 13.1

A portfolio consists of options on Microsoft and AT&T. The options on Microsoft have a delta of 1,000, and the options on AT&T have a delta of 20,000. The Microsoft share price is $120, and the AT&T share price is $30. From equation (13.5), it is approximately true that

$$\Delta P = 120 \times 1,000 \times \Delta x_1 + 30 \times 20,000 \times \Delta x_2$$

or

$$\Delta P = 120,000 \Delta x_1 + 600,000 \Delta x_2$$

where Δx_1 and Δx_2 are the returns from Microsoft and AT&T in one day and ΔP is the resultant change in the value of the portfolio. (The portfolio is assumed to be equivalent to an investment of $120,000 in Microsoft and $600,000 in AT&T.) Assuming that the daily volatility of Microsoft is 2% and that of AT&T is 1%, and that the correlation between the daily changes is 0.3, the standard deviation of ΔP (in $000s) is

$$\sqrt{(120 \times 0.02)^2 + (600 \times 0.01)^2 + 2 \times 120 \times 0.02 \times 600 \times 0.01 \times 0.3} = 7.099$$

Since $N(-1.65) = 0.05$, the 5-day 95% VaR is

$$1.65 \times \sqrt{5} \times 7,099 = \$26,193$$

Figure 13.1 Probability distribution for value of portfolio: (a) positive gamma; (b) negative gamma.

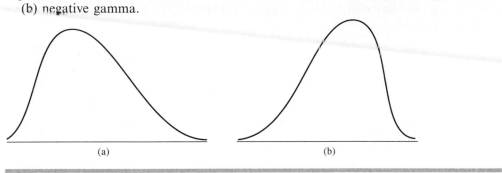

(a)   (b)

Weakness of Model

When a portfolio includes options, the linear model is an approximation. It does not take account of the gamma of the portfolio. As discussed in Chapter 6, delta is defined as the rate of change of the portfolio value with respect to an underlying market variable and gamma is defined as the rate of change of the delta with respect to the market variable. Gamma measures the curvature of the relationship between the portfolio value and an underlying market variable.

Figure 13.1 shows the impact of a nonzero gamma on the probability distribution of the value of the portfolio. When gamma is positive, the probability distribution tends to be positively skewed; when gamma is negative, it tends to be negatively skewed. Figures 13.2 and 13.3 illustrate the reason for this result. Figure 13.2 shows the

Figure 13.2 Translation of normal probability distribution for an asset into probability distribution for value of a long call on that asset.

Figure 13.3 Translation of normal probability distribution for an asset into probability distribution for value of a short call on that asset.

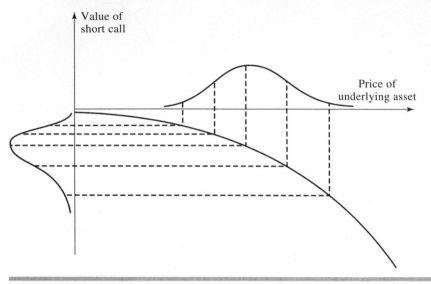

relationship between the value of a long call option and the price of the underlying asset. A long call is an example of an option position with positive gamma. The figure shows that, when the probability distribution for the price of the underlying asset at the end of one day is normal, the probability distribution for the option price is positively skewed.[8] Figure 13.3 shows the relationship between the value of a short call position and the price of the underlying asset. A short call position has a negative gamma. In this case, we see that a normal distribution for the price of the underlying asset at the end of one day gets mapped into a negatively skewed distribution for the value of the option position.

The VaR for a portfolio is critically dependent on the left tail of the probability distribution of the portfolio value. For example, when the confidence level used is 99%, the VaR is the value in the left tail below which only 1% of the distribution resides. As indicated in Figures 13.1(a) and 13.2, a positive gamma portfolio tends to have a less heavy left tail than the normal distribution. If the distribution is assumed to be normal, the calculated VaR will tend to be too high. Similarly, as indicated in Figures 13.1(b) and 13.3, a negative gamma portfolio tends to have a heavier left tail than the normal distribution. If the distribution is assumed to be normal, the calculated VaR will tend to be too low.

13.7 QUADRATIC MODEL

For a more accurate estimate of VaR than that given by the linear model, both delta and gamma measures can be used to relate ΔP to the Δx_i. Consider a portfolio dependent on a single asset whose price is S. Suppose δ and γ are the delta and gamma

---

[8] The normal distribution is a good approximation to the lognormal distribution for short time periods.

of the portfolio. As indicated in Chapter 6, a Taylor series expansion gives

$$\Delta P = \delta \, \Delta S + \tfrac{1}{2}\gamma(\Delta S)^2$$

as an improvement over the linear approximation $\Delta P - \delta \, \Delta S$.[9] Setting

$$\Delta x = \Delta S / S$$

reduces this to

$$\Delta P = S\delta \, \Delta x + \tfrac{1}{2}S^2\gamma(\Delta x)^2 \tag{13.7}$$

In this case, when Δx is assumed to be normal, we have

$$E(\Delta P) = 0.5S^2\gamma\sigma^2$$
$$E(\Delta P^2) = S^2\delta^2\sigma^2 + 0.75S^4\gamma^2\sigma^4$$
$$E(\Delta P^3) = 4.5S^4\delta^2\gamma\sigma^4 + 1.875S^6\gamma^3\sigma^6$$

where σ is the daily volatility of the variable.

For a portfolio with n underlying market variables, and with each instrument in the portfolio being dependent on only one of the market variables, equation (13.7) becomes

$$\Delta P = \sum_{i=1}^{n} S_i\delta_i \, \Delta x_i + \sum_{i=1}^{n} \tfrac{1}{2}S_i^2\gamma_i(\Delta x_i)^2$$

where S_i is the value of the ith market variable, and δ_i and γ_i are the delta and gamma of the portfolio with respect to the ith market variable. When some of the individual instruments in the portfolio are dependent on more than one market variable, this equation takes the more general form

$$\Delta P = \sum_{i=1}^{n} S_i\delta_i \, \Delta x_i + \sum_{i=1}^{n}\sum_{j=1}^{n} \tfrac{1}{2}S_iS_j\gamma_{ij} \, \Delta x_i\Delta x_j \tag{13.8}$$

where γ_{ij} is a "cross gamma" defined as

$$\gamma_{ij} = \partial^2 P / \partial S_i \partial S_j$$

Equation (13.8) is not as easy to work with as equation (13.6), but it can be used to calculate the first few moments of ΔP when the Δx_i are assumed to be multivariate normal, provided that n is not too large.

Cornish–Fisher Expansion

A result in statistics known as the Cornish–Fisher expansion can be used to estimate quantiles of a probability distribution from its moments. We illustrate this by showing how the first three moments can be used to produce a VaR estimate that takes account of

---

[9] A fuller Taylor series expansion suggests the approximation

$$\Delta P = \Theta \, \Delta t + \delta \, \Delta S + \tfrac{1}{2}\gamma(\Delta S)^2$$

when terms of higher order than Δt are ignored. In practice, the $\Theta \, \Delta t$ term is so small that it is usually ignored.

the skewness of ΔP. Define μ_P and σ_P as the mean and standard deviation of ΔP, so that

$$\mu_P = E(\Delta P) \quad \text{and} \quad \sigma_P^2 = E[(\Delta P)^2] - [E(\Delta P)]^2$$

The skewness ξ_P of the probability distribution of ΔP is defined as

$$\xi_P = \frac{1}{\sigma_P^3} E[(\Delta P - \mu_P)^3] = \frac{E[(\Delta P)^3] - 3E[(\Delta P)^2]\mu_P + 2\mu_P^3}{\sigma_P^3}$$

Using the first three moments of ΔP, the Cornish–Fisher expansion estimates the q-quantile of the distribution of ΔP as

$$\mu_P + w_q \sigma_P$$

where

$$w_q = z_q + \tfrac{1}{6}(z_q^2 - 1)\xi_P$$

and z_q is q-quantile of the standard normal distribution.

Example 13.2

Suppose that for a certain portfolio we calculate $\mu_P = -0.2$, $\sigma_P = 2.2$, and $\xi_P = -0.4$, and we are interested in the 0.01 quantile ($q = 0.01$). In this case, $z_q = -2.33$. If we assume that the probability distribution of ΔP is normal, then the 0.01 quantile is

$$-0.2 - 2.33 \times 2.2 = -5.326$$

In other words, we are 99% certain that

$$\Delta P > -5.326$$

Using the Cornish–Fisher expansion to adjust for skewness and setting $q = 0.01$, we obtain

$$w_q = -2.33 - \tfrac{1}{6}(2.33^2 - 1) \times 0.4 = -2.625$$

so that the 0.01 quantile of the distribution is

$$-0.2 - 2.625 \times 2.2 = -5.976$$

Taking account of skewness, therefore, changes the VaR from 5.326 to 5.976.

13.8 MONTE CARLO SIMULATION

As an alternative to the approaches described so far, we can implement the model-building approach using Monte Carlo simulation to generate the probability distribution for ΔP. Suppose we wish to calculate a 1-day VaR for a portfolio. The procedure is as follows:

1. Value the portfolio today in the usual way using the current values of market variables.

2. Sample once from the multivariate normal probability distribution of the Δx_i.[10]

---

[10] One way of doing so is given in Section 10.3.

3. Use the sampled values of the Δx_i to determine the value of each market variable at the end of one day.

4. Revalue the portfolio at the end of the day in the usual way.

5. Subtract the value calculated in Step 1 from the value in Step 4 to determine a sample ΔP.

6. Repeat Steps 2–5 many times to build up a probability distribution for ΔP.

The VaR is calculated as the appropriate percentile of the probability distribution of ΔP. Suppose, for example, that we calculate 5,000 different sample values of ΔP in the way just described. The 1-day 99% VaR is the value of ΔP for the 50th-worst outcome; the 1-day 95% VaR is the value of ΔP for the 250th-worst outcome; and so on.[11] The N-day VaR is usually assumed to be the 1-day VaR multiplied by $\sqrt{N}$.[12]

The drawback of Monte Carlo simulation is that it tends to be computationally slow because a company's complete portfolio (which might consist of hundreds of thousands of different instruments) has to be revalued many times.[13] One way of speeding things up is to assume that equation (13.8) describes the relationship between ΔP and the Δx_i. We can then jump straight from Step 2 to Step 5 in the Monte Carlo simulation and avoid the need for a complete revaluation of the portfolio. This is sometimes referred to as the *partial simulation approach*.

13.9 NONNORMAL ASSUMPTIONS

The approaches described so far in this chapter have assumed that the underlying market variables have a multivariate normal distribution. This is a serious weakness of the model-building approach. In practice, market variables have heavier tails than the normal distribution, so that the model-building approach tends to lead to VaR estimates that are too low.

When Monte Carlo simulation is used, there are ways of extending the model-building approach so that market variables are no longer assumed to be normal. One possibility is to assume that the variables have a multivariate t-distribution. As indicated by Figures 10.4 and 10.5, this has the effect of giving a higher value to the probability that extreme values for several variables occur simultaneously.

We can assume any set of distributions for the Δx_i in conjunction with a copula model.[14] Suppose, for example, that we assume a one-factor Gaussian copula model. As explained in Chapter 10, this means that, when the changes in market variables Δx_i are transformed on a percentile-to-percentile basis to normally distributed variables u_i, the u_i are multivariate normal. We can follow the five steps given earlier except that

---

[11] As in the case of historical simulation, extreme value theory can be used to "smooth the tails" so that better estimates of extreme percentiles are obtained.

[12] This is only approximately true when the portfolio includes options, but it is the assumption that is made in practice for most VaR calculation methods.

[13] An approach for limiting the number of portfolio revaluations is proposed in F. Jamshidian and Y. Zhu "Scenario Simulation Model: Theory and Methodology," *Finance and Stochastics*, 1 (1997): 43–67.

[14] See J. Hull and White, "Value at Risk When Daily Changes Are Not Normally Distributed," *Journal of Derivatives*, 5, 3 (Spring 1998): 9–19.

Step 2 is changed and a step is inserted between Steps 2 and 3 as follows:

2. Sample once from the multivariate probability distribution for the u_i.

2a. Transform each u_i to Δx_i on a percentile-to-percentile basis.

If a financial institution has already implemented the Monte Carlo simulation approach for calculating VaR assuming percentage changes in market variables to be normal, it should be relatively easy to implement the approach we describe here. The marginal distributions of the Δx_i can be calculated by fitting a more general distribution than the normal distribution to empirical data.

13.10   MODEL BUILDING vs. HISTORICAL SIMULATION

In the last chapter and in this one, we have discussed two methods for estimating VaR: the historical simulation approach and the model-building approach. The advantages of the model-building approach are that results can be produced very quickly and can easily be used in conjunction with volatility and correlation updating procedures such as those described in Chapters 9 and 10. As mentioned in Section 12.3, volatility updating can be incorporated into the historical simulation approach—but in a rather more artificial way. The main disadvantage of the model-building approach is that (at least in the simplest version of the approach) it assumes that the market variables have a multivariate normal distribution. In practice, daily changes in market variables often have distributions that are quite different from normal (see, for example, Table 9.2). A user of the model-building approach is hoping that some form of the central limit theorem of statistics applies, so that the probability distribution of daily gains and losses on a large portfolio is normally distributed—even though the gains or losses on the component parts of the portfolio are not normally distributed.

The historical simulation approach has the advantage that historical data determine the joint probability distribution of the market variables. It is also easier to handle interest rates in a historical simulation because, on each trial, a complete zero-coupon yield curve for both today and tomorrow can be calculated. The somewhat messy cash-flow mapping procedure described in Section 13.4 is avoided. The main disadvantage of historical simulation is that it is computationally much slower than the model-building approach. It is sometimes necessary to use an approximation such as equation (13.8) when using the historical simulation approach. This is because a full revaluation for each of the 500 different scenarios is not possible.[15]

The model-building approach is most often used for investment portfolios. (It is, after all, closely related to the popular Markowitz mean–variance method of portfolio analysis.) It is less commonly used for calculating the VaR for the trading operations of a financial institution. This is because, as explained in Chapter 6, financial institutions like to maintain their deltas with respect to market variables close to zero. Neither the linear model nor the quadratic model work well when deltas are low and portfolios are nonlinear (see Problem 13.22).

---

[15] This is particularly likely to be the case if Monte Carlo simulation is the numerical procedure used by the financial institution to value a deal. Monte Carlo simulations within historical simulations lead to extremely time-consuming computations.

SUMMARY

Whereas historical simulation lets the data determine the joint probability distribution of daily percentage changes in market variables, the model-building approach assumes a particular form for this distribution. The most common assumption is that percentage changes in the variables have a multivariate normal distribution. For situations where the change in the value of the portfolio is linearly dependent on percentage changes in the market variables, VaR can then be calculated exactly in a straightforward way. In other situations, approximations are necessary. One approach is to use a quadratic approximation for the change in the value of the portfolio as a function of percentage changes in the market variables. Another (much slower) approach is to use Monte Carlo simulation.

The model-building approach is frequently used for investment portfolios. It is less popular for the trading portfolios of financial institutions because it does not work well when deltas are low.

FURTHER READING

Frye, J., "Principals of Risk: Finding VaR through Factor-Based Interest Rate Scenarios," in: *VAR: Understanding and Applying Value at Risk*, pp. 275–288. London: Risk Publications, 1997.

Hull, J. C., and A. White, "Value at Risk When Daily Changes in Market Variables Are Not Normally Distributed," *Journal of Derivatives*, 5 (Spring 1998): 9–19.

Jamshidian, F., and Y. Zhu, "Scenario Simulation Model: Theory and Methodology," *Finance and Stochastics*, 1 (1997): 43–67.

Rich, D., "Second Generation VaR and Risk-Adjusted Return on Capital." *Journal of Derivatives*, 10, 4 (Summer 2003): 51–61.

PRACTICE QUESTIONS AND PROBLEMS (Answers at the End of the Book)

13.1. Consider a position consisting of a $100,000 investment in asset A and a $100,000 investment in asset B. Assume that the daily volatilities of both assets are 1% and that the coefficient of correlation between their returns is 0.3. What is the 5-day 99% VaR for the portfolio?

13.2. Describe three ways of handling interest-rate-dependent instruments when the model-building approach is used to calculate VaR.

13.3. Explain how an interest rate swap is mapped into a portfolio of zero-coupon bonds with standard maturities for the purposes of a VaR calculation.

13.4. A financial institution owns a portfolio of options on the US dollar–sterling exchange rate. The delta of the portfolio is 56.0. The current exchange rate is 1.5000. Derive an approximate linear relationship between the change in the portfolio value and the percentage change in the exchange rate. If the daily volatility of the exchange rate is 0.7%, estimate the 10-day 99% VaR.

13.5. Suppose that you know the gamma of the portfolio in Problem 13.4 to be 16.2. How does this change your estimate of the relationship between the change in the portfolio value and the percentage change in the exchange rate?

13.6. Suppose that the 5-year rate is 6%, the 7-year rate is 7% (both expressed with annual compounding), the daily volatility of a 5-year zero-coupon bond is 0.5%, and the daily volatility of a 7-year zero-coupon bond is 0.58%. The correlation between daily returns on the two bonds is 0.6. Map a cash flow of $1,000 received at 6.5 years into a position in a 5-year bond and a position in a 7-year bond. What cash flows in 5 and 7 years are equivalent to the 6.5-year cash flow?

13.7. Verify that the 0.3-year zero-coupon bond in the cash-flow mapping example in Table 13.9 is mapped into a $37,397 position in a 3-month bond and a $11,793 position in a 6-month bond.

13.8. Suppose that the daily change in the value of a portfolio is, to a good approximation, linearly dependent on two factors, calculated from a principal components analysis. The delta of a portfolio with respect to the first factor is 6 and the delta with respect to the second factor is −4. The standard deviations of the factor are 20 and 8, respectively. What is the 5-day 90% VaR?

13.9. The text calculates a VaR estimate for the example in Table 13.10 assuming two factors. How does the estimate change if you assume (a) one factor and (b) three factors.

13.10. A bank has a portfolio of options on an asset. The delta of the options is −30 and the gamma is −5. Explain how these numbers can be interpreted. The asset price is 20 and its volatility is 1% per day. Using the quadratic model, calculate the first three moments of the change in the portfolio value. Calculate a 1-day 99% VaR using (a) the first two moments and (b) the first three moments.

13.11. Suppose that in Problem 13.10 the vega of the portfolio is −2 per 1% change in the annual volatility. Derive a model relating the change in the portfolio value in 1 day to delta, gamma, and vega. Explain without doing detailed calculations how you would use the model to calculate a VaR estimate.

13.12. Explain why the linear model can provide only approximate estimates of VaR for a portfolio containing options.

13.13. Some time ago, a company entered into a forward contract to buy £1 million for $1.5 million. The contract now has 6 months to maturity. The daily volatility of a 6-month zero-coupon sterling bond (when its price is translated to dollars) is 0.06% and the daily volatility of a 6-month zero-coupon dollar bond is 0.05%. The correlation between returns from the two bonds is 0.8. The current exchange rate is 1.53. Calculate the standard deviation of the change in the dollar value of the forward contract in 1 day. What is the 10-day 99% VaR? Assume that the 6-month interest rate in both sterling and dollars is 5% per annum with continuous compounding.

13.14. The calculations in Section 13.3 assume that the investments in the DJIA, FTSE 100, CAC 40, and Nikkei 225 are $4 million, $3 million, $1 million, and $2 million, respectively. How does the VaR calculated change if the investment is $2.5 million in each index? Carry out calculations when (a) volatilities and correlations are estimated using the equally weighted model and (b) when they are estimated using the EWMA model with λ = 0.94. Use the spreadsheets on the author's website.

13.15. What is the effect of changing λ from 0.94 to 0.97 in the EWMA calculations in Section 13.3. Use the spreadsheets on the author's website.

FURTHER QUESTIONS

13.16. Consider a position consisting of a $300,000 investment in gold and a $500,000 investment in silver. Suppose that the daily volatilities of these two assets are 1.8% and 1.2%, respectively, and that the coefficient of correlation between their returns is 0.6. What is the 10-day 97.5% VaR for the portfolio? By how much does diversification reduce the VaR?

13.17. Consider a portfolio of options on a single asset. Suppose that the delta of the portfolio is 12, the value of the asset is $10, and the daily volatility of the asset is 2%. Estimate the 1-day 95% VaR for the portfolio from the delta.

13.18. Suppose that you know the gamma of the portfolio in Problem 13.17 to be −2.6. Derive a quadratic relationship between the change in the portfolio value and the percentage change in the underlying asset price in one day.
   (a) Calculate the first three moments of the change in the portfolio value.
   (b) Using the first two moments and assuming that the change in the portfolio is normally distributed, calculate the 1-day 95% VaR for the portfolio.
   (c) Use the third moment and the Cornish–Fisher expansion to revise your answer to (b).

13.19. A company has a long position in a 2-year bond and a 3-year bond as well as a short position in a 5-year bond. Each bond has a principal of $100 and pays a 5% coupon annually. Calculate the company's exposure to the 1-year, 2-year, 3-year, 4-year, and 5-year rates. Use the data in Tables 7.7 and 7.8 to calculate a 20-day 95% VaR on the assumption that rate changes are explained by (a) one factor, (b) two factors, and (c) three factors. Assume that the zero-coupon yield curve is flat at 5%.

13.20. A company has a position in bonds worth $6 million. The modified duration of the portfolio is 5.2 years. Assume that only parallel shifts in the yield curve can take place and that the standard deviation of the daily yield change (when yield is measured in percent) is 0.09. Use the duration model to estimate the 20-day 90% VaR for the portfolio. Explain carefully the weaknesses of this approach to calculating VaR. Explain two alternatives that give more accuracy.

13.21. A bank has written a call option on one stock and a put option on another stock. For the first option, the stock price is 50, the strike price is 51, the volatility is 28% per annum, and the time to maturity is 9 months. For the second option, the stock price is 20, the strike price is 19, the volatility is 25% per annum, and the time to maturity is 1 year. Neither stock pays a dividend, the risk-free rate is 6% per annum, and the correlation between stock price returns is 0.4. Calculate a 10-day 99% VaR (a) using only deltas, (b) using the partial simulation approach, (c) using the full simulation approach.

13.22. A common complaint of risk managers is that the model-building approach (either linear or quadratic) does not work well when delta is close to zero. Test what happens when delta is close to zero in using Sample Application E in the DerivaGem Application Builder software. (You can do this by experimenting with different option positions and adjusting the position in the underlying to give a delta of zero.) Explain the results you get.

13.23. The calculations in Section 13.3 assume that the investments in the DJIA, FTSE 100, CAC 40, and Nikkei 225 are $4 million, $3 million, $1 million, and $2 million, respectively. How does the VaR calculated change if the investments are $3 million, $3 million, $1 million, and $3 million, respectively? Carry out calculations when (a) volatilities and correlations are estimated using the equally weighted model and (b) when they are estimated using the EWMA model. What is the effect of changing λ from 0.94 to 0.90 in the EWMA calculations? Use the spreadsheets on the author's website.

CHAPTER

14

Credit Risk: Estimating Default Probabilities

Credit risk arises from the possibility that borrowers, bond issuers, and counterparties in derivatives transactions may default. As explained in Chapter 11, regulators have for a long time required banks to keep capital for credit risk. Under Basel II banks can, with approval from bank supervisors, use their own estimates of default probabilities to determine the amount of capital they are required to keep. This has led banks to devote a lot of resources to developing better ways of estimating default probabilities.

In this chapter, we discuss a number of different approaches to estimating default probabilities and explain the key difference between risk-neutral and real-world estimates. The material we cover will be used in Chapter 15 when we examine the nature of the credit risk in over-the-counter derivatives transactions and discuss the calculation of credit value at risk.

14.1 CREDIT RATINGS

Rating agencies such as Moody's, S&P, and Fitch are in the business of providing ratings describing the creditworthiness of corporate bonds. The best rating assigned by Moody's is Aaa. Bonds with this rating are considered to have almost no chance of defaulting. The next best rating is Aa. Following that come A, Baa, Ba, B, Caa, Ca, and C. Only bonds with ratings of Baa or above are considered to be *investment grade*. The S&P ratings corresponding to Moody's Aaa, Aa, A, Baa, Ba, B, Caa, Ca, and C are AAA, AA, A, BBB, BB, B, CCC, CC, and C, respectively. To create finer rating measures, Moody's divides the Aa rating category into Aa1, Aa2, and Aa3. It divides A into A1, A2 and A3, and so on. Similarly S&P divides its AA rating category into AA+, AA, and AA−; it divides its A rating category into A+, A, and A−; and so on. Moody's Aaa rating category and S&P's rating AAA are not subdivided, nor usually are the two lowest rating categories. Fitch's rating categories are similar to those of S&P.

A credit rating is designed to provide information about credit quality. As such, one might expect frequent changes in a company's credit rating as positive and negative information reaches the market.[1] In fact, ratings change relatively infrequently. One of

---

[1] In theory, a credit rating is an attribute of a bond issue, not a company. However, in most cases all bonds issued by a company have the same rating. A rating is therefore often referred to as an attribute of a company.

the objectives of ratings agencies when they assign ratings is ratings stability. For example, they want to avoid ratings reversals, such as where a company is downgraded and then upgraded a few weeks later. Ratings therefore change only when there is reason to believe that a long-term change in the company's creditworthiness has taken place. The reason for this is that bond traders are major users of ratings. Often they are subject to rules governing what the credit ratings of the bonds they hold must be. (For example, many bond funds are allowed to hold only investment-grade bonds.) If these ratings changed frequently, they might have to do a large amount of trading (and incur high transaction costs) just to satisfy the rules.

A related point is that rating agencies try to "rate through the cycle". Suppose that the economy exhibits a downturn and this has the effect of increasing the probability of a company defaulting in the next six months, but makes very little difference to the company's cumulative probability of defaulting over the next three to five years. A rating agency would not usually change the company's credit rating in these circumstances.

Internal Credit Ratings

Most banks have procedures for rating the creditworthiness of their corporate and retail clients. This is a necessity. The ratings published by rating agencies are available only for relatively large corporate clients. Many small and medium-sized businesses do not issue publicly traded bonds and therefore are not rated by rating agencies. As explained in Chapter 11, the internal ratings based (IRB) approach in Basel II allows banks to use their internal ratings in determining the probability of default (PD). Under the advanced IRB approach, they are also allowed to use their own internal procedures for estimating the loss given default (LGD), the exposure at default (EAD), and the maturity (M).

Internal ratings based approaches for PD typically involve profitability ratios, such as return on assets, and balance-sheet ratios, such as current assets divided by current liabilities (the current ratio) and debt to equity. Banks recognize that it is cash rather than profits that is necessary to repay a loan. They typically take the financial information provided by a company and convert it to a cash-flow statement that allows them to estimate how easy it will be for a company to service its debt.

Altman's Z-Score

Edward Altman has pioneered the use of accounting ratios to predict default. In 1968 he developed what has become known as the Z-score.[2] Using a statistical technique known as discriminant analysis, he attempted to predict defaults from five accounting ratios:

X_1: Working capital/Total assets

X_2: Retained earnings/Total assets

X_3: Earnings before interest and taxes/Total assets

X_4: Market value of equity/Book value of total liabilities

X_5: Sales/Total assets

---

[2] See E. I. Altman, "Financial Ratios, Discriminant Analysis, and the Prediction of Corporate Bankruptcy," *Journal of Finance*, 23, 4 (September 1968), 589–609.

The Z-score is calculated as

$$Z = 1.2X_1 + 1.4X_2 + 3.3X_3 + 0.6X_4 + 0.999X_5 \tag{14.1}$$

If the Z-score is greater than 3.0, then the company is unlikely to default. If it is between 2.7 and 3.0, we should be "on alert". If it is between 1.8 and 2.7, there is a good chance of default. If it is less than 1.8, the probability of a financial embarrassment is very high. The Z-score was calculated from a sample of 66 publicly traded manufacturing companies. Of these, 33 failed within one year and 33 did not fail within one year. The model proved to be fairly accurate when tested out of sample (i.e., on a set of firms different from that used to estimate equation (14.1)). Both Type I errors (companies that were predicted not to go bankrupt, but did so) and Type II errors (companies that were predicted to go bankrupt, but did not do so) were small.[3] Variations on the model have been developed for manufacturing companies that are not publicly traded and for companies not involved in manufacturing.

Example 14.1

Consider a company for which working capital is 170,000, total assets are 670,000, earnings before interest and taxes are 60,000, sales are 2,200,000, the market value of equity is 380,000, total liabilities are 240,000, and retained earnings are 300,000. In this case, $X_1 = 0.254$, $X_2 = 0.448$, $X_3 = 0.0896$, $X_4 = 1.583$, and $X_5 = 3.284$. The Z-score is

$$1.2 \times 0.254 + 1.4 \times 0.448 + 3.3 \times 0.0896 + 0.6 \times 1.583 + 0.999 \times 3.284 = 5.46$$

The Z-score indicates that the company is not in danger of defaulting in the near future.

14.2 HISTORICAL DEFAULT PROBABILITIES

Table 14.1 is typical of the data that are produced by rating agencies. It shows the default experience through time of companies that started with a certain credit rating. For example, Table 14.1 shows that a bond issue with an initial credit rating of Baa has a 0.170% chance of defaulting by the end of the first year, a 0.478% chance of defaulting by the end of the second year, and so on. The probability of a bond defaulting during a particular year can be calculated from the table. For example, the probability that a bond initially rated Baa will default during the second year of its life is $0.478 - 0.170 = 0.308\%$.

Table 14.1 shows that, for investment-grade bonds, the probability of default in a year tends to be an increasing function of time. (For example, the probability of a Aa-rated bond defaulting during years 1, 2, 3, 4, and 5 are 0.008%, 0.010%, 0.024%, 0.064%, and 0.072%, respectively.) This is because the bond issuer is initially considered to be creditworthy and, the more time that elapses, the greater is the possibility that its financial health will decline. For bonds with a poor credit rating, the probability of default is often a decreasing function of time. (For example the probabilities that a Caa-rated bond will default during years 1, 2, 3, 4, and 5 are 17.723%, 10.186%,

---

[3] Clearly Type I errors are much more costly to the lending department of a commercial bank than Type II errors.

Table 14.1   Average cumulative default rates (%), 1970–2007. *Source*: Moody's.

Rating	Time (years)								
	1	2	3	4	5	7	10	15	20
Aaa	0.000	0.000	0.000	0.026	0.100	0.252	0.525	1.004	1.204
Aa	0.008	0.018	0.042	0.106	0.178	0.344	0.521	1.094	1.884
A	0.020	0.094	0.218	0.342	0.467	0.762	1.308	2.396	4.082
Baa	0.170	0.478	0.883	1.360	1.835	2.794	4.353	7.601	10.510
Ba	1.125	3.019	5.298	7.648	9.805	13.465	18.426	27.533	34.852
B	4.660	10.195	15.566	20.325	24.692	32.527	40.922	50.212	52.375
Caa	17.723	27.909	36.116	42.603	47.836	54.539	64.928	70.298	72.783

8.207%, 6.487%, and 5.233%, respectively.) The reason here is that, for a bond with a poor credit rating, the next year or two may be critical. If the issuer survives this period, its financial health is likely to have improved.

Default Intensities

From Table 14.1 we can calculate the probability of a Caa bond defaulting during the third year as $36.116 - 27.909 = 8.207\%$. We will refer to this as the *unconditional default probability*. It is the probability of default during the third year as seen at time zero. The probability that the Caa-rated bond will survive until the end of year 2 is $100 - 27.909 = 72.091\%$. The probability that it will default during the third year conditional on no earlier default is therefore $0.08207/0.72091$, or 11.38%.

The 11.38% we have just calculated is a conditional default rate for a 1-year time period. When we consider a conditional default rate for a short time period of length Δt, we get a measure known as the *default intensity* or *hazard rate*. The default intensity $\lambda(t)$ at time t is defined so that $\lambda(t)\, \Delta t$ is the probability of default between time t and $t + \Delta t$ conditional on no default between time zero and time t. It is the instantaneous conditional default rate. If $V(t)$ is the cumulative probability of the company surviving to time t (i.e., no default by time t), the unconditional default probability between times t and $t + \Delta t$ is $V(t) - V(t + \Delta t)$. The probability of default between times t and $t + \Delta t$ conditional on no earlier default is $[V(t) - V(t + \Delta t)]/V(t)$. Hence,

$$\frac{V(t) - V(t + \Delta t)}{V(t)} = \lambda(t)\, \Delta t$$

or

$$\frac{V(t + \Delta t) - V(t)}{\Delta t} = -\lambda(t)\, V(t)$$

Taking limits, we obtain

$$\frac{dV(t)}{dt} = -\lambda(t)\, V(t)$$

from which

$$V(t) = e^{-\int_0^t \lambda(\tau)d\tau}$$

Defining $Q(t)$ as the probability of default by time t, so that $Q(t) = 1 - V(t)$, gives

$$Q(t) = 1 - e^{-\int_0^t \lambda(\tau)d\tau}$$

or

$$Q(t) = 1 - e^{-\bar{\lambda}(t)t} \tag{14.2}$$

where $\bar{\lambda}(t)$ is the average default intensity between time 0 and time t.

Example 14.2

Suppose that the default intensity is a constant 1.5% per year. The probability of a default by the end of the first year is $1 - e^{-0.015 \times 1} = 0.0149$. The probability of a default by the end of the second year is $1 - e^{-0.015 \times 2} = 0.0296$. The probability of a default by the end of the third, fourth, and fifth years are similarly 0.0440, 0.0582, and 0.0723. The unconditional probability of a default during the fourth year is $0.0582 - 0.0440 = 0.0142$. The probability of default for in the fourth year conditional on no earlier default is $0.0142/(1 - 0.0440) = 0.0149$.

14.3 RECOVERY RATES

When a company goes bankrupt, those that are owed money by the company file claims against the assets of the company.[4] Sometimes there is a reorganization in which these creditors agree to a partial payment of their claims. In other cases, the assets are sold by the liquidator and the proceeds are used to meet the claims as far as possible. Some claims typically have priorities over other claims and are met more fully.

The *recovery rate* for a bond is normally defined as the bond's market value a few days after a default as a percentage of its face value. As we saw in Chapter 11, the Basel II formulas are expressed in terms of the loss given default (LGD). The percentage recovery rate is 100 minus the percentage loss given default.

Table 14.2 provides historical data on average recovery rates for different categories of bonds in the United States. It shows that senior secured debt-holders had an average

Table 14.2 Recovery rates on corporate bonds as a percent of face value, 1982–2007, issuer weighted. *Source*: Moody's.

Class	Average recovery rate (%)
Senior secured	51.89
Senior unsecured	36.69
Senior subordinated	32.42
Subordinated	31.19
Junior subordinated	23.95

---

[4] In the United States, the claim made by a bondholder is the bond's face value plus accrued interest.

recovery rate of 51.89 cents per dollar of face value, while junior subordinated debt-holders had an average recovery rate of only 23.95 cents per dollar of face value.

Recovery rates are significantly negatively correlated with default rates. Moody's looked at average recovery rates and average default rates for unsecured bonds each year between 1982 and 2007 and compared it with the default rate for speculative-grade (i.e., non-investment-grade) bonds. It found that the following relationship provides a good fit to the data:[5]

$$\text{Average recovery rate (\%)} = 59.33 - 3.06 \times \text{Speculative-grade default rate (\%)}$$

This relationship means that a bad year for the default rate is usually doubly bad because it is accompanied by a low recovery rate. For example, when the default rate on speculative bonds in a year is 1%, we expect the average recovery rate to be relatively high at about 56%. When the default rate is relatively high at 10%, we expect the average recovery rate to be about 29%.

14.4 CREDIT DEFAULT SWAPS

An instrument that is very useful for estimating default probabilities is a *credit default swap* (CDS). As indicated in Business Snapshot 14.1, the market for this product has seen huge growth since the late 1990s. A CDS is an instrument that provides insurance against the risk of a default by particular company. The company is known as the *reference entity* and a default by the company is known as a *credit event*. The buyer of the insurance obtains the right to sell bonds issued by the company for their face value when a credit event occurs, and the seller of the insurance agrees to buy the bonds for their face value when a credit event occurs.[6] The total face value of the bonds that can be sold is known as the credit default swap's *notional principal*.

The buyer of the CDS makes periodic payments to the seller until the end of the life of the CDS or until a credit event occurs. These payments are typically made in arrears every quarter, every half year, or every year. The settlement in the event of a default involves either physical delivery of the bonds or a cash payment.

Figure 14.1 Credit default swap.

[5] See K. Emery, S. Ou, J. Tennant, F. Kim, and R. Cantor, "Corporate Default and Recovery Rates, 1920–2007," Moody's Investor's Services, February 2008. The R^2 of the regression is 0.499. The correlation is also identified and discussed in E. I. Altman, B. Brady, A. Resti, and A. Sironi, "The Link Between Default and Recovery Rates: Implications for Credit Risk Models and Procyclicality," *Journal of Business*, November 2005: 2203–2228.

[6] The face value (or par value) of a bond is the principal amount that the issuer will repay at maturity if it does not default.

Business Snapshot 14.1 The CDS Market

In 1998 and 1999, the International Swaps and Derivatives Association developed a standard contract for trading credit default swaps in the over-the-counter market. Since then the market has grown very fast. Banks and insurance companies are both buyers and sellers of protection. However, banks are net buyers of protection and insurance companies are net sellers of protection. One of the results of the popularity of credit default swaps (and other credit derivatives) is that the financial institution bearing the credit risk of a loan is often different from the financial institution that did the original credit checks. Whether this proves to be good for the overall health of the financial system remains to be seen.

During the credit turmoil that started in August 2007, regulators became very concerned about systemic risk (see Business Snapshot 11.1). They felt that credit default swaps were a source of vulnerability for financial markets. The danger is that a default by one financial institution might lead to big losses by its counterparties in CDS transactions and further defaults by other financial institutions. Regulatory concerns were fueled by troubles at insurance giant AIG. This was a big seller of protection on the AAA-rated tranches created from mortgages (see Chapter 16). The protection proved very costly to AIG and the company was bailed out by the US government.

Regulatory concerns have led to the development of a clearinghouse for CDS trades between financial institutions. The clearinghouse requires financial institutions to post margin on their CDS trades in much the same way that traders post margin on futures contracts (see Chapter 5).

During 2007 and 2008, trading ceased in many types of credit derivatives, but CDSs continued to trade actively (albeit with dramatically increased spreads). The advantage of CDSs over some other credit derivatives is that the way they work is straightforward. Other credit derivatives, such as those created from the securitization of household mortgages (see Chapter 16), lack transparency.

There were a huge number of CDS contracts outstanding with Lehman Brothers as the reference entity when Lehman Brothers declared bankruptcy in September 2008. The recovery rate was only about 8 cents on the dollar, so that the payout to the buyers of protection was equal to about 92% of the notional principal. There were predictions that some sellers of protection would be unable to pay and that further bankruptcies would occur, but on the settlement day (October 21, 2008) everything went smoothly.

An example will help to illustrate how a typical deal is structured. Suppose that two parties enter into a five-year credit default swap on March 1, 2009. Assume that the notional principal is $100 million and the buyer agrees to pay 90 basis points once a year in arrears for protection against default by the reference entity.

The CDS is shown in Figure 14.1. If the reference entity does not default (i.e., there is no credit event), the buyer receives no payoff and pays $900,000 on March 1 of each of the years 2010, 2011, 2012, 2013, and 2014. If there is a credit event, a substantial payoff is likely. Suppose that the buyer notifies the seller of a credit event on June 1, 2012 (a quarter of the way into the fourth year). If the contract specifies physical settlement, the buyer has the right to sell bonds issued by the reference entity with a face value

---

Business Snapshot 14.2   Is the CDS Market a Fair Game?

There is one important difference between credit default swaps and most other over-the-counter derivatives. The other over-the-counter derivatives depend on interest rates, exchange rates, equity indices, commodity prices, and so on. There is no reason to assume that any one market participant has better information than other market participants about these variables.

   Credit default swaps spreads depend on the probability that a particular company will default during a particular period of time. Arguably some market participants have more information to estimate this probability than others. A financial institution that works closely with a particular company by providing advice, making loans, and handling new issues of securities is likely to have more information about the creditworthiness of the company than another financial institution that has no dealings with the company. Economists refer to this as an *asymmetric information* problem.

   Whether asymmetric information will curtail the expansion of the credit default swap market remains to be seen. Financial institutions emphasize that the decision to buy protection against the risk of default by a company is normally made by a risk manager and is not based on any special information that may exist elsewhere in the financial institution about the company.

---

of $100 million for $100 million. If the contract requires cash settlement, an independent calculation agent will conduct a poll of dealers to determine, at a predesignated number of days after the credit event, the mid-market value of the cheapest deliverable bond. Suppose this bond is worth $35 per $100 of face value. The cash payoff would be $65 million.

   The regular quarterly, semiannual, or annual payments from the buyer of protection to the seller of protection cease when there is a credit event. However, because these payments are made in arrears, a final accrual payment by the buyer is usually required. In our example, where there is a default on June 1, 2012, the buyer would be required to pay to the seller the amount of the annual payment accrued between March 1, 2012, and June 1, 2012 (approximately $225,000), but no further payments would be required.

   The total amount paid per year, as a percentage of the notional principal, to buy protection is known as the *CDS spread*. Several large banks are market makers in the credit default swap market. When quoting on a new five-year credit default swap on a company, a market maker might bid 250 basis points and offer 260 basis points. This means that the market maker is prepared to buy protection by paying 250 basis points per year (i.e., 2.5% of the principal per year) and to sell protection for 260 basis points per year (i.e., 2.6% of the principal per year).

   Many different companies and countries are reference entities for the CDS contracts that trade. Under the most popular arrangement, payments are made quarterly in arrears. Contracts with maturities of 5 years are most popular, but other maturities such as 1, 2, 3, 7, and 10 years are not uncommon. Usually contracts mature on what are known as the IMM dates (March 20, June 20, September 20, and December 20). The effect of this is that the actual time to maturity of a contract when it is initiated is close to, but not necessarily the same as, the number of years to maturity that is specified. Suppose you call a dealer on November 15, 2009, to buy 5-year protection on a company. The contract would probably last until December 20, 2014. Your first payment would be due on December 20, 2009, and would equal an amount covering the November 15, 2009, to December 20, 2009, period.[7]

A key aspect of a CDS contract is the definition of default. In contracts on European reference entities restructuring is typically included as a credit event, whereas in contracts on North American reference entities it is not.

Some market participants think the CDS market will continue its meteoric growth. Others are less optimistic. As pointed out in Business Snapshot 14.2, there is a potential asymmetric information problem in the CDS market that is not present in most other over-the-counter derivatives markets.

The Cheapest-to-Deliver Bond

As explained in Section 14.3, the recovery rate on a bond is defined as the value of the bond immediately after default as a percentage of face value. This means that the payoff from a CDS is $L(1 - R)$, where L is the notional principal and R is the recovery rate.

Usually a CDS specifies that a number of different bonds can be delivered in the event of a default. The bonds typically have the same seniority, but they may not sell for the same percentage of face value immediately after a default.[8] This gives the holder of a CDS what is known as a *cheapest-to-deliver bond option*. When a default happens, the buyer of protection (or the calculation agent in the event of cash settlement) will review alternative deliverable bonds and choose for delivery the one that can be purchased most cheaply.

Credit Indices

Participants in credit markets have developed indices to track credit default swap spreads. In 2004, there were agreements between different producers of indices that led to some consolidation. Two important standard portfolios used by index providers are:

1. CDX NA IG, a portfolio of 125 investment grade companies in North America
2. iTraxx Europe, a portfolio of 125 investment grade names in Europe

These portfolios are updated on March 20 and September 20 each year. Companies that are no longer investment grade are dropped from the portfolios and new investment grade companies are added.[9]

Suppose that the 5-year CDX NA IG index is quoted by a market maker as bid 165 basis points, offer 166 basis points. Roughly speaking, this means that an investor

---

[7] If the time to the first IMM date is less than one month, the first payment is typically on the second IMM payment date; otherwise it is in the first IMM payment date.

[8] There are a number of reasons for this. The claim that is made in the event of a default is typically equal to the bond's face value plus accrued interest. Bonds with high accrued interest at the time of default therefore tend to have higher prices immediately after default. Also the market may judge that, in the event of a reorganization of the company, some bond-holders will fare better than others.

[9] On September 20, 2007, the Series 8 iTraxx Europe portfolio and the Series 9 CDX NA IG portfolio were defined. The series numbers indicate that, by the end of September 2007, the iTraxx Europe portfolio had been updated seven times and the CDX NA IG portfolio had been updated eight times.

can buy CDS protection on all 125 companies in the index for 166 basis points per company. Suppose an investor wants $800,000 of protection on each company. The total cost is $0.0166 \times 800,000 \times 125$, or $1,660,000 per year. The investor can similarly sell $800,000 of protection on each of the 125 companies for a total of $1,650,000 per annum. When a company defaults, the protection buyer receives the usual CDS payoff and the annual payment is reduced by $1,660,000/125 = \$13,280$. There is an active market in buying and selling CDS index protection for maturities of 3, 5, 7, and 10 years. The maturities for these types of contracts on the index are usually December 20 and June 20. (This means that a "five-year" contract lasts between $4\frac{3}{4}$ and $5\frac{1}{4}$ years.) Roughly speaking, the index is the average of the CDS spreads on the companies in the underlying portfolio.[10]

The precise way in which the contract works is a little more complicated than has just been described. A credit index trades similarly to a bond. For each index and each maturity a "coupon" is specified. If the quoted spread is greater than the coupon, the buyer of protection pays at the outset to the seller the expected present value of the excess of the spread over the coupon over the remaining life of the contract. If the quoted spread is less than the coupon, the seller of protection pays at the outset to the buyer the expected present value of the excess of the coupon over the spread. The buyer of protection then pays the coupon times the principal applicable to those companies in the index that have not yet defaulted to the seller. This arrangement facilitates trading.

14.5 CREDIT SPREADS

The credit spread is the extra rate of interest per annum required by investors for bearing a particular credit risk. CDS spreads, which we met in the previous section, are one type of credit spread. Another is the bond yield spread. This is the amount by which the yield on a corporate bond exceeds the yield on a similar risk-free bond.[11] We now show that the two should be approximately equal.

CDS Spreads and Bond Yields

A CDS can be used to hedge a position in a corporate bond. Suppose that an investor buys a 5-year corporate bond yielding 7% per year for its face value and at the same time enters into a 5-year CDS to buy protection against the issuer of the bond defaulting. Suppose that the CDS spread is 200 basis points (or 2%) per annum. The effect of the CDS is to convert the corporate bond to a risk-free bond (at least approximately). If the bond issuer does not default, the investor earns 5% per year

---

[10] More precisely, the index is slightly lower than the average of the credit default swap spreads for the companies in the portfolio. To understand the reason for this, consider a portfolio consisting of two companies, one with a spread of 1,000 basis points and the other with a spread of 10 basis points. To buy protection on the companies would cost slightly less than 505 basis points per company. This is because the 1,000 basis points is not expected to be paid for as long as the 10 basis points and should therefore carry less weight. Another complication for CDX NA IG, but not iTraxx Europe, is that the definition of default applicable to the index includes restructuring, whereas the definition for CDS contracts on the underlying companies does not.

[11] At this stage, we assume that the whole of an observed bond yield spread or CDS spread is attributable to credit risk. As will be discussed later, liquidity as well as credit risk affects these spreads. The lower the liquidity, the higher the spread.

(when the CDS spread is netted against the corporate bond yield). If the bond does default, the investor earns 5% up to the time of the default. Under the terms of the CDS, the investor is then able to exchange the bond for its face value. This face value can be invested at the risk-free rate for the remainder of the five years.

This argument shows that the n-year CDS spread should be approximately equal to the excess of the par yield on an n-year corporate bond over the par yield on an n-year risk-free bond.[12] If it is markedly less than this, an investor can earn more than the risk-free rate by buying the corporate bond and buying protection. If it is markedly greater than this, an investor can borrow at less than the risk-free rate by shorting the corporate bond and selling CDS protection. These are not perfect arbitrages, as we discuss later, but in normal markets they do give a good guide to the relationship between CDS spreads and bond yields.

The Risk-Free Rate

CDSs provide a direct estimate of the credit spread. To calculate a credit spread from a bond yield, it is necessary to make an assumption about the risk-free rate. When bond yield spreads are quoted by bond traders, the risk-free rate that is used is usually the yield on a Treasury bond of similar maturity. For example, a bond trader might quote the yield on a particular corporate bond as being a spread of 250 basis points over Treasuries.

A number of researchers have compared bond yields to CDS spreads to imply a risk-free rate. This involves matching the maturities of CDSs and bonds and implying a risk-free rate from the arbitrage arguments given above. For example, if the 5-year bond yield is 4.7% and the 5-year CDS spread is 80 basis points, the implied 5-year risk-free rate is 3.9%.

As discussed in Section 7.2, traders usually use LIBOR/swap rates as proxies for risk-free rates when valuing derivatives. The research indicates that this practice carries over to the credit market. Implied risk-free rates are much closer to the LIBOR/swap rates than to the Treasury rates. One estimate puts implied risk-free rates at about 10 basis points less than the LIBOR/swap rate.[13] This estimate is plausible. As explained in Section 7.2, the credit risk in a swap rate is the credit risk from making a series of short-term loans to AA-rated counterparties and 10 basis points is a reasonable credit spread for a short-term AA-rated instrument.

Asset Swaps

Asset swaps provide a convenient reference point for traders in credit markets because the asset swap spread for a bond is a direct estimate of the excess of the bond's yield over the LIBOR/swap rate.

To explain how asset swaps work, consider the situation where an asset swap spread for a particular bond is quoted as 150 basis points. There are three possible

---

[12] The par yield on an n-year bond is the coupon rate per year that causes the bond to sell for its par value (i.e., its face value).

[13] See J. Hull, M. Predescu, and A. White, "The Relationship Between Credit Default Swap Spreads, Bond Yields, and Credit Rating Announcements," *Journal of Banking and Finance*, 28 (November 2004), 2789–2811.

situations:

1. The bond sells for its par value of 100. The swap then involves one side (company A) paying the coupon on the bond and the other side (company B) paying LIBOR plus 150 basis points.[14]

2. The bond sells below its par value, say for $95. The swap is then structured so that company A pays $5 per $100 of notional principal at the outset. After that, company A pays the bond's coupons and company B pays LIBOR plus 150 basis points.

3. The underlying bond sells above par, say for 108. The swap is then structured so that Company B makes a payment of $8 per $100 of principal at the outset. After that, company A pays the bond's coupons and company B pays LIBOR plus 150 basis points.

The effect of all this is that the present value of the asset swap spread (150 basis points in our example) is the amount by which the price of the corporate bond is exceeded by the price of a similar risk-free bond, where the risk-free rate is assumed to be given by the LIBOR/swap curve (see Problem 14.16).

CDS–Bond Basis

The CDS–bond basis is the excess of the CDS spread over the asset swap spread for a company:

$$\text{CDS–bond basis} = \text{CDS spread} - \text{Asset swap spread}$$

The arbitrage argument given above suggests that this should be close to zero. In fact, there are a number of reasons why it deviates from zero. For example:

1. The underlying bond may sell for a price that is significantly different from par. (Bond prices above par tend to give rise to a positive basis; bond prices below par tend to give rise to a negative basis.)

2. There is counterparty default risk in a CDS. (This pushes the basis in a negative direction.)

3. There is a cheapest-to-deliver bond option in a CDS. (This pushes the basis in a positive direction.)

4. The payoff in a CDS does not include accrued interest on the bond that is delivered. (This pushes the basis in a negative direction.)

5. The restructuring clause in a CDS contract may lead to a payoff when there is no default. (This pushes the basis in a positive direction.)

6. LIBOR is greater than the risk-free rate being assumed by the market. (This pushes the basis in a positive direction.)

Prior to the market turmoil starting in 2007, the basis tended to be positive. For example, De Witt estimates that the average CDS–bond basis in 2004 and 2005 was 16 basis points.[15] During the credit crisis that started in August 2007, the basis has

---

[14] Note that it is the promised coupons that are exchanged. The exchanges take place regardless of whether the bond defaults.

[15] See J. De Witt, "Exploring the CDS–Bond Basis," Working Paper No. 104, National Bank of Belgium.

tended to be negative. Possibly counterparty default risk loomed large in the minds of investors. Finding the capital to fund the arbitrage might also have been a problem for some investors.

14.6 ESTIMATING DEFAULT PROBABILITIES FROM CREDIT SPREADS

We now discuss how default probabilities can be estimated from credit spreads.

Approximate Calculation

Suppose that a 5-year credit spread (CDS or asset swap) is 240 basis points and that the expected recovery rate in the event of a default is 40%. The holder of a corporate bond must be expecting to lose 240 basis points (or 2.4%) per year from defaults. Given the recovery rate of 40%, this leads to an estimate of the average probability of a default per year over the 5-year period, conditional on no earlier default, of $0.024/(1 - 0.4)$, or 4%. In general,

$$h = \frac{s}{1 - R} \tag{14.3}$$

where h is the default intensity (hazard rate) per year, s is the spread of the corporate bond yield over the risk-free rate, and R is the expected recovery rate.

If credit spreads are known for a number of different maturities, the term structure of the default intensity can be bootstrapped (at least approximately) as the following example illustrates.

Example 14.3

Suppose that the CDS spreads for 3-year, 5-year, and 10-year instruments are 50, 60, and 100 basis points and that the expected recovery rate is 60%. The average default intensity over 3 years is approximately $0.005/(1 - 0.6) = 0.0125$. The average default intensity over 5 years is approximately $0.006/(1 - 0.6) = 0.015$. The average default intensity over 10 years is approximately $0.01/(1 - 0.6) = 0.025$. From this we can estimate that the average default intensity between year 3 and year 5 is $(5 \times 0.015 - 3 \times 0.0125)/2 = 0.01875$. The average default intensity between year 5 and year 10 is $(10 \times 0.025 - 5 \times 0.015)/5 = 0.035$.

A More Exact Calculation

The calculation just given works well for CDS spreads. It also works well for asset swap spreads when the underlying bond is selling for close to its par value. We now present a more exact calculation that can be used when the bond's price is not close to par.

Suppose that the asset swap spread for a 5-year corporate bond is 200 basis points and that the risk-free (LIBOR/swap) rate of interest is 5% (with continuous compounding). The bond provides a coupon of 6% per year (paid semiannually). The expected recovery rate is 40%. For simplicity, we suppose that the unconditional probability of default per year is the same each year and equal to Q.[16] Furthermore, we assume

---

[16] An alternative assumption is that the default probability conditional on no default, rather than the unconditional default probability, is the same each year (see Problem 14.23). An iterative search is then necessary to determine the default intensity.

Table 14.3 Calculation of loss from default on a bond in terms of the default probabilities per year, Q. Notional principal = $100.

Time (years)	Default probability	Recovery amount ($)	Default-free value ($)	Loss ($)	Discount factor	PV of expected loss ($)
0.5	Q	40	106.73	66.73	0.9753	65.08Q
1.5	Q	40	105.97	65.97	0.9277	61.20Q
2.5	Q	40	105.17	65.17	0.8825	57.52Q
3.5	Q	40	104.34	64.34	0.8395	54.01Q
4.5	Q	40	103.46	63.46	0.7985	50.67Q
Total						288.48Q

defaults can happen only at times 0.5, 1.5, 2.5, 3.5, and 4.5 years, immediately before coupon payment dates. (The analysis can be extended so that defaults can occur more frequently than once a year.)

Table 14.3 calculates the expected loss from defaults in terms of Q. To illustrate the calculations, consider the 3.5-year row in Table 14.3. The expected value of the default-free bond at 3.5 years (calculated using the risk-free, LIBOR/swap, forward interest rates) is

$$3 + 3e^{-0.05 \times 0.5} + 3e^{-0.05 \times 1.0} + 103e^{-0.05 \times 1.5} = 104.34$$

Given the definition of recovery rates in the previous section, the amount recovered if there is a default is 40, so that the loss given default is $104.34 - 40$, or $64.34. The present value of this loss is 54.01, and the expected loss is therefore 54.01Q.

Table 14.3 shows that the total expected loss is 288.48Q. The expected loss is also equal to the present value of the asset swap spread payments. This is the present value of 2% per annum on $100 with payments being made semiannually. Payments are $1 every 6 months. Their present value is

$$1 \times e^{-0.05 \times 0.5} + 1 \times e^{-0.05 \times 1} + 1 \times e^{-0.05 \times 1.5} + \cdots + 1 \times e^{-0.05 \times 5} = 8.738$$

It follows that

$$288.48Q = 8.738$$

so that $Q = 8.738/288.48 = 0.0303$. An unconditional default probability of 3.03% per year is therefore consistent with the data.

The approximate approach would have estimated a default intensity of

$$0.02/(1 - 0.4) = 0.0333$$

or 3.33%. This is larger than the result given by the more accurate approach because, in this case, the bond would sell below par.[17]

If asset swap spreads for bonds with several different maturities are available, a bootstrap procedure can be used to determine term structure of default probabilities (see Problems 14.15 and 14.23). The approach is analogous to the bootstrap procedure in Appendix B for calculating a zero-coupon yield curve. Suppose, for example, the

---

[17] The bond would sell below par because the bond yield (about 7%) is greater than the coupon (which is 6%).

bonds mature in 3, 5, 7, and 10 years. We could use the first bond to estimate a default probability per year for the first 3 years, the second bond to estimate default probability per year for years 4 and 5, the third bond to estimate a default probability for years 6 and 7, and the fourth bond to estimate a default probability for years 8, 9, and 10.

14.7 COMPARISON OF DEFAULT PROBABILITY ESTIMATES

The default probabilities estimated from historical data are much less than those derived from bond prices. Table 14.4 illustrates this.[18] It shows, for companies that start with a particular rating, the average annual default intensity over 7 years calculated from (a) historical data and (b) bond prices.

The calculation of default intensities using historical data are based on equation (14.2) with $t = 7$ and Table 14.1. From equation (14.2), we have

$$\bar{\lambda}(7) = -\tfrac{1}{7}\ln[1 - Q(7)]$$

where $\bar{\lambda}(t)$ is the average default intensity (or hazard rate) up to time t, and $Q(t)$ is the cumulative probability of default by time t. The values of $Q(7)$ are taken directly from Table 14.1. Consider, for example, an A-rated company. The value of $Q(7)$ is 0.00762. The average 7-year default intensity is therefore

$$\bar{\lambda}(t) = -\tfrac{1}{7}\ln(1 - 0.00762) = 0.0011$$

or 0.11%.

The calculations of average default intensities from bond prices are based on equation (14.3) and bond yields published by Merrill Lynch. The results shown are averages between December 1996 and October 2007. The recovery rate is assumed to be 40% and, for the reasons discussed in the previous section, the risk-free interest rate is assumed to be the 7-year swap rate minus 10 basis points. For example, for A-rated bonds, the average Merrill Lynch yield was 5.993%. The average swap rate was 5.398%, so that the average risk-free rate was 5.298%. This gives the average 7-year default probability as

$$\frac{0.05993 - 0.05298}{1 - 0.4} = 0.0116$$

or 1.16%.

Table 14.4 shows that the ratio of the default probability backed out of bond prices to the default probability calculated from historical data is high for investment-grade bonds and tends to decline as the credit quality declines. By contrast, the difference between the two default probabilities tends to increase as credit quality declines.

Table 14.5 provides another way of looking at these results. It shows the excess return over the risk-free rate (still assumed to be the 7-year swap rate minus 10 basis points) earned by investors in bonds with different credit rating. Consider again an A-rated bond. The average spread over Treasuries is 112 basis points. Of this, 42 basis points are accounted for by the average spread between 7-year Treasuries and our proxy for the risk-free rate. A spread of 7 basis points is necessary to cover expected defaults. (This equals the real-world probability of default from Table 14.4 times 1 minus the assumed

---

[18] Tables 14.4 and 14.5 are updated versions of those in J. Hull, M. Predescu, and A. White, "Bond Prices, Default Probabilities, and Risk Premiums," *Journal of Credit Risk*, 1, 2 (Spring 2005): 53–60.

Table 14.4   Seven-year average default intensities (% per annum).

Rating	Historical default intensity	Default intensity from bonds	Ratio	Difference
Aaa	0.04	0.60	16.6	0.56
Aa	0.05	0.74	15.0	0.69
A	0.11	1.16	10.6	1.05
Baa	0.40	2.13	5.3	1.73
Ba	2.07	4.67	2.3	2.60
B	5.62	7.97	1.4	2.15
Caa	11.26	18.16	1.6	6.90

recovery rate of 0.4.) This leaves an expected excess return (after expected defaults have been taken into account) of 63 basis points.

Tables 14.4 and 14.5 show that a large percentage difference between default probability estimates translates into a relatively small expected excess return on the bond. For Aaa-rated bonds, the ratio of the two default probabilities is 16.6, but the expected excess return is only 34 basis points. The expected return tends to increase as credit quality declines.[19]

The excess return in Table 14.5 does not remain constant through time. Credit spreads, and therefore excess returns, were high in 2001, 2002, and the first half of 2003. After that they were fairly low until the start of the credit crisis in August 2007, when they started to increase rapidly. (See Chapter 16 for a discussion of the credit crunch.)

Real-World vs. Risk-Neutral Probabilities

The risk-neutral valuation argument is explained in Business Snapshot 14.3. It shows that we can value cash flows on the assumption that all investors are risk neutral (that is, on the assumption that they do not require a premium for bearing risks).

Table 14.5   Expected excess return on bonds in basis points (bps).

Rating	Bond yield spread over Treasuries (bps)	Spread of risk-free rate over Treasuries (bps)	Spread for historical defaults (bps)	Expected excess return (bps)
Aaa	78	42	2	34
Aa	87	42	3	42
A	112	42	7	63
Baa	170	42	24	104
Ba	323	42	124	157
B	521	42	337	142
Caa	1132	42	676	414

[19] The results for B-rated bonds in Tables 14.4 and 14.5 run counter to the overall pattern.

Business Snapshot 14.3 Risk-Neutral Valuation

The single most important idea in the valuation of derivatives is risk-neutral valuation. It shows that we can value a derivative by

1. Assuming that all investors are risk neutral
2. Calculating expected cash flows
3. Discounting the cash flows at the risk-free rate

As a simple example of the application of risk-neutral valuation, suppose that the price of a non-dividend-paying stock is $30 and consider a derivative that pays off $100 in one year if the stock price is greater than $40 at that time. (This is known as a binary cash-or-nothing call option.) Suppose that the risk-free rate (continuously compounded) is 5%, the expected return on the stock (also continuously compounded) is 10%, and the stock price volatility is 30% per annum. In a risk-neutral world, the expected growth of the stock price is 5%. It can be shown (with the usual Black–Scholes lognormal assumptions) that, when the stock price has this growth rate, the probability that the stock price will be greater than $40 in one year is 0.1730. The expected payoff from the derivatives is therefore $100 × 0.1730 = $17.30. The value of the derivative is calculated by discounting this at 5%. It is $16.46.

The real-world (physical) probability of the stock price being greater than $40 in one year is calculated by assuming a growth rate of 10%. It is 0.2190. The expected payoff in the real world is therefore $21.90. The problem with using this expected cash flow is that we do not know the correct discount rate. The stock price has risk associated with it that is priced by the market (otherwise the expected return on the stock would not be 5% more than the risk-free rate). The derivative has the effect of "leveraging this risk" so that a very high discount rate is required for its expected payoff. Because we know the correct value of the derivative to be $16.46, we can deduce that the correct discount rate to apply to the $21.90 real-world expected payoff must be 28.6%.

When we do this, we get the right answer in the real world as well as in the risk-neutral world.

The default probabilities implied from bond yields are risk-neutral probabilities of default (that is, they are the probabilities of default in a world where all investors are risk-neutral). To understand why this is so, consider the calculations of default probabilities in Table 14.3. The calculations assume that expected default losses can be discounted at the risk-free rate. The risk-neutral valuation principle shows that this is a valid procedure provided that the expected losses are calculated in a risk-neutral world. This means that the default probability Q in Table 14.3 must be a risk-neutral probability.

By contrast, the default probabilities implied from historical data are real-world default probabilities (sometimes also called *physical probabilities*). The expected excess return in Table 14.5 arises directly from the difference between real-world and risk-neutral default probabilities. If there was no expected excess return, the real-world and risk-neutral default probabilities would be the same, and vice versa.

Why do we see such big differences between real-world and risk-neutral default probabilities? As we have just argued, this is the same as asking why corporate bond traders earn more than the risk-free rate on average.

One reason for the results is that corporate bonds are relatively illiquid and the returns on bonds are higher than they would otherwise be to compensate for this. But this is a small part of what is going on. It explains perhaps 25 basis points of the excess return in Table 14.5. Another possible reason for the results is that the subjective default probabilities of bond traders are much higher than the those given in Tables 14.1. Bond traders may be allowing for depression scenarios much worse than anything seen during the period from 1970 to 2003. However, it is difficult to see how this can explain a large part of the excess return that is observed.[20]

By far the most important reason for the results in Tables 14.4 and 14.5 is that bonds do not default independently of each other. There are periods of time when default rates are very low and also periods when they are very high. Evidence for this can be obtained by looking at the default rates in different years. Moody's statistics show that between 1970 and 2007 the default rate per year for speculative-grade bonds ranged from a low of 0.418% in 1979 to a high of 9.978% in 2001. The year-to-year variation in default rates gives rise to systematic risk (i.e., risk that cannot be diversified away) and bond traders earn an excess expected return for bearing the risk. The variation in default rates from year to year may be because of overall economic conditions or because a default by one company has a ripple effect resulting in defaults by other companies. (The latter is referred to by researchers as *credit contagion*.)

In addition to the systematic risk we have just talked about, there is nonsystematic (or idiosyncratic) risk associated with each bond. If we were talking about stocks, we would argue that investors can diversify the nonsystematic risk by choosing a portfolio of, say, 30 stocks. They should not therefore demand a risk premium for bearing nonsystematic risk. For bonds the arguments are not so clear-cut. Bond returns are highly skewed with limited upside. (For example, on an individual bond, there might be a 99.75% chance of a 7% return in a year, and a 0.25% chance of a -60% return in the year, the first outcome corresponding to no default and the second to default.) This type of risk is difficult to "diversify away".[21] It requires tens of thousands of different bonds to be held. In practice, many bond portfolios are far from fully diversified. As a result, bond traders may earn an extra return for bearing unsystematic risk as well as for bearing the systematic risk mentioned in the previous paragraph.

Which Estimates Should Be Used?

At this stage it is natural to ask whether we should use real-world or risk-neutral default probabilities in the analysis of credit risk. The answer depends on the purpose of the analysis. When valuing credit derivatives or estimating the impact of default risk on the pricing of instruments, we should use risk-neutral default probabilities. This is because the analysis calculates the present value of expected future cash flows and almost invariably (implicitly or explicitly) involves using risk-neutral valuation. When carrying out scenario analyses to calculate potential future losses from defaults, we should use

---

[20] In addition to producing Table 14.1, which is based on the period from 1970 to 2007, Moody's produces a similar table based on the period from 1920 to 2007. When this table is used, historical default intensities for investment-grade bonds in Table 14.4 rise somewhat. However, the non-investment-grade historical default intensities decline.

[21] See J. D. Amato and E. M. Remolona, "The Credit Spread Puzzle," *BIS Quarterly Review*, 5 (December 2003): 51–63.

real-world default probabilities. The probability of default used to calculate regulatory capital is a real-world default probability.

14.8 USING EQUITY PRICES TO ESTIMATE DEFAULT PROBABILITIES

When we use a table such as Table 14.1 to estimate a company's real-world probability of default, we are relying on the company's credit rating. Unfortunately, credit ratings are revised relatively infrequently. This has led some analysts to argue that equity prices can provide more up-to-date information for estimating default probabilities.

In 1974, Merton proposed a model where a company's equity is an option on the assets of the company.[22] Suppose, for simplicity, that a firm has one zero-coupon bond outstanding and that the bond matures at time T. Define:

V_0: Value of company's assets today

V_T: Value of company's assets at time T

E_0: Value of company's equity today

E_T: Value of company's equity at time T

D: Amount of debt interest and principal due to be repaid at time T

σ_V: Volatility of assets (assumed constant)

σ_E: Instantaneous volatility of equity

If $V_T < D$, it is (at least in theory) rational for the company to default on the debt at time T. The value of the equity is then zero. If $V_T > D$, the company should make the debt repayment at time T and the value of the equity at this time is $V_T - D$. Merton's model, therefore, gives the value of the firm's equity at time T as

$$E_T = \max(V_T - D, 0)$$

This shows that the equity of a company is a call option on the value of the assets of the company with a strike price equal to the repayment required on the debt. The Black–Scholes formula (see Appendix E at the end of this book) gives the value of the equity today as

$$E_0 = V_0 N(d_1) - De^{-rT}N(d_2) \tag{14.4}$$

where

$$d_1 = \frac{\ln(V_0/D) + (r + \sigma_V^2/2)T}{\sigma_V\sqrt{T}}, \qquad d_2 = d_1 - \sigma_V\sqrt{T}$$

and N is the cumulative normal distribution function. The value of the debt today is $V_0 - E_0$.

The risk-neutral probability that the company will default on the debt is $N(-d_2)$. To calculate this, we require V_0 and σ_V. Neither of these is directly observable. However, if the company is publicly traded, we can observe E_0. This means that equation (14.4)

---

[22] See R. Merton "On the Pricing of Corporate Debt: The Risk Structure of Interest Rates," *Journal of Finance*, 29 (1974), 449–470.

provides one condition that must be satisfied by V_0 and σ_V. We can also estimate σ_E. From a result in stochastic calculus known as Itô's lemma, we have

$$\sigma_E E_0 = \frac{\partial E}{\partial V}\sigma_V V_0$$

Here, $\partial E/\partial V$ is the delta of the equity. From Appendix E, it is $N(d_1)$, so that

$$\sigma_E E_0 = N(d_1)\sigma_V V_0 \tag{14.5}$$

This provides another equation that must be satisfied by V_0 and σ_V. Equations (14.4) and (14.5) provide a pair of simultaneous equations that can be solved for V_0 and σ_V.[23]

Example 14.4

The value of a company's equity is \$3 million and the volatility of the equity is 80%. The debt that will have to be paid in one year is \$10 million. The risk-free rate is 5% per annum. In this case $E_0 = 3$, $\sigma_E = 0.80$, $r = 0.05$, $T = 1$, and $D = 10$. Solving equations (14.4) and (14.5) yields $V_0 = 12.40$ and $\sigma_V = 0.2123$. The parameter d_2 is 1.1408, so that the probability of default is $N(-d_2) = 0.127$ or 12.7%. The market value of the debt is $V_0 - E_0$, or 9.40. The present value of the promised payment on the debt is $10e^{-0.05 \times 1} = 9.51$. The expected loss on the debt is therefore $(9.51 - 9.40)/9.51$, or about 1.2% of its no-default value. Comparing this with the probability of default gives the expected recovery in the event of a default as $(12.7 - 1.2)/12.7$, or about 91%.

Distance to Default

The term *distance to default* has been coined to describe the output from Merton's model. This is the number of standard deviations by which the asset price must change for default to be triggered T years in the future. It is

$$\frac{\ln V_0 - \ln D + (r - \sigma_V^2/2)T}{\sigma_V \sqrt{T}}$$

As the distance to default decreases, the company becomes more likely to default. In Example 14.4, the one-year distance to default is 1.14 standard deviations.

Extensions of the Basic Model

The basic Merton model we have just presented has been extended in a number of ways. For example, one version of the model assumes that a default occurs whenever the value of the assets falls below a barrier level. Another allows payments on debt instruments to be required at more than one time. Many analysts have found the implied volatility of equity issued by a company to be a good predictor of the probability of default. (The higher the implied volatility, the higher the probability of default.) Hull *et al.* show that this is consistent with Merton's model.[24] They provide a

---

[23] To solve two nonlinear equations of the form $F(x, y) = 0$ and $G(x, y) = 0$, we can use the Solver routine in Excel to find the values of x and y that minimize $[F(x, y)]^2 + [G(x, y)]^2$.

[24] See J. Hull, I. Nelken, and A. White, "Merton's Model, Credit Risk, and Volatility Skews," *Journal of Credit Risk*, 1, 1 (2004), 1–27.

way of implementing Merton's model using two equity-implied volatilities and show that the resulting model gives results comparable with those provided by the usual implementation of the model.

Performance of the Model

How well do the default probabilities produced by Merton's model and its extensions correspond to actual default experience? The answer is that Merton's model and its extensions produce a good ranking of default probabilities for both the risk-neutral and real-world situations. This means that a monotonic transformation can be estimated to convert the probability of default output from Merton's model into a good estimate of either the real-world or risk-neutral default probability.[25] It may seem strange to use a default probability $N(-d_2)$ that is in theory a risk-neutral default probability (because it is calculated from an option pricing model) and use it to estimate a real-world default probability. Given the nature of the calibration process we have just described, the underlying assumption is that the ranking of the risk-neutral default probabilities of different companies is the same as the ranking of their real-world default probabilities.

SUMMARY

The estimation of default probabilities and recovery rates is an important activity for risk managers. If a company has issued publicly traded debt, then credit ratings provide one source of information. Rating agencies such as Moody's provide extensive statistics on default rates for companies that have been awarded particular credit ratings. The recovery rate is the fraction of a bond's principal that is recovered in the event of a default. Rating agencies also provide statistics on recovery rates for different types of bond.

There are a number of other sources of information for the estimation of default probabilities. The credit default swap (CDS) market is one such source. A CDS is an instrument where one company buys insurance against another company defaulting on its obligations. The payoff from the instrument is usually the difference between the face value of a bond issued by the second company and its value immediately after a default. The CDS spread, which can be directly related to the probability of default, is the amount paid per year for protection. Another source of information is the asset swap market. Asset swap spreads provide an estimate of the excess of a bond's yield spread over the LIBOR/swap rate. A third source of information is the equity market. A model developed by Robert Merton in 1974 can be used to estimate default probabilities from equity prices and equity volatilities.

The default probabilities that are based on historical data, such as those produced by rating agencies, are termed real-world or physical default probabilities. The default probabilities calculated from the prices of instruments that trade such as credit default swaps, bonds, or asset swaps are termed risk-neutral default probabilities. There are big differences between the two types of probability. This is mainly because bonds and related investments have systematic risk which cannot be diversified away. Traders

---

[25] Moody's KMV provides a service that transforms a default probability produced by Merton's model into a real-world default probability (which it refers to as an EDF, short for expected default frequency). CreditGrades uses Merton's model to estimate credit spreads, which are closely linked to risk-neutral default probabilities.

require compensation for more than just the real-world expected cost of defaults because of this. The default probabilities calculated from equity prices using Merton's model are in theory risk-neutral default probabilities. However, the output from the model can be calibrated so that either risk-neutral or real-world default probabilities are produced.

Real-world probabilities should be used for scenario analysis and the calculation of credit VaR. Risk-neutral probabilities should be used for valuing credit-sensitive instruments and evaluating price adjustments for counterparty default risk.

FURTHER READING

Altman, E. I., "Measuring Corporate Bond Mortality and Performance," *Journal of Finance*, 44 (1989): 902–922.

Duffie, D., and K. Singleton, "Modeling Term Structures of Defaultable Bonds," *Review of Financial Studies*, 12 (1999): 687–720.

Hull, J., M. Predescu, and A. White, "Relationship Between Credit Default Swap Spreads, Bond Yields, and Credit Rating Announcements," *Journal of Banking and Finance*, 28 (November 2004): 2789–2811.

Hull, J., M. Predescu, and A. White, "Bond Prices, Default Probabilities, and Risk Premiums," *Journal of Credit Risk*, 1, 2 (Spring 2005): 53–60.

Kealhofer, S., "Quantifying Default Risk I: Default Prediction," *Financial Analysts Journal*, 59, 1 (2003a): 30–44.

Kealhofer S., "Quantifying Default Risk II: Debt Valuation," *Financial Analysts Journal*, 59, 3 (2003b): 78–92.

Litterman, R., and T. Iben, "Corporate Bond Valuation and the Term Structure of Credit Spreads," *Journal of Portfolio Management*, Spring 1991: 52–64.

Merton, R. C., "On the Pricing of Corporate Debt: The Risk Structure of Interest Rates," *Journal of Finance*, 29 (1974): 449–470.

Rodriguez, R. J., "Default Risk, Yield Spreads, and Time to Maturity," *Journal of Financial and Quantitative Analysis*, 23 (1988): 111–117.

PRACTICE QUESTIONS AND PROBLEMS (Answers at the End of the Book)

14.1. How many investment-grade ratings does Moody's use? What are they?

14.2. How many investment-grade ratings does S&P use? What are they?

14.3. Calculate the average default intensity for B-rated companies during the first year from the data in Table 14.1.

14.4. Calculate the average default intensity for Ba-rated companies during the third year from the data in Table 14.1.

14.5. A credit default swap requires a semiannual payment at the rate of 60 basis points per year. The principal is $300 million and the credit default swap is settled in cash. A default occurs after 4 years and 2 months, and the calculation agent estimates that the price of the cheapest deliverable bond is 40% of its face value shortly after the default. List the cash flows and their timing for the seller of the credit default swap.

14.6. Explain the two ways a credit default swap can be settled.

14.7. Explain the difference between risk-neutral and real-world default probabilities.

14.8. What is the formula relating the payoff on a CDS to the notional principal and the recovery rate?

14.9. The spread between the yield on a 3-year corporate bond and the yield on a similar risk-free bond is 50 basis points. The recovery rate is 30%. Estimate the average default intensity per year over the 3-year period.

14.10. The spread between the yield on a 5-year bond issued by a company and the yield on a similar risk-free bond is 80 basis points. Assuming a recovery rate of 40%, estimate the average default intensity per year over the 5-year period. If the spread is 70 basis points for a 3-year bond, what do your results indicate about the average default intensity in years 4 and 5?

14.11. Should researchers use real-world or risk-neutral default probabilities for (a) calculating credit value at risk and (b) adjusting the price of a derivative for defaults?

14.12. How are recovery rates usually defined?

14.13. Verify (a) that the numbers in the second column of Table 14.4 are consistent with the numbers in Table 14.1, and (b) that the numbers in the fourth column of Table 14.5 are consistent with the numbers in Table 14.4 and a recovery rate of 40%.

14.14. A 4-year asset swap rate is 180 basis points (payable semiannually). The underlying corporate bond provides a coupon of 4% per year payable semiannually. The risk-free yield curve is flat at 3% with continuous compounding. Assume that defaults can take place at the end of each year (immediately before a coupon or principal payment) and the recovery rate is 30%. Estimate the risk-neutral default probability on the assumption that it is the same each year.

14.15. The 3-year and 5-year asset swaps for a company have spreads of 100 and 125 basis points (payable annually), respectively. The underlying bonds have a coupon of 4% per annum, payable annually. Risk-free interest rates are 3.5% with continuous compounding for all maturities. The recovery rate is 40%. Defaults can take place halfway through each year. The unconditional risk-neutral default rates per year are Q_1 for years 1 to 3 and Q_2 for years 4 and 5. Estimate Q_1 and Q_2.

14.16. Suppose that, in an asset swap, B is the market price of the bond per dollar of principal, B^* is the default-free value of the bond per dollar of principal, and V is the present value of the asset swap spread per dollar of principal. Show that $V = B^* - B$.

14.17. Show that, under Merton's model in Section 14.8, the credit spread on a T-year zero-coupon bond is $-\ln[N(d_2) + N(-d_1)/L]/T$, where $L = De^{-rT}/V_0$.

14.18. The value of a company's equity is $2 million and the volatility of its equity is 50%. The debt that will have to be repaid in 1 year is $5 million. The risk-free interest rate is 4% per annum. Use Merton's model to estimate the probability of default. [*Hint*: The Solver function in Excel can be used for this question.]

14.19. "The position of a buyer of a credit default swap is similar to the position of someone who is long a risk-free bond and short a corporate bond." Explain this statement.

14.20. Why is there a potential asymmetric information problem in credit default swaps?

14.21. Suppose that the LIBOR/swap curve is flat at 6% with continuous compounding and that a 5-year bond with a coupon of 5% (paid semiannually) sells for 90.00. How much would the bond be worth if it were a risk-free bond? What is the present value of the expected loss from defaults? How would an asset swap on the bond be structured? What is the asset swap spread that would be calculated in this situation?

FURTHER QUESTIONS

14.22. A 3-year asset swap spread is 100 basis points (payable semiannually). Suppose that a 3-year corporate bond provides a coupon of 7% per year payable semiannually. The yields for all maturities on risk-free bonds is 4% per annum (expressed with semiannual compounding). Assume that defaults can take place every 6 months (immediately before a coupon payment) and that the recovery rate is 45%. Estimate the default probabilities assuming (a) that the unconditional default probabilities are the same on each possible default date, and (b) that the default probabilities conditional on no earlier default are the same on each possible default date.

14.23. The 1-year and 2-year asset swap spreads for a company are 150 and 210 basis points, respectively. The underlying bonds provide a coupon of 8% per year payable annually. Risk-free rates are 4.5% for all maturities. The recovery rate is 35%. Defaults can take place halfway through each year. Estimate the risk-neutral default rate each year.

14.24. The value of a company's equity is $4 million and the volatility of its equity is 60%. The debt that will have to be repaid in 2 years is $15 million. The risk-free interest rate is 6% per annum. Use Merton's model to estimate the expected loss from default, the probability of default, and the recovery rate in the event of default. Explain why Merton's model gives a high recovery rate. [*Hint*: The Solver function in Excel can be used for this question.]

15

Credit Risk Losses and Credit VaR

This chapter is concerned with the quantification of credit risk in derivatives transactions and the calculation of credit VaR. It also covers various ways in which a financial institution can structure its transactions so as to reduce credit losses.

The chapter then covers the calculation of credit VaR. The 1996 amendment to Basel I allows banks to develop their own models for calculating VaR for market risk in the trading book. However, Basel II does not give banks quite the same freedom to calculate credit VaR for the banking book. The development of internal models for calculating credit VaR is nevertheless an important activity for banks. These models can potentially be used to determine regulatory capital for credit risk in the trading book (i.e., to determine the specific risk charge and the incremental risk charge). They can also be used when economic capital is calculated, as we will explain in Chapter 21.

Chapter 14 covered the important difference between real-world and risk-neutral default probabilities (see Sections 14.6 and 14.7). Real-world default probabilities can be estimated from historical data. Risk-neutral default probabilities can be estimated from credit default swap spreads or bond yields. When calculating expected credit losses, in the first part of this chapter, we will use risk-neutral default probabilities. This is because we are calculating the present value of future cash flows. Later in the chapter, when calculating credit VaR, we will use real-world default probabilities. This is because the purpose of this type of analysis is to evaluate future scenarios.

15.1 ESTIMATING CREDIT LOSSES

Credit losses on a loan depend primarily on the probability of default and the recovery rate. We covered ways these can be estimated in Chapter 14. In practice, a financial institution is likely to use a mixture of publicly available information and data that is based on its own experience.

Derivatives Transactions

The credit exposure on a derivatives transaction is more complicated than that on a loan. This is because the claim that will be made in the event of a default is more uncertain. Consider a financial institution that has one derivative instrument outstanding with a counterparty. We can distinguish three possible situations:

1. Derivative is always a liability to the financial institution.
2. Derivative is always an asset to the financial institution.
3. Derivative can become either an asset or a liability to the financial institution.

An example of a derivative in the first category is a short option position; an example in the second category is a long option position; an example in the third category is a forward or swap transaction.

Derivatives in the first category have no credit risk to the financial institution. If the counterparty goes bankrupt, there will be no loss. The derivative is one of the counterparty's assets. It is likely to be retained, closed out, or sold to a third party. The result is no loss (or gain) to the financial institution.

Derivatives in the second category always have credit risk to the financial institution. If the counterparty goes bankrupt, a loss is likely to be experienced. The derivative is one of the counterparty's liabilities. The financial institution has to make a claim against the assets of the counterparty and may eventually realize some percentage of the value of the derivative.[1]

Derivatives in the third category may or may not lead to a loss when there is a default. If the counterparty defaults when the value of the derivative is positive to the financial institution, a claim will be made against the assets of the counterparty and a loss is likely to be experienced. If the counterparty defaults when the value is negative to the financial institution, no loss is made because the derivative will be retained, closed out, or sold to a third party.[2]

Adjusting Derivatives' Valuations for Counterparty Default Risk

How should a financial institution adjust the value of a derivative to allow for counterparty credit risk? Consider a derivative that has a value of f_0 today assuming no defaults. Let us suppose that defaults can take place at times $t_1, t_2, \ldots, t_n$ and that the value of the derivative to the financial institution (assuming no defaults) at time t_i is f_i. Define the risk-neutral probability of default at time t_i as q_i and the expected recovery rate as R.[3]

The exposure at time t_i is the financial institution's potential loss. This is $\max(f_i, 0)$, as illustrated in Figure 15.1. Assume that the expected recovery in the event of a default is R times the exposure. Assume also that the recovery rate and the probability of default are independent of the value of the derivative. The risk-neutral valuation principle (see Business Snapshot 14.3) tells us that any future cash flow can be valued by calculating its expected value in a risk-neutral world and discounting at the risk-free

---

[1] Counterparties of derivatives transactions usually rank equally with unsecured creditors in the event of a liquidation.

[2] A company usually defaults because of the size of its liabilities and liquidity problems, not because of the value of any one transaction. At the time a company defaults, it is likely that some of its derivatives will have positive values.

[3] This probability of default can be calculated from asset swaps or bond prices in the way described in Section 14.6.

Figure 15.1   Exposure on a derivative as a function of its no-default value.

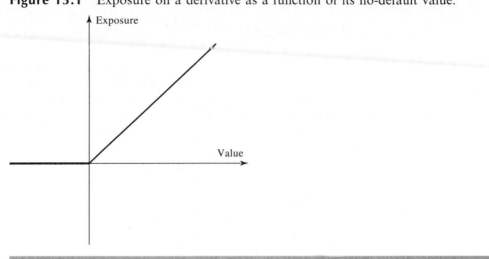

rate. The expected loss from defaults at time t_i in a risk-neutral world is[4]

$$q_i(1 - R)\hat{E}[\max(f_i, 0)]$$

where $\hat{E}$ denotes expected value in a risk-neutral world. The term $\max(f_i, 0)$ is the payoff from a "derivative of a derivative". The present value of the loss from defaults at time t_i is $u_i v_i$, where u_i equals $q_i(1 - R)$ and v_i is the result of discounting $\hat{E}[\max(f_i, 0)]$ from time t_i to the present at the risk-rate. (The variable v_i is the value of the derivative of a derivative.) Summing over all possible default times gives the total present value of the cost of defaults as

$$\sum_{i=1}^{n} u_i v_i \tag{15.1}$$

Consider again the three categories of derivatives mentioned earlier. The first category (where the derivative is always a liability to the financial institution) is easy to deal with. The value of f_i is always negative, so that v_i is always zero. The cost of counterparty defaults to the financial institution is zero, and the financial institution therefore needs to make no adjustments for this in its pricing. (Of course, the counterparty may want to take account of the possibility of the financial institution defaulting in its own analysis.)

For the second category (where the derivative is always an asset to the financial institution), f_i is always positive. This means than the expression $\max(f_i, 0)$ always equals f_i. Suppose that the only payoff from the derivative is at the end of its life, time T. In this case, f_0 must be the present value of f_i, so that $v_i = f_0$ for all i. The expression in equation (15.1) for the present value of the cost of defaults becomes

$$f_0 \sum_{i=1}^{n} q_i(1 - R)$$

---

[4] Note that this expression is not correct if the probability of default depends on the exposure.

If f_0^* is the actual value of the derivative (after allowing for possible defaults), it follows that

$$f_0^* = f_0 - f_0 \sum_{i=1}^{n} q_i(1 - R) = f_0 \left[1 - \sum_{i=1}^{n} q_i(1 - R) \right] \qquad (15.2)$$

One particular instrument that falls into the second category we are considering is an unsecured zero-coupon bond issued by the counterparty that promises \$1 at time T. Define B_0 as the value of the bond assuming no possibility of default and B_0^* as the actual value of the bond. Assuming that the bond ranks equally with the derivative in the event of a default, it will have the same recovery rate, so that

$$B_0^* = B_0 \left[1 - \sum_{i=1}^{n} q_i(1 - R) \right] \qquad (15.3)$$

From equations (15.2) and (15.3),

$$\frac{f_0^*}{f_0} = \frac{B_0^*}{B_0} \qquad (15.4)$$

If y is the yield on a risk-free zero-coupon bond maturing at time T and y^* is the yield on a zero-coupon bond issued by the counterparty that matures at time T, then $B_0 = e^{-yT}$ and $B_0^* = e^{-y^*T}$, so that equation (15.4) gives

$$f_0^* = f_0 e^{-(y^* - y)T} \qquad (15.5)$$

This shows that any derivative promising a payoff at time T can be valued by discounting the default-free value of the derivative by $y^* - y$.

Example 15.1

Consider a two-year over-the-counter option sold by a company with a value, assuming no possibility of default, of \$3. Suppose that two-year zero-coupon bonds issued by the company have a yield that is 1.5% greater than a similar risk-free zero-coupon bond. The value of the option is

$$3e^{-0.015 \times 2} = 2.91$$

or \$2.91.

For the third category of derivatives, the sign of f_i is uncertain. The variable v_i is a call option on f_i with a strike price of zero. One way of calculating all the v's with a single analysis is to simulate the underlying market variables over the life of the derivative. Sometimes it is possible to use analytic calculations, look-up tables, and algorithms to obtain an approximate answer.

Example 15.2

Suppose that a bank has just entered into a forward contract to buy 1 million ounces of gold from a mining company in two years. The forward price in the contract is \$800 per ounce. Suppose that only two default times are considered: one year from today and two years from today. The chance of the company defaulting one year from today is 2% and the chance of it defaulting two years from today is 3%. The risk-free rate is 5% per annum. The financial institution anticipates a 30% recovery in the event of a default. The volatility of the forward price of gold for a contract expiring in two years is 20%.

In this case,

$$u_1 = 0.02 \times (1 - 0.3) = 0.014 \quad \text{and} \quad u_2 = 0.03 \times (1 - 0.3) = 0.021$$

The value of the forward contract in one year is $(F_1 - 800)e^{-0.05 \times 1}$, where F_1 is the forward price for a one-year contract in one year (see Appendix C). The value of v_1 is therefore the value of a contract that pays $\max[(F_1 - 800)e^{-0.05 \times 1}, 0]$ million dollars in one year. This is the same as $e^{-0.05 \times 1} \max(F_1 - 800, 0)$ million dollars. The present value of this is $e^{-0.05 \times 1}$ times the value of a one-year call option on F_1. From DerivaGem, the value of a one-year call option on a futures contract when the initial future price is 800, the strike price is 800, the risk-free rate is 5%, the volatility is 20%, and the time to maturity is one year is \$60.62. The value of v_1 is therefore $60.62e^{-0.05}$, or \$57.66 million.

The value of the forward contract in two years is $F_2 - 800$, where F_2 is the forward price of gold in two years. (This is the same as the spot price.) The value of v_2 is therefore the value of a contract that pays off $\max(F_2 - 800, 0)$ in two years. This is the value of a two-year call option on F_2. From DerivaGem, the value of a two-year call option on a futures contract when the initial future price is 800, the strike price is 800, the risk-free rate is 5%, the volatility is 20%, and the time to maturity is two years is \$81.41. The value of v_1 is therefore \$81.41 million.

The expected cost of defaults is

$$u_1 v_1 + u_2 v_2 = 0.014 \times 57.66 + 0.021 \times 81.41 = 2.52$$

or \$2.52 million. This example can be extended to consider the situation where the mining company can default more frequently (see Problem 15.15).

The analysis we have presented assumes that the probability of default is independent of the value of the derivative. This is likely to be a reasonable approximation in circumstances where the derivative is a small part of the portfolio of the counterparty or where the counterparty is using the derivative for hedging purposes. When a counterparty wants to enter into a large derivatives transaction for speculative purposes, a financial institution should be wary. When the transaction has a large negative value for the counterparty (and a large positive value for the financial institution), the probability of counterparty declaring bankruptcy may be much higher than when the situation is the other way round.

Traders working for a financial institution use the term *right-way risk* to describe the situation where a counterparty is most likely to default when the financial institution has zero or very little exposure. They use the term *wrong-way risk* for the situation where the counterparty is most likely to default when the financial institution has a big exposure.

Interest Rate Swaps vs. Currency Swaps

The impact of default risk on interest rate swaps is considerably less than that on currency swaps. Figure 15.2 shows the reason for this. It compares the expected exposure for a bank on a pair of offsetting interest rate swaps entered into with different counterparties with the expected exposure on a pair of offsetting currency swaps entered into with different counterparties. The expected exposure on the interest rate swaps starts at zero, increases, and then decreases to zero. By contrast, expected exposure on

Figure 15.2   Expected exposure on a pair of offsetting interest rate swaps and a pair of offsetting currency swaps.

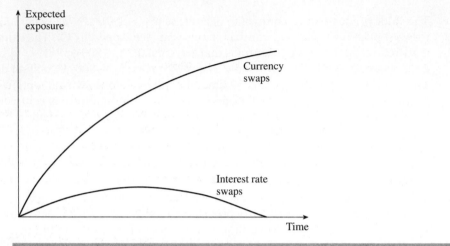

the currency swaps increases steadily with the passage of time.[5] The main reason for the difference is that principals are exchanged at the end of the life of a currency swap and there is uncertainty about the exchange rate at that time.[6]

Two-Sided Default Risk

One of the interesting aspects of derivatives in the third category (that is, derivatives that can become assets or liabilities) is that there is two-sided default risk. For example, if company X enters into a currency swap with company Y, company X may lose money if company Y defaults, and vice versa. Human nature being what it is, most financial and nonfinancial companies consider that there is no chance that they themselves will default, but they want to receive compensation for a possible default by their counterparty. In our example, company X wants to be compensated for the possibility that company Y will default, and company Y wants to be compensated for the possibility that company X will default. Unless they are both highly creditworthy, this can make it very difficult for the two companies to agree on terms.

In theory, the value of the currency swap to company X should be

$$f - y + x$$

where f is the value if both sides were default-free, y is the adjustment necessary for the possibility of company Y defaulting, and x is the adjustment necessary for company X itself defaulting. Similarly, the value to company Y should be

$$-f - x + y$$

In practice, company X is likely to calculate a value of $f - y$ and company Y is likely to

---

[5] The expected exposure affects the v_i in equation (15.1). The u_i are the same for both swaps.

[6] Currency swaps with no final exchange of principal have become more popular in recent years. These have less credit risk and market risk than traditional currency swaps.

calculate a value of $-f - x$. Unless x and y are small it is unlikely that the companies will be able to agree on a price.

Continuing with our currency swap example, suppose that interest rates in the foreign and domestic currency are the same and that company X and company Y are equally creditworthy. The swap is symmetrical in the sense that it has just as much chance of moving in the money for company X as for company Y. In this case, $x = y$ and neither side should in theory make any adjustment for credit risk.

15.2 CREDIT RISK MITIGATION

In many instances the analysis we have just presented overstates the credit risk in a derivatives transaction. This is because there are a number of clauses that derivatives dealers include in their contracts to mitigate credit risk.

Netting

We discussed netting in Section 11.5. Banks have master agreements with each of their counterparties that cover all outstanding transactions. A netting clause in the master agreement states that, if a company defaults on one transaction it has with a counterparty, it must default on all outstanding transactions with the counterparty. Netting has been successfully tested in the courts in most jurisdictions and can substantially reduce credit risk for a financial institution.

As explained in Section 11.5, without netting, the future exposure on a portfolio of transactions is the payoff from a portfolio of options. With netting, it is the payoff from an option on the portfolio. The latter is always either the same or less than the former. We can extend the analysis presented in the previous section so that equation (15.1) gives the present value of the expected loss from all transactions with a counterparty when netting agreements are in place. This is achieved by redefining v_i in the equation as the present value of a derivative that pays off the exposure at time t_i on the portfolio of all transactions with a counterparty.

A challenging task for a financial institution when considering whether it should enter into a new derivatives transaction with a counterparty is to calculate the incremental effect on expected credit losses. This can be done by using equation (15.1) in the way just described to calculate expected default costs with and without the new transaction, but this is liable to be too time-consuming if the trader has to make a quick decision on whether a certain trade is acceptable. If a Monte Carlo simulation (perhaps run over the weekend) has been used to calculate expected default costs for a counterparty's portfolio, the results from the simulation trials can be stored so that, when a new transaction is being considered, only it needs to be valued for each trial. It is interesting to note that, because of netting, the incremental effect of a new transaction on expected default losses can be negative. This tends to happen when the value of the new transaction is highly negatively correlated with the value of existing transactions.

It might be thought that, in well-functioning capital markets, a company wanting to enter into a derivatives transaction will get the same quote from all dealers. Netting shows that this is not necessarily the case. The company is likely to get the most favorable quote from a financial institution it has done business with in the past—particularly if that business gives rise to exposures for the financial institution that are opposite to the exposure generated by the new transaction.

Collateralization

Another clause frequently used in master agreements to mitigate credit risks is known as *collateralization*. Suppose that a company and a financial institution have entered into a number of derivatives transactions. A typical collateralization agreement specifies that the transactions be valued periodically. If the total value of the transactions to the financial institution is above a specified threshold level, the agreement requires the company to post collateral with the financial institution. The amount of collateral posted, when added to collateral already posted by the company, should be equal to the difference between the value of the transactions to the financial institution and the threshold level. When the total value of the transactions moves in favor of the company so that the difference between the value of the transactions to the financial institution and the threshold level is less than the total margin already posted, the company can reclaim collateral that has been posted. In the event of a default by the company, the financial institution can seize the collateral. If the company does not post collateral as required, it is in default and transactions are liable to be closed out by the financial institution. Long-Term Capital Management made extensive use of collateralization agreements (see Business Snapshot 15.1).

Suppose, for example, that the threshold level for the company is $10 million and transactions are valued daily for the purposes of collateralization. If, on a particular day, the value of the transactions to the financial institution rises from $9 million to $10.5 million, it can ask for $0.5 million of collateral. If on the next day the value of the transactions rises to $11.4 million, it can ask for a further $0.9 million of collateral. If the value of the transactions falls to $10.8 million on the following day, the company can ask for $0.6 million of the collateral to be returned. Note that the threshold ($10 million in this case) can be regarded as a line of credit that the financial institution is granting to the company.

Collateral must be deposited by the company with the financial institution in cash or in the form of acceptable securities such as bonds. Interest is normally paid on cash. The securities are subject to a discount known as a *haircut* applied to their market value for the purposes of collateral calculations.

If the collateralization agreement is a two-way agreement, a threshold will also be specified for the financial institution. The company can then ask the financial institution to post collateral when the value of the outstanding transactions to the company exceeds the threshold.

Collateralization agreements provide a great deal of protection against the possibility of default (just as the margin accounts discussed in Chapter 5 provide protection for people who trade on an exchange). However, the threshold amount is not subject to protection. Furthermore, even when the threshold is zero, the protection is not total. When a company gets into financial difficulties, it is likely to stop responding to requests to post collateral. By the time the counterparty exercises its right to close out transactions, their value may have moved further in its favor.

Downgrade Triggers

Another credit mitigation technique used by a financial institution is known as a *downgrade trigger*. This is a clause in the master agreement stating that if the credit

> **Business Snapshot 15.1** Long-Term Capital Management's Big Loss
>
> Long-Term Capital Management (LTCM), a hedge fund formed in the mid-1990s, always collateralized its transactions. The hedge fund's investment strategy was known as convergence arbitrage. A very simple example of what it might do is the following. It would find two bonds, X and Y, issued by the same company promising the same payoffs, with X being less liquid (i.e., less actively traded) than Y. The market always places a value on liquidity. As a result the price of X would be less than the price of Y. LTCM would buy X, short Y and wait, expecting the prices of the two bonds to converge at some future time.
>
> When interest rates increased, the company expected both bonds to move down in price by about the same amount, so that the collateral it paid on bond X would be about the same as the collateral it received on bond Y. Similarly, when interest rates decreased LTCM expected both bonds to move up in price by about the same amount, so that the collateral it received on bond X would be about the same as the collateral it paid on bond Y. It therefore expected that there would be no significant outflow of funds as a result of its collateralization agreements.
>
> In August 1998, Russia defaulted on its debt and this led to what is termed a "flight to quality" in capital markets. One result was that investors valued liquid instruments more highly than usual and the spreads between the prices of the liquid and illiquid instruments in LTCM's portfolio increased dramatically. The prices of the bonds LTCM had bought went down and the prices of those it had shorted increased. It was required to post collateral on both. The company was highly leveraged and unable to make the payments required under the collateralization agreements. The result was that positions had to be closed out and there was a total loss of about $4 billion. If the company had been less highly leveraged, it would probably have been able to survive the flight to quality and could have waited for the prices of the liquid and illiquid bonds to become closer.

rating of the counterparty falls below a certain level, say Baa, the financial institution has the option to close out all outstanding transactions. Typically, a financial institution will choose to close out transactions when their value is positive to the financial institution and negative to the counterparty.

Downgrade triggers do not provide protection from a big jump in a company's credit rating (for example, from A to default). Also, downgrade triggers work well only when relatively little use is made of them. If a company has downgrade triggers in its master agreements with many financial institutions, they are liable to provide relatively little protection to the financial institutions. The Enron bankruptcy illustrates this (see Business Snapshot 15.2).

15.3 CREDIT VaR

Credit value at risk is defined in the same way as market value at risk. For example, a credit VaR with a confidence level of 99.9% and a one-year time horizon is the credit

---

Business Snapshot 15.2 Downgrade Triggers and Enron's Bankruptcy

In December 2001 Enron, one of the largest companies in the United States, went bankrupt. Right up to the last few days, it had an investment-grade credit rating. The Moody's rating immediately prior to default was Baa3 and the S&P rating was BBB−. The default was, however, anticipated to some extent by the stock market because Enron's stock price fell sharply in the period leading up to the bankruptcy. The probability of default estimated by models such as the one described in Section 14.8 increased sharply during this period.

Enron had entered into a huge number of derivatives agreements with downgrade triggers. The downgrade triggers stated that, if its credit rating fell below investment grade (i.e., below Baa3/BBB−), its counterparties would have the option of closing out transactions. Suppose that Enron had been downgraded to below investment grade in, say, October 2001. Those counterparties whose transactions with Enron had a negative value to Enron (and positive value to the counterparties) would choose to close out. Other counterparties would not. As a result Enron would have been required to make huge cash payments to its counterparties. It would not have been able to do this and immediate bankruptcy would result.

This example illustrates that downgrade triggers provide protection only when relatively little use is made of them! When a company enters into a huge number of agreements with downgrade triggers, they may actually cause a company to go bankrupt prematurely. In Enron's case we could argue that it was going to go bankrupt anyway and accelerating the event by two months would not have done any harm. In fact, Enron did have a chance of survival in October 2001. Attempts were being made to work out a deal with another energy company, Dynergy, and so forcing bankruptcy in October 2001 was not in the interests of either creditors or shareholders.

The credit-rating companies found themselves in a difficult position. If they downgraded Enron to recognize its deteriorating financial position, they were signing its death warrant. If they did not do so, there was a chance of Enron surviving.

---

loss that we are 99.9% confident will not be exceeded over one year. Whereas the time horizon for market risk is usually between one day and one month, that for credit risk is usually much longer—often one year.

As explained in Chapter 11, banks do not have complete freedom in the way they calculate credit VaR for regulatory capital purposes. (Under the IRB approach they are allowed to use their own estimates for probabilities of default, and possibly for other parameters as well, but must use the Gaussian copula model and correlations prescribed by Basel II.) However, banks do have complete freedom in the models they choose when calculating economic capital. (As discussed in Chapter 21, this is a bank's own estimate of the capital it requires.) Banks are also given some freedom in the calculation of credit VaR for the purposes of determining the specific risk charge for credit-sensitive items in the trading book (see Section 11.6). Although standard rules for determining specific risk have been specified, banks can, with regulatory approval, use their own models. For a model to be approved, the bank supervisor must be satisfied that concentration risk, spread risk, downgrade risk, and default risk are appropriately captured. The confidence limit and time horizon is the same as for market risk (99% and ten days). The capital charge for specific risk is the product of a multiplier and the calculated VaR with the minimum multiplier being 4. Another regulatory credit risk VaR calculation where banks may have some freedom in their choice of model is the incremental risk charge (see Section 11.12). This is based on a VaR calculated with a one-year 99% confidence level and reflects the impact of defaults, downgrades, credit spread increases, and liquidity-related losses for certain items in the trading book.

15.4 THE VASICEK AND MERTON MODELS

Vasicek's model, which we discussed in Sections 10.5 and 11.8, provides an easy way to estimate credit VaR for a loan portfolio. From equation (10.12), the model leads to the result that the percentage of defaults on a large portfolio by time T will be less than

$$\text{WCDR}(T, X) = N\left(\frac{N^{-1}[Q(T)] + \sqrt{\rho}\, N^{-1}(X)}{\sqrt{1 - \rho}}\right)$$

with probability X, where $Q(T)$ is the cumulative probability of each loan defaulting by time T and ρ is the copula correlation. When multiplied by the average exposure per counterparty and by the average loss given default, this gives the T-year VaR for an $X\%$ confidence level. As explained in Chapter 11, the Basel committee has based the capital it requires under the IRB approach for credit risk in the banking book on this model. The time horizon T is one year, the confidence level X is 99.9%, and the value of ρ is prescribed by the Basel committee. The variation of the 99.9% worst-case probability of default with the average probability of default and ρ is shown in Table 11.5.

A key decision is the choice of ρ. Basel II specifies the value to be used when regulatory capital is determined for items in the banking book. When a portfolio of corporate defaults is being modeled, structural models of the type discussed in Section 14.8 can be used to show that ρ should be roughly equal to the correlation between asset prices. As an approximation, this is the same as the correlation between equity prices. One way of determining ρ for a portfolio of exposures to companies is therefore to calculate the average correlation between the equity prices of the companies. If the companies are not publicly traded, the average correlation between representative publicly traded companies can be used instead. For retail and other exposures, ρ can in theory be determined from historical experience. However, the model has limitations. Suppose we observe that the average one-year probability of default is 1% and that one year in ten this is greater than 3%. It turns out that there is no parameter ρ that is consistent with these observations. Other one-factor copula models of the time to default must be developed to provide a fit to data in this type of situation.[7]

Another way of examining the credit risk in a portfolio is by using Merton's model. This model was described in Section 14.8. It is a model where the value of the assets of a company is assumed to follow a stochastic process. The company defaults by time T if the value of the assets is less than a certain barrier level (theoretically the debt level) at time T.[8]

[7] In the context of pricing CDOs, Hull and White show that a wide range of alternative models can be developed by choosing nonnormal distributions for F and Z_i in equation (10.9). See J. Hull and A. White, "Valuation of a CDO and nth to Default CDS Without Monte Carlo Simulation," *Journal of Derivatives*, 12, 2 (Winter 2004), 8–23.

[8] As explained in Section 14.8, the basic Merton model can be extended in a number of ways.

In order to use the model to assess default risk on a portfolio, a multicompany version of Merton's model is necessary. The assets of different companies are assumed to follow correlated stochastic processes. A barrier is associated with each company and a default by a company occurs when its assets fall below its barrier. Moody's KMV uses this approach in conjunction with a factor model for the correlations between the stochastic processes driving asset prices. (See Section 10.3 for a discussion of factor models.) Vasicek's model can be viewed as a one-factor version of a multicompany Merton model.

15.5 CREDIT RISK PLUS

In 1997, Credit Suisse Financial Products proposed a methodology for calculating VaR that it termed *Credit Risk Plus*.[9] It utilizes ideas that are well established in the insurance industry. We will present a simplified version of the approach.

Suppose that a financial institution has N counterparties of a certain type and that the probability of default by each counterparty in time T is p. The expected number of defaults for the whole portfolio, μ, is given by $\mu = Np$. Assuming that default events are independent and p is small, the probability of n defaults is given by the Poisson distribution as

$$\frac{e^{-\mu}\mu^n}{n!}$$

This can be combined with a probability distribution for the losses experienced on a counterparty default (taking account of the impact of netting) to obtain a probability distribution for the total default losses from the counterparties. The probability distribution for losses from a counterparty default can be determined from (a) the current probability distribution of exposures to counterparties and (b) an estimate of the recovery rates.

In practice, it is likely to be necessary for the financial institution to consider several different counterparty categories. This means that the analysis just described must be carried out for each category and the results combined.

Another complication is that default rates vary significantly from year to year. As has been discussed, data from Moody's show that the probability of default on speculative-grade bonds during the 1970 to 2007 period varied from a low of 0.418% in 1979 to a high of 9.978% in 2001. To account for this, a probability distribution for the default rate per year can be assumed for each category of counterparties. One approach is to assume a probability distribution for the overall default rate (perhaps from data provided by one of the rating agencies) and then to assume that the default rate for each counterparty category is proportional to this. For example, one counterparty category might be assumed to have a default rate equal to 70% of the overall default rate; another might be assumed to have a default rate equal to 120% of the overall default rate, and so on.

Rating agency data show that the default rate in one year is not independent of the default rate in the previous year. One way of taking this into account is to fit overall default rate data to an autoregressive model.

---

[9] See Credit Suisse Financial Products, "Credit Risk Management Framework," October, 1997.

Figure 15.3 Probability distribution of default losses.

0   Loss

Credit Suisse Financial Products shows that, if certain assumptions are made, the total loss probability distribution can be calculated analytically. To accommodate more general assumptions, Monte Carlo simulation can be used. The procedure is

1. Sample an overall default rate
2. Calculate a probability of default for each counterparty category
3. Sample a number of defaults for each counterparty category
4. Sample a loss for each default
5. Calculate total loss
6. Repeat steps 1–5 many times to build up a probability distribution for the total loss
7. Calculate the required VaR from the total loss probability distribution

If the default rate is assumed to be the same each year, there is no default correlation between different companies and the loss probability distribution is roughly symmetrical. The effect of assuming a probability distribution for the overall default rate is to build in default correlation and make the probability distribution of total default losses positively skewed, as indicated in Figure 15.3. The default correlation arises because, when a high (low) overall default rate is sampled, all companies have a high (low) probability of default.

The model outlined above assumes that a single factor drives all default rates. It can be generalized to the situation where there are several factors driving company default rates.

15.6 CREDITMETRICS

Credit Risk Plus estimates the probability distribution of losses arising from defaults. An appealing feature of what is known as *CreditMetrics* is that it estimates the probability distribution of losses from both downgrades and default. (As indicated earlier, regulators like the models used for estimating credit risk in the trading book to have this property.)

CreditMetrics was proposed by J.P. Morgan in 1997. It is based on an analysis of credit migration. This is the probability of a company moving from one rating category to another during a certain period of time. A typical one-year *ratings transition matrix* is shown in Table 15.1. It indicates the percentage probability of a bond moving from one rating category to another during a one-year period. For example, a bond that starts with an A credit rating has a 90.23% chance of still having an A rating at the end of one year. It has a 0.08% chance of defaulting during the year, a 0.11% chance of dropping to B, and so on.

Consider a bank with a portfolio of corporate bonds. Calculating a one-year VaR for the portfolio using CreditMetrics involves carrying out a Monte Carlo simulation of ratings transitions for bonds in the portfolio over a one-year period. On each simulation trial the final credit rating of all bonds is calculated and the bonds are revalued to determine total credit losses for the year. The 99% worst result is the one-year 99% VaR for the portfolio.

It is interesting to note that, if both the CreditMetrics and the Credit Risk Plus models were based on the same set of assumptions, they would predict the same probability distribution for losses over the long term. It is the timing of losses that is different. Suppose for example that you hold a certain bond in your portfolio. In year 1 it gets downgraded from A to BBB; in year 2 it gets downgraded from BBB to B; in year 3 it defaults. You could assume that there are no losses in years 1 and 2 and calculate loss in year 3 (the Credit Risk Plus approach). Alternatively, you can calculate separate revaluation losses in years 1, 2, and 3 (the CreditMetrics approach). The losses under the second approach should in theory add up to the losses under the first approach.

There are two key issues in the implementation of CreditMetrics. One is handling correlations between bonds. The other is calculating credit spreads for valuing the bonds at the end of the year.

Table 15.1 One-year ratings transition matrix, 1970–2007, with probabilities expressed as percentages and adjustments for transition to the without-rating (WR) category. *Source*: Moody's.

Initial rating	*Rating at year end*								
	Aaa	Aa	A	Baa	Ba	B	Caa	Ca–C	Default
Aaa	91.37	7.59	0.85	0.17	0.02	0.00	0.00	0.00	0.00
Aa	1.29	90.84	6.85	0.73	0.19	0.04	0.00	0.00	0.07
A	0.09	3.10	90.23	5.62	0.74	0.11	0.02	0.01	0.08
Baa	0.05	0.34	4.94	87.79	5.54	0.84	0.17	0.02	0.32
Ba	0.01	0.09	0.54	6.62	82.76	7.80	0.63	0.06	1.49
B	0.01	0.06	0.20	0.73	7.10	81.24	5.64	0.57	4.45
Caa	0.00	0.03	0.04	0.24	1.04	9.59	71.50	3.97	13.58
Ca–C	0.00	0.00	0.14	0.00	0.55	3.76	8.41	64.19	22.96
Default	0.00	0.00	0.00	0.00	0.00	0.00	0.00	0.00	100.00

The CreditMetrics Correlation Model

In sampling to determine credit losses, the credit-rating changes for different counter-parties should not be assumed to be independent. A Gaussian copula model can be used to construct a joint probability distribution of rating changes (see Section 10.4 for a discussion of copula models). The copula correlation between the rating transitions for two companies is typically set equal to the correlation between their equity returns, with a factor model similar to that in Section 10.3 being assumed for the correlation structure of equity returns.

As an illustration of the CreditMetrics approach, suppose that we are simulating the rating change of an A-rated and a B-rated company over a one-year period using the transition matrix in Table 15.1. Suppose that the correlation between the equity returns of the two companies is 0.2. On each simulation trial, we would sample two variables x_A and x_B from standard normal distributions, so that their correlation is 0.2. The variable x_A determines the new rating of the A-rated company, and variable x_B determines the new rating of the B-rated company. Since

$$N^{-1}(0.0009) = -3.1214$$

$$N^{-1}(0.0009 + 0.0310) = -1.8536$$

$$N^{-1}(0.0009 + 0.0310 + 0.9023) = 1.5078$$

the A-rated company gets upgraded to Aaa if $x_A < -3.1214$, it becomes Aa-rated if $-3.1214 < x_A < -1.8536$, it stays A-rated if $-1.8536 < x_A < 1.5078$, and so on. Similarly, since

$$N^{-1}(0.0001) = -3.7190$$

$$N^{-1}(0.0001 + 0.0006) = -3.1947$$

$$N^{-1}(0.0001 + 0.0006 + 0.0020) = -2.7822$$

the B-rated company becomes Aaa-rated if $x_B < -3.7190$, it becomes Aa-rated if $-3.7190 < x_B < -3.1947$, it becomes A-rated if $-3.1947 < x_B < -2.7822$, and so on. The A-rated company defaults if $x_A > N^{-1}(0.9992)$, that is, when $x_A > 3.1559$. The B-rated company defaults when $x_B > N^{-1}(0.9555)$, that is, when $x_B > 1.7007$. This example is illustrated in Figure 15.4.

Spread Changes

In order to revalue the portfolio of bonds on each simulation trial, it is necessary to calculate spread changes. One way of proceeding is to use a one-factor regression model to divide the spread changes for each bond into a systematic component and an idiosyncratic component. The systematic component is the spread change that affects all bonds in the rating category being considered. The idiosyncratic component affects only one particular bond.

If the systematic component of spread changes is reflected in market risk VaR calculations, it is only necessary to take account of the idiosyncratic spread changes in specific risk VaR calculations. On each trial, we therefore calculate not only what happens to the rating of each bond but also an idiosyncratic spread change for the

Figure 15.4   The CreditMetrics correlation model: Transition of A-rated and
B-rated companies to a new rating after one year. The variables x_A and x_B are
sampled from standard normal distributions, with the correlation equal to the
correlation between the equity returns of the companies.

bond. For each bond on each simulation trial one of three things happen:

1. The credit rating of the bond stays the same. In this case the bond is revalued in a
    way that reflects the idiosyncratic spread change for the bond.
2. The credit rating of the bond changes. In this case the bond is revalued using a
    spread corresponding to the new rating category.
3. The bond defaults. In this case a recovery rate is sampled. Often the recovery rate
    is assumed to have a beta distribution centered on the mean recovery rate
    published by rating agencies (see Table 14.2).

Time Horizon

Regulators require a bank's credit VaR for specific risk to be a ten-day 99% VaR. In
practice, this means that a bank has two choices. One is to calculate a one-year 99%
VaR in the way we have just outlined and then use the square root rule to scale it to a
ten-day 99% VaR. If for convenience we assume 250 days in a year (rather than the
usual 252), this means that the calculated VaR is divided by about 5. The other is to
convert the transition matrix in Table 15.1 from a one-year transition matrix to a
ten-day transition matrix and use the procedure we have just described to calculate a

ten-day loss distribution directly. If we assume that ratings transitions in successive periods are independent, the second approach involves finding a matrix B such that $B^{25} = A$, where A is the matrix in Table 15.1. A procedure for doing this is outlined in Appendix J at the end of the book.

SUMMARY

The credit risk on a loan depends on the probability of default and the recovery rate (or equivalently the loss given default). The credit risk in a derivatives transaction is more complicated than that in a loan because the exposure at the time of default is uncertain. Some derivatives transactions (e.g., written options) are always liabilities and give rise to no credit risk. Some (e.g., long positions in options) are always assets and entail significant credit risks. The most difficult types of derivatives transaction to deal with from a credit risk perspective are those that may become either assets or liabilities during their life. Examples are forward and swap transactions.

The over-the-counter market has developed a number of ways of mitigating credit risk. The most important of these is netting. This is a clause in most agreements that are entered into by a financial institution stating that, if a counterparty defaults on one transaction it has with the financial institution, then it must default on all transactions with the financial institution. Another credit mitigation technique is collateralization. This requires a counterparty to post collateral. If the value of its outstanding transactions with the financial institution moves against the counterparty, more collateral is required. In the event that collateral is not posted in a timely fashion, the contract is closed out. A third credit mitigation technique is the downgrade trigger. This gives a company the option to close out transactions if the credit rating of the counterparty falls below a certain level.

Credit VaR can be defined in the same way that VaR is defined for market risk. It is the credit loss that will not be exceeded over some time horizon with a specified confidence level. The Basel II IRB methods calculate credit VaR for the banking book using a one-factor Gaussian copula model of time to default that was originally developed by Vasicek. An approach for calculating credit VaR that is similar to procedures used in the insurance industry is Credit Risk Plus which was proposed by Credit Suisse Financial Products in 1997. For specific risk in the trading book, most large banks use CreditMetrics which was proposed by J.P. Morgan in 1997. This involves simulating rating changes for companies. Default correlation is introduced by assuming a Gaussian copula model for rating changes.

FURTHER READING

Credit Suisse Financial Products, "Credit Risk Management Framework," October, 1997.

Finger, C.C., "The One-Factor CreditMetrics Model in the New Basel Capital Accord," *RiskMetrics Journal*, Summer 2001.

J.P. Morgan, "CreditMetrics—Technical Document," April 1997.

PRACTICE QUESTIONS AND PROBLEMS (Answers at the End of the Book)

15.1. A bank already has one transaction with a counterparty on its books. Explain why a new transaction by a bank with a counterparty can have the effect of increasing or reducing the bank's credit exposure to the counterparty.

15.2. What is meant by a haircut in a collateralization agreement? A company offers to post its own equity as collateral. How would you respond?

15.3. Explain the difference between Vasicek's model, the Credit Risk Plus model, and CreditMetrics as far as the following are concerned: (a) when a credit loss is recognized and (b) the way in which default correlation is modeled.

15.4. Suppose that a financial institution has entered into a swap dependent on the sterling interest rate with counterparty X and an exactly offsetting swap with counterparty Y. Determine which of the following statements are true and which are false. Explain your answers.
   (a) The total present value of the cost of defaults is the sum of the present value of the cost of defaults on the transaction with X plus the present value of the cost of defaults on the transaction with Y.
   (b) The expected exposure in one year on both transactions is the sum of the expected exposure on the transaction with X and the expected exposure on the transaction with Y.
   (c) The 95% upper confidence limit for the exposure in one year on both transactions is the sum of the 95% upper confidence limit for the exposure in one year on the transaction with X and the 95% upper confidence limit for the exposure in one year on the transaction with Y.

15.5. A US company enters into a one-year forward contract to sell 100 USD for 150 AUD. The contract is initially at the money. In other words, the forward exchange rate is 1.50. The one-year US dollar risk-free rate of interest is 5% per annum. The one-year US dollar rate of interest at which the counterparty can borrow is 6% per annum. The exchange rate volatility is 12% per annum. Estimate the present value of the cost of defaults on the contract. Assume that defaults are recognized only at the end of the life of the contract.

15.6. Suppose that in Problem 15.5, the six-month forward rate is also 1.50 and the six-month US dollar risk-free interest rate is 5% per annum. Suppose further that the six-month US dollar rate of interest at which the counterparty can borrow is 5.5% per annum. Estimate the present value of the cost of defaults assuming that defaults can occur either at the six-month point or at the one-year point. (If a default occurs at the six-month point, the company's potential loss is the market value of the contract.)

15.7. "A long forward contract subject to credit risk is a combination of a short position in a no-default put and a long position in a call subject to credit risk." Explain this statement.

15.8. Explain why the credit exposure on a pair of offsetting forward contracts with different counterparties resembles a straddle.

15.9. "When a bank is negotiating a pair of offsetting currency swaps with different counterparties, it should try to ensure that it is receiving the currency with the lower interest rate from the counterparty with the lower credit risk." Explain why.

15.10. Suppose that the spread between the yield on a three-year riskless zero-coupon bond and a three-year zero-coupon bond issued by a corporation is 1%. By how much do standard option pricing models such as Black–Scholes overstate the value a three-year option sold by the corporation?

15.11. Can the existence of default triggers increase default risk? Explain your answer.

FURTHER QUESTIONS

15.12. Explain carefully the distinction between real-world and risk-neutral default probabilities. Which is higher? A bank enters into a credit derivative where it agrees to pay $100 at the end of one year if a certain company's credit rating falls from A to Baa or lower during the year. The one-year risk-free rate is 5%. Using Table 15.1, estimate a value for the derivative. What assumptions are you making? Do they tend to overstate or understate the value of the derivative?

15.13. Suppose that a bank has a total of $10 million of exposures of a certain type. The one-year probability of default averages 1% and the recovery rate averages 40%. The copula correlation parameter is 0.2. Estimate the 99.5% one-year credit VaR.

15.14. Consider a European option on a non-dividend-paying stock where the stock price is $52, the strike price $50, the risk-free rate is 5%, the volatility is 30%, and the time to maturity is one year. Answer the following questions assuming no recovery in the event of default and that the probability of default is independent of the option valuation.
 (a) What is the value of the option assuming no possibility of a default?
 (b) What is the value of the option to the buyer if there is a 2% chance that the option seller will default at maturity?
 (c) Suppose that, instead of paying the option price up front, the option buyer agrees to pay the forward value of the option price at the end of option's life. By how much does this reduce the cost of default to the option buyer in the case where there is a 2% chance of the option seller defaulting?
 (d) If in case (c) the option buyer has a 1% chance of defaulting at the end of the life of the option, what is the default risk to the option seller? Discuss the two-sided nature of default risk in this case and the value of the option to each side.

15.15. Extend Example 15.2 so that default can happen at the end of each month. Assume that the default probability at the end of each month during the first year is 0.001667 and the default probability at the end of each month of the second year is 0.0025. Use the DerivaGem Applications Builder.

ABSs, CDOs, and the Credit Crunch of 2007

Starting in 2007, the United States experienced the worst financial crisis since the 1930s. The crisis spread rapidly from the United States to other countries and from financial markets to the real economy. Some financial institutions failed. Many more had to be bailed out by national governments. The first decade of the twenty-first century has been disastrous for the financial sector, and the risk management practices of financial institutions have been subjected to a great deal of criticism.

This chapter examines the origins of the crisis, what went wrong, and why it went wrong. It discusses what needs to be done to avoid similar crises in the future. In the course of the chapter, we will learn about the US mortgage market, asset-backed securities, and collateralized debt obligations.

16.1 THE US HOUSING MARKET

A natural starting point for any discussion of the credit crunch of 2007 is the US housing market. Figure 16.1 shows the S&P/Case–Shiller Composite-10 index for house prices in the US between January 1987 and November 2008. In about the year 2000, house prices started to rise much faster than they had in the previous decade. The very low level of interest rates between 2002 and 2005 was an important contributory factor, but the bubble in house prices was largely fueled by mortgage-lending practices.

The 2000 to 2006 period was characterized by a huge increase in what is termed subprime mortgage lending. Subprime mortgages are mortgages that are considered to be significantly more risky than average. Before 2000, most mortgages classified as subprime were second mortgages. After 2000, this changed as financial institutions became more comfortable with the notion of a subprime first mortgage.

The Relaxation of Lending Standards

Mortgage lenders started to relax their lending standards in about 2000. This made house purchase possible for many families that had previously been considered to be not sufficiently creditworthy to qualify for a mortgage. These families increased the demand for real estate and prices rose. To mortgage brokers and mortgage lenders the combination of more lending and higher house prices was attractive. More lending meant bigger

Figure 16.1   The S&P/Case–Shiller Composite-10 index of US real estate prices, 1987 to 2008.

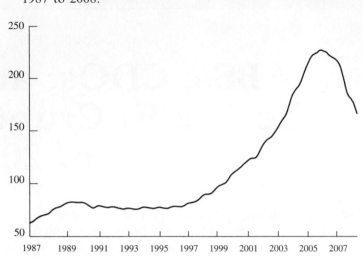

profits. Higher house prices meant that the lending was well covered by the underlying collateral. If the borrower defaulted, the resulting foreclosure would not lead to a loss.

How could mortgage brokers and mortgage lenders keep increasing their profits? Their problem was that, as house prices rose, it was more difficult for first-time buyers to afford a house. In order to continue to attract new entrants to the housing market, they had to find ways to relax their lending standards even more—and this is exactly what they did. The amount lent as a percentage of the house price increased. Adjustable rate mortgages (ARMS) were developed where there was a low "teaser" rate of interest that would last for two or three years and be followed by a rate that was much higher.[1] A typical teaser rate was about 6% and the rate after the end of the teaser-rate period was typically six-month LIBOR plus 6%.[2] However, teaser rates as low as 1% or 2% have been reported. Lenders also became more cavalier in the way they reviewed mortgage applications. Indeed, the applicant's income and other information reported on the application were frequently not checked.

Why was the government not regulating the behavior of mortgage lenders? The answer is that the US government has since the 1990s been trying to expand home ownership, and has been applying pressure to mortgage lenders to increase loans to people with low and moderate incomes. Some state legislators (such as those in Ohio and Georgia) were concerned about what was going on and wanted to curtail predatory lending.[3] However, the courts decided that national standards should prevail.

---

[1] If real estate prices increased, lenders expected the borrowers to prepay and take out a new mortgage at the end of the teaser rate period. However, prepayment penalties, often zero on prime mortgages, were quite high on subprime mortgages.

[2] A "2/28" ARM, for example, is an ARM where the rate is fixed for two years and then floats for the remaining 28 years.

[3] Predatory lending describes the situation where a lender deceptively convinces borrowers to agree to unfair and abusive loan terms.

A number of terms have been used to describe mortgage lending during the period leading up to the credit crunch. One is "liar loans", so-called because individuals applying for a mortgage, knowing that no checks would be carried out, sometimes chose to lie on the application form. Another term used to describe some borrowers is "NINJA" (no income, no job, no assets.) To quote from Krinsman (2007),[4] "In 2005 and 2006, lenders made it easier for borrowers to obtain subprime loans. For example, the typical subprime borrower with a (FICO) credit score between 450 and 680 could obtain a loan with little or no down payment, provide little or no documented proof of income or assets, obtain a loan with a low initial 'teaser' interest rate that reset to a new, higher rate after two or three years..." (Mortgages where the borrower had a FICO score less than 620 were typically classified as subprime, but when the down payment was low, 680 was sometimes used as the subprime cutoff.) Some people realized that the mortgages were risky, but pricing in the market for ABSs and ABS CDOs suggest that the full extent of the risks and their potential impact on markets was not appreciated until well into 2007. (ABSs and ABS CDOs will be discussed later in the chapter.)

Mian and Sufi have carried out research confirming that there was a relaxation of the criteria used for mortgage lending.[5] Their research defines "high denial zip codes" as zip codes where a high proportion of mortgage applicants had been turned down in 1996, and shows that mortgage origination grew particularly fast for these zip codes between 2000 to 2007. Moreover, their research shows that lending criteria were relaxed progressively through time rather than all at once because originations in high denial zip codes are an increasing function of time during the 2000 to 2007 period. Zimmerman (2007) provides some confirmation of this.[6] He shows that subsequent default experience indicates that mortgages made in 2006 were of a lower quality than those made in 2005 and that the latter were in turn of lower quality than the mortgages made in 2004. Standard & Poor's has estimated that subprime mortgage origination in 2006 alone totaled $421 billion. AMP Capital Investors estimates that there was a total of $1.4 trillion of subprime mortgages outstanding in July 2007.

The Bubble Bursts

The result of the relaxation of lending standards was a bubble in house prices. Prices increased very fast during the 2000 to 2006 period. All bubbles burst eventually, and this one was no exception. In 2007, many mortgage holders found that they could no longer afford their mortgages when teaser rates ended. This led to foreclosures and a large number of houses coming on the market, which in turn led to a decline in house prices. Other mortgage holders, who had borrowed 100%, or close to 100%, of the cost of a house found that they had negative equity.

One of the features of the US housing market is that mortgages are nonrecourse in many states. This means that, when there is a default, the lender is able to take possession of the house, but other assets of the borrower are off-limits. Consequently, the borrower has a free American-style put option. He or she can at any time sell the

[4] See A. N. Krinsman, "Subprime Mortgage Meltdown: How Did It Happen and How Will It End," *Journal of Structured Finance*, Summer 2007: 13–19.

[5] See A. Mian and A. Sufi, "The Consequences of Mortgage Credit Expansion: Evidence from the 2007 Mortgage Default Crisis," Working Paper, Graduate School of Business, University of Chicago, 2008.

[6] See T. Zimmerman, "The Great Subprime Meltdown," *Journal of Structured Finance*, Fall 2007: 7–20.

house to the lender for the principal outstanding on the mortgage. (During the teaser interest rate period this principal typically increased, making the option more valuable.) Market participants realized belatedly how costly the put option could be. If the borrower had negative equity, the optimal decision was to exchange the house for the outstanding principal on the mortgage. The house was then sold, adding to the downward pressure on house prices.

It would be a mistake to assume that all mortgage defaulters were in the same position. Some were unable to meet mortgage payments and suffered greatly when they had to give up their homes. But many of the defaulters were speculators who bought multiple homes as rental properties and chose to exercise their put options. It was their tenants who suffered. There are also reports that some house owners (who were not speculators) were quite creative in extracting value from their put options. After handing the keys of their houses to the lender, they turned around and bought (sometimes at a bargain price) other houses that were in foreclosure. Imagine two people owning identical houses next to each other. Both have mortgages of $250,000. Both houses are worth $200,000 and in foreclosure can be expected to sell for $170,000. What is the owners' optimal strategy? The answer is that each person should exercise the put option and buy the neighbor's house. (There were ways of doing this without getting a bad credit rating.)

As Figure 16.1 illustrates, the bubble burst during the 2006–2007 period. Many mortgage holders found they could no longer afford mortgages when teaser rates ended. Foreclosures increased. House prices declined. This resulted in other mortgage holders, who had borrowed 100%, or close to 100%, of the cost of a house having negative equity. Some exercised their implicit put options and "walked away" from their houses and their mortgage obligations. This reinforced the downward trend in house prices.

The United States was not alone in having declining real estate prices. Prices declined in many other countries as well. Real estate in the United Kingdom was particularly badly affected.

16.2 SECURITIZATION

The originators of mortgages did not in many cases keep the mortgages themselves. They sold portfolios of mortgages to companies that created products for investors from them. This process is known as *securitization*. Securitization has been an important and useful tool in financial markets for many years. It underlies the originate-to-distribute model that was widely used by banks prior to 2007 and is discussed in Chapter 2.

Securitization played a part in the creation of the housing bubble. The behavior of mortgage originators was influenced by their knowledge that mortgages would be securitized.[7] When considering new mortgage applications, the question was not, "Is this a credit we want to assume?" Instead it was, "Is this a mortgage we can make money on by selling it to someone else?"

When mortgages were securitized, the only information received about the mortgages by the buyers of the products that were created from them was the loan-to-value ratio

---

[7] Research by Keys *et al.* shows that there was a link between securitization and the lax screening of mortgages. See B. J. Keys, T. Mukherjee, A. Seru, and V. Vig, "Did Securitization Lead to Lax Screening? Evidence from Subprime Loans," Working Paper, University of Michigan, 2008.

(i.e., the ratio of the size of the loan to the assessed value of the house) and the borrower's FICO score. The reason why lenders did not check information on things such as the applicant's income, the number of years the applicant had lived at his or her current address, and so on, was that this information was considered irrelevant. The most important thing for the lender was whether the mortgage could be sold to others—and this depended primarily on the loan-to-value ratio and the applicant's FICO score.

It is interesting to note in passing that both the loan-to-value ratio and the FICO score were of doubtful quality. The property assessors who determined the value of a house at the time of a mortgage application sometimes succumbed to pressure from the lenders to come up with high values. Potential borrowers were sometimes counseled to take certain actions that would improve their FICO scores.[8]

We now consider the products that were created from the mortgages and sold in the market.

Asset-Backed Securities

An ABS (*asset-backed security*) is a security created from the cash flows of financial assets such as loans, bonds, credit card receivables, mortgages, auto loans, and aircraft leases. Sometimes, cash flow streams such as royalties from the future sales of a piece of music are even used. The way the security works is illustrated by Figure 16.2. A portfolio of assets (such as subprime mortgages) is sold by the originators of the assets to a special purpose vehicle (SPV) and the cash flows from the assets are allocated to tranches. In Figure 16.2, there are three tranches. These are the senior tranche, the mezzanine tranche, and the equity tranche. The portfolio has a principal of $100 million. This is

Figure 16.2 An asset-backed security (simplified).

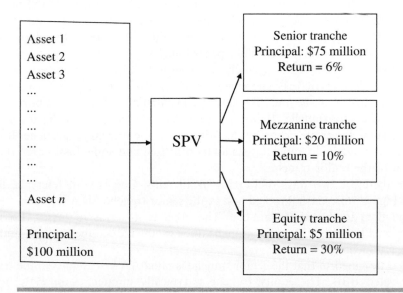

---

[8] One such action might be to make regular payments on a credit card for a few months.

Figure 16.3 The waterfall in an asset-backed security.

divided as follows: $75 million to the senior tranche, $20 million to the mezzanine tranche, and $5 million to the equity tranche. The senior tranche is promised a return of 6%, the mezzanine tranche is promised a return of 10%, and the equity tranche is promised a return of 30%.

It sounds as though the equity tranche has the best deal, but this is not necessarily the case. The equity tranche is much less likely to realize its return than the other two tranches. Cash flows are allocated to tranches by specifying what is known as a waterfall. The general way a waterfall works is illustrated in Figure 16.3. The cash flows from the assets are allocated to the senior tranche until the senior tranche has received its promised return. Assuming that the promised return to the senior tranche can be made, cash flows are then allocated to the mezzanine tranche. If the promised return to the mezzanine tranche can be made and cash flows are left over, they are allocated to the equity tranche. The precise waterfall rules are outlined in a legal document that is usually several hundred pages long.

The structure in Figure 16.2 typically lasts several years. At the end, principal payments are made to tranches. The extent to which the tranches get their principal back depends on losses on the underlying assets. The first 5% of losses are borne by the principal of the equity tranche. If losses exceed 5%, the equity tranche loses all its principal and some losses are borne by the principal of the mezzanine tranche. If losses exceed 25%, the mezzanine tranche loses all its principal and some losses are borne by the principal of the senior tranche.

There are therefore two ways of looking at an ABS. One is with reference to the waterfall in Figure 16.3. Cash flows go first to the senior tranche, then to the mezzanine tranche, and then to the equity tranche. The other is in terms of losses. Losses of principal are first borne by the equity tranche, then by the mezzanine tranche, and then by the senior tranche.

The ABS is designed so that the senior tranche is rated AAA. The mezzanine tranche is typically rated BBB. The equity tranche is typically unrated. Unlike the ratings assigned to bonds, the ratings assigned to the tranches of an ABS are what might be termed "negotiated ratings". The objective of the creator of the ABS is to make the senior tranche as big as possible without losing its AAA credit rating. (This maximizes the profitability of the structure.) The ABS creator examines information published by rating agencies on how tranches are rated and may present several structures to rating agencies for a preliminary evaluation before choosing the final one.

A particular type of ABS is a *collateralized debt obligation* (CDO). This is an ABS where the underlying assets are fixed-income securities.

ABS CDOs

Finding investors to buy the senior AAA-rated tranches created from subprime mortgages was not difficult. Equity tranches were typically retained by the originator of the mortgages or sold to a hedge fund. Finding investors for the mezzanine tranches was more difficult. This led financial engineers to be creative (arguably too creative). Financial engineers created an ABS from the mezzanine tranches of ABSs that were created from subprime mortgages. This is known as an *ABS CDO* or *Mezz ABS CDO* and is illustrated in Figure 16.4. The senior tranche of the ABS CDO is rated AAA. This means that the total of the AAA-rated instruments created in the example that is considered here is 90% (75% plus 75% of 20%) of the principal of the underlying mortgage portfolio. This seems high but, if the securitization were carried further with an ABS being created from the mezzanine tranches of ABS CDOs (and this did happen), the percentage would be pushed higher.

In the example in Figure 16.4, the AAA-rated tranche of the ABS would probably be downgraded in the second half of 2007. However, it would probably receive the promised return if losses on the underlying mortgage portfolio were less than 25% because all losses of principal would be absorbed by the more junior tranches. The AAA-rated tranche of the ABS CDO in Figure 16.4 is much more risky. It will get paid the promised return if losses on the underlying portfolio are 10% or less because in that case mezzanine tranches of ABSs have to absorb losses equal to 5% of the ABS principal or less. As they have a total principal of 20% of the ABS principal, their loss is at most 5/20, or 25%. At worst this wipes out the equity tranche and mezzanine tranche of the ABS CDO but leaves the senior tranche unscathed.

The senior tranche of the ABS CDO suffers losses if losses on the underlying portfolios are more than 10%. Consider, for example, the situation where losses

Figure 16.4   An ABS CDO (simplified).

Table 16.1   Losses to AAA-rated tranches of ABS CDO in Figure 16.4.

Losses to subprime portfolios	Losses to mezzanine tranche of ABS	Losses to equity tranche of ABS CDO	Losses to mezzanine tranche of ABS CDO	Losses to senior tranche of ABS CDO
10%	25%	100%	100%	0%
15%	50%	100%	100%	33%
20%	75%	100%	100%	67%
25%	100%	100%	100%	100%

are 20% on the underlying portfolios. In this case, losses on the mezzanine tranches are 15/20, or 75%, of their principal. The first 25% is absorbed by the equity and mezzanine tranches of the ABS CDO. The senior tranche of the ABS CDO therefore loses 50/75, or 67%, of its value. These and other results are summarized in Table 16.1.

Many banks have lost money investing in the senior tranches of ABS CDOs. The investments were typically financed at LIBOR and promised a return quite a bit higher than LIBOR. Because they were rated AAA, the capital requirements were minimal. Merrill Lynch is an example of a bank that lost a great deal of money from investments in ABS CDOs. In July 2008 Merrill Lynch agreed to sell senior tranches of ABS CDOs that had previously been rated AAA and had a principal of $30.6 billion to Lone Star Funds for 22 cents on the dollar.[9]

ABSs and ABS CDOs in Practice

Figure 16.4 illustrates the nature of the securitizations that were done. In practice, more tranches were created and many of the tranches were thinner (i.e., corresponded to a narrower range of losses) than those in Figure 16.4. Figure 16.5 shows a more realistic example of the structures that were created. This is adapted from an illustration by Gorton, which was taken from an article by UBS.[10]

It can be seen that two ABS CDOs might be created. One is created from the BBB-rated tranches of ABSs (as with the ABS CDO in Figure 16.4); the other is from the AAA, AA, and A tranches of ABSs. The figure shows a third level of securitization based on the A and AA tranches of the Mezz ABS CDO.

Many of the tranches in Figure 16.5 (e.g., the BBB tranches of the ABS that cover losses from 1% to 4% and are used to create the Mess ABS CDO) appear to be very risky. In fact, they are less risky than they appear when the details of the waterfalls of the underlying ABSs are taken into account. In the arrangement in Figure 16.5, there is some *over-collateralization* with the face value of the mortgages being greater than the face value of the instruments that are created by the ABSs. There is also some *excess spread* so that the aggregate of the returns promised to tranche holders is less

---

[9] In fact the deal was worse than it sounds for Merrill Lynch because Merrill Lynch agreed to finance 75% of the purchase price. Presumably, if the value of the tranches fell below 16.5 cents on the dollar, Merrill Lynch might find itself owning the assets again.

[10] G. Gorton, "The Panic of 2007," Working Paper, Yale School of Management, 2008.

Figure 16.5   More realistic example of subprime securitizations: ABS, Mezz ABS CDO, and CDO of CDO have some overcollateralization and excess spread.

than the aggregate of the interest payments due on the mortgages. If because of these features there are cash flows left over when all ABS tranches have received their promised returns, the cash flows are used to reduce the principal on the senior tranches.

16.3   VALUATION MISTAKES

The risks in the AAA-rated tranches of ABS CDOs and, to a lesser extent, ABSs were higher than either investors or rating agencies realized. The values of the tranches of ABSs depend on the default correlation of the underlying mortgages. The tranches of ABS CDOs are even more heavily dependent on these default correlations. If mortgages exhibit moderate default correlation (as they do in normal times), there is very little chance of a high overall default rate and the AAA-rated tranches are fairly safe. But, in stressed market conditions, the default correlation can be expected to increase so that very high default rates become possible. One way of recognizing this is to use a copula model for time to default that involves Student t-distributions rather than the usual normal distributions.

Business Snapshot 16.1   Not All BBBs Are the Same

Analysts tended to assume that the mezzanine tranche of an ABS, when rated BBB, can be considered to be identical to a BBB bond for the purposes of evaluating a CDO created from the mezzanine tranches. This is not a good assumption. The BBB tranche of an ABS may have the same probability of loss, or the same expected loss, as a BBB bond, but the probability distribution of the loss is different. For example, it is much more likely that an investor in the tranche of an ABS will lose 100% of the principal than that this will happen for a BBB-rated bond. (This is sometimes referred to as "cliff risk".) This means that the risk characteristics of ABS CDO tranches are quite different from the risk characteristics of similar CDO tranches created from bonds. This difference becomes more pronounced as tranches become thinner—and, as indicated by Figure 16.5, the mezzanine tranches in an ABS CDO were typically quite thin.

One lesson from this is that it is dangerous to interpret ratings for the tranches of an ABS—or any other structured product—in the same way that ratings for bonds are interpreted.

As explained in Business Snapshot 16.1, one mistake made by analysts was to assume that the BBB-rated tranches of an ABS could be treated in the same way as BBB-rated bonds. There are important differences between the two, and these differences can have a big effect on the risks of the tranches of ABS CDOs.

The ABSs and ABS CDOs that were created were complex instruments that were difficult to analyze. Many investors did not take the trouble to analyze the products they were buying. They made the mistake of relying on ratings without understanding the assumptions they were based on. The fact that AAA-rated tranches promised considerably higher returns than AAA-rated bonds should have served as a warning sign that there were risks that were not taken into account by the ratings.

16.4 AVOIDING FUTURE CRISES

Many factors contributed to the financial crisis that started in 2007. Mortgage originators used lax lending standards. Products were developed to enable mortgage originators to profitably transfer credit risk to investors. The products bought by investors were complex, and in many instances investors and rating agencies had inaccurate or incomplete information about the quality of the underlying assets. Rating agencies moved from their traditional business of rating bonds to rating structured products and assigned a AAA rating to tranches that were in some cases highly dependent on the default correlation between the underlying assets. Investors in the structured products that were created thought they had found a money machine and chose to rely on rating agencies rather than forming their own opinions about the underlying risks. The return earned by the products was high (e.g., LIBOR plus 120 basis points) and they required very little capital because of the AAA rating. (Typically the capital was 7% of the principal.) Traders loved the products because their returns on regulatory capital (and therefore their bonuses) were high.

How can future crises be avoided? Here are a few observations.

Agency Costs: Originators and Investors

Agency cost is a term used by economists to describe the cost in a situation where the interests of two parties in a business relationship are not perfectly aligned. It should be clear from the discussion earlier in this chapter that there were agency costs in the US mortgage market because the interests of the originators of mortgages and the interests of investors were not perfectly aligned. The present crisis might have been less severe if the originators of mortgages (and other assets where credit risk is transferred) were required by regulators to keep, say, 20% of each tranche created. This would have better aligned the interests of originators with the interests of the investors who bought the tranches. The market for structured products virtually disappeared during the credit crisis. However, the finance sector has a short memory. The market is likely to reappear at some future time. Regulators and rating agencies should be sensitive to situations where the interests of parties are not aligned.

The most important reason why originators should have a stake in all the tranches created is that this encourages the originators to make the same lending decisions that the investors would make. Another reason is that the originators often end up as administrators of the mortgages (collecting interest, making foreclosure decisions, etc.). It is important that their decisions as administrators are in the best interests of investors. The originators of mortgages did sometimes keep the equity tranches of ABSs. This aligned their interests somewhat with the interests of the investors who purchased tranches. However, the equity tranche was often regarded as free by an originator because it had obtained adequate compensation for the mortgages from the sales of the other tranches to investors. Furthermore, once the equity tranche had been wiped out, mortgage originators had no stake at all in the performance of the mortgages.

It is important to note that there is a difference between (a) a mortgage lender securitizing 80% of its portfolio and (b) a mortgage lender securitizing 100% of its portfolio while keeping 20% of each tranche. In the first case, there will always be a suspicion that the better loans have been retained by the originator and that screening was lax on the rest. Rating agencies might reasonably assign a higher rating to tranches of a portfolio where a percentage of each tranche has been retained. However, the regulatory capital for the whole portfolio of mortgages that are originated should be the same in both cases.

This idea might have reduced the market excesses during the period leading up to the credit crunch of 2007. However, it should be acknowledged that one of the ironies of the credit crunch is that securitization did not in many instances get the mortgages off the books of originating banks. Often AAA-rated senior tranches were bought by other parts of the bank. Because banks were both investors in and originators of mortgages, one might expect a reasonable alignment of the interests of investors and originators. But the part of the bank investing in the mortgages was usually far removed from the part of the bank originating the mortgages and there appears to have been little information flow from one to the other.

Some regulators have made proposals similar to the one here. Not surprisingly, they have been met with a great deal of opposition from the banks.[11] However, many banks have received huge capital injections from the government and may not be in a strong position to oppose the proposals.

---

[11] See W. Rhode, "Keep What You Sow," *Risk*, 21, 10 (October 2008): 56–58.

Agency Costs: Financial Institutions and Their Employees

Another source of agency costs concerns financial institutions and their employees. Employee compensation falls into three categories: regular salary, the end-of-year bonus, and stock or stock options. Many employees at all levels of seniority in financial institutions, particularly traders, receive much of their compensation in the form of end-of-year bonuses. This form of compensation is focused on short-term performance. If an employee generates huge profits one year and is responsible for severe losses the next, a big bonus will be paid at the end of the first year and the employee will not have to return it the following year. The employee might lose his or her job as a result of the second year losses, but even that is not a disaster. Financial institutions seem to be surprisingly willing to recruit individuals with losses on their résumés.

Imagine you are an employee of a financial institution investing in ABS CDOs in 2006. Almost certainly you would have recognized that there was a bubble in the US housing market and would expect that bubble to burst sooner or later. However, it is possible that you would decide to continue with your ABS CDO investments. If the bubble did not burst until after December 31, 2006, you would still get a nice bonus at the end of 2006.

It is not necessarily the case that salaries on Wall Street are too high. Instead, it is the case that they should be calculated differently. Politicians and regulators are urging financial institutions to base the performance-related component of an employee's remuneration on performance over a longer period of time than one year (say, five years). One idea is the following. At the end of each year a financial institution awards a "bonus accrual" (positive or negative) to each employee reflecting the employee's contribution to the business. The actual cash bonus received by an employee at the end of a year would be the average bonus accrual over the previous five years or zero, whichever is higher. For the purpose of this calculation, bonus accruals would be set equal to zero for years prior to the employee joining the financial institution and bonuses would not be paid after an employee leaves it. Although not perfect, this type of plan would motivate employees to use a multiyear time horizon when making decisions.

Transparency

An ABS or ABS CDO is typically defined by a legal document several hundred pages long. As already mentioned, many investors did not analyze this document carefully when they bought AAA-rated tranches of the structures. They relied on the "AAA" label. Once the tranches were perceived as risky, it became almost impossible to trade them. This was because potential investors did not understand enough about the underlying portfolio and the algorithm used to determine the cash flows received by the various tranches.

ABSs (and particularly ABS CDOs) are arguably the most complex credit derivatives that are traded. Lawyers should move with the times and define these instruments using software rather than words. In addition to providing a data file with the attributes of the mortgages or other instruments underlying the instruments, lawyers should provide software enabling the cash flows realized by different tranches in different circumstances to be calculated. The user's inputs to the software would define a possible outcome concerning interest and principal payments on the underlying instruments each year. The outputs would be the cash flows realized by each tranche holder each year. The problems of defining structures such as ABS CDOs where tranches are defined in terms of other tranches could be handled efficiently. The creators of tranches should be required to publish information about the performance of the underlying assets and tranches in a way that is compatible with the software produced by the originators and their lawyers.

There are companies that provide investors with detailed information about tranches of the sort suggested here. However, the information is expensive and not widely available to researchers and financial commentators. Ensuring that the information is widely available would be advantageous for the functioning of markets. Investors and independent researchers would have no difficulties in running scenario analyses and forming their own opinions about the values of different tranches. The illiquidity of the ABS and ABS CDO market in 2007 and 2008 might then not have been as severe as it was. (Indeed, investors might have better understood the risks in the ABS CDO market in the first place.) A good case can be made for defining many derivatives (particularly the more complex ones) using software rather than written confirmations because the latter are very cumbersome as a description of how the products work.

The Need for Models

Normally financial institutions do not trade instruments unless they have satisfactory models for valuing them. Typically there is a group within a financial institution that has the responsibility of vetting the model used for valuing a product, and the product cannot be traded in any volume until the model has been approved (see Chapter 20). What is surprising about the subprime crisis is that financial institutions were prepared to trade senior tranches of an ABS or an ABS CDO without a model. Possibly it was thought that a model is unnecessary for valuing a AAA-rated instrument. But the lack of a model makes risk management almost impossible and causes problems when the instrument is downgraded.

The readiness of financial institutions to trade ABS CDOs is particularly surprising. An ABS CDO is a similar structure to what is called a *CDO squared* in the synthetic CDO market. (This market is discussed in the next section.) CDO squareds are recognized by traders in the synthetic CDO market as highly risky products that are difficult to price. The market for them has disappeared largely for this reason. A tranche of an ABS CDO is no less risky and no less difficult to price than a tranche of a CDO squared, but it was nevertheless considered by many financial institutions to be a good investment. Because models were not developed, the key role of correlation in valuing ABSs and (particularly) ABS CDOs was not well understood.

How Models Are Used

Having the models to value ABSs and ABS CDOs would have helped, but it would not by itself have been enough to mitigate the subprime crisis. To understand how models might have helped, we have to consider how they should have been used. The risk measures used by regulators, and by financial institutions themselves, are largely based on historical experience. For example, value-at-risk measures for market risk are typically based on the movements in market variables seen over the last two to four years. Credit risk measures are based on default experience stretching back over a hundred years. Stress testing often involves looking at the largest market moves experienced over the last 10, 20, or 30 years.

There can be no question that historical data provides a useful guide for risk managers. But historical data cannot be used in conjunction with models in a mechanistic way to determine whether risks are acceptable. In risk management, it is important that models be supplemented with human judgment. A risk management committee consisting of senior managers should meet regularly to consider the key risks facing a financial institution. Stress tests should be based on the scenarios generated by these managers in addition to those generated from historical data. The risk committee should be particularly sensitive to situations where the market appears to be showing bouts of "irrational exuberance".[12] This is discussed further in Chapter 17.

One of the lessons from past financial crises is that correlations increase in stressed market conditions. Using standard value-at-risk techniques to estimate correlations from past data and assuming that those correlations will apply in stressed markets is not appropriate. One of the roles of the risk management committee should have been to recognize the bubble in house prices and insist that stress tests where default rates simultaneously rise in all parts of the country be carried out. Of course, it is also important that key decision makers within the bank actually listen to risk managers and the risk management committee—particularly during periods of irrational exuberance. There is some evidence that they are reluctant to do this.

16.5 SYNTHETIC CDOS

As already mentioned, when an ABS is created from bonds or other fixed-income instruments it is referred to as a CDO. More precisely, it is a *cash CDO* because the underlying instruments are instruments that trade in the cash market. To round off our description of ABSs and CDOs, we now describe what are known as *synthetic CDOs*.

A long position in a corporate bond has essentially the same credit risk as the seller of protection (i.e., the party with a short position) in a credit default swap (see Chapter 14 for a discussion of credit default swaps.) This observation has led to an alternative way of creating a CDO. Instead of forming a portfolio of corporate bonds, the originator of the CDO forms a portfolio consisting of short positions in credit default swaps. The credit risks are then passed on to tranches. A CDO created in this way is known as a *synthetic CDO*.

A synthetic CDO is structured so that default losses on the credit default swap portfolio are allocated to tranches and the tranche principals are reduced by the amount of the losses. Suppose that the total notional principal underlying the portfolio of credit default swaps is $100 million and that there are three tranches. The situation might be as follows:

1. Tranche 1 is responsible for the first $5 million of losses. As compensation for this, it earns 15% on the remaining Tranche 1 principal.

2. Tranche 2 is responsible for the next $20 million of losses. As compensation for this, it earns 100 basis points on the remaining Tranche 2 principal.

3. Tranche 3 is responsible for all losses in excess of $25 million. As compensation for this, it earns 10 basis points on the remaining Tranche 3 principal.

---

[12] Irrational exuberance was a term coined by Alan Greenspan during the bull market of the 1990s.

The principals for Tranches 1, 2, and 3 are initially $5 million, $20 million, and $75 million, respectively. The notional principal in a tranche is reduced by the payoffs on the underlying CDSs. Initially, the protection sellers for Tranche 1 receive 15% on a principal of $5 million. Suppose that, after six months, a default leads to a payoff of $1 million on an underlying CDS. This is paid by the protection seller to the protection buyer and the notional principal of Tranche 1 is reduced by $1 million, so that the protection seller then receives 15% on $4 million rather than $5 million. If payoffs on the CDSs exceed $5 million, Tranche 1 gets wiped out and Tranche 2 becomes responsible for payoffs. When payoffs reach $7 million, the notional principal in Tranche 2 is $18 million and Tranche 2 has by that time paid amounts totaling $2 million.[13]

Standard Portfolios and Single Tranche Trading

In Section 14.4 we discussed CDS indices such as CDX NA IG and iTraxx Europe. These track credit spreads on investment grade bonds in North America and Europe, respectively. The market uses the portfolios underlying these indices to define standard tranches. The CDX IG NA portfolio consists of 125 investment grade North American companies. The equity tranche covers losses between 0% and 3% of the principal. The mezzanine tranche covers losses between 3% and 7%. The remaining tranches cover losses from 7–10%, 10–15%, 15–30%, and 30–100%. In the case of iTraxx Europe, the tranches cover losses from 0–3%, 3–6%, 6–9%, 9–12%, 12–22%, and 22–100%.

Traders can trade a single tranche of a synthetic CDO, once it has been defined, without the structure being created. This is known as *single-tranche trading*. The synthetic CDO structure is simply used as a reference point to define cash flows between the trader who is buying protection and the trader who is selling protection.

Table 16.2 shows the quotes for iTraxx tranches at the end of January on three successive years. To understand the quotes, consider the January 31, 2007, row of the table. The index level of 23 basis points indicates that (ignoring bid–offer spreads) it would cost 23 basis points per year to buy five-year protection on all 125 companies underlying the index. (For example, if $1 million of protection was bought on each

Table 16.2 Mid-market quotes for five-year tranches of iTraxx Europe. Quotes are in basis points except for the 0–3% tranche where the quote equals the percent of the tranche principal that must be paid up front in addition to 500 basis points per year. *Source*: Creditex Group Inc.

| Date | \| *Tranche* | | | | | *iTraxx index* |
	0–3%	3–6%	6–9%	9–12%	12–22%	
January 31, 2007	10.34%	41.59	11.95	5.60	2.00	23
January 31, 2008	30.98%	316.90	212.40	140.00	73.60	77
January 30, 2009	64.28%	1185.63	606.69	315.63	97.13	165

---

[13] In practice, sellers of protection are required to post the initial tranche principal as collateral up front. This collateral earns LIBOR. When the tranche becomes responsible for the payoff on a CDS, the money is taken out of the collateral. The recovery amounts when defaults occur are usually used to retire principal on the most senior tranche. Note that the senior tranche does not lose the principal that is retired. It just fails to earn the spread (10 basis points in our example) on it.

company, the cost would be $0.0023 \times \$1,000,000 \times 125$, or \$287,500 per year.) A trader could buy five-year protection against losses on the underlying portfolio that are in the range 6–9% for 11.95 basis points. Suppose that the amount of protection bought is \$6 million. This is the initial tranche principal. Payoffs from the protection seller to the protection buyer depend on default losses on the iTraxx Europe portfolio. While the cumulative loss is less than 6% of the portfolio principal, there is no payoff. As soon as the cumulative loss exceeds 6% of the portfolio principal, payoffs start. If, at the end of year 3, the cumulative loss rises from 6% to 7% of the portfolio principal, the protection seller pays the protection buyer \$2 million and the tranche principal reduces to \$4 million. If, at the end of year 4, the cumulative loss increases from 7% to 9% of the portfolio principal, the protection seller pays the protection buyer an additional \$4 million and the tranche principal reduces to zero. Subsequent losses then give rise to no payments. Payments from the protection buyer to the protection seller are made quarterly in arrears and equal 0.001195% of the remaining tranche principal. Initially the payments are made at the rate of $0.001195 \times \$6,000,000 = \$7,170$ per year.

The equity (0–3%) tranche is quoted differently from other tranches. The market quote of 10.34% means that the protection seller receives an initial payment equal to 10.34% of the tranche principal and then receives 500 basis points per year on the remaining tranche principal.

What a difference two years makes in credit markets! The credit crunch has led to a huge increase in credit spreads. The iTraxx index rose from 23 basis points in January 2007 to 165 basis points in January 2009. The individual tranche quotes have also shown huge increases. One reason for the changes is that the market's assessment of default probabilities for investment-grade corporations has increased. However, it is also the case that protection sellers were in many cases experiencing liquidity problems. They became more averse to risk and increased the risk premiums they required.

The Role of Default Correlation

The standard model for valuing tranches of CDOs is the Gaussian copula model that we first met in Chapter 10. The role of default correlation in valuing the tranches of CDOs is interesting. When correlation is low, the equity tranche is almost certain to sustain losses and can easily get wiped out.[14] However, the senior tranches are relatively safe.

As the correlation increases, the senior tranches become more vulnerable, but the expected loss on the equity tranche actually goes down. To understand this, suppose that the probability of default is 10% and that the default correlation is perfect. We are then in an all-or-nothing position. There is a 10% probability that all the companies default and a 90% probability that none of them do so. As a result, there is a 90% probability that the equity tranche will escape unscathed.

SUMMARY

The credit crisis starting in 2007 had a devastating effect on financial markets throughout the world. Its origins can be found in the US housing market. The US government

---

[14] For example, if the default rate over the five years is 5% and the correlation is zero, the probability of zero defaults out of 125 companies is only 0.2% and the probability of six or more defaults is about 60%.

was keen to encourage home ownership. Interest rates were low. Mortgage brokers and mortgage lenders found it attractive to do more business by relaxing their lending standards. Products for securitizing mortgages had been developed so that the investors bearing the credit risk were not necessarily the same as the original lenders. Rating agencies were prepared to give a AAA rating to senior tranches that were created by securitization. There was no shortage of buyers for the AAA-rated securities that were created, because their yields were higher than the yields on other AAA-rated securities. Banks thought the "good times" would continue and, because compensation plans focused their attention on short-term profits, chose to ignore the housing bubble and its potential impact on some very complicated products they were trading.

House prices rose as both first-time buyers and speculators entered the market. Some mortgages had included a low "teaser rate" for two or three years. After the teaser rate ended, there was a significant increase in the interest rate for many borrowers. Unable to meet the higher interest rates, they had no choice but to default. This led to foreclosures and an increase in the supply of houses be sold. The price increases between 2000 and 2006 began to be reversed. Speculators and others who found that the amount owing on their mortgages was less than the value of their houses (i.e., they had negative equity) defaulted. This accentuated the price decline.

There are a number of steps that need to be taken to avoid future crises. The interests of the originators of loans should be aligned with the interests of those who ultimately bear the credit risk. This could be achieved by requiring originators of loans to keep some of the risk in each instrument created from the loans. The compensation plans within financial institutions should be changed so that there is much less emphasis on short-term performance. Some banks such as UBS moved in this direction in late 2008, and early in 2009 President Obama made it clear that he regards it as a priority to reform the freewheeling bonus culture within US financial institutions. The products that are traded should be made more transparent, so that their risks are widely understood. Risk management should involve a heavy dose of managerial judgment, as well as the mechanistic application of models.

The increase in credit spreads during the period following July 2007 has been dramatic. One reason is that the market's estimates of default probabilities increased. Another is that liquidity was in short supply and there were relatively few market participants that were willing to risk their capital by selling protection. The deleveraging that took place made market participants more risk averse, so that they required higher risk premiums.

FURTHER READING

Figlewski, S., "Viewing the Financial Crisis from 20,000 Feet Up," *Journal of Derivatives*, 16, 3 (Spring 2009): 53–61.

Gorton, G., "The Panic of 2007," Working Paper, Yale School of Management, 2008.

Hull, J C., "The Financial Crisis of 2007: Another Case of Irrational Exuberance," in: *The Finance Crisis and Rescue. What Went Wrong? Why? What Lessons Can Be Learned?* University of Toronto Press, 2008.

Hull, J.C., "The Credit Crunch of 2007: What Went Wrong? Why? What Lessons Can Be Learned?" *Journal of Credit Risk*, forthcoming, Summer 2009.

Hull, J.C., and A. White, "The Risk of Tranches Created from Residential Mortgages," Working Paper, University of Toronto, 2009.

Keys, B. J., T. Mukherjee , A. Seru, A., and V. Vig, "Did Securitization Lead to Lax Screening? Evidence from Subprime Loans," Working Paper, University of Michigan, 2008.

Krinsman, A. N., "Subprime Mortgage Meltdown: How Did it Happen and How Will It End," *Journal of Structured Finance*, Summer 2007: 13–19.

Mian, A., and A. Sufi, "The Consequences of Mortgage Credit Expansion: Evidence from the 2007 Mortgage Default Crisis," Working Paper, Graduate School of Business, University of Chicago, 2008.

Zimmerman, T., "The Great Subprime Meltdown," *Journal of Structured Finance*, Fall 2007: 7–20.

PRACTICE QUESTIONS AND PROBLEMS (Answers at the End of the Book)

16.1. Why did mortgage lenders frequently not check information in mortgage applications during the 2000 to 2007 period?

16.2. Why is the increase in house prices during the 2000 to 2007 period referred to as a bubble?

16.3. What are the numbers in Table 16.1 for a loss rate on the underlying assets of (a) 5% and (b) 12%?

16.4. In Figure 16.5, what proportion of the subprime mortgage principal ends up as AAA if: (a) there is no overcollateralization or excess spread and (b) there is 10% over-collateralization in the ABS, so that $110 of mortgages are used to create $100 of ABS securities.

16.5. Explain the difference between (a) an ABS, (b) a CDO, and (c) an ABS CDO.

16.6. Compare the risks in (a) the AAA-rated tranche of the ABS in Figure 16.4 and (b) the AAA-rated tranche of the ABS CDO in Figure 16.4 Which is riskier? Why?

16.7. What is meant by the term "agency costs"? How did agency costs play a role in the credit crisis?

16.8. "If the originator of mortgages securitizes all mortgages and keeps 10% of each tranche, it is in the same position as it would be if it had securitized 90% of the mortgages and kept no part of the tranches." Do you agree with this viewpoint? Discuss.

16.9. How is an ABS CDO created? What was the motivation to create ABS CDOs?

16.10. How did Mian and Sufi show that mortgage lenders relaxed their lending criteria during the 2000 to 2006 period?

16.11. What is the difference between a synthetic CDO and a cash CDO?

16.12. Explain the influence of default correlation on (a) the risks in the equity tranche of a CDO and (b) the risks in the senior tranches of a CDO.

16.13. Explain why the end-of-year bonus is regarded as short-term compensation.

FURTHER QUESTIONS

16.14. Suppose that the principal assigned to the senior, mezzanine, and equity tranches is 85%, 5%, and 10% instead of 75%, 20%, and 5% in Figure 16.4. How are the results in Table 16.1 affected? Discuss how the risks borne by investors change.

16.15. Suppose that a Gaussian copula model with a default correlation of 0.4 is used to define correlation in a 125-company synthetic CDO. The probability of default for each company during 5 years is 6%. What is the probability of more than 10 defaults during the 5-year period when the factor F in equation (10.9) is (a) -2, (b) -1, (c) 0, (d) $+1$, and (e) $+2$?

Scenario Analysis and Stress Testing

Stress testing involves valuing a financial institution's portfolio for extreme, but plausible, scenarios that are not considered by VaR models. If there is one lesson to be learned from the market turmoil that started in the summer of 2007, it is that more emphasis should be placed on stress testing and less emphasis should be placed on the mechanistic application of VaR models. VaR models are useful, but they are inevitably backward looking. Risk management is concerned with what might happen in the future. Managerial judgment is necessary to develop credible extreme scenarios that can form the basis of stress tests.

This chapter reviews the different approaches that can be used to generate scenarios for stress testing. It explains that the financial crisis of 2007 and 2008 has caused bank supervisors to place more emphasis on stress testing. It discusses some of the problems that have to be overcome for stress testing to become a useful and meaningful part of a financial institution's risk management procedures.

17.1 GENERATING THE SCENARIOS

The most popular approach for calculating VaR is the historical simulation approach covered in Chapter 12. This approach assumes that data from the last few years is a good guide to what will happen over the next one to ten days. If an event has not happened during the period covered by the data, it will not affect the VaR results when the basic VaR methodology (Section 12.1) is used. Incorporating volatility updating (Section 12.3) leads to more extreme outcomes being considered when the market is volatile. Extreme value theory (Section 12.4) provides a way of smoothing and extending the tails of the loss distribution. The stressed VaR calculation (Section 11.12) is a step in the right direction. But the nature of a VaR calculation is that it is backward looking. Events that could happen, but are quite different from those that occurred during the period covered by the data, are not taken into account. Stress testing is an attempt to overcome this weakness of the VaR measure.

Stress testing involves estimating how the portfolio of a financial institution would perform under extreme market moves. There are two steps in stress testing. The first is the development of scenarios involving plausible extreme market moves. The second is valuing the portfolio under these scenarios. Sometimes, the extreme market moves that are considered in stress testing are measured in standard deviations. (This approach corresponds to the approach used in our analysis of foreign exchange data in Table 9.2.) If daily changes are normally distributed, a 5-standard-deviation daily change in a market variable happens about once every 7,000 years. But in practice, it is not uncommon to see a 5-standard-deviation move once or twice every ten years. (This emphasizes that the assumption that variables are normally distributed is not a good one in risk management.)

A key issue in stress testing is the choice of the scenarios that are used. We now consider alternative procedures.

Stressing Individual Variables

One approach is to use scenarios where there is a large move in one variable while other variables are unchanged. Examples of scenarios of this type that are sometimes considered are:

1. A 100-basis-point parallel shift (up or down) in a yield curve
2. Increasing or decreasing all the implied volatilities used for an asset by 20% of current values
3. Increasing or decreasing an equity index by 10%
4. Increasing or decreasing the exchange rate for a major currency by 6%
5. Increasing or decreasing the exchange rate for a minor currency by 20%

The impact of small changes in a variable is measured by its delta, as explained in Chapter 6. The impact of larger changes can be measured by a combination of delta and gamma. Here we are considering changes which are so large that it is liable to be unreliable to estimate the change in the value of a portfolio using Greek letters.

Scenarios Involving Several Variables

Usually, when one market variable shows a big change, others do as well. This has led financial institutions to develop scenarios where several variables change at the same time. A common practice is to use extreme movements in market variables that have occurred in the past. For example, to test the impact of an extreme movement in US equity prices, a company might set the percentage changes in all market variables equal to those on October 19, 1987 (when the S&P 500 moved by 22.3 standard deviations). If this is considered to be too extreme, the company might choose January 8, 1988 (when the S&P 500 moved by 6.8 standard deviations). Other dates when there were big movements in equity prices are September 11, 2001, when terrorists attacked the World Trade Center in New York, and September 15, 2008, when Lehman Brothers declared bankruptcy. To test the effect of extreme movements in UK interest rates, the company might set the percentage changes in all market variables equal to those on April 10, 1992 (when 10-year bond yields moved by 8.7 standard deviations).

Some historical scenarios are one-day shocks to market variables. Others, particularly those involving credit and liquidity, involve shocks that take place over several days, several weeks, or even several months. It is important to include volatilities in the market variables that are considered. Typically, extreme movements in market variables such as interest rates and exchange rates are accompanied by large increases in implied volatilities for these variables and large increases in the volatility of a wide range of other variables. Some scenarios are likely to involve big movements in commodity prices. On September 22, 2008, oil posted its biggest one-day price increase ever. On September 27–28, 1999, the price of gold increased by 15.4%. Some scenarios are likely to involve a situation where there is a flight to quality combined with a shortage of liquidity and an increase in credit spreads. This was what happened in August 1998 when Russia defaulted on its debt and in July and August 2007 when investors lost confidence in the products created from the securitization of subprime mortgages (see Chapter 16).

Scenarios Generated by Management

History never repeats itself exactly. This may be partly because traders are aware of past financial crises and try to avoid making the same mistakes as their predecessors. The US mortgage market led to the credit crisis that started in 2007. It is unlikely that future credit crises will be a result of mortgage-lending criteria being relaxed—but it is also likely that there will be credit crises in the future.

In many ways, the scenarios that are most useful in stress testing are those generated by senior management. Senior management are in a good position to use their understanding of markets, world politics, the economic environment, and current global uncertainties to develop plausible scenarios that would lead to large losses. Sometimes, the scenarios produced by management are based on things that have happened in the past, but are adjusted to include key features of the current financial and economic environment.

One way of developing the scenarios is for a committee of senior management to meet periodically and "brainstorm" answers to the simple question: "What can go wrong?" Clemens and Winkler have done studies to investigate the optimal composition of a committee of this type.[1] Their conclusions are that (a) the committee should have three to five members, (b) the backgrounds of the committee members should be different, and (c) there should be a healthy dialogue between members of the committee. It is important that members of the committee are able step back from their day-to-day responsibilities to consider the big picture.

It is not always the case that senior management's thinking has to be highly innovative for it to come up with relevant scenarios. In 2005 and 2006, many commentators realized that the US housing market was experiencing a bubble and that sooner or later the bubble would burst. It is easy to be wise after the event, but one reasonable scenario for the stress-testing committee to propose during that period would have been a 10% or 20% decline in house prices in all parts of the country.

It is important that senior management and the board of directors understand and recognize the importance of stress testing. They have the responsibility for taking strategic decisions based on the stress-testing results. One advantage of involving senior management in the development of the scenarios to be used in stress testing is that it should naturally lead to a "buy in" by them to the idea that stress testing is important. The results generated from scenarios that are created by individuals who have middle management positions are unlikely to be taken as seriously.

---

[1] See R. Clemens and R. Winkler, "Combining Probability Distributions from Experts in Risk Analysis," *Risk Analysis*, 19, 2 (April 1999): 187–203.

If the scenarios generated by management involve extreme movements in only a few (core) market variables, one approach is to set changes in all other (peripheral) variables to zero. Another approach is to regress the peripheral variables on the core variables that are being stressed to obtain forecasts for them conditional on the changes being made to the core variables. These forecasts (as point forecasts or probability distributions) can be incorporated into the stress test. This is known as *conditional stress testing* and is discussed by Kupiec.[2] Kim and Finger carry this idea further by using what they call a "broken arrow" stress test. In this, the correlation between the core variables and the peripheral variables is based on what happens in stressed market conditions rather than what happens on average.[3]

Making Scenarios Complete

Scenarios should be carefully examined in an attempt to make sure that all the adverse consequences are considered. The scenarios should include not only the immediate effect of a shock to market variables on the financial institution's portfolio. They should also include any "knock-on" effect resulting from many different financial institutions being affected by the shock in the same way and responding in the same way. Many people have said that they recognized the real estate bubble in the United States would burst in 2007, but did not realize how bad the consequences would be. They did not appreciate that many financial institutions would experience losses at the same time with the result that there would be a flight to quality with severe liquidity problems and a huge increase in credit spreads.

Another example of knock-on effects is provided by the failure of Long-Term Capital Management (LTCM) in 1998 (see Business Snapshot 15.1). LTCM tended to have long positions in illiquid securities and short positions in liquid securities. Its failure was caused by a flight to quality following Russia's default on its debt. Many investors were only interested in buying liquid securities. Spreads between liquid and illiquid securities increased. LTCM contends that it had done stress tests looking at the impact of flights to quality similar to those that had occurred pre-1998. What it did not allow for was the knock-on effect. Many hedge funds were following similar trading strategies to those of LTCM in 1998. When the flight to quality started they were all forced to unwind their positions at the same time. Unwinding meant selling illiquid securities and buying liquid securities, reinforcing the flight to quality and making it more severe than previous flights to quality.

Scenarios should ideally be dynamic scenarios in which the response of the financial institution doing the stress test to the shock, as well as the response of other financial institutions, are considered. Consider, for example, the situation where a financial institution has sold options dependent on an underlying asset and maintains delta neutrality. A shock where there is a large increase (decrease) in the asset price will lead to an immediate loss on the option position (see Section 6.7). To maintain delta neutrality, large amounts of the asset will have to be bought (sold). The cost of subsequent delta hedging is liable to depend on the path followed by the asset price. The worst-case scenario, which should be the one considered by stress testers, is that

---

[2] P. Kupiec, "Stress Testing in a Value at Risk Framework," *Journal of Derivatives*, 6 (1999): 7–24.

[3] See J. Kim and C. C. Finger, "A Stress Test to Incorporate Correlation Breakdown," *Journal of Risk*, 2, 3 (Spring 2000), 5–19.

the asset price experiences wild swings (i.e., large increases and decreases) before it settles down.

Reverse Stress Testing

Reverse stress testing involves searching for scenarios that lead to a large loss. Many search procedures can be used. For example, if ten different key market variables can be identified, changes in other variables can be specified as dependent on changes in these ten variables. Standard algorithms can then be used to search in ten-dimensional space for the combination of movements in the ten variables that give really bad outcomes.

The disadvantage of reverse stress testing is that the scenarios generated might be totally unreasonable. For example, they might involve two variables moving in opposite directions when it is known that they are almost invariably positively correlated in stressed market conditions. However, the advantage of reverse stress testing is that it can uncover scenarios that would be disastrous for the financial institution, but had not occurred to senior management.

Reverse stress testing can be used as a tool to facilitate brainstorming by the stress-testing committee. Prior to a meeting of the stress-testing committee, analysts can use reverse stress testing to come up with several scenarios that would be disastrous to the financial institution. These scenarios, along with others they generate themselves, are then considered by the stress-testing committee. They use their judgment to eliminate some of the analysts' scenarios as implausible and modify others so that they become plausible and are retained for serious evaluation.

Example 17.1

As a simple example of reverse stress testing, suppose that a financial institution has positions in four European call options on an asset. The asset price is $50, the risk-free rate is 3%, the volatility is 20%, and there is no income on the asset. The positions, strike prices, and times to maturity are as indicated in the table below. The current value of the position (in $000s) is −29.00. The DerivaGem Application Builder can be used to search for one-day changes in the asset price and the volatility that will lead to the greatest losses. It is assumed that the asset price will not fall below $40 or rise above $60 and that the volatility will not decrease below 10% or increase above 30%.

Position (000s)	Strike price ($)	Life (years)	Position value ($000s)
+250	50	1.0	1174.20
−125	60	1.5	−293.56
−75	40	0.8	−843.72
−50	55	0.5	−65.30
Total			−29.00

Using the DerivaGem Application Builder in conjunction with Solver, the worst loss is found to be when the volatility decreases to 10% and the asset price falls to $45.99. The loss is $286.25. Reverse stress testing therefore shows that the financial institution is most exposed to a reduction of about 10% in the asset price combined with a sharp decline in volatility.

This might seem to be an unreasonable scenario. It is unlikely that volatility would go down sharply when the asset price declines by 10%. Solver could be run again with the lower bound to volatility being 20% instead of 10%. This gives a worst-case loss occurring when the volatility stays at 20% and the asset price falls to $42.61. The loss (in $000s) is then $85.17.

17.2 REGULATION

The Basel Committee requires market risk calculations that are based on a bank's internal VaR models to be accompanied by "rigorous and comprehensive" stress testing. Similarly, banks using the IRB approach in Basel II (advanced or foundation) to determine credit risk capital are required to conduct stress tests to determine the robustness of their assumptions.

In January 2009, the Basel Committee issued a consultative document on stress testing.[4] The document emphasizes the importance of stress testing in determining how much capital is necessary to absorb losses should large shocks occur. It makes the point that stress testing is particularly important after long periods of benign conditions because such conditions tend to lead to complacency.

The consultative document stresses the importance of top management and board involvement in stress testing. In particular top management and board members should be involved in setting stress-testing objectives, defining scenarios, discussing the results of stress tests, assessing potential actions, and decision making. It makes the point that the banks that fared well in the financial crisis that started in mid-2007 were the ones where senior management as a whole took an active interest in the development and operation of stress testing, with the results of stress testing serving as an input into strategic decision making. Stress testing should be conducted across all areas of the bank. It should not be the case that each area conducts its own stress test.

The consultative document makes the point that many of the scenarios chosen pre-2007 were based on historical data and much less severe than what actually happened. Specific recommendations for banks are:

1. Stress testing should form an integral part of the overall governance and risk management culture of the bank. Stress testing should be actionable, with the results from stress-testing analyses impacting decision making at the appropriate management level, including strategic business decisions of the board and senior management. Board and senior management involvement in the stress-testing program is essential for its effective operation.

2. A bank should operate a stress-testing program that promotes risk identification and control, provides a complementary risk perspective to other risk management tools, improves capital and liquidity management, and enhances internal and external communication.

3. Stress-testing programs should take account of views from across the organization and should cover a range of perspectives and techniques.

---

[4] See "Principles for Sound Stress Testing Practices and Supervision," Basel Committee on Banking Supervision, Consultative Document, January 2009.

4. A bank should have written policies and procedures governing the stress-testing program. The operation of the program should be appropriately documented.

5. A bank should have a suitably robust infrastructure in place that is sufficiently flexible to accommodate different and possibly changing stress tests at an appropriate level of granularity.

6. A bank should regularly maintain and update its stress-testing framework. The effectiveness of the stress-testing program, as well as the robustness of major individual components, should be assessed regularly and independently.

7. Stress tests should cover a range of risks and business areas, including at the firm-wide level. A bank should be able to integrate effectively across the range of its stress-testing activities to deliver a complete picture of firm-wide risk.

8. Stress-testing programs should cover a range of scenarios, including forward-looking scenarios, and aim to take into account system-wide interactions and feedback effects.

9. Stress tests should be geared towards the events capable of generating most damage whether through size of loss or through loss of reputation. A stress-testing program should also determine what scenarios could challenge the viability of the bank (reverse stress tests) and thereby uncover hidden risks and interactions among risks.

10. As part of an overall stress-testing program, a bank should aim to take account of simultaneous pressures in funding and asset markets, and the impact of a reduction in market liquidity on exposure valuation.

11. The efficacy of risk-mitigation techniques should be systematically challenged.

12. The stress-testing program should explicitly cover complex and bespoke products such as securitized exposures. Stress tests for securitized assets should consider the underlying assets, their exposure to systematic market factors, relevant contractual arrangements and embedded triggers, and the impact of leverage, particularly as it relates to the subordination level in the issue structure.

13. The stress-testing program should cover pipeline and warehousing risks. A bank should include such exposures in its stress tests regardless of their probability of being securitized.

14. A bank should enhance its stress-testing methodologies to capture the effect of reputational risk. The bank should integrate risks arising from off-balance-sheet vehicles and other related entities in its stress-testing program.

15. A bank should enhance its stress-testing approaches for highly leveraged counterparties in considering its vulnerability to specific asset categories or market movements and in assessing potential wrong-way risk related to risk-mitigating techniques.

The recommendations for bank supervisors are:

16. Supervisors should make regular and comprehensive assessments of a bank's stress-testing programs.

17. Supervisors should require management to take corrective action if material deficiencies in the stress-testing program are identified or if the results of stress tests are not adequately taken into consideration in the decision-making process.

18. Supervisors should assess and, if necessary, challenge the scope and severity of firm-wide scenarios. Supervisors may ask banks to use specific scenarios or to evaluate scenarios under which their viability is threatened (reverse stress-testing scenarios).

19. Under Pillar 2, supervisors should examine a bank's stress-testing results as part of a supervisory review of both the bank's internal capital assessment and its liquidity risk management. In particular, supervisors should consider the results of forward-looking stress testing for assessing the adequacy of capital and liquidity.

20. Supervisors should consider implementing stress-test exercises based on common scenarios.

21. Supervisors should engage in a constructive dialogue with other public authorities and the industry to identify systemic vulnerabilities. Supervisors should also ensure that they have the capacity and the skills to assess a bank's stress-testing program.

Key Problems Faced by Regulators

Bank regulators require banks to consider extreme scenarios and then make sure they have enough capital for those scenarios. There is an obvious problem here. Banks want to keep their regulatory capital as low as possible. They therefore have no incentive to consider extreme scenarios that would lead to a bank supervisor telling them that their capital requirements need to be increased. There is therefore a natural tendency for the scenarios they consider to be "watered down" and fairly benign.

One approach to overcoming this problem is for bank supervisors themselves to suggest scenarios. (Recommendations 20 and 21 suggest that the Basel Committee may be planning to move in this direction.) This imposes a huge burden on supervisors, but, if the scenarios were carefully chosen, it would undoubtedly have the effect of focusing a bank's attention on issues that were of concern to supervisors. In particular, if supervisors saw many banks taking positions with similar risks, they could insist that all banks consider a particular set of scenarios that gave rise to adverse results for the positions. A favorable result of the same supervisor-chosen scenarios being used across the banking system might be a lessening of the systemic risk in the financial system (see Business Snapshot 11.1 for an explanation of systemic risk). The downside is that part of the reason for the increased focus by supervisors on stress testing is that they want to encourage financial institutions to spend more time thinking about and worrying about extreme outcomes. If supervisors do the work in generating the scenarios, this may not happen. A compromise might be to insist on both management-generated scenarios and supervisor-generated scenarios being evaluated.

Systems put in place by regulators do not always have the results one expects. Business Snapshot 17.1 explains that, when regulators defined key scenarios for life insurance companies and pension funds in Europe, some of those companies responded by hedging against the particular scenarios used by regulators, and only against those scenarios.[5] This is probably not what regulators intended. Each scenario used in stress

---

[5] The information in Business Snapshot 17.1 is from P. L. Jorgensen, "Traffic Light Options," *Journal of Banking and Finance*, 31, 12 (December 2007): 3698–3719.

Business Snapshot 17.1   Traffic Light Options

In June 2001, the Danish Financial Supervisory Authority (DFSA) introduced a "traffic light" solvency stress-testing system. This requires life insurance companies and pension funds to submit semiannual reports indicating the impact on them of certain predefined shocks. The "red light scenario" involves a 70-basis-point decrease in interest rates, a 12% decline in stock prices, and an 8% decline in real estate prices. If capital falls below a specified critical level in this scenario, the company is categorized with "red light status" and is subject to more frequent monitoring with monthly reports being required. The "yellow light scenario" involves a 100-basis-point decrease in interest rates, a 30% decline in stock prices, and a 12% decline in real estate prices. If capital falls below the critical level in this scenario, the company is categorized with "yellow light status" and has to submit quarterly reports. When the company's capital stays above the critical levels for the red and yellow light scenarios, the company has "green light status" and is subject to normal semiannual reporting. Some other countries in Europe have adopted similar procedures.

Investment banks have developed products for helping life insurance and pension funds keep a green light status. These are known as traffic light options. They pay off in the traffic light scenarios so as to give a boost to the financial institution's capital when these scenarios are considered. Rather than hedge against interest rates, equities, and real estate prices separately, the financial institution buys a hedge that pays off only when the traffic light scenario occurs and there is an extreme movement in all three. This is much less expensive. (In practice, most of the financial institutions being regulated had very little exposure to real estate and the big moves that led to a payoff involved only interest rates and equity prices.)

---

testing should be viewed as representative of a range of things that might happen. Financial institutions should ensure that their capital will be in good shape not just for the specified scenarios but also for other similar or related scenarios. An extreme form of hedging against the red light scenario in Business Snapshot 17.1 would be to buy a security that pays off only if there is a decline in equity prices between 11% and 13% combined with a decline in interest rates between 65 and 75 basis points. This security would presumably cost very little and would be a ridiculous hedge, but would deal with the regulator-imposed stress tests.

Mechanistic hedging against particular adverse scenarios is not desirable. It is important for the financial institution to understand the range of risks represented by each stress scenario and to take sensible steps to deal with them. Risk management is not a game between regulators and financial institutions.

17.3   WHAT TO DO WITH THE RESULTS

The biggest problem in stress testing is knowing what to do with the results. All too often, the results of stress testing are ignored by senior management. A typical response is: "Yes, there are always one or two scenarios that will sink us. We cannot protect ourselves against everything that might happen." One way trying to avoid this sort of response is to involve senior management in the development of scenarios, as outlined earlier. A better response on the part of senior management would be: "Are the risks associated with these scenarios acceptable. If not, let's investigate what trades we can put on to make these types of risks more acceptable."

The problem for both senior management and the risk management group is that they have two separate reports on their desks concerning what could go wrong. One report comes from VaR models, the other from stress testing. Which one should they base their decision making on? There is a natural tendency to take the VaR results more seriously because they impact regulatory capital in a direct way.

Integrating Stress Testing and VaR Calculations

Berkowitz suggests that stress testing will be taken more seriously if its results are integrated into the calculation of VaR.[6] This can be done by assigning a probability to stressed scenarios. Suppose that a financial institution has considered n_s stressed scenarios and the total probability assigned to the stressed scenarios is p. Assume further that there are n_h scenarios generated using historical simulation. An analyst can assume that there are a total of $n_s + n_h$ scenarios. The n_s stressed scenarios have probability p, and the n_h historical scenarios have probability $1 - p$.

Unfortunately human beings are not good at estimating a subjective probability for the occurrence of a rare event. To make the task feasible for the stress-testing committee, one approach is to ask the stress-testing committee to allocate each scenario to categories with preassigned probabilities. The categories might be:

1. Probability = 0.05%. Extremely unlikely. One chance in 2,000.
2. Probability = 0.2%. Very unlikely, but the scenario should be given about the same weight as the 500 scenarios used in the historical simulation analysis.
3. Probability = 0.5%. Unlikely, but the scenario should be given more weight than the 500 scenarios used in the historical simulation analysis.

Example 17.2

Suppose that, in the example in Section 12.1, five stressed scenarios are considered. They lead to losses ($000s) of 235, 300, 450, 750, and 850. The subjective probabilities assigned to the scenarios are 0.5%, 0.2%, 0.2%, 0.05%, and 0.05%, respectively. The total probability of the stressed scenarios is, therefore, 1%. This means that the probability assigned to the scenarios generated by historical simulation is 99%. Assuming that equal weighting is used, each historical simulation scenario is assigned a probability of 0.99/500 = 0.00198. Table 12.4 is therefore replaced by Table 17.1. The probabilities assigned to scenarios are accumulated from the worst scenario to the best.[7] The VaR level when the confidence level is 99% is the first loss for which the cumulative probability is greater than 0.01. In our example this is $300,000.

---

[6] See J. Berkowitz, "A Coherent Framework for Stress Testing," *Journal of Risk*, 2, 2 (Winter 1999/2000): 5–15.

[7] This is the same procedure that we used when weights were assigned to historical simulation scenarios (see Table 12.5 in Section 12.3).

Table 17.1   Losses ranked from highest to lowest for Example 17.2: $s1, s2, \ldots$ are the stress scenarios; $h1, h2, \ldots$ are the historical simulation scenarios.

Scenario	Loss ($000s)	Probability	Cumulative probability
s5	850.000	0.00050	0.00050
s4	750.000	0.00050	0.00100
h494	499.395	0.00198	0.00298
s3	450.000	0.00200	0.00498
h339	359.440	0.00198	0.00696
h329	341.366	0.00198	0.00894
s2	300.000	0.00200	0.01094
h299	251.943	0.00198	0.01292
h487	247.571	0.00198	0.01490
h131	241.712	0.00198	0.01688
s1	235.000	0.00500	0.02188
h227	230.265	0.00198	0.02386
h495	227.332	0.00198	0.02584
h441	225.051	0.00198	0.02782
$\vdots$	$\vdots$	$\vdots$	$\vdots$

Subjective vs. Objective Probabilities

At this stage it is appropriate to discuss the types of probability estimates that can be made. An *objective probability* for an event is a probability calculated by observing the frequency with which the event happens in repeated trials. As an idealized example of an objective probability, consider an urn containing red balls and black balls in an unknown proportion. We want to know the probability of a ball drawn at random from the urn being red. We could draw a ball at random, observe its color, replace it in the urn, draw another ball at random, observe its color, replace it in the urn, and so on, until 100 balls have been drawn. If 30 of the balls that have been drawn are red and 70 are black, our estimate for the probability of drawing a red ball is 0.3. Unfortunately most objective probabilities calculated in real life are usually less reliable than the probability in this example, because the probability of the event happening does not remain constant during the trials and the trials are not independent.

A *subjective probability* is a probability derived from an individual's personal judgment about the chance of a particular event occurring. The probability is not based on historical data. It is a degree of belief. Different people are liable to have different subjective probabilities for the same event.

The probabilities assigned to historical simulation are objective, whereas the probabilities assigned to the scenarios in stress testing are subjective. Many analysts are uncomfortable with subjective probabilities because they are not based on data. Also, it is unfortunately the case that political consideration may play a part in a financial institution's decision to focus on historical data. If you use historical data and things go wrong, you can blame the data. If you use subjective judgments that have been provided by a group of people, those people are liable to be blamed.

However, if it is based only on objective probabilities, risk management is inevitably backward looking and fails to capitalize on the judgment and expertise of senior managers. It is the responsibility of those managers to steer the financial institution so that catastrophic risks are avoided.

SUMMARY

Stress testing is an important part of the risk management process. It leads to a financial institution considering the impact of extreme scenarios that are ignored by a traditional VaR analysis but that do happen from time to time. Once plausible scenarios have been evaluated, the financial institution can take steps to lessen the impact of the particularly bad ones. One advantage of a comprehensive stress-testing program is that a financial institution obtains a better understanding of the nature of the risks in its portfolio.

Scenarios can be generated in a number of different ways. One approach is to consider extreme movements in just one market variable while keeping others fixed. Another is to use the movements in all market variables that occurred during periods in the past when the market experienced extreme shocks. The best approach is to ask a committee of senior management to use their judgment and experience to generate the plausible extreme scenarios. Sometimes financial institutions carry out reverse stress testing where algorithms are used to search for scenarios that would lead to large losses. Scenarios should be as complete as possible and include the impact of knock-on effects as well as the initial shock to market variables. The market turmoil starting in summer 2007 shows that, in some cases, the knock-on effect can be significant and include a flight to quality, an increase in credit spreads, and a shortage of liquidity.

Regulators require banks to keep sufficient capital for stressed scenarios. In the case of pension funds and life insurance companies in Europe (which are primarily exposed to interest rates and equity prices), regulators have themselves developed scenarios that the financial institutions are required to consider.

If subjective probabilities are assigned to the extreme scenarios that are considered, stress testing can be integrated with a VaR analysis. This is an interesting idea, but was not one of the approaches outlined in the Basel Committee consultative document published in January 2009.

FURTHER READING

Alexander, C., and E. A. Sheedy, "Model-Based Stress Tests: Linking Stress Tests to VaR for Market Risk," Working Paper, 2008, Macquarie Applied Finance Center.

Aragonés, J. R., C. Blanco, and K. Dowd, "Incorporating Stress Tests into Market Risk Modeling," *Derivatives Quarterly*, 7 (Spring 2001): 44–49.

Aragonés, J. R., C. Blanco, and K. Dowd, "Stress Tests, Market Risk Measures, and Extremes: Bringing Stress Tests to the Forefront of Market Risk Management," in: *Stress Testing for Financial Institutions: Applications, Regulations, and Techniques* (D. Rösch and H. Scheule, eds.). London: Risk Books, 2008.

Basel Committee on Banking Supervision, "Principles for Sound Stress Testing Practices and Supervision," Consultative Document, January 2009.

Berkowitz, J., "A Coherent Framework for Stress Testing," *Journal of Risk*, 2, 2 (Winter 1999/2000): 5–15.

Bogle, J., "Black Monday and Black Swans," *Financial Analysts Journal*, 64, 2 (March/April 2008): 30–40.

Clemens, R., and R. Winkler, "Combining Probability Distributions from Experts in Risk Analysis," *Risk Analysis*, 19, 2 (April 1999): 187–203.

Hua, P., and P. Wilmott, "Crash Courses," *Risk*, 10, 6 (June 1997): 64–67.

Kim, J., and C. C. Finger, "A Stress Test to Incorporate Correlation Breakdown," *Journal of Risk*, 2, 3 (Spring 2000): 5–19.

Kupiec, P., "Stress Testing in a Value at Risk Framework," *Journal of Derivatives*, 6 (1999): 7–24.

Taleb, N. N., *The Black Swan: The Impact of the Highly Improbable*. New York: Random House, 2007.

PRACTICE QUESTIONS AND PROBLEMS (Answers at the End of the Book)

17.1. Explain three different ways that scenarios can be generated for stress testing.

17.2. What is reverse stress testing? How is it used?

17.3. Why might the regulatory environment lead to a financial institution underestimating the severity of the scenarios it considers?

17.4. What are traffic light options? What are their drawbacks?

17.5. Why is it important for senior management to be involved in stress testing. What form should this involvement take?

17.6. What are the advantages and disadvantages of bank supervisors choosing some of the scenarios that are considered for stress testing.

17.7. Explain the difference between subjective and objective probabilities. Which should be used in stress testing?

17.8. Suppose that, in the example in Section 12.1, seven stressed scenarios are considered. They lead to losses ($000s) of 240, 280, 340, 500, 700, 850, and 1050. The subjective probabilities assigned to the scenarios are 0.5%, 0.5%, 0.2%, 0.2%, 0.05%, 0.05%, and 0.05%, respectively. What is the new one-day 99% VaR that would be calculated using the procedure discussed in Section 17.3?

17.9. Suppose that the positions in the four options in Example 17.1 are changed to 200, −70, −120, and −60. Use the DerivaGem Application Builder and Solver to calculate the worst-case scenario for a daily change. Consider asset prices between $40 and $60 and volatilities between 10% and 30%.

FURTHER QUESTIONS

17.10. What difference does it make to the worst-case scenario in Example 17.1 if (a) the options are American rather than European and (b) the options are barrier options that are knocked out if the asset price reaches $65? Use the DerivaGem Applications Builder in conjunction with Solver to search over asset prices between $40 and $60 and volatilities between 18% and 30%.

17.11. What difference does it make to the VaR calculated in Example 17.2 if the exponentially weighted moving average model is used to assign weights to scenarios as described in Section 12.3?

CHAPTER 18

Operational Risk

In 1999, bank supervisors announced plans to assign capital for operational risk in the new Basel II regulations. This met with some opposition from banks. The chairman and CEO of one major international bank described it as "the dopiest thing I have ever seen". However, bank supervisors persisted. They listed more 100 operational risk losses by banks, each exceeding $100 million. Here are some of those losses:

Internal fraud: Allied Irish Bank, Barings, and Daiwa lost $700 million, $1 billion, and $1.4 billion, respectively from fraudulent trading.

External fraud: Republic New York Corp. lost $611 million because of fraud committed by a custodial client.

Employment practices and workplace safety: Merrill Lynch lost $250 million in a legal settlement regarding gender discrimination.

Clients, products, and business practices: Household International lost $484 million from improper lending practices; Providian Financial Corporation lost $405 million from improper sales and billing practices.

Damage to physical assets: Bank of New York lost $140 million because of damage to its facilities related to the September 11, 2001, terrorist attack.

Business disruption and system failures: Salomon Brothers lost $303 million from a change in computing technology.

Execution, delivery, and process management: Bank of America and Wells Fargo Bank lost $225 million and $150 million, respectively, from systems integration failures and transactions processing failures.

Most banks have always had some framework in place for managing operational risk. However, the prospect of new capital requirements has led them to greatly increase the resources they devote to measuring and monitoring operational risk.

It is much more difficult to quantify operational risk than credit or market risk. Operational risk is also more difficult to manage. Financial institutions make a conscious decision to take a certain amount of credit and market risk, and there are many traded instruments that can be used to reduce these risks. Operational risk, by contrast, is a necessary part of doing business. An important part of operational risk management is identifying the types of risk that are being taken and which should be insured against. There is always a danger that a huge loss will be incurred from taking an operational risk that *ex ante* was not even recognized as a risk.

367

It might be thought that a loss such as that suffered by Barings (see Business Snapshot 5.5) was a result of market risk because it was movements in market variables that led to it. However, it should be classified as an operational risk loss because it involved fraud. (Nick Leeson fraudulently hid his positions and, as a result, ended up spending a few years in a Singapore prison.) Suppose there was no fraud. If it was part of the bank's policy to let traders take huge risks, then the loss would be classified as market risk. But, if this was not part of the bank's policy and there was a breakdown in its controls, it would be classified as operational risk. The Barings Bank example illustrates that operational risk losses are often contingent on market movements. If the market had moved in Leeson's favor there would have been no loss. The fraud and the breakdown in control systems at Barings might then never have come to light.

There are some parallels between the operational risk losses of banks and the losses of insurance companies. Insurance companies face a small probability of a large loss from a hurricane, earthquake, or other natural disaster. Similarly, banks face a small probability of a large operational risk loss. But there is one important difference. When insurance companies lose a large amount of money because of a natural disaster, all companies in the industry tend to be affected and premiums rise the next year to cover losses. Operational risk losses tend to affect only one bank. Because it operates in a competitive environment, the bank does not have the luxury of increasing prices for the services it offers during the following year.

18.1   WHAT IS OPERATIONAL RISK?

There are many different ways in which operational risk can be defined. It is tempting to consider operational risk as a residual risk and define it as any risk faced by a financial institution that is not market risk or credit risk. To produce an estimate of operational risk, we could then look at the financial institution's financial statements and remove from the income statement (a) the impact of credit losses and (b) the profits or losses from market risk exposure. The variation in the resulting income would then be attributed to operational risk.

Most people agree that this definition of operational risk is too broad. It includes the risks associated with entering new markets, developing new products, economic factors, and so on. Another possible definition is that operational risk, as its name implies, is the risk arising from operations. This includes the risk of mistakes in processing transactions, making payments, etc. This definition of risk is too narrow. It does not include major risks such as the "rogue trader" risk.

We can distinguish between internal risks and external risks. Internal risks are those over which the company has control. The company chooses whom it employs, what computer systems it develops, what controls are in place, and so on. Some people define operational risks as all internal risks. Operational risk then includes more than just the risk arising from operations. It includes risks arising from inadequate controls such as the rogue trader risk and the risks of other sorts of employee fraud.

Bank regulators favor including more than just internal risks in their definition of operational risk. They include the impact of external events such as natural disasters (e.g., a fire or an earthquake that affects the bank's operations), political and regulatory risk (e.g., being prevented from operating in a foreign country by that country's government), security breaches, and so on. All of this is reflected in the following definition of operational risk produced by the Basel Committee on Banking Supervision in 2001:

> The risk of loss resulting from inadequate or failed internal processes, people, and systems or from external events.

Note that this definition includes legal risk but does not include reputation risk and the risk resulting from strategic decisions.

Some operational risks result in increases in the bank's operating cost or decreases in its revenue. Other operational risks interact with credit and market risk. For example, when mistakes are made in a loan's documentation, it is usually the case that losses result if and only if the counterparty defaults. When a trader exceeds limits and misreports positions, losses result if and only if the market moves against the trader.

18.2 DETERMINATION OF REGULATORY CAPITAL

Banks have three alternatives for determining operational risk regulatory capital. The simplest approach is the *basic indicator approach*. Under this approach, operational risk capital is set equal to 15% of annual gross income over the previous three years. Gross income is defined as net interest income plus noninterest income.[1] A slightly more complicated approach is the *standardized approach*. In this, a bank's activities are divided into eight business lines: corporate finance, trading and sales, retail banking, commercial banking, payment and settlement, agency services, asset management, and retail brokerage. The average gross income over the last three years for each business line is multiplied by a "beta factor" for that business line and the result summed to determine the total capital. The beta factors are shown in Table 18.1. The third alternative is the *advanced measurement approach* (AMA). In this, the operational risk regulatory capital requirement is calculated by the bank internally using qualitative and quantitative criteria.

Table 18.1   Beta factors in standardized approach.

Business line	*Beta factor*
Corporate finance	18%
Trading and sales	18%
Retail banking	12%
Commercial banking	15%
Payment and settlement	18%
Agency services	15%
Asset management	12%
Retail brokerage	12%

[1] Net interest income is the excess of income earned on loans over interest paid on deposits and other instruments that are used to fund the loans (see Section 2.2).

Figure 18.1 Calculation of VaR for operational risk.

The Basel Committee has listed conditions that a bank must satisfy in order to use the standardized approach or the AMA approach. It expects large internationally active banks to move toward adopting the AMA approach through time. To use the standardized approach a bank must satisfy the following conditions:

1. The bank must have an operational risk management function that is responsible for identifying, assessing, monitoring, and controlling operational risk.

2. The bank must keep track of relevant losses by business line and must create incentives for the improvement of operational risk.

3. There must be regular reporting of operational risk losses throughout the bank.

4. The bank's operational risk management system must be well documented.

5. The bank's operational risk management processes and assessment system must be subject to regular independent reviews by internal auditors. It must also be subject to regular review by external auditors or supervisors or both.

To use the AMA approach, the bank must satisfy additional requirements. It must be able to estimate unexpected losses based on an analysis of relevant internal and external data, and scenario analyses. The bank's system must be capable of allocating economic capital for operational risk across business lines in a way that creates incentives for the business lines to improve operational risk management.

The objective of banks using the AMA approach for operational risk is analogous to their objectives when they attempt to quantify credit risk. They would like to produce a probability distribution of losses such as that shown in Figure 18.1. Assuming that they can convince regulators that their expected operational risk cost is incorporated into their pricing of products, capital is assigned to cover unexpected costs. The confidence level is 99.9% and the time horizon is one year.

18.3 CATEGORIZATION OF OPERATIONAL RISKS

The Basel Committee on Banking Supervision has identified seven categories of operational risk.[2] These are:

1. *Internal fraud*: Acts of a type intended to defraud, misappropriate property or circumvent regulations, the law, or company policy (excluding diversity or discrimination events which involve at least one internal party). Examples include intentional misreporting of positions, employee theft, and insider trading on an employee's own account.

2. *External fraud*: Acts by third party of a type intended to defraud, misappropriate property or circumvent the law. Examples include robbery, forgery, check kiting, and damage from computer hacking.

3. *Employment practices and workplace safety*: Acts inconsistent with employment, health or safety laws or agreements, or which result in payment of personal injury claims, or claims relating to diversity or discrimination issues. Examples include workers compensation claims, violation of employee heath and safety rules, organized labor activities, discrimination claims, and general liability (e.g., a customer slipping and falling at a branch office).

4. *Clients, products, and business practices*: Unintentional or negligent failure to meet a professional obligation to specific clients and the use of inappropriate products or business practices. Examples are fiduciary breaches, misuse of confidential customer information, improper trading activities on the bank's account, money laundering, and the sale of unauthorized products.

5. *Damage to physical assets*: Loss or damage to physical assets from natural disasters or other events. Examples include terrorism, vandalism, earthquakes, fires, and floods.

6. *Business disruption and system failures*: Disruption of business or system failures. Examples include hardware and software failures, telecommunication problems, and utility outage.

7. *Execution, delivery, and process management*: Failed transaction processing or process management, and disputes with trade counterparties and vendors. Examples include data entry errors, collateral management failures, incomplete legal documentation, unapproved access given to clients accounts, nonclient counterparty misperformance, and vendor disputes.

Banks must estimate VaR for each of the $7 \times 8 = 56$ combinations of risk types and business lines. The way these VaRs can be combined into a single VaR measure for operational risk is explained in Section 21.5.

18.4 LOSS SEVERITY AND LOSS FREQUENCY

There are two distributions that are important in estimating potential operational risk losses. One is the *loss frequency distribution* and the other is the *loss severity distribution*.

---

[2] See Basel Committee on Bank Supervision, "Sound Practices for the Management and Supervision of Operational Risk." Bank for International Settlements, July 2002.

The loss frequency distribution is the distribution of the number of losses observed during the time horizon (usually one year). The loss severity distribution is the distribution of the size of a loss, given that a loss occurs. It is usually assumed that loss severity and loss frequency are independent (although this is questionable).

For loss frequency, the natural probability distribution to use is a Poisson distribution. This distribution assumes that losses happen randomly through time so that, in any short period of time Δt, there is a probability $\lambda \Delta t$ of a loss being sustained. The probability of n losses in time T is

$$e^{-\lambda T} \frac{(\lambda T)^n}{n!}$$

The parameter λ can be estimated as the average number of losses per unit time. For example, if during a ten-year period there were a total 12 losses, λ would be estimated as 1.2 per year, or 0.1 per month. A Poisson distribution has the property that the mean frequency of losses equals the variance of the frequency of losses.[3]

For the loss severity probability distribution, a lognormal probability distribution is often used. The parameters of this probability distribution are the mean and standard deviation of the logarithm of the loss.

The loss frequency distribution must be combined with the loss severity distribution for each loss type and business line to determine a total loss distribution. Monte Carlo simulation can be used for this purpose.[4] As mentioned earlier, the usual assumption is that loss severity is independent of loss frequency. On each simulation trial, we proceed as follows.

1. We sample from the frequency distribution to determine the number of loss events ($= n$).

2. We sample n times from the loss severity distribution to determine the loss experienced for each loss event ($L_1, L_2, \ldots, L_n$).

3. We determine the total loss experienced ($= L_1 + L_2 + \cdots + L_n$).

When many simulation trials are used, we obtain a total loss distribution.

Figure 18.2 illustrates the procedure. In this example, the expected loss frequency is 3 per year and the loss severity is drawn from a lognormal distribution. The logarithm of each loss ($ millions) is assumed to have a mean of zero and a standard deviation of 0.4. The Excel worksheet used to produce Figure 18.2 is on the author's website.

Data Issues

Unfortunately there is usually relatively little historical data available within a bank to estimate loss severity and loss frequency distributions. Many banks have not kept records of losses arising from different types of operational risk for different business lines. As a result of regulatory pressure, they are starting to do so, but it may be some

---

[3] If the mean frequency is greater than the variance of the frequency, a binomial distribution may be more appropriate. If the mean frequency is less than the variance, a negative binomial distribution (mixed Poisson distribution) may be more appropriate.

[4] Combining the loss severity and loss frequency distribution is a very common problem in insurance. Apart from Monte Carlo simulation, two approaches that are used are Panjer's algorithm and fast Fourier transforms. See H. H. Panjer, "Recursive Evaluation of a Family of Compound Distributions," *ASTIN Bulletin*, 12 (1981): 22–29.

Figure 18.2 Calculation of loss distribution from loss frequency and loss severity.

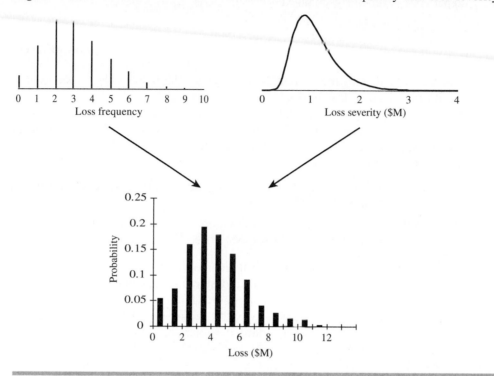

time before a reasonable amount of historical data is available. It is interesting to compare operational risk losses with credit risk losses in this respect. Traditionally, banks have done a much better job at documenting their credit risk losses than their operational risk losses. Also, in the case of credit risks, a bank can rely on a wealth of information published by credit rating agencies to assess probabilities of default and expected losses given default. Similar data on operational risk have not been collected in a systematic way. It may also be a problem that banks sometimes conceal a large operational risk loss from the market because they feel it will damage their reputation.

As indicated above, the Poisson distribution is often used for loss frequency and the lognormal distribution is often used for loss severity. Available data are usually used to estimate the parameters of these distributions. The loss frequency distribution should be estimated from a bank's own data as far as possible. For the loss severity distribution, regulators encourage banks to use their own data in conjunction with external data. There are two sources of external data. The first is data obtained through sharing arrangements between banks. (The insurance industry has had mechanisms for sharing loss data for many years and banks are now beginning to do this as well.) The second is publicly available data that have been collected in a systematic way by data vendors.

Both internal and external historical data must be adjusted for inflation. In addition, a scale adjustment should be made to external data. If a bank with a revenue of $10 billion reports a loss of $8 million, how should the loss be scaled for a bank with a revenue of $5 billion? A natural assumption is that a similar loss for a bank with a revenue of $5 billion would be $4 million. But this estimate is probably too small. For example, research by Shih *et al*. suggests that the effect of firm size on the size of a loss experience is relatively small.[5] Their estimate is

$$\text{Estimated loss for Bank A} = \text{Observed loss for Bank B} \times \left(\frac{\text{Bank A revenue}}{\text{Bank B revenue}}\right)^{\alpha}$$

where $\alpha = 0.23$. This means that in our example the bank with a revenue of \$5 billion would experience a loss of $8 \times 0.5^{0.23} = \$6.82$ million.

After the appropriate scale adjustment, data obtained through sharing arrangements with other banks can be merged with the bank's own data to obtain a larger sample for determining the loss severity distribution. Public data purchased from data vendors cannot be used in this way because they are subject to biases. For example:

1. Only large losses are publicly reported, and the larger the loss, the more likely it is to be reported.

2. Institutions with weak controls are more likely to be represented in the database because they suffer more losses. Moreover, their losses tend to be larger.

Public data are most useful for determining *relative* loss severity. Suppose that a bank has good information on the mean and standard deviation of the its loss severity distribution for internal fraud in corporate finance, but not for external fraud in corporate finance or for internal fraud in trading and sales. Suppose that the bank estimates its own mean and standard deviation of the loss severity distribution for internal fraud in corporate finance as \$50,000 and \$30,000. Suppose further that external data indicate that for external fraud in corporate finance the mean severity is twice that for internal fraud in corporate finance and the standard deviation of the severity is 1.5 times as great. In the absence of a better alternative, the bank might assume that its own severity for external fraud in corporate finance has a mean of $2 \times 50,000 = \$100,000$ and a standard deviation of severity equal to $1.5 \times 30,000 = \$45,000$. Similarly, if the external data indicate that the mean severity for internal fraud in trading and sales is 2.5 times that for internal fraud in corporate finance and that the standard deviation is twice as great, then the bank might assume that its own severity for internal fraud in trading and sales has a mean of $2.5 \times 50,000 = \$125,000$ and a standard deviation of $2 \times 30,000 = \$60,000$.

Scenario Analysis

Since historical data are relatively difficult to obtain, regulators encourage banks to use scenario analyses in addition to internal and external loss data. This involves using managerial judgment to generate scenarios where large losses occur and involves procedures similar to those discussed in Chapter 17 for carrying out stress tests to evaluate market and credit risks.

An operational risk committee consisting of senior managers who are knowledgeable about the bank's internal controls should be charged with the responsibility of generating scenarios. They should be asked to estimate the loss frequency parameter λ

---

[5] See J. Shih, A. Samad-Khan, and P. Medapa, "Is the Size of an Operational Loss Related to Firm Size," *Operational Risk Magazine*, 2, 1 (January 2000). Whether Shih *et al*.'s results apply to legal risks is debatable. The size of a settlement in a large lawsuit against a bank can be governed by how much the bank can afford.

associated with each scenario. As in Section 17.3, a number of categories of scenario can be defined, such as:

1. $\lambda = 0.0001$: scenario has one chance in 10,000 of happening.
2. $\lambda = 0.001$: scenario has one chance in 1,000 of happening
3. $\lambda = 0.01$: scenario has one chance in 100 of happening.

The operational risk committee can be asked to assign each scenario that is developed to one category. One difference between this scenario analysis and the one in Chapter 17 is that there is no model for determining losses. The parameters of the loss severity distribution have to be estimated by the committee. One approach is to ask the committee to estimate an average loss and a "high loss" that the committee is 99% certain will not be exceeded. A lognormal distribution can then be fitted to the estimates. Once the loss scenarios, their probabilities, and their severity have been estimated, a one-year 99.9% VaR can be calculated using Monte Carlo simulation.

Fortunately, the operational risk environment does not usually change as fast as the market or credit risk environment, so the development of scenarios should not be as onerous. Nevertheless, the approach we have described does require a great deal of senior management time. The relevant scenarios for one bank are often similar to those for other banks and, to lessen the burden on the operational risk committee, there is the potential for standard scenarios to be developed by consultants or by a banking industry association. However, the loss frequency and loss severity estimates should always be specific to a bank and reflect the controls in place in the bank and the type of business it is currently doing.

As in the case of market or credit risk stress testing, the advantage of generating scenarios using managerial judgment is that they include losses that the financial institution has never experienced, but could occur. The scenario analysis approach leads to management thinking actively and creatively about potential adverse events. This can have a number of benefits. In some cases, strategies for responding to an event so as to minimize its severity are likely to be developed. In other cases, proposals may be made for reducing the probability of the event occurring at all.

18.5 PROACTIVE APPROACHES

Risk managers should try to be proactive in preventing losses from occurring. One approach is to monitor what is happening at other banks and try and learn from their mistakes. When a $700 million rogue trader loss happened at a Baltimore subsidiary of Allied Irish Bank in 2002, risk managers throughout the world studied the situation carefully and asked: "Could this happen to us?" Business Snapshot 18.1 describes a situation concerning a British local authority in the late 1980s. It immediately led to all banks instituting procedures for checking that counterparties had the authority to enter into derivatives transactions.

Causal Relationships

Operational risk managers should try to establish causal relations between decisions taken and operational risk losses. Does increasing the average educational qualifications

---

Business Snapshot 18.1   The Hammersmith and Fulham Story

Between 1987 and 1989, the London Borough of Hammersmith and Fulham in Great Britain entered into about 600 interest rate swaps and related instruments with a total notional principal of about 6 billion pounds. The transactions appear to have been entered into for speculative rather than hedging purposes. The two employees of Hammersmith and Fulham that were responsible for the trades had only a sketchy understanding of the risks they were taking and how the products they were trading worked.

By 1989, because of movements in sterling interest rates, Hammersmith and Fulham had lost several hundred million pounds on the swaps. To the banks on the other side of the transactions, the swaps were worth several hundred million pounds. The banks were concerned about credit risk. They had entered into off-setting swaps to hedge their interest rate risks. If Hammersmith and Fulham defaulted, they would still have to honor their obligations on the offsetting swaps and would take a huge loss.

What actually happened was not a default. Hammersmith and Fulham's auditor asked to have the transactions declared void because Hammersmith and Fulham did not have the authority to enter into the transactions. The British courts agreed. The case was appealed and went all the way to the House of Lords, Britain's highest court. The final decision was that Hammersmith and Fulham did not have the authority to enter into the swaps, but that they ought to have the authority to do so in the future for risk management purposes. Needless to say, banks were furious that their contracts were overturned in this way by the courts.

---

of employees reduce losses arising from mistakes in the way transactions are processed? Will a new computer system reduce the probabilities of losses from system failures? Are operational risk losses correlated with the employee turnover rate? If so, can they be reduced by measures taken to improve employee retention? Can the risk of a rogue trader be reduced by the way responsibilities are divided between different individuals and by the way traders are motivated?

One approach to establishing causal relationships is statistical. If we look at 12 different locations where a bank operates and find a high negative correlation between the education of back-office employees and the cost of mistakes in processing transactions, it might well make sense to do a cost–benefit analysis of changing the educational requirements for a back-office job in some of the locations. In some cases a more qualitative analysis of the cause of losses may provide insights. For example, if 40% of computer failures can be attributed to the fact that the current hardware is several years old and less reliable than newer versions, a cost–benefit analysis of upgrading is likely to be useful.

RCSA and KRIs

Risk control and self-assessment (RCSA) is an important way in which banks try to achieve a better understanding of their operational risk exposures. It involves asking the managers of business units to identify their operational risks. Sometimes questionnaires designed by senior management or consultants are used.

A by-product of any program to measure and understand operational risk is likely to be the development of key risk indicators (KRIs). The most important indicators are prospective. They provide an early warning system to track the level of operational risk in the organization. Examples of key risk indicators are staff turnover and number of failed transactions. The hope is that key risk indicators can identify potential problems and allow remedial action to be taken before losses are incurred.

It is important for a bank to quantify operational risks, but it is even more important to take actions that control and manage those risks.

18.6 ALLOCATION OF OPERATIONAL RISK CAPITAL

General approaches to allocating risk capital are discussed in Section 21.6. Operational risk capital should be allocated to business units in a way that encourages them to improve their operational risk management. If a business unit can show that it has taken steps to reduce the frequency or severity of a particular risk, it should be allocated less capital. This will have the effect of improving the business unit's return on capital (and possibly lead to the business-unit manager receiving an increased bonus).

Note that it is not always optimal for a manager to reduce a particular operational risk. Sometimes the costs of reducing the risk outweigh the benefits of reduced capital, so that return on allocated capital decreases. A business unit should be encouraged to make appropriate calculations and determine the amount of operational risk that maximizes return on capital.

The overall result of operational risk assessment and operational risk capital allocation should be that business units become more sensitive to the need for managing operational risk. Hopefully operational risk management will be seen to be an important part of every manager's job. A key ingredient for the success of any operational risk program is the support of senior management. The Basel Committee on Banking Supervision is very much aware of this. It recommends that a bank's board of directors be involved in the approval of a risk management program and that it reviews the program on a regular basis.

Scorecard Approaches

Some banks use scorecard approaches to allocate operational risk capital. Experts identify the key determinants of each type of risk and then formulate questions for managers of business units to enable risk levels to be quantified. Scores are assigned to the answers. The total number of different business units is likely to be greater than the eight listed in Table 18.1, because each region of world in which the bank operates will often have to be considered separately. Example questions that might be used are:

1. What is the number of sensitive positions filled by temps?
2. What is the ratio of supervisors to staff?
3. Does your business have confidential client information?
4. What is the employee turnover rate per annum?
5. How many open employee positions are there at any time?

6. What percentage of your staff has a performance-based component to their remuneration?

7. What percentage of your staff did not take 10 consecutive days leave in the last 12 months?

The total score for a particular business unit indicates the amount of risk present in the business unit and can be used as a basis for allocating capital to the business unit. The scores given by a scorecard approach should be validated by comparing scores with actual loss experience whenever possible.

18.7 USE OF POWER LAW

In Section 9.4, we introduced the power law. This states that, for a wide range of variables,

$$\text{Prob}(v > x) = Kx^{-\alpha}$$

where v is the value of the variable, x is a relatively large value of v, and K and α are constants. We covered the theoretical underpinnings of the power law and maximum likelihood estimation procedures when we looked at extreme value theory in Section 12.4.

De Fountnouvelle *et al.*, using data on losses from external vendors, find that the power law holds well for the large losses experienced by banks.[6] This makes the calculation of VaR with high degrees of confidence such as 99.9% possible. Loss data (internal or external) are employed to estimate the power law parameters using the maximum likelihood approach in Chapter 12. The 99.9% quantile of the loss distribution is then estimated using equation (12.6).

When loss distributions are aggregated, the distribution with the heaviest tails tends to dominate. This means that the loss with the lowest α defines the extreme tails of the total loss distribution.[7] Therefore, if all we are interested in is calculating the extreme tail of the total operational risk loss distribution, it may only be necessary to consider one or two business-line/risk-type combinations.

18.8 INSURANCE

An important decision for operational risk managers is the extent to which operational risks should be insured against. Insurance policies are available on many different kinds of risk ranging from fire losses to rogue trader losses. Provided that the insurance company's balance sheet satisfies certain criteria, a bank using AMA can reduce the capital it is required to hold by entering into insurance contracts. In Section 3.7 we discussed the moral hazard and adverse selection risks faced by insurance companies. We now review these again in the context of operational risk.

---

[6] See P. De Fountnouvelle, V. DeJesus-Rueff, J. Jordan, and E. Rosengren, "Capital and Risk: New Evidence on Implications of Large Operational Risk Losses," Federal Reserve Board of Boston, Working Paper, September 2003.

[7] In Chapter 12 the parameter ξ equals $1/\alpha$, so it is the loss distribution with the largest ξ that defines the extreme tails.

Moral Hazard

One of the risks facing an insurance company is moral hazard. This is the risk that the existence of the insurance contract will cause the bank to behave differently than it otherwise would. This changed behavior increases the risks to the insurance company. Consider, for example, a bank that insures itself against robberies. As a result of the insurance policy, it may be tempted to be lax in its implementation of security measures—making a robbery more likely than it would otherwise have been.

Insurance companies have traditionally dealt with moral hazard in a number of ways. Typically there is a *deductible* in any insurance policy. This means that the bank is responsible for bearing the first part of any loss. Sometimes there is a *coinsurance provision* in a policy. In this case, the insurance company pays a predetermined percentage (less than 100%) of losses in excess of the deductible. In addition, there is nearly always a *policy limit*. This is a limit on the total liability of the insurer. Consider again a bank that has insured itself against robberies. The existence of deductibles, coinsurance provisions, and policy limits are likely to provide an incentive for a bank not to relax security measures in its branches. The moral hazard problem in rogue trader insurance in discussed in Business Snapshot 18.2.

Adverse Selection

The other major problem facing insurance companies is adverse selection. This is where an insurance company cannot distinguish between good and bad risks. It offers the same price to everyone and inadvertently attracts more of the bad risks. For example, banks without good internal controls are more likely to enter into rogue trader insurance contracts; banks without good internal controls are more likely to buy insurance policies to protect themselves against external fraud.

To overcome the adverse selection problem, an insurance company must try to understand the controls that exist within banks and the losses that have been experienced. As a result of its initial assessment of risks, it may not charge the same premium for the same contract to all banks. As time goes by, it gains more information about the bank's operational risk losses and may increase or reduce the premium charged. This is much the same as the approach adopted by insurance companies when they sell automobile insurance to a driver. At the outset the insurance company obtains as much information on the driver as possible. As time goes by, it collects more information on the driver's risk (number of accidents, number of speeding tickets, etc.) and modifies the premium charged accordingly.

18.9 SARBANES–OXLEY

Largely as a result of the Enron bankruptcy, the Sarbanes–Oxley Act was passed in the United States in 2002. This provides another dimension to operational risk management for financial and nonfinancial institutions in the United States. The Act requires boards of directors to become much more involved with day-to-day operations. They must monitor internal controls to ensure that risks are being assessed and handled well.

The Act specifies rules concerning the composition of the board of directors of public companies and lists the responsibilities of the board. It gives the SEC the power to

---

Business Snapshot 18.2   Rogue Trader Insurance

A rogue trader insurance policy presents particularly tricky moral hazard problems. An unscrupulous bank could enter into an insurance contract to protect itself against losses from rogue trader risk and then choose to be lax in its implementation of trading limits. If a trader exceeds the trading limit and makes a large profit, the bank is better off than it would be otherwise. If a large loss results a claim can be made under the rogue trader insurance policy. Deductibles, coinsurance provisions, and policy limits may mean that the amount recovered is less than the loss incurred by the trader. However, potential net losses to the bank are likely to be far less than potential profits, making the lax trading-limits strategy a good bet for the bank.

Given this problem, it is perhaps surprising that some insurance companies do offer rogue trader insurance policies. These companies tend to specify carefully how trading limits are implemented. They may also require that the existence of the insurance policy not be revealed to anyone on the trading floor. They are likely to want to retain the right to investigate the circumstances underlying any loss. In addition, it is worth pointing out that, from the bank's point of view, the lax trading-limits strategy we have outlined may be very short-sighted. The bank might well find that the costs of all types of insurance rise significantly as a result of a rogue trader claim. Moreover, a large rogue trader loss (even if insured) would cause its reputation to suffer.

---

censure the board or give it additional responsibilities. A company's auditors are not allowed to carry out any significant nonauditing services for the company.[8] Audit partners must be rotated. The audit committee of the board must be made aware of alternative accounting treatments. The CEO and CFO must prepare a statement to accompany the audit report to the effect that the financial statements are accurate. The CEO and CFO are required to return bonuses in the event that financial statements are restated. Other rules concern insider trading, disclosure, personal loans to executives, reporting of transactions by directors, and the monitoring of internal controls by directors.

SUMMARY

In 1999, bank supervisors indicated their intention to charge capital for operational risk. This has led banks to carefully consider how they should measure and manage operational risk. Bank supervisors have identified seven different types of operational risk and eight different business lines. They encourage banks to quantify risks for each of the 56 business-line/risk-type combinations.

One approach that has been developed is the statistical approach. This treats operational risk losses in much the same way as actuaries treat losses from insurance policies. A frequency of loss distribution and a severity of loss distribution is estimated and these are combined to form a total operational risk loss distribution. If possible,

---

[8] Enron's auditor, Arthur Andersen provided a wide range of services in addition to auditing. It did not survive the litigation that followed the downfall of Enron.

the frequency of loss distribution is estimated from internal data. The loss severity distribution is estimated from a combination of internal and external data.

There are two sources of external data. One is data obtained from other banks via sharing arrangements. The other is publicly available data on large losses collected by data vendors. Increasingly banks are augmenting loss data with scenario analyses where senior managers develop loss-event scenarios and use subjective judgment to estimate parameters describing loss frequency and loss severity.

Risk managers should try to be forward-looking in their approach to operational risk. They should try to understand what determines operational risk losses and try to develop key risk indicators to track the level of operational risk in different parts of the organization.

Once operational risk capital has been estimated, it is important to develop procedures for allocating it to business units. This should be done in a way that encourages business units to reduce operational risk when this can be done without incurring excessive costs. One approach to allocation is the use of scorecards.

The power law introduced in Chapter 9 seems to apply to operational risk losses. This makes it possible to use extreme value theory to estimate the tails of a loss distribution from empirical data. When several loss distributions are aggregated, it is the loss distribution with the heaviest tail that dominates. In principle, this makes the calculation of VaR for total operational risk easier.

Many operational risks can be insured against. However, most policies include deductibles, coinsurance provisions, and policy limits. As a result a bank is always left bearing part of any risk itself. Moreover, the way insurance premiums change as time passes is likely to depend on the claims made and other indicators that the insurance company has of how well operational risks are being managed.

The whole process of measuring, managing, and allocating operational risk is still in its infancy. As time goes by and data are accumulated, more precise procedures than those we have mentioned in this chapter are likely to emerge. One of the key problems is that there are two sorts of operational risk: high-frequency low-severity risks and low-frequency high-severity risks. The former are relatively easy to quantify, but operational risk VaR is largely driven by the latter.

Bank supervisors seem to be succeeding in their objective of making banks more sensitive to the importance of operational risk. In many ways, the key benefit of an operational risk management program is not the numbers that are produced, but the process that banks go through in producing the numbers. If handled well, the process sensitizes managers to the importance of operational risk and perhaps leads to them thinking about it differently.

FURTHER READING

Bank for International Settlements, "Sound Practices for the Management and Supervision of Operational Risk," February 2003.

Baud, N., A. Frachot, and T. Roncalli, "Internal Data, External Data and Consortium Data for Operational Risk Management: How to Pool Data Properly," Working Paper, Groupe de Recherche Opérationelle, Credit Lyonnais, 2002.

Chorafas, D. N., *Operational Risk Control with Basel II: Basic Principles and Capital Requirements*, Elsevier, 2003.

De Fountnouvelle, P., V. DeJesus-Rueff, J. Jordan, and E. Rosengren, "Capital and Risk: New Evidence on Implications of Large Operational Risk Losses," Federal Reserve Board of Boston, Working Paper, September 2003.

Lambrigger, D. D., P. V. Shevchenko, and M. V. Wüthrich, "The Quantification of Operational Risk Using Internal Data, Relevant External Data, and Expert Opinion," *Journal of Operational Risk*," 2, 3 (Fall 2007): 3–28.

Netter, J., and A,. Poulsen, "Operational Risk in Financial Service Providers and the Proposed Basel Accord: An Overview," Working Paper, Terry College of Business, University of Georgia.

Van Den Brink, G. J., *Operational Risk: The New Challenge for Banks*, Basingstoke, UK: Palgrave, 2001.

PRACTICE QUESTIONS AND PROBLEMS (Answers at the End of the Book)

18.1. What risks are included by regulators in their definition of operational risks? What risks are not included?

18.2. Suppose that external data shows that a loss of $100 million occurred at a bank with annual revenues of $1 billion. Your bank has annual revenues of $3 billion. What is the implication of the external data for losses that could occur at your bank.

18.3. Suppose that there is a 90% probability that operational risk losses of a certain type will not exceed $20 million. The power law parameter α is 0.8. What is the probability of losses exceeding (a) $40 million, (b) $80 million, and (c) $200 million.

18.4. Discuss how moral hazard and adverse selection are handled in car insurance.

18.5. Give two ways Sarbanes–Oxley affects the CEOs of public companies.

18.6. When is a trading loss classified as a market risk and when is it classified as an operational risk?

18.7. Discuss whether there is (a) moral hazard and (b) adverse selection in life insurance contracts.

18.8. What is external loss data? How is it obtained? How is it used in determining operational risk loss distributions for a bank?

18.9. What distributions are commonly used for loss frequency and loss severity?

18.10. Give two examples of key risk indicators that might be monitored by a central operational risk management group within a bank.

18.11. The worksheet used to produce Figure 18.2 is on the author's website. What is the mean and standard deviation of the loss distribution? Modify the inputs to the simulation to test the effect of changing the loss frequency from 3 to 4.

FURTHER QUESTIONS

18.12. Suppose that there is a 1% probability that operational risk losses of a certain type exceed $10 million. Use the power law to estimate the 99.97% worst-case operational risk loss when the parameter α equals (a) 0.25, (b) 0.5, and (c) 1.0.

18.13. Consider the following two events: (a) a bank loses $1 billion from an unexpected lawsuit relating to its transactions with a counterparty and (b) an insurance company loses $1 billion because of an unexpected hurricane in Texas. Suppose that you have the same investment in shares of the bank and the insurance company. Which loss are you more concerned about? Why?

18.14. The worksheet used to produce Figure 18.2 is on the author's website. How does the loss distribution change when the loss severity has a beta distribution with upper bound of 5, lower bound of 0, and the other parameters both 1?

CHAPTER 19

Liquidity Risk

The credit crisis that started in the middle of 2007 has emphasized the importance of liquidity risk for both financial institutions and their regulators. Many financial institutions that relied on wholesale deposits for their funding experienced problems as investors lost confidence in financial institutions. Moreover, financial institutions found that many instruments for which there had previously been a liquid market could only be sold at fire-sale prices during the crisis.

It is important to distinguish solvency from liquidity. Solvency refers to a company having more assets than liabilities, so that the value of its equity is positive. Liquidity refers to the ability of a company to make cash payments as they become due. Financial institutions that are solvent can—and sometimes do—fail because of liquidity problems. Consider a bank whose assets are mostly illiquid mortgages. Suppose the assets are financed 90% with deposits and 10% with equity. The bank is comfortably solvent. But it could fail if there is a run on deposits with 25% of depositors suddenly deciding to withdraw their funds. In this chapter we will examine how Northern Rock, a British bank specializing in mortgage lending, failed largely because of liquidity problems of this type.

It is clearly important for financial institutions to manage liquidity carefully. Liquidity needs are uncertain. Financial institutions must assess a worst-case liquidity scenario and make sure that they can survive that scenario by either converting assets into cash or borrowing funds externally.

Liquidity is also an important consideration in trading. A liquid position in an asset is one that can be unwound at short notice. As the market for an asset becomes less liquid, traders are more likely to take losses because they face bigger bid–offer spreads. For an option or other derivative, it is important for there to be a liquid market for the underlying asset so that the trader has no difficulty in doing the daily trades necessary to maintain delta neutrality (see Chapter 6).

This chapter discusses different aspects of liquidity risk. It considers liquidity trading risk and liquidity funding risk. It also looks at what are termed "liquidity black holes". These are situations where a shock to financial markets causes liquidity to dry up.

19.1 LIQUIDITY TRADING RISK

If a financial institution owns 100, 1,000, 10,000, or even 100,000 shares in IBM, liquidity risk is not a concern. Several million IBM shares trade on the New York

Stock Exchange every day. The quoted price of the shares is very close to the price that the financial institution would be able to sell the shares for. However, not all assets are as readily convertible into cash. For example, a $100 million investment in the bonds of a non-investment-grade US company might be quite difficult to sell at close to the market price in one day. Shares and debt of companies in emerging markets are likely to be even less easy to sell.

The price at which a particular asset can be sold depends on:

1. The mid-market price of the asset, or an estimate of its value
2. How much of the asset is to be sold
3. How quickly it is to be sold
4. The economic environment

When there is a market maker who quotes a bid and offer price for a financial asset, the financial institution can sell relatively small amounts of the asset at the bid and buy relatively small amounts at the offer. However, it is usually stated that a particular quote is good for trades up to a certain size. Above that size, the market maker is likely to increase the bid–offer spread. This is because it knows that, as the size of a trade increases, the difficulty of hedging the exposure created by the trade also increases.

When there is no market maker for a financial instrument, there is still an implicit bid–offer spread. If a financial institution approaches another financial institution (or an interdealer broker) to do a trade, the price depends on which side of the trade it wants to take. The bid–offer spread for an asset can vary from 0.05% of the asset's mid-market price to as much as 5%, or even 10%, of its mid-market price.

Bid–offer spreads depend on the size of the trade. The general nature of the relationship between bid quotes, offer quotes, and trade size is indicated in Figure 19.1. The bid price tends to decrease and the offer price tends to increase with the size of a trade. For an instrument where there is a market maker, the bid and offer lines are exactly parallel up to the market maker's size limit and then start to diverge.

Figure 19.1 describes the market for large deals between sophisticated financial institutions. It is interesting to note that bid–offer spreads in the retail market sometimes show the opposite pattern to that in Figure 19.1. Consider, for example, an individual who approaches a branch of a bank wanting to do a foreign exchange transaction or invest money for 90 days. As the size of the transaction increases, the individual is likely to get a better quote.

The price that can be realized for an asset often depends on how quickly it is to be liquidated and the economic environment. Suppose you want to sell your house. Sometimes the real estate market is referred to as a "seller's market". Almost as soon as you put the house on the market, you can expect to get several different offers and the house will be sold within a week. In other markets, it may take six months or more to sell the house. In the latter case, if you need to sell the house immediately, you will have to reduce the asking price well below the estimated market value.

Financial assets are similar to real assets as far as this is concerned. Sometimes liquidity is tight (e.g., after the Russian default of 1998 and after the subprime crisis of 2007). Liquidating even a relatively small position can then be time-consuming and is sometimes impossible. On other occasions, there is plenty of liquidity in the market and relatively large positions can be unwound without difficulty.

Figure 19.1   Bid and offer prices as a function of quantity transacted.

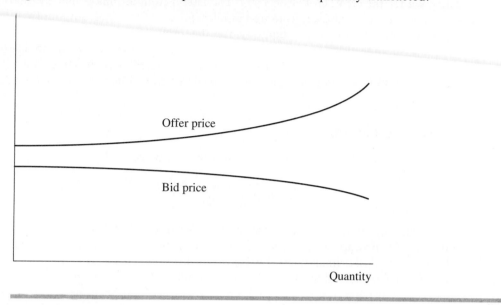

One of the problems in the market for financial assets is that, when one financial institution decides for whatever reason that it wants to unwind a position, it is often the case that many other financial institutions with similar positions decide they want to do the same thing. The liquidity normally present in the market then evaporates. This is the "liquidity black hole" phenomenon that will be discussed later in this chapter.

The Importance of Transparency

One thing that the market has learned from the credit crunch of 2007 is that transparency is important for liquidity. If the nature of an asset is uncertain, it is not likely to trade in a liquid market for very long.

As explained in Chapter 16, it had become common practice in the years prior to 2007 to form portfolios of subprime mortgages, credit card receivables, and other assets, and to create financial instruments by "tranching out" the credit risk. After August 2007, market participants realized that they knew very little about what was in these portfolios. Moreover, it was very difficult for them to find out very much about the portfolios. The situation was exacerbated by the fact that some of the assets in the portfolios were often tranches formed from other portfolios. Belatedly, market participants realized they had been using credit ratings as a substitute for an understanding of the instruments they had been trading.

After August 2007, the instruments created from subprime mortgages became illiquid. Financial institutions had no idea how to mark to market investments that they had been scrambling to buy a few months earlier. They realized that they had purchased highly complicated credit derivatives and that they did not have the tools to value them. They lacked both the necessary models and solid information about the assets in the portfolios underlying the derivatives.

Other well-defined credit derivatives, such as credit default swaps, continued to trade actively after the credit crunch of 2007. The lesson from all this is that the market can sometimes get carried away trading complex products that are not transparent, but, when it comes to its senses, liquidity for the products soon disappears. When the products do trade again, prices are likely to be low and bid–offer spreads are likely to be high. As mentioned in Chapter 16, in July 2008 Merrill Lynch agreed to sell $30.6 billion of ABS CDO tranches (previously rated AAA) to Lone Star Funds for 22 cents on the dollar.

Measuring Liquidity

The proportional bid–offer spread for an asset can be defined as

$$s = \frac{\text{Offer price} - \text{Bid price}}{\text{Mid-market price}}$$

where the mid-market price is halfway between the bid and the offer price. In liquidating a position in the asset, a financial institution incurs a cost equal to $\frac{1}{2}s\alpha$, where α is the dollar (mid-market) value of the position. This reflects the fact that trades are not done at the mid-market price. A buy trade is done at a proportional amount $\frac{1}{2}s$ above the mid-market price and a sell trade is done at a proportional amount $\frac{1}{2}s$ below the mid-market price.

One measure of the liquidity of a book is how much it would cost to liquidate the book in normal market conditions within a certain time. Suppose that s_i is an estimate of the relevant proportional bid–offer spread in normal market conditions for the ith financial instrument held by a financial institution and α_i is the dollar value of the position in the instrument. Then

$$\text{Cost of liquidation (normal market)} = \sum_{i=1}^{n} \frac{1}{2}s_i\alpha_i \qquad (19.1)$$

where n is the number of positions. Note that although diversification reduces market risk it does not automatically reduce liquidity trading risk. However, as explained earlier, s_i increases with the size of position i. Holding many small positions rather than a few large positions therefore tends to entail less liquidity risk. Setting position limits is one way of reducing liquidity trading risk.

Example 19.1

Suppose that a financial institution has bought 10 million shares of one company and 50 million ounces of a commodity. The shares are bid $89.5, offer $90.5. The commodity is bid $15, offer $15.1. The mid-market value of the position in the shares is $90 \times 10 = \$900$ million. The mid-market value of the position in the commodity is $15.05 \times 50 = 752.50$ million. The proportional bid–offer spread for the shares is $1/90$, or 0.01111. The proportional bid–offer spread for the commodity is $0.1/15.05$, or 0.006645. The cost of liquidation in a normal market is

$$900 \times 0.01111/2 + 752.5 \times 0.006645/2 = 7.5$$

or $7.5 million.

Another measure of liquidity is the cost of liquidation in stressed market conditions within a certain time period. Define μ_i and σ_i as the mean and standard deviation of the proportional bid–offer spread. Then

$$\text{Cost of liquidation (stressed market)} = \sum_{i=1}^{n} \tfrac{1}{2}(\mu_i + \lambda_i \sigma_i)\alpha_i \qquad (19.2)$$

The parameters λ_i give the required confidence level for the spread. If, for example, we are interested in a considering "a 99% worst case", in the sense that the bid–offer spreads are exceeded only 1% of the time, and if it is assumed that spreads are normally distributed, then $\lambda_i = 2.33$ for all i.

Example 19.2

Suppose that in Example 19.1 the mean and standard deviation for the bid–offer spread for the shares is 1.0 and 2.0, respectively. Suppose further that the mean and standard deviation for the bid–offer spread for the commodity are both 0.1. The mean and standard deviation for the proportional bid–offer spread for the shares are 0.01111 and 0.02222, respectively. The mean and standard deviation for the proportional bid–offer spread for the commodity are both 0.006645. Assuming that the spreads are normally distributed, the cost of liquidation that we are 99% confident will not be exceeded is

$$900 \times \tfrac{1}{2}(0.01111 + 2.33 \times 0.02222) + 752.5 \times (0.006645 + 2.33 \times 0.006645)$$
$$= 73.25$$

or $73.25. This is almost ten times the cost of liquidation in normal market conditions.

In practice, bid–offer spreads are not normally distributed, and it may be appropriate to use a value of λ that reflects their empirical distribution. For example, if it is found that the 99 percentile point of the distribution is 3.6 standard deviations above the mean for a particular category of financial instruments, λ_i can be set equal to 3.6 for those instruments.

Equation (19.1) assumes that spreads in all instruments are perfectly correlated. This may seem overly conservative, but it is not. When liquidity is tight and bid–offer spreads widen, they tend to do so for all instruments.

It makes sense for a financial institution to monitor changes in the liquidity of its book by calculating the measures in equations (19.1) and (19.2) on a regular basis. As we have seen, the bid–offer spread depends on how quickly a position is to be liquidated. The measures in equations (19.1) and (19.2) are therefore likely to be decreasing functions of the time period assumed for the liquidation.

Liquidity-Adjusted VaR

Value at risk, which we discussed in Chapters 8, 12, and 13, is designed to calculate an estimate of the "worst change" in the mark-to-market valuation of the trading book. The measures in equations (19.1) and (19.2) are designed to calculate the cost of liquidating a book if market prices do not change. Although VaR and liquidity risk measures deal with different types of risks, some researchers have proposed combining them into a *liquidity-adjusted VaR* measure. Assume that the mark-to-market process discussed in Section 19.1 values all instruments at the mid-marketprice. One definition of liquidity-adjusted VaR is regular VaR plus the cost of unwinding positions in a normal market. From equation (19.1), this gives

$$\text{Liquidity-adjusted VaR} = \text{VaR} + \sum_{i=1}^{n} \tfrac{1}{2} s_i \alpha_i \qquad \textbf{(19.3)}$$

Alternatively, it can be defined as regular VaR plus the cost of unwinding positions in a stressed market. From equation (19.2), this gives[1]

$$\text{Liquidity-adjusted VaR} = \text{VaR} + \sum_{i=1}^{n} \tfrac{1}{2} (\mu_i + \lambda \sigma_i) \alpha_i$$

Unwinding a Position Optimally

A trader wishing to unwind a large position in a financial instrument has to decide on the best trading strategy. If the position is unwound quickly, the trader will face large bid–offer spreads, but the potential loss from the mid-market price moving against the trader is small. If the trader chooses to take several days to unwind the position, the bid–offer spread the trader faces each day will be lower, but the potential loss from the mid-market price moving against the trader is larger.

This type of problem is discussed by Almgren and Chriss.[2] Suppose that the size of a position is V units and that a trader has to decide how to liquidate it over an n-day period. Define the bid–offer spread (measured in dollars per unit) when the trader trades q units in one day as $p(q)$. Define q_i as the units traded on day i and x_i as the size of the trader's position at the end of day i, with $1 \leqslant i \leqslant n$. It follows that $x_i = x_{i-1} - q_i$ for $1 \leqslant i \leqslant n$, where x_0 is defined as the initial position size V.

Each trade costs half the bid–offer spread. The total of the costs related to the bid–offer spread is therefore

$$\sum_{i=1}^{n} \tfrac{1}{2} q_i p(q_i)$$

Suppose that the mid-market price changes are normally distributed with a standard deviation of σ per day and trading takes place at the beginning of a day. The variance of the change in the value of the trader's position on day i is $\sigma^2 x_i^2$. The variance of the price change applicable to the unwind is therefore

$$\sum_{i=1}^{n} \sigma^2 x_i^2$$

A trader might reasonably wish to minimize VaR after trading costs have been considered. This corresponds to minimizing something a little similar to the liquidity-adjusted VaR measure in equation (19.3). The trader's objective is to choose the q_i so that

$$\lambda \sqrt{\sum_{i=1}^{n} \sigma^2 x_i^2} + \sum_{i=1}^{n} \tfrac{1}{2} q_i p(q_i)$$

[1] This was suggested in A. Bangia, F. Diebold, T. Schuermann, and J. Stroughair, "Liquidity on the Outside," *Risk*, 12 (June): 68–73.

[2] See R. Almgren and N. Chriss, "Optimal Execution of Portfolio Transactions," *Journal of Risk*, 3 (Winter 2001): 5–39.

is minimized subject to

$$\sum_{i=1}^{n} q_i = V$$

with the x_i being calculated from V and the q_i, as explained above. The parameter λ measures the confidence level in the VaR estimate. For example, when the confidence level is 99%, and daily price changes are assumed to be normally distributed, $\lambda = 2.33$. Once the $p(q)$ function has been estimated, Excel's Solver can be used for the optimization.

Example 19.3

A trader wishes to unwind a position of 100 million units in an asset over five days. Suppose that the bid–offer spread, measured in dollars, as a function of the daily trading volume, is

$$p(q) = a + be^{cq}$$

where $a = 0.1$, $b = 0.05$, and $c = 0.03$, and the amount traded, q, is measured in millions of units.

The standard deviation of the price change per day is \$0.1. A spreadsheet for calculating the optimal strategy can be downloaded from the author's website. When the confidence level is 95%, the amounts that should be traded on days 1, 2, 3, 4, 5 are 48.9, 30.0, 14.1, 5.1, 1.9 million units, respectively. As the VaR confidence level is reduced, the amounts traded per day show less variability. For example, when the confidence level is 90%, they are 45.0, 29.1, 15.6, 7.0, 3.3 million units, respectively. When the confidence level is 75%, they are 36.1, 26.2, 17.7, 11.6, 8.4 million units, respectively. In the limit when the confidence level is set equal to 50%, so that the trader is interested only in expected costs, not in the standard deviation of costs, 20 million units should be traded each day.

Example 19.3 illustrates that, when a position is to be closed out over n days, more than $1/n$ of the position should be traded on the first day. This is because the longer any part of the position is held, the greater is the risk of adverse market moves.

19.2 LIQUIDITY FUNDING RISK

We now move on to consider liquidity funding risk. This is the financial institution's ability to meet its cash needs as they arise. As mentioned at the outset of this chapter, liquidity is not the same as solvency. Financial institutions that are solvent (i.e., have positive equity) can, and sometimes do, fail because of liquidity problems. Northern Rock, a British mortgage lender, is a case in point (see Business Snapshot 19.1).

Some cash needs are predictable. For example, if a bank has issued a bond, it knows when coupons will have to be paid. Others, such as those arising from withdrawals of deposits by retail customers and draw-downs by corporations on lines of credit that the bank has granted, are less predictable. As the financial instruments entered into by financial institutions have become more complex, cash needs have become more difficult to predict. For example, credit triggers (see Section 15.2 and Business Snapshot 15.2), guarantees provided by a financial institution, and possible defaults by counterparties in derivative transactions can have an unexpected impact on cash resources.

Business Snapshot 19.1 Northern Rock

Northern Rock, a British bank, was founded in 1997 when the Northern Rock Building Society floated shares on the London Stock Exchange. In 2007 it was one of the top five mortgage lenders in the United Kingdom. It had 76 branches and offered deposit accounts, savings accounts, loans, and house and contents insurance. The bank grew rapidly between 1997 and 2007. Some of its mortgages were securitized through a subsidiary, Granite, that was based in the Channel Islands.

Northern Rock relied for about 75% of its funding on debt instruments it sold in wholesale markets. Following the subprime crisis of August 2007, the bank found it very difficult to replace maturing instruments. This is because institutional investors became very nervous about lending to banks that were heavily involved in the mortgage business. The bank's assets were sufficient to cover its liabilities, so it was not insolvent. To quote from the Financial Services Authority (FSA) in September 2007: "The FSA judges that Northern Rock is solvent, exceeds its regulatory capital requirement, and has a good quality loan book." But Northern Rock's inability to fund itself was a serious problem. It approached the Bank of England for funding on September 12, 2007, and borrowed about £3 billion from the Tripartite Authority (Bank of England, Financial Services Authority, and HM Treasury) in the following few days.

On September 13, 2007, the BBC business editor Robert Peston broke the news that the bank had requested emergency support from the Bank of England. On Friday, September 14, there was a run on the bank. Thousands of people lined up for hours to withdraw their funds. This was the first run on a British bank for 150 years. Some customers held their funds in an "internet-only" account, which they were unable to access due to the volume of customers trying to log on. On Monday, September 17, worried savers continued to withdraw their funds. An estimated £2 billion was withdrawn between September 12 and September 17, 2007.

Depositor insurance in the UK guaranteed 100% of the first £2,000 and 90% of the next £33,000. Late on September 17, 2007, the Chancellor of the Exchequer, Alistair Darling, announced that the British Government and the Bank of England would guarantee all deposits held at Northern Rock. As a result of this announcement and subsequent advertisements in major UK newspapers, the queues outside Northern Rock's branches gradually disappeared. Northern Rock's shares, which had fallen from £12 earlier in the year to £2.67, rose 16% on Mr. Darling's announcement.

During the months following September 12, 2007 Northern Rock's emergency borrowing requirement increased. The Bank of England insisted on a penalty rate of interest to discourage other banks from taking excessive risks and collateral requirements were strict. By October, borrowing had risen to £16 billion and collateral requirements were relaxed somewhat. There were takeover offers from the Virgin Group (headed by colorful entrepreneur Sir Richard Branson) and a number of other companies, but they were rejected. Northern Rock raised some funds by selling assets, but by February 2008 the emergency borrowing reached £25 billion and the bank was nationalized with the management of the bank being changed.

The Northern Rock story illustrates just how quickly liquidity problems can lead to a bank spiraling downward.

Liquidity funding risk is related to liquidity trading risk, considered in the previous section. This is because one way a financial institution can meet its funding requirements is by liquidating part of its trading book.

Sources of Liquidity

The main sources of liquidity for a financial institution are:

1. Holdings of cash and securities such as Treasury bills that can be readily convertible into cash
2. The ability to liquidate trading book positions
3. The ability to borrow money in the wholesale market at short notice
4. The ability to offer favorable terms to attract retail deposits at short notice
5. The ability to securitize assets (such as loans) at short notice
6. Borrowings from the central bank

Liquid Assets

Cash and marketable securities are relatively expensive sources of liquidity. This is because the interest earned on securities that can be readily converted into cash is less than the interest earned on other less liquid assets. For example, it is usually more profitable for a bank to allocate assets to loans than to Treasury bills, and more profitable for an insurance company to allocate assets to corporate bonds rather than Treasury bills. There is a trade-off between the liquidity of an asset and the return it provides. We see this in the market for Treasury bonds in the United States. On-the-run bonds are recently issued bonds that trade fairly actively. Off-the-run bonds are bonds that were issued some time ago and are relatively illiquid. The yield on off-the-run bonds is up to 20 basis points higher than the yield on similar on-the-run bonds.

Assessing which assets in the trading book are liquid (readily convertible into cash) and which are not is a key activity for a financial institution. It is important to base this assessment on stressed market conditions, not normal market conditions. When one financial institution is in need of liquidity, many other financial institutions are likely to be in a similar position. Assets that are highly liquid in normal market conditions are liable to become very difficult to sell during stressed market conditions. One result of the credit crisis that started in the summer of 2007 was that the trading books of all financial institutions suddenly became much less liquid.

Wholesale and Retail Deposits

Wholesale deposits are a more volatile source of funding than retail deposits. When markets are unstressed, a creditworthy bank usually has no problem in borrowing money in wholesale markets, but, in stressed market conditions, there is a heightened aversion to risk. This leads to higher interest rates, shorter maturities for loans in the wholesale market, and in some cases a refusal to provide funds at all. Financial institutions should monitor the assets that can be pledged as collateral for loans at short notice. A financial institution can (at a cost) mitigate its funding risks somewhat by arranging lines of credit. For example, Countrywide, an originator of mortgages in the United States, had a syndicated loan facility of $11.5 billion which it was able to use during the credit crisis of 2007. (This helped keep the company afloat, but it still experienced significant problems and was taken over by Bank of America in January 2008.) As Business Snapshot 19.1 shows, Northern Rock, a similar British mortgage lender, did not fare so well.

Deposits from retail clients are a less volatile source of funding than borrowings in the wholesale market. But retail deposits are not as stable as they used to be. Depositors now find it very easy to compare interest rates offered by different financial institutions and make transfers via the internet. Unfortunately, liquidity problems tend to be market-wide rather than something that affects one or two financial institutions. When one financial institution wants to increase its retail deposit base for liquidity reasons, others usually do as well and the desired increase is likely to be difficult to achieve.

Securitization

As mentioned in Chapter 2, banks have found the "originate to distribute" model attractive. Rather than keep illiquid assets such as loans on their balance sheet, they have securitized them. The structures developed for doing this were discussed in Chapter 16. Prior to August 2007, securitization was an important source of liquidity for banks. However, this source of liquidity dried up almost overnight in August 2007 as investors decided that the securitized products were too risky. "Originate to distribute" had to be replaced by "originate and fund"! Not surprisingly, banks became a lot less willing to lend.

Securitization led to other liquidity problems in August 2007. Banks had entered into liquidity backstop arrangements on the asset-backed commercial paper (ABCP) that was used to fund debt instruments such as mortgages prior to their securitization. When buyers could not be found, they had to buy the instruments themselves. In some cases, in order to avoid their reputations being adversely impacted, they had to provide financial support to conduits and other off-balance-sheet vehicles that were involved in securitization, even though not legally required to do so.

Central Bank Borrowing

Central banks (e.g., the Federal Reserve Board in the US, the Bank of England in the UK, or the European Central Bank) are often referred to as "lenders of last resort". When commercial banks are experiencing financial difficulties, central banks are prepared to lend money to maintain the health of the financial system. Collateral has to be posted by the banks and the central bank typically applies a haircut (i.e., it lends less than 100% of the value of the collateral) and may charge a relatively high rate of interest. In March 2008, after the failure of Bear Stearns (which was taken over by J. P. Morgan Chase), the Federal Reserve Board extended its borrowing facility to investment banks as well as commercial banks.[3] Later, it also made the facility available to Fannie Mae and Freddie Mac (which were taken over by the government in September 2008).

Different central banks apply different rules. Following the credit crisis of August 2007, the haircuts used by the European Central Bank (ECB) were lower than those of

[3] Central banks are concerned about the failure of investment banks because of systemic risk (see Business Snapshot 11.1). Investment banks have derivatives contracts with other investment banks and with commercial banks. There is a danger that, because of the huge amount of trading between banks, a failure by an investment bank will have a ripple effect throughout the financial sector leading to a failure by commercial banks.

> ### Business Snapshot 19.2 Ashanti Goldfields
>
> Ashanti Goldfields, a West African gold-mining company based in Ghana, experienced problems resulting from its hedging program in 1999. It had sought to protect its shareholders from gold price declines by selling gold forward. On September 26, 1999, 15 European central banks surprised the market with an announcement that they would limit their gold sales over the following five years. The price of gold jumped up over 25%. Ashanti was unable to meet margin calls and this resulted in a major restructuring that included the sale of a mine, a dilution of the interest of its equity shareholders, and a restructuring of its hedge positions.

other central banks. As a result, some British banks preferred to borrow from the European Central Bank (ECB) rather than the Bank of England. (There are even stories of North American banks contemplating the setting up of subsidiaries in Ireland to access the ECB.) By September 2008, the ECB had lent 467 billion euros and it then announced that it would apply larger haircuts in the future.

Banks try to keep their borrowings from a central bank a secret. There is a danger that the borrowings will be interpreted by the market as a sign that the bank is experiencing financial difficulties, with the result that other sources of liquidity dry up. As Business Snapshot 19.1 discusses, news that Northern Rock required emergency borrowing led to an immediate run on the bank, exacerbating its liquidity problems.

Hedging Issues

Liquidity problems are liable to arise when companies hedge illiquid assets with contracts that are subject to margin requirements. As indicated in Business Snapshot 6.1, gold-mining companies often hedge their risks by entering into agreements with financial institutions to sell gold forward for two or three years. Often the gold-mining company is required to post margin, and the amount of the margin required is calculated every day to reflect the value of its forward agreements. If the price of gold rises fast, the forward agreements lose money and result in big margin calls being made by the financial institution on the gold-mining company. The losses on the forward agreements are offset by gold in the ground—but this is an illiquid asset. As discussed in Business Snapshot 19.2, Ashanti Goldfields was forced to undertake a major restructuring when it could not meet margin calls after a sharp rise in the price of gold.

Another extreme example of a liquidity funding problem caused by hedging is provided by a German company, Metallgesellschaft, that entered into profitable fixed-price oil and gas contracts with its customers (see Business Snapshot 19.3). The lesson of the Ashanti and Metallgesellschaft episodes is not that the companies should not have used forward and futures contracts for hedging, but rather that they should have ensured they had access to funding to handle the cash-flow mismatches that might arise in extreme circumstances.

Reserve Requirements

In some countries there are *reserve requirements* that require banks to keep a certain percentage of deposits as cash in the bank's vault or on deposit with the central bank.

Business Snapshot 19.3   Metallgesellschaft

In the early 1990s, Metallgesellschaft (MG) sold a huge volume of 5- to 10-year heating oil and gasoline fixed-price supply contracts to its customers at 6 to 8 cents above market prices. It hedged its exposure with long positions in short-dated futures contracts that were rolled forward. As it turned out, the price of oil fell and there were margin calls on the futures positions. Considerable short-term cash-flow pressures were placed on MG. The members of MG who devised the hedging strategy argued that these short-term cash outflows were offset by positive cash flows that would ultimately be realized on the long-term fixed-price contracts. However, the company's senior management and its bankers became concerned about the huge cash drain. As a result, the company closed out all the hedge positions and agreed with its customers that the fixed-price contracts would be abandoned. The outcome was a loss to MG of $1.33 billion.

The reserve requirement applies only to transaction deposits (in essence, those made to a checking account). For large banks in the United States, the reserve requirement is currently 10%. Some countries, such as Canada and the United Kingdom, have no compulsory reserve requirements; others have higher compulsory reserve requirements than the United States.

In addition to ensuring that banks keep a minimum amount of liquidity, reserve requirements affect the money supply. When the reserve requirement is 10%, a $100 deposit leads to $90 of lending, which leads to a further $90 of deposits in the banking system, which leads to further $81 of lending, and so on. As this process continues, the total money supply (M1) that is created is $90 + 81 + 72.9 + \cdots$, or $900 of M1. If the reserve requirement is 20%, a $100 deposit leads to $80 of lending, which leads to $64 of lending, and so on. The total increase in the money supply is $80 + 64 + 51.2 + \cdots$, or $400. Most countries do not use the reserve requirement as a way of controlling the money supply. An exception appears to be China, where the reserve requirement is changed frequently.

Regulatory Principles

Following the liquidity crunch of 2007, bank regulators issued a revised set of principles on how banks should manage liquidity.[4] These can be summarized as follows:

1. A bank must take responsibility for sound liquidity management, establishing a framework to ensure that it maintains a cushion of highly liquid assets. Bank supervisors (i.e., regulators) should monitor the liquidity risk of a bank as carefully as they monitor other risks and intervene when necessary.

2. A bank should clearly articulate a liquidity risk tolerance that is appropriate for its business strategy and its role in the financial system.

3. Senior management should develop a strategy to monitor liquidity in accordance with the risk tolerance, and this strategy should be approved by the board

---

[4] See Bank for International Settlements, "Principles for Sound Liquidity Risk Management and Supervision," June 2008.

annually. Senior management should review information on liquidity developments continuously and report regularly to the board.

4. When new products or new lines of business are being considered the liquidity costs and benefits should be explicitly quantified and taken into account.

5. A bank should have procedures for projecting cash flows from assets, liabilities and off-balance-sheet instruments in different circumstances, including stressed market conditions. The extent to which liquidity needs and liquidity sources are matched for different future horizons should be assessed and early-warning indicators designed. The procedures should consider the "stickiness" of funding sources, commitments the bank has made, actions that could be necessary to maintain its reputation, and so on.

6. A bank should manage liquidity both within each of its legal entities (i.e., subsidiaries) and on a consolidated basis, taking account of legal, regulatory, and operational limitations on the transferability of liquidity from one legal entity to another.

7. A bank should develop a funding strategy that provides diversification in the sources and the maturity of funding that it has access to. It should regularly gauge its ability to raise funds quickly from each source.

8. A bank should actively manage its intraday liquidity positions and risks to meet payment and settlement obligations under normal and stressed market conditions.

9. A bank should actively manage the collateral it has pledged. It should keep track of encumbered assets (already pledged) and unencumbered assets (available to be pledged) for each of its legal entities.

10. A bank should conduct stress tests on a regular basis for a variety of scenarios. Some scenarios should involve problems faced by particular financial institutions or specific to certain types of asset, and some should involve market-wide stress scenarios. The results of this stress testing should be used to develop effective contingency plans.

11. A bank should have a contingency plan for addressing liquidity shortfalls in emergency situations, including lines of responsibility.

12. A bank should maintain a cushion of unencumbered high-quality liquid assets for insurance against liquidity stress scenarios. There should be no legal, regulatory, or operational impediment to using these assets to obtain funding.

13. A bank should publicly disclose information about the soundness of its liquidity positions and risk management policies.

14. Supervisors should regularly assess a bank's liquidity risk management procedures to ensure that they are adequate given the bank's role in the financial system.

15. Supervisors should supplement their regular assessments by monitoring internal reports and market information.

16. Supervisors should intervene in an effective and timely way to address liquidity risk management deficiencies in a bank.

17. Supervisors should share information with other supervisors and public authorities to facilitate cooperation in the oversight of liquidity risk management.

There can be little doubt that regulators will pay far more attention to liquidity risk management than they have in the past. This in turn is likely to lead to more resources being devoted to the monitoring and management of liquidity by banks.

19.3 LIQUIDITY BLACK HOLES

It is sometimes argued that technological and other developments have led to an improvement in the liquidity of financial markets. This is questionable. It is true that bid–offer spreads have on average declined. But there has also been an increasing tendency for situations to develop where almost everyone wants to do the same type of trade at the same time. The result has been that what are referred to as "liquidity black holes" occur with increasing frequency.[5] A liquidity black hole is situation where liquidity has dried up in a particular market because everyone wants to sell and no one wants to buy or vice versa.

In a well-functioning market, the market may change its opinion about the price of an asset because of new information. However, the price does not overreact. If a price decrease is too great, traders will quickly move in and buy the asset and a new equilibrium price will be established. A liquidity black hole is created when a price decline causes more market participants to want to sell, driving prices well below where they will eventually settle. During the sell-off, liquidity dries up and the asset can be sold only at a fire-sale price.[6]

Positive and Negative Feedback Traders

Changes in the liquidity of financial markets are driven by the behavior of traders. There are two sorts of trader in the market: negative feedback traders and positive feedback traders.[7] Negative feedback traders buy when prices fall and sell when prices rise; positive feedback traders sell when prices fall and buy when prices rise. In liquid markets, negative feedback traders dominate the trading. If the price of an asset gets unreasonably low, traders will move in and buy. This creates demand for the asset that restores the price to a more reasonable level. Similarly, if the price of an asset gets unreasonably high, traders will sell. This creates supply of the asset that also restores the price to a more reasonable level. The result is that the market is liquid with reasonable prices and a good balance of buyers and sellers. When positive feedback traders dominate the trading, market prices are liable to be unstable and the market may become one-sided and illiquid. A reduction in the price of an asset causes traders to sell. This results in the price falling further, which leads to more selling. An increase in the price of an asset causes traders to buy. This results in the price of the asset increasing further, which leads to more buying.

---

[5] See A.D. Persaud (ed.), *Liquidity Black Holes: Understanding, Quantifying and Managing Financial Liquidity Risk*. London: Risk Books, 1999.

[6] Liquidity black holes tend to be associated with price decreases, but it is possible for them to occur when there are price increases.

[7] This is simplification of reality to help understand the dynamics of markets. Some traders follow complicated strategies that cannot be classified as positive feedback or negative feedback.

There are a number of reasons why positive feedback trading exists. For example:

1. *Stop-loss rules*. Traders often have rules to limit their losses. When the price of an asset that is owned falls below a certain level, they automatically sell to limit their losses. These rules are known as "stop-loss" rules and are a source of positive feedback trading that is always present in the market.

2. *Dynamic hedging*. Chapter 6 explains how options traders maintain a delta-neutral position using dynamic hedging. In particular, Tables 6.2 and 6.3 show how a trader would hedge a short position in an option over a 20-week period. Hedging a short option position (call or put) involves buying after a price rise and selling after a price decline. This is positive feedback trading that has the potential to reduce liquidity. (By contrast dynamically hedging a long position in a call or put option involves selling after a price rise and buying after a price decline. This is negative feedback trading and should not interfere with market liquidity.) Any situation where banks have a large short option position has the potential to destabilize the market and cause illiquidity. As discussed in Business Snapshot 3.1, at one point banks sold a huge volume of options on long-term interest rates to British insurance companies. As the banks hedged their risks, the behavior of long-term interest rates in the UK was dramatically affected.

3. *Creating options synthetically*. Hedging a short position in an option is equivalent to creating a long position in the same option synthetically. It follows that a financial institution can create a long option position synthetically by doing the same sort of trading as it would do if it were hedging a short option position. This leads to positive feedback trading that can cause market instability and illiquidity. The classic example here is the stock market crash of October 1987. In the period leading up to the crash, the stock market had done very well. Increasing numbers of portfolio managers were using commercially available programs to synthetically create put options on their portfolios. These programs told them to sell part of their portfolio immediately after a price decline and buy it back immediately after a price increase. The result, as indicated in Business Snapshot 19.4, was a liquidity black hole where prices plunged on October 19, 1987. In this case, the liquidity black hole was relatively short-lived. Within four months the market recovered close to its precrash level.

4. *Margins*. A big movement in market variables, particularly for traders who are highly leveraged, may lead to margin calls that cannot be met. This forces traders to close out their positions, which is a form of positive feedback trading. The failure of the hedge fund Long-Term Capital Management (LTCM), as outlined in Business Snapshot 15.1, provides an example here. One type of LTCM trade was "relative value fixed income". LTCM would take short position in a liquid bond and a long position in a similar illiquid bond, and wait for the prices to move close together. After the Russian default of 1998, the prices of illiquid instruments declined relative to similar liquid instruments. LTCM (and other companies that were following strategies similar to LTCM's) were highly leveraged and unable to meet margin calls. They were forced to close out their positions. This involved buying the liquid bonds and selling the illiquid bonds. This reinforced the flight to quality and made the prices of illiquid and liquid bonds diverge even further.

Business Snapshot 19.4   The Crash of 1987

On Monday, October 19, 1987, the Dow Jones Industrial Average dropped by more than 20%. Portfolio insurance played a major role in this crash. In October 1987, portfolios with over $60 billion of equity assets were being managed with trading rules that were designed to synthetically create put options on the portfolios. These trading rules involved selling equities (or selling index futures) when the market declined and buying equity (or buying equity futures) when the market rose.

During the period Wednesday, October 14, 1987, to Friday, October 16, 1987, the market declined by about 10%, with much of the fall taking place on Friday afternoon. The portfolio insurance rules should have generated at least $12 billion of equity or index futures sales as a result of this decline. In fact, portfolio insurers had time to sell only $4 billion and they approached the following week with huge amounts of selling already dictated by their models. It is estimated that, on Monday, October 19, sell programs by three portfolio insurers accounted for almost 10% of the sales on the New York Stock Exchange, and that portfolio insurance sales amounted to 21.3% of all sales in index futures markets. It is likely that the decline in equity prices was exacerbated by investors other than portfolio insurers selling heavily because they anticipated the actions of portfolio insurers.

Because the market declined so fast and the stock exchange systems were overloaded, many portfolio insurers were unable to execute the trades generated by their models and failed to obtain the protection they required. Needless to say, the popularity of portfolio insurance schemes has declined significantly since 1987. One of the lessons from this story is that it is dangerous to follow a particular trading strategy—even a hedging strategy—when many other market participants are doing the same thing. To quote from the Brady report on the crash, "Liquidity sufficient to absorb the limited selling demands of investors became an illusion of liquidity by massive selling, as everyone showed up on the same side of the market at once. Ironically, it was this illusion of liquidity which led certain similarly motivated investors, such as portfolio insurers, to adopt strategies which call for liquidity far in excess of what the market could supply."

Leveraging and Deleveraging

A common phenomenon in economics is leveraging and deleveraging. This is illustrated in Figures 19.2 and 19.3. When banks are awash with liquidity (e.g., because they have developed ways of securitizing assets or because deposit levels are higher than usual), they make credit easily available to businesses, investors, and consumers. Credit spreads decrease. The easy availability of credit increases demand for both financial and nonfinancial assets and the prices of these assets rise. Assets are often pledged as collateral for the loans that are used to finance them. When the prices of the assets rise, the collateral underlying loans (when measured at market prices) is greater and borrowing can increase further. This leads to further asset purchases and a repeat of the cycle. This cycle is referred to as "leveraging" because it leads to more borrowing throughout the economy.

Deleveraging is the opposite process to leveraging. Banks find themselves less liquid for some reason (e.g., because there is less demand for the products of securitization).

Figure 19.2   Leveraging.

They become more reluctant to lend money. Credit spreads increase. There is less demand for both nonfinancial and financial assets and their prices decrease. The value of the collateral supporting loans decreases and banks reduce lines of credit. This leads to asset sales being necessary and a further reduction in asset prices.

The period leading up to 2007 was characterized by leveraging for many of the world's economies. Credit spreads declined and it was relatively easy to borrow money for a wide range of different purposes. From the middle of 2007 onward, the situation changed and the deleveraging process shown in Figure 19.3 started. Credit spreads increased, it became much less easy to borrow money, and asset prices decreased.

Hedge funds are particularly affected by the leveraging–deleveraging cycle. Consider a hedge fund that is able to borrow 20 times its equity during the pre-2007 period. Soon after the middle of 2007, the hedge fund might get a call from its prime broker telling it to reduce leverage to, say, 5 times equity. It can only do this by selling assets. Asset prices decrease as a result of what the hedge fund, and other hedge funds, are doing. The hedge fund's equity declines and further sales are necessary.

Figure 19.3   Deleveraging.

The Impact of Capital Requirements

In many ways, it is a laudable goal on the part of regulators to seek to ensure that banks and other financial institutions throughout the world are regulated in the same way. As explained in Chapter 11, capital requirements and the extent to which they were enforced varied from country to country prior to Basel I. Banks were competing globally and, as a result, a bank subject to low capital requirements, or capital requirements that were not strictly enforced, had a competitive edge.

However, a uniform regulatory environment comes with costs. All banks tend to respond in the same way to external events. Consider, for example, market risk. When volatilities and correlations increase, market VaR and the capital required for market risks increase. Banks then take steps to reduce their exposures. Since banks often have similar positions to each other, they try to do similar trades. A liquidity black hole can develop.

There is a similar issue as far as credit risk is concerned. This is a similar phenomenon to that in Figures 19.2 and 19.3. During the low point of the economic cycle, default probabilities are relatively high and capital requirements for loans under the Basel II internal-ratings-based models tend to be high. As a result, banks may be less willing to make loans, creating a liquidity black hole for small and medium-sized businesses. The Basel Committee has recognized this problem and has dealt with it by asserting that the probability of default should be an average of the probability of default through the economic or credit cycle, rather than an estimate applicable to one particular point in time.

Irrational Exuberance

The term *irrational exuberance* was used by Alan Greenspan, Federal Reserve Board chairman, in a speech in December 1996, when, in reference to the stock market, he said: "How do we know when irrational exuberance has unduly escalated asset values?"

The phrase has been remembered because the speech was followed by declines in stock prices worldwide. Most liquidity black holes can be traced to irrational exuberance of one sort or another. What happens is that traders working for many different financial institutions become irrationally exuberant about a particular asset class or a particular market variable. The balance sheets of financial institutions then become overextended through the accumulation of exposure to this asset class or market variable. Often the process is self-reinforcing. When many financial institutions choose to take a particular position, prices increase, making the position look profitable. This creates extra desire on the part of financial institutions to take the position and yet more profits. Risk managers working for the financial institution should (and probably will) complain about the risks being taken, but in many instances senior management are likely to ignore their concerns because high profits are being made. To quote Chuck Prince, ex-CEO of Citigroup, on July 10, 2007: "When the music stops, in terms of liquidity, things will be complicated. But as long as the music is playing, you've got to get up and dance. We're still dancing."

At some stage the bubble must burst. Many traders then try to get out of their positions at the same time causing illiquid markets and huge losses. Volatility increases and the risk management procedures used within the financial institution (e.g., the calculation of market VaR from historical data) can cause many financial institutions to try to unwind a wide range of risky positions at the same time. This can lead to further losses and more serious illiquidity problems. There may be failures (or rumors of failures) by some banks. Most banks are likely to experience liquidity funding problems and as a result lending may be curtailed.

The classic example of what has been described is the subprime crisis that started in 2007. Other examples are provided by the 1987 stock market crash, the 1994 bond market crash, the 1997–8 Asian monetary crisis, and the 1998 Long-Term Capital Management failure. Irrational exuberance is part of human nature and to some extent is inevitable. As discussed in Chapter 16, it is exacerbated by the way traders are paid. A large part of the compensation comes from a bonus at year-end, which depends on performance during the year. A trader may be savvy enough to know that a market is irrationally exuberant and that there will be a correction. However, if there is a good chance that the correction will be delayed until next year, the trader is motivated continue building up his or her position to maximize short-term compensation.

The Importance of Diversity

Models in economics usually assume that market participants act independently of each other. We have argued that this is often not the case. It is this lack of independence that causes liquidity black holes. Traders working for financial institutions tend to want to do the same trades at the same time. To solve the problem of liquidity black holes, we need more diversity in financial markets.

One conclusion from the arguments we have put forward is that a contrarian investment strategy has some merit. If markets overreact, an investor can do quite well by buying when everyone else is selling and there is very little liquidity. However, it can be quite difficult for a fund to follow such a strategy if it is subject to the VaR-based risk management measures that have become standard.

Volatilities and correlations tend to be "mean-reverting". They sometimes increase but over time they get pulled back to long-run average levels. One way of creating diversity is to recognize that in regulation, and in risk management practices, not all market participants should be concerned about short-term changes in volatilities and correlations. Asset managers, for example, should base their decisions on long-term average volatilities and correlations. They should not join the herd when liquidity holes develop.

Hedge funds have become important market participants. They are unregulated and can follow any trading strategy they like. To some extent they do add diversity (and therefore liquidity) to the market. But, as mentioned earlier, hedge funds tend to be highly leveraged. When liquidity tightens, as it did in the second half of 2007, all hedge funds have to unwind positions, accentuating the liquidity problems.

SUMMARY

There are two types of liquidity risk: liquidity trading risk and liquidity funding risk. Liquidity trading risk is concerned with the ease with which positions in the trading book can be unwound. The liquidity trading risk of an asset depends on the nature of the asset, how much of the asset is to be traded, how quickly it is to be traded, and the economic environment. The credit crunch of 2007 emphasizes the importance of transparency. Assets that are not well defined or well understood are unlikely to trade in a liquid market for long. The liquidity of an asset at a particular time can be measured as the proportional bid–offer spread. This is the difference between the bid and offer price divided by the average of the bid and offer price. The cost of unwinding a position in the asset as a percentage of the value of the position is half of the proportional bid–offer spread. Financial institutions should monitor the cost of unwinding the whole trading book in both normal market conditions and stressed market conditions.

A trader, when faced with the problem of unwinding a large position in an asset, has a trade-off between the bid–offer spread and market risk. Unwinding quickly leads to high bid–offer spreads, but low market risk. Unwinding slowly leads to lower bid–offer spreads, but more market risk. The optimal trading strategy depends on (a) the dollar bid–offer spread as a function of the quantity traded in a day and (b) the probability distribution for daily changes in the asset price. For any particular unwind strategy, the trader can choose a confidence level and calculate the unwind cost that will not be exceeded with the confidence level. The unwind strategy that minimizes this cost can then be determined.

Liquidity funding risk management is concerned with being able to meet cash needs as they arise. It is important for a financial institution to forecast its cash needs in both normal and stressed market conditions to ensure that they can be met. Cash needs depend on depositor withdrawals, draw-downs on lines of credit, guarantees that have been made, defaults by counterparties, and so on. Sources of cash are instruments that can be readily converted into cash, borrowings in the wholesale market, asset securitizations, new depositors, cash itself, and (as a last resort) borrowings from a central bank. In June 2008, bank regulators issued a list of 17 principles describing how banks should manage their liquidity and indicated that they would be monitoring the liquidity management procedures of banks more carefully in the future.

The most serious liquidity risks arise from what are sometimes termed liquidity black holes. These occur when all traders want to be on the same side of the market at the same time. This may be because they have similar positions and manage risks in similar ways. It may also be because they become irrationally exuberant, overexposing themselves to particular risks. What is needed is more diversity in the trading strategies followed by market participants. Traders that have long-term objectives should avoid allowing themselves to be influenced by the short-term overreaction of markets.

FURTHER READING

Almgren, R., and N. Chriss, "Optimal Execution of Portfolio Transactions," *Journal of Risk*, 3 (Winter 2001): 5–39.

Bangia, A., F. Diebold, T. Schuermann, and J. Stroughair, "Liquidity on the Outside," *Risk*, 12, June: 68–73.

Bank for International Settlements, "Liquidity Risk Management and Supervisory Challenges," February 2008.

Bank for International Settlements, "Principles for Sound Liquidity Risk Management and Supervision," June 2008.

Persaud, A. D. (ed.), *Liquidity Black Holes: Understanding, Quantifying and Managing Financial Liquidity Risk*. London: Risk Books, 1999.

PRACTICE QUESTIONS AND PROBLEMS (Answers at the End of the Book)

19.1. What was the transparency problem in the subprime crisis of 2007?

19.2. An asset is quoted bid 50, offer 55. What does this mean? What is the proportional bid–offer spread?

19.3. Suppose that an investor has shorted shares worth $5000 of company A and bought shares worth $3000 of company B. The proportional bid–offer spread for company A is 0.01 and the proportional bid–offer spread for company B is 0.02. What does it cost the investor to unwind the portfolio?

19.4. Suppose that in Problem 19.3 the bid–offer spreads for the two companies are normally distributed. For company A, the bid–offer spread has a mean of 0.01 and a standard deviation of 0.01. For company B, the bid–offer spread has a mean of 0.02 and a standard deviation of 0.03. What is the cost of unwinding that the investor is 95% confident will not be exceeded?

19.5. A trader wishes to unwind a position of 60 million units in an asset over 10 days. The dollar bid–offer spread as a function of daily trading volume q is $a + be^{cq}$, where $a = 0.2$, $b = 0.1$, and $c = 0.08$, and q is measured in millions. The standard deviation of the price change per day is $0.1. What is the optimal strategy that minimizes the 95% confidence level for the costs?

19.6. Why does a bank need to keep track of the assets it has pledged as collateral as part of its procedures for managing liquidity funding risk?

19.7. Why is it risky to rely on borrowings in the wholesale market for funding?

19.8. What were the nature of the funding risk problems of Ashanti Goldfields and Metallgesellschaft?

19.9. What is meant by (a) positive feedback trading and (b) negative feedback trading? Which is liable to lead to liquidity problems?

19.10. What is meant by liquidity-adjusted VaR?

19.11. Explain how liquidity black holes occur. How can regulation lead to liquidity black holes?

19.12. Why is it beneficial to the liquidity of markets for traders to follow diverse trading strategies?

FURTHER QUESTIONS

19.13. Discuss whether hedge funds are good or bad for the liquidity of markets.

19.14. Suppose that a trader has bought some illiquid shares. The trader has 100 shares of A, quoted at bid $50 and offer $60, and 200 shares of B, quoted at bid $25 and offer $35. What are the proportional bid–offer spreads? What is the impact of the high bid–offer spreads on the amount it would cost the trader to unwind the portfolio. If the bid–offer spreads are normally distributed with mean $10 and standard deviation $3, what is the 99% worst-case cost of unwinding in the future as a percentage of the value of the portfolio?

19.15. A trader wishes to unwind a position of 200,000 units in an asset over eight days. The dollar bid–offer spread, as a function of daily trading volume q, is $a + be^{cq}$, where $a = 0.2$, $b = 0.15$, and $c = 0.1$, and q is measured in thousands. The standard deviation of the price change per day is $1.50. What is the optimal trading strategy for minimizing the 99% confidence level for the costs? What is the average time the trader waits before selling? How does this average time change as the confidence level changes?

Model Risk

20

Models are approximations to reality. They are necessary for determining the price at which an instrument should be traded. They are also necessary for marking to market a financial institution's position in an instrument once it has been traded.

There are two main types of model risk. One is the risk that the model will give the wrong price at the time a product is bought or sold. This can result in a company buying a product for a price that is too high or selling it for a price that is too low. The other risk concerns hedging. If a company uses the wrong model, the Greek letters it calculates—and the hedges it sets up based on those Greek letters—are liable to be wrong.

The art of building a model for valuing a financial product is to capture the key features of the product without allowing the model to become so complicated that it is difficult to use. This chapter contrasts the way models are used in finance with the way they are used by physicists and other scientists. It discusses how models are used for products that are traded actively and how they are used for customized products for which there are no market prices. It describes different types of model risk and how they can be managed.

20.1 MARKING TO MARKET

We start with a discussion of marking to market. As explained in Sections 2.7 and 11.6, a financial institution is required to mark to market its trading book each day. This means that it has to estimate a value for each financial instrument in its trading portfolio and then calculate the total value of the portfolio. The valuations are used in value-at-risk calculations to determine capital requirements and by accountants to calculate quarterly financial statements. Accountants refer to marking to market as "fair-value accounting".

How is the mark-to-market price of an asset calculated? In practice, a number of different approaches are used. For example:

1. When there are market makers for an asset, or an asset is traded on an exchange, the price of the asset can be based on the most recent quotes. Suppose that a financial instrument has a long position in a particular financial instrument and

that a market maker quotes "bid $20, offer $21". (This means that the market maker is prepared to buy at $20 and sell at $21.) In most cases, the financial institution will choose to mark to the mid-market price. This is the average of the bid price and the offer price, or $20.5 in this case. However, sometimes financial institutions choose to be more conservative and mark a long position to the bid and a short position to the offer.

2. When the financial institution itself has traded the asset in the last day, the price of the asset can be based on the price it paid or received.

3. When interdealer brokers provide information on the prices at which the asset has been traded by other financial institutions in the over-the-counter market, the financial institution can base the price of the asset on this information.

4. When interdealer brokers provide price indications (not the prices of actual trades), the financial institution will (in the absence of anything better) base its prices on this information.

5. For exotic deals and structured products, the price is usually based on a model developed by the financial institution. Using a model instead of a market price for the daily marking to market is sometimes referred to as *marking to model*.

The interdealer brokers being referred to here are intermediaries in the over-the-counter market. Examples are ICAP, Tullett Prebon, and GFI. Instead of approaching other potential counterparties directly to do a trade, a financial institution will often approach an interdealer broker to find a counterparty. (The broker earns a fee for deals it arranges.) One advantage of this is that the identity of the financial institution wanting to do the trade is not disclosed until after the trade has been finalized. Another is that the broker has in many cases more information than the financial institution about who wants to trade what. Brokers collect bid and offer quotes from their clients and relay this price information back to their clients on a regular basis.

When broker quotes are used by a financial institution for marking to market, it is important that the broker be not too closely involved with the financial institution's traders. There have been a few scandals where a trader has managed to conceal losses by persuading a broker to provide favorable quotes to the financial institution's middle office. Financial institutions should, whenever possible, try and get quotes from several different brokers.

Financial institutions usually want to be sure that they are pricing deals consistently with the rest of the market. For this reason, they like to periodically obtain a consensus price for a selection of test deals. Markit Group is a company that works in conjunction with large banks to provide consensus pricing. Each month, it presents the banks with a number of over-the-counter deals and asks them to provide quotes. After eliminating outliers, average quotes are calculated and sent back to the banks.

Accounting

The fair-value accounting rules of the Financial Accounting Standards Board in the United States (FASB 157) and the International Accounting Standards Board in Europe (IASB 39) require banks to classify instruments as "held for sale" or "held to maturity". Those classified as "held to maturity" are in the banking book and their values are not changed unless they become impaired. Those classified as "held for sale" are in the trading book and have to be marked to market. Three types of valuation are reported under FASB 157 for instruments that are "held for sale". Level 1 instruments are those for which there are quoted prices in active markets. Level 2 instruments are those for which there are quoted prices for similar assets in active markets or quoted prices for the same assets in markets that are not active. Level 3 instruments require some valuation assumptions by the bank.

Under the original IASB and FASB proposals, the classification of assets and liabilities could not be changed from "held to maturity" to "held for sale" or vice versa. A financial institution had to decide on how an asset or a liability was to be classified when it was first created. During the credit crisis that started in the summer of 2007, many bankers argued that fair-value accounting exacerbated their problems. High market volatility, high credit spreads, and low prices for products created from the securitization of mortgages led to banks having to recognize huge losses on a wide range of instruments that they held. Toward the end of 2008, both the Financial Accounting Standards Board and the International Accounting Standards Board bowed to pressure from bankers and politicians and allowed banks to reclassify "in rare circumstances" some of the instruments in their books from "held for sale" to "held to maturity". This meant that they did not have to record an immediate loss and equity capital did not decline by as much as it would otherwise have done.

In April 2009, another change was made that allowed financial institutions to use model prices in preference to market prices when they judge that market prices do not represent fair value. This could be because the market prices observed were from distressed sales—but it could be for other less defensible reasons as well. This change was also made in response to pressure from banks and politicians.

Many accountants are uncomfortable with these changes. They feel that they allow banks and other financial institutions to use fair-value accounting only when it suits them. They also suggest that bank regulation and the calculation of acceptable capital levels should be less reliant on accounting numbers.

The rest of this chapter considers how models are used for marking to market and trading, and looks at the risks that the use of models can entail.

20.2 MODELS FOR LINEAR PRODUCTS

The simplest types of pricing model in finance are the ones used for linear products such as forward contracts and swaps. There is usually very little disagreement in the market on the correct pricing models for these products and the model parameters that are used. The models are accurate and rely on little more than present-value arithmetic.

However, this does not mean that there is no model risk. Mistakes can be made. As indicated in Business Snapshot 20.1, Kidder Peabody's computer system did not account correctly for funding costs when a linear product was traded. As a result, the system indicated that one of the company's traders was making a large profit when in fact he was making a huge loss.

Another type of model risk arises when a financial institution makes a faulty assumption in a model. Consider the interest rate swap market. A plain vanilla interest rate swap, such as the one described in Section 5.4, can be valued by assuming that forward interest rates will be realized. This is explained in Appendix D. For example, if the forward interest rate for the period between 2 and 2.5 years is 4.3% per annum, the

---

Business Snapshot 20.1   Kidder Peabody's Embarrassing Mistake

Investment banks have developed a way of creating a zero-coupon bond, called a *strip*, from a coupon-bearing Treasury bond by selling each of the cash flows underlying the coupon-bearing bond as a separate security. Joseph Jett, a trader working for Kidder Peabody, had a relatively simple trading strategy. He would buy strips and sell them in the forward market. The forward price of the strip was always greater than the spot price, and so it appeared that he had found a money-making machine! In fact, the difference between the forward price and the spot price represents nothing more than the cost of funding the purchase of the strip. Suppose, for example, that the three-month interest rate is 4% per annum and the spot price of a strip is $70. The three-month forward price of the strip is $70e^{0.04 \times 3/12} = \$70.70$.

Kidder Peabody's computer system reported a profit on each of Jett's trades equal to the excess of the forward price over the spot price ($0.70 in our example). By rolling his contracts forward, Jett was able to prevent the funding cost from accruing to him. The result was that the system reported a profit of $100 million on Jett's trading (and Jett received a big bonus) when in fact there was a loss in the region of $350 million. This shows that even large financial institutions can get relatively simple things wrong.

---

swap is valued on the assumption that the floating rate that is exchanged for a fixed rate at the 2.5-year point is calculated using this rate. It is tempting to generalize from this and argue that any swap agreement to exchange cash flows in the future can be valued on the assumption that forward rates are realized. This is not so. Consider, for example, what is known as a *LIBOR-in-arrears swap*. In this instrument, the floating rate that is observed on a particular date is paid on that date, not one accrual period later as is the case for a plain vanilla swap. A LIBOR-in-arrears swap should be valued on the assumption that the realized interest rate equals the forward interest rate plus a "convexity adjustment". As indicated in Business Snapshot 20.2, financial institutions that did not understand this lost money in the mid-1990s.

20.3   PHYSICS vs. FINANCE

We now move on to consider the models used for nonlinear products. Many individuals who were trained in physics work in the front and middle office of banks and many of the models they use for nonlinear products are similar to those they encountered during their physics training. For example, the differential equation that leads to the famous Black–Scholes–Merton option pricing model is the heat-exchange equation that has been used by physicists for many years. However, as Derman has pointed out, there is an important difference between the models of physics and the models of finance.[1] The models of physics describe physical processes and are highly accurate. By contrast, the models of finance describe the behavior of market variables. This behavior depends on the actions of human beings. As a result, the models are, at

---

[1] See E. Derman, *My Life as a Quant: Reflections on Physics and Finance.* Wiley, 2004; E. Derman, "Model Risk," *Risk*, 9, 2 (May 1996): 139–145.

Business Snapshot 20.2 Exploiting the Weaknesses of a Competitor's Model

A LIBOR-in-arrears swap is an interest rate swap where the floating interest rate is paid on the day it is observed, not one accrual period later. Whereas a plain vanilla swap is correctly valued by assuming that future rates will be today's forward rates, a LIBOR-in-arrears swap should be valued on the assumption that the future rate is today's forward interest rate plus a "convexity adjustment".

In the mid-1990s sophisticated financial institutions understood the correct approach for valuing a LIBOR-in-arrears swap. Less sophisticated financial institutions used the naive "assume that forward rates will be realized" approach. The result was that, by choosing trades judiciously, sophisticated financial institutions were able to make substantial profits at the expense of their less sophisticated counterparties.

The derivatives business is one where traders do not hesitate to exploit the weaknesses of their competitors' models!

---

best, approximate descriptions of the market variables. This is the reason that the use of models in finance entails what is referred to as "model risk".

One important difference between the models of physics and the models of finance concerns model parameters. The parameters of models in the physics generally do not change. For example, the gravitational pull on the surface of the earth is always about 32 feet per second per second. By contrast, parameters in finance models change daily. The volatility used to price an option might be 20% one day, 22% the next day, and 19% the following day. The parameters used on a day are usually chosen to fit prices observed in the market on that day as closely as possible. The procedure for doing this is known as *calibration*.

The general approach usually used for valuing a financial instrument that is similar to, but not exactly the same as, other financial instruments that trade is illustrated in Figure 20.1. One or more other financial instruments whose prices can be observed in the market are chosen as the "calibrating instruments". These instruments are chosen so that they are as similar as possible to the financial instrument of interest. They are then used to imply model parameters that are appropriate for the instrument being valued.

The approach works particularly well if there is only one unknown model parameter. It is not designed to value a financial instrument in an absolute way. Instead it is designed for relative valuation. The objective is to value the financial instrument consistently with other similar financial instruments whose prices can be observed. The next section illustrates the procedure by showing how it is operationalized for actively traded options.

20.4 HOW MODELS ARE USED FOR PRICING STANDARD PRODUCTS

When a financial instrument trades actively, we do not need a model to know what its price is. The market tells us this. Suppose, for example, that a certain option on a stock index trades actively and is quoted by market makers as "bid $30, offer $30.5". Our best estimate of its current value is the mid-market price of $30.25.

Figure 20.1   How models are usually used for valuing a financial instrument.

A situation that is common in the over-the-counter market is one where a financial instrument that has to be valued is a standard product such as an option, but not exactly the same as one that trades in the market. For example, it might be an option with a strike price or time to maturity (or both) different from the options whose prices can be observed. The model is then used as a tool to ensure that the way an instrument is priced is consistent with the observed market prices of other similar instruments. A good example of how this is done is provided by the way the Black–Scholes–Merton model is used in practice. (See Appendix E for a description of the Black–Scholes–Merton model.)

The Black–Scholes–Merton Model

The Black–Scholes–Merton model was published in 1973 and is very widely used in trading rooms throughout the world.[2] The model (and its extensions) relate the price of a European option on an asset to:

1. The price of the asset
2. The strike price
3. The time to option maturity
4. The risk-free interest rate applicable to an investment lasting for the life of the asset
5. The asset price volatility
6. The income (if any) expected from the asset during the life of the option

The model is easy to use because most of the inputs are directly observable. The current price of an asset on which an option is written is normally known. The strike price and time to maturity are properties of the option and therefore known. The risk-free interest rates are also known. The income expected from the asset may not be known for certain, but in many instances it can be estimated reasonably accurately. Furthermore, if there are forward contracts trading on the asset, it turns out that the forward price

[2] See F. Black and M. Scholes, "The Pricing of Options and Corporate Liabilities," *Journal of Political Economy*, 81 (May–June 1973): 637–659; and R.C. Merton, "Theory of Rational Option Pricing," *Bell Journal of Economics and Management Science*, 4 (Spring 1973): 141–183.

captures everything the model needs to know about the income on the asset.[3] There is only one input that cannot be observed. This is the volatility.

An estimate of volatility can be made from historical data on the price on the underlying asset as described in Chapter 9. If there is no market at all for options on the asset, traders and risk management might base their pricing on such an estimate. But, if there is a market for options on the asset, traders and risk managers follow the practice outlined in Figure 20.1 and calculate the volatilities that match market prices. This does not mean that a trader always agrees with market prices. Traders can (and are paid to) take a view that the market price is too high or too low. But it is important that a financial institution's "official model" for valuing options match the market when market prices are available.

The volatility of an asset that matches an option price is known as the option's *implied volatility*, as explained in Section 9.2. Implied volatilities vary from option to option. We now describe how traders cope with this and choose a volatility for the option being valued.

Volatility Smiles

The variation of implied volatility with strike price for options with a particular maturity on a particular day is known as the *volatility smile*.[4] If the Black–Scholes–Merton model provided an accurate description of the assumptions made by the market, the implied volatility would be the same for all options and the volatility smile would be flat. In fact, this is rarely the case.

The volatility smile used by traders to price foreign currency options has the general form shown in Figure 20.2. The volatility is relatively low for at-the-money options. It

Figure 20.2 Volatility smile for foreign currency options.

---

[3] In practice, the market often uses a variant of the Black–Scholes model known as Black's model. This was published in 1976. It involves the forward or futures price, and the income on the asset is not an input. See F. Black, "The Pricing of Commodity Contracts," *Journal of Financial Economics*, 3 (1976): 167–179.

[4] It can be shown that the relationship between strike price and implied volatility should be exactly the same for calls and puts in the case of European options and approximately the same in the case of American options.

Figure 20.3   Volatility smile for equity options.

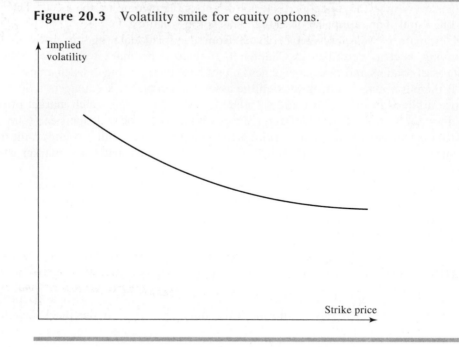

becomes progressively higher as an option moves either in the money or out of the money. The reason for the volatility smile is that Black–Scholes–Merton assumes:

1. The volatility of the asset is constant.
2. The price of the asset changes smoothly with no jumps.

In practice, neither of these conditions is satisfied for an exchange rate. The volatility of an exchange rate is far from constant, and exchange rates frequently exhibit jumps.[5] It turns out that the effect of both a nonconstant volatility and jumps is that extreme outcomes become more likely. This leads to the volatility smile in Figure 20.2.

The volatility smile used by traders to price equity options (both those on individual stocks and those on stock indices) has the general form shown in Figure 20.3. This is sometimes referred to as a *volatility skew*. The volatility decreases as the strike price increases. The volatility used to price an option with a low strike price (i.e., a deep-out-of-the-money put or a deep-in-the-money call) is significantly higher than that used to price an option with a high strike price (i.e., a deep-in-the-money put or a deep-out-of-the-money call). One possible explanation for the smile in equity options concerns leverage. As a company's equity declines in value, the company's leverage increases. This means that the equity becomes more risky and its volatility increases. As a company's equity increases in value, leverage decreases. The equity then becomes less risky and its volatility decreases. This argument shows that we can expect the volatility of equity to be a decreasing function of price and is consistent with Figure 20.3. Another explanation is crashophobia (see Business Snapshot 20.3).

---

[5] Often the jumps are in response to the actions of central banks.

Business Snapshot 20.3   Crashophobia

It is interesting that the pattern in Figure 20.3 for equities has existed only since the stock market crash of October 1987. Prior to October 1987 implied volatilities were much less dependent on strike price. This has led Mark Rubinstein to suggest that one reason for the equity volatility smile may be "crashophobia". Traders are concerned about the possibility of another crash similar to October 1987 and assign relatively high prices (and therefore relatively high implied volatilities) for deep-out-of-the-money puts.

There is some empirical support for this explanation. Declines in the S&P 500 tend to be accompanied by a steepening of the volatility skew, perhaps because traders become more nervous about the possibility of a crash. When the S&P increases, the skew tends to become less steep.

Volatility Surfaces

Figures 20.2 and 20.3 are for options with a particular maturity. Traders like to combine the volatility smiles for different maturities into a *volatility surface*. This shows implied volatility as a function of both strike price and time to maturity. Table 20.1 shows a volatility surface for currency options. The table indicates that the volatility smile becomes less pronounced as the time to maturity increases. This is what is usually observed in practice.[6]

The volatility surface is produced primarily from information provided by brokers in the interdealer market (see Section 20.1). These brokers have more information on the implied volatilities at which transactions are being done on any given day than individual derivatives dealers. Some of the points on a volatility surface such as that in Table 20.1 are calculated from transactions observed by brokers; others are calculated

Table 20.1   Volatility surface.

Time to maturity	Strike price				
	0.90	0.95	1.00	1.05	1.10
1 month	14.2	13.0	12.0	13.1	14.5
3 months	14.0	13.0	12.0	13.1	14.2
6 months	14.1	13.3	12.5	13.4	14.3
1 year	14.7	14.0	13.5	14.0	14.8
2 years	15.0	14.4	14.0	14.5	15.1
5 years	14.8	14.6	14.4	14.7	15.0

---

[6] Some traders choose to define the volatility smile as the relationship between implied volatility and

$$\frac{1}{\sqrt{T}} \ln \frac{K}{F_0}$$

where T is the time to maturity, K is the strike price, and F_0 as the forward price of the asset, rather than as the relationship between the implied volatility and K. The smile is then usually much less dependent on the time to maturity.

by interpolation between the implied volatilities for observed transactions. Both brokers and option traders develop an understanding of what the volatility surface for a particular underlying asset should look like and how it might change.

When a new option has to be valued, traders look up the appropriate volatility in the table using interpolation. For example, when valuing a 9-month option with a strike price of 1.05, a trader would interpolate between 13.4 and 14.0 in Table 20.1 to obtain a volatility of 13.7%. This is the volatility that would be used in the Black–Scholes–Merton formula. When valuing a 1.5-year option with a strike price of 0.925, a two-dimensional interpolation would be used to give an implied volatility of 14.525%.

Variation Through Time

The volatility smiles in Figures 20.2 and 20.3, and the volatility surface in Table 20.1 are at a particular point in time. They are recalculated at least once a day. The volatility smile for an asset tends to retain the same general shape, but the level of the volatility changes through time. The VIX index, which we discussed in Section 9.2, is a measure of the implied volatility of 30-day options on the S&P 500.[7] It can be seen from Figure 9.1 that the index varies from about 10% to about 30% in normal markets and was much higher during the credit crisis that started in 2007.

Why Is Black–Scholes–Merton So Popular?

Many people would argue that any model where the value of a key parameter can easily change by a factor of 3 (from 10% to 30%)—and sometimes by even more—is of no use at all. (Certainly this would be true for models in physics.) But, as explained, models for valuing financial instruments are used in a quite different way from the models of physics. The Black–Scholes–Merton model is popular because:

1. It can be used in the way we have described for interpolation in conjunction with a volatility surface and ensures that prices are consistent with observed market prices.

2. It is a communication tool. Traders often prefer quoting implied volatilities to quoting option prices because implied volatilities are more stable than option prices and, as a result, their quotes do not change as frequently. When the price of the underlying asset changes or the interest rate changes the option price changes but the implied volatility may not.

3. The model is sufficiently simple that a trader can develop intuition about the model and use it to structure his or her thinking about option markets.

But there is nothing unique about the Black–Scholes–Merton model. Another reasonable model, if used in a similar way to Black–Scholes–Merton, would probably lead to similar prices in markets where options trade actively. The fact that the model has only one free (i.e., unobservable) parameter, the volatility, is very appealing to traders because it creates less ambiguity. There is a one-to-one correspondence between an option price and a volatility. If there were two or more free parameters (as there are in some more complicated option pricing models), the model would be less easy to use.

[7] For more information on the VIX index, see J. Hull, *Options, Futures, and Other Derivatives*, 7th edn. Pearson, 2009.

Other Models

Valuing options on assets such as stocks, exchange rates, stock indices, and commodities involves modeling the behavior of a single variable, such as a stock price, and the Black–Scholes–Merton model has become the standard tool. During the 1980s, researchers turned their attention to valuing interest rate derivatives. It turns out that caps, floors, European bond options, and European swap options can be valued with an extension to the Black–Scholes–Merton model, and so procedures similar to those we have described can be used to find an appropriate volatility to substitute into the model to value these deals.

Bermudan swap options and other interest rate derivatives are more complicated because they require the behavior of the full term structure of interest rate to be modeled.[8] Instead of describing the behavior of a single variable, the model has to describe the behavior of the zero-coupon interest rate as a function of maturity. Subtle no-arbitrage conditions restrict the assumptions that can be made by the model. Most of the models that have been developed involve more than one parameter. They are designed to match the current term structure of interest rates exactly and the calibration procedure involves finding values for parameters that match observed option prices as closely as possible.

Toward the end of the 1990s, researchers turned their attention to valuing credit derivatives. This involves a sort of challenge different from valuing equity derivatives or interest rate derivatives. The value of a credit derivative depends on whether a particular discrete event (the default of a company) occurs. When the default of only one entity is involved (as is the case with a credit default swap), models are relatively straightforward. The term structure of the probability of default is estimated from actively traded instruments, and this is used to value other deals. When the defaults of several entities are involved (as is the case with a collateralized debt obligation), models are more complicated. The standard market model is the Gaussian copula model (see Section 10.5). It is used to imply and interpolate between default correlation measures in the same way that the Black–Scholes–Merton model is used to imply and interpolate between volatilities.

Official vs. Research Models

The models we have been talking about so far are a financial institution's "official models" that are used for valuing trades each day and calculating a trader's profit or loss. It is important that the official model matches the market very closely. A financial institution's external auditors will insist on this. Moreover, traders could—and probably would—take advantage of situations where the official model deviated from market prices. If the official model gave a price higher (lower) than the market for a product, they could buy (sell) the product in the market to record a profit.

In addition to official models, financial institutions sometimes use research models. These are typically more complicated than the official models and designed to determine trading strategies. When run in parallel with the official models, research models can test whether market prices are too high or too low.

---

[8] A Bermudan swap option is an option to enter into an interest rate swap that can be exercised on two or more payment dates.

20.5 HEDGING

So far we have focused on the use of models for pricing. Models also have an important role to play in hedging. Traders must manage risks such as delta, gamma, and vega (see Chapter 6). A model is necessary to assess these risks.

We can distinguish between *within-model hedging* and *outside-model hedging*. Within-model hedging is designed to deal with the risk of changes in variables that are assumed to be uncertain by the model. Outside-model hedging deals with the risk of changes in variables that are assumed to be constant (or deterministic) by the model. For Black–Scholes–Merton, hedging against movements in the underlying stock price (delta and gamma hedging) is within-model hedging, because the model assumes that stock price changes are uncertain. However, hedging against volatility changes (vega hedging) is outside-model hedging because the model assumes that volatility is constant.

In practice, traders almost invariably do outside-model hedging as well as within-model hedging. This is because, as we have explained, the calibration process results in parameters such as volatilities (which are assumed by a model to be constant) changing daily. A good options trader will monitor the exposure of a trading book to the sorts of shifts in the volatility surface that are typically seen.[9]

A natural assumption is that, if hedging is implemented for all the variables that could change in a day (both those that are assumed to be constant by the model and those that are assumed to be stochastic), then the value of the hedger's position will not change. In fact, this is not necessarily the case. If the model used to calculate the hedge is a poor representation of reality, there may be an unexpected gain or loss. The good news here is that, on average, the gain or loss from hedging using the wrong model may be small because there is a good chance that this type of risk is to some extent diversified away across the portfolio of a large financial institution.

Many financial institutions carefully evaluate the effectiveness of their hedging. They find it revealing to decompose the day-to-day change in a portfolio's value into:

1. A change resulting from risks that were unhedged
2. A change resulting from the hedging model being imperfect
3. A change resulting from new trades done during the day

This is sometimes referred to as a *P&L Decomposition*. If the day-to-day change is unacceptable, the analysis indicates the areas where more effort should be expended.

20.6 MODELS FOR NONSTANDARD PRODUCTS

As we have explained, standard products are valued by observing market prices, implying model parameters, and interpolating as necessary between those parameters. Although the model chosen does have a significant influence on hedging, it does not affect pricing to any great extent. Nonstandard products are products that are tailored to the needs of specific clients or are not yet sold in sufficient quantity for a standard

---

[9] A principal components analysis, as described in Chapter 7, can be used. If exposure to each of the major principal components is small, the exposure to the shifts that have been observed in practice should also be small.

model to have been established. They are sometimes referred to as exotic products or structured products. Because they do not trade actively, the model used by a financial institution is liable to influence the price it charges a client. Note the important difference between nonstandard products and standard products. A standard product usually trades actively and there is very little uncertainty about its price, so that the choice of model primarily affects how hedging is done. In the case of nonstandard products, model risk is much greater because there is the potential for both pricing and hedging being impacted.

A financial institution should not rely on a single model for pricing nonstandard products. Instead it should, whenever possible, use several different models. This leads to a price range for the instrument and a better understanding of the model risks being taken.

Suppose that three different models give prices of $6 million, $7.5 million, and $8.5 million for a particular product that a financial institution is planning to sell to a client. Even if the financial institution believes that the first model is the best one and plans to use that model as its standard model for daily repricing and hedging, it should ensure that the price it charges the client is at least $8.5 million. Moreover, it should be conservative about recognizing profits. If the product is sold for $9 million, it is tempting to recognize an immediate profit of $3 million ($9 million less the believed-to-be-accurate price of $6 million). However, this is overly aggressive. A better, more conservative, practice is to put the $3 million into a reserve account and transfer it to profits slowly during the life of the product.[10]

An example of model risk in the pricing of structured products is provided by Business Snapshot 16.1. This makes the point that the assumption that the BBB-rated tranche of an ABS is similar to a BBB bond is not a good one when tranches of an ABS CDO are being priced.

Model Audit Groups

Most large financial institutions have model audit groups as part of their risk management teams. These groups are responsible for vetting new models proposed by traders for particular products. A model cannot usually be used to any significant extent until the model audit group has approved it. Vetting typically includes the following:

1. Checking that a model has been correctly implemented
2. Examining whether there is a sound rationale for the model
3. Comparing the model with other models that can accomplish the same task
4. Specifying the limitations of the model
5. Assessing uncertainties in the prices and hedge parameters given by the model

20.7 DANGERS IN MODEL BUILDING

The art of model building is to capture what is important for valuing and hedging an instrument without making the model more complex than it needs to be. Sometimes

---

[10] This is also likely to have sensible implications for the way bonuses are paid.

models have to be quite complex to capture the important features of a product, but this is not always the case.

One danger in model building is *overfitting*. Consider the problem posed by the volatility surface in Table 20.1. We can exactly match the volatility surface with a single model by extending the Black–Scholes–Merton model so that volatility is a complex function of the underlying asset price and time.[11] But, when we do this, we may find that other properties of the model are less reasonable than those of simpler models. In particular, the joint probability distribution of the asset price at two or more times might be less than ideal and, in some circumstances, future volatility surfaces might look quite different from those observed in the market today.[12]

Another danger in model building is *overparameterization*. The Black–Scholes–Merton model can be extended to include features such as stochastic volatility or jumps in the asset price. This invariably introduces extra parameters that have to be estimated. It is usually claimed that the parameters in complex models are more stable than those in simpler models and do not have to be adjusted very much from day to day. This may be true, but we should remember that we are not dealing with physical processes. The parameters in a complex model may remain relatively constant for a period of time and then change, perhaps because there has been what economists refer to as a *regime shift*. A financial institution may find that a more complicated model is an improvement over a simple model until the parameters change. At that time, the more complicated model may not have the flexibility to cope with changing market conditions.[13]

As we have seen, traders like simple models that have just one unobservable parameter. They are skeptical of more complex models because they are "black boxes" and it is very difficult to develop intuition about them. In some situations, their skepticism is well founded for the reasons we have just mentioned.

20.8 DETECTING MODEL PROBLEMS

The risk management function within a financial institution should carefully monitor the financial institution's trading patterns. In particular, it should keep track of the following:

1. The type of trading the financial institution is doing with other financial institutions

---

[11] This is the implied volatility function model proposed by B. Dupire, "Pricing with a Smile," *Risk*, 7 (February 1994): 18–20; E. Derman and I. Kani, "Riding on a Smile," *Risk*, 7 (February 1994): 32–39; M. Rubinstein, "Implied Binomial Trees," *Journal of Finance*, 49, 3 (July 1994): 771–818.

[12] Models that fit the volatility surface at all future times accurately price instruments where there is a payoff at one future time that is dependent only on the asset price at that time. However, it is liable to be less accurate for instruments such as barrier options and compound options that depend on the joint probability distribution of the asset price at two or more times. Hull and Suo find that the implied volatility function model works reasonably well for compound options, but is less accurate for barrier options. See J. C. Hull and W. Suo, "A Methodology for the Assessment of Model Risk and its Application to the Implied Volatility Function Model," *Journal of Financial and Quantitative Analysis*, 37, 2 (June 2002), 297–318.

[13] The nature of this type of problem in the social sciences is discussed in the famous Lucas critique, which was propounded by the economist Robert Lucas in 1976. See R. Lucas, "Economic Policy Evaluation: A Critique," in: *The Phillips Curve and Labor Markets* (K. Brunner and A. H. Meltzer, eds.), Carnegie-Rochester Conference Series on Public Policy 1 (1976), pp. 19–46.

2. How competitive it is in bidding for different types of structured transactions
3. The profits being recorded from the trading of different products

Getting too much of a certain type of business, or making huge profits from relatively simple trading strategies, can be a warning sign. If a financial institution finds that its prices are out of line with the market, it must make adjustments to its mark-to-market procedures to bring them into line.

The high profits being recorded for Joseph Jett's trading at Kidder Peabody (see Business Snapshot 20.1) should have indicated to the bank that something was amiss.[14] Likewise, if in the mid-1990s a financial institution's risk management team discovered that traders were entering into a large number of LIBOR-in-arrears swaps with other financial institutions (see Business Snapshot 20.2) where they were receiving fixed and paying floating, they could have alerted modelers to a potential problem and directed that trading in the product be temporarily stopped.

SUMMARY

Since the publication of the Black–Scholes model in 1973, a huge amount of effort has been devoted to the development of improved models for the behavior of asset prices. It might be thought that it is just a matter of time before the perfect model is produced. Unfortunately, this is not the case. Models in finance are different from those in the physical sciences because they are ultimately models of human behavior. They are always likely to be at best approximations to the way market variables behave. Furthermore, from time to time there are regime shifts where there are fundamental changes in the behavior of market variables.

For products that trade actively, models are used primarily for communicating prices, interpolating between market prices, and hedging. When hedging, traders use both within-model hedging and outside-model hedging. This means that they hedge against movements in variables that the model assumes to be constant (or deterministic) as well as against those in variables that are assumed to be stochastic. This type of hedging is imperfect, but hopefully the unhedged risks are largely diversified in a large portfolio.

For products that are highly structured or do not trade actively, models are used for pricing. In this case, choosing the right model is often more of an art than a science. It is a good practice to use several models and assumptions about the underlying parameters in order to obtain a realistic range for pricing and to understand the accompanying model risk.

FURTHER READING

Bates, D. S., "Post '87 Crash Fears in the S&P Futures Market," *Journal of Econometrics*, 94 (January/February 2000): 181–238.

---

[14] Barry Finer, risk manager for the government bond desk, did point out the difficulty of making large arbitrage profits from a market as efficient as the US government bond market, but his concerns were dismissed out of hand.

Derman, E., *My Life as a Quant: Reflections on Physics and Finance*. New Jersey: Wiley, 2004.

Derman, E., "Model Risk," *Risk*, 9, 5 (May 1996): 139–145.

Hull, J. C., and W. Suo, "A Methodology for the Assessment of Model Risk and Its Application to the Implied Volatility Function Model," *Journal of Financial and Quantitative Analysis*, 37, 2 (June 2002): 297–318.

PRACTICE QUESTIONS AND PROBLEMS (Answers at the End of the Book)

20.1. Explain what is meant by (a) marking to market and (b) marking to model.

20.2. Give two explanations for the volatility skew observed for options on equities

20.3. Give two explanations for the volatility smile observed for options on a foreign currency.

20.4. "The Black–Scholes model is nothing more than a sophisticated interpolation tool." Discuss this viewpoint.

20.5. Using Table 20.1, calculate the volatility a trader would use for an eight-month option with a strike price of 1.04.

20.6. What is the key difference between the models of physics and the models of finance?

20.7. How is a financial institution likely to find that it is using a model different from its competitors for a particular type of derivatives product.

20.8. Distinguish between within-model and outside-model hedging.

20.9. The price of a certain stock is currently $20. Tomorrow, news is expected to be announced that will either increase its price by $5 or decrease it by $5. What is the problem in using Black–Scholes to value 1-month options on the stock?

20.10. What is meant by "fair-value" accounting? What changes were made to fair-value accounting in 2008 and 2009?

20.11. Suppose that a central bank's policy is to allow an exchange rate to fluctuate between 0.97 and 1.03. What pattern of implied volatilities for options on the exchange rate would you expect to see?

20.12. "For structured products, traders mark to model. They do not mark to market." Explain this remark.

FURTHER QUESTIONS

20.13. Suppose that all options traders decide to switch from Black–Scholes to another model that makes different assumptions about the behavior of asset prices. What effect do you think this would have on (a) the pricing of standard options and (b) the hedging of standard options?

20.14. Using Table 20.1, calculate the volatility a trader would use for an 11-month option with a strike price of 0.98.

20.15. Suppose that a financial institution uses an imprecise model for pricing and hedging a particular type of structured product. Discuss how, if at all, it is likely to realize its mistake.

20.16. A futures price is currently at $40. The risk-free interest rate is 5%. Some news is expected tomorrow that will cause the volatility over the next three months to be either 10% or 30%. There is a 60% chance of the first outcome and a 40% chance of the second outcome. Use the DerivaGem software to calculate a volatility smile for three-month options.

21

Economic Capital and RAROC

As we saw in Chapter 2, the role of capital in a bank is to provide a cushion against losses so that depositors are protected. The capital of a bank consists of common shareholder's equity, preferred shareholder's equity, subordinated debt, and other similar items.

In Chapter 11, we discussed the rules that the Basel Committee uses to determine regulatory capital. These rules are the same for all banks and, however carefully they have been chosen, it is inevitable that they will not be exactly appropriate for any particular bank. This has led banks to calculate *economic capital* (sometimes also referred to as *risk capital*). Economic capital is a bank's own internal estimate of the capital it needs for the risks it is taking. Economic capital can be regarded as a "currency" for risk-taking within a bank. A business unit can take a certain risk only when it is allocated the appropriate economic capital for that risk. The profitability of a business unit is measured relative to the economic capital allocated to the unit.

In this chapter, we discuss the approaches a financial institution uses to arrive at estimates of economic capital for particular risk types and particular business units, and how these estimates are aggregated to produce a single economic capital estimate for the whole financial institution. We also discuss risk-adjusted return on capital, or RAROC. This is the return earned by a business unit on the capital assigned to it. RAROC can be used to assess the past performance of business units. It can also be used to forecast future performance of the units and decide on the most appropriate way of allocating capital in the future. It provides a basis for determining whether some activities should be discontinued and others expanded.

21.1 DEFINITION OF ECONOMIC CAPITAL

Economic capital is defined as the amount of capital a financial institution needs in order to absorb losses over a certain time horizon with a certain confidence level. The time horizon is usually chosen as one year. The confidence level depends on the financial institution's objectives. A common objective for a large international bank is to maintain a AA credit rating. Corporations rated AA have a one-year probability of default of less than 0.1% (see Table 14.1). This suggests that the confidence level should be 99.9%, or even higher. Some banks use confidence levels as high as 99.97%. For a

Figure 21.1 Calculation of economic capital from one-year loss distribution: X is 99.8, 99.9, and in some cases as high as 99.97.

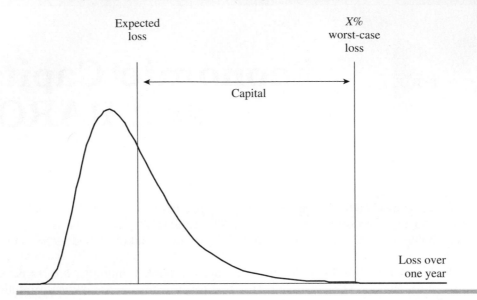

bank wanting to maintain a BBB credit rating, the confidence level can be lower. A BBB-rated corporation has a probability of about 0.2% of defaulting in one year, so that an appropriate confidence level, if the objective is to maintain the credit rating, would be about 99.80%.

Capital is required to cover unexpected loss. This is defined as the difference between the actual loss and the expected loss. As explained in Chapter 11, the idea here is that expected losses should be accounted for in the way a financial institution prices its products, so that only unexpected losses require capital. As indicated in Figure 21.1, the economic capital is the difference between expected losses and the X percentile point on the probability distribution of losses, where X% is the confidence level.

Example 21.1

When lending in a certain region of the world a AA-rated bank estimates its losses as 1% of outstanding loans per year on average. The 99.9% worst-case loss (i.e., the loss exceeded only 0.1% of the time) is estimated as 5% of outstanding loans. The economic capital required per $100 of loans made is therefore $4.0 (this is difference between the 99.9% worst-case loss and the expected loss).

Approaches to Measurement

There are two broad approaches to measuring economic capital: the "top-down" and "bottom-up" approaches. In the top-down approach, the volatility of the financial institution's assets is estimated and then used to calculate the probability that the value of the assets will fall below the value of the liabilities by the end of the time horizon. A theoretical framework that can be used for the top-down approach is Merton's model, which was discussed in Section 14.8.

Figure 21.2 Categorization of risks faced by a bank and the Basel II regulatory environment.

The approach most often used is the bottom-up approach, where loss distributions are estimated for different types of risk and different business units and then aggregated. The first step in the aggregation can be to calculate probability distributions for losses by risk type or losses by business unit. A final aggregation gives a probability distribution of total losses for the whole financial institution.

The various risks facing a bank or other financial institution are summarized in Figure 21.2. As we saw in Chapter 18, bank regulators have chosen to define operational risk as "the risk of loss resulting from inadequate or failed internal processes, people, and systems or from external events". Operational risk includes model risk and legal risk, but it does not include risk arising from strategic decisions or reputational risk. We will collectively refer to this type of risk as *business risk*. Regulatory capital is not required for business risk under Basel II, but some banks do assess economic capital for business risk.

21.2 COMPONENTS OF ECONOMIC CAPITAL

In earlier chapters, we covered approaches used to calculate loss distributions for different types of risk. This section reviews some of the key issues.

Market Risk Economic Capital

In Chapters 12 and 13, we discussed the historical simulation and model-building approaches for estimating the probability distribution of the losses or gains from market risk. As explained, this distribution is usually calculated in the first instance with a one-day time horizon. Regulatory capital for market risk is calculated as a multiple (at least 3.0) of the ten-day/99% VaR and bank supervisors have indicated that they are comfortable calculating the ten-day/99% VaR as $\sqrt{10}$ times the one-day/99%VaR.

When calculating economic capital, we usually want to use the same time horizon and confidence level for all risks. The time horizon is usually one year and, as already discussed, the confidence level is usually between 99.8% and 99.97%. The simplest assumptions are (a) that the probability distribution of gains and losses for each day during the next year will be the same as that estimated for the first day and (b) that the distributions are independent. We can then use the central limit theorem to argue that the one-year loss or gain distribution is approximately normal. Assuming 252 business days in the year, the standard deviation of the one-year loss or gain equals the standard deviation of the daily loss or gain multiplied by $\sqrt{252}$. The mean loss or gain is much more difficult to estimate than the standard deviation. A reasonable, if somewhat conservative assumption, is that the mean loss or gain is zero. The 99.9% worst-case loss is then 3.09 times the standard deviation of the one-year loss or gain, and the 99.8% worst-case loss is 2.88 times the standard deviation of the one-year loss or gain.

Example 21.2

Suppose that the one-day standard deviation of market risk losses or gains for a bank is \$5 million. The one-year 99.8% worst-case loss is

$$2.88 \times \sqrt{252} \times 5 = 228.6$$

or \$228.6 million.

Note that we are not assuming that the daily losses or gains are normal. All we are assuming is that they are independent and identically distributed. The central limit theorem of statistics tells us that the sum of many independent identically distributed variables is approximately normal.

Market risk regulatory capital for banks that are assigned the lowest multiplicative factor of 3.0 is

$$3 \times \sqrt{10} \times \text{one-day 99\% VaR} = 9.49 \times \text{one-day 99\% VaR}$$

Economic capital, when calculated in the way just outlined with a 99.9% confidence level, is

$$\sqrt{252} \times 3.09 \times \text{SD of daily change} = 49.06 \times \text{SD of daily change}$$

If the daily change in the portfolio value is normal, the one-day 99% VaR is 2.33 times the standard deviation of daily changes and the above analysis suggests that the ratio of economic capital to regulatory capital is about $49.06/(9.49 \times 2.33) = 2.22$. Nonnormality of daily changes is likely to reduce this ratio. However, autocorrelation between the returns is likely to increase it (see Section 8.6).

Credit Risk Economic Capital

Although Basel II gives banks that use the internal-ratings-based approach for regulatory capital a great deal of freedom, it does not allow them to choose their own credit correlation model and correlation parameters. When calculating economic capital, banks are free to make the assumptions they consider most appropriate for their situation. As explained in Section 15.6, CreditMetrics is often used to calculate the specific risk capital charge and incremental risk charge for credit risk in the trading book. It is also a popular approach for calculating economic capital for the banking book.

Another approach that is sometimes used is Credit Risk Plus, which is described in Section 15.5. This approach borrows a number of ideas from actuarial science to calculate a probability distribution for losses from defaults. Whereas CreditMetrics calculates the loss from downgrades and defaults, Credit Risk Plus calculates losses from defaults only.

In calculating credit risk economic capital, a financial institution can choose to adopt a conditional or unconditional model. In a conditional (cycle-specific) model, the expected and unexpected losses take account of current economic conditions. In an unconditional (cycle-neutral) model, they are calculated by assuming economic conditions that are in some sense an average of those experienced through the cycle. Rating agencies aim to produce ratings that are unconditional. In addition, when regulatory capital is calculated using the internal-ratings-based approach, the PD and LGD estimates should be unconditional. Obviously, it is important to be consistent when economic capital is calculated. If expected losses are conditional, unexpected losses should also be conditional. If expected losses are unconditional, the same should be true of unexpected losses.

Whatever the approach used, a Monte Carlo simulation is usually necessary to calculate the probability distribution of credit losses. Derivatives are difficult to handle because of the uncertainty about the exposure at the time of a default or downgrade. Sometimes, financial institutions make the simplifying assumption that this exposure is always equal to the expected exposure. The latter is usually known by the financial institution for each of its counterparties, as explained in Section 15.1.

Operational Risk Economic Capital

Banks are given a great deal of freedom in the assessment of regulatory capital for operational risk under the advanced measurement approach. It is therefore likely that most banks using this approach will calculate operational risk economic capital and operational risk regulatory capital in the same way. As noted in Chapter 18, methods for calculating operational risk capital are still evolving. Some approaches are statistical and some are more subjective.

Business Risk Economic Capital

As mentioned earlier, business risk includes strategic risk (relating to a bank's decision to enter new markets and develop new products) and reputational risk. Business risk is even more difficult to quantify than operational risk and estimates are likely to be largely subjective. However, it is important that senior risk managers within a financial institution have a good understanding of the portfolio of business risks being taken. This enables them to assess the marginal impact on total risk of new strategic initiatives that are being contemplated.

21.3 SHAPES OF THE LOSS DISTRIBUTIONS

The loss probability distributions for market, credit, and operational risk are very different. Rosenberg and Schuermann used data from a variety of different sources to estimate typical shapes for these distributions.[1] These are shown in Figures 21.3 to 21.5. The market risk loss distribution (see Figure 21.3) is symmetrical but not perfectly normally distributed. A t-distribution with 11 degrees of freedom provides a good fit. The credit risk loss distribution in Figure 21.4 is quite skewed, as one would expect. The

---

[1] See J. V. Rosenberg and T. Schuermann, "A General Approach to Integrated Risk Management with Skewed, Fat-tailed Risks," Federal Reserve Bank of New York, Staff Report No. 185, May 2004.

Figure 21.3   Loss probability density function for market risk.

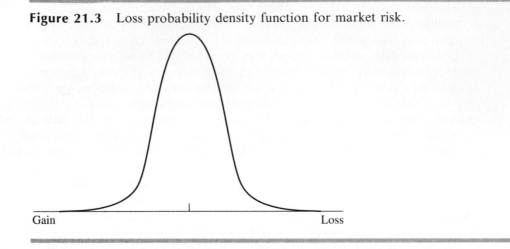

Gain   Loss

operational risk distribution in Figure 21.5 has a quite extreme shape. Most of the time, losses are modest, but occasionally they are very large.

We can characterize a distribution by its second, third, and fourth moments. Loosely speaking, the second moment measures standard deviation (or variance), the third moment measures skewness, and the fourth moment measures kurtosis (i.e., the heaviness of tails). Table 21.1 summarizes the properties of typical loss distributions for market, credit, and operational risk.

21.4   RELATIVE IMPORTANCE OF RISKS

The relative importance of different types of risk depends on the business mix. For a bank whose prime business is taking deposits and making loans, credit risk is of paramount importance. For an investment bank, both credit risk and market risk are important. For an asset manager, the greatest risk is operational risk.

Figure 21.4   Loss probability density function for credit risk.

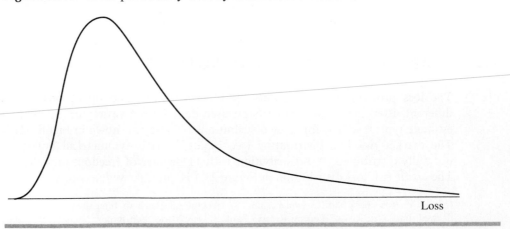

Loss

Figure 21.5 Loss probability density function for operational risk.

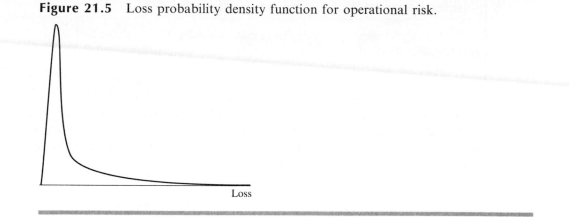

Loss

If an asset manager is found to be negligent in some way, there are liable to be expensive investor lawsuits. Business Snapshot 21.1 gives one example of this. Another high-profile example is provided by the Unilever's pension plan. Mercury Asset Management, owned by Merrill Lynch, pledged not to underperform a benchmark index by more than 3%. Between January 1997 and March 1998, it underperformed the index by 10.5%. Unilever sued Merrill Lynch for $185 million and the matter was settled out of court. The Spanish bank Santander incurred operational risk losses in 2009 on funds it managed for investors and placed with Bernard Madoff, who it transpired was running a $50 billion Ponzi scheme.

Interactions Between Risks

There are interactions between the different types of risks. For example, when a derivative such as a swap is traded, there are interactions between credit and market risk. If a financial institution's counterparty defaults, credit risk exists only if market variables have moved so that the value of the derivative to the financial institution is positive. Another interaction is that the probability of default by a counterparty may depend on the value of a financial institution's contract (or contracts) with the counterparty.[2] As mentioned in Section 15.1, if the counterparty has entered into the contract for hedging purposes, the dependence should be small. However, if the contract has been entered into for speculative purposes and the contract is large in relation to the size of the counterparty, the dependence should be considered.

Table 21.1 Characteristics of loss distributions for different risk types.

Type of risk	Second moment (standard deviation)	Third moment (skewness)	Fourth moment (kurtosis)
Market risk	High	Zero	Low
Credit risk	Moderate	Moderate	Moderate
Operational risk	Low	High	High

[2] When calculating the expected cost of counterparty default risk in Section 15.1, we assumed no dependence.

Business Snapshot 21.1   The EGT Fund

In 1996 Peter Young was fund manager at Deutsche Morgan Grenfell, a subsidiary of Deutsche Bank. He was responsible for managing a fund called the European Growth Trust (EGT). It had grown to be a very large fund and Young had responsibilities for managing over £1 billion of investors' money.

  Certain rules applied to EGT. One of these was that no more than 10% of the fund could be invested in unlisted securities. Peter Young violated this rule in a way that, it can be argued, benefited him personally. When the facts were uncovered, he was fired and Deutsche Bank had to compensate investors. The total cost to Deutsche Bank was over £200 million.

As the Long-Term Capital Management saga clearly shows, there can be interactions between liquidity risks and market risks (see Business Snapshot 15.1). There are also interactions between operational risks and market risks. It is unlikely that we would know about the activities of Nick Leeson at Barings Bank if he had guessed right about the Nikkei index (see Business Snapshot 5.5). Also, we are unlikely to hear about a violation of the rules for a fund (such as the one in Business Snapshot 21.1) if the violation leads to a gain rather than a loss.

21.5 AGGREGATING ECONOMIC CAPITAL

A financial institution typically calculates market, credit, operational, and (possibly) business risk loss distributions for a number of different business units. It is then faced with the problem of aggregating the loss distributions to calculate a total economic capital for the whole enterprise.

The simplest approach is to assume that the total economic capital for a set of n different risks is the sum of the economic capital amounts for each risk considered separately, so that

$$E_{\text{total}} = \sum_{i=1}^{n} E_i \tag{21.1}$$

where E_{total} is the total economic capital for the financial institution facing n different risks and E_i is the economic capital for the ith risk considered on its own. This is what the Basel Committee does for regulatory capital. The total regulatory capital a bank is required to keep under Basel II is the sum of the regulatory capital amounts for credit, market, and operational risks.

Equation (21.1) is clearly a very conservative assumption. It assumes perfect correlation. In the context of economic capital calculations where the confidence level is 99.9%, it would mean that, if a financial institution experiences the 99.9% worst-case loss for market risk, it also experiences the 99.9% worst-case loss for credit risk and operational risk. Rosenberg and Schuermann estimate the correlation between market risk and credit risk to be approximately 50% and the correlation between each of these risks and operational risk to be approximately 20%. They estimate that equation (21.1) when used as a way of aggregating market, credit, and operational risk overstates the total capital required by about 40%.

Assuming Normal Distributions

A simple assumption when aggregating loss distributions is that they are normally distributed. The standard deviation of the total loss from n sources of risk is then

$$\sigma_{\text{total}} = \sqrt{\sum_{i=1}^{n}\sum_{j=1}^{n} \sigma_i\, \sigma_j\, \rho_{ij}} \qquad (21.2)$$

where σ_i is the standard deviation of the loss from the ith source of risk and ρ_{ij} is the correlation between risk i and risk j. The capital requirement can be calculated from this. For example, the excess of the 99.9% worst-case loss over the expected loss is 3.09 times the number calculated in equation (21.2).

This approach tends to underestimate the capital requirement because it takes no account of the skewness and kurtosis of the loss distributions. Rosenberg and Schuermann estimate that, when the approach is applied to aggregating market, credit, and operational risk, the total capital is underestimated by about 40%.

Using Copulas

A more sophisticated approach to aggregating loss distributions is by using copulas. Copulas were discussed in Chapter 10. Each loss distribution is mapped on a percentile to percentile basis to a standard well-behaved distribution. A correlation structure between the standard distributions is defined and this indirectly defines a correlation structure between the original distributions.

Many different copulas can be defined. In the Gaussian copula, the standard distributions are assumed to be multivariate normal. An alternative is to assume that they are multivariate t. This leads to the joint probability of the extreme values of two variables being higher than in the Gaussian copula. This is discussed further in Section 10.4.

The Hybrid Approach

A simple approach that seems to work well is known as the *hybrid approach*. This involves calculating the economic capital for a portfolio of risks from the economic capital for the individual risks using

$$E_{\text{total}} = \sqrt{\sum_{i=1}^{n}\sum_{j=1}^{n} E_i\, E_j\, \rho_{ij}} \qquad (21.3)$$

When the distributions are normal, this approach is exactly correct. When distributions are nonnormal, the hybrid approach gives an approximate answer—but one that reflects any heaviness in the tails of the individual loss distributions. Rosenberg and Schuermann find that the answers given by the hybrid approach are reasonably close to those given by copula models.

Example 21.3

Suppose that the estimates for economic capital for market, credit, and operational risk for two business units are as shown in Table 21.2. The correlations between the losses are shown in Table 21.3. The correlation between credit risk and market risk within the same business unit is 0.5, and the correlation between operational risk and either credit or market risk within the same business unit is 0.2. (These correspond to the estimates of Rosenberg and Schuermann mentioned above.)

Table 21.2 Economic capital estimates for Example 21.3.

Type of risk	Business Unit 1	Business Unit 2
Market risk	30	40
Credit risk	70	80
Operational risk	30	90

Table 21.3 Correlations between losses in Example 21.3: MR, CR, and OR refer to market risk, credit risk, and operational risk; 1 and 2 refer to the business units.

	MR–1	CR–1	OR–1	MR–2	CR–2	OR–2
MR–1	1.0	0.5	0.2	0.4	0.0	0.0
CR–1	0.5	1.0	0.2	0.0	0.6	0.0
OR–1	0.2	0.2	1.0	0.0	0.0	0.0
MR–2	0.4	0.0	0.0	1.0	0.5	0.2
CR–2	0.0	0.6	0.0	0.5	1.0	0.2
OR–2	0.0	0.0	0.0	0.2	0.2	1.0

The correlation between two different risk types in two different business units is zero. The correlation between market risks across business units is 0.4. The correlation between credit risks across business units is 0.6. The correlation between operational risks across business units is zero.

We can aggregate the economic capital using the hybrid approach. The total market risk economic capital is

$$\sqrt{30^2 + 40^2 + 2 \times 0.4 \times 30 \times 40} = 58.8$$

The total credit risk economic capital is

$$\sqrt{70^2 + 80^2 + 2 \times 0.6 \times 70 \times 80} = 134.2$$

The total operational risk economic capital is

$$\sqrt{30^2 + 90^2} = 94.9$$

The total economic capital for Business Unit 1 is

$$\sqrt{30^2 + 70^2 + 30^2 + 2 \times 0.5 \times 30 \times 70 + 2 \times 0.2 \times 30 \times 30 + 2 \times 0.2 \times 70 \times 30}$$
$$= 100.0$$

The total economic capital for Business Unit 2 is

$$\sqrt{40^2 + 80^2 + 90^2 + 2 \times 0.5 \times 40 \times 80 + 2 \times 0.2 \times 40 \times 90 + 2 \times 0.2 \times 80 \times 90}$$
$$= 153.7$$

The total enterprise-wide economic capital is the square root of

$$30^2 + 40^2 + 70^2 + 80^2 + 30^2 + 90^2 + 2 \times 0.4 \times 30 \times 40 + 2 \times 0.5 \times 30 \times 70$$
$$+ 2 \times 0.2 \times 30 \times 30 + 2 \times 0.5 \times 40 \times 80 + 2 \times 0.2 \times 40 \times 90$$
$$+ 2 \times 0.6 \times 70 \times 80 + 2 \times 0.2 \times 70 \times 30 + 2 \times 0.2 \times 80 \times 90$$

or 203.224.

There are significant diversification benefits. The sum of the economic capital estimates for market, credit, and operational risk is $58.8 + 134.2 + 94.9 = 287.9$ and the sum of the economic capital estimates for two business units is $100 + 153.7 = 253.7$. Both of these are greater than the total economic capital estimate of 203.2.

21.6 ALLOCATION OF ECONOMIC CAPITAL

Suppose that the sum of the economic capital for the business units, $\sum_{i=1}^n E_i$, is \$2 billion and that the total economic capital for the whole bank, after taking less-than-perfect correlations into account, is \$1.3 billion ($= 65\%$ of the sum of the E_i). The \$0.7 billion is a diversification gain to the bank. How should the total economic capital be allocated to the business units?

A simple approach is to allocate $0.65 E_i$ to business unit i. However, this is probably not the best approach. Consider a situation where there are 50 business units and that two particular units both have an economic capital of \$100 million. Suppose that, when the first business unit is excluded from the calculations, the bank's economic capital decreases by \$60 million and that, when the second business unit is excluded from the calculation, the bank's economic capital decreases by \$10 million. Arguably, the first business unit should have more economic capital than the second, because its incremental impact on the bank's total economic capital is greater.

The issues here are analogous to those we discussed in Section 8.7 with allocating VaR. One approach is to calculate incremental economic capital for each business unit and then allocate economic capital to business units in proportion to their incremental capital. (Incremental capital is the difference between the total economic capital with and without the business unit.) Another approach is to work with the component economic capital. This involves allocating

$$x_i \frac{\partial E_{\text{total}}}{\partial x_i}$$

to the ith business unit, where x_i is the investment in the ith business unit. As we pointed out in Section 8.7, a result known as Euler's theorem ensures that the total of the allocated capital is the total economic capital E_{total}.

Define Q_i as the increase in the total economic capital when we increase x_i by a small amount Δx_i. A discrete approximation for the component economic capital for business unit i is

$$Q_i / y_i \tag{21.4}$$

where $y_i = \Delta x_i / x_i$.

Example 21.4

Consider again Example 21.3. The total economic capital is 203.2. The economic capital calculated for Business Unit 1 is 100 and that calculated for Business Unit 2 is 153.7. The simple approach would allocate 100/253.7 of the total economic capital to Business Unit 1 and 153.7/253.7 of the economic capital to Business Unit 2. This would result in 80.1 for Business Unit 1 and 123.1 to Business Unit 2.

The incremental effect of Business Unit 1 on the total economic capital is $203.2 - 153.7 = 49.5$. Similarly, the incremental effect of Business Unit 2 on the total economic capital is $203.2 - 100 = 103.2$. The two incremental capitals do not add up to the total capital (as is usually the case). However, we could use them as a basis for allocating the total capital. We would then allocate $49.5/(49.5 + 103.2)$ of the capital to Business Unit 1 and $103.2/(49.5 + 103.2)$ of it to Business Unit 2. This would result in 65.9 for Business Unit 1 and 137.3 for Business Unit 2.

To apply equation (21.4) and allocate component economic capital to each unit, we could calculate the partial derivative analytically. Alternatively, we can use a numerical calculation. When we increase the size of Business Unit 1 by 1%, its economic capital amounts for market, credit, and operational risk in Table 21.2 increase to 30.3, 70.7, and 30.3, respectively. The total economic capital becomes 203.906, so that $Q_1 = 203.906 - 203.224 = 0.682$. When we increase the size of Business Unit 2 by 1%, its economic capital amounts for market, credit, and operational risk in Table 21.2 increase to 40.4, 80.8, and 90.9, respectively. The total economic capital becomes 204.577, so that $Q_2 = 204.577 - 203.224 = 1.353$. In this case, because we are considering 1% increases in the size of each unit, $y_1 = y_2 = 0.01$. From equation (21.4), the economic capital allocations to the two business units are 68.2 and 135.3. (These do not quite add up to the total economic capital of 203.2, because we approximated the partial derivative.)

21.7 DEUTSCHE BANK'S ECONOMIC CAPITAL

Deutsche Bank publishes the results of its economic capital calculations in its annual financial statements. Table 21.4 summarizes the economic capital and regulatory capital reported at the end of 2007. Capital is calculated for credit risk, market risk, operational risk, and business risk. Deutsche Bank calculated a diversification benefit reflecting the lack of perfect correlation between credit, market, and operational risk, but assumed that no diversification benefits were associated with business risk. The total economic capital is about 13.6 billion euros. This is considerably less than the total regulatory capital, which is 8% of risk-weighted assets, or about 25.2 billion euros. The actual capital held is 11.6% of risk-weighted assets, or about 36.5 billion euros. Deutsche Bank appears well capitalized relative to the risks it is taking at the end of 2007. Table 21.5 shows how the capital was allocated to business units.

21.8 RAROC

Risk-adjusted performance measurement (RAPM) has become an important part of how business units are assessed. There are many different approaches, but all have one

Table 21.4 Deutsche Bank's economic capital and regulatory capital (millions of euros).

Credit risk	8,506
Market risk	3,481
Operational risk	3,974
Diversification benefit across credit, market, and operational risk	(2,651)
Business risk	301
Total economic capital	13,611
Total risk-weighted assets	314,845
Tier 1 capital held (% of risk-weighted assets)	8.6%
Tier 2 capital held (% of risk-weighted assets)	3.0%
Total capital held (% of risk-weighted assets)	11.6%

thing in common. They compare return with capital employed in a way that incorporates an adjustment for risk.

The most common approach is to compare expected return with economic capital. This is usually referred to as RAROC (risk-adjusted return on capital). The formula is

$$RAROC = \frac{\text{Revenues} - \text{Costs} - \text{Expected losses}}{\text{Economic capital}} \tag{21.5}$$

The numerator may be calculated on a pre-tax or post-tax basis. Sometimes, a risk-free rate of return on the economic capital is calculated and added to the numerator.

Example 21.5

When lending in a certain region of the world, a AA-rated bank estimates its losses as 1% of outstanding loans per year on average. The 99.9% worst-case loss (i.e., the loss exceeded only 0.1% of the time) is 5% of outstanding loans. As shown in Example 21.1, the economic capital required per $100 of loans is $4, which is the difference between the 99.9% worst-case loss and the expected loss. (This ignores diversification benefits that would in practice be allocated to the lending unit.) The spread between the cost of funds and the interest charged is

Table 21.5 Allocation of Deutsche Bank's economic capital (millions of euros).

Corporate banking and securities	10,533
Global transaction banking	430
Asset and wealth management	871
Private business clients	1,566
Corporate investments	207
Consolidation and adjustments	5
Total	13,611

2.5%. Subtracting from this the expected loan loss of 1%, the expected contribution per $100 of loans is $1.50. Assuming that the lending unit's administrative costs total 0.7% of the amount loaned, the expected profit is reduced to $0.80 per $100 in the loan portfolio. RAROC is therefore

$$\frac{0.80}{4} = 20\%$$

An alternative calculation would add the interest on the economic capital to the numerator. Suppose that the risk-free interest rate is 2%. Then $0.02 \times 4 = 0.08$ is added to the numerator, so that RAROC becomes

$$\frac{0.88}{4} = 22\%$$

As pointed out by Matten, it is more accurate to refer to the approach in equation (21.5) as RORAC (return on risk-adjusted capital) rather than RAROC, because it is the capital not the return that reflects risk.[3] In theory, RAROC should involve adjusting the return (i.e., the numerator) for risk. In equation (21.5), it is the capital (i.e., the denominator) that is adjusted for risk.

RAROC can be calculated *ex-ante* (before the start of the year) or *ex-post* (after the end of the year). *Ex-ante* calculations are based on estimates of expected profit. *Ex-post* calculations are based on actual profit results. *Ex-ante* calculations are typically used to decide whether a particular business unit should be expanded or contracted. *Ex-post* calculations are typically used for performance evaluation and bonus calculations.

It is usually not appropriate to base a decision to expand or contract a particular business unit on an *ex-post* analysis (although there is a natural temptation to do this). It may be that results were bad for the most recent year because credit losses were much larger than average or because there was an unexpectedly large operational risk loss. Key strategic decisions should be based on expected long-term results.

SUMMARY

Economic capital is the capital that a bank or other financial institution deems necessary for the risks it is bearing. When calculating economic capital, a financial institution is free to adopt any approach it likes. It does not have to use the one proposed by regulators. Typically, it estimates economic capital for credit risk, market risk, operational risk, and (possibly) business risk for its business units and then aggregates the estimates to produce an estimate of the economic capital for the whole enterprise. The risks are usually assumed to be less than perfectly correlated. The benefits of diversification are estimated and allocated to business units. Usually the approach used is designed to reflect the contributions of the business units to the total economic capital.

The one-year loss distributions for market risk, credit risk, and operational risk are quite different. The loss distribution for market risk is symmetrical, for credit risk it is skewed, and for operational risk it is highly skewed with very heavy tails.

[3] See C. Matten, *Managing Bank Capital: Capital Allocation and Performance Measurement*, 2nd edn. Chichester, UK: Wiley, 2000

The total economic capital for a financial institution is allocated to business units so that a return on capital can be calculated. There are a number of possible allocation procedures. The best are those that reflect the incremental impact of the business unit on the total economic capital. The amount of capital allocated to a business unit is generally less than the capital estimated for the business unit as a stand-alone entity because of the diversification benefits

FURTHER READING

Dev, A., *Economic Capital: A Practitioner's Guide*. London: Risk Books, 2004.

Matten, C., *Managing Bank Capital: Capital Allocation and Performance Measurement*, 2nd edn. Chichester, UK: Wiley, 2000.

Rosenberg, J. V., and T. Schuermann, "A General Approach to Integrated Risk Management with Skewed, Fat-tailed Risks," Federal Reserve Bank of New York, Staff Report No. 185, May 2004.

PRACTICE QUESTIONS AND PROBLEMS (Answers at End of Book)

21.1. What is the difference between economic capital and regulatory capital?

21.2. What determines the confidence level used by a financial institution in its economic capital calculations?

21.3. What types of risk are included in business risk?

21.4. In what respects are the models used to calculate economic capital for market risk, credit risk, and operational risk likely to be different from those used to calculate regulatory capital?

21.5. Suppose that the credit loss in a year has a lognormal distribution. The logarithm of the loss is normal with mean 0.5 and standard deviation 4. What is the economic capital requirement if a confidence level of 99.97% is used?

21.6. Suppose that the economic capital estimates for two business units are as follows:

Type of risk	Business Unit 1	Business Unit 2
Market risk	20	40
Credit risk	40	30
Operational risk	70	10

The correlations are as in Table 21.3. Calculate the total economic capital for each business unit and the two business units together.

21.7. In Problem 21.6, what is the incremental effect of each business unit on the total economic capital? Use this to allocate economic capital to business units. What is the impact on the economic capital of each business unit increasing by 0.5%? Show that your results are consistent with Euler's theorem.

21.8. A bank is considering expanding its asset management operations. The main risk is operational risk. It estimates the expected operational risk loss from the new venture in one year to be $2 million and the 99.9% worst-case loss (arising from a large investor law suit) to be $40 million. The expected fees it will receive from investors for the funds under administration are $12 million per year and administrative costs are expected to be $5 million per year. Estimate the before-tax RAROC.

21.9. RAROC can be used in two different ways. What are they?

FURTHER QUESTIONS

21.10. Suppose that daily gains and losses are normally distributed with standard deviation of $5 million.
   (a) Estimate the minimum regulatory capital the bank is required to hold (assume a multiplicative factor of 4.0).
   (b) Estimate the economic capital using a one-year time horizon and a 99.9% confidence limit, assuming that there is a correlation of 0.05 between gains or losses on successive days.

21.11. Suppose that the economic capital estimates for two business units are as follows:

Type of risk	Business Unit 1	Business Unit 2
Market risk	10	50
Credit risk	30	30
Operational risk	50	10

The correlation between market risk and credit risk in the same business unit is 0.3. The correlation between credit risk in one business unit and credit risk in the other is 0.7. The correlation between market risk in one business unit and market risk in the other is 0.2. All other correlations are zero. Calculate the total economic capital. How much should be allocated to each business unit?

21.12. Suppose that a bank's sole business is to lend in two regions of the world. The lending in each region has the same characteristics as in Example 21.5 of Section 21.8. Lending to Region A is three times as great as lending to Region B. The correlation between loan losses in the two regions is 0.4. Estimate the total RAROC.

CHAPTER **22**

Risk Management Mistakes to Avoid

Since the mid-1980s, there have been some spectacular losses in financial markets. This chapter explores the lessons we can learn from them and reviews key points made in earlier chapters. The losses that we will consider are listed in Business Snapshot 22.1.

One remarkable aspect of the list in Business Snapshot 22.1 is the number of times huge losses were caused by the activities of a single person. In 1994, Robert Citron's trading led to Orange County, a municipality in California, losing about $2 billion. Joseph Jett's trading for Kidder Peabody caused losses of $350 million in the same year. In 1995, Nick Leeson's trading brought about the collapse of Barings, Britain's oldest investment bank. John Rusnak's losses of $700 million at Allied Irish Bank came to light in 2002. Jérôme Kerviel lost over $7 billion for Société Générale in 2008.

22.1 RISK LIMITS

The first and most important lesson from the losses concerns risk limits. It is essential that all companies (financial and nonfinancial) define in a clear and unambiguous way limits to the financial risks that can be taken. They should then set up procedures for ensuring that the limits are adhered to. Ideally, overall risk limits should be set at board level. These should then be converted to limits applicable to the individuals responsible for managing particular risks. Daily reports should indicate the gain or loss that will be experienced for particular movements in market variables. These should be checked against the actual gains and losses that are experienced to ensure that the valuation procedures underlying the reports are accurate.

It is particularly important that companies monitor risks carefully when derivatives are used. This is because derivatives can be used for hedging or speculation or arbitrage. Without close monitoring, it is impossible to know whether a derivatives trader has switched from being a hedger or arbitrageur to being a speculator. Barings is a classic example of what can go wrong. Nick Leeson's mandate was to carry out low-risk arbitrage between the Singapore and Osaka markets on Nikkei 225 futures. Unknown to his superiors in London, Leeson switched from being an arbitrageur to taking huge bets on the future direction of the Nikkei 225. Systems within Barings were so inadequate that nobody knew what he was doing.

441

Business Snapshot 22.1   Big Losses

Allied Irish Bank
This bank lost about $700 million from the unauthorized speculative activities of one of its foreign exchange traders, John Rusnak, that lasted a number of years. Rusnak covered up his losses by creating fictitious options trades.

Barings (*see Business Snapshot* 5.5)
This 200-year-old British bank was wiped out in 1995 by the $1 billion loss of a single trader, Nick Leeson, in Singapore. The trader's mandate was to arbitrage between Nikkei 225 futures quotes in Singapore and Osaka. Instead he made big bets on the future direction of the Nikkei 225 using futures and options.

Enron's Counterparties
Enron managed to conceal its true situation from its shareholders with some creative contracts. Several financial institutions that allegedly helped Enron do this have each had to settle shareholder lawsuits for over $1 billion dollars.

Hammersmith and Fulham (*see Business Snapshot* 18.1)
This British Local Authority lost about $600 million on sterling interest rate swaps and options in 1988. The two traders responsible for the loss knew surprisingly little about the products they were trading.

Kidder Peabody (*see Business Snapshot* 20.1)
The activities of a single trader, Joseph Jett, led to this New York investment dealer losing $350 million trading US government securities. The loss arose because of a mistake in the way the company's computer system calculated profits.

Long-Term Capital Management (*see Business Snapshot* 15.1)
This hedge fund lost about $4 billion in 1998 carrying out convergence arbitrage strategies. The loss was caused by a flight to quality after Russia defaulted on its debt.

National Westminster Bank
This British bank lost about $130 million from using an inappropriate model to value swap options in 1997.

Orange County (*see Appendix B*)
The activities of the treasurer, Robert Citron, led to this California municipality losing about $2 billion in 1994. The treasurer was using derivatives to speculate that interest rates would not rise.

Procter and Gamble (*see Business Snapshot* 5.4)
The treasury department of this large US company lost about $90 million in 1994 trading highly exotic interest rate derivatives contracts with Bankers Trust. It later sued Bankers Trust and settled out of court.

Société Générale
Jérôme Kerviel, an equity trader in the Paris office, lost over $7 billion speculating on movements in equity indices in January 2008. He is alleged to have concealed his exposure by creating fictitious trades.

Subprime Mortgage Losses (*see Chapter* 16)
In 2007, investors lost confidence in the structured products created from US subprime mortgages. This led to a "credit crunch" with losses of tens of billions of dollars by financial institutions and the worst recession since the 1930s.

The argument here is not that no risks should be taken. A trader in a financial institution or a fund manager should be allowed to take positions on the future direction of relevant market variables. What we are arguing is that the sizes of the positions that can be taken should be limited and the systems in place should accurately report the risks being taken.

A Difficult Situation

What happens if an individual exceeds risk limits and makes a profit? This is a tricky issue for senior management. It is tempting to ignore violations of risk limits when profits result. However, this is shortsighted. It leads to a culture where risk limits are not taken seriously, and it paves the way for a disaster. The classic example here is Orange County. Robert Citron's activities in 1991–1993 had been very profitable for Orange County, and the municipality had come to rely on his trading for additional funding. People chose to ignore the risks he was taking because he had produced profits. Unfortunately, the losses made in 1994 far exceeded the profits from previous years.

The penalties for exceeding risk limits should be just as great when profits result as when losses result. Otherwise, traders who make losses are liable to keep increasing their bets in the hope that eventually a profit will result and all will be forgiven.

Do Not Assume You Can Outguess the Market

Some traders are quite possibly better than others. But no trader gets it right all the time. A trader who correctly predicts the direction in which market variables will move 60% of the time is doing well. If a trader has an outstanding track record (as Robert Citron did in the early 1990s), it is likely to be a result of luck rather than superior trading skill. As our discussion of mutual fund performance in Chapter 4 shows, it appears that fund managers usually produce superior returns as a result of luck rather than skill.

Suppose that a financial institution employs 16 traders and one of those traders makes profits in every quarter of a year. Should the trader receive a good bonus? Should the trader's risk limits be increased? The answer to the first question is that the trader will inevitably receive a good bonus. The answer to the second question should be no. The chance of making a profit in four consecutive quarters from random trading is 0.5^4, or 1 in 16. This means that just by chance one of the 16 traders will "get it right" every single quarter of the year. We should not assume that the trader's luck will continue and we should not increase the trader's risk limits.

Do Not Underestimate the Benefits of Diversification

When a trader appears good at predicting a particular market variable there is a tendency to increase the trader's risk limits. We have just argued that this is a bad idea because it is quite likely that the trader has been lucky rather than clever. However, let us suppose that we are really convinced that the trader has special talents. How undiversified should we allow ourselves to become in order to take advantage of the trader's special skills? As indicated in Section 1.1, the benefits from diversification are large. A trader has to be very good for it to be worth foregoing these benefits to speculate heavily on just one market variable.

An example will illustrate the point here. Suppose that there are 20 stocks, each of which has an expected return of 10% per annum and a standard deviation of return of 30%. The correlation between the returns from any two of the stocks is 0.2. By dividing an investment equally among the 20 stocks, an investor has an expected return of 10% per annum and standard deviation of returns of 14.7%. Diversification enables the investor to reduce risks by over half. Another way of expressing this is that diversification enables an investor to double the expected return per unit of risk taken. The investor would have to be very good at stock picking to get a better risk–return trade-off by investing in just one stock.

Carry out Scenario Analyses and Stress Tests

As discussed in Chapter 17, the calculation of risk measures such as VaR should always be accompanied by scenario analyses and stress testing to obtain an understanding of what can go wrong. Without the discipline of stress testing, human beings have an unfortunate tendency to anchor on one or two scenarios when evaluating decisions. In 1993 and 1994, for example, Procter and Gamble was so convinced that interest rates would remain low that, in its decision making, it ignored the possibility of a 100-basis-point increase.

Once stress-testing results have been produced, they should become inputs to a financial institution's strategic decision making. All too often, particularly when times are good, the results of stress testing are ignored. This happened at a number of financial institutions prior to July 2007.

22.2   MANAGING THE TRADING ROOM

In trading rooms there is a tendency to regard high-performing traders as "untouchable" and not to subject their activities to the same scrutiny as other traders. Apparently Joseph Jett, Kidder Peabody's star trader of Treasury instruments, was often "too busy" to answer questions and discuss his positions with the company's risk managers.

All traders—particularly those making high profits—should be fully accountable. It is important for the financial institution to know whether the high profits are being made by taking unreasonably high risks. It is also important to check that the financial institution's computer systems and pricing models are correct and are not being manipulated in some way.

Separate the Front, Middle, and Back Office

The *front office* in a financial institution consists of the traders who are executing trades, taking positions, etc. The *middle office* consists of risk managers who are monitoring the risks being taken. The *back office* is where the record keeping and accounting takes place. Some of the worst derivatives disasters have occurred because these functions were not kept separate. Nick Leeson controlled both the front and back office for Barings in Singapore and was, as a result, able to conceal the disastrous nature of his trades from his superiors in London for some time.

Do Not Blindly Trust Models

We discussed model risk in Chapter 20. Some of the large losses experienced by financial institutions arose because of the models and computer systems being used. Kidder Peabody was misled by its own systems. Another example of an incorrect model leading to losses is provided by National Westminster Bank. This bank had an incorrect model for valuing swap options that led to significant losses.

If large profits are reported when relatively simple trading strategies are followed, there is a good chance that the models underlying the calculation of the profits are wrong. Similarly, if a financial institution appears to be particularly competitive on its quotes for a particular type of deal, there is a good chance that it is using a different model from other market participants. This almost certainly means that, before too long, it will have to change its model and report a loss. Getting too much business of a certain type can be just as worrisome to the head of a trading room as getting too little business of that type.

Be Conservative in Recognizing Inception Profits

When a financial institution sells a highly exotic instrument to a nonfinancial corporation, the valuation can be highly dependent on the underlying model. For example, instruments with long-dated embedded interest rate options can be highly dependent on the interest rate model used. In these circumstances, a phrase used to describe the daily marking to market of the deal is *marking to model*. This is because there are no market prices for similar deals that can be used as a benchmark.

Suppose that a financial institution manages to sell an instrument to a client for $10 million more than it is worth—or at least $10 million more than its model says it is worth. The $10 million is known as an *inception profit*. When should it be recognized? There appears to be a lot of variation in what different derivatives dealers do. Some recognize the $10 million immediately, whereas others are much more conservative and recognize it slowly over the life of the deal.

Recognizing inception profits immediately is very dangerous. It encourages traders to use aggressive models, take their bonuses, and leave before the model and the value of the deal come under close scrutiny. It is much better to recognize inception profits slowly, so that traders are motivated to investigate the impact of several different models and several different sets of assumptions before committing themselves to a deal.

Do Not Sell Clients Inappropriate Products

It is tempting to sell corporate clients inappropriate products, particularly when they appear to have an appetite for the underlying risks. But this is shortsighted. A dramatic illustration is provided by the activities of Bankers Trust (BT) in the period leading up to the spring of 1994. Many of BT's clients were persuaded to buy high-risk and totally inappropriate products. A typical product would give the client a good chance of saving a few basis points on its borrowings and a small chance of costing a large amount of money. The products worked well for BT's clients in 1992 and 1993, but blew up in 1994 when interest rates rose sharply. The bad publicity that followed hurt BT greatly. The years it had spent building up trust among corporate clients and developing an enviable reputation for innovation in derivatives were largely lost as a result of the activities of a few overly aggressive salesmen. BT was forced to pay large amounts of money to its clients to settle lawsuits out of court. It was taken over by Deutsche Bank in 1999.

Beware of Easy Profits

Enron provides an example of how overly aggressive deal makers can cost their banks billions of dollars. Doing business with Enron seemed very profitable and banks competed with each other for this business. But the fact that many banks push hard to get a certain type of business should not be taken as an indication that the business will ultimately be profitable. The business that Enron did with banks resulted in many very expensive shareholder lawsuits. In general, transactions where high profits seem easy to achieve should be looked at closely for potential operational, credit, or market risks.

Investing in the AAA-rated tranches of ABSs and ABS CDOs that were created from subprime mortgages (see Chapter 16) seemed like a money-making machine for many banks. The promised returns were higher than the returns normally earned on AAA-rated instruments. Few investors stopped to ask whether this was because there were risks that had not been taken into account.

22.3 LIQUIDITY RISK

We discussed liquidity risk in Chapter 19. Financial engineers usually base the pricing of exotic instruments, and other instruments that trade relatively infrequently, on the prices of actively traded instruments. For example:

1. A trader often calculates a zero curve from actively traded government bonds (known as on-the-run bonds) and uses it to price bonds that trade less frequently (off-the-run bonds).

2. A trader often implies the volatility of an asset from actively traded options and uses it to price less actively traded options.

3. A trader often implies information about the behavior of interest rates from actively traded interest rate caps and swap options and uses it to price products that are highly structured.

These practices are not unreasonable. However, it is dangerous to assume that less actively traded instruments can always be traded at close to their theoretical price. When financial markets experience a shock of one sort or another, liquidity black holes may develop (see Section 19.3). Liquidity then becomes very important to investors, and illiquid instruments often sell at a big discount to their theoretical values. It is dangerous to adopt trading strategies that assume large volumes of relatively illiquid instruments to be sellable at short notice at close to their theoretical values.

An example of liquidity risk is provided by the investment strategy of Long-Term Capital Management (LTCM), which is the subject of Business Snapshot 15.1. This hedge fund followed a strategy known as *convergence arbitrage*. It attempted to identify two securities (or portfolios of securities) that should in theory sell for the same price. If the market price of one security was less that of the other, it would buy that security and sell the other. The strategy is based on the idea that, if two securities have the same theoretical price, their market prices should eventually be the same.

In the summer of 1998, LTCM made a huge loss. This was largely because a default by Russia on its debt caused a flight to quality. LTCM tended to be long illiquid instruments and short the corresponding liquid instruments. (For example, it was long off-the-run bonds and short on-the-run bonds.) The spreads between the prices of illiquid instruments and the corresponding liquid instruments widened sharply after the Russian default. LTCM was highly leveraged. It experienced huge losses and there were margin calls on its positions that it was unable to meet.

The LTCM story reinforces the importance of carrying out scenario analyses and stress testing to look at what can happen in extreme scenarios. As discussed in Chapter 17, it is important to consider not only immediate losses but also losses created by knock-on effects.

Beware When Everyone Is Following the Same Trading Strategy

It sometimes happens that many market participants are following essentially the same trading strategy. This creates a dangerous environment where there are liable to be big market moves, liquidity black holes, and large losses for the market participants.

We gave one example of this in Business Snapshot 19.4, which discussed portfolio insurance and the market crash of October 1987. In the months leading up to the crash, increasing numbers of portfolio managers were attempting to insure their portfolios by creating synthetic put options. They bought stocks or stock index futures after a rise in the market and sold them after a fall. This created an unstable market. A relatively small decline in stock prices could lead to a wave of selling by portfolio insurers. The latter would lead to a further decline in the market, which could give rise to another wave of selling, and so on. There is little doubt that, without portfolio insurance, the crash of October 1987 would have been much less severe.

Another example is provided again by LTCM in 1998. Its position was made more difficult by the fact that many other hedge funds were following similar convergence arbitrage strategies. After the Russian default and the flight to quality, LTCM tried to liquidate part of its portfolio to meet margin calls. Unfortunately, other hedge funds were facing similar problems to LTCM and trying to do similar trades. This exacerbated the situation, causing liquidity spreads to be even higher than they would otherwise have been and reinforcing the flight to quality. Consider, for example, LTCM's position in US Treasury bonds. It was long the illiquid off-the-run bonds and short the liquid on-the-run bonds. When a flight to quality caused spreads between yields on the two types of bond to widen, LTCM had to liquidate its positions by selling off-the-run bonds and buying on-the-run bonds. Other large hedge funds were doing the same. As a result, the price of on-the-run bonds rose relative to off-the-run bonds and the spread between the two yields widened even more than it had already.

A further example is provided by British insurance companies in the late 1990s. This is discussed in Business Snapshot 3.1. All insurance companies decided to hedge their exposure to a fall in long-term rates at about the same time. The result was a fall in long-term rates!

The chief lesson to be learned from these stories is that it is important to see the big picture of what is going on in financial markets and to understand the risks inherent in situations where many market participants are following the same trading strategy.

Do Not Finance Long-Term Assets with Short-Term Liabilities

As discussed in Section 7.1, it is important for a financial institution to match the maturities of assets and liabilities. If it does not do this, it is subjecting itself to significant interest rate risk. Savings and Loans in the United States ran into difficulties in the 1960s, 1970s, and 1980s because they financed long-term mortgages with short-term deposits. Continental Bank failed in 1984 for a similar reason (see Business Snapshot 7.1).

During the period leading up to the credit crunch of 2007, there was a tendency for subprime mortgages and other long-term assets to be financed by commercial paper while they were in a portfolio waiting to be packaged into structured products. Conduits and special purpose vehicles had an ongoing requirement for this type of financing. The commercial paper would typically be rolled over every month. For example, the purchasers of commercial paper issued on April 1 would be redeemed with the proceeds of a new commercial paper issue on May 1; this new commercial paper issue would in turn be redeemed with another new commercial paper issue on June 1; and so on. When investors lost confidence in subprime mortgages in August 2007, it became impossible to roll over commercial paper. In many instances, banks had provided guarantees and had to provide financing. This led to a shortage of liquidity. As a result, the credit crunch was more severe than it would have been if longer-term financing had been arranged.

Market Transparency Is Important

One of the lessons from the credit crunch of 2007 is that market transparency is important. During the period leading up to 2007, investors had been trading highly structured products without any real knowledge of the underlying assets. All they knew was the credit rating of the security being traded. With hindsight, we can say that investors should have demanded more information about the underlying assets and should have more carefully assessed the risks they were taking.

The subprime meltdown of August 2007 caused investors to lose confidence in all structured products and withdraw from that market. This led to a market breakdown where tranches of structured products could only be sold at prices well below their theoretical values. There was a flight to quality and credit spreads increased. If there had been market transparency, so that investors understood the asset-backed securities they were buying, there would still have been subprime losses, but the flight to quality and disruptions to the market would have been less pronounced.

22.4 LESSONS FOR NONFINANCIAL CORPORATIONS

We conclude with some lessons applicable primarily to nonfinancial corporations.

Make Sure You Fully Understand the Trades You Are Doing

Corporations should never undertake a trade or a trading strategy that they do not fully understand. This is a somewhat obvious point, but it is surprising how often a trader working for a nonfinancial corporation will, after a big loss, admit to not really understanding what was going on and claim to have been misled by investment bankers. Robert Citron, the treasurer of Orange County did this. So did the traders working for Hammersmith and Fulham, who in spite of their huge positions were surprisingly uninformed about how the swaps and other interest rate derivatives they traded really worked.

If a senior manager in a corporation does not understand a trade proposed by a subordinate, the trade should not be approved. A simple rule of thumb is that if a trade and the rationale for entering into it are so complicated that they cannot be understood by the manager, it is almost certainly inappropriate for the corporation. The trades undertaken by Procter and Gamble would have been vetoed under this criterion.

One way of ensuring that you fully understand a financial instrument is to value it. If a corporation does not have the in-house capability to value an instrument, it should not trade it. In practice, corporations often rely on their investment bankers for valuation advice. This is dangerous, as Procter and Gamble found out. When it wanted to unwind its transactions, it found it was facing prices produced by Bankers Trust's proprietary models, which it had no way of checking.

Make Sure a Hedger Does Not Become a Speculator

One of the unfortunate facts of life is that hedging is relatively dull, whereas speculation is exciting. When a company hires a trader to manage foreign exchange risk, commodity price risk, or interest rate risk there is a danger that the following happens. At first the trader does the job diligently and earns the confidence of top management. He or she assesses the company's exposures and hedges them. As time goes by, the trader becomes convinced that he or she can outguess the market. Slowly the trader becomes a speculator. At first things go well, but then a loss is made. To recover the loss, the trader doubles up the bets. Further losses are made, and so on. The result is likely to be a disaster.

As mentioned earlier, clear limits to the risks that can be taken should be set by senior management. Controls should be put in place to ensure that the limits are obeyed. The trading strategy for a corporation should start with an analysis of the risks facing the corporation in foreign exchange, interest rate, commodity markets. A decision should then be taken on how the risks are to be reduced to acceptable levels. It is a clear sign that something is wrong within a corporation if the trading strategy is not derived in a very direct way from the company's exposures.

Be Cautious about Making the Treasury Department a Profit Center

In the last 20 years there has been a tendency to make the treasury department within a corporation a profit center. This seems to have much to recommend it. The treasurer is motivated to reduce financing costs and manage risks as profitably as possible. The problem is that the potential for the treasurer to make profits is limited. When raising funds and investing surplus cash, the treasurer is facing an efficient market. The treasurer can usually improve the bottom line only by taking additional risks. The company's hedging program gives the treasurer some scope for making shrewd decisions that increase profits. But it should be remembered that the goal of a hedging program is to reduce risks, not to increase expected profits. The decision to hedge will lead to a worse outcome than the decision not to hedge roughly 50% of the time. The danger of making the treasury department a profit center is that the treasurer is motivated to become a speculator. An Orange County or Procter and Gamble type of outcome is then liable to occur.

SUMMARY

The key lesson to be learned from the losses is the importance of *internal controls*. The risks taken by traders, the models used, and the amounts of different types of business done should all be controlled. It is important to "think outside the box" about what could go wrong. LTCM, Enron's bank counterparties, and many other financial institutions failed to do this on occasion, with huge adverse financial consequences.

FURTHER READING

Dunbar, N., *Inventing Money: The Story of Long-Term Capital Management and the Legends Behind It*. Chichester, UK: John Wiley & Sons, 2000.

Jorion, P., *Big Bets Gone Bad: Derivatives and Bankruptcy in Orange County*. New York: Academic Press, 1995.

Jorion, P., "How Long-Term Lost Its Capital," *Risk*, September 1999: 31–36.

Ju, X., and N. Pearson. "Using Value at Risk to Control Risk Taking: How Wrong Can You Be?" *Journal of Risk*, 1 (1999): 5–36.

Thomson, R., *Apocalypse Roulette: The Lethal World of Derivatives*. London: Macmillan, 1998.

Zhang, P. G., *Barings Bankruptcy and Financial Derivatives*. Singapore: World Scientific Publishing, 1995.

Compounding Frequencies for Interest Rates

A statement by a bank that the interest rate on one-year deposits is 10% per annum sounds straightforward and unambiguous. In fact, its precise meaning depends on the way the interest rate is measured.

If the interest rate is measured with annual compounding, the bank's statement that the interest rate is 10% means that $100 grows to

$$\$100 \times 1.1 = \$110$$

at the end of one year. When the interest rate is measured with semiannual compounding, it means that we earn 5% every six months, with the interest being reinvested. In this case, $100 grows to

$$\$100 \times 1.05 \times 1.05 = \$110.25$$

at the end of one year. When the interest rate is measured with quarterly compounding, the bank's statement means that we earn 2.5% every three months, with the interest being reinvested. The $100 then grows to

$$\$100 \times 1.025^4 = \$110.38$$

at the end of one year. Table A.1 shows the effect of increasing the compounding frequency further.

The compounding frequency defines the units in which an interest rate is measured. A rate expressed with one compounding frequency can be converted into an equivalent rate with a different compounding frequency. For example, from Table A.1, we see that 10.25% with annual compounding is equivalent to 10% with semiannual compounding. We can think of the difference between one compounding frequency and another to be analogous to the difference between kilometers and miles. They are two different units of measurement.

To generalize our results, suppose that an amount A is invested for n years at an interest rate of R per annum. If the rate is compounded once per annum, the terminal value of the investment is

$$A(1 + R)^n$$

Table A.1   Effect of the compounding frequency on the value of $100 at the end of one year when the interest rate is 10% per annum.

Compounding frequency	Value of $100 at end of year ($)
Annually ($m = 1$)	110.00
Semiannually ($m = 2$)	110.25
Quarterly ($m = 4$)	110.38
Monthly ($m = 12$)	110.47
Weekly ($m = 52$)	110.51
Daily ($m = 365$)	110.52

If the rate is compounded m times per annum, the terminal value of the investment is

$$A\left(1 + \frac{R}{m}\right)^{mn} \tag{A.1}$$

When $m = 1$, the rate is sometimes referred to as the *equivalent annual interest rate*.

Continuous Compounding

The limit as the compounding frequency, m, tends to infinity is known as *continuous compounding*.[1] With continuous compounding, it can be shown that an amount A invested for n years at rate R grows to

$$Ae^{Rn} \tag{A.2}$$

where $e = 2.71828$. The function e^x is built into most calculators, so the computation of the expression in equation (A.2) presents no problems. In the example in Table A.1, $A = 100$, $n = 1$, and $R = 0.1$, so that the value to which A grows with continuous compounding is

$$100e^{0.1} = \$110.52$$

This is (to two decimal places) the same as the value with daily compounding. For most practical purposes, continuous compounding can be thought of as being equivalent to daily compounding. Compounding a sum of money at a continuously compounded rate R for n years involves multiplying it by e^{Rn}. Discounting it at a continuously compounded rate R for n years involves multiplying by e^{-Rn}.

Suppose that R_c is a rate of interest with continuous compounding and that R_m is the equivalent rate with compounding m times per annum. From the results in equations (A.1) and (A.2), we have

$$Ae^{R_c n} = A\left(1 + \frac{R_m}{m}\right)^{mn}$$

---

[1] Actuaries sometimes refer to a continuously compounded rate as the *force of interest*.

or

$$e^{R_c} = \left(1 + \frac{R_m}{m}\right)^m$$

This means that

$$R_c = m \ln\left(1 + \frac{R_m}{m}\right) \qquad\qquad \text{(A.3)}$$

and

$$R_m = m(e^{R_c/m} - 1) \qquad\qquad \text{(A.4)}$$

These equations can be used to convert a rate with a compounding frequency of m times per annum to a continuously compounded rate and vice versa. The function ln is the natural logarithm function and is built into most calculators. It is defined such that if $y = \ln x$ then $x = e^y$.

Example A.1

Consider an interest rate that is quoted as 10% per annum with semiannual compounding. From equation (A.3), with $m = 2$ and $R_m = 0.1$, the equivalent rate with continuous compounding is

$$2 \ln\left(1 + \frac{0.1}{2}\right) = 0.09758$$

or 9.758% per annum.

Example A.2

Suppose that a lender quotes the interest rate on loans as 8% per annum with continuous compounding and that interest is actually paid quarterly. From equation (A.4), with $m = 4$ and $R_c = 0.08$, the equivalent rate with quarterly compounding is

$$4(e^{0.08/4} - 1) = 0.0808$$

or 8.08% per annum. This means that on a $1,000 loan, interest payments of $20.20 would be required each quarter.

Zero Rates, Forward Rates, and Zero-Coupon Yield Curves

The n-year zero-coupon interest rate is the rate of interest earned on an investment that starts today and lasts for n years. All the interest and principal is realized at the end of n years. There are no intermediate payments. The n-year zero-coupon interest rate is sometimes also referred to as the n-year *spot rate*, the n-year *zero rate*, or just the n-year *zero*. The zero rate as a function of maturity is referred to as the *zero curve*. Suppose that a five-year zero rate with continuous compounding is quoted as 5% per annum. (See Appendix A for a discussion of compounding frequencies.) This means that $100, if invested for five years, grows to

$$100 \times e^{0.05 \times 5} = 128.40$$

A forward rate is the future zero rate implied by today's zero rates. Consider the zero rates shown in Table B.1. The forward rate for the period between six months and one year is 6.6%. This is because 5% for the first six months combined with 6.6% for the next six months gives an average of 5.8% for the two years. Similarly the forward rate for the period between 12 months and 18 months is 7.6%, because this rate when combined with 5.8% for the first 12 months gives and average of 6.4% for the 18 months. In general, the forward rate F for the period between times T_1 and T_2 is

$$F = \frac{R_2 T_2 - R_1 T_1}{T_2 - T_1} \tag{B.1}$$

Table B.1 Zero rates.

Maturity (years)	Zero rate (% cont. comp.)
0.5	5.0
1.0	5.8
1.5	6.4
2.0	6.8

Table B.2 Forward rates for zero rates in
Table B.1.

Period (years)	Forward rate (% cont. comp.)
0.5 to 1.0	6.6
1.0 to 1.5	7.6
1.5 to 2.0	8.0

where R_1 is the zero rate for maturity of T_1 and R_2 is the zero rate for maturity T_2. This formula is exactly true when rates are measured with continuous compounding and approximately true for other compounding frequencies. The results from using this formula on the rates in Table B.1 are in Table B.2. For example, substituting $T_1 = 1.5$, $T_2 = 2.0$, $R_1 = 0.064$, and $R_2 = 0.068$ gives $F = 0.08$ showing that the forward rate for the period between 18 months and 24 months is 8.0%.

Investors who think that future interest rates will be markedly different from forward rates have no difficulty in finding trades that reflect their beliefs. Consider an investor who can borrow or lend at the rates in Table B.1. Suppose the investor thinks that the six-month interest rates will not change much over the next two years. The investor can borrow six-month funds and invest for two years. The six-month borrowings can be rolled over at the end of 6, 12, and 18 months. If interest rates do stay about the same, this strategy will yield a profit of about 1.8% per year because interest will be received at 6.8% and paid at 5%. This type of trading strategy is known as a *yield curve play*. The investor is speculating that rates in the future will be quite different from the forward rates shown in Table B.2.

Robert Citron, the Treasurer at Orange County, used yield curve plays similar the one we have just described very successfully in 1992 and 1993. The profit from Mr. Citron's trades became an important contributor to Orange County's budget and he was re-elected. In 1994, he used the same strategy more aggressively. If short-term interest rates had remained the same or declined, he would have done very well. As it happened, interest rates rose sharply during 1994. On December 1, 1994, Orange County announced that its investment portfolio had lost $1.5 billion and several days later it filed for bankruptcy protection.

Bond Pricing

Most bonds provide coupons periodically. The bond's principal (which is also known as its par value or face value) is received at the end of its life. The theoretical price of a bond can be calculated as the present value of all the cash flows that will be received by the owner of the bond. The most accurate approach is to use a different zero rate for each cash flow. To illustrate this, consider the situation where zero rates are as in Table A.1. Suppose that a two-year bond with a principal of $100 provides coupons at the rate of 6% per annum semiannually. To calculate the present value of the first coupon of $3, we discount it at 5.0% for six months; to calculate the present value of the second coupon of $3, we discount it at 5.8% for one year; and so on. The theoretical price of the bond is therefore

$$3e^{-0.05\times0.5} + 3e^{-0.058\times1.0} + 3e^{-0.064\times1.5} + 103e^{-0.068\times2.0} = 98.39$$

or \$98.39.

Bond Yields

A bond's yield is the discount rate that, when applied to all cash flows, gives a bond price equal to its market price. Suppose that the theoretical price of the bond we have been considering, \$98.39, is also its market price (i.e., the market's price of the bond is in exact agreement with the data in Table A.1). If y is the yield on the bond, expressed with continuous compounding, we have

$$3e^{-y\times0.5} + 3e^{-y\times1.0} + 3e^{-y\times1.5} + 103e^{-y\times2.0} = 98.39$$

This equation can be solved using Excel's Solver or in some other way to give $y = 6.76\%$.

Treasury Rates

Treasury rates are the rates an investor earns on Treasury bills and Treasury bonds. These are the instruments used by a government to borrow in its own currency. Japanese Treasury rates are the rates at which the Japanese government borrows in yen, US Treasury rates are the rates at which the US government borrows in US dollars, and so on. It is usually assumed that there is no chance that a government will default on an obligation denominated in its own currency.[1] Treasury rates are therefore totally risk-free in the sense that an investor who buys a Treasury bill or Treasury bond is certain that interest and principal payments will be made as promised.

Determining Treasury Zero Rates

One way of determining Treasury zero rates such as those in Table B.1 is to observe the yields on "strips". These are zero-coupon bonds that are artificially created by traders when they sell the coupons on a Treasury bond separately from the principal.

Table B.3 Rates in Table B.1 after 2.5-year rate has been determined using the bootstrap method.

Maturity (years)	Zero rate (% cont. comp.)
0.5	5.00
1.0	5.80
1.5	6.40
2.0	6.80
2.5	7.05

[1] The reason for this is that the government can always meet its obligation by printing more money.

Figure B.1 Zero curve for data in Table B.3.

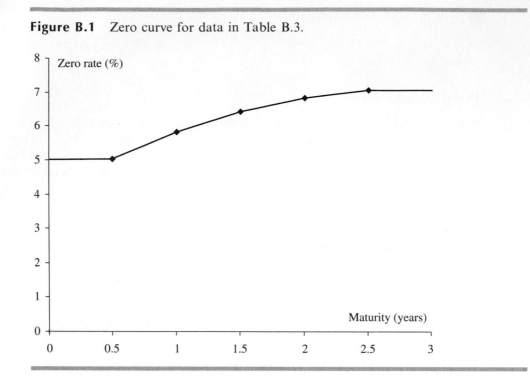

Another way of determining Treasury zero rates is from regular Treasury bills and bonds. The most popular approach is known as the *bootstrap method*. This involves working from short maturities to successively longer maturities matching prices. Suppose that Table B.1 gives the Treasury rates determined so far and that a 2.5-year bond providing a coupon of 8% sells for $102 per $100 of principal. We would determine the 2.5-year zero-coupon interest rate as the rate which, when used in conjunction with the rates in Table B.1, gives the correct price for this bond. This involves solving

$$4e^{-0.05 \times 0.5} + 4e^{-0.058 \times 1.0} + 4e^{-0.064 \times 1.5} + 4e^{-0.068 \times 2.0} + 104e^{-R \times 2.5} = 102$$

which gives $R = 7.05\%$. The complete set of zero rates is shown in Table B.3. The zero curve is usually assumed to be linear between the points that are determined by the bootstrap method. (In our example the 2.25-year zero rate would be 6.9025%.) It is also assumed to be constant prior to the first point and beyond the last point. The zero curve for our example is shown in Figure B.1.

LIBOR/Swap Rates

The LIBOR/swap zero curve is determined using a similar bootstrap method to that used for determining the Treasury zero curve. LIBOR deposit rates define the zero curve out to a maturity of one year. Eurodollar futures quotes are sometimes used for the next two or three years of maturities. Swap rates are used after that. The *n*-year swap rate is the yield on an *n*-year bond that sells for par.

APPENDIX C

Valuing Forward and Futures Contracts

The forward or futures price of an investment asset that provides no income is given by

$$S_0 e^{rT}$$

where S_0 is the spot price of the asset today, T is the time to maturity of the forward or futures contract, and r is the continuously compounded risk-free rate for maturity T. When the asset provides income during the life of the contract that has a present value I, this becomes

$$(S_0 - I)e^{rT}$$

When it provides a yield at rate q, it becomes

$$S_0 e^{(r-q)T}$$

A foreign currency can be regarded as an investment asset that provides a yield equal to the foreign risk-free rate, so that the forward or futures price for a foreign currency is

$$S_0 e^{(r-r_f)T}$$

where r_f is the foreign risk-free rate (continuously compounded) and S_0 is the spot exchange rate.

The value of a forward contract where the holder has the right to buy the asset for a price of K is, in all cases,

$$(F - K)e^{-rT}$$

where F is the forward price. The value of a forward contract where the holder has the right to sell the asset for a price of K is similarly

$$(K - F)e^{-rT}$$

Example C.1

Consider a six-month futures contract on the S&P 500. The current value of the index is 1200, the six-month risk-free rate is 5% per annum, and the average dividend yield on the S&P 500 over the next six months is expected to be 2% per annum (both rates continuously compounded). The futures price is $1,200e^{(0.05-0.02)\times 0.5}$, or 1,218.14.

459

Example C.2

The current forward price of gold for a contract maturing in nine months is $550. A company has a forward contract to buy 1,000 ounces of gold for a delivery price of $530 in nine months. The nine-month risk-free rate is 4% per annum continuously compounded. The value of the forward contract is $1,000 \times (550 - 530)e^{-0.04 \times 9/12}$, or $19,409.

Valuing Swaps

APPENDIX D

An interest rate swap can be valued by assuming that the interest rates that are realized in the future equal today's forward interest rates. As an example, consider an interest rate swap that has 14 months remaining and a notional principal of $100 million. A fixed rate of 5% per annum is received and LIBOR is paid, with exchanges taking place every six months. Assume that (a) four months ago the six-month LIBOR rate was 4%, (b) the forward LIBOR interest rate for a six-month period starting in two months is 4.6%, and (c) the forward LIBOR for a six-month period starting in eight months is 5.2%. All rates are expressed with semiannual compounding. Assuming that forward rates are realized, the cash flows on the swap are as shown in Table D.1. (For example, in eight months the fixed-rate cash flow received is $0.5 \times 0.05 \times 100$, or $2.5 million; the floating-rate cash flow paid is $0.5 \times 0.046 \times 100$, or $2.3 million.) The value of the swap is the present value of the net cash flows in the final column.[1]

An alternative approach (which gives the same valuation) is to assume that the swap principal of $100 million is paid and received at the end of the life of the swap. This makes no difference to the value of the swap but allows it to be regarded as the exchange of interest and principal on a fixed-rate bond for interest and principal on a floating-rate bond. The fixed-rate bond's cash flows can be valued in the usual way. A general rule is that the floating-rate bond is always worth an amount equal to the principal immediately after an interest payment. In our example, the value of the floating-rate bond is worth $100 million immediately after the payment in two months.

Table D.1 Valuing an interest rate swap by assuming forward rates are realized.

Time	Fixed cash flow ($ million)	Floating cash flow ($ million)	Net cash flow ($ million)
2 months	2.5	−2.0	0.5
8 months	2.5	−2.3	0.2
14 months	2.5	−2.6	−0.1

[1] Note that this is not perfectly accurate because it does not take account of day count conventions and holiday calendars.

461

Table D.2   Valuing a currency swap by assuming forward exchange rates are realized. (All cash flows in millions.)

Time	USD cash flow	GBP cash flow	Forward exchange rate	USD value of GBP cash flow	Net cash flow in USD
1	−0.6	0.2	1.8000	0.360	−0.240
2	−0.6	0.2	1.8400	0.368	−0.232
3	−0.6	0.2	1.8800	0.376	−0.224
3	−10.0	5.0	1.8800	9.400	−0.600

This payment (determined four months ago) is $2 million. The value of the floating-rate bond is therefore $102 million immediately before the payment at the two-month point. The value of the swap is therefore the present value of the fixed-rate bond less the present value of a cash flow of $102 million in two months.

Currency Swaps

A currency swap can be valued by assuming that exchange rates in the future equal today's forward exchange rates. As an example, consider a currency swap in which 4% will be received in GBP and 6% will be paid in USD once a year. The principals in the two currencies are 10 million USD and 5 million GBP. The swap will last for another three years. The swap cash flows are shown in the second and third columns of Table D.2. The forward exchange rates are (we assume) those shown in the fourth column. These are used to convert the GBP cash flows to USD. The final column shows the net cash flows. The value of the swap is the present value of these cash flows.

An alternative approach (which gives the same valuation) is to regard the swap as a long position in a GBP bond and a short position in a USD bond. Each bond can be valued in its own currency in the usual way and the current exchange rate can be used to convert the value of the GBP bond from GBP to USD.

Valuing European Options

The Black–Scholes–Merton formulas for valuing European call and put options on an investment asset that provides no income are

$$c = S_0 N(d_1) - K e^{-rT} N(d_2)$$

and

$$p = K e^{-rT} N(-d_2) - S_0 N(-d_1)$$

where

$$d_1 = \frac{\ln(S_0/K) + (r + \sigma^2/2)T}{\sigma\sqrt{T}}$$

$$d_2 = \frac{\ln(S_0/K) + (r - \sigma^2/2)T}{\sigma\sqrt{T}} = d_1 - \sigma\sqrt{T}$$

The function $N(x)$ is the cumulative probability distribution function for a standardized normal distribution (see the tables at the end of the book). The variables c and p are the European call and European put price, S_0 is the stock price at time zero, K is the strike price, r is the continuously compounded risk-free rate, σ is the stock price volatility, and T is the time to maturity of the option.

When the underlying asset provides a cash income, the present value of the income during the life of the option should be subtracted from S_0. When the underlying asset provides a yield at rate q, the formulas become

$$c = S_0 e^{-qT} N(d_1) - K e^{-rT} N(d_2)$$

and

$$p = K e^{-rT} N(-d_2) - S_0 e^{-qT} N(-d_1)$$

where

$$d_1 = \frac{\ln(S_0/K) + (r - q + \sigma^2/2)T}{\sigma\sqrt{T}}$$

$$d_2 = \frac{\ln(S_0/K) + (r - q - \sigma^2/2)T}{\sigma\sqrt{T}} = d_1 - \sigma\sqrt{T}$$

Options on a foreign currency can be valued by setting q equal to the foreign risk-free rate.

Table E.1 Greek letters for options on an asset that provides a yield at rate q.

Greek letter	Call option	Put option
Delta	$e^{-qT}N(d_1)$	$e^{-qT}[N(d_1) - 1]$
Gamma	$\dfrac{N'(d_1)e^{-qT}}{S_0\sigma\sqrt{T}}$	$\dfrac{N'(d_1)e^{-qT}}{S_0\sigma\sqrt{T}}$
Theta (per year)	$-S_0N'(d_1)\sigma e^{-qT}/(2\sqrt{T})$ $+qS_0N(d_1)e^{-qT}$ $-rKe^{-rT}N(d_2)$	$-S_0N'(d_1)\sigma e^{-qT}/(2\sqrt{T})$ $-qS_0N(-d_1)e^{-qT}$ $+rKe^{-rT}N(-d_2)$
Vega (per %)	$\dfrac{S_0\sqrt{T}\,N'(d_1)e^{-qT}}{100}$	$\dfrac{S_0\sqrt{T}\,N'(d_1)e^{-qT}}{100}$
Rho (per %)	$\dfrac{KTe^{-rT}N(d_2)}{100}$	$-\dfrac{KTe^{-rT}N(-d_2)}{100}$

Table E.1 gives formulas for the Greek letters. $N'(x)$ is the standard normal density function:

$$N'(x) = \frac{1}{\sqrt{2\pi}}e^{-x^2/2}$$

Example E.1

Consider a six-month European call option on a stock index. The current value of the index is 1,200, the strike price is 1,250, the risk-free rate is 5%, the dividend yield on the index is 2%, and the index volatility is 20%. In this case, $S_0 = 1,200$, $K = 1,250$, $r = 0.05$, $q = 0.02$, $\sigma = 0.2$, and $T = 0.5$. The value of the option is 53.44, the delta of the option is 0.45, the gamma is 0.0023, the theta is -0.22, the vega is 3.33, and rho is 2.44. Note that the formula in Table E.1 gives theta per year. The theta quoted here is per calendar day.

The calculations in this appendix can be done with the DerivaGem software by selecting Option Type: Analytic European. Option valuation is described more fully in Hull (2009).[1]

---

[1] See J.C. Hull, *Options, Futures, and Other Derivatives*, 7th edn. Pearson, 2009.

Valuing American Options

To value American-style options, we divide the life of the option into n time steps of length Δt. Suppose that the asset price at the beginning of a step is S. At the end of the time step, it moves up to Su with probability p and down to Sd with probability $1 - p$. For an investment asset that provides no income, the values of u, d, and p are given by

$$u = e^{\sigma\sqrt{\Delta t}}, \quad d = \frac{1}{u}, \quad p = \frac{a - d}{u - d}$$

with

$$a = e^{r\Delta t}$$

Figure F.1 shows the tree constructed for valuing a five-month American put option on a non-dividend-paying stock, where the initial stock price is 50, the strike price is 50, the risk-free rate is 10%, and the volatility is 40%. In this case there are five steps, so that $\Delta t = 0.08333$, $u = 1.1224$, $d = 0.8909$, $a = 1.0084$, and $p = 0.5073$. The upper number at each node is the stock price and the lower number is the value of the option.

At the final nodes of the tree, the option price is its intrinsic value. For example, at node G the option price is $50 - 35.36 = 14.64$. At earlier nodes, we first calculate a value assuming that the option is held for a further time period of length Δt and then check to see whether early exercise is optimal. Consider first node E. If the option is held for a further time period, it will be worth 0.00 if there is an up move (probability: p) and 5.45 if there is a down move (probability: $1 - p$). The expected value in time Δt is therefore $0.5073 \times 0 + 0.4927 \times 5.45$, or 2.686, and the 2.66 value at node E is calculated by discounting this at the risk-free rate of 10% for one month. The option should not be exercised at node E as the payoff from early exercise would be zero. Consider next node A. A calculation similar to that just given shows that, assuming it is held for a further time period, the option's value at node A is 9.90. If exercised, its value is $50 - 39.69 = 10.31$. In this case, it should be exercised and the value of being at node A is 10.31.

Continuing to work back from the end of the tree to the beginning, the value of the option at the initial node D is found to be 4.49. As the number of steps on the tree is increased, the accuracy of the option price increases. With 30, 50, and 100 time steps we get values for the option of 4.263, 4.272, and 4.278.

To calculate delta, we consider the two nodes at time Δt. In our example, as we move from the lower node to the upper node, the option price changes from 6.96 to 2.16 and

Figure F.1   Binomial tree from DerivaGem for an American put on a non-dividend-paying stock.

At each node:
 Upper value = Underlying Asset Price
 Lower value = Option Price
Shading indicates where option is exercised

Strike price = 50
Discount factor per step = 0.9917
Time step, dt = 0.0833 years, 30.42 days
Growth factor per step, a = 1.0084
Probability of up move, p = 0.5073
Up step size, u = 1.1224
Down step size, d = 0.8909

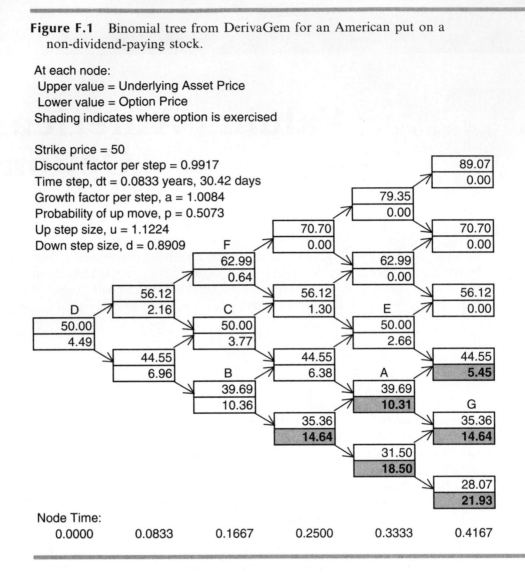

Node Time:
   0.0000   0.0833   0.1667   0.2500   0.3333   0.4167

the stock price changes from 44.55 to 56.12. The estimate of delta is the change in the option price divided by the change in the stock price:

$$\text{Delta} = \frac{2.16 - 6.96}{56.12 - 44.55} = -0.41$$

To calculate gamma, we consider the three nodes at time $2\Delta t$. The delta calculated from the upper two nodes (C and F) is −0.241. This can be regarded as the delta for a stock price of $(62.99 + 50)/2 = 56.49$. The delta calculated from the lower two nodes (B and C) is −0.639. This can be regarded as the delta for a stock price of $\frac{1}{2}(50 + 39.69) = 44.84$. The estimate of gamma is the change in delta divided by the change in the stock price:

$$\text{Gamma} = \frac{-0.241 - (-0.639)}{56.49 - 44.84} = 0.034$$

We estimate theta from nodes D and C as

$$\text{Theta} = \frac{3.77 - 4.49}{2 \times 0.08333}$$

or −4.30 per year. This is −0.0118 per calendar day. Vega is estimated by increasing the volatility, constructing a new tree and observing the effect of the increased volatility on the option price. Rho is calculated similarly.

When the asset underlying the option provides a yield at rate q, the procedure is exactly the same except that $a = e^{(r-q)\Delta t}$ instead of $e^{r\Delta t}$ in the equation for p. The calculations we have described can be done using the DerivaGem software by selecting Option Type: Binomial American. Binomial trees and other numerical procedures are described more fully in Hull (2009).[1]

---

[1] See J.C. Hull, *Options, Futures, and Other Derivatives*, 7th edn. Pearson, 2009.

APPENDIX G

Taylor Series Expansions

Consider a function $z = F(x)$. When a small change Δx is made to x, there is a corresponding small change Δz in z. A first approximation to the relationship between Δz and Δx is

$$\Delta z = \frac{dz}{dx}\Delta x \tag{G.1}$$

This relationship is exact if z is a linear function of x and approximate in other situations. A more accurate approximation is

$$\Delta z = \frac{dz}{dx}\Delta x + \tfrac{1}{2}\frac{d^2 z}{dx^2}(\Delta x)^2 \tag{G.2}$$

This relationship is exact if z is a quadratic function of x and approximate in other situations. By adding more terms in the series we can increase accuracy. The full expansion is

$$\Delta z = \frac{dz}{dx}\Delta x + \frac{1}{2!}\frac{d^2 z}{dx^2}(\Delta x)^2 + \frac{1}{3!}\frac{d^3 z}{dx^3}(\Delta x)^3 + \frac{1}{4!}\frac{d^4 z}{dx^4}(\Delta x)^4 + \cdots$$

Example G.1

Consider the function $z = \sqrt{x}$ so that

$$\frac{dz}{dx} = \frac{1}{2x^{1/2}}, \qquad \frac{d^2 z}{dx^2} = -\frac{1}{4x^{3/2}}, \qquad \frac{d^3 z}{dx^3} = \frac{3}{8x^{5/2}}$$

Suppose that $x = 2$ and $\Delta x = 0.1$, so that $\Delta z = \sqrt{2.1} - \sqrt{2} = 0.034924$. When $x = 2$,

$$\frac{dz}{dx} = 0.35355, \qquad \frac{d^2 z}{dx^2} = -0.08839, \qquad \frac{d^3 z}{dx^3} = 0.06629$$

The first-order approximation to Δz, given by equation (G.1), is

$$\Delta z = 0.35355 \times 0.1 = 0.035355$$

The second-order approximation, given by equation (G.2), is

$$\Delta z = 0.35355 \times 0.1 + \tfrac{1}{2} \times (-0.08839) \times 0.1^2 = 0.034913$$

The third-order approximation is

$$\Delta z = 0.35355 \times 0.1 + \tfrac{1}{2} \times (-0.08839) \times 0.1^2 + \tfrac{1}{6} \times 0.06629 \times 0.1^3$$

It can be seen that the series expansion quickly converges to the correct answer of 0.034924.

Functions of Two Variables

Consider next a function of two variables, $z = F(x, y)$. Suppose that Δx and Δy are small changes in x and y, respectively, and that Δz is the corresponding small change in z. In this case, the first-order approximation is

$$\Delta z = \frac{\partial z}{\partial x} \Delta x + \frac{\partial z}{\partial y} \Delta y \tag{G.3}$$

The second-order approximation is

$$\Delta z = \frac{\partial z}{\partial x} \Delta x + \frac{\partial z}{\partial y} \Delta y + \tfrac{1}{2} \frac{\partial^2 z}{\partial x^2} (\Delta x)^2 + \tfrac{1}{2} \frac{\partial^2 z}{\partial y^2} (\Delta y)^2 + \frac{\partial^2 z}{\partial x \partial y} (\Delta x \, \Delta y) \tag{G.4}$$

Example G.2

Consider the function $z = \sqrt{xy}$ so that

$$\frac{\partial z}{\partial x} = \frac{y^{1/2}}{2x^{1/2}}, \qquad \frac{\partial z}{\partial y} = \frac{x^{1/2}}{2y^{1/2}}$$

and

$$\frac{\partial^2 z}{\partial x^2} = -\frac{y^{1/2}}{4x^{3/2}}, \qquad \frac{\partial^2 z}{\partial y^2} = -\frac{x^{1/2}}{4y^{3/2}}, \qquad \frac{\partial^2 z}{\partial x \, \partial y} = \frac{1}{4(xy)^{1/2}}$$

Suppose that $x = 2$, $y = 1$, $\Delta x = 0.1$, and $\Delta y = 0.1$, so that

$$\Delta z = \sqrt{2.1 \times 1.1} - \sqrt{2 \times 1} = 0.10565$$

When $x = 2$ and $y = 1$,

$$\frac{\partial z}{\partial x} = 0.35355, \qquad \frac{\partial z}{\partial y} = 0.70711$$

and

$$\frac{\partial^2 z}{\partial x^2} = -0.08839, \qquad \frac{\partial^2 z}{\partial y^2} = -0.35355, \qquad \frac{\partial^2 z}{\partial x \partial y} = 0.17678$$

The first-order approximation to Δz, given by equation (G.3), is

$$\Delta z = 0.35355 \times 0.1 + 0.70711 \times 0.1 = 0.10607$$

The second-order approximation, given by equation (G.4), is

$$\Delta z = 0.35355 \times 0.1 + 0.70711 \times 0.1 + \tfrac{1}{2} \times (-0.08839) \times 0.1^2$$
$$+ \tfrac{1}{2} \times (-0.35355) \times 0.1^2 + 0.17678 \times 0.1 \times 0.1 = 0.10562$$

The series expansion is converging to the correct answer of 0.10565.

General Result

For a function z of n variables, $x_1, x_2, \ldots, x_n$, the Taylor series expansion of Δz is

$$\Delta z = \sum_{m_1=0}^{\infty} \cdots \sum_{m_n=0}^{\infty} \frac{1}{m_1! \cdots m_n!} \frac{\partial^m z}{\partial x_1^{m_1} \cdots \partial x_n^{m_n}} \Delta x_1^{m_1} \cdots \Delta x_m^{m_n}$$

where $m = m_1 + \cdots + m_n$ and the term where all the m_i are zero is zero.

APPENDIX **H**

Eigenvectors and Eigenvalues

Consider an $n \times n$ matrix A and suppose that x is an $n \times 1$ vector. Consider the equation

$$Ax = \lambda x \qquad \text{(H.1)}$$

The equation can be written

$$(A - \lambda I)x = 0$$

where I is the $n \times n$ identity matrix (which is the $n \times n$ matrix with diagonal elements equal to 1 and all other elements equal to zero). Clearly $x = 0$ is a solution to equation (H.1). Under what circumstances are there other solutions? A theorem in linear algebra tells us that there are other solutions when the determinant of $A - \lambda I$ is zero. The values of λ that lead to solutions of equation (H.1) are therefore the values of λ that we get when we solve the equation that sets the determinant of $A - \lambda I$ equal to zero. This equation is an nth-order polynomial in λ. In general, it has n solutions. The solutions are the *eigenvalues* of the matrix A. The vector x that solves equation (H.1) for a particular eigenvalue is an *eigenvector*. In general, there are n eigenvectors, one corresponding to each eigenvalue.

As a simple example, suppose that

$$A = \begin{bmatrix} 1 & -1 \\ 2 & 4 \end{bmatrix}$$

In this case,

$$A - \lambda I = \begin{bmatrix} 1 - \lambda & -1 \\ 2 & 4 - \lambda \end{bmatrix}$$

The determinant of this matrix is

$$(1 - \lambda)(4 - \lambda) - (-1) \times 2 = \lambda^2 - 5\lambda + 6$$

The solutions to this equation are $\lambda = 3$ and $\lambda = 2$. These are the two eigenvalues of the matrix.

To determine the eigenvectors corresponding to $\lambda = 3$, we solve equation (G.1):

$$\begin{bmatrix} 1 & -1 \\ 2 & 4 \end{bmatrix} x = 3x$$

473

Setting

$$x = \begin{bmatrix} x_1 \\ x_2 \end{bmatrix}$$

the equation to be solved becomes

$$\begin{bmatrix} 1 & -1 \\ 2 & 4 \end{bmatrix} \begin{bmatrix} x_1 \\ x_2 \end{bmatrix} = 3 \begin{bmatrix} x_1 \\ x_2 \end{bmatrix}$$

The simultaneous equations corresponding to this are

$$x_1 - x_2 = 3x_1$$

and

$$2x_1 + 4x_2 = 3x_2$$

Both these equations are equivalent to

$$x_2 + 2x_1 = 0$$

It follows that any pair of numbers x_1 and x_2 solve the equation when $\lambda = 3$, provided that $x_2 = -2x_1$. By convention, the values of x_1 and x_2 that are reported are those for which the length of the vector x is 1. This means that $x_1^2 + x_2^2 = 1$. In this case, the solution where x has a length of 1 is $x_1 = \sqrt{0.2} = 0.447$ and $x_2 = -2\sqrt{0.2} = -0.894$. (An alternative is $x_1 = -0.447$ and $x_2 = 0.894$.) The solution

$$x = \begin{bmatrix} 0.447 \\ -0.894 \end{bmatrix}$$

is the eigenvector corresponding to the first eigenvalue ($\lambda = 3$).

A similar calculation shows that equation (H.1) is satisfied for $\lambda = 2$ when $x_1 + x_2 = 0$. The solution where x has a length of 1 is $x_1 = \sqrt{0.5} = 0.707$ and $x_2 = -\sqrt{0.5} = -0.707$. (An alternative is $x_1 = -0.707$ and $x_2 = 0.707$.) The eigenvector corresponding to the second eigenvalue ($\lambda = 2$) is therefore

$$x = \begin{bmatrix} 0.707 \\ -0.707 \end{bmatrix}$$

For matrices of larger size, a numerical procedure must be used to determine eigenvectors and eigenvalues. One such numerical procedure is provided by Press et al.[1]

Applications of eigenvalues and eigenvectors are in Appendices I and J.

---

[1] See W. H. Press, S. A. Teukolsky, W. T. Vetterling, and B. P. Flannery, *Numerical Recipes: The Art of Scientific Computing*, 3rd edn. Cambridge University Press, 2007.

Principal Components Analysis

A principal components analysis is concerned with understanding the structure of data on n correlated variables. The aim of the analysis is to replace the n variables by a smaller number of uncorrelated variables. In the example in Section 7.8, there are ten variables. These are the daily changes in the 3-month, 6-month, 12-month, 2-year, 3-year, 4-year, 5-year, 7-year, 10-year, and 30-year rates.

The first step in the analysis to collect data on the n variables and calculate the mean of each variable. The mean of a variable is then subtracted from the data on the variable. The result is data on n variables where the mean of each variable is zero. We will refer to these as the *adjusted data*.

The next step is to calculate a covariance matrix from the adjusted data. As explained in Section 13.3, this is an $n \times n$ matrix where the (i, j) entry is the covariance between the adjusted data for variable i and the adjusted data for variable j. The entries on the diagonal (where $i = j$) are variances.

The next step is to calculate the eigenvalues and eigenvectors for this matrix (see Appendix H). The eigenvectors are chosen to have length 1. (As explained in Appendix H, this means that the sum of the squares of their elements is 1.) The eigenvector corresponding the highest eigenvalue is the first principal component, the eigenvector corresponding the second highest eigenvalue is the second principal component, and so on. The principal components for the example in Section 7.8 are shown in Table 7.7.

The eigenvalue for the ith principal component, as a percentage of the sum of all the eigenvalues, is the percentage of the overall variance explained by the ith principal component. The percentages of the variance explained by the principal components for the example in Section 7.8 are shown in Table 7.8.

APPENDIX

Manipulation of Credit Transition Matrices

J

Suppose that A is an $N \times N$ matrix of credit rating changes in one year. This is a matrix such as the one shown in Table 15.1. The matrix of credit rating changes in m years is A^m. This can be readily calculated using the normal rules for matrix multiplication.

The matrix corresponding to a period shorter than one year, say six months or one month, is more difficult to compute. We first calculate eigenvectors $x_1, x_2, \ldots, x_N$ and the corresponding eigenvalues $\lambda_1, \lambda_2, \ldots, \lambda_N$ of the matrix A. These are explained in Appendix H. They have the property that

$$Ax_i = \lambda_i x_i \qquad \text{(J.1)}$$

Define X as a matrix whose ith column is x_i, and Λ as a diagonal matrix where the ith diagonal element is λ_i. From equation (J.1), we have

$$AX = X\Lambda$$

so that

$$A = X\Lambda X^{-1}$$

Define Λ^* as a diagonal matrix where the ith diagonal element is $\lambda_i^{1/n}$. Then

$$(X\Lambda^* X^{-1})^n = (X\Lambda^* X^{-1})(X\Lambda^* X^{-1})(X\Lambda^* X^{-1}) \cdots (X\Lambda^* X^{-1}) = X(\Lambda^*)^n X^{-1} = X\Lambda X^{-1} = A$$

showing that the nth root of A is $X\Lambda^* X^{-1}$.

Some authors, such as Jarrow, Lando, and Turnbull, prefer to handle this problem in terms of what is called a *generator matrix*.[1] This is a matrix Γ such that the transition matrix for a short period of time, Δt, is $I + \Gamma \Delta t$ and the transition matrix for a longer period of time, t, is

$$\exp(t\Gamma) = \sum_{k=0}^{\infty} \frac{(t\Gamma)^k}{k!}$$

where I is the $N \times N$ identity matrix (with ones on the diagonal and zeros elsewhere).

---

[1] See R. A. Jarrow, D. Lando, and S. M. Turnbull, "A Markov Model for the Term Structure of Credit Spreads," *Review of Financial Studies*, 10 (1997): 481–523.

Answers to Practice Questions and Problems

CHAPTER 1

1.1. The expected return is 12.5%. The standard deviation of returns is 17.07%.

1.2. From equations (1.1) and (1.2), the expected return is 12.5%. SD of return is

$$\sqrt{0.5^2 \times 0.1707^2 + 0.5^2 \times 0.1707^2 + 2 \times 0.15 \times 0.5^2 \times 0.1707^2} = 0.1294$$

or 12.94%.

1.3.

w_1	w_2	μ_P	$\sigma_P\ (\rho = 0.3)$	$\sigma_P\ (\rho = 1)$	$\sigma_P\ (\rho = -1)$
0.0	1.0	15%	24.00%	24.00%	24.00%
0.2	0.8	14%	20.39%	22.40%	16.00%
0.4	0.6	13%	17.42%	20.80%	8.00%
0.6	0.4	12%	15.48%	19.20%	0.00%
0.8	0.2	11%	14.96%	17.60%	8.00%
1.0	0.0	10%	16.00%	16.00%	16.00%

1.4. Nonsystematic risk can be diversified; systematic risk cannot. Systematic risk is most important to an equity investor. Either type of risk can lead to the bankruptcy of a corporation.

1.5. We assume that investors trade off mean return and standard deviation of return. For a given mean return, they want to minimize standard deviation of returns. All make the same estimates of means, standard deviations, and coefficients of correlation for returns on individual investments. Furthermore, they can borrow or lend at the risk-free rate. The result is that they all want to be on the "new efficient frontier" in Figure 1.4. They choose the same portfolio of risky investments combined with borrowing or lending at the risk-free rate.

1.6. (a) 7.2%; (b) 9%; (c) 14.4%.

1.7. The capital asset pricing theory assumes that there is one factor driving returns. Arbitrage pricing theory assumes multiple factors.

1.8. In many jurisdictions, interest on debt is deductible to the corporation whereas dividends are not deductible. It can therefore more tax-efficient for a company to fund itself with debt. However, as debt increases the probability of bankruptcy increases.

1.9. Risk decomposition refers to a procedure where risks are handled one by one. Risk aggregation refers to a procedure where a portfolio of risks is considered. Risk decomposition requires an in-depth understanding of individual risks. Risk aggregation requires an understanding of the correlations between risks.

1.10. When potential losses are large, we cannot aggregate them and assume that they will be diversified away. It is necessary to consider them one by one and handle them with insurance contracts, tighter internal controls, etc.

1.11. This is the probability that profit is no worse than -4% of assets. This profit level is $4.6/1.5 = 3.067$ standard deviations from the mean. The probability that the bank will have a positive equity is therefore $N(3.067)$, where N is the cumulative normal distribution function. This is 99.89%.

1.12. Banks are allowed to accept deposits from the general public. Companies in retailing and manufacturing are not.

1.13. Professional fees ($10 million per month), lost sales (people are reluctant to do business with a company that is being reorganized), and loss of key senior executives (lack of continuity).

1.14. The return earned by the hedge fund manager with zero alpha would be $0.05 + 0.6 \times (0.10 - 0.05) = 0.08$, or 8%. Because the alpha equals 4%, the hedge fund manager's return was 8% plus 4%, or 12%.

CHAPTER 2

2.1. The banking system became more concentrated, with large banks having a bigger share of the market. The total number of banks declined from 14,483 to 7,450.

2.2. In the early twentieth century, many states passed laws restricting banks from opening more than one branch. The McFadden Act of 1927 restricted banks from opening branches in more than one state.

2.3. The risk is that interest rates will rise, so that, when deposits are renewed, the bank has to pay a higher rate of interest. The rate received on loans will not change. The result will be a reduction in the bank's net interest margin.

2.4. DLC's loss is more than its equity capital and it would probably be liquidated. The subordinated long-term debt holders would incur losses on their $5 million investment. The depositors should get their money back.

2.5. The net interest income of a bank is interest received minus interest paid.

2.6. Credit risk primarily affects loan losses. Noninterest income includes trading gains and losses. Market risk therefore affects noninterest income. It also affects net interest income if assets and liabilities are not matched. Operational risk primarily affects noninterest expense.

2.7. A private placement is a new issue of securities that is sold to a small number of large institutional investors. A public offering is a new issue of securities that is offered to the general public. In a best-efforts deal, the investment bank does as well as it can to place securities with investors, but does not guarantee that they can be sold. In a firm commitment, the investment bank agrees to buy the securities from the issuing company for a particular price and attempts to sell them in the market for a higher price.

2.8. The bidders when ranked from the highest bid to the lowest are: H, C, F, A, B, D, E, G. Bidders H, C, and F have bid for 140,000 shares. A has bid for 20,000. The price that clears the market is the price that was bid by A, or $100. H, C, and F get their orders filled at this price. Half of A's order is filled at this price.

2.9. A Dutch auction potentially attracts a wide range of bidders. If all interested market participants bid, the price paid should be close to the market price immediately after the IPO. The usual IPO situation where the price turns out to be well below the market price should therefore be avoided. Also, investment banks are not able to restrict purchasers to their best current and potential clients. The Google IPO was different from a standard Dutch auction in that Google reserved the right to choose the number of shares that would be issued, and the percentage allocated to each bidder, when it saw the bids.

2.10. Poison pills can give management a negotiation tool, particularly if the board has the right to overturn a poison pill or make it ineffective. When it is confronted with a potential acquirer, the poison pill can buy the company time to bargain for a better purchase price or find other bidders. However, there is the danger that the poison pill will discourage potential buyers from approaching the company in the first place.

2.11. The brokerage subsidiary of a bank might recommend securities that the investment banking subsidiary is trying to sell. The commercial banking subsidiary might pass confidential information about its clients to the investment banking subsidiary. When a bank does business with a company (or wants to do business with the company), it might persuade the brokerage subsidiary to recommend the company's shares as a "buy". The commercial banking subsidiary might persuade a company to which it has lent money to do a bond issue because it is worried about its exposure to the client. (It wants the investment banking subsidiary persuade its clients to take on the credit risk.) These conflicts of interest are handled by what are known as Chinese walls. They prevent the flow of information from one part of the bank to another.

2.12. The interest is no longer accrued. The before-tax income will be reduced by 8% of $10 million or $800,000 per year.

2.13. The provision for loan losses reflects the losses the bank expects in the future It is updated periodically. When the provision is increased in a year by X, there is a charge to the income statement of X. Actual loan losses, when they are recognized, are charged against the balance in the loan loss provision account.

2.14. In the originate-to-distribute model, a bank originates loans and then securitizes them so that they are passed on to investors. This was done extensively with household mortgages during the seven-year period leading up to July 2007. In July 2007, investors lost confidence in the securitized products and banks were force to abandon the originate-to-distribute model, at least temporarily.

CHAPTER 3

3.1. Term life insurance lasts a fixed period (e.g., five years or ten years). The policyholder pays premiums. If the policyholder dies during the life of the policy, the policyholder's beneficiaries receive a payoff equal to the principal amount of the policy. Whole life insurance lasts for the whole life of the policyholder. The policyholder pays premiums (usually the same each year), and the policyholder's beneficiaries receive a payoff equal to the principal amount of the policy when the policyholder dies. There is an investment element to whole life insurance because the premiums in early years are high relative to the expected payoff in those years. (The reverse is true in later years.) Tax on the investment income is deferred until death.

3.2. Variable life insurance is whole life insurance where the policyholder can specify how the funds generated in early years (the excess of the premiums over the actuarial cost of the insurance) are invested. There is a minimum payoff on death, but the payoff can be more than the minimum if the investments do well. Universal life insurance is whole life insurance where the premium can be reduced to a specified minimum level without the policy lapsing. The insurance company chooses the investments (generally fixed income) and guarantees a minimum return. If the investments do well, the return provided on the policyholder's death may be greater than the guaranteed minimum.

3.3. Annuity contracts have exposure to longevity risk. Life insurance contracts have exposure to mortality risk.

3.4. The lifetime annuity created from an accumulated value was calculated using an interest rate that was the greater of (a) the market interest rate and (b) a prespecified minimum interest rate.

3.5. The probability that the woman will die during the first year is 0.003198. The probability that she will die during the second year is $0.003431 \times (1 - 0.003198) = 0.003420$. Suppose that the break-even premium is X. We must have

$$1,000,000 \times (0.003198 + 0.03420) = X + (1 - 0.003198)X$$

so that $X = 3,314.31$. The break-even premium is therefore \$3,314.31.

3.6. The probability of a male surviving to 30 is 0.97146. The probability of a male surviving to 90 is 0.13988. The probability of male surviving to 90 conditional on 30 being reached is therefore $0.13988/0.97146 = 0.14399$. The probability of a female surviving to 90 conditional on 30 being reached is $0.25660/0.98442 = 0.26066$.

3.7. The biggest risks are those arising from catastrophes such as earthquakes and hurricanes and those arising from liability insurance (e.g., claims related to asbestos in the US). This is because there is no "law of large numbers" working in the insurance company's favor. Either the event happens and there are big payoffs or the event does not happen and there are no payoffs.

3.8. CAT bonds (catastrophe bonds) are an alternative to reinsurance for an insurance company that has taken on a certain catastrophic risk (e.g., the risk of a hurricane or an earthquake) and wants to get rid of it. CAT bonds are issued by the insurance company. They provide a higher rate of interest than risk-free bonds. However, the bondholders agree to forgo interest, and possibly principal, to meet any claims against the insurance company that are within a prespecified range.

3.9. The CAT bond has very little systematic risk. Whether a particular type of catastrophe occurs is independent of the return on the market. The risks in the CAT bond are likely to be largely "diversified away" by the other investments in the portfolio. A B-rated bond does have systematic risk that cannot be diversified away. It is likely therefore that the CAT bond is a better addition to the portfolio.

3.10. In Canada and the United Kingdom, health care is provided by the government. In the United States, publicly funded health care is limited and most individuals buy private health-care insurance of one sort or another. In the United Kingdom, a private health-care system operates alongside the public system.

3.11. Both moral hazard and adverse selection are potential problems. The insurance might lead to an individual not trying to keep a job as much as he or she otherwise would. Indeed, an individual might purposely lose his or her job to collect the insurance payoff! Also, individuals that are most at risk for losing their jobs would be the ones that choose to buy the insurance.

3.12. The payoffs of property–casualty insurers show more variability than the payoffs of life insurers. This is because of the possibility of catastrophes such as earthquakes and hurricanes and liability insurance claims such as those related to asbestos in the United States.

3.13. The loss ratio is the ratio of payoffs to premiums in a year. The expense ratio is the ratio of expenses (e.g., sales commissions and expenses incurred in validating losses) to premiums in a year. The statement is not true, because investment income is usually significant. Premiums are received at the beginning of the year, and payoffs are made during the year or after the end of the year.

3.14. A defined contribution plan is a plan where the contributions of each employee (together with contributions made by the employer for that employee) are kept in a separate account and invested for the employee. When retirement age is reached, the accumulated amount is usually converted into an annuity. In a defined benefit plan, all contributions for all employees are pooled and invested. Employees receive a predefined pension that is based on their years of employment and final salary. At any given time, a defined benefit plan may be in surplus or in deficit.

3.15. The employee's wages are constant in real terms. Suppose that they are X per year. (The units for X do not matter for the purposes of our calculation.) The pension is $0.75X$. The real return earned is zero. Because employees work for 40 years, the present value of the contributions made by one employee is $40XR$, where R is the contribution rate as a percentage of the employee's wages. The present value of the benefits is $20 \times 0.75X = 15X$. The value of R that is necessary to adequately fund the plan must therefore satisfy

$$40XR = 15X$$

The solution to this equation is $R = 0.375$. The total of the employer and employee contributions should therefore be 37.5% of salary.

CHAPTER 4

4.1. The number of shares of an open-end mutual fund increases as investments in the fund increase and decreases as investors withdraw their funds. A closed-end fund is like any other corporation with a fixed number of shares that trade.

4.2. The NAV of an open-ended mutual fund is calculated at 4 p.m. each day as the value of the assets held by the fund divided by the number of shares outstanding.

4.3. The investor is deemed to have made capital gains of $300 and $100 in 2009 and 2010, respectively. In 2011, the investor is deemed to have made a capital loss of $200.

4.4. An index fund is a fund that is designed so that its value tracks the performance of an index such as the S&P 500. It can be created by buying all the stocks (or a representative subset of the stocks) that underly the index. Sometimes futures contracts on the index are used.

4.5. The front-end load is the amount an investor pays, as a percentage of his or her investment, when shares of the fund are purchased. The back-end load is the amount an investor pays, as a percentage of his or her investment, when shares of the fund are redeemed.

4.6. An exchange-traded fund (ETF) that tracks the S&P 500 is created when an institutional investor deposits a portfolio of shares that is designed to track the S&P 500 and receives shares in the ETF. Institutional investors can at any time exchange shares in the ETF for the underlying shares held by the ETF or deposit the portfolio of shares that is designed to track the S&P 500 and receive shares in the ETF. The advantage over an open-end mutual fund that tracks the S&P 500 is that the fund can be traded at any time, the fund can be shorted, and the fund does not have to be partially liquidated to accommodate redemptions. The advantage over a closed-end mutual fund is that there is very little difference between the ETF share price and the net asset value per share of the fund.

4.7. The arithmetic average, or mean, of a set of *n* numbers is the sum of the numbers divided by *n*. The geometric mean is the *n*th root of the product of the numbers. The arithmetic mean is always greater than or equal to the geometric mean. The return per year realized when an investment is held for several years is calculated using a geometric, not an arithmetic average. (The procedure is to calculate the geometric average of one plus the return in each year and then subtract one.)

4.8. Late trading is the illegal practice of putting in an order to buy or sell an open-end mutual fund at the 4 p.m. price after 4 p.m. Market timing is a practice where favored clients are allowed to buy and sell a mutual fund frequently to take advantage of the fact that some prices used in the calculation of the 4 p.m. net asset value are stale. Front running is the practice of trading by individuals ahead of a large institutional trade that is expected to move the market. Directional brokerage describes the situation where a mutual fund uses a brokerage house for trades when the brokerage house recommends the fund to clients.

4.9. Mutual funds must disclose their investment policies; their use of leverage is limited; they cannot take short positions; they cannot use derivatives.

4.10. If a hedge fund is making money out of trading convertible bonds, it must be doing so at the expense of its counterparties. If most of the traders are hedge funds, they cannot all be making money.

4.11. Hurdle rate is the minimum return necessary for an incentive fee to be applicable. High water mark refers to the previous losses that must be recouped before incentive fees are applicable. Clawback refers to investors being able to apply a percentage of incentive fees against a percentage of future losses.

4.12. If the return is X, the investors pay $0.03 + 0.3X$ in fees. It must therefore be the case that

$$X - (0.03 + 0.3X) = 0.2$$

so that $0.7X = 0.23$ or $X = 0.3286$. A return of 32.86% is necessary.

4.13. Short-term gains and losses do matter if the hedge fund is highly leveraged. Short-term losses can lead to margin calls that destroy the hedge fund.

4.14. Prime brokers decide on the amount of leverage that they are prepared to let hedge funds have. This influences the risks that hedge funds can take.

CHAPTER 5

5.1. When a trader enters into a long forward contract, she is agreeing to *buy* the underlying asset for a certain price at a certain time in the future. When a trader enters into a short forward contract, she is agreeing to *sell* the underlying asset for a certain price at a certain time in the future.

5.2. A trader is *hedging* when she has an exposure to the price of an asset and takes a position in a derivative to offset the exposure. In a *speculation* the trader has no exposure to offset. She is betting on the future movements in the price of the asset. *Arbitrage* involves taking a position in two or more different markets to lock in a profit.

5.3. In the first case, the trader is obligated to buy the asset for $50. (The trader does not have a choice.) In the second case, the trader has an option to buy the asset for $50. (The trader does not have to exercise the option.)

5.4. Selling a call option involves giving someone else the right to buy an asset from you for a certain price. Buying a put option gives you the right to sell the asset to someone else.

5.5. (a) The investor is obligated to sell pounds for 1.9000 when they are worth 1.8900. The gain is $(1.9000 - 1.8900) \times 100{,}000 = \$1{,}000$.
(b) The investor is obligated to sell pounds for 1.9000 when they are worth 1.9200. The loss is $(1.9200 - 1.9000) \times 100{,}000 = \$2{,}000$.

5.6. (a) The trader sells for 50 cents per pound something that is worth 48.20 cents per pound. Gain $= (\$0.5000 - \$0.4820) \times 50{,}000 = \$900$.
(b) The trader sells for 50 cents per pound something that is worth 51.30 cents per pound. Loss $= (\$0.5130 - \$0.5000) \times 50{,}000 = \$650$.

5.7. You have sold a put option. You have agreed to buy 100 shares for $40 per share if the party on the other side of the contract chooses to exercise the right to sell for this price. The option will be exercised only when the price of stock is below $40. Suppose, for example, that the option is exercised when the price is $30. You have to buy at $40 shares that are worth $30; you lose $10 per share, or $1,000 in total. If the option is exercised when the price is $20, you lose $20 per share, or $2,000 in total. The worst that can happen is that the price of the stock declines to almost zero during the three-month period. This highly unlikely event would cost you $4,000. In return for the possible future losses, you receive the price of the option from the purchaser.

5.8. The over-the-counter (OTC) market is a telephone- and computer-linked network of financial institutions, fund managers, and corporate treasurers where two participants can enter into any mutually acceptable contract. An exchange-traded market is a market organized by an exchange where traders either meet physically or communicate electronically and the contracts that can be traded have been defined by the exchange. (a) OTC; (b) exchange; (c) both; (d) OTC; (e) OTC.

5.9. One strategy would be to buy 200 shares. Another would be to buy 2,000 options. If the share price does well, the second strategy will give rise to greater gains. For example, if the share price goes up to $40 you gain $[2{,}000 \times (\$40 - \$30)] - \$5{,}800 = \$14{,}200$ from the second strategy and only $200 \times (\$40 - \$29) = \$2{,}200$ from the first strategy. However, if the share price does badly, the second strategy gives greater losses. For example, if the share price goes down to $25, the first strategy leads to a loss of $200 \times (\$29 - \$25) = \$800$, whereas the second strategy leads to a loss of the whole $5,800 investment. This example shows that options contain built-in leverage.

5.10. You could buy 5,000 put options (or 50 contracts) with a strike price of $25 and an expiration date in four months. This provides a type of insurance. If, at the end of four months, the stock price proves to be less than $25, you can exercise the options and sell the shares for $25 each. The cost of this strategy is the price you pay for the put options.

5.11. A stock option provides no funds for the company. It is a security sold by one trader to another. The company is not involved. By contrast, a stock, when it is first issued, is a claim sold by the company to investors and does provide funds for the company.

5.12. Ignoring the time value of money, the holder of the option will make a profit if the stock price in March is greater than $52.50. This is because the payoff to the holder of the option is, in these circumstances, greater than the $2.50 paid for the option. The option will be exercised if the stock price at maturity is greater than $50.00. Note that, if the stock price is between $50.00 and $52.50, the option is exercised but the holder of the option takes a loss overall.

5.13. Ignoring the time value of money, the seller of the option will make a profit if the stock price in June is greater than $56.00. This is because the cost to the seller of the option is, in these circumstances, less than the price received for the option. The option will be exercised if the stock price at maturity is less than $60.00. Note that, if the stock price is between $56.00 and $60.00, the seller of the option makes a profit even though the option is exercised.

5.14. A long position in a four-month put option can provide insurance against the exchange rate falling below the strike price. It ensures that the foreign currency can be sold for at least the strike price.

5.15. The company could enter into a long forward contract to buy 1 million Canadian dollars in six months. This would have the effect of locking in an exchange rate equal to the current forward exchange rate. Alternatively the company could buy a call option giving it the right (but not the obligation) to purchase 1 million Canadian dollars at a certain exchange rate in six months. This would provide insurance against a strong Canadian dollar in six months while still allowing the company to benefit from a weak Canadian dollar at that time.

5.16. The payoff from an ICON is the payoff from:
(a) A regular bond
(b) A short position in call options to buy 169,000 yen with an exercise price of 1/169
(c) A long position in call options to buy 169,000 yen with an exercise price of 1/84.5

This is demonstrated by the following table:

	Terminal value of regular bond	Terminal value of short calls	Terminal value of long calls	Terminal value of whole position
$S_T > 169$	1,000	0	0	1,000
$84.5 \leqslant S_T \leqslant 169$	1,000	$-169{,}000\left(\dfrac{1}{S_T} - \dfrac{1}{169}\right)$	0	$2{,}000 - \dfrac{169{,}000}{S_T}$
$S_T < 84.5$	1,000	$-169{,}000\left(\dfrac{1}{S_T} - \dfrac{1}{169}\right)$	$169{,}000\left(\dfrac{1}{S_T} - \dfrac{1}{84.5}\right)$	0

5.17. (a) The trader buys a 180-day call option and takes a short position in a 180-day forward contract.

(b) The trader buys 90-day put options and takes a long position in a 90-day forward contract.

5.18. It enters into a 5-year swap where it pays 6.51% and receives LIBOR. Its investment is then at LIBOR minus 1.51%.

5.19. It enters into a 5-year swap where it receives 6.47% and pays LIBOR. Its net cost of borrowing is LIBOR plus 0.53%.

5.20. It enters into a three-year swap where it receives LIBOR and pays 6.24%. Its net borrowing cost for the three years is then 7.24% per annum.

5.21. Suppose that the weather is bad and the farmer's production is lower than expected. Other farmers are likely to have been affected similarly. Corn production overall will be low and as a consequence the price of corn will be relatively high. The farmer is likely to be overhedged relative to actual production. The farmer's problems arising from the bad harvest will be made worse by losses on the short futures position. This problem emphasizes the importance of looking at the big picture when hedging. The farmer is correct to question whether hedging price risk while ignoring other risks is a good strategy.

5.22. It may well be true that there is just as much chance that the price of oil in the future will be above the futures price as that it will be below the futures price. This means that the use of a futures contract for speculation would be like betting on whether a coin comes up heads or tails. But it might make sense for the airline to use futures for hedging rather than speculation. The futures contract then has the effect of reducing risks. It can be argued that an airline should not expose its shareholders to risks associated with the future price of oil when there are contracts available to hedge the risks.

5.23. Microsoft is choosing an option on a portfolio of assets instead of the corresponding portfolio of options. The former is always less expensive because there is the potential for an increase in the price of one asset to be netted off against a decrease in the price of another asset. Compare (a) an option with a strike price of $20 on a portfolio of two assets each worth $10 and (b) a portfolio of two options with a strike price of $10, one on each of the assets. If both assets increase in price or both assets decrease in price, the payoffs are the same. But if one decreases and the other increases, the payoff from (a) is less than that from (b). Both the Asian feature and the basket feature in Microsoft's options help to reduce the cost of the options because of the possibility of gains and loss being netted.

5.24. The two calculations are necessary to determine the initial margin. The first gives

$$500 \times (3.5 + 0.2 \times 57 - 3) = 5,950$$

The second gives

$$500 \times (3.5 + 0.1 \times 57) = 4,600$$

The initial margin is the greater of these, or $5,950. Part of this can be provided by the initial amount of $500 \times 3.5 = \$1,750$ received for the options.

5.25. It means that the price of the energy source can go up or down but will tend over time to get pulled back to its long-run average level. Electricity has the highest rate of mean reversion; oil has the lowest.

5.26. As we increase the frequency with which the asset price is observed, it becomes more likely to hit the barrier, and the value of a knock-out call goes down.

5.27. The average of the highest and lowest temperature each day is 75° Fahrenheit. The CDD each day is therefore 10 and the cumulative CDD for the month is $10 \times 31 = 310$. The payoff from the call option is therefore $(310 - 250) \times \$5,000 = \$300,000$.

5.28. A 5×8 contract for May, 2010, is a contract to provide electricity for five days per week during the off-peak period (11 p.m. to 7 a.m.). When daily exercise is specified, the holder of the option is able to choose each weekday whether he or she will buy electricity at the strike price. When there is monthly exercise, he or she chooses once at the beginning of the month whether electricity is to be bought at the strike price for the whole month. The option with daily exercise is worth more.

5.29. The cost of the shares is 500×50, or \$25,000. When shares are shorted, the proceeds of the sale form part of the margin. In this case the total margin required is $1.6 \times 25,000$, or \$40,000. The extra margin required is therefore \$15,000. This can be in the form of cash or marginable securities. When the share price rises to S, the value of the underlying stock is $500S$. There is a margin call when

$$40,000 < 1.3 \times 500S$$

or $S > 61.54$.

CHAPTER 6

6.1. The value of the portfolio decreases by \$10,500.

6.2. The value of the portfolio increases by \$400.

6.3. In both cases it increases by $0.5 \times 30 \times 2^2$, or \$60.

6.4. A delta of 0.7 means that, when the price of the stock increases by a small amount, the price of the option increases by 70% of this amount. Similarly, when the price of the stock decreases by a small amount, the price of the option decreases by 70% of this amount. A short position in 1,000 options has a delta of -700 and can be made delta neutral with the purchase of 700 shares.

6.5. A theta of -100 per day means that, if one day passes with no change in either the stock price or its volatility, the value of the option position declines by $-\$100$. If a trader feels that neither the stock price nor its implied volatility will change, she should write an option with as big a negative theta as possible so that her position has a high positive theta. At-the-money options with a relatively short life have the biggest negative theta.

6.6. The gamma of an option position is the rate of change of the delta of the position with respect to the asset price. For example, a gamma of 0.1 would indicate that, when the asset price increases by a certain small amount, delta increases by 0.1 of this amount. When the gamma of an option writer's position is large and negative and the delta is zero, the option writer will lose significant amounts of money if there is a large movement (either an increase or a decrease) in the asset price.

6.7. To hedge an option position, it is necessary to create the opposite option position synthetically. For example, to hedge a long position in a put, it is necessary to create a short position in a put synthetically. It follows that the procedure for creating an option position synthetically is the reverse of the procedure for hedging the option position.

6.8. A long position in either a put or a call option has a positive gamma. From Figure 6.9, when gamma is positive, the hedger gains from a large change in the stock price and loses from a small change in the stock price. Hence the hedger will fare better in case (b). When the portfolio contains short option position, the hedger will similarly fare better in (a).

6.9. The delta indicates that, when the value of the euro exchange rate increases by $0.01, the value of the bank's position increases by $0.01 × 30,000 = $300. The gamma indicates that, when the euro exchange rate increases by $0.01, the delta of the portfolio decreases by 0.01 × 80,000 = 800. For delta neutrality, 30,000 euros should be shorted. When the exchange rate moves up to 0.93, we expect the delta of the portfolio to decrease by (0.93 − 0.90) × 80,000 = 2,400, so that it becomes 27,600. To maintain delta neutrality, it is therefore necessary for the bank to unwind its short position by 2,400 euros so that a net 27,600 have been shorted. When a portfolio is delta neutral and has a negative gamma, a loss is experienced when there is a large movement in the underlying asset price. We can conclude that the bank is likely to have lost money.

6.10. When used in the way described in the text, it does assume volatility is constant. In theory we could implement a static options replication strategy where there are three dimensions: time, the stock price, and volatility. Prices are then matched on a surface in the three-dimensional space.

6.11. Ten regular options are likely to be needed. This is because there are ten equations to be satisfied, one for each point on the boundary.

6.12. The payoff from an Asian option becomes more certain with the passage of time. As a result, the amount of uncertainty that needs to be hedged decreases with the passage of time.

6.13. Consider a portfolio of options dependent on a single market variable. A single trade is all that is necessary to make the position delta neutral regardless of the number of options in the portfolio.

6.14. The price, delta, gamma, vega, theta, and rho are 0.0217, −0.396, 5.415, 0.00203, −0.0000625, and −0.00119. Delta predicts that the option price should decrease by approximately 0.000396 when the exchange rate increases by 0.001. This is what we find. When the exchange rate is increased to 0.751, the option price decreases to 0.0213.

CHAPTER 7

7.1. The liabilities with a maturity over one year were about $5 billion less than the assets with a maturity of more than one year. Equivalently, about $5 billion of liabilities (deposits) with a maturity less than one year were financing assets (loans) with a maturity of more than one year. This indicates a mismatch. If interest rates rise, the interest paid on deposits will rise, but that received on loans will not. The net interest margin will come under pressure.

7.2. S&Ls were financing long-term mortgages with short-term deposits. They lost money during periods when interest rates rose sharply.

7.3. In this case, the interest rate mismatch is $10 billion. The bank's net interest income declines by $100 million each year for the next three years.

7.4. If long-term rates were simply a reflection of expected future short-term rates, we would expect the long rates to be less than short rates as often as they are greater than short rates. (This is based on the assumption that half of the time investors expect rates to increase and half of the time investors expect rates to decrease). Liquidity preference theory argues that long-term rates are high relative to expected future short-term rates. This means that long rates are greater than short rates most of the time. When long rates are less than short rates, the market is expecting a relatively steep decline in rates.

7.5. There are three reasons:
  (1) Treasury bills and Treasury bonds must be purchased by financial institutions to fulfill a variety of regulatory requirements. This increases demand for these Treasury instruments driving the price up and the yield down.
  (2) The amount of capital a bank is required to hold to support an investment in Treasury bills and bonds is substantially smaller than the capital required to support a similar investment in other very-low-risk instruments.
  (3) In the United States, Treasury instruments are given a favorable tax treatment compared with most other fixed-income investments, because they are not taxed at the state level.

7.6. Duration provides information about the effect of a small parallel shift in the yield curve on the value of a bond portfolio. The percentage decrease in the value of the portfolio equals the duration of the portfolio multiplied by the amount by which interest rates are increased in the small parallel shift. Its limitation is that it applies only to parallel shifts in the yield curve that are small.

7.7. (a) The bond's price is 86.80; (b) the bond's duration is 4.256 years; (c) the duration formula shows that, when the yield decreases by 0.2%, the bond's price increases by 0.74; (d) recomputing the bond's price with a yield of 10.8% gives a price of 87.54, which is approximately consistent with (a) and (c).

7.8. (a) The bond's price is 88.91; (b) the bond's modified duration is 3.843 years; (c) the duration formula shows that, when the yield decreases by 0.2%, the bond's price increases by 0.68; (d) recomputing the bond's price with a yield of 10.8% (annually compounded) gives a price of 89.60, which is approximately consistent with (a) and (c).

7.9. The bond price is 104.80. The duration of the bond is 5.35. The convexity is 30.60. The effect of a 1% increase in the yield is estimated by equation (4.14) as

$$104.80 \times (-0.01 \times 5.35 + 0.5 \times 30.60 \times 0.0001) = -5.44$$

The bond price actually changes to 99.36, which is consistent with the estimate.

7.10. We can (a) perturb points on the yield curve (see Figure 4.4), (b) perturb sections of the yield curve (see Figure 4.6), and (c) perturb the market quotes used to create the yield curve.

7.11. The deltas are 10.7 and -190.1.

7.12. The impact on the portfolio, measured as a proportion of the value of the portfolio, is

$$-(2.0 \times 0.001 + 1.6 \times 0.0008 + 0.6 \times 0.0007 + 0.2 \times 0.0006$$
$$- 0.5 \times 0.0005 - 1.8 \times 0.0003 - 1.9 \times 0.0.0001) = -0.00284$$

The portfolio decreases by 0.284%.

7.13. Dollar duration is defined as the product of the duration of a portfolio and its price. Dollar convexity is defined as the product of the convexity of a portfolio and its price.

7.14. The partial durations add up to the total duration. The DV01 is the total duration times the portfolio value times 0.0001.

CHAPTER 8

8.1. VaR is the loss that is not expected to be exceeded with a certain confidence level. Expected shortfall is the expected loss conditional on the loss being worse than the VaR level. Expected shortfall has the advantage that it always satisfies the subadditivity (diversification is good) condition.

8.2. A spectral risk measure is a risk measure that assigns weights to the quantiles of the loss distribution. For the subadditivity condition to be satisfied, the weight assigned to the qth quantile must be a nondecreasing function of q.

8.3. There is a 5% chance that you will lose \$6,000 or more during a one-month period.

8.4. Your expected loss during a "bad month" is \$6,000. Bad months are defined as the months where returns are less than the 5-percentile point on the distribution of monthly returns.

8.5. (a) \$1 million.
   (b) The expected shortfall is $0.9 \times 10 + 0.1 \times 1$, or \$9.1 million.
   (c) There is a probability of $0.009^2 = 0.000081$ of a loss of \$20 million, a probability of $2 \times 0.009 \times 0.991 = 0.017838$ of a loss of \$11 million, and a probability of $0.991^2 = 0.982081$ of loss of \$2 million. The VaR when the confidence level is 99% is therefore \$11 million.
   (d) The expected shortfall is $(0.000081 \times 20 + 0.009919 \times 11)/0.01 = \$11.07$ million.
   (e) Since $1 + 1 < 11$, the subadditivity condition is not satisfied for VaR. Since $9.1 + 9.1 > 11.07$, it is satisfied for expected shortfall.

8.6. $2 \times 1.96 = \$3.92$m, (b) $\sqrt{5} \times 2 \times 1.96 = \$8.77$m, (c) $\sqrt{5} \times 2 \times 2.33 = 10.40$m.

8.7. In this case, (b) becomes \$9.96 million and (c) becomes \$11.82 million.

8.8. Marginal VaR is the rate of change of VaR with the amount invested in the ith asset. Incremental VaR is the incremental effect of the ith asset on VaR (i.e., the difference between VaR with and without the asset). Component VaR is the part of VaR that can be attributed the ith asset (the sum of component VaRs equals the total VaR).

8.9. The probability of 17 or more exceptions is $1 - \text{BINOMDIST}(16, 1000, 0.01, \text{TRUE})$, or 2.64%. The model should be rejected at the 5% confidence level.

8.10. Bunching is the tendency for exceptions to be bunched rather than occurring randomly throughout the time period considered.

8.11. We are interested in the variance of $\Delta P_1 + \Delta P_2 + \cdots + \Delta P_T$ This is $\sum_{i=1}^{T} \sigma_i^2 + 2 \sum_{i>j} \rho_{ij} \sigma_i \sigma_j$ where σ_i is the standard deviation of ΔP_i and ρ_{ij} is the correlation between ΔP_i and ΔP_j. In this case, $\sigma_i = \sigma$ for all i, and $\rho_{ij} = \rho^{i-j}$ when $i > j$. After further algebraic manipulation, this leads directly to equation (8.3).

CHAPTER 9

9.1. $30/\sqrt{52}$, or 4.16%.

9.2. The standard deviation of the percentage price change in one day is $25/\sqrt{252}$, or 1.57%. The 95% confidence limits are from -3.09% to $+3.09\%$.

9.3. Volatility is much higher when markets are open than when they are closed. Traders therefore measure time in trading days rather than calendar days.

9.4. Implied volatility is the volatility that leads to the option price equaling the market price when Black–Scholes assumptions are used. It is found by "trial and error". Since different options have different implied volatilities, traders are not using the same assumptions as Black–Scholes. (See Chapter 20 for a further discussion of this.)

9.5. The approach in Section 9.3 gives 0.547% per day. The simplified approach in equation (9.4) gives 0.530% per day.

9.6. The power law gives $0.01 = K \times 500^{-2}$, so that $K = 2{,}500$. (a) $2{,}500 \times 1000^{-2} = 0.0025$, or 0.25%; (b) $2{,}500 \times 2000^{-2} = 0.000625$, or 0.0625%.

9.7. The variance rate estimated calculated at the end of day $n-1$ for day n equals λ times the variance rate calculated at the end of day $n-2$ for day $n-1$ plus $1-\lambda$ times the squared return on day $n-1$.

9.8. GARCH(1,1) adapts the EWMA model by giving some weight to a long-run average variance rate. Whereas the EWMA has no mean reversion, GARCH(1,1) is consistent with a mean-reverting variance-rate model.

9.9. In this case, $\sigma_{n-1} = 0.015$ and $u_{n-1} = 0.5/30 = 0.01667$, so that equation (9.8) gives

$$\sigma_n^2 = 0.94 \times 0.015^2 + 0.06 \times 0.01667^2 = 0.0002281$$

The volatility estimate on day n is therefore $\sqrt{0.0002281} = 0.015103$, or 1.5103%.

9.10. Reducing λ from 0.95 to 0.85 means that more weight is given to recent observations of u_i^2, and less weight is given to older observations. Volatilities calculated with $\lambda = 0.85$ will react more quickly to new information and will "bounce around" much more than volatilities calculated with $\lambda = 0.95$.

9.11. With the usual notation, $u_{n-1} = 20/1040 = 0.01923$, so that

$$\sigma_n^2 = 0.000002 + 0.06 \times 0.01923^2 + 0.92 \times 0.01^2 = 0.0001162$$

This gives $\sigma_n = 0.01078$. The new volatility estimate is therefore 1.078% per day.

9.12. The proportional daily change is $-0.005/1.5000 = -0.003333$. The current daily variance estimate is $0.006^2 = 0.000036$. The new daily variance estimate is

$$0.9 \times 0.000036 + 0.1 \times 0.003333^2 = 0.000033511$$

The new volatility is the square root of this, i.e., 0.00579, or 0.579%.

9.13. The weight given to the long-run average variance rate is $1 - \alpha - \beta$, and the long-run average variance rate is $\omega/(1 - \alpha - \beta)$. Increasing ω increases the long-run average variance rate. Increasing α increases the weight given to the most recent data item, reduces the weight given to the long-run average variance rate, and increases the level of the long-run average variance rate. Increasing β increases the weight given to the previous variance estimate, reduces the weight given to the long-run average variance rate, and increases the level of the long-run average variance rate.

9.14. The long-run average variance rate is $\omega/(1 - \alpha - \beta)$, or $0.000004/0.03 = 0.0001333$. The long-run average volatility is $\sqrt{0.0001333}$, or 1.155%. The equation describing the way the variance rate reverts to its long-run average is

$$E[\sigma_{n+k}^2] = V_L + (\alpha + \beta)^k (\sigma_n^2 - V_L)$$

In this case,

$$E[\sigma_{n+k}^2] = 0.0001333 + 0.97^k (\sigma_n^2 - 0.0001333)$$

If the current volatility is 20% per year, $\sigma_n = 0.2/\sqrt{252} = 0.0126$. The expected variance rate in 20 days is

$$0.0001333 + 0.97^{20}(0.0126^2 - 0.0001333) = 0.0001471$$

The expected volatility in 20 days is therefore $\sqrt{0.0001471} = 0.0121$, or 1.21% per day.

9.15. The FTSE expressed in dollars is XY, where X is the FTSE expressed in sterling and Y is the exchange rate (value of one pound in dollars). Define x_i as the proportional change in X on day i, and y_i as the proportional change in Y on day i. The proportional change in XY is approximately $x_i + y_i$. The standard deviation of x_i is 0.018 and the standard deviation of y_i is 0.009. The correlation between the two is 0.4. The variance of $x_i + y_i$ is therefore

$$0.018^2 + 0.009^2 + 2 \times 0.018 \times 0.009 \times 0.4 = 0.0005346$$

so that the volatility of $x_i + y_i$ is 0.0231, or 2.31%. This is the volatility of the FTSE expressed in dollars. Note that it is greater than the volatility of the FTSE expressed in sterling. This is the impact of the positive correlation. When the FTSE increases, the value of sterling measured in dollars also tends to increase. This creates an even bigger increase in the value of FTSE measured in dollars, and likewise for a decrease in the FTSE.

9.16. In this case, $V_L = 0.000003/0.02 = 0.00015$, and equation (9.14) gives the expected variance rate in 30 days as

$$0.00015 + 0.98^{30}(0.01^2 - 0.00015) = 0.000123$$

The volatility is $\sqrt{0.000123} = 0.0111$ or 1.11% per day.

9.17. In this case, $V_L = 0.000002/0.02 = 0.0001$. In equation (9.15), $V_L = 0.0001$, $a = 0.0202$, $T = 20$, and $V(0) = 0.000169$, so that the volatility is 19.88%.

CHAPTER 10

10.1. You need the standard deviations of the two variables.

10.2. Loosely speaking, correlation measures the extent of linear dependence. It does not measure other types of dependence. When $y = x^2$, there is perfect dependence between x and y. However, $E(xy) = E(x^3)$ and $E(x) = 0$. Both $E(xy)$ and $E(x)E(y)$ are zero when x is normal (or when it has any symmetrical distribution centered at zero). The coefficient of correlation between x and y is therefore zero.

10.3. In a factor model, the correlation between two variables arises entirely because of their correlation with other variables known as factors. A factor model reduces the number of estimates that have to be made when correlations between large numbers of variables are being produced.

10.4. A positive-semidefinite matrix is a matrix that satisfies equation (10.4) for all vectors $\boldsymbol{w}$. If a correlation matrix is not positive-semidefinite, the correlations are internally inconsistent.

10.5. (a) The volatilities and correlation imply that the current estimate of the covariance is

$$0.25 \times 0.016 \times 0.025 = 0.0001$$

(b) If the prices of the assets at close of trading are \$20.5 and \$40.5, the proportional changes are $0.5/20 = 0.025$ and $0.5/40 = 0.0125$. The new covariance estimate is

$$0.95 \times 0.0001 + 0.05 \times 0.025 \times 0.0125 = 0.0001106$$

The new variance estimate for asset A is

$$0.95 \times 0.016^2 + 0.05 \times 0.025^2 = 0.00027445$$

so that the new volatility is 0.0166. The new variance estimate for asset B is

$$0.95 \times 0.025^2 + 0.05 \times 0.0125^2 = 0.000601562$$

so that the new volatility is 0.0245. The new correlation estimate is

$$\frac{0.0001106}{0.0166 \times 0.0245} = 0.272$$

10.6. The most recent returns for X and Y are $1/30 = 0.03333$ and $1/50 = 0.02$, respectively. The previous covariance is $0.01 \times 0.012 \times 0.50 = 0.00006$. The new estimate of the covariance is

$$0.000001 + 0.04 \times 0.03333 \times 0.02 + 0.94 \times 0.00006 = 0.0000841$$

The new estimate of the variance of X is

$$0.000003 + 0.04 \times 0.03333^2 + 0.94 \times 0.01^2 = 0.0001414$$

so that the new volatility of X is $\sqrt{0.0001414} = 0.01189$, or 1.189%. The new estimate of the variance of Y is

$$0.000003 + 0.04 \times 0.02^2 + 0.94 \times 0.012^2 = 0.0001544$$

so that the new volatility of Y is $\sqrt{0.0001544} = 0.01242$, or 1.242%. The new estimate of the correlation between the assets is therefore $0.0000841/(0.01189 \times 0.01242) = 0.569$.

10.7. Continuing with the notation in the answer to Problem 9.15, define z_i as the proportional change in the value of the S&P 500 on day i. The covariance between x_i and z_i is

$$0.7 \times 0.018 \times 0.016 = 0.0002016$$

The covariance between y_i and z_i is

$$0.3 \times 0.009 \times 0.016 = 0.0000432$$

The covariance between $x_i + y_i$ and z_i equals the covariance between x_i and z_i plus the covariance between y_i and z_i, which is

$$0.0002016 + 0.0000432 = 0.0002448$$

The volatility of $x_i + y_i$ is 2.31% from Problem 9.15. The correlation between $x_i + y_i$ and z_i is

$$\frac{0.0002448}{0.016 \times 0.0231} = 0.662$$

Note that the volatility of the S&P 500 drops out in this calculation.

10.8.

V_1	V_2		
	0.25	0.5	0.75
0.25	0.095	0.163	0.216
0.5	0.163	0.298	0.413
0.75	0.216	0.413	0.595

10.9. The formulas are:

$$\epsilon_1 = z_1, \qquad \epsilon_2 = \rho_{12}z_1 + z_2\sqrt{1 - \rho_{12}^2}, \qquad \epsilon_3 = \alpha_1 z_1 + \alpha_2 z_2 + \alpha_3 z_3$$

where

$$\alpha_1 = \rho_{13}, \qquad \alpha_1\rho_{12} + \alpha_2\sqrt{1 - \rho_{12}^2} = \rho_{23}, \qquad \alpha_1^2 + \alpha_2^2 + \alpha_3^2 = 1$$

This means that

$$\alpha_1 = \rho_{13}, \qquad \alpha_2 = \frac{\rho_{23} - \rho_{13}\rho_{12}}{\sqrt{1 - \rho_{12}^2}}, \qquad \alpha_3 = \sqrt{1 - \alpha_1^2 - \alpha_2^2}$$

10.10. Tail dependence is the tendency for extreme values for two or more variables to occur together. The choice of the copula affects tail dependence. For example, the Student t-copula gives more tail dependence than the Gaussian copula.

10.11. Sample from a bivariate Student t-distribution as in Figure 10.5. Convert each sample to a normal distribution on a "percentile-to-percentile" basis.

10.12. The probability that $V_1 < 0.1$ is 0.05. The conditional probability that $V_2 < 0.1$ is $0.006/0.05 = 0.12$. The conditional probability that $V_2 < 0.2$ is $0.017/0.05 = 0.34$, etc.

10.13. When $V_1 = 0.2$, $U_1 = -0.84$. From the properties of the bivariate normal distribution, the median of U_2 is $-0.5 \times 0.84 = -0.42$. This translates into a median value of 0.458 for V_2.

10.14. In this case,

$$\text{WCDR}(T, X) = N\left(\frac{N^{-1}(0.015) + \sqrt{0.2}N^{-1}(0.995)}{\sqrt{1 - 0.2}}\right) = 0.127$$

The 99.5% worst case is that there is a loss of $500 \times 0.7 \times 0.127 = 44.62$, or $44.62 million.

CHAPTER 11

11.1. The removal of a competitor may be beneficial. However, banks enter into many contracts with each other. When one bank goes bankrupt, other banks are liable to lose money on the contracts they have with the bank. Furthermore, other banks will be adversely affected if the bankruptcy reduces the public's overall level of confidence in the banking system.

11.2. Deposit insurance means that depositors are safe regardless of the risks taken by their financial institution. It is liable to lead to financial institutions taking more risks than they otherwise would, because they can do so without the risk of losing deposits. This in turn leads to more bank failures and more claims under the deposit insurance system. Regulation requiring the capital held by a bank to be related to the risks taken is necessary to avoid this happening.

11.3. The credit risk on the swap is the risk that the counterparty defaults at some future time when the swap has a positive value to the bank.

11.4. The value of a currency swap is liable to deviate further from zero than the value of an interest rate swap, because of the final exchange of principal. As a result, the potential loss from a counterparty default is higher.

11.5. There is some exposure. If the counterparty defaulted now, there would be no loss. However, interest rates could change so that at a future time the swap has a positive value to the financial institution. If the counterparty defaulted at that time, there would be a loss to the financial institution. The capital under Basel I would, from Table 11.2, be 0.5% of the swap's principal.

11.6. The risk-weighted assets for the three transactions are (a) $1.875 million, (b) $2 million, and (c) $3 million for a total of $6.875 million. The capital required is 0.08×6.875, or $0.55 million.

11.7. The NRR is $2.5/4.5 = 0.556$. The credit equivalent amount is

$$2.5 + (0.4 + 0.6 \times 0.556) \times 9.25 = \$9.28 \text{ million}$$

The risk-weighted assets total $4.64 million and the capital required is $0.371 million.

11.8. In this case, there is no value to the netting provisions.

11.9. This converts the estimated capital requirement to an estimate of risk-weighted assets. Capital required equals 8% of risk-weighted assets.

11.10. The trading book consists of instruments that are actively traded and marked to market daily. The banking book consists primarily of loans and is not marked to market daily. The effect of the change is to move the clients' borrowings from the banking book to the trading book. The bank will keep specific risk capital for the securities, reflecting the credit exposure, as well as market risk capital, reflecting the market risk exposure.

11.11. Under Basel I, the capital charged for lending to a corporation is the same regardless of the credit rating of the corporation. This leads to a bank's return on capital being relatively low for lending to highly creditworthy corporations. Under Basel II, the capital requirements of a loan are tied much more carefully to the creditworthiness of the borrower. As a result, lending to highly creditworthy companies may become attractive again.

11.12. Regulatory arbitrage involves entering into a transaction or series of transactions solely to reduce regulatory capital requirements.

11.13. EAD is the estimated exposure at default. LGD is the loss given default, that is, the proportion of the exposure that will be lost if a default occurs. WCDR is the one-year probability of default in a bad year that occurs only one time in 1,000. PD is the probability of default in an average year. MA is the maturity adjustment. The latter allows for the fact that, in the case of instruments lasting longer than a year, there may be losses arising from a decline in the creditworthiness of the counterparty during the year as well as from a default during the year.

11.14. Under the simple approach, the risk weight of the counterparty is replaced by the risk weight of the collateral for the part of the exposure covered by the collateral. Under the comprehensive approach, the exposure is adjusted for possible increases and the collateral is adjusted for possible decreases in value. The counterparty's risk weight is applied to the excess of the adjusted exposure over the adjusted collateral.

11.15. The standardized approach uses external ratings to determine capital requirements (but in a more sophisticated way than in Basel I). In the IRB approach, the Basel II correlation model is used with PD being determined by the bank. In the advanced IRB approach, the Basel II correlation model is used with PD, LGD, EAD, and MA being determined by the bank.

11.16. In the basic indicator approach, total capital is 15% of the average total annual gross income. In the standardized approach, gross income is calculated for different business lines and capital as a percentage of gross income is different for different business lines. In the advanced measurement approach, the bank uses internal models to determine the 99.9% worst-case loss in one year.

11.17. The correlation $\rho = 0.1216$, WCDR $= 0.0914$, and the capital requirement is $200 \times 0.7 \times 0.0814$, or \$11.39 million. At least half of this must be Tier 1.

11.18. The probability of 5 or more exceptions is $1 - \text{BINOMDIST}(4, 250, 0.01, \text{TRUE})$, or 10.8%. It could be argued that regulators are using a confidence level of about 10% (rather than the more usual 5%) in choosing to reject a VaR model.

CHAPTER 12

12.1. The assumption is that the statistical process driving changes in market variables over the next day is the same as that over the last 500 days.

12.2.

$$\lambda^{i-1}(1 - \lambda)/(1 - \lambda^n) = \frac{\lambda^{i-1}}{1 + \lambda + \lambda^2 + \cdots + \lambda^{n-1}}$$

This shows that as λ approaches 1 the weights approach $1/n$.

12.3. The standard error of the estimate is

$$\frac{1}{0.01} \sqrt{\frac{0.05 \times 0.95}{1000}} = 0.69$$

The standard error of the VaR estimate is \$0.69 million.

12.4. The one-day 95% VaR is the 25th-worst loss. This is \$168,612. The one-day 97% VaR is the 15th-worst loss. This is \$188,758.

12.5. In the "Scenarios" worksheet, the portfolio investments are changed to 2,500 in cells L2:O2. The losses are then sorted from the largest to the smallest. The fifth-worst loss is \$258,355. This is the one-day 99% VaR.

12.6. The value of λ in cell F2 of the "Scenarios with Weights" worksheet is changed from 0.995 to 0.99. The losses are then sorted from the largest to the smallest. The cumulative weight for the largest loss (Scenario 494) is 0.00948. The cumulative weight for the second-largest loss (Scenario 339) is 0.01147. The one-day 99% VaR is therefore the second-worst loss, or \$359,440.

12.7. The value of λ in cell A2 of the "Data with Vol Ests" worksheet is changed from 0.94 to 0.96. The losses in the "Vol Adjusted Scenarios" worksheet are then sorted from the highest to the lowest. The fifth-worst loss is \$557,815. This is the new one-day 99% VaR.

12.8. This is

$$\frac{13}{500}\left(1 + 0.371\frac{400 - 200}{43.526}\right)^{-1/0.371}$$

or 0.001779.

12.9. The VaR (\$000s) is

$$200 + \frac{43.526}{0.371}\left[\left(\frac{500}{13}(1 - 0.97)\right)^{-0.371} - 1\right] = 193.9$$

or \$193,900.

12.10. The maximum likelihood estimates of ξ and β become 0.302 and 44.22. The one-day 99% VaR becomes \$251,112, and the one-day 99.9% VaR becomes \$474,512.

12.11. The losses from the volatility updating procedure must be transferred to the "Extreme Val Theory" worksheet. With $u = 400$, we have $n_u = 21$ and the maximum likelihood values of ξ and β are 0.470 and 78.293. The one-day 99% VaR is $560,405. The one-day 99.9% VaR is $1,198,223. The probability of a loss greater than $600,000 is

$$\frac{21}{500}\left(1 + 0.470\frac{600 - 400}{78.293}\right)^{-1/0.470} = 0.00784$$

CHAPTER 13

13.1. The standard deviation of the daily change in the investment in each asset is $1,000. The variance of the portfolio's daily change is

$$1,000^2 + 1,000^2 + 2 \times 0.3 \times 1,000 \times 1,000 = 2,600,000$$

The standard deviation of the portfolio's daily change is the square root of this, or $1,612.45. The five-day 99% VaR is therefore $2.33 \times \sqrt{5} \times 1,612.45 = \$8,401$.

13.2. The three alternative procedures mentioned in the chapter for handling interest rates when the model-building approach is used to calculate VaR involve (a) the use of the duration model, (b) the use of cash-flow mapping, and (c) the use of principal components analysis.

13.3. When a final exchange of principal is added in, the floating side is equivalent a zero-coupon bond with a maturity date equal to the date of the next payment. The fixed side is a coupon-bearing bond, which is equivalent to a portfolio of zero-coupon bonds. The swap can therefore be mapped into a portfolio of zero-coupon bonds with maturity dates corresponding to the payment dates. Each of the zero-coupon bonds can then be mapped into positions in the adjacent standard-maturity zero-coupon bonds.

13.4. $\Delta P = 56 \times 1.5\Delta x$. The standard deviation of ΔP is $56 \times 1.5 \times 0.007 = 0.588$. It follows that the ten-day 99% VaR for the portfolio is $0.588 \times 2.33 \times \sqrt{10} = 4.33$.

13.5. The relationship is
$$\Delta P = 56 \times 1.5\Delta x + 0.5 \times 1.5^2 \times 16.2 \times \Delta x^2$$
or $\Delta P = 84\Delta x + 18.225\Delta x^2$.

13.6. The 6.5-year cash flow is equivalent to a position of $48.56 in a 5-year zero-coupon bond and a position of $605.49 in a 7-year zero-coupon bond. The equivalent 5-year and 7-year cash flows are $48.56 \times 1.06^5 = 64.98$ and $605.49 \times 1.07^7 = 972.28$.

13.7. A calculation similar to that in the text shows that $37,397 of the value is allocated to the three-month bond and $11,793 of the value is allocated to the six-month bond.

13.8. The daily variance of the portfolio is

$$6^2 \times 20^2 + 4^2 \times 8^2 = 15,424$$

and the daily standard deviation is $\sqrt{15,424} = \$124.19$. Since $N(-1.282) = 0.9$, the five-day 90% VaR is

$$124.19 \times \sqrt{5} \times 1.282 = \$356.01$$

13.9. (a) 3.26; (b) 63.87.

13.10. The delta of the options is the rate of change of the value of the options with respect to the price of the asset. When the asset price increases by a small amount, the value of the options decrease by 30 times this amount. The gamma of the options is the rate of change of their delta with respect to the price of the asset. When the asset price increases by a small amount, the delta of the portfolio decreases by five times this amount.

In this case, $E(\Delta P) = -0.1$, $E[(\Delta P)^2] = 36.03$, and $E[(\Delta P)^3] = -32.415$. The mean change in the portfolio value in one day is -0.1 and the standard deviation of the change in one day is $\sqrt{36.03 - 0.1^2} = 6.002$. The skewness is

$$\frac{-32.415 - 3 \times 36.03 \times (-0.1) + 2 \times (-0.1)^3}{6.002^3} = -\frac{21.608}{216.180} = -0.10$$

Using only the first two moments, the one-day 99% VaR is $14.08. When three moments are considered in conjunction with a Cornish–Fisher expansion, it is $14.53.

13.11. Define σ as the volatility (%) per year, $\Delta\sigma$ as the change in σ in one day, and Δw and the proportional change in σ in one day. The current value of σ is $1 \times \sqrt{252} = 15.87$. The delta–gamma–vega model is

$$\Delta P = -30\Delta S - 0.5 \times 5 \times (\Delta S)^2 - 2\Delta\sigma$$

or

$$\Delta P = -30 \times 20 \times \Delta x - 0.5 \times 5 \times 20^2 \times (\Delta x)^2 - 2 \times 15.87 \times \Delta w$$

where $\Delta x = \Delta S/S$, which simplifies to

$$\Delta P = -600\Delta x - 1,000 \times (\Delta x)^2 - 31.74 \times \Delta w$$

The change in the portfolio value now depends on two market variables.

13.12. The change in the value of an option is not linearly related to the changes in the values of the underlying variables. When the changes in the values of underlying variables are normal, the change in the value of the option is nonnormal. The linear model assumes that it is normal and is therefore only an approximation.

13.13. The contract is a long position in a sterling bond combined with a short position in a dollar bond. The value of the sterling bond is $1.53e^{-0.05 \times 0.5}$, or $1.492 million. The value of the dollar bond is $1.5e^{-0.05 \times 0.5}$, or $1.463 million. The variance of the change in the value of the contract in one day is

$$1.492^2 \times 0.0006^2 + 1.463^2 \times 0.0005^2 - 2 \times 0.8 \times 1.492 \times 0.0006 \times 1.463 \times 0.0005$$

$$= 0.000000288$$

The standard deviation is therefore $0.000537 million. The ten-day 99% VaR is $0.000537 \times \sqrt{10} \times 2.33 = 0.00396 million.

13.14. The alpha's should be changed to 2,500. This changes the one-day 99% VaR to $238,022 when volatilities and correlations are estimated using the equally weighted model and to $519,932 when EWMA with $\lambda = 0.94$ is used.

13.15. This changes the one-day 99% VaR from $496,610 to $406,753.

CHAPTER 14

14.1. The investment-grade ratings used by Moody's are: Aaa, Aa1, Aa2, Aa3, A1, A2, A3, Baa1, Baa2, and Baa3

14.2. The investment-grade ratings used by S&P are: AAA, AA+, AA, AA−, A+, A, A−, BBB+, BBB, and BBB−.

14.3. From equation (14.2), the average default intensity, $\bar{\lambda}$ satisfies $0.04660 = 1 - e^{-\bar{\lambda} \times 1}$, so that $\bar{\lambda} = -\ln 0.95340 = 0.0477$. The average default intensity is 4.77% per year.

14.4. Conditional on no default by year 2, the probability of a default in year 3 is

$$0.05298/0.95856 = 0.05527$$

Average default intensity for the third year, $\bar{\lambda}$, satisfies $1 - e^{-\bar{\lambda} \times 1} = 0.05527$. It is 5.69% per year.

14.5. The seller receives $\$300,000,000 \times 0.0060 \times 0.5 = \$900,000$ at times 0.5, 1.0, 1.5, 2.0, 2.5, 3.0, 3.5, and 4.0 years. The seller also receives a final accrual payment of about \$300,000 ($= \$300,000,000 \times 0.060 \times 2/12$) at the time of the default (4 years and 2 months). The seller pays $\$300,000,000 \times 0.6 = \$180,000,000$ at the time of the default.

14.6. Sometimes there is physical settlement and sometimes there is cash settlement. In the event of a default when there is physical settlement, the buyer of protection sells bonds issued by the reference entity for their face value. Bonds with a total face value equal to the notional principal can be sold. In the event of a default when there is cash settlement, a calculation agent estimates the value of the cheapest-to-deliver bonds issued by the reference entity a specified number of days after the default event. The cash payoff is then based on the excess of the face value of these bonds over the estimated value.

14.7. Risk-neutral default probabilities are calculated from credit default swaps, asset swaps, or bond prices. Real-world default probabilities are calculated from historical data. Risk-neutral default probabilities should be used for valuation. Real-world default probabilities should be used for scenario analysis and credit VaR calculations.

14.8. The payoff is $L(1 - R)$, where L is the notional principal and R is the recovery rate.

14.9. From equation (14.3), the average default intensity over the three years is $0.0050/(1 - 0.3) = 0.0071$, or 0.71% per year.

14.10. From equation (14.3), the average default intensity over five years is $0.0080/(1 - 0.4)$, or 1.333% per year. Similarly, the average default intensity over three years is 1.1667% per year. This means that the average default intensity for years 4 and 5 is

$$\tfrac{1}{2}(5 \times 1.333 - 3 \times 1.1667) = 1.58\%$$

14.11. Real-world probabilities of default should be used for calculating credit value at risk. Risk-neutral probabilities of default should be used for adjusting the price of a derivative for default.

14.12. The recovery rate for a bond is the value of the bond immediately after the issuer defaults as a percentage of its face value.

14.13. The first number in the second column of Table 14.4 is calculated from the numbers in the seven-year column of Table 14.1 as

$$-\tfrac{1}{7}\ln(1 - 0.00252) = 0.0004$$

or 0.04% per year. The second number in the second column of Table 14.4 is calculated from the numbers in the seven-year column of Table 14.1 as

$$-\tfrac{1}{7}\ln(1 - 0.00344) = 0.0005$$

Other numbers in the column are calculated in a similar fashion. The numbers in the fourth column of Table 14.5 are the numbers in the second column of Table 14.4

multiplied by one minus the expected recovery rate. In this case the expected recovery rate is 0.4.

14.14. The present value of the asset swap payments per $100 face value is

$$0.9e^{-0.03 \times 0.5} + 0.9e^{-0.03 \times 1.0} + \cdots + 0.9e^{-0.03 \times 4.0} = 6.73$$

This is also the present value of the cost of default. An analysis similar to that in Table 14.3 shows that, if Q is the default probability per year, then the loss from defaults is $272.69Q$. The implied probability of default is therefore given by solving $6.73 = 272.69Q$. It is 2.47% per year.

14.15. If Q_1 is the default probability at times 0.5, 1.5, and 2.5 years, an analysis similar to that in Table 14.3 shows that the present value of the loss from defaults for the first bond is $178.31Q_1$ per $100 of face value. The present value of the asset swap spreads for this bond is

$$1 \times e^{-0.035 \times 1} + 1 \times e^{-0.035 \times 2} + 1 \times e^{-0.035 \times 3} = 2.798$$

It follows that $178.31Q_1 = 2.798$, so that $Q_1 = 0.0157$, or 1.57%. If Q_2 is the probability of default at times 3.5 and 4.5, an analysis similar to that in Table 14.3 gives the present value of the loss from default for the second bond to be $180.56Q_1 + 108.53Q_2$. The present value of the asset swap spreads for the second bond is

$$1.25e^{-0.035 \times 1} + 1.25 \times e^{-0.035 \times 2} + \cdots + 1.25 \times e^{-0.035 \times 2} = 5.634$$

It follows that $180.56Q_1 + 108.53Q_2 = 5.634$. Substituting for Q_1, we find that $Q - 2 = 0.0258$, or 2.58%.

14.16. We can assume that the principal is paid and received at the end of the life of the swap without changing the swap's value. If the spread were zero, the present value of the floating payments per dollar of principal would be 1. The payment of LIBOR plus the spread therefore has a present value of $1 + V$. The payment of the bond cash flows has a present value per dollar of principal of B^*. The initial payment required from the payer of the bond cash flows per dollar of principal is $1 - B$. (This may be negative; an initial amount of $B - 1$ is then paid by the payer of the floating rate.) Because the asset swap is initially worth zero, we have

$$1 + V = B^* + 1 - B$$

so that

$$V = B^* - B$$

14.17. The value of the debt in Merton's model is $V_0 - E_0$, or

$$V_0 - V_0N(d_1) + De^{-rT}N(d_2) = De^{-rT}N(d_2) + V_0N(-d_1)$$

If the credit spread is s, this should equal $De^{-(r+s)T}$, so that

$$De^{-(r+s)T} = De^{-rT}N(d_2) + V_0N(-d_1)$$

Substituting $De^{-rT} = LV_0$, we get

$$Le^{-sT} = LN(d_2) + N(-d_1)$$

so that

$$s = -\ln[N(d_2) + N(-d_1)/L]/T$$

14.18. In this case, $E_0 = 2$, $\sigma_E = 0.50$, $D = 5$, $r = 0.04$, and $T = 1$. Solving the simultaneous equations gives $V_0 = 6.80$ and $\sigma_V = 14.82$. The probability of default is $N(-d_2)$, or 1.15%.

14.19. A credit default swap insures a corporate bond issued by the reference entity against default. Its approximate effect is to convert the corporate bond into a risk-free bond. The buyer of a credit default swap has therefore chosen to exchange a corporate bond for a risk-free bond. This means that the buyer is long a risk-free bond and short a similar corporate bond.

14.20. Payoffs from credit default swaps depend on whether a particular company defaults. Arguably some market participants have more information about this than other market participants. (See Business Snapshot 14.2.)

14.21. Suppose that the principal is $100. The present value of the bond if it were risk-free would be

$$2.5e^{-0.06\times0.5} + 2.5e^{-0.06\times1} + \cdots + 2.5e^{-0.06\times5} + 100e^{-0.06\times5} = 95.3579$$

The present value of the expected loss from defaults is therefore $95.3579 - 90 = 5.3579$. The asset swap is structured so that the $10 is paid initially. After that, $2.50 is paid every six months. In return, LIBOR plus a spread is received on the principal of $100. The present value of the fixed payments is

$$10 + 2.5e^{-0.06\times0.5} + 2.5e^{-0.06\times1} + \cdots + 2.5e^{-0.06\times5} + 100e^{-0.06\times5} = 105.3579$$

The spread over LIBOR must therefore have a present value of $5.3579. The present value of $1 received every six months for five years is $8.5105. The spread received every six months must therefore be $5.3579/8.5105 = \$0.6296$. The asset swap spread is therefore $2 \times 0.6296 = 1.2592\%$ per annum. This problem provides an illustration of the result in Problem 14.16.

CHAPTER 15

15.1. The new transaction will increase the bank's exposure to the counterparty if it tends to have a positive value whenever the existing contract has a positive value, and a negative value whenever the existing contract has a negative value. However, if the new transaction tends to offset the existing transaction, it is likely to have the incremental effect of reducing credit risk.

15.2. When securities are pledged as collateral, the haircut is the discount applied to their market value for margin calculations. A company's own equity would not be good collateral. When the company defaults on its contracts, its equity is likely to be worth very little.

15.3. In Vasicek's model and Credit Risk Plus, a credit loss is recognized when a default occurs. In CreditMetrics, both downgrades and defaults lead to credit losses. In Vasicek's model, a Gaussian copula model of time to default is used. In Credit Risk Plus, a probability distribution is assumed for the default rate per year. In CreditMetrics, a Gaussian copula model is used to define rating transitions.

15.4. The statements in (a) and (b) are true. The statement in (c) is not. Suppose that v_X and v_Y are the exposures to X and Y. The expected value of $v_X + v_Y$ is the expected value of v_X plus the expected value of v_Y. The same is not true of 95% confidence limits.

15.5. The cost of defaults is uv, where u is percentage loss from defaults during the life of the contract and v is the value of an option that pays off $\max(150S_T - 100, 0)$, where S_T is the exchange rate in one year (USD per AUD). The value of u is

$$u = 1 - e^{-(0.06-0.05)\times1} = 0.009950$$

The variable v is 150 times the value of a call option to buy 1 AUD for 0.6667. This is 4.545. It follows that the cost of defaults is 4.545×0.009950, or 0.04522.

15.6. In this case, the costs of defaults is $u_1 v_1 + u_2 v_2$, where

$$u_1 = 1 - e^{-(0.055 - 0.05) \times 0.3} = 0.002497$$

$$u_2 = e^{-(0.055 - 0.05) \times 0.5} - e^{-(0.06 - 0.05) \times 1} = 0.007453$$

v_1 is the value of a six-month call option on 150 AUD with a strike price of $100, and v_2 is the value of a similar one-year option. Evaluating the options gives $v_1 = 3.300$ and $v_2 = 4.545$. The cost of defaults is 0.04211.

15.7. Assume that defaults happen only at the end of the life of the forward contract. In a default-free world, the forward contract is the combination of a long European call and a short European put where the strike price of the options equals the delivery price and the maturity of the options equals the maturity of the forward contract. If the no-default value of the contract is positive at maturity, the call has a positive value and the put is worth zero. The impact of defaults on the forward contract is the same as that on the call. If the no-default value of the contract is negative at maturity, the call has a zero value and the put has a positive value. In this case, defaults have no effect. Again the impact of defaults on the forward contract is the same as that on the call. It follows that the contract has a value equal to a long position in a call that is subject to default risk and short position in a default-free put.

15.8. Suppose that the forward contract provides a payoff at time T. With our usual notation, the value of a long forward contract is $S_T - Ke^{-rT}$ (see Appendix C). The credit exposure on a long forward contract is therefore $\max(S_T - Ke^{-rT}, 0)$; that is, it is a call on the asset price with strike price Ke^{-rT}. Similarly the credit exposure on a short forward contract is $\max(Ke^{-rT} - S_T, 0)$; that is, it is a put on the asset price with strike price Ke^{-rT}. The total credit exposure is, therefore, a straddle with strike price Ke^{-rT}.

15.9. As time passes, there is a tendency for the currency which has the lower interest rate to strengthen. This means that a swap where we are receiving this currency will tend to move in the money (i.e., have a positive value). Similarly a swap where we are paying the currency will tend to move out of the money (i.e., have a negative value). From this it follows that our expected exposure on the swap where we are receiving the low-interest currency is much greater than our expected exposure on the swap where we are receiving the high-interest currency. We should therefore look for counterparties with a low credit risk on the side of the swap where we are receiving the low-interest currency. On the other side of the swap, we are far less concerned about the creditworthiness of the counterparty.

15.10. The Black–Scholes–Merton price must be multiplied by $e^{-0.01 \times 3} = 0.97$. Black–Scholes–Merton overstates the price by about 3%.

15.11. If many contracts entered into by company X are subject to the same default trigger, the effect of the default trigger may be to increase risk. If the company is downgraded so that the default trigger is activated, those of its counterparties who have contracts with negative values to company X will try to close out the contracts. As a result, company X is likely to experience liquidity problems and may be forced into bankruptcy. (See Business Snapshot 15.2.)

CHAPTER 16

16.1. Mortgages were frequently securitized. The only information that was retained during the securitization process was the applicant's FICO score and the loan-to-value ratio of the mortgage.

16.2. There was a short-term imbalance between supply and demand because many people were persuaded to take out mortgages that they could not afford.

16.3. When the loss rate on the mortgages is 5%, there are no losses on the mezzanine tranche of the ABS and therefore there are no losses on any of the tranches of the ABS CDO. When the loss rate on the mortgages is 12%, the loss on the mezzanine tranche of the ABS is 7/20, or 35%. The loss rate on the equity and mezzanine tranches of the ABS CDO is 100%. The loss rate on the senior tranche of the ABS CDO is $10/75 = 13.333\%$.

16.4 (a) $96\% \times 93\% + 3\% \times 76\% + 3\% \times 14\% \times 87\% = 91.9\%$.
(b) In this case, the answer is $91.9\% \times (100/110) = 83.6\%$

16.5. An ABS is a set of tranches created from a portfolio of loans, bonds, credit card receivables, etc. A CDO is an ABS created from fixed-income instruments such as bonds. An ABS CDO is an ABS created from particular tranches (e.g., the BBB-rated tranches) of a number of different ABSs.

16.6. The AAA-rated tranche of the ABS will experience losses when the loss rate on the underlying portfolio is greater than 25%. The AAA-rated tranche of the ABS CDO will experience losses when the loss rates on the mezzanine ABS tranches that are used to create the ABS CDO average more than 25%. This happens when the average loss rate on the underlying portfolios of mortgages is more than $5\% + 0.25 \times 20\%$, or 10%. The AAA-rated tranche of the ABS CDO is therefore much riskier.

16.7. "Agency costs" is a term used to describe the costs in a situation where the interests of two parties are not perfectly aligned.

16.8. If the mortgages to be securitized were chosen at random from all mortgages originated, there would be no difference. However, the originator is likely to be tempted to choose less creditworthy mortgages as the ones that are securitized. Moreover, when the originator has a stake in all the securitized products and is also the administrator of the mortgages, it has an incentive to administer the mortgages in the best interests of the investors.

16.9. Typically an ABS CDO is created from the BBB-rated tranches of an ABS. This is because it is difficult to find people to invest in the BBB-rated tranches of an ABS.

16.10. Mian and Sufi showed that regions where mortgage application denials were highest in the US in 1996 were also regions where mortgage origination grew particularly fast during the 2000 to 2007 period.

16.11. A cash CDO is created from bonds (or other fixed-income securities). A synthetic CDO is created from CDSs.

16.12. As default correlation increases, the senior tranche of a CDO becomes more risky because it is more likely to suffer losses. The equity tranche becomes less risky as the default correlation increases. To understand this, note that in the limit, when there is perfect correlation (and assuming no recoveries), all tranches have the same losses because either (a) all companies default or (b) no companies default.

16.13. The end-of-year bonus usually reflects performance during the year. Traders and other employees of banks are liable to be always focusing on their next end-of-year bonus and therefore have a short-term time horizon for their decision-making.

CHAPTER 17

17.1. Scenarios can be generated by (a) making large changes to key variables such as interest rates, equity prices, etc., (b) making percentage changes in all market variables that are the same as those that occurred on particular extreme days in the past, and (c) asking a committee of senior management to generate the scenarios.

17.2. Reverse stress testing involves using an algorithm to search for scenarios that lead to big losses. It is used to help identify appropriate scenarios for stress testing.

17.3. Financial institutions might consider that regulators will require more capital if scenarios leading to large losses are considered.

17.4. Traffic light options were options that provided payoffs when the scenarios considered by insurance company regulators occurred. The danger is that, when it buys a traffic light option, the financial institution is protecting itself against a too narrow range of adverse scenarios. The financial institution might not be protected against a scenario that is similar to, but not exactly the same as, the scenarios covered by the traffic light option.

17.5. Senior management are in the best position to develop scenarios for stress testing. The involvement of senior management in the development of scenarios makes it more likely that they will take the results of stress testing seriously and incorporate stress testing in their strategic decision making.

17.6. The advantage is that the same scenarios are considered by different banks and systemic risks can be evaluated. The scenarios might be worse than those considered by the banks themselves (see Problem 17.3). The disadvantage is that it might lead to the banks themselves not developing their own stress scenarios.

17.7. An objective probability is calculated from data. A subjective probability is a "degree of belief" and reflects a person's judgment.

17.8. The total probability of the stressed scenarios is 1.55%. The probability associated with the historical simulation scenarios is therefore 98.45%. Each historical simulation scenario has a probability of 0.001969. When the scenarios and their probabilities are ranked, we see that the VaR with a 99% confidence limit is $340,000. (For a loss of $341,366, the cumulative probability is 0.00941. For a loss of $340,000, the cumulative probability is 0.01141.)

17.9. In this case, the position values are 941.34, −164.39, −1,349.94 and −78.36. The worst-case scenario is where the asset price is 60 and its volatility is 30%. This leads to a loss of $341.39.

CHAPTER 18

18.1. The definition includes all internal risks and external risks except those related to reputation risk and risks resulting from strategic decisions.

18.2. Based on the results reported in Section 18.4, the loss would be $100 \times 3^{0.23}$, or $128.7 million.

18.3. $\text{Prob}(v > x) = Kx^{-0.8}$. When $x = 20$, the probability is 0.1. This means that $K = 1.0986$. The probability of the specified losses being exceeded are (a) 5.74%, (b) 3.30%, and (c) 1.58%.

18.4. Moral hazard is handled by deductibles and by making premiums dependent on past claims. Adverse selection is handled by finding out as much as possible about a driver before insurance is granted, and then modifying premiums as more information on the driver becomes available.

18.5. CEOs must prepare a statement asserting that the financial statements are accurate. They must return bonuses in the event that there is a restatement of financial statements.

18.6. If a trader operates within established risk limits and takes a loss, this is part of market risk. If risk limits are violated, the loss becomes classified as an operational risk.

18.7. (a) It is unlikely that an individual would not look after his or her health because of the existence of a life insurance contract, but it has been known for the beneficiary of a life insurance contract to commit murder to receive the payoff from the contract!

   (b) Individuals with short life expectancies are more likely to buy life insurance than individuals with long life expectancies.

18.8. External loss data is data relating to the losses of other banks. It is data obtained from sharing agreements with other banks or from data vendors. Vendor data is used to determine relative loss severity. It can be a useful indicator of the ratio of mean losses in Business Unit A to mean losses in Business Unit B or the ratio of the standard deviation of losses in Business Unit A to the standard deviation of losses in Business Unit B.

18.9. The Poisson distribution is commonly used for loss frequency. The lognormal distribution is commonly used for loss severity.

18.10. Two examples of key risk indicators are staff turnover and number of failed transactions.

18.11. When the loss frequency is 3, the mean total loss is about 3.3 and the standard deviation is about 2.0. When the loss frequency is increased to 4, the mean loss is about 4.4 and the standard deviation of the loss is about 2.4.

CHAPTER 19

19.1. Investors did not know very much about the mortgages underlying the tranches that were created and the waterfalls were complex.

19.2. The company or individual providing the quotes is prepared to buy at 50 and sell at 55. the mid-market quote is 52.5. The proportional bid–offer spread is 5.0/52.5, or 0.0952.

19.3. The bid–offer spread for the holding in company A is $0.01 \times 5000 = \$50$. The bid–offer spread for the holding in company B is $0.02 \times 3,000 = \$60$. The cost of unwinding the portfolio is $(50 + 60)/2$, or 55.

19.4. The bid–offer spread for the first holding that we are 95% confident will not be exceeded is $5,000 \times (0.01 + 1.645 \times 0.01) = \$132.24$. The bid–offer spread for the second holding that we are 95% confident will not be exceeded is $3,000 \times (0.02 + 1.645 \times 0.03) = \$208.04$. The total cost of unwinding that we are 95% confident will not be exceeded is

$$\tfrac{1}{2}(132.24 + 208.04) = \$170.14$$

19.5. The amount traded on successive days should be 15.9, 12.9, 10.0, 7.4, 5.2, 3.4, 2.2, 1.4, 0.9, 0.7. The bid–offer spread cost is $13.4. The total price variance is 36.6, so that the VaR for the market risk with a 95% confidence level is $1.645 \times \sqrt{36.6} = \$9.9$. (The value of the objective function that is minimized is the sum of these two, or $23.3.)

19.6. This is necessary because these assets cannot be converted into cash and cannot be pledged as collateral for additional loans.

19.7. Wholesale deposits are more liable to disappear in stressed market conditions.

19.8. Their hedging led to a loss on the hedge and a gain on the position being hedged. The loss on the hedge gave rise to margin calls. Unfortunately, the position being hedged, although it increased in value to the company, was illiquid.

19.9. Positive feedback trading refers to situations where traders accentuate market movements. They buy when prices increase and sell when prices decrease. Negative feedback trading is when traders do the reverse, that is, they buy when prices decline and sell when prices increase.

19.10. This is a VaR measure that includes an adjustment for the bid–offer spread costs that are incurred in a close-out of the position.

19.11. Liquidity black holes occur when most market participants want to be on one side of a market. Regulation is liable to lead to liquidity black holes. This is because, when all financial institutions are regulated in the same way, they tend to want to respond to external economic events in the same way.

19.12. Liquidity black holes are typically caused by too many traders following the same trading strategy. If traders follow diverse trading strategies, liquidity black holes are less likely to occur.

CHAPTER 20

20.1. Marking to market involves valuing a position using the prices at which the same or similar positions are trading in the market. Marking to model occurs when a model plays a key role in determining the price of an instrument.

20.2. Leverage and crashophobia.

20.3. Uncertain volatility and jumps.

20.4. When plain vanilla call and put options are being priced, traders do use the Black–Scholes–Merton model as an interpolation tool. They calculate implied volatilities for the options that are actively traded. By interpolating between strike prices and between times to maturity, they estimate implied volatilities for other options. These implied volatilities are then substituted into Black–Scholes–Merton to calculate prices for these options. Black–Scholes–Merton is more than an interpolation tool when used for hedging.

20.5. 13.45%. We get the same answer (a) by interpolating between strike prices of 1.00 and 1.05 and then between maturities of 6 months and 1 year, and (b) by interpolating between maturities of 6 months and 1 year and then between strike prices of 1.00 and 1.05.

20.6. The models of physics describe the behavior of physical processes. The models of finance ultimately describe the behavior of human beings.

20.7. It might notice that it is getting a large amount of business of a certain type because it is quoting prices different from its competitors. The pricing differences might also become apparent if it decides to unwind transactions and approaches competitors for quotes. In addition, it might subscribe to a service where once a month it obtains the average-price quotes by dealers for particular transactions.

20.8. Within-model hedging involves hedging against changes in variables that the model assumes to be stochastic. Outside-model hedging involves hedging against parameters that the model assumes to be constant.

20.9. The Black–Scholes–Merton model assumes that the probability distribution of the stock price in one month is lognormal. In this case, it is clearly not lognormal. Possibly, it consists of two lognormal distributions superimposed on each other and is bimodal. Black–Scholes is clearly inappropriate.

20.10. Fair-value accounting distinguishes between assets and liabilities that are expected to be held to maturity and assets and liabilities that are held for trading. Assets and liabilities in the second category have to be revalued each time financial statements are produced. In 2008, rules were eased so that financial institutions were, in exceptional cases, allowed to move an item from the "held for trading" to "held to maturity" category or vice versa. In 2009, rules were eased again so that internal models could be used in place of market prices in some situations.

20.11. In this case, the probability distribution of the exchange rate has a thin left tail and a thin right tail relative to the lognormal distribution. We are in the opposite situation to that described for foreign currencies in Section 20.4. Both out-of-the-money and in-the-money calls and puts can be expected to have lower implied volatilities than at-the-money calls and puts.

20.12. The term "marking to market" refers to the practice of revaluing instruments (usually daily) so that their prices are consistent with the market. The prices calculated for actively traded products do reflect market prices. The model is used merely as an interpolation tool. The term "marking to market" is therefore accurate for these products. The prices for structured products and exotic options depend on the model being used. Hence the term "marking to model".

CHAPTER 21

21.1. Economic capital is a bank's own estimate of the capital it requires. Regulatory capital is the capital it is required to keep by bank supervisors.

21.2. Often the confidence level is chosen to be consistent with the financial institution's credit rating. For example, if the credit rating is AA and a company with a AA rating has 0.03% chance of defaulting in one year, the confidence level is 99.97%.

21.3. Business risk includes risks relating to strategic decisions and reputation.

21.4. The models used for economic capital are likely to be broadly similar to those used to calculate regulatory capital in the case of market risk and operational risk. When calculating credit risk economic capital, a bank may consider it appropriate to use a different credit correlation model and different correlation parameters from those used in regulatory capital calculations.

21.5. The 99.97% worst-case value of the logarithm of the loss is $0.5 + 4 \times 3.43 = 14.23$. The 99.97% worst-case loss is therefore $1.510 million. From the properties of the log-normal distribution, the expected loss is $\exp(0.5 + 4^2/2)$, or $4,915. The capital requirement is therefore $1.505 million.

21.6. The economic capital for Business Unit 1 is 96.85. The economic capital for Business Unit 2 is 63.87. The total capital is 124.66.

21.7. The incremental effect of Business Unit 1 on total economic capital is 60.78. The incremental effect of Business Unit 2 on total economic capital is 27.81. This suggests that $60.78/(60.78 + 27.81)$, or 68.61%, of economic capital should be allocated to Business Unit 1 and $27.81/(60.78 + 27.81)$, or 31.39%, to Business Unit 2. The marginal effect of increasing the size of Business Unit 1 by 0.5% is 0.4182. The marginal effect of increasing the size of Business Unit 2 by 0.5% is 0.2056. Euler's theorem is satisfied because the total economic capital is approximately equal to the sum of 0.4182/0.005 and 0.2056/0.005.

21.8. The capital is $38 million and the return before tax is $7 million. The before-tax RAROC is therefore 18.4%. In practice the allocation of diversification benefits to this venture might reduce capital and increase RAROC.

21.9. RAROC can be used to compare the past performance of different business units or to project the expected future performance of business units.

Glossary of Terms

ABS *See* Asset-backed Security

ABS CDO Security created from the tranches of different ABSs.

Accrued Interest The interest earned on a bond since the last coupon payment date.

Add-on Factor When the credit equivalent amount for a derivatives transaction is being calculated, this is the percentage of principal added to the current exposure to allow for possible future changes in the value of the derivative.

Advanced Measurement Approach The way in which the most sophisticated banks are allowed to calculate regulatory capital for operational risk under Basel II.

Adverse Selection The phenomenon that, if an insurance company offers the same premiums to everyone, it tends to end up providing coverage for the worst risks.

Agency Costs Costs in a business relationship where the interests of the two parties are not perfectly aligned.

Alternative Investments *See* Hedge Funds.

Alpha Return earned on a portfolio in excess of that predicted by the capital asset pricing model.

American Option An option that can be exercised at any time during its life.

Analytic Result Result where answer is in the form of an equation.

Arbitrage A trading strategy that takes advantage of two or more securities being mispriced relative to each other.

Arbitrage Pricing Theory A theory where the return from an investment is assumed to depend on several factors.

Arbitrageur An individual engaging in arbitrage.

Asian Option An option with a payoff dependent on the average price of the underlying asset during a specified period.

Ask Price *See* Offer Price.

Asked Price *See* Offer Price.

Asset-backed Security Security created from the cash flows from bonds, mortgages, credit card receivables, or other instruments.

511

Asset Swap   Exchanges the promised coupon on a bond for LIBOR plus a spread.

At-the-Money Option   An option in which the strike price equals the price of the underlying asset.

Autocorrelation   The correlation between the value of a variable and the value of the same variable k days later. (k is referred to as the time lag.)

Average Price Call Option   An option giving a payoff equal to the greater of zero and the amount by which the average price of the asset exceeds the strike price.

Average Price Put Option   An option giving a payoff equal to the greater of zero and the amount by which the strike price exceeds the average price of the asset.

Back-end Load   Fee charged when an investment in a mutual fund is terminated.

Back-testing   Testing a value-at-risk or other model using historical data.

Backwards Induction   A procedure for working from the end of a tree to its beginning in order to value an option.

Banking Book   Part of a bank's portfolio that consists of instruments that are expected to be held to maturity.

Bankruptcy Costs   Costs such as lost sales, loss of key managers, and professional fees arising from a declaration of bankruptcy. These costs are not associated with the adverse events leading to bankruptcy.

Barrier Option   An option whose payoff depends on whether the path of the underlying asset has reached a barrier (i.e., a certain predetermined level).

Basel I   The first international agreement on the regulation of banks in 1988.

Basel II   New international regulations for calculating bank capital that came into effect in 2007.

Basic Indicator Approach   The simplest way of calculating regulatory capital for operational risk under Basel II.

Basis   The difference between the spot price and the futures price of a commodity.

Basis Point   When used to describe an interest rate, a basis point is one hundredth of one percent (= 0.01%)

Basis Risk   The risk to a hedger arising from uncertainty about the basis at a future time.

Basket Credit Default Swap   Credit default swap where there are several reference entities.

Basket Option   Option on a portfolio of assets.

Bermudan Options   An option that can be exercised on certain dates during its life.

Best Efforts   Phrase used to describe the situation where an investment bank agrees that it will do the best it can to sell a new issue of securities at a certain price, but does not guarantee that it will be able to do so.

Beta   A measure of the systematic risk of an asset.

Bid–Ask Spread   *See* Bid–Offer Spread

Bid–Offer Spread   The amount by which the offer price exceeds the bid price.

Bid Price   The price that a dealer is prepared to pay for an asset.

Binary Credit Default Swap Instrument where there is a fixed dollar payoff in the event of a default by a particular company.

Binary Option Option with a discontinuous payoff; for example, an option that pays off $100 if an asset price is greater than $20 on a certain date.

Binomial Model A model where the price of an asset is monitored over successive short periods of time. In each short period, it is assumed that only two price movements are possible.

Binomial Tree A tree that represents how an asset price can evolve under the binomial model.

BIS Accord Agreement reached in 1988 between the central banks of 12 countries concerning how banks should be regulated.

Bivariate Normal Distribution A distribution for two correlated variables, each of which is normal.

Black's Model An extension of the Black–Scholes–Merton model for valuing European options on futures contracts. It is used extensively in practice to value European options when the distribution of the asset price at maturity is assumed to be lognormal.

Black–Scholes–Merton Model A model for pricing European options on stocks, developed by Fischer Black, Myron Scholes, and Robert Merton.

Bond Option An option where a bond is the underlying asset.

Bond Yield Discount rate which, when applied to all the cash flows of a bond, causes the present value of the cash flows to equal the bond's market price.

Bootstrap Method A procedure for calculating the zero-coupon yield curve from market data. Also a statistical procedure for calculating confidence levels when distributions are determined empirically.

Bunching A tendency for days when the loss is greater than the value at risk to be bunched close together.

Business Risk When used for a bank this refers to strategic risk (related to a bank's decision to enter new markets and develop new products) and reputation risk.

Calendar Days Includes every day.

Calibration Method for implying a model's parameters from the prices of actively traded instruments.

Callable Bond A bond containing provisions that allow the issuer to buy it back at a predetermined price at certain times during its life.

Call Option An option to buy an asset at a certain price by a certain date.

Cancelable Swap Swap that can be canceled by one side on prespecified dates.

Cap *See* Interest Rate Cap.

Cap Rate The rate determining payoffs in an interest rate cap.

Capital Adequacy The adequacy of the capital held by a bank or other financial institution.

Capital Asset Pricing Model A model relating the expected return on an asset to its beta.

Caplet   One component of an interest rate cap.

Cash-flow Mapping   A procedure for representing an instrument as a portfolio of zero-coupon bonds for the purpose of calculating value at risk.

Case–Shiller Index   Index of house prices in US.

Cash Settlement   Procedure for settling a contract in cash rather than by delivering the underlying asset.

CAT Bond   Bond where the interest and, possibly, the principal paid are reduced if a particular category of "catastrophic" insurance claims exceed a certain amount.

CDD   Cooling degree days. The maximum of zero and the amount by which the daily average temperature is greater than $65°$ Fahrenheit. The average temperature is the average of the highest and lowest temperatures (midnight to midnight).

CDO   *See* Collateralized Debt Obligation.

CDO Squared   An instrument in which the default risks in a portfolio of CDO tranches are allocated to new securities.

CDS–Bond Basis   The excess of the CDS spread over the asset swap spread.

CDX   An index of the credit quality of 125 North American investment grade companies.

Cheapest-to-Deliver Bond   Bond that is cheapest to buy and then deliver in a futures contract or a credit default swap contract.

Chinese Walls   Phrase used to describe the policies in place within a financial institution that prevent information flowing from one part of the financial institution to another when this would be disadvantageous to one or more of the financial institution's clients.

Cholesky Decomposition   Method of sampling from a multivariate normal distribution.

Clawback Clause   Clause where a percentage of previous incentive fees can be recouped to compensate for a percentage of current losses.

Clean Price of Bond   The quoted price of a bond. The cash price paid for the bond (or dirty price) is calculated by adding the accrued interest to the clean price.

Clearinghouse   A firm that guarantees the performance of the parties in an exchange-traded derivatives transaction. (Also referred to as a clearing corporation.)

Clearing margin   A margin posted by a member of a clearinghouse.

Closed-end Fund   A mutual fund where there is a fixed number of shares.

Coherent Risk Measure   A risk measure satisfying a number of conditions.

Collar   *See* Interest Rate Collar

Collateralization   A system for posting collateral by one or both parties in a derivatives transaction.

Collateralized Debt Obligation   A way of packaging credit risk. Several classes of securities (known as tranches) are created from a portfolio of bonds and there are rules for determining how cash flows are allocated to classes.

Commercial Bank   A bank that takes deposits and makes loans.

Component Value at Risk VaR corresponding to a component of a portfolio. Defined so that the sum of the component VaRs for the components of a portfolio equals the VaR for the whole portfolio.

Compounding Frequency This defines how an interest rate is measured.

Compound Option An option on an option.

Compounding Swap Swap where interest compounds instead of being paid.

Conditional Value at Risk (C-VaR) *See* Expected Shortfall.

Confirmation Contract confirming verbal agreement between two parties to a trade in the over-the-counter market

Consumption Asset An asset held for consumption rather than investment.

Continuous Compounding A way of quoting interest rates. It is the limit as the assumed compounding interval is made smaller and smaller.

Convenience Yield A measure of the benefits from ownership of an asset that are not obtained by the holder of a long futures contract on the asset.

Conversion Factor Factor multiplied by principal to convert an off-balance sheet item to its credit equivalent amount.

Convertible Bond A corporate bond that can be converted into a predetermined amount of the company's equity at certain times during its life.

Convexity A measure of the curvature in the relationship between bond prices and bond yields.

Convexity Adjustment An overworked term. For example, it can refer to the adjustment necessary to convert a futures interest rate to a forward interest rate. It can also refer to the adjustment to a forward rate that is sometimes necessary when instruments are valued.

Cooke Ratio Ratio of capital to risk weighted assets under Basel I.

Copula A way of defining the correlation between variables with known distributions.

Cornish–Fisher Expansion An approximate relationship between the fractiles of a probability distribution and its moments.

Correlation Measure of the extent to which there is a linear relation between two variables.

Correlation Matrix A matrix showing correlations between a number of different market variables.

Cost of Carry The storage costs plus the cost of financing an asset minus the income earned on the asset.

Counterparty The opposite side in a financial transaction.

Coupon Interest payment made on a bond.

Covariance Measure of the linear relationship between two variables (equals the correlation between the variables times the product of their standard deviations)

Covered Call A short position in a call option on an asset combined with a long position in the asset.

Crashophobia The fear of a stock market crash similar to that in 1987 that some people claim causes market participants to increase the value of deep-out-of-the-money put options.

Credit Contagion The tendency of a default by one company to lead to defaults by other companies.

Credit Default Swap An instrument that gives the holder the right to sell a bond for its face value in the event of a default by the issuer.

Credit Derivative A derivative whose payoff depends on the creditworthiness of one or more companies or countries.

Credit Equivalent Amount Size of loan that is considered equivalent to an off-balance-sheet transaction in Basel I.

Credit Index Index that tracks the cost of buying protection for each company in a particular portfolio.

Credit Rating A measure of the creditworthiness of a bond.

Credit Ratings Transition Matrix A table showing the probability that a bond will move from one credit rating to another during a certain period of time.

Credit Risk The risk that a loss will be experienced because of a default by a company.

Credit Risk Migration Movement of a company from one rating category to another.

Credit Risk Plus A procedure for calculating credit value at risk.

Credit Spread Cost of buying credit protection. Also, the difference between the yield on a bond that might default and the yield on a risk-free bond.

Credit Value at Risk The credit loss that will not be exceeded at some specified confidence level.

CreditMetrics A procedure for calculating credit value at risk.

Cumulative Distribution Function The probability that a variable will be less than x as a function of x.

Currency Swap A swap where interest and principal in one currency are exchanged for interest and principal in another currency.

Day Count A convention for quoting interest rates.

Day Trade A trade that is entered into and closed out on the same day.

Default Correlation Measures the tendency of two companies to default at about the same time.

Default Intensity *See* Hazard Rate.

Deferred Annuity Annuity where time elapses between the payment of the funds that will provide the annuity and the start of the annuity

Defined Benefit Plan Pension plan where there is a formula defining the pension that will be received. Typically, the formula depends on the number of years of service and the salary during the final years of service.

Defined Contribution Plan Pension plan where an employee's contributions plus the contributions made for the employee by the employer are kept in a separate account and invested. On retirement the funds in the account are usually converted into an annuity. Sometimes, they can be taken out as a lump sum.

Deleveraging   Individuals and companies reducing their borrowings.

Delivery Price   Price that will be paid or received in a forward contract.

Delta   The rate of change of the price of a derivative with the price of the underlying asset.

Delta Hedging   A hedging procedure that is designed to make the price of a portfolio of derivatives insensitive to small changes in the price of the underlying asset.

Delta-neutral Portfolio   A portfolio with a delta of zero, so that there is no sensitivity to small changes in the price of the underlying asset.

Dependence   Variable X is dependent on variable Y if knowing the value of Y affects the probability density function of X.

Deposit Insurance   Government programs for providing restitution to the depositors of a bank in the event that the bank fails.

DerivaGem   Software for valuing options, available with this book.

Derivative   An instrument whose price depends on, or is derived from, the price of another asset.

Deterministic Variable   A variable whose future value is known.

Directed Brokerage   Phrase used to describe the situation where a fund directs its trades to a brokerage house in return for the brokerage house advising its clients to buy the fund.

Dirty Price of Bond   Cash price of bond.

Discount Bond   *See* Zero-Coupon Bond.

Discount Instrument   An instrument, such as a Treasury bill, that provides no coupons.

Discount Rate   The annualized dollar return on a Treasury bill or similar instrument expressed as a percentage of the final face value.

Distance to Default   The number of standard deviations that the value of a company's assets must move for a default to be triggered.

Diversification   Reducing risk by dividing a portfolio between many different assets.

Dividend   A cash payment made to the owner of a stock.

Dividend Yield   The dividend as a percentage of the stock price.

Dollar Convexity   The convexity of an interest-rate-dependent portfolio multiplied by the value of the portfolio.

Dollar Duration   The duration of an interest-rate-dependent portfolio multiplied by the value of the portfolio.

Down-and-In Option   An option that comes into existence when the price of the underlying asset declines to a prespecified level.

Down-and-Out Option   An option that ceases to exist when the price of the underlying asset declines to a prespecified level.

Downgrade Trigger   A clause in a contract that states that the contract can be terminated by one side if the credit rating of the other side falls below a certain level.

Duration   A measure of the average life a bond. It is also an approximation to the ratio of the proportional change in the bond price to the absolute change in its yield.

Duration Matching   A procedure for matching the durations of assets and liabilities.

Dutch Auction   A process where investors provide bids indicating the number of shares they are prepared to buy and the price they are prepared to pay. Suppose that there are N shares on offer. The price that clears the market is the highest price, P, such that investors are prepared to buy at least N shares at either P or a higher price than P. The investors who have bid more than P get their orders filled at a price of P. The investors who have bid P get part of their orders filled at P.

DV01   The impact of a 1-basis-point increase in all interest rates.

Dynamic Hedging   A procedure for hedging an option position by periodically changing the position held in the underlying asset. The objective is usually to maintain a delta-neutral position.

Dynamic Scenarios   Scenarios involving adverse movements in market variables that consider the way companies will respond to the adverse movements.

EAD   *See* Exposure at Default.

Early Exercise   Exercise prior to the maturity date.

Economic Capital   The capital that a bank's own calculation indicates it needs.

Efficient Frontier   The optimal trade-offs for an investor between expected return and standard deviation of return.

Efficient Market Hypothesis   A hypothesis that asset prices reflect relevant information.

Electronic Trading   System of trading where a computer is used to match buyers and sellers.

Embedded Option   An option that is an inseparable part of another instrument.

Empirical Research   Research based on historical market data.

Endowment Life Insurance   Insurance that pays out a predetermined amount on maturity of the contract or on the policyholder's death, whichever is earlier.

Equity Swap   A swap where the return on an equity portfolio is exchanged for either a fixed or a floating rate of interest.

Equity Tranche   Tranche which is first to be affected by losses on the underlying portfolio.

Eurocurrency   A currency that is outside the formal control of the issuing country's monetary authorities.

Eurodollar   A dollar held in a bank outside the United States.

Eurodollar Futures Contract   A futures contract written on a Eurodollar deposit.

Eurodollar Interest Rate   The interest rate on a Eurodollar deposit.

European Option   An option that can be exercised only at the end of its life.

EWMA   *See* Exponentially Weighted Moving Average Model.

Excess Cost Layers   The costs for an insurance company on a particular type of business that are within a certain range.

Excess Spread   Situation where the aggregate return promised to the tranches is less than the promised return on the underlying assets.

Exchange-traded Fund Fund that is created in such a way that units of the can be exchanged for the underlying shares and vice versa by institutional investors.

Exchange-traded Market Market organized by an exchange such as the New York Stock Exchange or Chicago Board Options Exchange.

Ex-dividend Date When a dividend is declared, an ex-dividend date is specified. Investors who own shares of the stock just before the ex-dividend date receive the dividend.

Exercise Price The price at which the underlying asset may be bought or sold in an option contract. Also called the strike price.

Exotic Option A nonstandard option.

Expected Shortfall Expected loss during N days conditional on being in the $(100 - X)\%$ right tail of the distribution of losses. The variable N is the time horizon and $X\%$ is the confidence level.

Expectations Theory The theory that forward interest rates equal expected future spot interest rates.

Expected Value of a Variable The average value of the variable obtained by weighting the alternative values by their probabilities.

Expiration Date The end of life of a contract.

Exponential Weighting A weighting scheme where the weight given to an observation depends on how recent it is. The weight given to an observation t time periods ago is λ times the weight given to an observation $t - 1$ time periods ago, where $\lambda < 1$.

Exponentially Weighted Moving Average (EWMA) Model A model where exponential weighting is used to provide forecasts for a variable from historical data. It is sometimes applied to variances and covariances in value at risk calculations.

Exposure at Default The maximum amount that could be lost (assuming no recovery) when a default occurs.

Extreme Value Theory A theory enabling the shape of the tails of a distribution to be estimated from data.

Factor Source of uncertainty.

Factor Analysis An analysis aimed at finding a small number of factors that describe most of the variation in a large number of correlated variables. (Similar to a principal components analysis.)

Factor Copula A copula involving several variables where a factor model describes the correlation structure of the transformed variables.

Factor Loadings The values of variables in a factor model when we have one unit of a particular factor and no units of other factors.

Factor Model Model where a set of correlated variables are assumed to depend linearly on a number of uncorrelated factors.

Factor Score In a factor model, this is the amount of a factor present in a particular observation on the variables.

FICO A credit score developed by Fair Isaac Corporation.

Fair-Value Accounting Involves showing financial instruments on the balance sheet at their market value.

Financial Intermediary A bank or other financial institution that facilitates the flow of funds between different entities in the economy.

Firm Commitment Phrase used to describe the situation where an investment bank guarantees that a new issue of securities will be sold at a certain price. If investors do not want to buy the securities, the investment bank will have to do so.

Fixed Annuity Annuity where payments that will be received are fixed in advance.

Floor *See* Interest Rate Floor.

Floor–Ceiling Agreement *See* Collar.

Floorlet One component of a floor.

Floor Rate The rate in an interest rate floor agreement.

Foreign Currency Option An option on a foreign exchange rate.

Forward Contract A contract that obligates the holder to buy or sell an asset for a predetermined delivery price at a predetermined future time.

Forward Exchange Rate The forward price of one unit of a foreign currency.

Forward Interest Rate The interest rate for a future period of time implied by the rates prevailing in the market today.

Forward Price The delivery price in a forward contract that causes the contract to be worth zero.

Forward Rate Can refer to a forward interest rate or a forward exchange rate.

Forward Rate Agreement (FRA) Agreement that a certain interest rate will apply to a certain principal amount for a certain time period in the future.

Front-end Load Fee charged when mutual fund is purchased.

Front Running Trading a stock on a personal account before a fund trades a large volume of the stock.

Fund of Funds A fund that invests in a portfolio of different hedge funds.

Futures Contract A contract that obligates the holder to buy or sell an asset at a predetermined delivery price during a specified future time period. The contract is settled daily.

Futures Option An option on a futures contract.

Futures Price The delivery price currently applicable to a futures contract.

G-30 Policy Recommendations A set of recommendations concerning derivatives issued by nonregulators in 1993.

Gamma The rate of change of delta with respect to the asset price.

Gamma-neutral Portfolio A portfolio with a gamma of zero.

GARCH Model A model for forecasting volatility where the variance rate follows a mean-reverting process.

Gaussian Copula Model A copula model based on the multivariate normal distribution.

Glass–Steagall Act An act passed in the United States separating commercial and investment banks.

Greek Letters *See* Greeks.

Greeks   Hedge parameters such as delta, gamma, vega, theta, and rho.

Group Life Insurance   Life insurance arranged for a group of people, usually by their employer.

Haircut   Discount applied to the value of an asset when it is used as collateral.

Hazard Rate   Measures probability of default in a short period of time conditional on no earlier default.

HDD   Heating degree days. The maximum of zero and the amount by which the daily average temperature is less than 65° Fahrenheit. The average temperature is the average of the highest and lowest temperatures (midnight to midnight).

Hedge   A trade designed to reduce risk.

Hedge Funds   Funds that are subject to less restrictions and less regulation than mutual funds. They can take short positions and use derivatives, but they cannot publicly offer their securities.

Hedger   An individual who enters into hedging trades.

Hedge Ratio   The ratio of the size of a position in a hedging instrument to the size of the position being hedged.

High Water Mark Clause   Clause stating that gains equal to previous losses must be made before incentive fees apply.

Historical Default Probabilities   Default probabilities estimated from historical default experience.

Historical Simulation   A simulation based on historical data.

Historical Volatility   A volatility estimated from historical data.

Holiday Calendar   Calendar defining which days are holidays for the purposes of determining payment dates in a financial transaction.

Hurdle Rate   Return that must be earned by a hedge fund before the incentive fee applies.

Hybrid Approach   Approach to aggregating different types of economic capital.

Implied Volatility   Volatility implied from an option price using the Black–Scholes–Merton or similar model.

Inception Profit   Profit created by selling a derivative for more than its theoretical value.

Incremental Value at Risk   The difference between the value at risk with and without a particular component of the portfolio.

Independence   Variable X is independent of variable Y if knowing the value of variable Y does not affect the probability density function for variable X.

Index Fund   A fund that is designed to match the performance of a particular stock index.

Initial Margin   The cash required from a futures trader at the time of the trade.

Instantaneous Forward Rate   Forward rate for a very short period of time in the future.

Interest Rate Cap   An option that provides a payoff when a specified interest rate is above a certain level. The interest rate is a floating rate that is reset periodically.

Interest Rate Collar   A combination of an interest rate cap and an interest rate floor.

Interest Rate Derivative   A derivative whose payoffs are dependent on future interest rates.

Interest Rate Floor   An option that provides a payoff when an interest rate is below a certain level. The interest rate is a floating rate that is reset periodically.

Interest Rate Option   An option where the payoff is dependent on the level of interest rates.

Interest Rate Swap   An exchange of a fixed rate of interest on a certain notional principal for a floating rate of interest on the same notional principal.

Internal Credit Rating   Credit rating produced by a financial institution rather than by a outside agency such as Moody's or S&P.

In-the-Money Option   Either (a) a call option where the asset price is greater than the strike price or (b) a put option where the asset price is less than the strike price.

Intrinsic Value   For a call option, this is the greater of the excess of the asset price over the strike price and zero. For a put option, it is the greater of the excess of the strike price over the asset price and zero.

Investment Asset   An asset held by a significant number of individuals for investment purposes.

Investment Bank   A bank that helps companies issue debt and equity securities.

Investment Grade   Bond or other instrument with a credit rating of BBB (Baa) or above.

IPO   Initial Public Offering. An offering to investors of shares in a company for the first time. Prior to an IPO, shares are typically held only by the company's founders, its employees, and the providers of venture capital.

iTraxx   An index of the credit quality of 125 European investment grade companies.

IRB Approach   Internal ratings based approach for assessing credit risk capital in Basel II.

IRC   Incremental Risk Charge. A possible extra capital charge for credit sensitive instruments in the trading book.

Junk Bond   Non-investment-grade bond.

Key Risk Indicators   Indicators to track the level of operational risk.

Kurtosis   A measure of the fatness of the tails of a distribution.

Late Trading   Trading a mutual fund after 4 p.m. at the 4 p.m. price.

Leveraging   Individuals and companies increasing their borrowings.

LGD   *See* Loss Given Default.

Liar Loan   Loan where the borrower does not tell the truth on the application form.

LIBID   London interbank bid rate. The rate bid by banks on Eurocurrency deposits (i.e., the rate at which a bank is willing to borrow from other banks).

LIBOR   London interbank offered rate. The rate offered by banks on Eurocurrency deposits (i.e., the rate at which a bank is willing to lend to other banks).

LIBOR Zero Curve   *See* LIBOR/Swap Zero Curve.

LIBOR-in-Arrears Swap Swap where the interest paid on a date is determined by the interest rate observed on that date (not by the interest rate observed on the previous payment date).

LIBOR/Swap Zero Curve Zero rates that are calculated from LIBOR rates, eurodollar futures, and swap rates.

Life Insurance Insurance where payouts depend on when a person dies.

Linear Model A model where the change in the portfolio value depends linearly on the returns of the underlying market variables.

Linear Product Derivative product whose price depends linearly on one or more underlying variables.

Liquidity-adjusted VaR A value at risk calculation that takes account of the impact of the bid–offer spread when positions are unwound.

Liquidity Black Holes The risk that liquidity will dry up because everyone wants to be on the same side of the market.

Liquidity Preference Theory A theory leading to the conclusion that forward interest rates are above expected future spot interest rates.

Liquidity Premium The amount that forward interest rates exceed expected future spot interest rates.

Liquidity Funding Risk The risk that sources of funding will dry up.

Liquidity Trading Risk The risk that it will not be possible to unwind positions in financial instruments at their theoretical price.

Lognormal Distribution A variable has a lognormal distribution when the logarithm of the variable has a normal distribution.

Longevity Risk Risk that people will live longer than expected.

Long Position A position involving the purchase of an asset.

Long-tail Risk Risk in property–casualty insurance that claims will be made well after the end of the life of a policy.

Lookback Option An option whose payoff is dependent on the maximum or minimum of the asset price achieved during a certain period.

Loss Given Default The percentage of the exposure to a counterparty that is lost when a default by the counterparty occurs.

MacCaulay's Duration The weighted average of the times when cash flows are received where the weight applied to a cash flow is proportional to the present value of the cash flow.

Maintenance Margin When the balance in a trader's margin account falls below the maintenance margin level, the trader receives a margin call requiring the account to be topped up.

Margin The cash or traded securities required from a trader to reduce potential losses in the event that the trader defaults.

Margin Call A request for extra margin when the balance in the margin account falls below the maintenance margin level.

Marginal Value at Risk   The rate of change of the value at risk with the size of one component of the portfolio.

Market Maker   A trader who is willing to quote both bid and offer prices for an asset.

Market Model   A model most commonly used by traders.

Market Portfolio   A portfolio consisting of the universe of all possible investments.

Market Risk   Risk relating to movements in market variables.

Market Timing   Frequent trading of a mutual fund to benefit from stale prices or to do late trading.

Marking to Market   The practice of revaluing a financial instrument to reflect the current values of the relevant market variables.

Marking to Model   Use of a model to determine the current value of a financial instrument.

Maturity Date   The end of the life of a contract.

Maximum Likelihood Method   A method for choosing the values of parameters by maximizing the probability of a set of observations occurring.

Mean Reversion   The tendency of a market variable (such as a volatility or an interest rate) to revert back to some long-run average level.

Merton's Model   Model using equity prices to estimate default probabilities. (Other models developed by Merton are also sometimes referred to as Merton's model.)

Mezzanine Tranche   Tranche which experiences losses after equity tranche but before the senior tranches.

Model-building Approach   The use of a model to estimate value at risk.

Model Risk   The risk relating to the use of models to price derivative products.

Moral Hazard   The possibility that the behavior of an insured entity will change because of the existence of an insurance contract.

Modified Duration   A modification to the standard duration measure so that it more accurately describes the relationship between proportional changes in a bond price and actual changes in its yield. The modification takes account of the compounding frequency with which the yield is quoted.

Money Center Banks   Banks with a global presence that fund themselves to a significant extent in wholesale markets.

Monte Carlo Simulation   A procedure for randomly sampling changes in market variables.

Mortality Risk   Risk that people will die earlier than expected.

Multibank Holding Company   A holding company owning several banks. This structure was used in the US for getting round some bank regulations.

Multivariate Normal Distribution   The joint distribution of many variables, each of which is normal.

Mutual Fund   A vehicle for investing the funds of many small investors. (Also called a *unit trust* in some countries.)

Naked Position   A short position in an option that is not combined with a position in the underlying asset.

National Association of Insurance Commissioners National body that provides services to the insurance regulators in each state in the US.

Negative Feedback Trading Trading where assets are sold after a price increase and bought after a price decrease.

Net Asset Value Value of a fund's investments divided by the number of shares in the fund.

Net Interest Income The excess of interest earned over interest paid for a bank.

Net Replacement Ratio The ratio of current exposure with netting to current exposure without netting.

Netting The ability to offset instruments with positive and negative values in the event of a default by a counterparty

NINJA Term used to describe a poor credit risk: no income, no job, no assets.

Noninvestment Grade Bond or other instrument with a credit rating below BBB (Baa).

Nonlife Insurance *See* Property–Casualty Insurance

Nonlinear product Derivative product that is not linearly dependent on the underlying variables.

Nonperforming Loan A loan where interest is more than 90 days' overdue.

Nonsystematic Risk Risk that can be diversified away.

Normal Distribution The standard bell-shaped distribution of statistics.

Normal Market A market where futures prices increase with maturity.

Notional Principal The principal used to calculate payments in an interest rate swap. The principal is "notional" because it is neither paid nor received.

Numerical Procedure A method of calculation when no formula is available.

Objective Probability Probability based on data.

Offer Price The price that a dealer is offering to sell an asset.

Open-end Fund Mutual fund where the number of shares outstanding increases and decreases as investors deposit and withdraw funds.

Open Interest The total number of long positions outstanding in a futures contract (equals the total number of short positions).

Open Outcry System of trading where traders meet on the floor of the exchange

Operational Risk The risk of loss arising from inadequate or failed internal processes, people, and systems or from external events.

Option The right to buy or sell an asset.

Originate-to-Distribute Model Phrase used to describe the practice where a bank originates loans, credit card receivables, etc., and securitizes them so that the credit risks are distributed to other investors.

Out-of-the-Money Option Either (a) a call option where the asset price is less than the strike price or (b) a put option where the asset price is greater than the strike price.

Outside-Model Hedging   Hedging against parameters that are assumed to be constant rather than stochastic by a model (cf. Within-Model Hedging).

Overcollateralization   Situation where total principal of the underlying assets is greater than the sum of the principals of the tranches that are created from the assets.

Over-the-Counter Market   A market where traders deal by phone. The traders are usually financial institutions, corporations, and fund managers.

Par Value   The principal amount of a bond.

Par Yield   The coupon on a bond that makes its price equal the principal.

Parallel Shift   A movement in the yield curve where each point on the curve changes by the same amount.

Partial Duration   Percentage change in value of a portfolio for a small change in one point on the zero-coupon yield curve.

Payoff   The cash realized by the holder of an option or other derivative at the end of its life.

PD   Probability of default.

Performing Loan   A loan where interest is not more than 90 days' overdue.

Physical Default Probability   *See* Historical Default Probability.

Plain Vanilla   A term used to describe a standard deal.

Poison Pill   Action taken by a company to make a takeover of the company more difficult.

Poisson Distribution   Distribution for number of events in a certain time period in a Poisson process.

Poisson Process   A process describing a situation where events happen at random. The probability of an event in time Δt is $\lambda \Delta t$, where λ is the intensity of the process.

Policyholder   Holder of an insurance policy.

Portfolio Immunization   Making a portfolio relatively insensitive to interest rates.

Portfolio Insurance   Entering into trades to ensure that the value of a portfolio will not fall below a certain level.

Positive Feedback Trading   Trading where assets are sold after a price decline and bought after a price increase.

Positive Semidefinite   Condition that must be satisfied by a variance–covariance matrix for it to be valid.

Power Law   Law describing the tails of many probability distributions that are encountered in practice.

Premium   The price of an instrument.

Prime Broker   A bank that clears a hedge fund's trades, provides it with borrowings, and provides other services.

Principal   The par or face value of a debt instrument.

Principal Components Analysis   An analysis aimed at finding a small number of factors that describe most of the variation in a large number of correlated variables. (Similar to a factor analysis.)

Private Placement   Selling a new issue of securities to a small number large financial institutions without offering it to the general public.

Property–Casualty Insurance   Property insurance provides a payout in the event of loss of property or damage to property. Casualty insurance provides protection against legal liabilities or damage to the property of others.

Proprietary Trading   Trading for a financial institution's own account rather than the account of one of the financial institution's clients.

Public Offering   Attempting to sell a new issue of securities to the general public.

Put–Call Parity   The relationship between the price of a European call option and the price of a European put option when they have the same strike price and maturity date.

Put Option   An option to sell an asset for a certain price by a certain date.

Puttable Bond   A bond where the holder has the right to sell it back to the issuer at certain predetermined times for a predetermined price.

Puttable Swap   A swap where one side has the right to terminate early.

Quadratic Model   Quadratic relationship between change in portfolio value and percentage changes in market variables.

Quantitative Impact Studies   Studies by the Basel committee of the effect of proposed new regulations on capital of banks.

RAROC   Risk-adjusted return on capital.

RCSA   Risk control and self-assessment. An approach to assessing operational risk.

Rebalancing   The process of adjusting a trading position periodically. Usually the purpose is to maintain delta neutrality.

Recovery Rate   Amount recovered in the event of a default as a percent of the face value.

Regulatory Arbitrage   Transactions designed to reduce the total regulatory capital of the financial institutions involved.

Regulatory Capital   Capital a financial institution is required by regulators to keep.

Reinsurance   Situation where an insurance company passes on some of its risks to another company. Of course, it has to pay the other company for taking on the risks.

Repo   Repurchase agreement. A procedure for borrowing money by selling securities to a counterparty and agreeing to buy them back later at a slightly higher price.

Repo Rate   The rate of interest in a repo transaction.

Reset Date   The date in a swap or cap or floor when the floating rate for the next period is set.

Reserve Requirement   Percentage of deposits that must be kept in cash or on deposit with the central bank.

Retail Banking   Taking relatively small deposits from retail customers and making relatively small loans to them.

Reverse Stress Testing   Using an algorithm to search for scenarios that lead to large losses.

Reversion Level The level to which the value of a market variable (e.g., a volatility) tends to revert.

Rho Rate of change of the price of a derivative with the interest rate.

Risk-free Rate The rate of interest that can be earned without assuming any risks.

Risk-neutral Valuation The valuation of an option or other derivative assuming the world is risk neutral. Risk-neutral valuation gives the correct price for a derivative in all worlds, not just in a risk-neutral world.

Risk-neutral World A world where investors are assumed to require no extra return on average for bearing risks.

Risk-weighted Amount *See* Risk-weighted Assets.

Risk-weighted Assets Quantity calculated in Basel I and Basel II. Total capital must be at least 8% of risk-weighted assets.

Roll Back *See* Backwards Induction.

Sarbanes–Oxley Act passed in the United States in 2002 increasing the responsibilities of directors, CEOs, and CFOs of public companies.

Scenario Analysis An analysis of the effects of possible alternative future movements in market variables on the value of a portfolio. Also used to evaluate possible future operational risk losses.

Scorecard Approach A self-assessment procedure used for operational risk.

SEC Securities and Exchange Commission.

Securitization Process whereby securities are created from future cash flow streams.

Senior Tranche Tranche which is the last to experience losses arising from defaults on the underlying assets.

Short Position A position assumed when traders sell shares they do not own.

Short Selling Selling in the market shares that have been borrowed from another investor.

Simulation *See* Monte Carlo simulation.

Solvency I Current regulatory framework for insurance companies in the European Union.

Solvency II A new regulatory framework for insurance companies proposed by the European Union.

Solvency Risk The risk that liabilities will be greater than assets.

Specific Risk Charge Capital requirement for idiosyncratic risks in the trading book.

Spectral Risk Measure Risk measure that assigns weights to the quantiles of the loss distribution.

Speculative Grade *See* Noninvestment Grade.

Speculator An individual who is taking a position in the market. Usually the individual is betting that the price of an asset will go up or that the price of an asset will go down.

Spot Interest Rate *See* Zero-Coupon Interest Rate.

Spot Price The price for immediate delivery.

Spot Volatilities The volatilities used to price a cap when a different volatility is used for each caplet.

Static Hedge A hedge that does not have to be changed once it is initiated.

Static Options Replication A procedure for hedging a portfolio that involves finding another portfolio of approximately equal value on some boundary.

Stochastic Variable Variable whose future value is uncertain.

Stock Index An index monitoring the value of a portfolio of stocks.

Stock Index Futures Futures on a stock index.

Stock Index Option An option on a stock index.

Stock Option Option on a stock.

Stop-Loss Rule A trading rule where a position is unwound when losses on the position reach a certain level.

Storage Costs The costs of storing a commodity.

Stress Testing Testing of the impact of extreme market moves on the value of a portfolio.

Strike Price The price at which the asset may be bought or sold in an option contract. (Also called the exercise price.)

Structured Product Derivative designed by a financial institution to meet the needs of clients.

Student *t*-Copula Copula based on the multivariate Student *t*-distribution.

Student *t*-Distribution Distribution with heavier tails than the normal distribution.

Subjective Probability Probability that reflects a person's opinion, rather than data.

Subprime Mortgage Mortgages that are more risky than the average mortgage.

Supplemental Capital *See* Tier 2 Capital.

Swap An agreement to exchange cash flows in the future according to a prearranged formula.

Swap Rate The fixed rate in an interest rate swap that causes the swap to have a value of zero.

Swap Zero Curve *See* LIBOR/Swap Zero Curve.

Swaption An option to enter into an interest rate swap where a specified fixed rate is exchanged for floating.

Synthetic CDO A CDO created by selling credit default swaps.

Synthetic Option An option created by trading the underlying asset.

Systematic Risk Risk that cannot be diversified away.

Systemic Risk Risk that a default by one financial institution will lead to defaults by other financial institutions.

Tail Correlation Correlation between the tails of two distributions. Measures the extent to which extreme values tend to occur together.

Tail Loss *See* Expected Shortfall.

Taylor Series Expansion   For a function of several variables, this relates changes in the value of the function to changes in the values of the variables when the changes are small.

Teaser Rate   A low interest rate offered for the first two or three years on a mortgage.

Term Life   Life insurance that pays off if death occurs before a certain date.

Term Structure of Interest Rates   The relationship between interest rates and their maturities.

Terminal Value   The value at maturity.

Threshold   The credit advanced to a counterparty in a collateralization agreement.

Theta   The rate of change of the price of an option or other derivative with the passage of time.

Tier 1 Capital   Equity and similar sources of capital.

Tier 2 Capital   Subordinated debt (life greater than 5 years) and similar sources of capital.

Tier 3 Capital   Short term subordinated debt (life between 2 and 5 years).

Time Decay   *See* Theta.

Time Value   The value of an option arising from the time left to maturity (equals an option's price minus its intrinsic value).

Total Expense Ratio   Ratio of total expenses to premiums for a property–casualty insurance company.

Total Return Swap   A swap where the return on an asset such as a bond is exchanged for LIBOR plus a spread. The return on the asset includes income such as coupons and the change in value of the asset.

Trading Days   Days when markets are open for trading.

Trading Book   Part of a bank's portfolio that consists of instruments that are held for resale.

Tranche   One of several securities that have different risk attributes. Examples are the tranches of a CDO.

Transaction Costs   The cost of carrying out a trade (commissions plus the difference between the price obtained and the midpoint of the bid–offer spread).

Treasury Bill   A short-term non-coupon-bearing instrument issued by the government to finance its debt.

Treasury Bond   A long-term coupon-bearing instrument issued by the government to finance it debt.

Treasury Note   Treasury bond lasting less than ten years.

Tree   Representation of the evolution of the value of a market variable for the purposes of valuing an option or other derivative.

Underlying Variable   A variable that the price of an option or other derivative depends on.

Unit Trust   *See* Mutual Fund.

Universal Life Insurance   A form of whole life insurance where the premium payments can be varied from year to year. The final payout is determined from the premiums, the performance of investments, and costs.

Unsystematic Risk   *See* Nonsystematic Risk.

Up-and-In Option   An option that comes into existence when the price of the underlying asset increases to a prespecified level.

Up-and-Out Option   An option that ceases to exist when the price of the underlying asset increases to a prespecified level.

Value at Risk   A loss that will not be exceeded at some specified confidence level.

Variable Annuity   A typical arrangement is that the policyholder deposits a lump sum with an insurance company and chooses from a number of options on how it is to be invested. At some future time (the maturity date), the accumulated value is converted into an annuity. If the policyholder dies before the maturity date, his or her beneficiaries receive the accumulated value.

Variable Life Insurance   A form of whole life insurance where the policyholder decides how funds will be invested. If the investments do well, the proceeds can be used to reduce premiums. There is a guaranteed minimum payout on death, but the payout may be higher if the investments do well.

Variance–Covariance Matrix   A matrix showing variances of, and covariances between, a number of different market variables.

Variance Rate   The square of volatility.

Vasicek's Model   Model of default correlation based on the Gaussian copula. (Other models developed by Vasicek are also sometimes referred to as Vasicek's model.)

Vega   The rate of change in the price of an option or other derivative with volatility.

Vega-neutral Portfolio   A portfolio with a vega of zero.

VIX Index   Index of the implied volatilities of options on the S&P 500.

Volatility   A measure of the uncertainty of the return realized on an asset.

Volatility Skew   A term used to describe the volatility smile when it is nonsymmetrical.

Volatility Smile   The variation of implied volatility with strike price.

Volatility Surface   A table showing the variation of implied volatilities with strike price and time to maturity.

Volatility Term Structure   The variation of implied volatility with time to maturity.

Waterfall   Rules for determining how cash flows from the underlying portfolio are distributed to tranches. In a typical arrangement, cash flows are first used to pay the senior tranche its promised return. The cash flows (if any) that are left over are used to provide the mezzanine tranche with its promised return. The cash flows (if any) that are left over are then used to provide the equity tranche with its promised return. Any residual cash flows are used to pay down the principal on the senior tranches.

Weather Derivative   Derivative where the payoff depends on the weather.

Whole Life Insurance   Life insurance that lasts for the whole life of the insured and so is certain to provide a payout.

Wholesale Banking   Taking large deposits and making large loans.

Within-Model Hedging   Hedging against those variables that the model considers to be stochastic (cf. Outside-Model Hedging).

Writing an Option   Selling an option.

Yield   A return provided by an instrument.

Yield Curve   *See* Term Structure.

Zero-Coupon Bond   A bond that provides no coupons.

Zero-Coupon Interest Rate   The interest rate that would be earned on a bond that provides no coupons.

Zero-Coupon Yield Curve   A plot of the zero-coupon interest rate against time to maturity.

Zero Curve   *See* Zero-Coupon Yield Curve.

Zero Rate   *See* Zero-Coupon Interest Rate.

Z-Score   A number indicating how likely a company is to default.

DerivaGem Software

The software accompanying this book is DerivaGem for Excel, Version 1.53. It requires Excel 2000 or later and Windows 2000 or later. The software consists of three files: dg153.dll, DG153.xls, and DG153 functions.xls. A setup routine is provided with the software. This will load dg153.dll into Windows/System or WINNT/System32 and create icons.[1]

Before using the software, Office 2007 users must click on the Options button to *Enable Macros*. If you are not using Office 2007, you should ensure that Security for Macros is set at *Medium* or *Low*. To change the security setting in Excel, check *Tools*, followed by *Macros*, followed by *Security*. While using the software, you may be asked whether you want to enable macros. You should click *Enable Macros*.

Updates to the software can be downloaded from the author's website:

http://www.rotman.utoronto.ca/~hull

There are two parts to the software: the Options Calculator (DG153.xls) and the Applications Builder (DG153 functions.xls). Both parts of the software require dg153.dll to be loaded into the Windows/System or WINNT/System32 folder. New users are advised to start with the Options Calculator.

THE OPTIONS CALCULATOR

DG153.xls is a user-friendly options calculator. It consists of three worksheets. The first worksheet is used to carry out computations for stock options, currency options, index options, and futures options; the second is used for European and American bond options; the third is used for caps, floors, and European swap options.

The software produces prices, Greek letters, and implied volatilities for a wide range of different instruments. It displays charts showing the way that option prices and the Greek letters depend on inputs. It also displays binomial and trinomial trees showing how the computations are carried out.

---

[1] Sometimes Windows Explorer is set up so that *.dll files are not displayed. (This does not appear to be a problem in Windows Vista.) To change the setting so that the *.dll files can be seen, proceed as follows. Click *Tools*, followed by *Folder Options*, followed by *View*, followed by *Show Hidden Files and Folders*.

General Operation

To use the options calculator, you should choose a worksheet and click on the appropriate buttons to select the Option Type, Underlying Type, and so on. You should then enter the parameters for the option you are considering, hit *Enter* on your keyboard, and click on *Calculate*. DerivaGem will then display the price or implied volatility for the option you are considering, together with Greek letters. If the price has been calculated from a tree, and you are using the first or second worksheet, you can then click on *Display Tree* to see the tree. If a tree is to be displayed, there should be no more than ten steps. An example of the tree that is displayed is in Appendix F. Many different charts can be displayed in all three worksheets. To display a chart, you must first choose the variable you require on the vertical axis, the variable you require on the horizontal axis, and the range of values to be considered on the horizontal axis. Following that, you should hit *Enter* on your keyboard and click on *Draw Graph*. Note that, whenever the values in one or more cells are changed, it is necessary to hit *Enter* on your keyboard before clicking on one of the buttons.

Options on Stocks, Currencies, Indices, and Futures

The first worksheet (Equity_FX_Index_Futures) is used for options on stocks, currencies, indices, and futures. To use it, you should first select the Underlying Type (Equity, Currency, Index, or Futures). You should then select the Option Type. The alternatives are: Analytic European (i.e., Black–Scholes for a European option), Binomial European (i.e., European option using a binomial tree), Binomial American (i.e., American option using a binomial tree), Asian, Barrier Up and In, Barrier Up and Out, Barrier Down and In, Barrier Down and Out, Binary Cash or Nothing, Binary Asset or Nothing, Chooser, Compound Option on Call, Compound Option on Put, or Lookback. You should then enter the data on the underlying asset and data on the option. Note that all interest rates are expressed with continuous compounding.

In the case of European and American equity options, a table pops up allowing you to enter dividends. Enter the time of each ex-dividend date (measured in years from today) in the first column and the amount of the dividend in the second column. Dividends must be entered in chronological order.

You must click on buttons to choose whether the option is a call or a put and whether you wish to calculate an implied volatility. If you do wish to calculate an implied volatility, the option price should be entered in the cell labeled Price.

Once all the data has been entered you should hit *Enter* on your keyboard and click on *Calculate*. If Implied Volatility was selected, DerivaGem displays the implied volatility in the Volatility (% per year) cell. If Implied Volatility was not selected, it uses the volatility you entered in this cell and displays the option price in the Price cell.

Once the calculations have been completed, the tree (if used) can be inspected and charts can be displayed.

When Analytic European is selected, DerivaGem uses the equations in Appendix E to calculate prices and Greek letters. When Binomial European or Binomial American is selected, a binomial tree is constructed as described in Appendix F. Up to 500 time steps can be used.

The input data are largely self-explanatory. In the case of an Asian option, the Current Average is the average price since inception. If the Asian option is new (Time since Inception equals zero), then the Current Average cell is irrelevant and can be left blank. In the case of a Lookback Option, the Minimum to Date is used when a Call is valued and the Maximum to Date is used when a Put is valued. For a new deal, these should be set equal to the current price of the underlying asset.

Bond Options

The second worksheet (Bond_Options) is used for European and American options on bonds. You should first select a pricing model (Black-European, Normal-Analytic European, Normal-Tree European, Normal-American, Lognormal-European, or Lognormal-American; these models are explained in John Hull's book *Options, Futures, and Other Derivatives*). You should then enter the Bond Data and the Option Data. The coupon is the rate paid per year and the frequency of payments can be selected as Quarterly, Semi-Annual or Annual. The zero-coupon yield curve is entered in the table labeled Term Structure. Enter maturities (measured in years) in the first column and the corresponding continuously compounded rates in the second column. The maturities should be entered in chronological order. DerivaGem assumes a piecewise linear zero curve similar to that in Figure B.1 of Appendix B. Note that, when valuing interest rate derivatives, DerivaGem rounds all times to the nearest whole number of days.

When all data have been entered, hit *Enter* on your keyboard. The quoted bond price per $100 of Principal, calculated from the zero curve, is displayed when the calculations are complete. You should indicate whether the option is a call or a put and whether the strike price is a quoted (clean) strike price or a cash (dirty) strike price. (The cash price is the quoted price plus accrued interest.) Note that the strike price is entered as the price per $100 of principal. You should indicate whether you are considering a call or a put option and whether you wish to calculate an implied volatility. If you select implied volatility and the normal model or lognormal model is used, DerivaGem implies the short-rate volatility keeping the reversion rate fixed.

Once all the inputs are complete, you should hit *Enter* on your keyboard and click *Calculate*. After that, the tree (if used) can be inspected and charts can be displayed. Note that the tree displayed lasts until the end of the life of the option. DerivaGem uses a much larger tree in its computations to value the underlying bond.

Note that Black's model is similar to Black–Scholes–Merton and assumes that the bond price is lognormal at option maturity. The approximate duration relationship in Chapter 7 is used to convert bond-yield volatilities to bond-price volatilities. This is the usual market practice.

Caps and Swap Options

The third worksheet (Caps_and_Swap_Options) is used for caps and swap options. You should first select the Option Type (Swap Option or Cap/Floor) and Pricing Model (Black-European, Normal-European, or Lognormal-European; these products and the alternative models are explained in John Hull's book *Options, Futures, and Other Derivatives*). You should then enter data on the option you are considering. The Settlement Frequency indicates the frequency of payments and can be Annual, Semi-Annual, Quarterly, or Monthly. The software calculates payment dates by working backward from the end of the life of the cap or swap option. The initial accrual period may be a nonstandard length between 0.5 and 1.5 times a normal accrual period. The software can be used to imply either a volatility or a cap rate/swap rate from the price. When a normal model or a lognormal model is used, DerivaGem implies the short-rate volatility keeping the reversion rate fixed. The zero-coupon yield curve is entered in the table labeled Term Structure. Enter maturities (measured in years) in the first column and the corresponding continuously compounded rates in the second column. The maturities should be entered in chronological order. DerivaGem assumes a piecewise linear zero curve similar to that in Figure B.1 of Appendix B.

Once all the inputs are complete, you should click *Calculate*. After that, charts can be displayed. Note that, when Black's model is used, DerivaGem assumes (a) that future interest rates are lognormal when caps are valued and (b) that future swap rates are lognormal when swap options are valued.

Greek Letters

In the Equity_FX_Index_Futures worksheet, the Greek letters are calculated as follows:

Delta: Change in option price per dollar increase in underlying asset

Gamma: Change in delta per dollar increase in underlying asset

Vega: Change in option price per 1% increase in volatility (e.g., volatility increases from 20% to 21%)

Rho: Change in option price per 1% increase in interest rate (e.g., interest increases from 5% to 6%)

Theta: Change in option price per calendar day passing

In the Bond_Options and Caps_and_Swap_Options worksheets, the Greek letters are calculated as follows:

DV01: Change in option price per one basis point upward parallel shift in the zero curve

Gamma01: Change in DV01 per one basis point upward parallel shift in the zero curve, multiplied by 100

Vega: Change in option price when volatility parameter increases by 1% (e.g., volatility increases from 20% to 21%)

THE APPLICATIONS BUILDER

The Application Builder is DG153 functions.xls. It is a set of 21 functions and seven sample applications from which users can build their own applications.

The Functions

The following is a list of the 21 functions included in the Applications Builder. Full details are on the first worksheet (FunctionSpecs).

1. Black_Scholes. This carries out Black–Scholes–Merton calculations for a European option on a stock, stock index, currency or futures contract.

2. TreeEquityOpt. This carries out binomial tree calculations for a European or American option on a stock, stock index, currency, or futures contract.

3. BinaryOption. This carries out calculations for a binary option on a stock, stock index, currency, or futures contract.

4. BarrierOption. This carries out calculations for a barrier option on a non-dividend-paying stock, stock index, currency, or futures contract.

5. AverageOption. This carries out calculations for an Asian option on a non-dividend-paying stock, stock index, currency, or futures contract.

6. ChooserOption. This carries out calculations for a chooser option on a non-dividend-paying stock, stock index, currency, or futures contract.

7. CompoundOption. This carries out calculations for compound options on non-dividend-paying stocks, stock indices, currencies, and futures.

8. LookbackOption. This carries out calculations for a lookback option on a non-dividend-paying stock, stock index, currency, or futures contract.

9. EPortfolio. This carries out calculations for a portfolio of options on a stock, stock index, currency, or futures contract.

10. BlackCap. This carries out calculations for a cap or floor using Black's model.

11. HullWhiteCap. This carries out calculations for a cap or floor using the Hull–White model.

12. TreeCap. This carries out calculations for a cap or floor using a trinomial tree.

13. BlackSwapOption. This carries out calculations for a swap option using Black's model.

14. HullWhiteSwap. This carries out calculations for a swap option using the Hull–White model.

15. TreeSwapOption. This carries out calculations for a swap option using a trinomial tree.

16. BlackBondOption. This carries out calculations for a bond option using Black's model.

17. HullWhiteBondOption. This carries out calculations for a bond option using the Hull–White model.

18. TreeBondOption. This carries out calculations for a bond option using a trinomial tree.

19. BondPrice. This values a bond.

20. SwapPrice. This values a plain vanilla interest rate swap. Note that it ignores cash flows arising from reset dates prior to start time.

21. IPortfolio. This carries out calculations for a portfolio of interest rate derivatives.

Sample Applications

DG153 functions.xls includes seven worksheets with sample applications:

A. Binomial Convergence. This investigates the convergence of the binomial model in Appendix F.

B. GreekLetters. This provides charts showing the Greek letters in Chapter 6.

C. Delta Hedge. This investigates the performance of delta hedging as in Tables 6.2 and 6.3.

D. Delta and Gamma Hedge. This investigates the performance of delta plus gamma hedging for a position in a binary option.

E. Value at Risk. This calculates Value at Risk for a portfolio consisting of three options on a single stock using three different approaches.

F. Barrier Replication. This carries out calculations for static options replication (see Chapter 6).

G. Trinomial Convergence. This investigates the convergence of a trinomial tree model (not covered in this book).

Tables for Cumulative Normal Distribution

Table for $N(x)$ When $x \leqslant 0$

This table shows values of $N(x)$ for $x \leqslant 0$. The table should be used with interpolation. For example,

$$N(-0.1234) = N(-0.12) - 0.34[N(-0.12) - N(-0.13)]$$
$$= 0.4522 - 0.34 \times (0.4522 - 0.4483)$$
$$= 0.4509$$

x	.00	.01	.02	.03	.04	.05	.06	.07	.08	.09
−0.0	0.5000	0.4960	0.4920	0.4880	0.4840	0.4801	0.4761	0.4721	0.4681	0.4641
−0.1	0.4602	0.4562	0.4522	0.4483	0.4443	0.4404	0.4364	0.4325	0.4286	0.4247
−0.2	0.4207	0.4168	0.4129	0.4090	0.4052	0.4013	0.3974	0.3936	0.3897	0.3859
−0.3	0.3821	0.3783	0.3745	0.3707	0.3669	0.3632	0.3594	0.3557	0.3520	0.3483
−0.4	0.3446	0.3409	0.3372	0.3336	0.3300	0.3264	0.3228	0.3192	0.3156	0.3121
−0.5	0.3085	0.3050	0.3015	0.2981	0.2946	0.2912	0.2877	0.2843	0.2810	0.2776
−0.6	0.2743	0.2709	0.2676	0.2643	0.2611	0.2578	0.2546	0.2514	0.2483	0.2451
−0.7	0.2420	0.2389	0.2358	0.2327	0.2296	0.2266	0.2236	0.2206	0.2177	0.2148
−0.8	0.2119	0.2090	0.2061	0.2033	0.2005	0.1977	0.1949	0.1922	0.1894	0.1867
−0.9	0.1841	0.1814	0.1788	0.1762	0.1736	0.1711	0.1685	0.1660	0.1635	0.1611
−1.0	0.1587	0.1562	0.1539	0.1515	0.1492	0.1469	0.1446	0.1423	0.1401	0.1379
−1.1	0.1357	0.1335	0.1314	0.1292	0.1271	0.1251	0.1230	0.1210	0.1190	0.1170
−1.2	0.1151	0.1131	0.1112	0.1093	0.1075	0.1056	0.1038	0.1020	0.1003	0.0985
−1.3	0.0968	0.0951	0.0934	0.0918	0.0901	0.0885	0.0869	0.0853	0.0838	0.0823
−1.4	0.0808	0.0793	0.0778	0.0764	0.0749	0.0735	0.0721	0.0708	0.0694	0.0681
−1.5	0.0668	0.0655	0.0643	0.0630	0.0618	0.0606	0.0594	0.0582	0.0571	0.0559
−1.6	0.0548	0.0537	0.0526	0.0516	0.0505	0.0495	0.0485	0.0475	0.0465	0.0455
−1.7	0.0446	0.0436	0.0427	0.0418	0.0409	0.0401	0.0392	0.0384	0.0375	0.0367
−1.8	0.0359	0.0351	0.0344	0.0336	0.0329	0.0322	0.0314	0.0307	0.0301	0.0294
−1.9	0.0287	0.0281	0.0274	0.0268	0.0262	0.0256	0.0250	0.0244	0.0239	0.0233
−2.0	0.0228	0.0222	0.0217	0.0212	0.0207	0.0202	0.0197	0.0192	0.0188	0.0183
−2.1	0.0179	0.0174	0.0170	0.0166	0.0162	0.0158	0.0154	0.0150	0.0146	0.0143
−2.2	0.0139	0.0136	0.0132	0.0129	0.0125	0.0122	0.0119	0.0116	0.0113	0.0110
−2.3	0.0107	0.0104	0.0102	0.0099	0.0096	0.0094	0.0091	0.0089	0.0087	0.0084
−2.4	0.0082	0.0080	0.0078	0.0075	0.0073	0.0071	0.0069	0.0068	0.0066	0.0064
−2.5	0.0062	0.0060	0.0059	0.0057	0.0055	0.0054	0.0052	0.0051	0.0049	0.0048
−2.6	0.0047	0.0045	0.0044	0.0043	0.0041	0.0040	0.0039	0.0038	0.0037	0.0036
−2.7	0.0035	0.0034	0.0033	0.0032	0.0031	0.0030	0.0029	0.0028	0.0027	0.0026
−2.8	0.0026	0.0025	0.0024	0.0023	0.0023	0.0022	0.0021	0.0021	0.0020	0.0019
−2.9	0.0019	0.0018	0.0018	0.0017	0.0016	0.0016	0.0015	0.0015	0.0014	0.0014
−3.0	0.0014	0.0013	0.0013	0.0012	0.0012	0.0011	0.0011	0.0011	0.0010	0.0010
−3.1	0.0010	0.0009	0.0009	0.0009	0.0008	0.0008	0.0008	0.0008	0.0007	0.0007
−3.2	0.0007	0.0007	0.0006	0.0006	0.0006	0.0006	0.0006	0.0005	0.0005	0.0005
−3.3	0.0005	0.0005	0.0005	0.0004	0.0004	0.0004	0.0004	0.0004	0.0004	0.0003
−3.4	0.0003	0.0003	0.0003	0.0003	0.0003	0.0003	0.0003	0.0003	0.0003	0.0002
−3.5	0.0002	0.0002	0.0002	0.0002	0.0002	0.0002	0.0002	0.0002	0.0002	0.0002
−3.6	0.0002	0.0002	0.0001	0.0001	0.0001	0.0001	0.0001	0.0001	0.0001	0.0001
−3.7	0.0001	0.0001	0.0001	0.0001	0.0001	0.0001	0.0001	0.0001	0.0001	0.0001
−3.8	0.0001	0.0001	0.0001	0.0001	0.0001	0.0001	0.0001	0.0001	0.0001	0.0001
−3.9	0.0000	0.0000	0.0000	0.0000	0.0000	0.0000	0.0000	0.0000	0.0000	0.0000
−4.0	0.0000	0.0000	0.0000	0.0000	0.0000	0.0000	0.0000	0.0000	0.0000	0.0000

Table for $N(x)$ When $x \geqslant 0$

This table shows values of $N(x)$ for $x \geqslant 0$. The table should be used with interpolation. For example,

$$N(0.6278) = N(0.62) + 0.78[N(0.63) - N(0.62)]$$
$$= 0.7324 + 0.78 \times (0.7357 - 0.7324)$$
$$= 0.7350$$

x	.00	.01	.02	.03	.04	.05	.06	.07	.08	.09
0.0	0.5000	0.5040	0.5080	0.5120	0.5160	0.5199	0.5239	0.5279	0.5319	0.5359
0.1	0.5398	0.5438	0.5478	0.5517	0.5557	0.5596	0.5636	0.5675	0.5714	0.5753
0.2	0.5793	0.5832	0.5871	0.5910	0.5948	0.5987	0.6026	0.6064	0.6103	0.6141
0.3	0.6179	0.6217	0.6255	0.6293	0.6331	0.6368	0.6406	0.6443	0.6480	0.6517
0.4	0.6554	0.6591	0.6628	0.6664	0.6700	0.6736	0.6772	0.6808	0.6844	0.6879
0.5	0.6915	0.6950	0.6985	0.7019	0.7054	0.7088	0.7123	0.7157	0.7190	0.7224
0.6	0.7257	0.7291	0.7324	0.7357	0.7389	0.7422	0.7454	0.7486	0.7517	0.7549
0.7	0.7580	0.7611	0.7642	0.7673	0.7704	0.7734	0.7764	0.7794	0.7823	0.7852
0.8	0.7881	0.7910	0.7939	0.7967	0.7995	0.8023	0.8051	0.8078	0.8106	0.8133
0.9	0.8159	0.8186	0.8212	0.8238	0.8264	0.8289	0.8315	0.8340	0.8365	0.8389
1.0	0.8413	0.8438	0.8461	0.8485	0.8508	0.8531	0.8554	0.8577	0.8599	0.8621
1.1	0.8643	0.8665	0.8686	0.8708	0.8729	0.8749	0.8770	0.8790	0.8810	0.8830
1.2	0.8849	0.8869	0.8888	0.8907	0.8925	0.8944	0.8962	0.8980	0.8997	0.9015
1.3	0.9032	0.9049	0.9066	0.9082	0.9099	0.9115	0.9131	0.9147	0.9162	0.9177
1.4	0.9192	0.9207	0.9222	0.9236	0.9251	0.9265	0.9279	0.9292	0.9306	0.9319
1.5	0.9332	0.9345	0.9357	0.9370	0.9382	0.9394	0.9406	0.9418	0.9429	0.9441
1.6	0.9452	0.9463	0.9474	0.9484	0.9495	0.9505	0.9515	0.9525	0.9535	0.9545
1.7	0.9554	0.9564	0.9573	0.9582	0.9591	0.9599	0.9608	0.9616	0.9625	0.9633
1.8	0.9641	0.9649	0.9656	0.9664	0.9671	0.9678	0.9686	0.9693	0.9699	0.9706
1.9	0.9713	0.9719	0.9726	0.9732	0.9738	0.9744	0.9750	0.9756	0.9761	0.9767
2.0	0.9772	0.9778	0.9783	0.9788	0.9793	0.9798	0.9803	0.9808	0.9812	0.9817
2.1	0.9821	0.9826	0.9830	0.9834	0.9838	0.9842	0.9846	0.9850	0.9854	0.9857
2.2	0.9861	0.9864	0.9868	0.9871	0.9875	0.9878	0.9881	0.9884	0.9887	0.9890
2.3	0.9893	0.9896	0.9898	0.9901	0.9904	0.9906	0.9909	0.9911	0.9913	0.9916
2.4	0.9918	0.9920	0.9922	0.9925	0.9927	0.9929	0.9931	0.9932	0.9934	0.9936
2.5	0.9938	0.9940	0.9941	0.9943	0.9945	0.9946	0.9948	0.9949	0.9951	0.9952
2.6	0.9953	0.9955	0.9956	0.9957	0.9959	0.9960	0.9961	0.9962	0.9963	0.9964
2.7	0.9965	0.9966	0.9967	0.9968	0.9969	0.9970	0.9971	0.9972	0.9973	0.9974
2.8	0.9974	0.9975	0.9976	0.9977	0.9977	0.9978	0.9979	0.9979	0.9980	0.9981
2.9	0.9981	0.9982	0.9982	0.9983	0.9984	0.9984	0.9985	0.9985	0.9986	0.9986
3.0	0.9986	0.9987	0.9987	0.9988	0.9988	0.9989	0.9989	0.9989	0.9990	0.9990
3.1	0.9990	0.9991	0.9991	0.9991	0.9992	0.9992	0.9992	0.9992	0.9993	0.9993
3.2	0.9993	0.9993	0.9994	0.9994	0.9994	0.9994	0.9994	0.9995	0.9995	0.9995
3.3	0.9995	0.9995	0.9995	0.9996	0.9996	0.9996	0.9996	0.9996	0.9996	0.9997
3.4	0.9997	0.9997	0.9997	0.9997	0.9997	0.9997	0.9997	0.9997	0.9997	0.9998
3.5	0.9998	0.9998	0.9998	0.9998	0.9998	0.9998	0.9998	0.9998	0.9998	0.9998
3.6	0.9998	0.9998	0.9999	0.9999	0.9999	0.9999	0.9999	0.9999	0.9999	0.9999
3.7	0.9999	0.9999	0.9999	0.9999	0.9999	0.9999	0.9999	0.9999	0.9999	0.9999
3.8	0.9999	0.9999	0.9999	0.9999	0.9999	0.9999	0.9999	0.9999	0.9999	0.9999
3.9	1.0000	1.0000	1.0000	1.0000	1.0000	1.0000	1.0000	1.0000	1.0000	1.0000
4.0	1.0000	1.0000	1.0000	1.0000	1.0000	1.0000	1.0000	1.0000	1.0000	1.0000

Index

Page numbers in **bold** refer to the Glossary of Terms

DATA DISK LICENSE AGREEMENT AND LIMITED WARRANTY

READ THIS LICENSE CAREFULLY BEFORE USING THIS PACKAGE. BY USING THIS PACKAGE, YOU ARE AGREEING TO THE TERMS AND CONDITIONS OF THIS LICENSE. IF YOU DO NOT AGREE, DO NOT USE THE PACKAGE. PROMPTLY RETURN THE UNUSED PACKAGE AND ALL ACCOMPANYING ITEMS TO THE PLACE YOU OBTAINED THEM. *THESE TERMS APPLY TO ALL LICENSED SOFTWARE ON THE DISK EXCEPT THAT THE TERMS FOR USE OF ANY SHARE-WARE OR FREEWARE ON THE DISKETTES ARE AS SET FORTH IN THE ELECTRONIC LICENSE LOCATED ON THE DISK:*

1. GRANT OF LICENSE and OWNERSHIP: The enclosed data disk ("Software") is licensed, not sold, to you by Pearson Education, Inc., publishing as Prentice Hall ("We" or the "Company") for academic purposes and in consideration of your purchase or adoption of the accompanying Company textbooks and/or other materials, and your agreement to these terms. This license allows instructors and students enrolled in the course using the Company textbook that accompanies this Software (the "Course") to use, display and manipulate the data for academic use only, so long as you comply with the terms of this Agreement. We reserve any rights not granted to you. You own only the disk(s) but we and our licensors own the Software itself.

2. RESTRICTIONS ON USE AND TRANSFER: You may not transfer, distribute or make available the Software or the Documentation, except to instructors and students in your school in connection with the Course. You may not reverse engineer, disassemble, decompile, modify, adapt, translate or create derivative works based on the Software or the Documentation. You may be held legally responsible for any copying or copyright infringement that is caused by your failure to abide by the terms of these restrictions.

3. TERMINATION: This license is effective until terminated. This license will terminate automatically without notice from the Company if you fail to comply with any provisions or limitations of this license. Upon termination, you shall destroy the Documentation and all copies of the Software. All provisions of this Agreement as to limitation and disclaimer of warranties, limitation of liability, remedies or damages, and our ownership rights shall survive termination.

4. DISCLAIMER OF WARRANTY: THE COMPANY AND ITS LICENSORS MAKE NO WARRANTIES ABOUT THE SOFTWARE, WHICH IS PROVIDED "AS-IS." IF THE DISK IS DEFECTIVE IN MATERIALS OR WORKMANSHIP, YOUR ONLY REMEDY IS TO RETURN IT TO THE COMPANY WITHIN 30 DAYS FOR REPLACEMENT UNLESS THE COMPANY DETERMINES IN GOOD FAITH THAT THE DISK HAS BEEN MISUSED OR IMPROPERLY INSTALLED, REPAIRED, ALTERED OR DAMAGED. THE COMPANY DISCLAIMS ALL WARRANTIES, EXPRESS OR IMPLIED, INCLUDING WITHOUT LIMITATION, THE IMPLIED WARRANTIES OF MERCHANTABILITY AND FITNESS FOR A PARTICULAR PURPOSE. THE COMPANY DOES NOT WARRANT, GUARANTEE OR MAKE ANY REPRESENTATION REGARDING THE ACCURACY, RELIABILITY, CURRENTNESS, USE, OR RESULTS OF USE, OF THE SOFTWARE.

5. LIMITATION OF REMEDIES AND DAMAGES: IN NO EVENT, SHALL THE COMPANY OR ITS EMPLOYEES, AGENTS, LICENSORS OR CONTRACTORS BE LIABLE FOR ANY INCIDENTAL, INDIRECT, SPECIAL OR CONSEQUENTIAL DAMAGES ARISING OUT OF OR IN CONNECTION WITH THIS LICENSE OR THE SOFTWARE, INCLUDING, WITHOUT LIMITATION, LOSS OF USE, LOSS OF DATA, LOSS OF INCOME OR PROFIT, OR OTHER LOSSES SUSTAINED AS A RESULT OF INJURY TO ANY PERSON, OR LOSS OF OR DAMAGE TO PROPERTY, OR CLAIMS OF THIRD PARTIES, EVEN IF THE COMPANY OR AN AUTHORIZED REPRESENTATIVE OF THE COMPANY HAS BEEN ADVISED OF THE POSSIBILITY OF SUCH DAMAGES. SOME JURISDICTIONS DO NOT ALLOW THE LIMITATION OF DAMAGES IN CERTAIN CIRCUMSTANCES, SO THE ABOVE LIMITATIONS MAY NOT ALWAYS APPLY.

6. GENERAL: THIS AGREEMENT SHALL BE CONSTRUED IN ACCORDANCE WITH THE LAWS OF THE UNITED STATES OF AMERICA AND THE STATE OF NEW YORK, APPLICABLE TO CONTRACTS MADE IN NEW YORK, AND SHALL BENEFIT THE COMPANY, ITS AFFILIATES AND ASSIGNEES. This Agreement is the complete and exclusive statement of the agreement between you and the Company and supersedes all proposals, prior agreements, oral or written, and any other communications between you and the company or any of its representatives relating to the subject matter. If you are a U.S. Government user, this Software is licensed with "restricted rights" as set forth in subparagraphs (a)–(d) of the Commercial Computer-Restricted Rights clause at FAR 52.227-19 or in subparagraphs (c)(1)(ii) of the Rights in Technical Data and Computer Software clause at DFARS 252.227-7013, and similar clauses, as applicable.

Should you have any questions concerning this agreement or if you wish to contact the Company for any reason, please contact in writing:

Director, Media Production
Prentice Hall
1 Lake Street
Upper Saddle River, NJ 07458